Pascal Mansmann

Interaktion von Unternehmen mit Kunden in sozialen Netzwerken

Eine Untersuchung der deutschen Facebook-Seiten von Automobilherstellern

Bachelor + Master
Publishing

Mansmann, Pascal: Interaktion von Unternehmen mit Kunden in sozialen Netzwerken. Eine Untersuchung der deutschen Facebook-Seiten von Automobilherstellern, Hamburg, Diplomica Verlag GmbH 2013

Originaltitel der Abschlussarbeit: Interaktion von Unternehmen mit Kunden in sozialen Netzwerken: Eine Untersuchung der deutschen Facebook Seiten von Automobilherstellern

ISBN: 978-3-95549-014-0
Druck: Bachelor + Master Publishing, ein Imprint der Diplomica® Verlag GmbH, Hamburg, 2013
Zugl. BiTS Business and Information Technology School, Iserlohn, Deutschland, Bachelorarbeit, September 2011

Bibliografische Information der Deutschen Nationalbibliothek:
Die Deutsche Nationalbibliothek verzeichnet diese Publikation in der Deutschen Nationalbibliografie; detaillierte bibliografische Daten sind im Internet über http://dnb.d-nb.de abrufbar.

Die digitale Ausgabe (eBook-Ausgabe) dieses Titels trägt die ISBN 978-3-95549-514-5 und kann über den Handel oder den Verlag bezogen werden.

Inhaltsverzeichnis

Abkürzungsverzeichnis

Abb.   Abbildung

IR   Interaktionsrate

SFI   Summe der Fan-Interaktionen

SUI   Summe der Unternehmens-Interaktionen

Abbildungsverzeichnis

Tabellenverzeichnis

Vorwort

Liken, posten, adden, sharen – Es sind Wörter, die man immer öfter zu hören bekommt. Hierbei handelt es sich aber nicht um reine Jugendsprache. Es ist Facebook- Vokabular. Und es wird sowohl von jungen Leuten genutzt, aber auch Leuten jenseits des 30. Lebensjahres sind die Bedeutungen dieser Begriffen bekannt. Die Online-Welt hält mehr und mehr Einzug in das alltägliche reale Leben. Mittlerweile nutzen über 51 Mio. Personen in Deutschland im Alter von 14 Jahre oder älter das Internet, dies entspricht über 73% dieser Bevölkerungsgruppe. Über alle Altersgruppen hinweg sind Zuwächse sind zu verzeichnen.

Geschehnisse und Dialoge werden online angefangen und offline weitergeführt oder andersherum. Die Inhalte verschmelzen in beiden Welten. Einen großen Anteil daran haben sozialen Netzwerke, denen Facebook als weltweit größtes dieser Art voran steht. Ganze 42% der deutschen Internetnutzer über 14 Jahren besitzen ein Profil in einem sozialen Netzwerk. Die Nutzungsfrequenz ist dabei sehr hoch, denn über die Hälfte der Nutzer halten sich dort täglich auf. Vorbei sind die Zeiten in denen im Internet anonym gesurft wurde und mit Ausschalten des Computers das dortige Treiben ruhte und abgeschlossen war. Durch Profile wird die eigene Identität in Netzwerken in Auszügen Preis gegeben und es findet ein Teil des eigenen Lebens dort statt. Dieser persönliche Einzug in die sozialen Netzwerke bezieht sich aber nicht nur auf die Kommunikation mit Mitmenschen und Freunden. Auch kommerzielle Aspekte finden mehr und mehr ihren Platz. Zur Bekennung der gekauften und genutzten Marken bietet sich im eigenen Facebook-Profil genügend Platz und Gelegenheit. Die Motive sind unterschiedlich. So kann es nur als Statussymbol und Kennzeichnung des eigenen Konsumprofils dienen, aber auch als Chance persönlich mit den Marken und Unternehmen dahinter in Kontakt zu treten. Hier bietet sich Unternehmen die Chance mehr über die eigenen Kunden zu erfahren, die Bindungen zu ihnen zu verstärken und vor allem ihnen zuzuhören und daraus zu lernen. Daher ist es zurzeit sehr im Trend als Unternehmen auf Facebook vertreten zu sein. Doch wie geht man nun mit der eigenen Facebook Seite adäquat um?

1 Einleitung

1.1 Relevanz der Arbeit

Nach dem Facebook sich als das weltweit größte soziale Netzwerk im Internet etabliert hat und zu dem immer weiter an Funktionen und Verwendungsmöglichkeiten gewinnt, bietet sich seit einiger Zeit für Unternehmen des B2C-Bereichs die Möglichkeit auf dieser Plattform mit Kunden in Kontakt zu treten und mit diesen zu interagieren. Diese Arbeit macht sich die Beobachtung jener Interaktionen zum Thema und untersucht, analysiert und bewertet diese. Hierzu wurden die Pinnwandaktivitäten auf Facebook-Unternehmensseiten miteinander verglichen und gegenüber gestellt. Dabei wurde die Automobilbranche ausgewählt. Dabei wurde die Automobilbranche ausgewählt. Das Auto als High-Involvement-Produkt unterliegt komplexeren Auswahlvorgängen als Güter mit niedrigeren Preisen, kürzerer Nutzungsdauer und höherer Kauffrequenz. Somit ist das Werben neuer Kunden durch beispielsweise Produktproben nicht möglich über Social Media nicht möglich, außer vielleicht durch buchbare Probefahrten, und durch die Autohäuser als Zwischenhändler sind Preisangebote und Rabatte ebenfalls nicht anbietbar. Direkte absatzsteigernde Maßnahmen, abgesehen von der Reproduzierung klassischer Werbung können über diesen Kommunikationskanal nicht getätigt werden, dies liegt in der Natur des Produkts. Den Autoherstellern bietet das Engagement in Social Media also vor allem die Chance der Steigerung der Kundenzufriedenheit durch persönlichen Kontakt.

Es gibt noch eine Menge anderer Kommunikationsziele aus den Bereichen Public Relations und Marketing die sich über Social Media und Facebook erreichen lassen. Themen wie Nachhaltigkeit, Umweltfreundlichkeit und Corporate Social Responsibility spielen beispielsweise für die Bekleidungs- und Lebensmittel eine große Rolle. Andere Gewerbe können auch Brücken zu ihrem E-Commerce über die Social Media schlagen. Aber solche Konversions spielen ebenfalls keine tragende Rolle für die Automobilindustrie auf Facebook.

Die zunehmende Wichtigkeit von Social Media ist von den Unternehmen bereits realisiert worden. Jedoch ist es noch nicht eindeutig geklärt, was eine erfolgreiche Facebook Seite ausmacht und in welchem Maße die Unternehmen von ihrem Engagement profitieren können. Diese Arbeit erörtert den Nutzen von Facebook Seiten für Automobilhersteller hinsichtlich der Pflege von Kundenbeziehung. Dieser brancheninterne Vergleich will eine Wertung vornehmen und anhand der beobachteten Vorgehensweise gute und schlechte Vorgehensweise bei der Führung einer Facebook Seite darstellen, da hierfür zurzeit noch kein Patentrezept herausgestellt wurde.

1.2 Vorgehensweise

Diese Arbeit schafft im ersten Teil eine theoretische Grundlage um zu verstehen was Social Media bedeutet und was zu dieser neuen Mediengattung zugezählt wird. Darauf aufbauend wird der Begriff der sozialen Netzwerke erläutert und beschrieben, aus denen dann Facebook speziell nochmal gesondert vorgestellt wird, da es das zu untersuchende Netzwerk und damit Hauptbestandteil dieser Arbeit ist. Im Zuge dessen werden zunächst die Geschichte und die Funktionen dieses sozialen Netzwerkes beschrieben, woran sich die Erklärung der kommerziellen Zwecke und besonders der Facebook Seiten anschließt. Des Weiteren vermittelt die Arbeit Grundlagen für das Verständnis von Kundenzufriedenheit und Kundenbindung, denn dies sind die vorwiegenden Nutzenfelder, in Verbindung mit dem Aufbau von Vertrauen und Identifizierung seitens des Kunden, für die Automobilbranche auf Facebook.

Das Thema der Arbeit findet sich dann in empirischen Teil wieder. Nach der Erklärung der Forschungsmethodik folgen die Ergebnisse der empirischen Untersuchung der deutschsprachigen Facebook Seiten von Autoherstellern, genauer gesagt der jeweiligen Pinnwände und dort stattgefundenen Aktivitäten. Es wurden hierbei die Einträge, Kommentare und Gefällt-mir-Klicks der Betreiber der Facebook Seite und der Fans in einem Zeitraum von zwei Wochen erfasst. Zunächst fand eine quantitative Untersuchung statt in der die Anzahl der Beiträge, Kommentare und Gefällt-mir-Klicks gemessen wurden. Anhand dieser wurden dann statistische Werte errechnet wie beispielsweise die Menge an Fan-Interaktionen pro Unternehmensbeitrag. Zudem wurden die Beiträge auf ihre medialen Anhänge untersucht, soll heißen ob sie mit Fotos, Videos oder Links versehen sind. Des Weiteren stellt diese Arbeit Interaktionsraten heraus, die die Anzahl der Pinnwandaktivitäten von Unternehmen und Fans in ein Verhältnis zur Fan-Menge setzt.

Ebenso wurden Kategorien ermittelt, in die sich sowohl die Beiträge der Fans als auch vom Unternehmen jeweils einordnen lassen um zu messen für welche Zwecke die beiden Parteien diese Plattform nutzen. Zudem werden noch weitere Daten erfasst die Rückschlüsse auf die Arbeit der Unternehmen auf Facebook zulassen.

Im Rahmen der qualitativen Inhaltsanalyse werden zur Verdeutlichung der unterschiedlichen inhaltlichen Kategorien der Pinnwand-Beiträge einzelne Beispiele herausgenommen und genauer betrachtet. Hierbei wird untersucht wie die Unternehmen auf verschiedene Sachlagen reagieren und was für Auswirkungen dies hat oder haben könnte.

Im weiteren Verlauf gibt diese Arbeit Handlungsempfehlungen und Wertungen für die verglichenen Automobilhersteller, wobei die besonders gut geführten Beispiel e für Interaktion mit Kunden als Best Practice für die gesamte Industrie angesehen werden.

Im abschließenden Fazit resümiert die Arbeit noch einmal die wichtigsten Befunde in kompakter Form.

2 Theoretische Grundlagen

2.1 Social Media

Der Begriff Social Media ist ein Konglomerat aus zwei Wörtern, die zu sich zu einer neuen Bedeutung zusammenschließen. Diese neue Bedeutung beschreibt die technologischen Möglichkeiten, die es Menschen ermöglicht im Internet ihre Meinung kund zu tun, diese selber zu veröffentlichen und zu verbreiten sowie sich auszutauschen (Safko, 2010, S. 4).

Sind die klassischen Medien noch als Massenmedien mit asymmetrischer Einweg-Kommunikation anzusehen, sind Social Media ein Sprachrohr für jedermann. Der ursprüngliche Rezipient kann nun zum Kommunikator werden, der sich selber ein Publikum aufbaut. Diese Ermöglichung neuer Kommunikationswege ist der Basisgedanke von Social Media und wird von Lon Safko als fundamentaler Machtwechsel bezeichnet. Die von Nutzern publizierten Meinungen sind durch ihre eigenen Erfahrungen und Eindrücke geprägt und erzeugen dadurch eine höhere Glaubwürdigkeit, derer sich die die Informationssuchenden lieber annehmen als den kommerziellen Werbebotschaften (Safko, 2010, S. 5). Der betriebene Meinungs- und Informationsaustausch unterliegt weder institutioneller Zensur noch Selektionsprozessen durch Agenda-Setting (Esch, 2009, S. 342). Somit avancieren Social Media zu einer Sammlung von unverfälschten Medien, welche nichts als die Wahrheit darstellen. Diese freie Kommunikation birgt jedoch auch eine Gefahr, wie etwa die fehlende Kontrolle über die Inhalte (Zarrella, 2010, S. 5).

Laut Weinberg (2010, S. 1) stehen Social Media für den Austausch von Informationen, Erfahrungen und Sichtweisen mit Hilfe von Community-Websites. Geographische Barrieren werden überwunden und Personen finden Leute mit gleichen Interessen auf dem ganzen Globus verteilt und treten in Kontakt miteinander.

In welche Kategorien und Formen sich Social Media nun einteilen lassen, variiert in der Literatur, jedoch sind sie im groben Blick übereinstimmend.

Kategorien von Social Media

Category Title
Social Networking
Publish
Photo Sharing
Audio
Video
Microblogging
Livecasting
Virtual Worlds
Gaming
Productivity Applications
Aggregators
RSS
Search
Mobile
Interpersonal

Tabelle 1: Social Media Categories (Safko, 2010, S. 9)

All diese Kategorien sind technologische Möglichkeiten, die dem Nutzer via Social Media zur Verfügung stehen. Aus technologischer Sicht sind viele der Kategorien keine Innovation, jedoch setzen Social Media sie in einen sozialen Kontext, verbinden Nutzer dabei und schaffen somit neuen Nutzen. Zarrella benutzt den Begriff Media-Sharing-Site, mit dem dann die Kategorien Photo, Video und Audio zu einer zusammengefasst werden (Zarrella, 2010, S. 7).

Neben den sozialen Netzwerken ist Microblogging eine der bekanntesten und meistgenutzt Social Media Kategorien, die die Kommunikation und Vernetzung von Inhalten online verändert hat. Microblogging leitet sich vom Begriff Blog ab, also das Publizieren eigener Texte online. Beim Microblogging geschieht dies aber nur in sehr komprimierter Form, daher der Name. Twitter steht als weltweit meistgenutzte Microblogging-Plattform stellvertretend für diesen Social Media Kanal. Nach Anlegung eines eigenen Profils können Twitter-Nachrichten maximal 140 Zeichen, sogenannte *Tweets*, veröffentlicht werden. Daher eignet es sich vor allem als Sprachrohr für Verkündungen, Kurzmeldungen und Verlinkungen. Die Nutzung von Twitter hat charakteristische Eigenheiten, die die Online-Kommunikation nachhaltig beeinflusst hat. Wie schon erwähnt, haben die Nachrichten ihren eigenen Namen und selbst Tätigkeit des Nachrichtenverfassens hat mit dem Verb *tweeten* mittlerweile gebrauchsfähigen Status erreicht. Um die Tweets einer Person zu lesen und über dessen Aktivitäten benachrichtigt zu werden, muss man ein *Follower* werden, also der Person sozusagen folgen. Man kann auf Tweets antworten, Personen in ihnen samt Profil erwähnen oder sie zitieren bzw. *retweeten* wie es dort genannt wird. Twitter bietet die Funktion die momentan meist verwendeten Wörter und Phrase der gesamten Community darzustellen, die durch einen Algorithmus ermittelt werden. Um im Mikrokosmos Twitter zielführender zu kommunizieren gibt es sogenannte *Hashtags*, damit werden Wörter kenntlich gemacht die die Nachricht einem bestimmten Thema zuordnen sollen. Somit werden die sich darauf beziehenden Tweets besser miteinander verknüpft und auffindbar gemacht. Durch diese Verwendungsmöglichkeiten als Sprachrohr, zum Weitersagen und themenorientierte Kommunikation hat Twitter auch für das Online-Marketing große Relevanz erlangt. Viele zusätzliche Anwendungen erweitern das Arsenal an Funktionen und helfen beim Umgang und bei der Auswertung (Zarrella, 2010, S. 39-57).

Eine Verwendung Twitters als Service-Kanal haben bereits mehrere Konzerne wie etwa die Deutsche Bahn oder die Deutsche Telekom bereits umgesetzt (Kolbrück, 2011).

Social Media können Unternehmen in vielen Bereichen wertvolle Dienste erweisen wie etwa dem Marketing, dem Verkauf, den Public Relations, der Unternehmenskommunikation, dem Krisenmanagement, dem Kundendienst, der Marktforschung, der Konkurrenzanalyse oder der Rekrutierung (Stuber, 2010, S. 30). Durch die soziale und verstärkte Interaktion zwischen Kunden und Unternehmen, werden deren Marken intensiver erlebt, ein höherer Identifikationsgrad erreicht sowie die Markenbindung ausgebaut und Wechselbarrieren geschaffen (Esch, 2009, S. 326).

Der Begriff Web 2.0 stand lange Zeit in einem umstrittenen Verhältnis zum Begriff Social Media. So gab es die Meinung, dass die beiden Begriffe lediglich als Synonyme für einander stehen würden, jedoch schließen die Definitionen zu Web 2.0 auf Unterschiede. So besagt Tim O'Reilly, der Begründer dieses Terminus, in einem Artikel zur Entstehung dieses Begriffs, dass das Web 2.0 als eine Plattform anzusehen ist um die sich ein System aus Praktiken und Prinzipien anordnet, die es vom Web 1.0 unterscheiden. Zudem stellte er Kernkompetenzen heraus, die Unternehmen gehabt haben, welche sie die Dot-Com-Krise überstehen ließen (O'Reilly, 2005).

Mittlerweile wird der Begriff aber mehr und mehr vernachlässigt, da es schwierig ist anhand von Versionsnummern ein sich stetig weiterentwickelndes Medium wie das Internet zu beziffern und zu kategorisieren. Es fehlen schlichtweg die klaren, objektiven Grenzen der einzelnen Versionen um sich eindeutig festlegen zu können (Alby, 2008, S. 18).

2.2   Soziale Netzwerke

Soziale Bindungen und Interkationen gibt es bereits seit dem Ursprung der Menschheit. Sozialen Beziehungen verknüpfen und vernetzen sich, aus denen wiederum Gesellschaften entstehen. Somit sind das Zusammenleben von Menschen und der Austausch zwischen Personen keine Neuheit.

Soziale Netzwerke, wie sie Gegenstand dieser Arbeit sind, meinen nach Weber mitgliederbasierte Online-Communities die Nutzer mit gleichen Interessen zusammenbringen. Der dort bereitgestellte Content ist größtenteils, aber nicht ausschließlich, von Nutzern generiert worden. Auch Unternehmen machen Gebrauch von sozialen Netzwerken um ihre Inhalte dort zu publizieren (Weber, 2009, S. 195). Laut Hettler versteht man unter sozialen Netzwerken im Kontext von Social Media Plattformen und Onlinepräsenzen die dem Aufbau und der Pflege von Beziehungen dienen und den dabei betriebenen Informationsaustausch und die zwischenmenschliche Kommunikation im Internet erleichtern (Hettler, 2010, S. 54).

Jeder Nutzer erstellt sich sein eigenes Profil, welches die Basis zur Interaktion mit anderen Nutzern darstellt. Je nach Art des sozialen Netzwerkes kann das Profil mit verschiedenen Funktionen versehen werden. Grundlegende Funktionen sind das Veröffentlichen von Fotos, Texten, Links und Videos, die mit anderen Nutzern geteilt werden können. Ebenso kann über private oder öffentliche Nachrichten mit anderen Nutzern kommuniziert werden. Dieses Interagieren zwischen Mitgliedern verleiht der Community den Titel soziales Netzwerk (Schwindt, 2010, S. 15) (Zarrella, 2010, S. 66).

Das bekannteste und größte soziale Netzwerk ist zurzeit Facebook. Jedoch gab es schon andere Vorgänger die sich einer großen Beliebtheit annehmen konnten. Auf internationaler Ebene war dies MySpace, welches bis auf eine Größe von 100 Mio. Nutzern heranwachsen konnte und jahrelang Marktführer gewesen ist, ehe Facebook die Spitzenposition einnahm. Nach dem Abgang vieler Nutzer schlug man bei MySpace in die Sparte des Social Entertainments ein, da sich dieses Netzwerk ohnehin bei Musikern einen große Beliebtheit durch die profilintegrierten Musikplayer erarbeiten konnte (Spiegel Online Netzwelt, 2011) (Weinberg, 2010, S. 13). Mittlerweile wurde MySpace von Besitzer News Corp. für 35 Mio. US-$ verkauft im Juni 2011, nach dem es fünf Jahre zuvor noch für 580 Mio. US-$ übernommen wurde (Focus Online Money, 2011).

Ein ganz ähnliches Schicksal holte hierzulande die VZ-Netzwerke ein. Das ehemals größte deutsche soziale Netzwerk, welches sich in die drei Netzwerken StudiVZ, SchülerVZ und MeinVZ aufteilt, musste seine Spitzenposition an Facebook abtreten. Auch andere ehemals erfolgreiche deutsche soziale Netzwerke wie wer-kennt-wen.de und lokalisten.de verlieren an Nutzern und somit an Bedeutung (Hutter, 2011) (Schröder, 2011).

Es bleibt abzuwarten ob auch hier einen Nischenbesetzung die Rettung sein kann und für die betreibenden Unternehmen in Frage kommt. Für den allgemeinen, privaten Gebrauch scheint

Facebook immer mehr das globale Monopol zu erlangen wie die folgenden Graphiken aus dem Herbst 2010 zeigen, deren Grundmenge für die Untersuchung die Gesamtheit aller deutschen Internetnutzer ist. Die Kluften zwischen Facebook und den Mitbewerbern sind aller Wahrscheinlichkeit nach im Laufe der Zeit noch weiter auseinander gegangen.

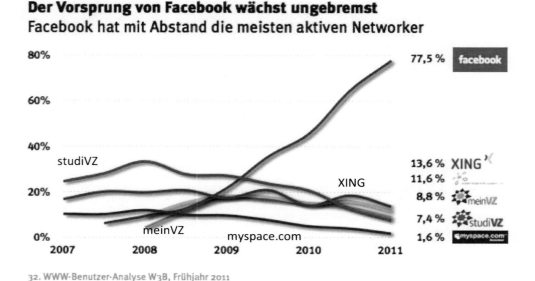

Abbildung 1: Der Vorsprung von Facebook wächst ungebremst
(Fittkau & Maaß Consulting, 2011)

Neben der privaten Nutzung gibt es auch Bedarf für berufliche soziale Netzwerke. Auch hier gibt es einen Wettstreit zwischen dem größten globalen Vertreter, LinkedIn, und seinem deutschen Pendant, Xing. Jedoch unterliegt dieses Duell anderen Voraussetzungen. Zunächst ist Xing auch in anderen Ländern und Sprachen verfügbar und somit in einer besseren Lage zu expandieren als es etwa die VZ-Netzwerke waren. Des Weiteren besitzen beide beruflichen sozialen Netzwerke die Erlösquelle der kostenpflichtigen Premium-Mitgliedschaften. Sie ähneln sich ebenfalls im Funktionsumfang. So kann neben der Profilerstellung und dem persönlichen Vernetzen auch von Gruppen und Foren Gebrauch gemacht werden, in denen konstruktiv und themengebunden diskutiert wird (Weinberg, 2010, S. 13). Xing hatte im Juni 2011 11,1 Mio. Mitglieder, 4,9 Mio., davon in Deutschland, Österreich und der Schweiz (Gross-Selbeck, 2011). LinkedIn lag am 4. August 2011 bei über 120 Mio. Mietgliedern, davon über 1 Mio. in der D-A-CH-Region (LinkedIn Press Center, 2011).

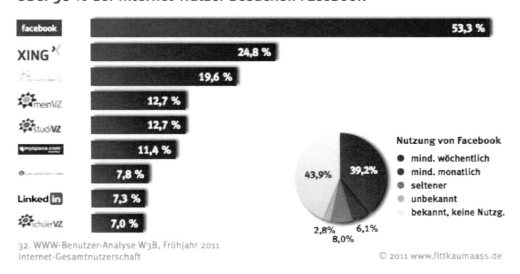

Facebook ist das am häufigsten genutzte Social Network
Über 50 % der Internet-Nutzer besuchen Facebook

Abbildung 2: Facebook ist das am meisten genutzte Social Network
(Fittkau & Maaß Consulting, 2011)

Am 28. Juli 2011 launchte Google sein eigenes soziales Netzwerk namens Google Plus. Es hat bereits für Aufsehen gesorgt, in dem es auf eine Größe von über 25 Mio. Nutzern anwuchs und dafür weniger als einen ganzen Monat benötigte. Dies ist zwar noch ein Bruchteil der Mitglieder-anzahl Facebooks, zeigt jedoch das allemal vorhandene Potenzial dieses neuen Netzwerks an. Auch in Deutschland ist das Interesse groß. Es gibt bereits knapp 1 Mio. deutsche Nutzer was schon einem Anteil von 5% der deutschen Facebook-Nutzerschaft von 20 Mio. Mitgliedern entspricht (Schönherr, 2011).

Bisher befindet es sich noch in der Betaphase und ist kommerziellen Angeboten wie Werbung oder Unternehmensseiten nicht zugänglich bis auf Ausnahmen zu Testzwecken wie es zurzeit mit einem Ford-Profil durchgeführt wird (Gardener, 2011). Wie schnell es weiterhin wachsen wird, ob es Facebook wirklich Konkurrenz machen kann und sogar Nutzer sich daher bei Facebook abmelden sind interessante Fragen die sich im Laufe der Zeit klären dürften. Die Vergangenheit zeigte, dass die vorherigen Netzwerke Zyklen unterlagen und von einem besseren Nachfolger abgelöst wurden. Google hat große Kompetenzen und ein noch größere Ressourcen um dieses Duell anzutreten.

2.3 Facebook

2.3.1 Geschichte von Facebook

Bekannt als das mittlerweile weitreichendste soziale Netzwerk weltweit hat Facebook innerhalb von sieben Jahren eine wahre Erfolgsgeschichte hervorgebracht. Gegründet wurde Facebook im Jahre 2004 vom damaligen Harvard-Studenten Mark Zuckerberg mit Hilfe einiger Studienkollegen. Zunächst war der Zugang zu diesem Netzwerk nur eingeschriebenen Studenten der Universität vorbehalten. Nach und nach wurde das Netzwerk immer mehr Leuten zugänglich gemacht. Zuerst bekamen auch Studenten der Universitäten von Columbia, Stanford und Yale Zutritt. Später waren alle Studenten in den USA zugangsberechtigt bis man 2005 auch High-School-Schüler in Facebook zuließ. Zwei Jahre nach Gründung Facebooks wurden die Restriktionen dann komplett entfernt und der explosionsartige Zuwachs nahm seinen Lauf nach dem es nun frei zugänglich gemacht wurde (Stuber, 2010, S. 147). Laut dem offiziellen Facebook-Blog wurde im Juli 2010 die Grenze von 750 Mio. aktiven Nutzern überschritten (Facebook Inc., 2011). Wenn man diese Menge anteilig auf die Weltbevölkerung von rund 6,9 Mrd. betrachtet, kommt man auf einen Schätzwert von 11%. Auch wenn es sich hier um grobe Werte handelt, ist dies allemal ein beachtlicher Anteil und stellt eine dermaßen große verbundene Nutzerschaft dar, wie sie in diesem Ausmaß vorher noch nie existierte. Diese Größe in Kombination mit der hohen Nutzungsfrequenz vieler User, die Hälfte loggt sich jeden Tag ein (Facebook Inc., 2011), macht den momentanen Hype aus der sich um soziale Netzwerke und Facebook als Zugpferd aufgebaut hat.

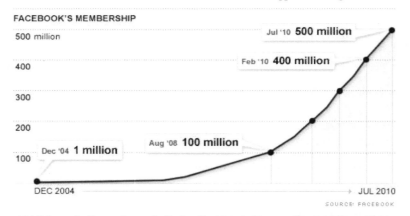

Abbildung 3: Zuwachsstatistik der Facebook-Nutzer (Social eCart, 2011)

2.3.2 Funktionen auf Facebook

Wie schon in Kapitel 2.2 beschrieben, startet auch bei Facebook die Nutzung mit der Erstellung eines persönlichen Profils. Die Struktur eines persönlichen Facebook-Profils setzt sich dabei wie folgt zusammen: Pinnwand, Info, Fotos, Notizen und Freunde (Schwindt, 2010, S. 29).

Die Pinnwand hat dabei die Funktion, dem Nutzer selbst wie auch seinen Freunden Platz für Veröffentlichungen jeder Art zu bieten. Hier können alle zugelassenen medialen Formen *gepostet* werden. Reine Textbeiträge können kommentiert werden oder einem *gefallen*. Fotos, Videos und URL-Links können zudem noch geteilt werden, das heißt an andere Nutzer kommuniziert werden.

Pascal Mansmann
Deutschland macht seinem Ruf als Bürokratie-bessene Nation mal wieder alle Ehre.

YouTube Live muss draußen bleiben
www.wuv.de

Ärger in Deutschland: Youtbe kann seine Livestream-Experiment nicht in Deutschcland starten. Denn das deutsche Rundfunkrecht macht dem Portal das Leben schwer.

Gefällt mir · Kommentieren · Teilen · 12. Juli um 16:06

▢ gefällt das.

▢ Auf der einen Seite wirklich blamabel und extrem innovations-hemmmend. Im Bereich des Antrags, von dem gesprochen wird ist es aber auch International Marketing 1x1. Legal Environment in Deutschland. Also ist google auch nicht allzu gut aufgestellt.
12. Juli um 16:28 · Gefällt mir

▢ Agree, wie schwierig/aussichtsreich das Durchbringen dieses Antrags ist weiß ich nicht. Aber ihn nicht mal auszufüllen ist natürlich eigene Doofheit.
12. Juli um 16:36 · Gefällt mir

▢ die regulierung des deutschen mediensystems ist aber auch im allgemeinen nicht gerade innovationsförderlich ;)
14. Juli um 09:00 · Gefällt mir

▢ true
14. Juli um 11:15 · Gefällt mir

Schreibe einen Kommentar ...

Abbildung 4: Pinnwand-Post (Mansmann, 2011)

Dieses Weiterkommunizieren kann auf der eigenen Pinnwand oder der eines Freundes stattfinden sowie in einer Nachricht an eine Gruppe oder einen Freund (Schwindt, 2010, S. 29).

Der Reiter Infos beinhaltet alle vom Nutzer eingetragenen Angaben über seine Person wie unter anderem Kontaktdaten, Interessen und Informationen über Ausbildung und Beruf (Schwindt, 2010, S. 30f).

Der *Reiter* Fotos zeigt eine Übersicht alle Fotos und Videos, die der Nutzer hochgeladen oder in denen er markiert wurde (Schwindt, 2010, S. 73-79).

Der *Reiter* Notizen ist als eine Art profileigener Facebook-Blog zu sehen. Der Nutzer kann hier Blog Posts schreiben und auf seiner Pinnwand veröffentlichen. Hierbei ist seinem Text mehr Platz gegeben als der beschränkten Zeichenanzahl in einer Statusnachricht (Schwindt, 2010, S. 95).

Der *Reiter* Freunde zeigt dem Nutzer alle Kontakte an mit denen er auf Facebook befreundet ist. Zudem besteht hier die Möglichkeit Listen zu erstellen, denen Freunde zugeordnet werden können. Diese können dann auch durch entsprechende Einstellungen beim Veröffentlichen von Beiträgen etc. ein- oder ausgeschlossen werden, genauso wie einzelne Freunde (Schwindt, 2010, S. 83).

So viel zum Grundraster des persönlichen Profils.

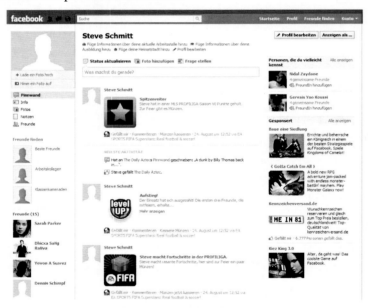

Abbildung 5: Facebook Profil (Schmitt, 2011)

Wenn ein Nutzer sich bei Facebook einloggt, gelangt er auf seine persönliche Startseite. In der linken Spalte befindet sich Verlinkungen zu den Hauptfunktionen wie Nachrichten, Veranstaltungen, Freunde, Gruppen sowie genutzte Applikationen und Spiele (Schwindt, 2010, S. 99). Ebenfalls in der linken Spalte befindet sich die Chatfunktion. Hier kann der Nutzer in Echtzeit mit seinen Freunden schreiben, die zur gleichen Zeit online sind wie er. Diese Funktion kann je nach Nutzerwunsch über einen Button ein- oder ausgeschaltet werden (Schwindt, 2010, S. 111).

Das zentrale Element der Startseite ist die Spalte Neuigkeiten, oder auch *Newsfeed* genannt. Hier werden dem Nutzer die Neuigkeiten aus seinem Netzwerk angezeigt. Darunter zu verstehen sind: Eigene Posts, Neuigkeiten von Facebook Pages und Aktivitäten von Freunden; also Posts, neue Freundschaften, Gefällt-mir-Klicks neuer Seiten, abgegebene Kommentare und Installation von Facebook-Anwendungen (Schwindt, 2010, S. 100f).

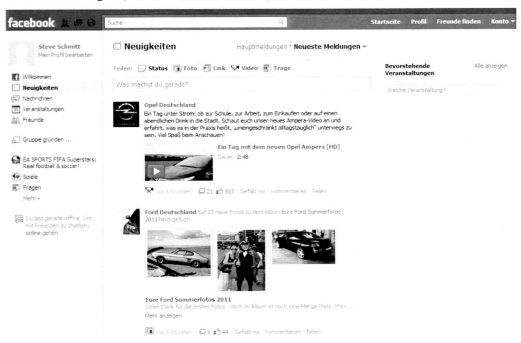

Abbildung 6: Facebook Startseite (Schmitt, 2011)

Der Nutzer kann hierbei zwischen dem Anzeigen der Neueste Meldungen oder der Hauptmeldungen auswählen (Stuber, 2010, S. 190). Während erstere Option die Meldungen rein chronologisch sortiert, ermittelt Facebook bei der Auswahl der Hauptmeldungen mit dem sogenannten Edgerank Algorithmus welche kürzlich veröffentlichten Neuigkeiten die größte Relevanz für den Nutzer haben. In einem Video erklärt Dag Holmboe, ein Social Media Analytiker, die ungefähre Funktionsweise und Zusammensetzung. Der Algorithmus ist eine Summe aus den drei ermittelten Kriterien für die Affinität zwischen Nutzer und Freund/Fan-Page, die Gewichtung der Beiträge und dem Alter des Beitrags. Die Affinität ergibt sich aus der Häufigkeit der Klicks des Nutzers auf die Beiträge des Freundes bzw. der Fan-Page. Bewertet Facebook die Affinität eines Nutzers zum Ersteller eines Beitrags als hoch, so werden Beiträge von diesem Autor dem Nutzer eher oben im Newsfeed angezeigt. Die Gewichtung der Beiträge ergibt sich aus der Summe an Klicks, Likes und Kommentaren, die je nach Art des medialen Anhangs (Link, Foto, Video) größeres Potenzial hat. Je größer die Summe ausfällt, desto höher ist die Wertung Facebooks für dieses Kriterium. Je älter ein Beitrag ist, desto irrelevanter stuft Facebook diesen ein. Das Zusammenspiel dieser drei

Kriterien entscheidet über Facebooks Einstufung der Relevanz für den Nutzer (Holmboe, 2011). Unternehmen müssen also möglichst hohe Punktzahlen in den Kriterien erreichen, damit ihre Beiträge auch wirklich dem Nutzer angezeigt werden und dieser sich angesprochen fühlt und daraufhin mit dem Unternehmen interagiert.

Über dem Newsfeed befindet sich die Suchleiste. Hier kann der Nutzer nach Personen suchen um auf ihr Profil zu gelangen, aber auch nach Seiten, Gruppen, Veranstaltungen, Anwendungen (Schwindt, 2010, S. 55) und mittlerweile auch nach Inhalten in Beiträgen verschiedener Art. Damit erweiterte Facebook sein Funktionsarsenal um eine *soziale Suchmaschine.*

Weitere Kommunikationsfunktionen sind private Nachrichten und Echtzeit-Chats. Mittlerweile ergänzt Facebook diese Funktionen um weitere Features. So können Nachrichten und Chats auch mit mehreren Personen gleichzeitig geführt. Der Chat bietet seit Juli 2011 die Möglichkeit auch Videotelefonate zu halten. Dies wird durch eine Kooperation Facebooks mit dem Voice-over-IP-Anbieter Skype sichergestellt (Frickel, 2011).

Durch die Sharing-Funktion innerhalb Facebooks und durch Plug-Ins auf externen Websites wird virale Distribution betrieben und es wird somit virtuelle Mundpropaganda betrieben durch Weiter-empfehlungen.

2.3.3   Kommerzielle Zwecke von Facebook

Da die Nutzung von Facebook gratis für den Nutzer ist, benötigt es andere Erlösquellen als Nutzungsgebühren. Facebook bietet Unternehmen jeder Größe eine Vielzahl an nutzvollen Möglichkeiten.

Angefangen beim Schalten von gezielter personalisierte Werbung, den sogenannten *FacebookAds,* die seit Ende 2007 gebucht werden können (Stuber, 2010, S. 148). Dies ist der Name für kleine Werbeflächen, die dem Nutzer in der rechten Spalte auf der Startseite angezeigt werden.

Abbildung 7: Beispiel einer FacebookAd

Durch sogenanntes *Targeting*, lässt sich bei der Buchung von *FacebookAds* sehr detailliert auswählen, welcher Zielgruppe die Werbung angezeigt werden soll, um so die Streuverluste auf ein Minimum zu reduzieren. Die Auswahl geht über demographische Kriterien hin zu anderen Angaben, die Nutzer in ihren Profilen machen wie Hobbies, Interessen und Vorlieben, somit wird eine sehr spezifische Zielgruppenfestlegung gewährleistet. Dazu bietet Facebook einen kostenlosen *Ads Manager* an, mit dem sich Werbekampagnen planen lassen hinsichtlich ihrer Laufzeit und dem einzusetzenden Budget. Ebenso kann das Abrechnungsmodell ausgewählt werden zwischen CPC (Cost Per Click) und CPM (Cost Per Mill), danach gilt es im Auktionsverfahren seinen Maximalpreis für die ausgewählte Abrechnungseinheit zu bestimmen, in dem der Höchstbietende den Zuschlag bekommt. Weitere Funktionsweisen und Ratschläge stellt Facebook den Werbern kostenlos zur Verfügung (Facebook Inc., 2011).

Man sieht dabei, dass die Betreiber von Facebook Seiten die Werbeplanung in eigener Hand haben und mehrere Glieder der Wertschöpfungskette in der Online-Werbeschaltung überspringt: Die Werbeagenturen, die Mediaagenturen und die Vermarkter. Diese drei Zwischenstationen entfallen, da die Werbemittel bei FacebookAds simpel und leicht zu gestalten sind und man mit dem Ads Manager selber die Planung übernimmt und direkt Facebook als Werbeträger zusammenarbeitet. Somit entstehen weniger Kosten für die Wertschöpfung mehrerer Zwischenglieder und so können Werbetreibende auch kleinere Budgets besser ausnutzen.

Abbildung 8: Wertschöpfungskette beim Ablauf einer Online-Kampagne (Kopp, 2008, S. 29)

Ein weiteres sehr stark expandierendes Geschäftsfeld innerhalb Facebook sind Spieleanwendungen. Diese in Facebook integrierten Browser-Spiele zeichnen sich durch einfache Handhabung und leichte Zugänglichkeit aus, da sie über das eigene Facebook-Profil gesteuert werden. Die Mehrheit der Spiele basiert auf dem Freemium-Prinzip. Dies bedeutet, dass die Nutzung des Spiels kostenlos nutzbar ist, die Spieler jedoch durch den Kauf sogenannter *Virtual Goods* sich im Spiel schneller verbessern können als durch zeitlich aufwendige kostenfreie Spielweise. Die Spieler können ihre Fortschritte in den Spielen auf ihrer Pinnwand *sharen/mitteilen,* um ihre Freunde und gleichzeitigen Konkurrenten um Hilfe zu bitten, bewerben dabei auch das Spiel für die Unternehmen völlig gratis. Bekanntester Vertreter dieses Genres ist das kalifornische Unternehmen Zynga, welches eine Vielzahl an Facebookspielen entwickelt hat, allen voran das größte Spiel von allen auf Facebook: FarmVille. Durch die zahlreichen Verkäufe an Spielgütern verdienen Spielehersteller wie auch Facebook gutes Geld (Patalong, 2010). Zynga erfreut sich sogar einer dermaßen großen

Beliebtheit, dass es auch für Werbezwecke in Frage kommt. So gab es bereits Testaktionen, bei denen werbetreibende Unternehmen sowohl online wie auch offline in das Spiel eingebracht wurden. Dies geschah etwa durch gebrandete Spielelandschaften oder Verkaufsaktionen, die dem Kunden die Einlösung von Gutscheinen für Spielgüter einbrachten beim Kauf ausgewählter Artikel (Fancher, 2010).

Es gibt auch weitere installierbare Anwendungen auf Facebook die keinen Spielecharakter haben. Hierbei profitieren die Entwickler vor allem durch den Gewinn von Nutzerdaten, wofür Facebook auch teilweise kritisiert wird (Stuber, 2010, S. 148).

2.3.4 Facebook Seiten

Eine weitere kommerzielle Sparte sind die sogenannten *Seiten*, auch bekannt als *Facebook Pages* oder *Fan Pages*, die Unternehmen, Marken, Organisationen, Produkten und Künstlern einen eigenen kommerziellen Auftritt in dem sozialen Netzwerk bieten (Schwindt, 2010, S. 175). Offizielle Facebook Seiten dürfen nur von den Unternehmen selbst gegründet und betrieben werden. Die Facebook Seiten ähneln in ihrem Aufbau sehr den privaten Profilen, jedoch gibt es ein paar kleine Unterschiede. Zunächst verbinden sich die Seiten über Gefällt-mir-Klicks und nicht über Freundschaftseinladung, des Weiteren lassen sich die Reiter auf einer Facebook Seite bearbeiten und neue hinzufügen (Joshi & Rutledge, 2011, S. 243ff). Sie kann von einem oder mehreren Administratoren betrieben werden (Joshi & Rutledge, 2011, S. 256).

Die Nutzer können, nach dem sie auf der Facebook Seite den Gefällt-mir-Button geklickt haben, auf die Pinnwand schreiben, sofern es vom Administrator zugelassen wurde, um sich mit der Marke und anderen Fans auszutauschen. Zudem können sie Unternehmensinformationen einsehen, von den verschiedenen auf der Seite angebotenen Anwendungen Gebrauch machen und kriegen von ab an die Beiträge der Marke als Neuigkeiten in ihrem Newsfeed angezeigt. Ebenfalls können weitere Freunde eingeladen werden sich ebenfalls als Fan der Seite und somit des Unternehmens zu bekennen (Schwindt, 2010, S. 181). Größeren Unternehmen und Konzerne bieten Facebook Seiten die Chance sich am virtuellen Aufenthaltsort ihrer Kunden zu präsentieren und ihre Online-Kommunikation zu ergänzen (Hettler, 2010, S. 201f). Kleinen und lokalen Unternehmen können die Facebook Pages sogar als kostengünstiger Ersatz einer eigenen Website und virtuelles Prospekt für Sonderangebote dienen. Unabhängig von der Unternehmensgröße, bietet das Engagement der Fans auf den Facebook Seiten die Markenbindung zu erhöhen, sofern die Erwartungen nicht enttäuscht werden (Hettler, 2010, S. 209).

Die Facebook Seiten gewinnen somit immer mehr an Bedeutung und Anerkennung als Kommunikationsinstrument für Marken und die dort stattfindenden Dialoge sollten ernst genommen werden, egal ob sie positiver oder negativer Natur sind. Durch die uneingeschränkte Einsehbarkeit der Dialoge für alle Fans ist es wichtig, den nötigen Einsatz und Willen zu demonstrieren sich mit den Fans austauschen zu wollen (Hettler, 2010, S. 209f).

Über zusätzliche Reiter können spezielle Unterseiten in die Facebook Seite integriert werden. Der Vielfalt an Funktionalitäten sind kaum Grenzen gesetzt. Über Spieleanwendungen Wettbewerbe, Produktprobenbestellung,… bis hin zu Angebotsseiten zur Verkaufsförderung kann dort alles vertreten sein. (Hettler, 2010, S. 212). Daher werden die Praktiken zur Administration dieser Unternehmensseiten zurzeit sehr aktiv erforscht und beobachtet um die besten Methoden zu bestimmen. Consultingunternehmen sowie Kommunikationsagenturen bereiten dazu Studien auf, von denen hier nun ein paar samt ihrer Ergebnisse aufgeführt werden.

Da dieses Betätigungsfeld aber noch sehr jung ist, treten die Marken auf ihren Präsenzen recht unterschiedlich auf hinsichtlich der Kommunikation mit ihren Fans. Hierzu wurde bereits im zweiten Jahr in Folge eine Studie durchgeführt, der Trendreport Juli 2011: Facebook, Marken & TV in Deutschland. Diese Studie, erstellt durch die Zucker.Kommunikation GmbH und die pilot media GmbH & Co. KG, stellt unter anderem eine Typologie heraus, in die sich die Facebook Seiten einteilen lassen gemessen am administrativen Verhalten der Unternehmen und der Interaktionen auf den Pinnwänden. Die verschiedenen Typen sind folgende:

Passive Brands sind wie der Name sagt passive Marken, die gar keine Interaktion mit den ihren Fans betreiben.

Sender Brands sind Marken die ihre Pinnwand als Sprachrohr benutzen, in dem nur sie selber Beiträge auf ihrer Pinnwand veröffentlichen können und dies den Fans vorenthalten, sondern ihnen nur einräumen die Unternehmensbeiträge zu kommentieren oder zu *liken*. Die Inhalte der Beiträge sind Informationen zu Sponsorenaktivitäten, Kampagnen, Events, Neuigkeiten oder Aktionen auf den anderen Plattformen des Unternehmens. Es wird eine Push-Strategie verfolgt.

Host Brands posten wenig selber auf die Pinnwand und suchen nicht den Dialog mit den Fans, von denen die meiste Aktivität auf Pinnwand ausgeht, dies wiederum in großem Maße durch Foto-Uploads mit einem Produkt der Marke. Die Unternehmen verleihen den anderen Reitern mehr Priorität. Es wird eine Pull-Strategie verfolgt.

Friend Brands bauen eine persönliche Bindung mit den Fans auf die über die Produkte der Marke hinausgehen. Das Unternehmen bringt sich sehr aktiv in den Pinnwand-Dialog ein und animiert die Fans dazu mit ihr in Kontakt zu treten. Die Aussagen und Anfragen der Fans werden von der Marke ernst genommen. Es wird eine Interaktions-Strategie verfolgt.

Service Brands nutzen die Pinnwand zum Dialog mit den Fans um Probleme zu lösen, Kundenservice zu betreiben und echten Nutzen zu erschaffen für beide Seiten. Die Kunden haben eine Alternative zur Kundenhotline oder dem Email-Kontaktformular und die Unternehmen betreiben ihr Customer-Relationship-Management in einem öffentlichen Kanal. Die Problemlösung findet zeitnah und teilweise auch durch andere Fans unterstützt statt (Zucker.Kommunikation, 2011).

Im Trendreport 2011 stellten sich dazu noch branchenspezifische Unterschiede bei den Interaktionsraten heraus. Die Hersteller von Fast Moving Consumer Goods (FMCG) boten dabei die niedrigsten Interaktionsraten auf mit Werten von 1,1% im Schnitt, die Automobilhersteller mit durchschnittlich 2,3% die höchsten. Diese größere Aktivität könnte darauf zurückzufuhren sein, dass Konsumenten sich mit High-Involvement Gütern viel intensiver beschäftigen als mit Alltagsprodukten, also Low Involvement Gütern, und bei Zufriedenheit eine höhere Loyalität entwickeln. Ebenso ist anzunehmen, dass sich die Differenzen auf der realen Markenbindung basieren. Somit schaffen es die Automobilhersteller besonders gut die reale Markenbindung in die sozialen Netzwerke zu transferieren. Auf High-Involvement Käufe geht Kapitel 2.4 noch weiter ein im Laufe der Arbeit.

Die Altimeter Group aus Kalifornien hat mit Hilfe einer Vielzahl an Agenturen, Vermarktern und Experten acht Erfolgskriterien für das Betreiben eine Unternehmensseite auf Facebook herausgestellt und die Facebook Pages von 34 Unternehmen in den jeweiligen Kriterien benotet. Die Ergebnisse werden nun nicht erwähnt, jedoch die aufgestellten Kriterien:

1. Erwartungen an die Community festlegen
2. Zusammenhängendes Branding bieten
3. Aktuell zu sein
4. Glaubwürdigkeit ausstrahlen
5. Am Dialog teilnehmen
6. Fan-zu-Fan Interaktionen ermöglichen
7. Befürwortung fördern
8. Zur Handlung aufrufen

(Altimeter Group, 2011)

Ein Beispiel für mangelnde Authentizität und versuchte Manipulation bietet ein Vorfall auf der amerikanischen Facebook Seite von Honda. Nach dem kritische Fan-Äußerungen über das Design eines neuen Modells verfasst wurden, versuchte ein Honda Produktmanager die Meinungen zu beeinflussen in dem er sich für das Modell aussprach durch und angebliches Interesse bekundete. Er machte sich dabei nicht als Produktmanager kenntlich und wurde von Fans enttarnt als die sein Profil auf LinkedIn entdeckten und im Dialog verlinkten. Dies sorgte für Aufruhe, weil sich die Fans einer Täuschung ausgesetzt fühlten. Honda löschte den Kommentar mit Angabe von Gründen (Stuber, 2010, S. 54).

Auch Facebook selbst gibt den Administratoren von Facebook Seiten einige Ratschläge an die Hand. Im Facebook Pages Guide werden in dem Kapitel der Dialogführung unter anderem folgende Vorgehensweisen:

– Teilen Sie Neuigkeiten und exklusive Inhalte

– Ermutigen Sie Fans zur Teilnahme

– Belohne Sie die Fans

– Behandeln Sie negatives Feedback

(Facebook Inc., 2011)

2.4 High-Involvement Käufe

Diese Art von Erwerben meint Kaufentscheidungen für Güter und Dienstleistungen mit denen ein hoher Suchaufwand sowie ein persönliches Risiko einhergehen. Der Konsument durchläuft hierbei die Bewertungs- und Vergleichsprozesse mit einer größeren Tiefe und Gründlichkeit als es bei Low-Involvement Erwerben der Fall ist. Dabei werden mehr Zeit und Aufmerksamkeit in die Suchphase vor der Kaufentscheidung investiert um das Produkt bzw. die Dienstleistung zu finden, das die subjektiven Anspruchskriterien am besten erfüllt. Hierbei findet eine Bestimmung / Abgleichung der Zielerreichungsgrade eines jeden zu vergleichenden Produktes statt anhand der vom Konsumenten persönlich gewichteten Prioritäten einzelner Attribute (Lake, 2009, S. 34). Die Preisniveaus für solche Produkte und Dienstleistung sind in der Regel hoch, da sie eines der Hauptrisiken für den Konsumenten darstellen.

Die Automobilindustrie hat gesamtwirtschaftlich gesehen eine große Bedeutung und den Produkten dieses Wirtschaftszweiges wird daher viel Aufmerksamkeit seitens der Gesellschaft und der Endverbraucher entgegen gebracht (Peter, 2001, S. 151).

2.5 Kundenzufriedenheit und Kundenbindung in der Automobil-Branche

Der Aufbau von Beziehungen zu Neukunden ist für Unternehmen fünfmal so teuer wie die Pflege und der Ausbau von Beziehungen zu Bestandskunden (Safko, 2010, S. 6). Diese empirische Erkenntnis kombiniert mit der hohen Marktsättigung und Konkurrenzintensität in der Automobilbranche verdeutlicht wie wichtig es für Unternehmen ist seine Kunden zu binden und zu halten (Peter, 2001, S. 151). Nach Bruhn & Homburg ist die Bindung des Kunden und daraus resultierender ökonomischer Erfolg ein mehrstufiger Prozess der sich in einer Wirkungskette darstellen lässt (Bruhn & Homburg, 2010, S. 10).

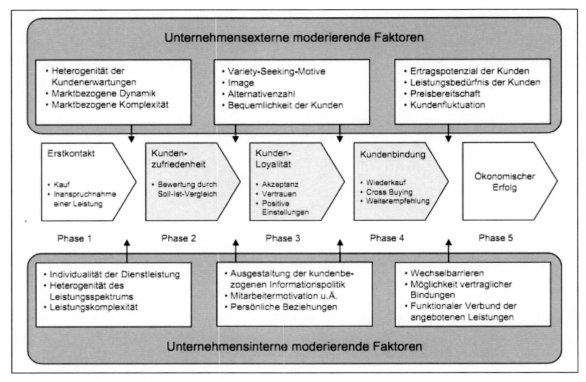

Abbildung 9: Wirkungskette der Kundenbindung (Bruhn & Homburg, 2010, S. 10)

Erfolgreiche und langfristige Bindung lässt sich demnach nur durch vorher eingetretene Zufriedenheit und Loyalität beim Kunden erzeugen. Einer der unternehmensinternen moderierenden Faktoren ist die persönliche Beziehung. Hier gilt es das Vertrauen des Kunden zu gewinnen und sowohl mit dem eigenen Produkt als auch dem angebotenen Service zu überzeugen. Social Media kann für Unternehmen ein Hilfsmittel sein, diese persönliche Beziehung aufzubauen und zu verstärken.

Nach umfassender wissenschaftlicher Prüfung hat Sybille Isabelle Peter eine auf Automobilhersteller angepasste Anwendung eines Basismodells zur Erklärung von Kundenbindung dargestellt und die Hypothesen zu den Ursachen-Wirkungszusammenhängen umformuliert.

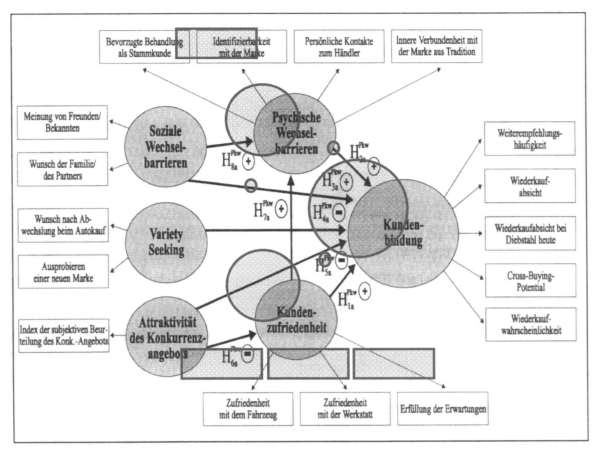

Abbildung 5: Kausalmodell zur Erklärung von Kundenbindung bei einem Automobilhersteller

(Peter, 2001, S. 198) mit eigenen Hervorhebungen

Es wurden im Verlauf des Buches Varianten erstellt um einzelne Hypothese zu ergänzen oder zu entfernen, doch die daraus gewonnen Kenntnisse sind für diese Arbeit nicht relevant. Beachtung schenkt die Arbeit nur der Kundenbindung, der Kundenzufriedenheit und den psychischen Wechselbarrieren sowie Beziehungen und die sich darauf beziehenden Hypothesen.

Bezeich-nung	Ursache-Wirkungszusammenhang
H_{1a}^{Pkw}	Je höher die Zufriedenheit eines Abnehmers mit der Leistung des betreffenden Pkw-Herstellers ist, als desto stärker erweist sich seine Bindung an diesen Anbieter.
H_{2a}^{Pkw}	Je höher die psychischen Wechselbarrieren sind, die ein Kunde gegenüber dem betreffenden Hersteller empfindet, desto stärker ist seine Bindung an das Unternehmen.
H_{3a}^{Pkw}	Je höher die sozialen Wechselbarrieren sind, denen sich ein Abnehmer in der Geschäftsbeziehung zu dem Pkw-Hersteller ausgesetzt sieht, desto stärker ist seine Bindung an den betreffenden Anbieter.
H_{4a}^{Pkw}	Je stärker ein Kunde beim Erwerb eines Fahrzeugs den Wunsch nach Abwechslung verspürt, desto geringer ist seine Bindung an den Hersteller seines derzeitigen Wagens.
H_{5a}^{Pkw}	Je attraktiver das Konkurrenzangebot in den Augen eines Kunden erscheint, als desto niedriger erweist sich seine Bindung an das betrachtete Automobilunternehmen.
H_{6a}^{Pkw}	Als je attraktiver ein Abnehmer ein Konkurrenzangebot erachtet, desto niedriger ist seine Zufriedenheit mit der Leistung des betrachteten Pkw-Herstellers.
H_{7a}^{Pkw}	Je zufriedener ein Abnehmer mit dem Leistungsangebot des Pkw-Anbieters ist, desto stärker ausgeprägt sind seine psychischen Wechselbarrieren gegenüber diesem Unternehmen.
H_{8a}^{Pkw}	Je stärker ausgeprägt die sozialen Wechselbarrieren eines Abnehmers gegenüber dem Pkw-Hersteller sind, als desto höher erweisen sich seine psychischen Wechselhemmnisse.

Abbildung 61: Hypothesen der Modellvariante für Automobilhersteller (Peter, 2001, S. 199)

Die markierten Hypothesen und Ursachen-Wirkungszusammenhänge lassen sich die Tätigkeiten der Unternehmen auf ihren Facebook Seiten übertragen.

H1: Die Leistung des Pkw-Herstellers wird durch den Service auf der Facebook Seite ergänzt. Wenn der Hersteller sich hier gut zu vertreten weiß, dem Abnehmer bei Fragen und Problemen hilfreich zur Seite steht und sich der Beschwerden annimmt, kann dies die Zufriedenheit mit Leistung steigern und somit die Bindung an das Unternehmen stärken. Somit sind ein gewisses Engagement und der Einsatz ausreichender Ressourcen notwendig, um dieses Potenzial auszuschöpfen.

H2: Die psychischen Wechselbarrieren werden noch im Verlauf dieses Kapitels erläutert. Um sich auf das Kausalmodell zu beziehen, ist für Unternehmen auf Facebook vor allem der Faktor Identifizierbarkeit mit der Marke beeinflussbar. Durch persönlichen Umgang und Zuwendung sowie der Aufbau eines Gemeinschaftsgefühls in einer Brand Community können die Kunden stärker an das Unternehmen gebunden werden. Wie sich in der Untersuchung der Fallbeispiele später herausstellen wird, können auch die persönlichen Kontakte zum Händler nachträglich beeinflusst werden, so etwa im Falle eines Fehlverhaltens Wiedergutmachung betrieben werden.

H7: Das Ausmaß an Kundenzufriedenheit wirkt sich ebenfalls auf den Aufbau von psychischen Wechselbarrieren aus. Die schon H1 erwähnten Maßnahmen führen zur Steigerung der Zufriedenheit. Im Umkehrschluss resultiert aus nicht erfüllten Erwartungen an das Produkt und den Service, der auf Facebook eingeschlossen, ein sinkende Zufriedenheit. Diese schwächt wiederum die Bindung an die Marke und die Wirkung der psychischen Wechselbarrieren, das Risiko eines Abgangs des Kunden wächst.

Unter Wechselbarrieren versteht man generell Hemmnisse jeglicher Art, die einem Kunden das Wechseln des Anbieters bzw. Geschäftspartner erschweren oder unmöglich machen. Wechselbarrieren lassen sich in drei Verschiedene Kategorien einteilen: Ökonomische, soziale und psychische Wechselbarrieren. Letztere beiden gehen vom Kunden aus und haben sind somit emotional bedingt, ökonomische Wechselbarrieren hingegen sind auf Wechselkosten zurückzuführen und der daher nötigen Abwägung des Kunden über Rentabilität eines Wechsels (Peter, 2001, S. 117f). Das Eingehen auf die Ausprägungen von Wechselbarrieren, Lock-in-Effekte und die Unterscheidung zwischen Gebundenheit und Verbundenheit des Kunden würde zu sehr vom Thema abweichen und es werden somit nur die relevanten Faktoren erörtert.

Psychische Wechselbarrieren resultieren aus einer positiven emotionalen Affinität zum Anbieter. Daraus folgt, dass der Kunde aus eigener Überzeugung nicht eigenmächtig wechseln will. Ein wichtiger Faktor dafür ist Vertrauen. Es bewirkt, dass der Kunde sich nicht den Anbieter und seine Aktivitäten nicht kritisch kontrolliert. Vertrauen wird in einem aufbauen Prozess gewonnen durch mehrere Geschäftsabwicklungen und den daraus entstehenden positiven Erfahrungen. Andere Gründe für psychische Wechselbarrieren sind unter anderem von Kunden geführte Traditionen einer Marke treu zu bleiben oder hohe Identifikationsgrade mit dem Image des Unternehmens, der Marke und der Produkte, vor allem wenn diese Statussymbol dienen (Peter, 2001, S. 120f).

Eben jene Wechsel psychischer Art lassen sich durch kommunikativen Kontakt mit derzeitigen oder potenziellen Kunden aufbauen. Kommunikation mit derzeitigen und potenziellen Kunden kann sowohl die psychischen Wechselbarrieren aufbauen als auch beim Beschwerdemanagement behilflich sein, was den Abbau von Unzufriedenheit ermöglicht (Peter, 2001, S. 248).

Wie sowohl aus der Wirkungskette nach Bruhn & Homburg als auch aus dem Kausalmodell nach Peter hervorgeht, ist ein gewisses Maß an Kundenzufriedenheit notwendig um die Kunden zu binden. Durch eine hohe Bindung können weitere Transaktionen folgen, entweder vom gleichen Kunden durch Wiederkauf oder Cross-Buying, oder durch einen neuen Kunden, den der Bestandskunde durch Weiterempfehlungen auf das Unternehmen aufmerksam gemacht und dazu bewogen hat. Aus diesen Transaktionen resultiert wiederum ökonomischer Erfolg für das Unternehmen durch größere Umsätze.

Daraus erschließt sich folgendes: Unternehmen müssen sich zunächst bemühen und in die Maximierung der Kundenzufriedenheit investieren, wie nun auch durch den Einsatz von Social Media, um später daraus Gewinne und Profite zu erzielen.

2.6   Forschungsleitende Annahmen

Facebook kann Unternehmen ein brauchbares Werkzeug sein in deren Repertoire der Kommunikations-Kanäle und im Kundenbeziehungsmanagement, wenn es richtig eingesetzt wird. Doch was macht diesen richtigen Einsatz überhaupt aus? Ist eine hohe Anzahl an Fans ein Erfolgskriterium für eine gute Fan-Page? Vielleicht sogar eins der entscheidenden? Sind Unternehmen mit großen Fan-Mengen aktiver als die mit weniger Anhängern? Wie sehr sollte man sich um den Fan-Zuwachs bemühen? Welche Informationen geben die Unternehmen ihren Fans Preis? Wo liegen die Unterschiede und Mehrwerte zur Unternehmenswebsite? Wie verhalten sich die Unternehmen im Dialog mit den Fans? Für welche Zwecke benutzen die Unternehmen den Facebookauftritt? Welche Art von Beiträgen verfassen die Unternehmen? Wie oft veröffentlich sie etwas? Wie sieht die Reaktion der Fans auf die Beiträge aus? Was schreiben die Fans auf die Pinnwände der Unternehmen? Loben oder kritisieren die Fans die Marke? Wie reagieren die Unternehmen auf Beschwerden? Treten die Unternehmen den Fans anonym gegenüber auf oder sind die zuständigen Mitarbeiter bekannt? Zu welchen Tageszeiten schreiben und antworten die Unternehmen?

Hierzu wurden die Pinnwände auf den Facebook Seiten untersucht und ausgewertet, um zu erfahren ob und wie die Unternehmen mit ihren Fans interagieren. Da bei der Auswahl ausschließlich Unternehmen ausgewählt wurden, die es ihren Fans genehmigt hat selber Beiträge auf der Pinnwand zu veröffentlichen, ist die Grundvoraussetzung für Interaktion gegeben.

3 Empirische Forschung

3.1 Forschungsmethodik

3.1.1 Vorgehensweise

Bei der Auswahl der zu untersuchenden Facebookauftritte von Unternehmen wurde zunächst die Entscheidung getroffen sich auf eine einzige Branche zu konzentrieren. Dies grenzt sowohl das Feld an möglichen Untersuchungsobjekten ein und soll durch die Ähnlichkeit der Produkte und die daraus resultierende Konkurrenz der Unternehmen eine bessere Vergleichbarkeit der Forschungsergebnisse der Arbeit gewährleisten. Zunächst wurde die Branche der Fast Moving Consumer Goods in Betracht gezogen, genauer gesagt die Schokoladenhersteller/-marken Lindt, Ritter Sport und Milka. Jedoch wurde dies umgeändert und die Automobilbranche als zu untersuchende Branche ausgewählt.

Daraufhin galt es alle gängigen Automobilhersteller auf Facebook ausfindig zu machen mit der Einschränkung, dass es sich hierbei um einen ausschließlichen deutschsprachigen Auftritt handeln sollte. Diese Limitierung wurde auferlegt, um die Größe der Fan-Communities in einem annähernd vergleichbaren Rahmen zu halten und bei der Untersuchung der Interaktionen Sprachbarrieren auf internationalen Facebook Pages aus dem Weg zu gehen.

Diverse Automobilhersteller-Auflistungen aus dem Internet wurden abgeglichen und daraufhin auf Facebook über die Sucheingabe gesucht. Die Eingabekombination von *Herstellername + Deutschland* brachte hierbei weitestgehend Erfolge, alternativ waren eine Vielzahl der Seiten auch über einen Link auf den internationalen Facebook Pages der Hersteller aufzufinden. Das Untersuchungsfeld reduzierte sich somit auf eine Anzahl von 20 Herstellern. Unerwarteter Weise bietet Volkswagen seinen Kunden in der Konzernheimat keine eigene deutsche Facebook Page auf Facebook an. Für sie ist die Nutzung des internationalen Profils vorgesehen, wo hingegen eine Vielzahl anderer Nationen eine eigene Facebook Page gewidmet bekommt. Die Anfrage auf der Pinnwand der internationalen Volkswagen Facebook Page wurde zügig beantwortet mit der Erklärung, dass eine deutsche Facebook Seite sich noch in der Planungsphase befinde und bald online gehen werde (Schmitt, 2011).

Abbildung 72: Frage nach deutscher Facebook Seite (Volkswagen International, 2011)

Weitere bedeutende Hersteller, die keine eigene Facebook Seite für den deutschen Markt während des Untersuchungszeitraums hatten, sind Porsche, Alfa Romeo, Nissan, Suzuki und Toyota. Skoda bietet zwar eine deutschsprachige Facebook Seite, doch ist diese klar dem Markt Österreich zugeschrieben und wurde somit außen vorgelassen bei der Untersuchung.

Der Zeitraum für die Untersuchung war mit einer Dauer von zwei Wochen abgesteckt, welche um 00:00 Uhr am 11.07.2011 begannen und um 23:59 Uhr am 24.07.2011 zu Ende gingen. Hierbei wurde zunächst quantitativ gemessen, in dem alle Pinnwand-Einträge, die von den Fans der Seite sowie vom betreibenden Unternehmen selbst veröffentlicht wurden, erfasst wurden samt aller darauf folgenden Kommentare und Gefällt-mir-Klicks. Die seit einigen Monaten verfügbare Funktion auch bei Kommentaren den Gefällt-mir-Button betätigen zu können, wurde in der Untersuchung nicht berücksichtigt. Zudem erfasst die Untersuchung ob und mit welchen Zusatzmedien ein Beitrag verfasst wurde. Hier zu stehen den Unternehmen und ihren Anhängern die Möglichkeit zur Verfügung Fotos, Videos oder Links an ihre Textbeiträge anzuhängen. Unternehmen können zudem noch Umfragen starten und diese von den Anhängern beantworten lassen, jedoch haben davon nur wenige Unternehmen Gebrauch gemacht, weshalb diese Beitragsform nicht beachtet wurde.

Da sich die Fan-Mengen der Unternehmen in ihrer Größe sehr unterscheiden wird zur Vergleichbarkeit der Aktivitäten eine Interaktionsrate ermittelt. Diese ermittelt wie viele Interaktionen, sprich eigene Beiträge, Kommentare und Gefällt-mir-Klicks zu Beiträgen des Unternehmens und anderer Teilnehmer pro 100 Fans erfolgten und bietet somit eine Vergleichbarkeit unabhängig von der Gesamtgröße der Fan-Menge. Des Weiteren stellt die Arbeit mehrere Statistikwerte und Verhältnisse dar, die aus den gemessenen Interaktionen errechnet wurden. Diese werden in Tortendiagrammen oder Tabellen dargestellt. In den Tabellen sind die Ranglisten durch Farbverläufe in Dreiergruppen eingeteilt. Leuchtend grün markiert dabei die Spitzengruppe, leuchtend rot die letzten drei Marken.

3.1.2 Forschungsmethodik

Bei der Erforschung von Medieninhalten erweist es sich als nützlich aufgrund der hohen Komplexität sich bewährter Methodiken zu bedienen. In dieser Arbeit wird daher die Inhaltsanalyse verwendet. Für die Analyse von Dialogen auf Facebook-Pinnwänden wie es sich diese Arbeit zur Aufgabe gemacht hat, gelten folgende Charakteristika, die die Inhaltsanalyse als passende Methode bestätigen.

1. „Die Inhaltsanalyse erlaubt die Aussagen über Kommunikatoren und Rezipienten, die nicht bzw. nicht mehr erreichbar sind.
2. Der Forscher ist nicht auf die Kooperationen von Versuchspersonen angewiesen.
3. Der Faktor Zeit spielt für die Untersuchung eine untergeordnete Rolle; man ist in der Regel nicht an bestimmte Termine zur Datenerhebung und Datenanalyse gebunden.
4. Es tritt keine Veränderung des Untersuchungsobjekts durch die Untersuchung auf.
5. Die Untersuchung ist beliebig reproduzierbar oder mit einem modifizierten Analyseinstrument am selben Gegenstand wiederholbar.
6. Inhaltsanalysen sind meist billiger als andere Datenerhebungsmethoden." (Früh, 2007)

Der Nutzen der Inhaltsanalyse ist die Reduktion der Komplexität, wobei nicht benötigte Informationen verloren gehen und sich auf forschungsrelevante Mitteilungsmerkmale konzentriert wird. Durch die bewusst eingeschränkte Perspektive werden neue Zusammenhänge erschlossen und neue Informationen gewonnen, die vorher nicht in der Form vorlagen (Früh, 2007, S. 42).

Nach den Definitionen von Rössler erfolgte die Zerlegung und Einteilung in die vier Typen der Einheiten (Rössler, 2005, S. 40). Als Auswahleinheiten wurden alle deutschsprachigen Facebook-Seiten von Automobilherstellern festgelegt. Als Analyseeinheiten gelten alle während des Untersuchungszeitraums veröffentlichten Pinnwandbeiträge. Zu den Codiereinheiten gehören die Inhalte der Beiträge (formal und inhaltlich), deren medialen Anhänge (formal), Gefällt-mir-Klicks (formal) und Kommentare (formal) sowie die inhaltlichen Kategorien (inhaltlich).

Die Beiträge auf den Pinnwänden lassen sich zunächst in zwei Dimensionen einteilen. (Früh, 2007, S. 83). Entweder sie wurden vom Unternehmen veröffentlicht oder von den Fans. Für beide Dimensionen gilt es daraufhin Unterkategorien zu bilden. Sie dienen der thematischen Zuordnung der inhaltlichen Codiereinheiten *Inhalte der Beiträge*. Die aufgestellten Kategorien können jeweils nur zwei Ausprägungen annehmen, ob der Beitrag zu dieser Kategorie gehört oder nicht, die somit als dichotome Variablen bezeichnet werden können (Früh, 2007, S. 84). Die Trennschärfe der Kategoriensysteme ist in der Inhaltsanalyse der Arbeit gegeben, jedoch sind die in den Codiereinheiten zu findenden Indikatoren nicht immer disjunkt einer Kategorie zuweisbar gewesen (Früh, 2007, S. 87f). Bei der Kategorienzuordnung werden sowohl diagnostische als auch prognostische Ansätze verfolgt. Somit interpretiert diese Arbeit sowohl die Absichten der Beitragsverfasser als auch die möglich eintretenden Wirkungen beim Leser der Beiträge (Früh, 2007, S. 44). Objektivität bei der Interpretation gewährleistet theoretisch die Nachvollziehbarkeit von Forschungsergebnissen. Jedoch ist faktisch betrachtet Objektivität nicht sicherzustellen, da die Wahrnehmung verschiedener Mensch nie in vollem Umfang komplett identisch sein kann. Daher lautet die Prämisse für Inhaltsanalysen intersubjektiv nachvollziehbare Interpretationen zu tätigen (Rössler, 2005, S. 20f).

Es wurde hieraus resultierend folgende inhaltliche Kategorien erstellt für die Pinnwandbeiträge der Fans:

Lob & Sympathiebekundung (Abkürzung - LS): Der Fan verfasst ein Lob über den Hersteller, die Marke oder einzelne Produkte. Er bekennt sich zu dem Gebrauch und identifiziert sich mit der Marke. Neben rein verbalen Bekundungen können dies auch Fotos sein von Fahrzeugen, die der Fan besitzt oder die ihm gefallen.

Beschwerde, Kritik oder Verbesserungsvorschlag (BK): Der Fan verkündet seine Unzufriedenheit gegenüber dem Hersteller. Dies kann durch einen Defekt beim Fahrzeug sein oder ein Mangel beim Service durch die Händler oder die Kundenbetreuung sein. Ebenso äußert er Verbesserungsvorschläge zum Produkt oder der Leistungserstellung.

Informationsbedarf & Fragen (IF): Hierbei stellt der Fan explizite Fragen an das Unternehmen bzw. die zuständigen Angestellten. Dies können Fakten zu einem Produkt sein, der Status verschiedener Prozesse und Vorgänge oder zu anderen Dingen.

Werbung in eigener Sache (WS): Zu dieser Kategorie gehören Beiträge, in denen Fans auf Internetseiten und -artikel verlinken oder den Verkauf eines Fahrzeugs bewerben als auch andere Beiträge, die nicht die anderen drei Kategorien eingeordnet werden können.

Für die Beiträge der Unternehmen wurden folgende sechs Kategorien gebildet:

Rennsport, Events und Sponsoring (RES): In dieser Kategorie finden sich Beiträge des Unternehmens die Neuigkeiten aus der eigenen Rennsportsparte, zu veranstalteten Events oder Sponsoring-Partnern betreffen.

Gewinnspiele und Verlosungen (GWV): Dies umfasst sowohl Ankündigungen von Gewinnspielen und Verlosungen als auch die Bekanntgabe der Gewinner dieser Aktionen.

Marktforschung (MaFo): Diese Beiträge nutzen dem Unternehmen zu Zwecken der Marktforschung. Hierbei werden die Fans durch eine explizite Fragestellung zur Meinungsäußerung bezüglich eines Produkts oder ähnlichem aufgefordert.

Reine Informationsbeiträge (Info): Hierbei werden den Fans relativ nüchtern und objektiv Informationen vermittelt. Das Unternehmen fordert nicht zum Dialog auf, noch versucht es besonders auf subjektive Art und Weise die eigenen Produkte zu bewerben.

Marketingzwecke (MK): Mit Verfassung dieser Beiträge versuchen Unternehmen durch Branding die Kundenbindung zu erhöhen und die eigene Marke samt Produkte zu präsentieren und zu bewerben.

Dialog (DIA): In diesen Beiträgen sucht das Unternehmen den Dialog mit seinen Fans in dem es sie durch explizite Fragestellung zur Abgabe von Kommentaren animiert. Thema dieser Dialoge sind jedoch nicht zwangsläufig die Produkte des Unternehmens wie bei der Kategorie Marktforschung. Es können auch Danksagungen an die Fans darin enthalten sein.

Für die quantitative Inhaltsanalyse in dieser Arbeit wurden somit folgende Kategorien aufgestellt:

- Wie viele Fans haben die Unternehmensseiten? (Zahl der Fans)
- Wie groß ist der Zuwachs in den zwei Wochen gewesen? (Zuwachs an Fans)
- Verlinken die Unternehmen von ihrer Website aus auf die Fan-Page? (Ja/Nein)
- Wie viele Beiträge veröffentlichen die Unternehmen selbst? (Anzahl an Beiträgen der Unternehmen)
- Wozu nutzen Unternehmen die Beiträge? (RES, GWV, MaFo, Info, MK, DIA)
- Welche Medien nutzen die Unternehmen in ihren Beiträgen? (Anzahl an Beiträgen mit Links, Fotos, Videos oder ohne Anhang)
- In welchem Umfang interagieren die Fans mit dem Unternehmen? (Beiträge, Kommentare und Gefällt-mir-Klicks)
- Wie aktiv sind die Unternehmen gemessen an ihrer Fan-Anzahl? (Unternehmens-Interaktionsrate)
- Antworten sie anonym oder werden Personen/Autoren bekannt gegeben? (Ja/Nein)
- Zu welchen Tageszeiten antworten diese? (Früheste und späteste gemessene Uhrzeit einer Aktivität)
- Wozu nutzen die Fans die Beiträge? (LS, BK, WS, IF)

Im Anschluss erfolgt noch eine qualitative Inhaltsanalyse, in der Fallbeispiele präsentiert und untersucht werden. Die eingefügten Screenshots bilden zunächst den stattgefundenen Dialog ab, danach geht die Analyse auf die Inhalte, Problemstellungen und möglichen Folgen ein. Dabei wird bewertet wie die Marke durch die Autoren bzw. Administratoren vertreten wurde und wie sich dabei um die Anliegen der Fans kümmerten.

3.2 Ergebnisse der empirischen Forschung

3.2.1 Quantitative Forschung

Zunächst ist zu erwähnen, dass sich im Laufe der Untersuchung die Anzahl der Unternehmen von 20 auf 18 reduziert hat. Die Facebook Seiten der Hersteller Jaguar und Lexus boten nicht genug Pinnwandbeiträge für die Untersuchung. Im Falle von Jaguar lässt sich dies durch die geringe Fan-Zahl von 92 Fans und dem Startdatum der Seite erklären. Sie wurde am 5. Mai 2011 öffentlich erstellt und hat in der Zwischenzeit noch nicht in großem Maße wachsen können, was vermutlich auch mit der Zielgruppe der Marke zusammenhängt. Lexus hingegen hatte zum Ende der Untersuchungszeit 13.095 Fans, was einen Platz 9 unter den 20 untersuchten Unternehmen bedeuten würde. Ein Mangel an Markensympathisanten besteht also nicht. Stattdessen ist auf fehlende Initiative seitens des Unternehmens zu schließen, die Anhänger zum interaktiven Dialog und Austausch mit der Marke zu animieren.

Die Betrachtung der Fan-Zahlen der anderen 18 Hersteller stellt enorme Größenunterschiede dar. Audi führt das Untersuchungsfeld mit fast 200.000 Fans und hat damit mehr als hundertzwanzigmal so viele Anhänger wie smart mit einer Menge von 1.644 Fans. BMW, Mercedes-Benz und Opel setzen sich auch noch deutlich vom Rest des Feldes ab. Daher liegt das arithmetische Mittel von 30.780 Fans weit höher als der Median bei 10.805 Fans. Insgesamt hatten zwölf Hersteller jeweils als weniger 20.000 Fans, acht befanden sich sogar unter der Marke von 10.000. Die größten und kleinsten Zuwachsraten über die Dauer des Untersuchungszeitraumes verteilen sich unabhängig von der Fan-Menge.

Name	Fan-Menge	relativer Zuwachs
Audi	199.799	3,4
Mercedes-Benz	92.344	4,3
BMW	84.416	2,4
Opel	54.778	1,4
Ford	24.246	1,2
Mazda	19.533	0,1
MINI	18.932	2,6
Citroen	14.065	6,0
Peugeot	11.061	1,1
Volvo	10.548	1,0
KIA	9.641	0,3
Chevrolet	9.483	18,0
Renault	8.866	0,9
Fiat	3.802	13,2
Seat	3.442	2,7
Honda	2.707	
Hyundai	2.418	11,1
smart	1.644	69,5
Mittelwerte	**31.763**	**8,2**

Tabelle 2: Fan-Mengen und relative Zuwächse (Stand: 25.07.2011)

Um diese Mengenunterschiede ausgleichen und relativieren zu können, wurden Interaktionsraten errechnet. Sie geben an wie viel Interaktion vom Unternehmen ausgegangen ist auf 10.000 Fans hochgerechnet. Unter Interaktionen werden in diesem Fall das Verfassen von Beiträgen vom Unternehmen selbst gezählt, sowie Kommentare und Gefällt-mir-Klicks zu den eigenen Beiträgen und denen der Fans. Hierbei ist die Tendenz zu erkennen, dass die Interaktionsrate der Unternehmen mit steigenden Fan-Zahlen abnimmt. Inaktivster Automobilhersteller ist Mercedes-Benz mit einer IR von 0,76. Ebenfalls auffällig ist der Vergleich zwischen Honda und Hyundai. Die Fan-Menge unterscheidet sich nur um wenige 100 Zähler, jedoch ist Honda mit einer IR von 110 das aktivste Unternehmen pro 10.000 Fans, wo hingegen Hyundai mit einer IR von 37 nah am Mittelwert liegt.

Jedoch ist dieser Befund alleine noch nicht aussagekräftig über die Unternehmensaktivität im Pinnwanddialog. Hier bringt die Arbeit noch zwei weitere Messdaten für jede Facebook Page hervor: Die Summe an Unternehmens- Interaktionen (SUI) und die prozentuale Verteilung von Posts, Kommentaren und Gefällt-mir-Klicks.

Die SUI gibt an wie viele Interaktionen vom Unternehmen in den zwei Wochen getätigt wurden, wohin gegen die prozentuale Verteilung Aufschluss darüber gibt in welcher Form dies geschah. Sowohl bei den Interaktionen der Unternehmen als auch der Fans sind Posts und Kommentare als hochwertiger einzustufen aufgrund ihres Aussagewertes und der daran gebundenen intensiveren

Auseinandersetzung mit der Marke bzw. dem Kunden. Honda hat fast ausschließlich nur Beiträge verfasst oder Gefällt-mir geklickt und dabei nur einen einzigen Kommentar zu den Fan-Posts abgegeben. KIA hingegen als Autohersteller mit der höchsten SUI-Summe hat über die Hälfte seiner Interaktionen in Form von Kommentare erfolgen lassen. Ford als Unternehmen mit den zweitmeisten Interaktionen hat diese ungefähr zu je einem Drittel auf die drei Arten verteilt und damit am meisten *gepostet* und *gelinkte* zugleich. Fünf der Hersteller unterließen hingegen das *Ligen* komplett, wodurch der Anschein entsteht sie interagieren nur hochwertig durch Posts und Kommentare. Jedoch liegen diese Unternehmen auch allesamt in der unteren Hälfte der SUI-Rangliste und haben mäßige bis schlechte Interaktionsraten. Somit zeigt die quantitative Messung, dass alle drei Messwerte zusammen betrachtet erst wirklich Aufschluss geben können wie aktiv und aussagekräftig ein Unternehmen auf seiner Pinnwand mit den Kunden interagiert.

In Tabelle 4 sind die Fan-Interaktionsraten aufgeführt, ergänzt durch die Summen an Fan-Interaktionen (SFI) und deren prozentuale Verteilung. Die IR der Fans gibt an welcher prozentuale Anteil der Fans im Untersuchungszeitraum mit dem Unternehmen auf der Pinnwand interagiert hat. Wie auch beim Vergleich der IR der Unternehmen, ergänzen die Summe an Fan-Aktionen sowie die Verteilungen dieser die Wertung.

Marke	Unt.-IR	Sum. Unt-Interak.	rel - P/K/L
Honda	110,8	30	47% / 3% / 50%
KIA	83,0	80	10% / 58% / 33%
Chevrolet	58,0	55	31% / 50% / 19%
smart	48,7	8	54% / 31% / 15%
Seat	46,5	16	29% / 24% / 47%
Fiat	44,7	17	41% / 41% / 18%
Hyundai	37,2	9	67% / 33% / 0%
Ford	31,3	76	30% / 34% / 36%
Renault	25,9	23	52% / 48% / 0%
Peugeot	25,3	28	21% / 68% / 11%
Volvo	14,2	15	27% / 53% / 20%
Mazda	9,2	18	56% / 33% / 11%
MINI	9,0	17	71% / 29% / 0%
Opel	6,4	35	29% / 51% / 20%
Citroën	4,3	6	67% / 33% / 0%
BMW	1,5	13	46% / 38% / 15%
Audi	1,4	28	25% / 75% / 0%
Mercedes-Benz	0,8	7	86% / 14% / 0%
Mittelwerte	**31,0**	**26,7**	**4% / 20% / 76%**

Tabelle 3: Unternehmens-Interaktionsraten, Summen an Unternehmens-Interaktionen und Interaktionsverteilungen

Mit Honda, smart und Seat bringen drei der vier Marken mit den wenigsten Fans die besten Fan-IRs hervor. Die drei schlechtesten Fan-IRs stellen im Umkehrschluss aber nicht die Marken mit den größten Fan-Mengen. Die kleinste Fan-IR hat Mercedes-Benz, die Marke mit den zweitmeisten Fans. Die zweit- und drittschlechtesten Fan-IRs bringen mit Citroën und Volvo jedoch Marken hervor die von der Fan-Menge her im Mittelfeld des Untersuchungsrangliste stehen. Ein negativer Zusammenhang zwischen Fan-Menge und Fan-IR liegt also nicht so stark wie es beim Vergleich Fan-Menge und Unternehmens-IR der Fall ist.

Marke	Fan-IR	Sum. Fan-Interak.	Post / Komm. / Like
Honda	13,1	354	5% / 23% / 72%
smart	10,6	174	5% / 17% / 78%
Seat	9,7	335	2% / 25% / 73%
Fiat	7,8	295	5% / 56% / 39%
MINI	6,9	1.314	2% / 4% / 94%
Renault	6,5	579	2% / 14% / 84%
Chevrolet	6,2	588	3% / 18% / 79%
Hyundai	6,1	148	4% / 16% / 80%
KIA	6,1	584	12% / 33% / 55%
Audi	4,8	9.646	3% / 13% / 84%
Peugeot	4,5	495	3% / 23% / 74%
Mazda	4,2	826	7% / 17% / 76%
BMW	4,1	3.475	1% / 8% / 91%
Opel	4,1	2.240	3% / 18% / 79%
Ford	2,9	700	5% / 28% / 67%
Volvo	2,0	209	9% / 6% / 66%
Citroën	1,3	188	3% / 18% / 79%
Mercedes-Benz	1,2	1.130	1% / 7% / 92%
Mittelwerte	**5,7**	**1.293**	**4% / 20% / 76%**

Tabelle 4: Fan-Interaktionsraten, Summen an Fan-Interaktionen und Interaktionsverteilungen

Die Untersuchung der Interaktion kann noch weiter ins Detail heruntergebrochen werden. Der Resonanzindex ist im Grunde einer Interaktionsrate ähnlich. Aber der Übersichtlichkeit halber wird hier ein anderer Name gewählt. Dem Resonanzindex gehen mehrere Rechnungen voraus. Zunächst werden für alle Pinnwand-Beiträge einer Marke die Likes und Kommentare der Fans erfasst, ehe diese Summe durch die Anzahl der Beiträge dividiert wird. Im Anschluss wird dieser Quotient mit dem 1.000 multipliziert und durch die Menge der Fans dividiert. Somit erhält man den Anteil an Fans der durchschnittlich auf einen Unternehmens-Beitrag reagiert hat in Promille, dem eigens benannten Resonanzindex. Auch hier für diesen Statistikwert lässt sich kein klarer negativer Zusammenhang mit der Fan-Menge beobachten. Die fünf Marken mit den kleinsten Fan-Mengen, allesamt unter 4.000 Fans, besitzen zwar die größten Resonanzindizes, jedoch ist das Feld der darauf folgenden Marken durchmischt. Audi und BMW als die erst- bzw. drittgrößten Marken liegen im oberen Mittelfeld auf Platz sieben und neun in der Resonanzindex-Rangliste.

Name	Resonanzindex	Fan-Menge	Anzahl Posts
Seat	12,0	3.442	5
smart	11,6	1.644	7
Fiat	9,4	3.802	7
Hyundai	8,3	2.418	6
Honda	7,8	2.707	14
Peugeot	6,7	11.061	6
BMW	6,6	84.416	5
MINI	5,2	18.932	12
Audi	4,9	199.799	7
Renault	4,8	8.866	12
Opel	3,4	54.778	10
Chevrolet	3,3	9.483	17
Mazda	3,3	19.533	10
KIA	3,1	9.641	8
Citroën	3,0	14.065	4
Volvo	2,9	10.548	4
Mercedes-Benz	2,0	92.344	6
Ford	1,6	24.246	23
Mittelwerte	**5,6**	**31.763**	**9**

Tabelle 5: Resonanzindex

Die prozentuale Verteilung der inhaltlichen Kategorien für die Fan-Posts ergibt die Aufteilung wie sie in Abb. 10 zu sehen ist. Die für Unternehmen besonders relevanten Beiträge sind allgemein betrachtet vor allem jene, in denen Fans Kritik, Beschwerden & Verbesserungsvorschläge äußern (Kat. BK) oder Informationsbedarf & Fragen stellen, die sich in der Regel an die Marke richten und demnach auch von dieser beantwortet werden sollten (Kat. IF). Hier zeigt sich nämlich das wahre Engagement der Marken im Kundenkontakt. Es sind Kunden, die Probleme oder Fragen klären wollen, welche wiederum von Marken ernst genommen und entsprechenden Service geboten bekommen wollen. Der Durchschnitt für alle Seiten zusammen genommen ergibt einen Anteil von 7% an Kat. BK und 14% an Kat. IF. Addiert machen diese Kategorien nur ein Fünftel der Fan-Beiträge aus.

Kategorien Fan-Posts

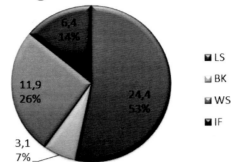

Abbildung 83: Kategorien Fan-Posts

Jedoch verfälschen die großen Mengen an Lob & Sympathiebekundungen (Kat. LS) auf der Audi-Pinnwand diese Durchschnittswerte. Dies geschah zum Großteil durch Fotos der Fans von ihrem eigenen oder einem anderen Audi-Modell. Daher wurden zur Berechnung der Durchschnittsverteilungen die Werte der Fan-Posts auf Audis Pinnwand nicht miteinbezogen. Die neuen Verteilungen sind in Abbildung 11 zu sehen. Die Anteile für Kat. BK sind auf 9% und für Kat. IF auf 21% gestiegen, was addiert etwas weniger als ein Drittel der Fan-Posts ausmachte.

Kategorien Fan-Posts ohne Audi

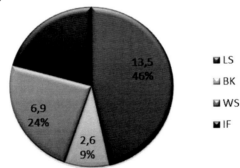

Abbildung 94: Kategorien Fan-Posts ohne Audi

Im Umkehrschluss bedeutet dies, dass Administratoren sich die wirklich wichtigen Beiträge, in denen die Kundenzufriedenheit gesteigert und verärgerte Fans besänftigt können, auf der Pinnwand heraussuchen müssen um dann im besten Sinne die Marke zu vertreten. Auf den Facebook Seiten mit besonders vielen Fans und Fan-Beiträgen ist diese Extraktion mit einem gewissen Such- und Zeitaufwand verbunden. Von daher sind große Fan-Mengen nicht immer ein pauschal ein erstrebenswertes Ziel.

Kategorien Unternehmens-Posts

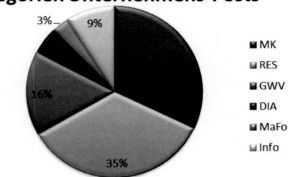

- MK
- RES
- GWV
- DIA
- MaFo
- Info

Abbildung 105: Kategorien Unternehmens-Posts

Das Diagramm in Abb. 14 gibt die Verteilung der Kategorien auf die Unternehmens- Beiträge wieder. Dabei sind Kategorien MK und RES die dominanten beiden mit jeweils rund einem Drittel Anteil. Und dabei haben einige der Hersteller gar keine Verbindung zum Rennsport, sonst würde der Anteil an RES wahrscheinlich noch größer ausfallen. Die Unternehmen benutzen also die Beiträge in großem Maße als Sprachrohr und verfolgen somit eine Push-Strategie um ihre Nachrichten zu verbreiten. Die eher dialogorientierten Kategorien DIA und MaFo werden kumuliert in weniger als 10% der Beiträge verwendet. Die Verteilungen sind für die einzelnen Hersteller jedoch höchst unterschiedlich, sodass diese Durchschnittswerte sich kaum in einem der Einzelfälle wiederspiegeln.

Von der Anzahl der veröffentlichten Posts im Untersuchungszeitraum liegen die Automarken ebenfalls weit auseinander. Das Feld führt Ford klar an mit 23 Beiträgen, Chevrolet kann noch 17 Beiträgen folgen. Dies sind aber auch die einzigen beiden Marken die damit im Schnitt mehr als zwei Beiträge pro Tag verfasst haben. Beide haben dabei jeweils unterschiedliche Anhänge favorisiert. Ford benutzte in über der Hälfte seiner Beiträge Videos, die Anhangsform die neben reinem Text am wenigsten benutzt wurde. Fotos und Links sind hier klar populärer. Zehn Marken kamen auf einen Tagesschnitt von einem verfassten Beitrag oder weniger im Untersuchungszeitraum, darunter auch die drei größten (Audi, BMW und Mercedes-Benz) und zwei kleinsten (smart und Hyundai) Facebook Seiten. Somit scheint die Frequenz beim Verfassen von Beiträgen nicht ausschlaggeben zu sein für den Erfolg gemessen in Fan-Zahlen.

Marke	Links	Fotos	Text	Videos	Posts Gesamt
Ford	1	9	0	13	23
Chevrolet	10	6	1	0	17
Honda	8	3	3	0	14
MINI	7	4	1	0	12
Renault	5	5	0	2	12
Mazda	4	4	2	0	10
Opel	1	6	1	2	10
KIA	5	1	0	2	8
Audi	3	4	0	0	7
Fiat	2	3	2	0	7
smart	2	3	1	1	7
BMW	3	2	0	1	6
Hyundai	0	6	0	0	6
Mercedes-Benz	5	1	0	0	6
Peugeot	1	5	0	0	6
Seat	3	1	0	1	5
Citroën	2	2	0	0	4
Volvo	2	1	1	0	4
Mittelwerte	**3,6**	**3,7**	**0,7**	**1,2**	**9,1**

Tabelle 6: Unternehmens-Posts und ihre medialen Anhänge

Ein weiterer Untersuchungspunkt auf den Facebook Seiten sollte zunächst auch zeitliche Messungen miteinbeziehen. Das empirische Statistikmaterial hat den frühesten und spätesten Zeitpunkt gemessen, zu denen die Administratoren durch Beiträge oder Antworten aktiv waren. Dies lässt zwar eine Zeitspanne errechnen, jedoch lässt sich davon nicht auf die Arbeitszeiten der Administratoren schließen. Sie lassen sich schlichtweg nicht einschätzen, da ebenso nicht erforscht werden konnte, ob sie für ihre Tätigkeit hauptberuflich zuständig sind oder es als zusätzliche Aufgabe aufgetragen bekommen haben. Eine externe Übernahme dieser Aufgaben durch Kommunikationsagenturen ist ebenso denkbar. Es wurde bei allen Marken angefragt wie dies bei ihnen geregelt wurde. Doch leider gab es nur von wenigen Marken Auskunft darüber und somit wurde dieser Punkt nicht in der Arbeit aufgeführt. Ebenso war zunächst geplant zu messen, wie lange die Marken brauchen auf Beiträge zu reagieren auf welche sie antworten müssen. Auch hier ist die fehlende Information über die Arbeitszeit ein Hindernis und lässt aussagekräftige Messungen nicht zu.

Abgesehen von den Pinnwänden galt es noch andere Dinge auf den Facebook Seiten zu erfassen, die eine Relevanz für das Thema der Arbeit haben.

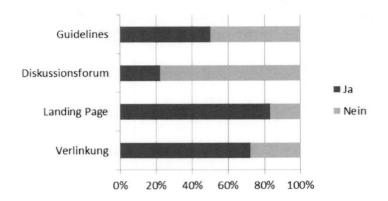

Abbildung 116: Vorhandensein von Foren, Landing Pages, Guidelines sowie Verlinkungen von der Unternehmenswebsite zur Facebook Seite

So wurden auch die Unternehmenswebsites angeschaut um festzustellen ob sie von dort aus auf die Facebook Seiten verlinken. Dies geschah bei fünf der untersuchten Marken nicht. Darunter auch BMW und Mercedes-Benz und somit zwei der Hersteller mit den größten Fan-Mengen. Die Gründe können verschiedene sein, jedenfalls scheinen sie nicht zusätzlichen Traffic von ihrer Website auf die Facebook Seite bringen zu müssen, da sie auch so in großer Häufigkeiten gefunden werden.

Landing Pages sind die Unterseite auf denen Noch-nicht-Fans zuerst gelangen wenn sie eine Facebook Seite aufrufen. Hier wird versucht den Facebook Nutzer dazu zu bewegen den Gefällt-mir-Button zu drücken und Fan der Seite zu werden. Außerdem können hier auch noch Hinweise auf Inhalte der Seite oder momentane Aktionen aufmerksam gemacht werden. Bis auf Fiat, Peugeot und Renault hatten alle anderen Marken ein Landing Page in ihre Facebook Seite eingebaut.

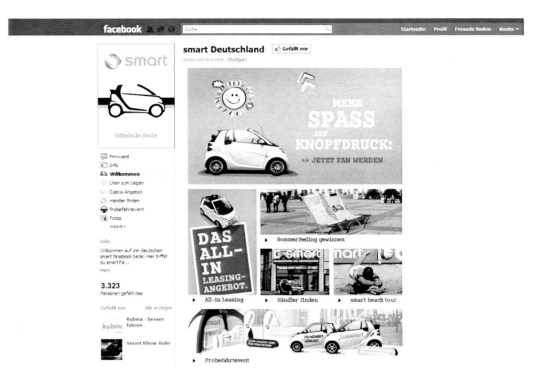

Abbildung 127: Landing Page (smart Deutschland, 2011)

Die in Abb.17 dargestellte Landing Page von smart Deutschland wird als Musterbeispiel empfunden, da sie graphisch ansprechend gestaltet ist und mehrere Themen unterbringt. Dazu gehören auch Angebote für Probefahrten und Auto-Leasing, also transaktionsorientierte Vorgänge. Somit gelingt es smart direkt von der Facebook Seite aus Konversions zu erstellen.

Wie in der qualitativen Forschung später noch aufgezeigt wird, benötigen Unternehmen Guidelines die ihre Fans in den Social Media aufklärt und sie bittet gewisse Regeln im Umgang mit anderen Fans zu befolgen. Diese Richtlinien wurden jedoch nur von neun der 18 Marken auf ihren Facebook Seiten ausgewiesen. Dies fand zumeist im Reiter Info statt oder im Falle Volvos in einem eigens dafür angelegten Reiter. Somit stellt die Hälfte der Unternehmen keine Social Media Guidelines bereit, was jedoch eine Pflicht darstellt, um zu gewähren, dass sich die Fans auch ohne zensierende Kontrolle nicht beleidigend oder diskriminierend auf der Markenpräsenz äußern und damit das Image der Marke beschmutzen könnten.

Eine weitere Funktion der Facebook Seiten ist die Einrichtung eines Reiters namens Diskussionen. Dieser funktioniert wie ein herkömmliches Internet-Forum, eine bereits sehr alte- Art der Online-Kommunikation. Die Foren wurden vermutlich eingerichtet um längere Diskussionen nicht auf der Pinnwand führen zu müssen und diese besser auffindbar zu machen, da sie auf der Pinnwand durch die anderen Beiträge schnell aus dem Beachtungsbereich verschwinden. Die Fans nutzten die Foren vor allem für technische Fragen, Hilfestellungen bei Problemen mit Fahrzeugen oder Beschwerden. Somit werden auch hier Inhalte aus den sehr relevanten Kategorien BK und IF veröffentlicht.

In dieser Arbeit wurden sie nicht erfasst und untersucht, da sich die Threads über sehr lange Zeiträume erstrecken. Außerdem nutzen nur Audi, BMW und Opel diese Forumsfunktion. Dies kann verschiedene Gründe haben, einerseits die Ansammlung und dadurch bessere Auffindbarkeit von negativen Inhalten über Produkte und Marke. Wenn die Marken nicht als Service Brand auftreten und sich im nötigen Maße um diese Beschwerden und Probleme kümmern, kann dies sehr schädlich sein. Daher werden sich wohlmöglich viele der untersuchten Autohersteller gedacht haben kein Forum anzubieten. Dies ist legitim, denn die Fans können ihre Anliegen eben auch auf der Pinnwand veröffentlichen. Durch das schnelle Herunterrutschen durch die ständige Bewegung auf der Pinnwand wird es aber nicht zu solchen Beschwerdeansammlungen wie in einem Forum kommen. Diese können zu einem Abschrecken und Abwandern von Kunden führen, weil die Bindung zur Marke geschwächt wurde. Solch einer potenziellen Gefahr wollen sich die Marken anscheinend nicht aussetzen und verzichten daher auf diese Funktion auf ihrer Facebook Seite.

3.2.2   Qualitative Forschung

Abbildung 138: Beschwerde eines Fans I (Audi Deutschland, 2011)

Der Kunde bemängelt in diesem Fall die Langlebigkeit eines Bauteiles an seinem Wagen, die im Katalog noch explizit als Stärke beworben wurde. Die Reparaturen waren seiner Meinung nach schon zu oft fällig und nahmen dabei zu viel Zeit in Anspruch, weil der Vorgang dabei zu aufwendig ist. Dieser deutlichen Kritik und dem schon fast als ironisch geltenden Produktmangel tritt Audi auf unpersönlichste Art und Weise entgegen. Der verärgerte Fan wird weder begrüßt noch vertröstet. Es wird ihm keine richtige Hilfe angeboten, stattdessen weist Audi ihn auf eine als zynisch aufzufassende Weise auf die Kontaktdaten im Info-Tab hin. Der Fan reagiert aufgebracht und sieht keinen Sinn in diesem Ratschlag noch in den Möglichkeiten der Kundenbetreuung. Audi reagiert daraufhin nicht mehr. Mit dieser misslungenen Hilfestellung signalisiert Audi mangelnde Wertschätzung des Kundenkontakts auf Facebook und zeigt keinerlei proaktive Bereitschaft zur Problemlösung. Der Fan wird nüchtern und unfreundlich abgespeist und seinem Schicksal alleine überlassen Hilfe an anderer Stelle bei Audi zu finden. Der Nutzen eines Service-Brand wurde hier klar verfehlt.

Abbildung 149: Antwort von der Autorin (Ford Deutschland, 2011)

Mit dieser Antwort auf einen Fan-Beitrag beweist das Ford Social Media Team, das es sich stets bemüht zeitnah zu antworten, auch wenn es nicht unmittelbar die Informationen und Antworten liefern kann. Den Fans wird signalisiert, wie ernst der Kontakt zu ihnen via Facebook genommen wird und mit welcher Sorgfalt gearbeitet wird. Der Fan weiß nun wie lange er ungefähr auf seine Antwort warten muss und wieso es zu der Verzögerung kommt. Dies zeugt von hoher Transparenz, die Ford mit seinen personalisierten Autoren ohnehin schon beispielhaft an den Tag legt.

Abbildung 20: Hinweis auf Social Media Guidelines (Opel Deutschland, 2011)

Dieser Aufruf zur Achtung der Social Media Guidelines und der darin enthaltenen Bitte um respektvollen Umgang miteinander erfolgte nach dem im Laufe einer Pinnwand-Diskussion sich ein Nutzer abfällig gegen Opel äußerte und er darauf mit ausländerfeindlichen Beschimpfungen diskriminiert wurde. In solch einem Härtefall stehen dem Seitenbetreiber zwei Handlungsoptionen zur Verfügung: Entweder die Kommentare löschen und damit die im Internet herrschen Meinungsfreiheit verletzen oder, die bessere Variante wie sie auch gewählt wurde, auf die geltenden Richtlinien zur Kommunikation auf dieser Plattform hinweisen. Somit befreit sich Opel von jeglichem Zusammenhang mit den Beleidigungen, da es im Info-Tab die Guidelines für jedermann sichtbar und leicht zugänglich aufgeführt hat. Kommentare zu zensieren hätte ein größeres Unheil anrichten können als die beleidigenden Äußerungen selbst (Stuber, 2010, S. 21).

Abbildung 151: Beschwerde eines Fans II (KIA Motors Deutschland, 2011)

Bei der Beschwerde dieses Fans über das mangelhafte Verhalten eines KIA-Händlers bei der Abwicklung einer Probefahrt reagiert der Administrator gut. Die Antwort folgte in weniger als einer Stunde auf die Beschwerde. Die Anrede und der Umgang mit dem Fan sind höflich und es wird sich dem Problem angenommen, in dem nach den Kontaktdaten des Händlers gefragt wird. Es wäre interessant gewesen zu sehen, in welcher Form KIA dem Fan Wiedergutmachung anbietet. Daher wurde bei dem betroffenen Fan nachgefragt, zu welchem Ergebnis der Kontakt mit KIA führte. Wie in Abb. 17 zu lesen ist, hat KIA sich um die Abwicklung einer Probefahrt gekümmert.

Die potenzielle Kundin ist also noch nicht verloren gegangen nach dem Vorfall, da sie vom Produkt nach wie vor überzeugt zu sein scheint und der schlechte Service durch einen Händler, also nur von einem Zwischenmann, erbracht wurde. Somit hat KIA als Marke selbst nur einen kleinen Schaden genommen, der wieder auszugleichen ist.

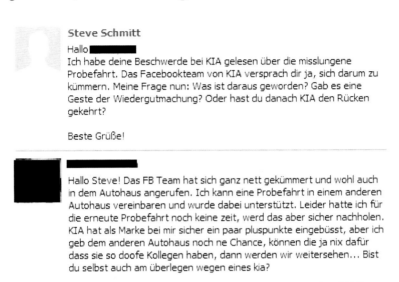

Abbildung 162: Nachricht des betroffenen Fans (Schmitt, 2011)

Für die Auto-Händler kann der Bericht eines solchen Vorfalls auch seine Folgen haben. Durch die Social Media haben verärgerte und enttäusche Kunden nun einen Kanal ihre Enttäuschung öffentlich Kund zu tun und es andere Kunden sowie die Marke erfahren zu lassen. Den Herstellern bietet sich somit auch eine Möglichkeit schwarze Schafe unter den Händlern ausfindig zu machen und dementsprechend zu reagieren und sie zurechtzuweisen, womit sich der Service weiter verbessern dürfte.

Abbildung 173: Fanaufrufe (Opel Deutschland, 2011)

In diesen beiden Beiträgen wird das Design eines neuen Opel-Modells kritisiert. Die Anzahl der Bestätigungen und Zustimmungen ist zwar weder repräsentativ noch besonders alarmierend, jedoch kann Opel aus der Kritik durchaus Schlüsse ziehen und darüber nachdenken, im Falle eines tatsächlichen Ausbleiben des Verkaufserfolgs entsprechende Maßnahmen zu betreiben. Solche übereinstimmenden Kritiken und Verbesserungsvorschläge, die eigenständig vom Kunden getätigt werden, können Anstöße zu weiteren Marktforschungstätigkeiten geben.

Es gibt zurzeit branchenübergreifend einige Versuche den Kunden mehr in die Produktentwicklung einzubeziehen. Beide Parteien profitieren davon gleichermaßen. Die Kunden haben ein Mitspracherecht, setzen sich somit noch mehr mit Produkt und Marke auseinander was die Markenbindung verstärkt. Die Unternehmen kriegen von der Zielgruppe gesagt auf was sie achtet, was ihr gefällt und verringert so das Risiko Flops zu produzieren. Wie sehr nun dieses neue Verfahren Einkehr in die Automobilindustrie finden kann, bleibt abzuwarten. Aber in Sachen Design bietet sich dies es sich wie dieser Fall, zeigt sicher an Meinungen der Kundschaft einzuholen und dem Dialog in den Social Media Gehör zu schenken.

 Renault Deutschland
Renault ist der neue Programmsponsor der ARD-Sportschau. Morgen geht's los. Die Premiere der Sponsor-Trailer gibt es aber bereits heute und exklusiv bei facebook. Wir wünschen euch ein schönes Wochenende!

 **22. Juli 2011 16:13**
Dauer: 0:09

22. Juli um 16:13 · Gefällt mir · Kommentieren · Teilen

68 Personen gefällt das.

Tor des Monats :)
22. Juli um 16:15 · Gefällt mir · 2 Personen

dos auto
22. Juli um 16:27 · Gefällt mir

D Cooles Video!
22. Juli um 16:36 · Gefällt mir

Geiles Video und super Idee mit dem Drift Bälle zu treffen :)
22. Juli um 18:21 · Gefällt mir

geil =) renault sport ♥
22. Juli um 19:09 · Gefällt mir · 1 Person

das is top!!! sehr gute idee
22. Juli um 19:25 · Gefällt mir · 1 Person

Abbildung 18: Preview des neuen Sponsor-Trailers (Renault Deutschland, 2011)

Renault präsentierte seinen Fans auf Facebook einen Blick auf den neuen Sponsor-Trailer bevor er zum ersten Mal im Fernsehen ausgestrahlt wurde. Auch wenn es sich hier um einen Werbespot handelt, zeigt dieses Beispiel auf wie man den Fans einen Mehrwert bieten kann in dem man ihnen exklusive Informationen anbietet und es sich für sie lohnt Renault auf Facebook zu folgen. Den Fans wurde dabei die Chance geboten als auserwählte Menge den Spot bereits früher zu sehen, was einen psychologischen Reiz setzt, nämlich Exklusivität. Diesen Weg sollte man weiterhin einschlagen in dem man auch andere Informationen den Facebook-Fans eher zugänglich macht. Sei dies nur durch ein kleines Zeitfenster, wenn beispielsweise Neuigkeiten auf der Website oder in einer Pressemitteilung veröffentlicht werden sollen und die Fans einen Auszug oder den kompletten Inhalt Stunden vorher mitgeteilt bekämen. Die Fans würden dies als Geste der Wertschätzung empfinden und die emotionale Bindung zum Unternehmen sich verstärken. Zudem würde sich dieser Mehrwert durch Word-oft-Muth Empfehlungen der Fans online wie auch offline weitersprechen und zum Zuwachs führen.

Honda Deutschland Automobile

Jetzt ist eure Meinung gefragt: Was fällt euch zum Thema Start-Stopp-Automatik ein? Wünschenswertes Feature oder unnützer Schnickschnack?

23. Juli um 12:04 · Gefällt mir · Kommentieren

👍 14 Personen gefällt das.

"unnützer Schnickschnack!!!!!!"
23. Juli um 12:04 · Gefällt mir · 👍 2 Personen

unnötig wie ein Kropf.....
23. Juli um 12:05 · Gefällt mir

unnötig !
23. Juli um 12:05 · Gefällt mir

Ist es wirklich soooo sparsam???
23. Juli um 12:06 · Gefällt mir

an längeren Ampelphasen ist es vllt sinnvoll 1,2% Sprit zusparen ansonsten eher unütz
23. Juli um 12:06 · Gefällt mir

VTEC!
23. Juli um 12:06 · Gefällt mir · 👍 2 Personen

Mein Fall is das nicht, es mag zwar sein das man damit etwas Sprit spart, aber es verlängert die Reaktionszeit in Notfällen da erst nochmal der Motor gestartet werden muss. Daher : Flop
23. Juli um 12:06 · Gefällt mir · 👍 1 Person

gibt nix besseres :)
23. Juli um 12:06 · Gefällt mir

so unnötig, wie automatik.... so macht autofahren dann ja keinen spaß mehr!
23. Juli um 12:07 · Gefällt mir · 👍 3 Personen

die start-stop automatik erfolgt ja in der regel erst, wenn der motor die erforderliche betriebstemperatur erreicht hat. aus sicherheitsgründen wird darüber hinaus bei bestimmten bedingungen drauf verzichtet, zb wenn die batterie zu stark entladen ist oder temperaturen um den nullpunkt herrschen... zb im winter. eine vernünftige fahrweise bringt meiner meinung nach viel mehr, als einen haufen geld in solch einen schnickschnack zu investieren! für mich persöhnlich ist das zumindest mehr schein als sein ^^
23. Juli um 12:12 · Gefällt mir

nööö ist nichts.... sorgt ml lieber dafür das hier in deutschland mal die neuen si civic und die fd2 eingefürt werden:D
23. Juli um 12:12 · Gefällt mir

Abbildung 195: Marktforschung auf der Facebook Seite (Honda Deutschland, 2011)

Honda nutzte wie einige der anderen Marken auch die Möglichkeit um die Fans nach ihrer Meinung zu fragen und somit kostenlos Marktforschung im kleinen Rahmen zu betreiben. Dieses Beispiel wurde gewählt, weil Honda Deutschland hier schon durch die Fragestellung polarisierende Antworten bei den Fans herbei beschwört, welche dann auch so erfolgen. Es kann sein das man damit die Fans schon im Voraus beeinflusst hat, jedoch äußern sich vereinzelte Fans auch konstruktiv zu dieser Frage.

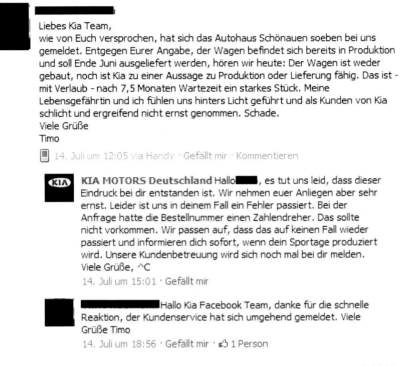

Liebes Kia Team,
wie von Euch versprochen, hat sich das Autohaus Schönauen soeben bei uns gemeldet. Entgegen Eurer Angabe, der Wagen befindet sich bereits in Produktion und soll Ende Juni ausgeliefert werden, hören wir heute: Der Wagen ist weder gebaut, noch ist Kia zu einer Aussage zu Produktion oder Lieferung fähig. Das ist - mit Verlaub - nach 7,5 Monaten Wartezeit ein starkes Stück. Meine Lebensgefährtin und ich fühlen uns hinters Licht geführt und als Kunden von Kia schlicht und ergreifend nicht ernst genommen. Schade.
Viele Grüße
Timo

14. Juli um 12:05 via Handy · Gefällt mir · Kommentieren

KIA MOTORS Deutschland Hallo██, es tut uns leid, dass dieser Eindruck bei dir entstanden ist. Wir nehmen euer Anliegen aber sehr ernst. Leider ist uns in deinem Fall ein Fehler passiert. Bei der Anfrage hatte die Bestellnummer einen Zahlendreher. Das sollte nicht vorkommen. Wir passen auf, dass das auf keinen Fall wieder passiert und informieren dich sofort, wenn dein Sportage produziert wird. Unsere Kundenbetreuung wird sich noch mal bei dir melden.
Viele Grüße, ^C
14. Juli um 15:01 · Gefällt mir

████████████Hallo Kia Facebook Team, danke für die schnelle Reaktion, der Kundenservice hat sich umgehend gemeldet. Viele Grüße Timo
14. Juli um 18:56 · Gefällt mir · 👍 1 Person

Abbildung 206: Beschwerde eines Fans III (KIA MOTORS Deutschland, 2011)

In dieser Beschwerde auf KIA MOTORS Deutschland bemängelt ein Fan die Verzögerung bei der Produktion und Lieferung seines bestellten Wagens. Wie es sich herausstellt, wurde er von den Facebook Administratoren falsch informiert und muss weiter warten. KIA MOTORS Deutschland antwortet innerhalb von drei Stunden auf den Beitrag und entschuldigt sich dafür mit der Erklärung es wäre ein Zahlendreher unterlaufen und verspricht Besserung. Der Fan scheint durch die umgehende Antwort und den schnellen Service besänftigt worden zu sein. Der Pflicht als Service Brand auf Facebook wurde erfüllt.

Armutszeugnis für Kia-Deutschland

Seit 2Wochen versuche ich den Liefertermin für meinen im Januar bestellten Sportage zu erfahren, der Liefertermin sollte im Juli sein. Mein Händler kann mir leider keine Info geben, da er selber keine erhält.

So habe ich mich telefonisch an Kia Deutschland gewandt. Die anfangs noch freundliche Dame, wechselte die Tonlage nach meiner Frage zum Liefertermin. Es gibt hier niemand der Auskunft geben könne und ich soll mich an Korea wenden! Mir ist fast der Hörer aus der Hand gefallen, zumal der Sportage ja in Europa gebaut wird.

Da ich Ende diesem Monats in Urlaub fahre, hilft mir nun mein freundlicher Kia-Händler weiter und trägt die Kosten aus eigener Tasche.

Ein absolutes Armutszeugnis für Kia-Deutschland!!!

Derzeit überlegen wir ob wir vom Kaufvertrag zurücktreten werden...

15. Juli um 20:22 · Gefällt mir · Kommentieren

████ Mach dass. Besser wird der Kia Service nicht.
18. Juli um 13:01 · Gefällt mir

KIA MOTORS Deutschland @Dirk: Ich kann gut verstehen, dass du mit der Situation unzufrieden bist. Ich habe deine Bestellung in unserer Disposition prüfen lassen. Leider kann ich dir noch keinen genauen Liefertermin nennen. Wir möchten erst nach einer werksseitigen Bestätigung Termine mitteilen. Wir geben alles damit dein Sportage bald kommt. Sobald das Autohaus Engbert oder ich Neuigkeiten haben, melden wir uns bei dir. Liebe Grüße, ^A
18. Juli um 15:49 · Gefällt mir

Hallo ████ ... ich kann Dir nur raten geduldig zu sein. Das Warte wird sich lohnen. Ich habe meinen Sporty seit 2 Monaten (auch im Januar bestellt) und bin begeistert von dem Auto.
18. Juli um 19:56 · Gefällt mir · 👍 1 Person

████ @KIA MOTORS Deutschland Danke für die Rückinfo und die Bemühungen. Dennoch kann ich nicht nachvollziehen, wie die Planungen beim Werk gemacht werden, denn bei anderen Automobilherstellern bekommt man, wenn der Liefertermin nicht eingehalten werden kann, zumindest eine Info zum neuen Liefertermin.

Zudem wird ein Ersatzfahrzeug zur Verfügung gestellt.

Wenn uns das Autohaus Engbert (auf eigene Kosten) nicht weiterhelfen würde, könnten wir erst mal zusehen wie wir überhaupt in den Urlaub kommen!

Für die Dame am Telefon bei Kia Motors Deutschland, würde ich mal einen Stresstest empfehlen. Es kann nicht angehen, das man sehr unfreundlich und mit patzigen Antworten auf eine freundliche Nachfrage zum Liefertermin abgespeist wird. Zudem als letztes noch gebeten widr in Korea anzurufen. Da ich der Dame gesagt habe, das es sich um einen Sportage handelt, hätte sie wissen müssen das dieses Fahrzeug in Europa gebaut wird.

Mit freundlichen Grüßen
18. Juli um 20:31 · Gefällt mir

████ @████ Kann ich mir vorstellen, ist ja ein tolles Fahrzeug. Aber von anderen Automobilherstellern bin ich anderen Service gewohnt!

Übrigens: Wir haben das Fahrzeug Mitte Januar bestellt. Wieso hast Du Dein Fahrzeug schon seit 2 Monaten???
18. Juli um 20:35 · Gefällt mir

Abbildung 217: Beschwerde eines Fans IV (KIA MOTORS Deutschland, 2011)

Bei dieser getätigten Beschwerde werden gleich mehrere Missstände offen gelegt. Zunächst die bisher nicht geschehene Lieferung laut Terminabgabe. Dies ist noch das kleinste Unheil, da dies jedem Hersteller passieren kann. Der nächste Mangel liegt in der Kundenbetreuung, genauer gesagt bei der Telefonauskunft. Der Kunde wollte hierüber den Termin nachfragen und wurde keineswegs mit einer Lösung bedient. Die Service-Mitarbeiterin entgegnete ihm höchst unfreundlich und dazu noch inkompetent, da sie nicht zu wissen schien wo das gefragte Modell produziert wird. Der Kunde erhielt keinerlei Information über den Status seiner Fahrzeuglieferung. Stattdessen wird er der Unwissenheit überlassen, obwohl er dringend ein Auto benötigt um in den Urlaub fahren zu können. Dies führt zum dritten Kritikpunkt.

Der betreuende KIA-Händler stellt ihm auf eigene Kosten ein Fahrzeug bereit. Dies wird vom Kunden sehr positiv bewertet, jedoch ging dies nicht von KIA Motors Deutschland aus, was er dabei auch bemängelt. Der Administrator kann dem Kunden auch nicht weiterhelfen, da er die Information ohne eine Bestätigung vom Werk nicht herausgeben darf. Dies wird zwar noch anerkannt, doch äußert sein generelles Unverständnis über den mangelhaften Lieferablauf bei KIA MOTORS Deutschland und weist auf besseren Service bei anderen Herstellern hin.

Die schwerwiegendste Kritik betrifft jedoch nochmal das Verhalten des Telefonkontakts. Er beklagt ein unprofessionelles Verhalten und weist nochmal auf die extreme Unfreundlichkeit hin, Wie schon im genannten Beispiel zum schlechten Verhalten eines KIA-Händlers könnten hier Konsequenzen für den negativ aufgefallenen Mitarbeiter daraus hervorgehen. Solch ein Verhalten ist sehr schädlich allein in der Beziehung mit dem betroffenen Kunden, aber wenn es öffentlich auch noch dargelegt wird, könnte daraus eine schlechte Publicity entstehen. Gerade die Anstellung in eine von der Hierarchie-Ebene eher unten anzusiedelnde Position wie diese könnte durch solche Verfehlungen in Gefahr geraten und zu einer Mahnung oder gar schlimmerem führen.

Als ob dies noch nicht genug verkündeter Unmut gewesen wäre, stellt sich im Dialog auch noch heraus, das ein anderer KIA-Kunde das gleiche Modell zum ähnlichen Zeitpunkt bestellt hat, dies jedoch bereits vor zwei Monaten erhalten hat. Auf die Frage wie dies denn sein könnte reagiert KIA MOTORS Deutschland nicht, genauso wie resümierende Bemängelung des Services im Vergleich mit anderen Herstellern. KIA Motors Deutschland ist es nicht gelungen auch nur einen einzigen der vielen Missstände zu klären oder zu beschwichtigen.

hahaha, mein auto gehört endlich MIR :D
hab heute den Fzg-brief bekommen :)

ich bin sooo happy, endlich isses MEIN baby :D

21. Juli um 00:00 · Gefällt mir · Kommentieren

👍 4 Personen gefällt das.

Ich bekomme meine Autos immer ohne Brief, die
Bank will den immer behalten :-)
Viel Spass mit Deinem .... was ist eigentlich für einer ?
21. Juli um 13:54 · Gefällt mir

Ford Deutschland ███ fährt einen Ford Escort. Den will er noch
ca. vier Jahre fahren - das hat er sich vorgenommen :-) Danach
plant er sich einen Ford Fusion (letzte Generation) zu kaufen. ;-) Und
wenn ich mich nicht täusche besitzt seine Mutter bereits einen Ford
Fusion - aber korrigier mich, Yves, wenn ich da falsch liege. Liebe
Grüße, Janette | Ford Social Media Team
21. Juli um 15:46 · Gefällt mir · 👍 2 Personen

Janette, Du bist ja voll der Stalker *grins*
Was Du alles weißt :-))
21. Juli um 15:48 · Gefällt mir

Ford Deutschland ███, ich bin aufmerksam. Ich weiß ja auch,
welches Modell du fährst und wie lange du auf deinen Ford Mondeo
warten musstest, weil er beim Händler gestohlen wurde. :-(Janette
| Ford Social Media Team
21. Juli um 15:57 · Gefällt mir · 👍 1 Person

Jetzt reißt Du die alte Wunde wieder auf ;-))
So habe ich wenigstens immer eine schöne Geschichte parat *hihi*
21. Juli um 16:06 · Gefällt mir · 👍 1 Person

hehe, ja Janette, das ist alles richtig :D
aber du hast den Focus meiner Schwester vergessen ;)

Find ich aber interessant dass ihr euch das so notiert ;)
21. Juli um 23:50 · Gefällt mir · 👍 1 Person

und ██████, wenn du es genau wissen willst: es ist
ein Escort Classic Turnier ;)
22. Juli um 00:03 · Gefällt mir

So einen hatte ich von 2000 bis 2002 auch, in
Salsarot mit 90PS Diesel.
22. Juli um 10:25 · Gefällt mir

Der Escort ist mein Traum, den wollte ich schon als
Kind haben. Bin ja damit aufgewachsen :)

meiner ist Spanischrot (ich glaub das hieß beim Escort so, wenn nich
isses Coloradorot XD)
22. Juli um 10:36 · Gefällt mir

Ford Deutschland ███ Ich hab mir das nicht notiert. Ich hatte
das noch im Kopf. ;-) Liebe Grüße, Janette | Ford Social Media Team
22. Juli um 11:50 · Gefällt mir

Abbildung 228: Sympathiebekundung eines Fans (Ford Deutschland, 2011)

Der Dialog in Abb. 28 zeigt besonders deutlich wie Marken über Facebook Seiten ganz persönliche Beziehungen und Kontakte zu den Kunden aufbauen können. Ford erwies sah in diesem Punkt als stärkste Marke im Untersuchungsfeld. Neben der stets erfolgenden Nennung des antwortenden Autors und dem netten Umgang, zeigt sich das Engagement auf Kunden auch ohne Aufforderung oder Sachklärung einzugehen. Die Autoren haben, wie es hier der Fall zu sein scheint, einen Zugriff auf Kundendatenbanken und können somit selber in deren Käufe und weitere Geschehnisse Einblick bekommen. Diese vermittelt den Kunden Aufmerksamkeit, Interesse und Initiative, was im Laufe des Dialogs auch anerkannt und positiv kommentiert wurde.

Es ging hier lediglich um eine Sympathiebekundung wie sie bei allen Marken in mehr oder weniger häufig stattfindet und es entwickelte sich eine Darbietung der Kundenzuwendung seitens von Ford, wo hingegen viele andere Marken dies komplett ignorieren und unbeantwortet stehen lassen.

Liebe Seat Mitarbeiter ... Ich finde es durchaus ärgerlich, dass ich für meinen Altea XL für viel Geld eine Zusatzgarantie abschließe, ein Garantiefall eintritt, das Ersatzteil nicht lieferbar ist und ich noch nicht einmal einen Leihwagen gestellt bekomme. Das Angebot, mir für mehrere Wochen (bisher zwei Wochen, Liefertermin weiterhin auf unbestimmte Zeit nicht festlegbar) ein Auto für 35 EUR am Tag zu mieten empfinde ich als Frechheit!

11. Juli um 09:32 · Gefällt mir · Kommentieren

👍 ██████ gefällt das.

SEAT Deutschland Hallo lieber ████, wie unsere Kundenbetreuung dir bereits am 08.07. bestätigt hat, haben wir immer noch Lieferschwierigkeiten beim Klimakompressor. Der Prozess lässt sich leider nicht beschleunigen. Unsere Empfehlung: halte bitte weiterhin Kontakt zu deinem SEAT Partner oder zur unserer Kundenbetreuung. Dort bekommst du alle relevanten Informationen und Neuigkeiten zu diesem Thema. Solltest du aber noch Rückfragen an uns haben, so kannst du gerne eine E-Mail an social@seat.de schicken. Viele Grüße, dein SEAT Facebook Team.

11. Juli um 15:32 · Gefällt mir

 ████████████████ Hallo Seat Team
Es geht mir nur darum, dass ich eine Garantie abgeschlossen habe, damit so etwas nicht vorkommt. Für die Lieferengpässe können Sie nichts, das ist klar, dass ich aber fast 250 Eur für einen Kleinwagen pro Woche zahlen soll, ist für mich nicht nachzuvollziehen.

Und klar ist ja auch, dass der Händler vor Ort auf Sie verweist und Sie auf den Händler vor Ort. Auch ist nicht nachzuvollziehen, warum ein lagernder passender Klimakompressor im KFZ Teile Laden um die Ecke nicht genommen werden kann, nur weil er von einer Fremdfirma ist? Ich hatte sogar angeboten den Kompressor selber zu bezahlen, aber selbst das ging nicht....

Ich werde jetzt das Auto wohl aus der Werkstatt holen, den Kompressor und die Reparatur selber zahlen und mich nach zwei Seat Neuwagen von Ihnen verabschieden.

11. Juli um 15:43 · Gefällt mir

SEAT Deutschland Hallo ████, wie bereits geschrieben, ist unsere Kundenbetreuung hier der richtige Ansprechpartner. In Kürze erhältst du erneut eine Rückmeldung von unseren Kollegen aus der Kundenbetreuung. Viele Grüße, dein SEAT Facebook Team.

11. Juli um 16:27 · Gefällt mir

 ████████████████ ... und wieder sind 4 Tage verstrichen ... das macht dann mal so 140 EUR zusätzlich an Wagenmiete. Macht ja nichts... nach 16 Tagen sind das ja nur 560 EUR. Mittlerweile könnte ich von diesem Geld den Kompressor selber bezahlen - und nächste Woche wäre dann auch der Einbau mit drin. Da merke ich, wie groß kundenzufriedenheit geschrieben wird...

14. Juli um 09:01 · Gefällt mir · 👍 1 Person

 ████████████████ So, heute ist der 20.07. - das Auto ist jetzt seit 21 Tagen in der Werkstatt, Die Kompressoren von Drittfirmen sind massenweise vor Ort, dürfen aber immer noch nicht wegen der Garantie verbaut werden. Seat hat sich entgegen der letzten Aussage hier nicht mehr bei gemeldet!
Ich merke, Seat hat einen weiteren Schritt in seinem ewig währenden Kampf gegen die Kundenfreundlichkeit erfolgreich hinter sich gebracht...

20. Juli um 09:58 · Gefällt mir

Abbildung 239: Beschwerde eines Fans V (SEAT Deutschland, 2011)

Der Beschwerdefall der auf der Pinnwand von SEAT diskutiert wurde, war der wohl negativste und aus Unternehmenssicht verheerendste von allen untersuchten Beiträgen. Nach dem der Kunde eine Zusatzgarantie abgeschlossen hat und es beim Liefern des Ersatzteils zu Komplikationen gab, wurde ihm ein Ersatzwagen angeboten, jedoch nur gegen Entgeltzahlung. Hierüber beschwert sich der Kunde, da er wohl dachte, eine solche Leistung wäre wohl für in der Garantie kostenlos enthalten. Das SEAT Facebook Team bestätigt in der ersten Antwort die Lieferschwierigkeiten und kann sich dabei nur als Vermittler zu Partnern und Kundenbetreuung anbieten. Daraufhin bemängelt der Kunde die Schuldzuweisung zwischen Hersteller und Händler, sowie die Leistung der Garantie, die in diesem Fall ihren Zweck total verfehlt und ihn dabei noch aufhält sein Auto schnell nutzen zu können, in dem die Garantie es untersagt Teil von Drittanbietern einzubauen. Genau dies kündigt er dann antun zu wollen auf eigene Kosten und sich danach von der Marke SEAT zu trennen. Der Kunde ist zu diesem Zeitpunkt dermaßen verärgert, dass SEAT ihn nun komplett verloren zu haben scheint.

In der nächsten Antwort seitens SEATs wird erneut auf die Kundenbetreuung verwiesen mit dem Versprechen, der Kunde würde zeitnah von dieser kontaktiert werden. Der Kunde schreibt jeweils drei und neun Tage später wieder mit noch schlechteren Nachrichten. Die Reparatur konnte immer noch nicht durchgeführt werden, die Ausgaben für den Mietwagen steigen stetig und die Kundenbetreuung hat sich nicht an ihn gewendet.

Ein Versagen auf ganzer Linie, denn nun wird dazu auch noch die Glaubwürdigkeit des SEAT Facebook Teams angezweifelt. Der Kunde avanciert zum absoluten Negativbotschafter. Er spricht

SEAT auf deren eigener Pinnwand jegliche Kundenfreundlichkeit ab aus für jeden Fan einsehbaren Gründen. Erst einen Tag später reagiert das SEAT Facebook Team mit dem Hinweis, dass ein Schreiben auf dem Weg zum Kunden sei. Dieser meldet sich im Laufe des gleichen Tages und zitiert aus dem Schreiben. SEAT antwortete ihm, dass sie nicht der richtige Ansprechpartner seien für diese Art von Vorfall und bitten den Kunden sich an Anbieter der Garantie zu wenden. Wie sich in der weiteren Ausführung des Kunden herausstellt, wird die Garantie aber mit Seat als Hersteller direkt abgeschlossen und nicht mit dem Händler.

Damit hat SEAT sich nun endgültig sein eigenes Grab geschaufelt. Sie haben einen Kunden verloren, ungenügende Kundenbetreuung bewiesen und die erwähnte Zusatzgarantie hat sich als untauglich erwiesen. So ein Vorfall wird SEAT nicht in den Ruin treiben, das Ansehen des Services wird bei allen Lesern jedoch für Aufsehen sorgen. Am meisten bemerkbar machen wird sich vermutlich der Rückgang an Abschlüssen dieser Garantie.

4   Handlungsempfehlungen

Eine weitere Empfehlung wäre das Bekanntmachen der Gesichter hinter dem jeweiligen Team das für die Seite zuständig ist. Dies kann sowohl durch Fotos der Mitglieder gemacht wie bei Ford, sollte aber zumindest durch Kennzeichnung von Namen oder Initialen in den Beiträge durchgeführt werden. Ein pauschaler oder gar kein Gruß vom Team mindert die Nähe zwischen Kunden und Unternehmen, womit einer der Vorteile von Social Media, nämlich der persönliche Kontakt, nicht genutzt wird. Ebenso ist bietet es sich für die im Rennsport tätigen Hersteller an, ihre Mitarbeiter auch am Wochenende zeitnah etwas zu Geschehen zu posten um Aktualität und Bereitschaft zu signalisieren und den Dialog zur interessantesten Zeit, also unmittelbar nach dem Ereignis, zu führen. So ist es vereinzelt auch schon geschehen bei einigen Marken, aber nicht durchgängig.

Ein weiterer wichtiger Nutzen eine Facebook-Facebook Page für Unternehmen ist die Möglichkeit sie zum Kundenservice zu nutzen. Fragen zum Produkt und anderen Leistungen sowie Beschwerden und Kritiken sollten ernst genommen und schnell beantwortet melden. Kunden die ihren Unmut äußern sind für Unternehmen wertvoller, da sie Missstände darstellen und nicht durch Unzufriedenheit wortlos abwandern. Stattdessen bieten sie den Unternehmen die Chance zur Wiedergutmachung und gleichzeitig zur Verbesserung der Reputation bei den mitlesenden Fans. Problemlösungen direkt auf Facebook anzubieten hat dabei noch einen weiteren positiven Aspekt, da die anderen Kunden den Prozess verfolgen, was bei einer Weiterleitung an andere Stellen im Unternehmen nicht der Fall ist.

Interaktion mit Kunden auf Facebook bedeutet nicht sich pseudo-aktiv zu zeigen, in dem das Unternehmen jeden noch so aussageschwachen Fan-Beitrag mit einem Gefällt-mir-Klick oder einer simplen Danksagung versieht. Die Community-Manager bzw. Facebook-Beauftragten sollen Fan-Gemeinschaft moderieren und sich der Fans auch unaufgefordert annehmen. Ein gutes Beispiel lieferte hier Ford Deutschland, in dem die Autorin selber die Kaufhistorie des Fans und seiner Familie nachschaute und somit ohne vorhergegangene Anfrage oder Aufforderung im Bilde war. Um diese Art von Zuwendung zu gewährleisten Bedarf es gewisser Ressourcen, demnach sollten sich die Unternehmen der strategischen Frage stellen: Wie groß soll unsere Community? Wie viel Ressourcen sollen dafür bereitgestellt werden?

Ab einer gewissen Größe und Menge an Beiträge ist ein abgestellter Mitarbeiter sicherlich nicht mehr ausreichend und es bedarf weiterer Verstärkung. Der alternative Einsatz wäre es, wirklich involvierte Fans auf die Facebook Seite zu holen und nicht durch Gewinnspiele die Fan-Zahlen zur Inflation zu bringen und schweigende, nicht involvierte Fan-Massen anzusammeln. Ein noch viel

55

schlimmeres Vergehen ist der Gebrauch von mittlerweile entstandenen Dienstleistungen des Fan-Kaufs. Dienste wie FanSlave oder FanBuy bieten es Administratoren an gegen ein Entgelt ein festgelegtes Kontingent an Fans der Seite einzubringen. Diese fragwürdigen Methoden sollten von keinem authentischen Seitenbetreiber in Anspruch genommen werden.

Bei Audi und BMW ist zu beobachten, dass eine große Zahl der Fan-Beiträge reine Lob und Sympathiebekundungen sind in dem lediglich das eigene Fahrzeug des Fans dargestellt wird. Diese bringen dem Unternehmen nicht sonderlich viel Nutzen, da die Person allein durch das Gefällt-mir-Klicken der Facebook Seite ihren Besitz eines Fahrzeugs oder zumindest vorhandene Vorliebe für die Marke bereits geäußert hat. Es ist natürlich nur ein theoretischer Idealfall einen große Menge an Fans zu haben, die sich zu einem Großteil auch in der Community einbringen. Marken mit großer Beliebtheit können es gar nicht umgehen, dass viele Leute nur Fan werden um ihr Profil damit zu schmücken und dann in der Community nicht partizipieren. Aber für kleineren, weniger populären Hersteller bieten Facebook Seiten eine Chance wirklich starke Communities organisch aufzubauen und sich somit auch ein Alleinstellungsmerkmal zu erarbeiten.

5   Fazit

Die Arbeit stellt heraus, dass Facebook Seiten Unternehmen viel Nutzen bringen können. Der untersuchten Automobilindustrie hilft dieser neue Kommunikationskanal vor allem zur Verbesserung der persönlichen Beziehung mit den Kunden, die Fans geworden sind in dem sozialen Netzwerk. Somit kann eine noch höhere Identifikation mit der Marke geschaffen werden, was die Kunden noch mehr bindet und sie somit vor dem Abwandern abhält. Genauso wichtig haben sich die Facebook Seiten als Bestandteil des Kundenservices und des Beschwerdemanagements bewiesen. Das interaktive und partizipierende Internet führt dazu, dass Kunden nun einer Vielzahl anderer Kunden ihre Probleme mit dem Fahrzeug oder dem Service mitteilen können. Hier sind die Marken gefragt, entsprechend zu reagieren und den drohenden Verlust des Kunden aber auch des eigenen Images zu retten. Dies gelang den untersuchten Autoherstellern weniger gut. KIA MOTORS Deutschland und SEAT Deutschland sind in den Fallbeispielen offensichtlich Kunden verloren gegangen, weil die aufgetreten Defizite nicht behoben werden und der verärgerte Kunde nicht vertröstet werden konnte.

Die Facebook Seiten unterschieden sich sehr was die Größe der Fan-Mengen anging. Jedoch konnte nicht festgestellt werden, dass die Größe auch gleich mit einer besseren Führung einhergeht. Die Marken unterschieden sich auch in Aspekten wie Interaktionsraten, sowohl was die eigenen betrifft als auch die der Fans. Die Untersuchung der Facebook Seiten ergab aber auch das reine Statistiken allein noch nichts über den Wert der betriebenen Interaktionen aussagen. Ohne sich mit dem Inhalt zu beschäftigen, sind keine Aussagen über die Qualität und den Wert zu treffen.

Durch die Untersuchung der Führungsstile der Facebook Seiten stellte sich heraus, dass die Marken mit unterschiedlichen Ansätzen dies angehen. Dies reicht von einem sehr hohen persönlichen Grad wie es beispielsweise Ford tut, in dem es mehrere Autoren hat dessen Namen und Fotos auf der Seite veröffentlicht werden. Sie kommunizierten pro-aktiv und arbeiteten mit hoher Eigeninitiative. Sie sind hier ein Paradebeispiel für den Typ Friend Brand aus dem Trendreport 2011.

Premiumhersteller wie Audi, BMW und Mercedes-Benz schienen an einem dermaßen persönlichen Umgang nicht so interessiert gewesen zu sein. Sie schätzen diesen Kanal entweder nicht so wichtig ein oder halten ihr begrenztes Engagement für ausreichend, da sie ihr Image von den Produkten und dem Markenmythos ohne weiteres in das soziale Netzwerk übertragen können. Sie haben den Typus der Service Brand oder Friend Brand nicht verkörpert und scheinen dies auch nicht tun zu wollen.

Resümierend kann gesagt werden, dass die Marken zusammengenommen als gesamte Industrie bereits in großer Anzahl mit deutschsprachigen Seiten auf Facebook vertreten sind und im Umgang damit schon einen gewissen Standard erreicht haben. Die Präsenzen waren vom Aufbau her alle auf einem anspruchsvollem Niveau, auch was die Funktionalitäten anging. Jedoch muss der Dialog auf der Pinnwand, die dafür eine gesetzten Mitarbeiter und die Einbettung dieses Kanals in andere Prozesse der Konzerne noch verbessert werden. Zu oft wirkten die Facebook Autoren zwar freundlich und bemüht, aber in einigen Problemstellungen entweder überfordert oder machtlos waren. Die Branche ist jedoch auf einem guten Weg sich Facebook immer besser zunutze zu machen und die Potenziale in dem Rahmen auszuschöpfen wie es die Produktkategorie Automobil zulässt. So kann Facebook für die Hersteller zum Customerbook bzw. Servicebook avancieren.

Literaturverzeichnis

LinkedIn Press Center. (5. August 2011). Abgerufen am 19. August 2011 von LinkedIn:

    http://press.linkedin.com/about

MySpace-Verkauf: Murdoch verspekuliert sich mit Online-Netzwerk. (30. Juni 2011).

    Abgerufen am 15. Juli 2011 von Focus Online:

    http://www.focus.de/finanzen/news/unternehmen/myspace-verkauf-murdoch-verspekuliert-sich-mit-online-netzwerk_aid_641641.html

Soziales Netzwerk: MySpace entlässt die Hälfte seiner Mitarbeiter. (11. Januar 2011).

    Abgerufen am 15. Juli 2011 von Spiegel Online:
    http://www.spiegel.de/netzwelt/web/0,1518,739009,00.html

Volkswagen International. (2011). Abgerufen am 8. August 2011 von Facebook:

    http://www.facebook.com/volkswagen

Alby, T. (2008). *Web 2.0: Konzepte, Anwendungen und Technologien* (3. Ausg.).

    München: Carl Hanser Verlag.

Altimeter Group. (27. Juli 2011). *The 8 Success Criteria For Facebook Page Marketing.*

    Abgerufen am 7. August 2011 von Slideshare:

    http://www.slideshare.net/jeremiah_owyang/the-8-success-criteria-for -facebookpage-marketing

Bruhn, M., & Homburg, C. (2010). *Handbuch Kundenbindungsmanagement* (7. Ausg.).

    Wiesbaden: Gabler.

Esch, F.-R. (2009). *Strategie und Technik der Markenführung* (6. Ausg.). München: Vahlen.

Facebook Inc. (2011). *Facebook Ads.* Abgerufen am 2. August 2011 von Facebook:

    http://www.facebook.com/adsmarketing/index.php?sk=home

Facebook Inc. (16. Mai 2011). *Facebook Pages Guide.* Abgerufen am 7. August 2001 von

    Facebook: http://ads.ak.facebook.com/ads/FacebookAds/FB_PagesGuide_MediaKit_051611.pdf

Facebook Inc. (2011). *Facebook Statistics.* Abgerufen am 12. Juli 2011 von Facebook:

    https://www.facebook.com/press/info.php?statistics

Fancher, E. (8. Oktober 2010). *McDonalds plants brand in Zynga's Farmville* . Abgerufen am 18.

   Juli 2011 von San Francisco Business Times:

   http://www.bizjournals.com/sanfrancisco/stories/2010/10/04/daily57.html

Fittkau & Maaß Consulting. (29. Juni 2011). Abgerufen am 20. Juli 2011 von W3B-Umfrage:

   http://www.w3b.org/web-20/an-facebook-fuhrt-kein-weg-mehr-vorbei.html

Frickel, C. (6. Juli 2011). *Skype-Integration: Facebook startet Videochats.* Abgerufen am 20. Juli

   2011 von Focus Online: http://www.focus.de/digital/internet/facebook/skypeintegration-

   facebook-startet-videochats_aid_643133.html

Früh, W. (2007). *Inhaltsanalyse* (6. Ausg.). Konstanz: UVK.

Gardener, M. (27. Juli 2011). *Google Plus Blog.* Abgerufen am 14. August 2011 von Google Plus

   Blog: http://googleplusblog.de/google-plus-neuigkeiten/google-plus-business-in-dertestphase-

   offizieller-start-unbekann

Gross-Selbeck, D. S. (10.. August 2011). *net.work.xing.* Abgerufen am 13.. August 2011 von

   Xing: http://blog.xing.com/2011/08/halbjahreszahlen-2011/

Hettler, U. (2010). *Social Media Marketing.* München: Oldenbourg.

Holmboe, D. (3. Januar 2011). *Facebook Edgerank Algorithm Explained* . Abgerufen am 2.

   August 2011 von YouTube: http://youtu.be/kI4YIYInou0

Hutter, T. (18.. Juli 2011). Abgerufen am 20.. Juli 2011 von Thomas Hutter:

   http://www.thomashutter.com/index.php/2011/07/social-media-social-networksstatistiken-

   deutschland-gewinner-und-verlierer-update-juli-2011/

Joshi, K., & Rutledge, P.-A. (2011). *Using Facebook.* Indianapolis: QUE.

Kolbrück, O. (7. Juni 2011). *Deutsche Bahn: Twitter soll Kundenservice verbessern.* Abgerufen

   am 2. August 2011 von Horizont.net:

   http://www.horizont.net/aktuell/digital/pages/protected/Deutsche-Bahn-Twitter-soll-

   Kundenservice-verbessern_100593.html

Kopp, G. (2008). *Behavioral Targeting: Identifizierung verhaltensorientierter Zielgruppen im*

   Rahmen der Online-Werbung. Norderstedt: GRIN Verlag.

Lake, L. (2009). *Consumer Behavior for Dummies.* Indianapolis: Wiley.

O'Reilly, T. (30. September 2005). *What Is Web 2.0?* Abgerufen am 14. Juli 2011 von O'Reilly

  Verlag: http://www.oreilly.de/artikel/web20.html

Patalong, F. (15. Mai 2010). *Spiele in Social Networks: Das Zynga-Dilemma.* Abgerufen am 18.

  Juli 2011 von Spiegel Online:

http://www.spiegel.de/netzwelt/games/0,1518,694205,00.html

Peter, S. I. (2001). *Kundenbindung als Marketingziel* (2. aktualisierte Ausg.). Wiesbaden:

  Gabler.

Rössler, P. (2005). *Inhaltsanalyse.* Konstanz: UVK.

Safko, L. (2010). *The Social Media Bible* (2. Ausg.). Hoboken: Wiley.

Schmitt, S. (August. 7 2011). *Volkswagen International.* Abgerufen am 8. August 2011 von

  Facebook: http://www.facebook.com/volkswagen

Schönherr, K. (4. August 2011). Google Plus hat 25 Millionen Nutzer. Abgerufen am 4. August

  2011 von Werben & Verkaufen:
  http://www.wuv.de/nachrichten/digital/google_plus_hat_25_millionen_nutzer

Schröder, J. (28. Mai 2011). Wie Facebook die Konkurrenz auffrisst. Abgerufen am 15. Juli 2011

  von ZDF Blog: http://blog.zdf.de/hyperland/2011/05/wie-facebook-die konkurrenzauffrisst/

Schwindt, A. (2010). Das Facebook Buch. Köln: O'Reilly.

Social eCart. (15. Januar 2011). Social eCart Blog. Abgerufen am 15. Juli 2011 von Social eCart:

  http://www.socialecart.com/blog/

Stuber, R. (2010). Erfolgreiches Social Media Marketing mit Facebook, Twitter, Xing & Co.

  Düsseldorf: DATA BECKER.

Unabhängiges Landeszentrum für Datenschutz Schleswig-Holstein. (19. August 2011). ULD an

  Webseitenbetreiber: "Facebook-Reichweitenanalyse abschalten". Abgerufen am 20.

  August 2011 von Unabhängiges Landeszentrum für Datenschutz Schleswig-Holstein:

  https://www.datenschutzzentrum.de/presse/20110819-facebook.htm

Weber, L. (2009). Marketing to the Social Web. Hoboken: Wiley.

Weinberg, T. (2010). Social Media Marketing. Köln: O'Reilly.

Zarrella, D. (2010). Das Social Media Marketing Buch. Köln: O'Reilly.

Zucker.Kommunikation. (Juli 2011). Trendreport Juli 2011: Facebook, Marken & TV in

Deutschland. Abgerufen am 7. August 2011 von Slideshare:

http://www.slideshare.net/zuckerberlin/trendreport-juli-2011-facebook-marken-tv-in-

deutschland

Lipid Rafts and Caveolae

Edited by
Christopher J. Fielding

Related Titles

Tamm, L. K. (Ed.)

Protein-Lipid Interactions

From Membrane Domains to Cellular Networks

2005

ISBN 3-527-31151-3

Wedlich, D. (Ed.)

Cell Migration in Development and Disease

2005

ISBN 3-527-30587-4

Benz, R. (Ed.)

Bacterial and Eukaryotic Porins

Structure, Function, Mechanism

2004

ISBN 3-527-30775-3

Krauss, G.

Biochemistry of Signal Transduction and Regulation

2003

ISBN 3-527-30591-2

Yawata, Y.

Cell Membrane

The Red Blood Cell as a Model

2003

ISBN 3-527-30463-0

Lipid Rafts and Caveolae

From Membrane Biophysics to Cell Biology

Edited by
Christopher J. Fielding

WILEY-VCH Verlag GmbH & Co. KGaA

The Editor

Prof. Dr. Christopher J. Fielding
Cardiovascular Research Institute and
Department of Medicine
University of California San Francisco
San Francisco, CA 94143
USA

■ All books published by Wiley-VCH are carefully produced. Nevertheless, authors, editor, and publisher do not warrant the information contained in these books, including this book, to mind that statements, data, illustrations, procedural details or other items may inadvertently be inaccurate.

Library of Congress Card No.:
applied for

British Library Cataloguing-in-Publication Data:
A catalogue record for this book is available from the British Library.

Bibliographic information published by Die Deutsche Bibliothek
Die Deutsche Bibliothek lists this publication in the Deutsche Nationalbibliografie; detailed bibliographic data is available in the Internet at <http://dnb.ddb.de>

© 2006 WILEY-VCH Verlag GmbH & Co. KGaA, Weinheim

Typesetting: Typomedia GmbH, Ostfildern
Printing: betz-Druck GmbH, Darmstadt
Binding: J. Schäffer GmbH, Grünstadt
Cover Design: Grafik-Design Schulz, Fußgönheim

Printed in the Federal Republic of Germany
Printed on acid-free paper

ISBN-13:   978-3-527-31261-0
ISBN-10:   3-527-31261-7

Table of Contents

Lipid Rafts and Caveolae. Christopher J. Fielding
Copyright © 2006 WILEY-VCH Verlag GmbH & Co. KGaA, Weinheim
ISBN: 3-527-31261-7

Preface

This volume is the first book-length survey of caveolae and lipid rafts. Interest has developed rapidly in the role of these surface microdomains in such diverse fields as transmembrane signaling, cell locomotion, vascular relaxation, senescence, and the uptake and exit from cells of viruses and bacteria. Individual chapters in this volume cover areas as diverse as the forces that induce and maintain membrane invaginations, and the clinical relevance of multiprotein complexes at the cell surface, defects in which are associated with cancer, and Alzheimer's and prion-dependent diseases.

The book includes contributors from twelve countries. This reflects the growth and spread of these studies over the last twenty-five years, since the recognition of free cholesterol/sphingolipid (FC/SPH) rich cell microdomains as a distinct class of cell-surface structures. The historical origin of this concept is presented in the Overview by Drs Meder and Simons. Their chapter places caveolar and lipid rafts in context as biological membranes with special roles in information transfer across the plasma membrane, and between cell compartments. Other contributions described research, in a number of cases for the first time, in key areas of the molecular physiology of lipid-protein complexes in rafts and caveolae.

One area addressed in several chapters is the physical nature of FC/SPH-rich microdomains, their origin, and their lifetimes as independent structures within the cell membrane. Are planar lipid rafts, and invaginated caveolae, variations of a common theme? Can they be interconverted? Contributions by Dr Mayor and colleagues and by Drs Sens and Turner on the biophysics of lipid rafts and caveolae respectively, break new ground in describing the techniques now available to analyze these structures. They also summarize the physical forces sustaining them in the cell membrane.

A second group of chapters describes how these physical forces at the surface regulate cell behaviour. The chapter by Dr van Deurs and colleagues addresses one of the most important of these, the significance of caveolae in endocytosis, a pathway alternate to that mediated by clathrin-coated pits. The balance of evidence indicates that though caveolae are usually relatively stable, they can be induced to bud off by a variety of physiological and pathological stimuli. The chapter by Drs Park and Cho reviews the role of caveolae in maintaining cell shape, and promoting locomotion, though their interaction with the actin skeleton.

Lipid Rafts and Caveolae. Christopher J. Fielding
Copyright © 2006 WILEY-VCH Verlag GmbH & Co. KGaA, Weinheim
ISBN: 3-527-31261-7

A third group of contributions deals with recent research on the factors controlling the level of lipid (especially FC) and protein (especially the structural protein caveolin) in cell surface caveolae. Drs Everson and Smart summarizes research indicating that caveolins play key roles in FC homeostasis and intracellular transport, in addition to promoting caveola formation at the cell surface. The chapter by Drs C. and P. Fielding describes mechanisms by which the level of FC at the cell surface affects the structure and function of caveolae, and re-examines the concept of caveolin as scaffold. Data from these and other laboratories have shown that the composition of caveolae is dynamically regulated, and can respond to the extracellular environment as well as the current internal needs of the cell.

One of the best characterized functions of FC/SPH-rich domains is to serve as an assembly point for the multiprotein complexes that promote signal transduction. Recent research has identified structural features that contribute to the assembly of these complexes. These include reversible covalent modifications, such as changes in protein phosphorylation and acylation, that promote assembly and disassembly, leading to signal propagation to the nucleus. The chapter by Dr Damjanovitch and colleagues gives a detailed review of the most recent data on these events in lipid rafts. Dr Mastick and colleagues dissect the regulatory role of caveolin within caveolae during signaling via transmembrane growth factor receptors.

Perhaps the most detailed of all investigation in the field of caveolae has concerned the mechanism by which the activity of endothelial nitric oxide synthase (eNOS) a major determinant of vascular relaxation, is regulated by its association with caveolae. The chapter by Dr Feron, based on the work of his own and other laboratories, describes in detail the complex relationship between e-nos, caveolin and FC.

A final group of chapters discusses the roles of FC/SPH rich domains in human disease. Drs David and Liscovitch discuss the roles of caveolin and caveolin in cancer cells, and show that under different conditions both positive and negative pathways can be identified. The chapter by Dr Zurzolo and colleagues describes the recently identified roles of FC/SPH domains in the pathophysiology of prion-based and Alzheimer's diseases.

The present volume has two main purposes. It brings together current hypotheses about the structure and functions of lipid rafts and caveolae by leading experts. These ideas will be of interest to biophysicists, biochemists, cell biologists and clinicians who study biological membranes. The book also provides a convenient reference work summarizing published work in this rapidly growing area. We hope that this will assist the research of a new generation of investigators drawn to this subtle but fascinating field, with its ramifications in many areas of current biology.

San Francisco, December 2005   Christopher J. Fielding

Author List

Andrea Bodnár
Cell Biophysics Research Group of the
Hungarian Academy of Sciences
Medical and Health Science Center
Research Center for Molecular
Medicine
University of Debrecen
Nagyerdei krt. 98
4012 Debrecen
Hungary

Vincenza Campana
Dipartimento di Biologia e Patologia
Cellulare e Molecolare
Centro di Endocrinologia ed Oncologia
Sperimentale del Consiglio Nazionale
delle Ricerche
Università degli Studi di Napoli
Federico II
80131 Napoli
Italy
and
Unité de Trafic Membranaire et
Pathogénèse
Institut Pasteur
25 rue du Dr. Roux
75724 Paris Cedex 15
France

Haiming Cao
Department of Biochemistry and
Molecular Biology
School of Medicine and College of
Agriculture, Biotechnology, and Natural
Resources
University of Nevada
Reno
NV 89557
USA

Kyung A. Cho
Department of Biochemistry and
Molecular Biology
Seoul National University Medical
School
28 Yon Gon Dong
Chong-No Ku
Seoul 110–799
Korea

Sándor Damjanovich
Cell Biophysics Research Group of the
Hungarian Academy of Sciences and
Department of Biophysics and Cell
Biology
Medical and Health Science Center
Research Center for Molecular
Medicine
University of Debrecen
Nagyerdei krt. 98
4012 Debrecen
Hungary

William V. Everson
Department of Pediatrics
University of Kentucky
423 Sanders-Brown Center on Aging
800 South Limestone Street
Lexington
KY 40536–0230
USA

Olivier Feron
University of Louvain Medical School
Unit of Pharmacology and
Therapeutics
UCL-FATH 5349
53 Avenue E. Mounier
1200 Brussels
Belgium

Christopher J. Fielding
Cardiovascular Research Institute
and Department of Physiology
University of California San Francisco
San Francisco
CA 94143
USA

Phoebe E. Fielding
Cardiovascular Research Institute
and Department of Medicine
University of California San Francisco
San Francisco
CA 94143
USA

Anette M. Hommelgaard
Structural Cell Biology Unit
Department of Medical Anatomy
The Panum Institute
University of Copenhagen
2200 Copenhagen N
Denmark

Mordechai Liscovitch
Department of Biological Regulation
Weizmann Institute of Science
Rehovot 76100
Israel

Cynthia Corley Mastick
Department of Biochemistry and
Molecular Biology
School of Medicine and College of
Agriculture, Biotechnology, and Natural
Resources
University of Nevada
Reno
NV 89557
USA

Satyajit Mayor
National Centre for Biological Sciences
UAS-GKVK Campus
Bangalore 560065
India

Doris Meder
Max Planck Institute of Molecular Cell
Biology and Genetics
Pfotenhauerstr. 108
01307 Dresden
Germany

Sang Chul Park
Department of Biochemistry and
Molecular Biology
Seoul National University Medical
School
28 Yon Gon Dong
Chong-No Ku
Seoul 110–799
Korea

Dana Ravid
Department of Biological Regulation
Weizmann Institute of Science
Rehovot 76100
Israel

Kirstine Roepstorff
Structural Cell Biology Unit
Department of Medical Anatomy
The Panum Institute
University of Copenhagen
2200 Copenhagen N
Denmark

Kirsten Sandvig
Institute for Cancer Research
Department of Biochemistry
The Norwegian Radium Hospital
Montebello
0310 Oslo
Norway

Amy Sanguinetti
Department of Biochemistry and
Molecular Biology
School of Medicine and College of
Agriculture, Biotechnology, and Natural
Resources
University of Nevada
Reno
NV 89557
USA

Daniela Sarnataro
Dipartimento di Biologia e Patologia
Cellulare e Molecolare
Centro di Endocrinologia ed Oncologia
Sperimentale del Consiglio Nazionale
delle Ricerche
Università degli Studi di Napoli
Federico II
80131 Napoli
Italy

Pierre Sens
Phisico-Chimie Theorique
ESPCI
10 rue Vauquelin
75231 Paris cedex 05
France

Pranav Sharma
Cold Spring Harbor Laboratories
Cold Spring Harbor
New York 11724
USA

Kai Simons
Max Planck Institute of Molecular Cell
Biology and Genetics
Pfotenhauerstr. 108
01307 Dresden
Germany

Eric J. Smart
Barnstable-Brown Endowed Chair
of Diabetes
University of Kentucky
429 Sanders Brown Center on Aging
800 South Limestone Street
Lexington
KY 40536–0230
USA

János Szöllősi
Cell Biophysics Research Group of the
Hungarian Academy of Sciences and
Department of Biophysics and Cell
Biology
Medical and Health Science Center
Research Center for Molecular
Medicine
University of Debrecen
Nagyerdei krt. 98
4012 Debrecen
Hungary

Suhani Thakker
Department of Biochemistry
and Molecular Biology
School of Medicine and College
of Agriculture, Biotechnology,
and Natural Resources
University of Nevada
Reno
NV 89557
USA

Maria Torgersen
Institute for Cancer Research
Department of Biochemistry
The Norwegian Radium Hospital
Montebello
0310 Oslo
Norway

Matthew S. Turner
Department of Physics
Warwick University
Coventry CV4 7AL
UK

György Vámosi
Cell Biophysics Research Group of the
Hungarian Academy of Sciences
Medical and Health Science Center
Research Center for Molecular
Medicine
University of Debrecen
Nagyerdei krt. 98
4012 Debrecen
Hungary

Bo van Deurs
Structural Cell Biology Unit
Department of Medical Anatomy
The Panum Institute
University of Copenhagen
2200 Copenhagen N
Denmark

Rajat Varma
Program in Molecular Pathogenesis
Skirball Institute for Biomolecular
Medicine
New York University School of
Medicine
540 First Avenue
New York 10016
USA

György Vereb
Department of Biophysics
and Cell Biology
Medical and Health Science Center
Research Center for Molecular
Medicine
University of Debrecen
Nagyerdei krt. 98
4012 Debrecen
Hungary

Frederik Vilhardt
Structural Cell Biology Unit
Department of Medical Anatomy
The Panum Institute
University of Copenhagen
2200 Copenhagen N
Denmark

Chiara Zurzolo
Dipartimento di Biologia e Patologia
Cellulare e Molecolare
Centro di Endocrinologia ed Oncologia
Sperimentale del Consiglio Nazionale
delle Ricerche
Università degli Studi di Napoli
Federico II
80131 Napoli
Italy
and
Unité de Trafic Membranaire et
Pathogénèse
Institut Pasteur
25 rue du Dr. Roux
75724 Paris Cedex 15
France

1
Lipid Rafts, Caveolae, and Membrane Traffic

Doris Meder and Kai Simons

1.1
Introduction

Cell membranes are dynamic assemblies of a variety of lipids and proteins. They form a protective layer around the cell, but also mediate the communication with the outside world – that is, neighboring cells in a tissue, hormones and growth factors arriving with the blood supply, or pathogens trying to enter the system. The unique feature of cell membranes is that their lipid and protein constituents can self-assemble into 5 nm-thin, two-dimensional fluids composed of two apposing lipid monolayers that form a hydrophobic interior and two polar interfacial regions oriented towards the aqueous medium. This organizing principle – the lipid bilayer – is the oldest, still valid molecular model of biological structures. The first model that incorporated proteins was proposed by Danielli and Davson, and assumed that the bilayer was made up entirely of lipids and that proteins covered the two polar surfaces [1]. Some 40 years later, the fluid mosaic model of the cell membrane proposed by Singer and Nicolson [2] was a conceptual breakthrough. Amphipathic membrane proteins were recognized to reside within, and even span, the whole bilayer that was depicted as a dynamic structure, the components of which are laterally mobile. However, the view that the lipids in the bilayer mainly serve as a homogeneous solvent for proteins [2] has been proven to be too simplistic. Lipids are not only distributed asymmetrically between the two leaflets of the bilayer, but also within the leaflet they are heterogeneously arranged [3]. This chapter will recapitulate the history and recent advances in membrane biology including the lipid raft concept, and then summarize current views on the functions of rafts and caveolae in membrane traffic.

1.2
Basic Organization Principles of a Cell Membrane

The lipid bilayer is a two-dimensional fluid, where lipid molecules exchange slowly between leaflets but are mobile within the leaflet. This mobility consists of two parts:

Lipid Rafts and Caveolae. Christopher J. Fielding
Copyright © 2006 WILEY-VCH Verlag GmbH & Co. KGaA, Weinheim
ISBN: 3-527-31261-7

- the "translational freedom" of a molecule – that is, its lateral mobility; and
- the "configurational freedom" that is, the ability to flex parts of the molecule and to rotate bonds in its carbon backbone.

Synthetic bilayers change from a liquid state with high translational and configurational freedom into a rigid gel state at a characteristic freezing point. Cell membranes at physiological temperatures are almost always in the liquid state, but can contain regions with high configurational order, as will be described later. Importantly, the lipid bilayer of cell membranes is asymmetric, with a different lipid composition in the two leaflets. The main lipid components of cellular membranes are glycerophospholipids, with the most abundant species being phosphatidylcholine (PC) in the exoplasmic leaflet and phosphatidylethanolamine (PE) and phosphatidylserine (PS) in the inner leaflet, as well as sphingolipids with glycosphingolipids and sphingomyelin (SM) mostly localized to the exoplasmic leaflet. Sterols make up the third lipid class, and are present in both leaflets. Mammalian cell membranes contain only one sterol, namely cholesterol, but probably more than thousand different glyco- and sphingolipid species, emerging from the combinatorial propensity to assemble lipids from different backbones linked in different ways with two varying hydrocarbon chains and a vast number of headgroups. A large number of flippases and translocators tightly control the asymmetric distribution of all these lipids across the bilayer [4].

Lipids are differentially distributed between cellular organelles. The endoplasmic reticulum and the Golgi-complex contain mainly glycerophospholipids and only small amounts of sphingolipids, whereas the plasma membrane is relatively enriched in SM and glycosphingolipids [5]. Also within the membrane plane of one organelle, lipids are believed to be heterogeneously arranged. Caveolae – small invaginations of the plasma membrane – are enriched in glycosphingolipids [6], and phosphatidylinositol-3'-phosphate (PI(3)P) is concentrated in subdomains of early endosome membranes [7]. Recently, vacuole-fusion in yeast has been shown to be controlled by microdomains of ergosterol, diacylglycerol and phosphoinositide-3-and-4-phosphate [8]. Furthermore, membranes are differentially susceptible to extraction by detergents such as Triton X-100 or CHAPS at 4 °C, with some proteins and lipids being completely solubilized and others forming so-called "detergent-resistant membranes" (DRM; for a review, see [9]). These findings suggested that cell membranes contained microdomains in which lipids were more tightly packed and thus not accessible to the detergent, although it is widely accepted that DRMs do not have an exact *in-vivo* correlate but are defined by being formed during the detergent treatment [10]. These microdomains were later termed "rafts" and were described as sphingolipid-cholesterol assemblies containing a subset of membrane proteins [11]. Currently, the raft hypothesis is heavily debated [12–14], with the main discussion points being the methodologies to study rafts and the size of the domains (see below). The core of the raft concept is that cell membranes phase-separate into different domains and that this is a lipid-driven process. In light of the ongoing discussion in the field, the following sections will provide an overview about what is known about phase separation, first discussing the studies conducted in model membrane systems and later in cell membranes.

1.3
Evidence for Phase Separation in Model Membrane Systems:
Liquid-Ordered and Liquid-Disordered Phases

Various model membrane systems have been used by physicists and chemists to study phase separation in lipid mixtures. They are either monolayers or bilayers. Monolayers are either assembled at an air-water interface with the packing density of the lipids being adjusted by applying lateral pressure, or on a supporting lipid monolayer that is fixed to a solid support. Bilayers are used in the supported version as described above, or in the form of vesicles. The most commonly used vesicles are large or giant unilamellar vesicles (LUV or GUV, respectively) composed of only a single bilayer, but also multilamellar vesicles (MLV) are used. The basic principles were first established in simple binary lipid mixtures, but recently ternary mixtures which more closely mimic the composition of the cell plasma membrane have been used. The mixtures usually contain one lipid with a high melting temperature (T_m), one with a low T_m, and cholesterol. GUVs are probably the system closest to a cell membrane, because artifacts from a support are excluded. Still, cell membranes are asymmetric with different lipid compositions of the outer versus the inner leaflet, while the GUVs used so far were all symmetric. Since maintaining an asymmetric lipid distribution is energy-consuming, perhaps by reconstituting lipid translocators into liposomes this drawback can be overcome in the future. Although model membrane systems produce very simplified pictures of cell membranes, there are many examples of a close correlation with experimental data obtained in living cells [14].

Ipsen et al. were the first to describe the formation of a liquid-ordered phase by cholesterol and saturated phospholipids [15,16]. This phase can coexist with other lipid phases, and its characteristics are described as follows: the translational order of lipid molecules within the liquid-ordered phase is similar to that in a fluid bilayer state, whereas the configurational order of the hydrocarbon chains compares more to that in a gel state. The formation of the liquid-ordered phase was attributed to the unique chemical nature of cholesterol (for a review, see [17]), but later it was shown that all natural sterols promote domain formation and that also small amounts of ceramide (3%) can stabilize domains formed in vesicles [18]. Leventis and Silvius showed that the interaction of cholesterol with different lipid species is dependent on the nature of their hydrocarbon chains and, to a lesser extent, also on their headgroup. The interaction preference decreases with SM > PS > PC > PE and with increasing unsaturation of the acyl chains [19]. Whereas the kink in unsaturated hydrocarbon chains is likely to hinder tight packing with the flat sterol ring of cholesterol, the reason for the preferential interaction of cholesterol with SM is still a debated issue.

The first visualization of "raft-like domains" in model membranes was achieved by Dietrich et al. [20]. They visualized liquid ordered domains in supported bi-layers and GUVs composed not only of synthetic lipid mixtures but also of lipid extracts from brush border membrane, the apical membrane of intestinal cells. Domain formation was cholesterol-dependent, since domains disappeared after treatment with the cholesterol-extracting drug methyl-β-cyclodextrin. Another big step forward was the establishment of a ternary phase diagram of SM/PC/choles-terol at the physiological temperature of 37 °C [21]. This predicts the coexistence of liquid-ordered and liquid-disordered phases for a wide range of compositions mimicking those occurring in the plasma membrane of cells. Most domains ob-served in model membranes are rather large (i.e., several micrometer in diameter) or they start small when they are being formed and then grow continuously by collision and fusion as the system reaches equilibrium [22]. Contrary to this, raft domains in cells are believed to be small, most likely because the cell membrane is not at equilibrium (see below). Interestingly, fluorescence resonance energy trans-fer (FRET) measurements on vesicles composed of a ternary lipid mixture mimick-ing the outer leaflet of the plasma membrane revealed heterogeneities (i.e., do-mains) of sizes in the tens of nanometer range at 37 °C [23]. Large domains were observed with the same lipid mixture only below 20 °C.

A slightly different interpretation of liquid-liquid immiscibility observed in model membranes was proposed by McConnell and colleagues. These authors argue for the formation of "condensed complexes" between cholesterol and SM rather than a liquid-ordered phase or domain. The name originates from the ob-servation that cholesterol and SM occupy less surface area when mixed together compared to the sum of the areas occupied by each component alone before mix-ing. Such a complex is supposed to contain 15–30 molecules with a fixed stoichio-metry of 2:1 (SM:cholesterol). These complexes could exist in quite high concen-tration without necessarily leading to a phase separation (for a review, see [24]). However, the condensed complex theory was developed on monolayer membranes and has not yet been validated for bilayers.

Taken together, there is clear evidence for lipid-driven domain formation in model membrane systems mimicking the outer leaflet of the plasma membrane. On the contrary, domain formation could not be observed in lipid mixtures mim-icking the inner leaflet of the plasma membrane [25]. The intermolecular forces leading to phase separation are van der Waals interactions between saturated acyl chains and cholesterol, as well as forces such as hydrophobic shielding or the "umbrella effect", described for cholesterol filling the holes left between the acyl chains of glycosphingolipids with large headgroups [26]. However, none of the systems described so far has included proteins in their analysis, and the question remains whether proteins choose the domain they partition into, or whether they organize a domain around them.

Partitioning experiments have been performed, in which proteins were reconsti-tuted into model membranes, and their phase distribution was analyzed. In this way, glycosyl-phosphatidyl-inositol (GPI)-anchored placental alkaline phosphatase (PLAP; [27,28] and Thy-1 [29] were shown to partition into the liquid-ordered phase, and the chain length of the GPI-anchor was shown to be important for partitioning of the protein [30]. Similarly, peptides modified with prenyl groups were excluded from liquid-ordered domains, while peptides modified with cholesterol or palmityl chains partitioned significantly into the ordered phase [31]. Partitioning studies with synthetic transmembrane peptides revealed that longer transmembrane domains are incorporated better into liquid-ordered domains than shorter versions [32]. Another important determinant for the partitioning of a molecule is the size and orientation of its dipole moment [33]. The membrane dipole moment is stronger in ordered phases where the dipoles are better aligned. Only molecules displaying a dipole moment with the same orientation as the dipolar potential of the membrane, are predicted to be able to enter the ordered phase. Nevertheless, our knowledge about lipid-transmembrane protein interactions is still scarce and this area of research is a major challenge.

1.4
Evidence for Phase Separation in Cell Membranes: The "Raft Concept"

There are several indications for cell membranes being inhomogeneous fluids and for the existence of lipid-driven phase separation. One key finding was the selective co-clustering of certain membrane components and segregation from others upon application of antibodies to living cells. Co-clustering of lipids was first observed in lymphocytes, where one ganglioside species was capped with antibodies and another species was found to redistribute into the cap [34]. It was then shown that simultaneous addition of two antibodies against apparently homogeneously distributed surface antigens could, in selected cases, lead to their co-clustering and in other cases to their segregation [35]. These findings were explained by certain proteins residing in small raft domains that are below the light microscopic resolution in size, and others residing outside the raft domains. Upon cross-linking by antibodies the small raft domains coalesce into visible, stable clusters that contain several different raft proteins. The antigens that were previously in the non-raft environment are excluded from the coalescing domains and thus form separate clusters upon cross-linking. How these large-scale domains containing multiple raft components could be formed in a homogeneous membrane without the occurrence of phase separation is not obvious, and an alternative explanation for this phenomenon has not been put forward. Since then, two techniques have been used to directly assess liquid order in living cells. Gidwani et al. measured the steady-state anisotropy of the lipid-probe DPH-PC, which is sensitive to cholesterol-induced liquid order. With this approach, they found that approximately 40% of the plasma membrane of mast cells is in a liquid-ordered state [36]. More recently, Gaus et al. were able to directly visualize liquid-ordered domains in living macrophages on the light microscopic level. They applied two-photon imaging of the amphiphilic dye LAURDAN, which changes its emission peak depending on the state of its lipid environment [37].

Other techniques have also been employed for assessing raft domains in living cells, most of them analyzing the distribution and dynamics of membrane proteins rather than lipids. Pralle et al. measured the local diffusion of a bead attached to a single protein molecule in the plasma membrane of fibroblasts within an area smaller than 100 nm in diameter [38]. In this way, diffusion was not hindered by cytoskeletal constraints but was supposed to be free. Proteins previously shown to be resistant to detergent extraction diffused three times slower than detergent-soluble proteins. After cholesterol depletion, the former diffused as fast as the latter. The first group of proteins was thus assumed to reside in a raft environment and to diffuse together with the whole raft entity. After destruction of this entity by cholesterol extraction the proteins behaved as if they were diffusing in a non-raft environment. From the viscous drag and from the diffusion coefficient, the size of the raft entities was calculated to be approximately 50 nm in diameter. Extrapolated from average protein and lipid densities in cell membranes, one raft entity was calculated to contain roughly 3000 lipid molecules and 10–20 proteins.

Remarkably, Prior et al. come to a very similar size for raft domains formed in the cytoplasmic leaflet of the plasma membrane using a completely different technique [39]. They ripped plasma membrane sheets off adherent cells and labeled them with gold-coupled antibodies against H-Ras and K-Ras, supposed to reside inside and outside of raft domains, respectively. Statistical analysis of the distribution of the gold particles revealed that 35% of H-Ras labels were clustered in domains of roughly 44 nm diameter. These domains were cholesterol-dependent. Furthermore, cross-linking of GPI-anchored green fluorescent protein (GFP-GPI) in the exoplasmic leaflet resulted in co-localization of the H-Ras clusters with the formed GPI-patches, but did not change their size. However, 20% of the non-raft protein K-Ras was also found to be clustered in domains of 32 nm diameter, although these domains were cholesterol-independent. H- and K-Ras had been reported to occupy distinct domains in the plasma membrane before [40]. Recently, single molecule imaging of H-Ras revealed cholesterol and actin dependent domains as large as 250 nm [41].

An often-applied technique trying to visualize raft domains *in vivo* is that of FRET. Hetero-FRET, which detects energy transfer between two different fluorophores, has not proven successful [42–44], most likely because the probability that donor and acceptor are in the same microdomain is very low. Even cross-linking one raft marker by antibodies does not lead to appreciable recruitment of others [45]. Recently, Mayor and coworkers refined their previous analysis [46] using homo-FRET (i.e., energy transfer between two fluorophores of the same kind) to study clustering of GPI-anchored proteins in the plasma membrane [47]. By measuring the anisotropy decay over time, these authors found that 20–40% of the GPI-anchored proteins are present in small complexes of two to four molecules, while the remainder is randomly distributed as monomers. The limitation of FRET measurements becomes obvious in these studies. The technique provides information about "closeness" on a very small scale (5 nm), but is not suited for visualizing bigger entities.

The fact that raft domains are difficult to visualize *in vivo* has led to a number of alternative explanations, mostly describing smaller entities and, most importantly, describing the formation of these entities as a protein-driven, induced event. The smallest entity was proposed by Kusumi and colleagues, who have pioneered single-particle tracking with ultra-high sampling frequencies of 40 000 Hz. The spatial resolution achieved with this frequency is 20 nm, meaning that if the domains were significantly larger and the probe resided either inside or outside the domain for several consecutive steps, then different diffusion behaviors could be observed. Since however raft and non-raft markers displayed the same diffusion characteristics, it was postulated that rafts are extremely small, namely molecular complexes of at least three membrane components, one of which comprises a saturated acyl chain or cholesterol. Stabilized raft domains accessible to diffusion measurements would only form by clustering following stimulation (for a review, see [48]). Anderson and Jacobson have put forward the lipid shell hypothesis, in which roughly 80 lipid molecules are supposed to surround a raft protein and form a shell of 7 nm diameter [49]. The shells would be thermodynamically stable structures resulting from specific binding interactions between proteins and lipids, and could target the protein into larger raft-domains. How the larger raft domains form and why the raft-protein must assemble a shell of raft-lipids around it before it can enter a raft-domain remain open questions.

The size of raft domains is heavily debated and, as a consequence of the different measurements, their existence is questioned. Consensus is reached in that the proposed domain sizes of 200 nm or larger based on single-particle tracking experiments [50,51] were most likely clustered rafts, formed and stabilized by the multi-valent beads used for the tracking. Also, the 50-nm raft calculated from the viscous drag experiments by Pralle et al. [38] could have been a stabilized raft in which the altered dynamics due to optical trap led to enlargement of a previously smaller structure. This leaves us with a domain size between the 5 nm derived from the FRET measurements [47] and the <20 nm derived from the high-speed single particle tracking studies [52]. Better estimates will have to await the development of new methods which can finally assess the size of isolated raft domains *in vivo*.

In light of the co-clustering data [35], the visualization of distinct liquid-ordered domains in living cells [37], and the evidence that isolated cell membranes phase separate *in vitro* [20], it seems reasonable to assume that native cell membranes can display phase separation. One explanation for the formation of small and transient domains in the plasma membrane lies in its composition. In contrast to ternary lipid mixtures in model systems, the plasma membrane is composed of hundreds of different lipid species and, in addition to that, a variety of proteins. Viewed over a large scale, the complexity of the plasma membrane should counteract phase separation, buffer fluctuations, and in fact protect the cell against rapid phase transitions in response to small changes in the environment. If every fusion or budding event led to a phase transition, it would be difficult to prevent leakages through the bilayer and keep the membrane tight. Viewed on a smaller scale however, the picture can appear very different. Local impurities or changes in membrane composition can allow coalescence and separation of domains containing reaction partners and thus provide a regulatory principle.

1.5
Raft Domains are Clustered to Exert their Function

While the steady-state existence, size and shape of liquid-ordered domains in cells remains the subject of debate, agreement has been reached on the fact that raft domains coalesce upon cross-linking to form signaling and possibly also sorting platforms [53–55]. Cross-linking is achieved by multivalent ligands binding to surface receptors or by cytoplasmic scaffolding proteins. The initial cross-linking event is thought to increase the number of contact sites between raft proteins and lipids, which leads to a potentiation of the formerly weak interactions. The previously small raft domains coalesce and form large, more stable entities. It is the clustered state in which rafts are accessible to microscopy.

Cross-linking of raft antigens not only leads to co-clustering of raft components within one leaflet, but also influences the organization of the opposing monolayer. Cross-linking of the exoplasmic GPI-anchored PLAP led to partial co-clustering of the src-kinase fyn in the cytoplasmic leaflet of Jurkat cells [35, 56]. Cross-correlation analysis revealed co-distribution of an inner leaflet raft protein with FceRI transmembrane receptors that were cross-linked by binding of their multivalent ligand IgE, as well as with antibody cross-linked raft markers of the exoplasmic leaflet, such as the GPI-anchored protein Thy-1 or the ganglioside GD_{1b} [57]. The finding that clustering not only leads to lateral coalescence of small raft domains in the exoplasmic leaflet, but also in the cytoplasmic leaflet, strengthens the hypothesis that clustered raft domains provide a platform for bringing together signaling complexes and propagating signals into the cell (reviewed in [58]). Interestingly, also in symmetric model bilayers, liquid-ordered domains have always been observed to coincide in both leaflets [20, 59]. How the connection of the inner leaflet and the outer leaflet is achieved, remains an open question. Interdigitation of the often long fatty acid chains of glycosphingolipids has been proposed to enforce a higher order also in the cytoplasmic leaflet. Alternatively, or additionally, transmembrane proteins could mediate transbilayer coupling.

Many signaling processes have been proposed to depend on the clustering of raft domains [60,61] (see also Chapter 7), the T-cell synapse being the prime example [62,63]. According to a recent study by Douglass et al., the initial stage of signaling complex assembly does not require rafts but is rather dependent on protein-protein interactions [64]. Studies by Magee et al., on the other hand, have shown that raft clustering independent of protein-protein interactions can activate signaling pathways downstream of the T-cell receptor [65]. These authors observed that incubating T cells at 0 °C leads to coalescence of raft components into visible domains on the plasma membrane. At the same time, chilling activates the signaling cascade, leading to increased tyrosine phosphorylation and ERK activation. The cold-induced, protein-independent coalescence of raft domains is a clear indicator for a phase separation phenomenon, since it is well established that the phase-separated domains are larger at lower temperature and fragment at higher temperature due to the increase in Brownian motion [66]. However, it is not yet clear which role this raft coalescence would play in T-cell signaling under physiological conditions.

The formation of large, clustered raft domains is easiest imagined to occur by coalescence of pre-existing, small rafts. However, a recent study on model membranes of different compositions argued that phase separation can be induced by cross-linking one component in a previously homogeneous membrane [67]. GUVs composed of PC, SM and cholesterol exhibit phase separation into a liquid-ordered and a liquid-disordered phase, depending on the ratio of the components. When a small amount of the ganglioside GM1 is included in the vesicles, its cross-linking with the pentavalent cholera toxin B subunit leads to coalescence of the GM1-containing phase into larger, visible domains. Hammond et al. showed that domains can not only be formed at GUV compositions that displayed phase separation prior to clustering, but also at compositions very close to the phase transition boundary in which no previous phase separation was detected [67]. The local increase in GM1 concentration following the cross-linking might have been enough to cross the boundary and cause the membrane to phase separate.

1.6
The Apical Membrane of Epithelial Cells: A Percolating Raft Membrane at 25 °C

Columnar epithelia lining the kidney, intestine or pancreas are composed of a single layer of polarized cells. They have evolved to create stable apical and basolateral membrane domains, which are sealed off from each other by a tight junction barrier. While the basolateral domain of columnar epithelia faces the underlying extracellular matrix and the blood supply, the apical membrane is the one facing the lumen of the renal tubules, of the intestine, or of the pancreas. It has long been known that apical and basolateral membrane domains have a distinct protein composition [68,69]. However, lipids are also distributed differently between the apical and the basolateral membrane. The lipids found in the basolateral membrane resemble those found in the plasma membrane of an unpolarized cell, whereas the apical membrane contains much more glycosphingolipids [70]. In the brush border membrane of the intestine, glycosphingolipids account for more than 30 % of the total lipid amount [71]. Considering that they reside exclusively in the exoplasmic leaflet, more than 50 % of the lipids in the exoplasmic leaflet should be glycosphingolipids, and together with cholesterol they should leave very little space for glycerophospholipids. Glycosphingolipids mainly contain two long, saturated hydrocarbon chains, as opposed to glycerophospholipids which usually contain unsaturated acyl chains [72], and have been proposed to form a liquid-ordered phase together with cholesterol. It was this segregation of raft lipids in the outer leaflet of the apical membrane from the more phosphatidylcholine-enriched basolateral membrane that prompted Simons and van Meer to postulate the existence of lipid platforms involved in the biogenesis of the apical membrane [70] and has led to the formulation of the raft hypothesis [11].

Recently, we have experimentally explored the domain organization of the apical membrane of epithelial cells in comparison to that of a fibroblast plasma membrane by measuring long-range diffusion of several fluorescent membrane proteins using fluorescence recovery after photobleaching (FRAP) [73]. By using this technique, the diffusion of millions of proteins can be examined at the same time in a noninvasive manner. As previously reported [74], all proteins display free diffusion with 100% recovery in the fibroblast plasma membrane. In the apical membrane of epithelial cells, however, we could distinguish two populations of proteins on the basis of their distinct diffusion characteristics at 25 °C. One group displayed free diffusion with recoveries close to 100%, whereas the other group displayed anomalous diffusion [75, 76] with limited recovery. This is indicative of a phase-separated system, in which there are (at least) two coexisting phases – one which has a mass fraction just high enough to be continuous (percolating) over the entire membrane surface, and the other being present in isolated domains [77]. Within the percolating phase, long-range diffusion is unconstrained, results in complete recovery, and can be described with a single apparent diffusion coefficient [78, 79] – as observed for the first group of proteins. In the non-percolating phase, proteins will be obstructed in their long-range diffusion, resulting in either incomplete or extremely slow recovery [78, 79] – as observed for the second group of proteins. Strikingly, all proteins falling into the first group have been proposed to reside in rafts, while all members of the second group have been proposed to reside outside of rafts. This may suggest that at 25 °C the apical membrane of epithelial cells is a percolating raft phase with isolated non-raft domains.

Phase separation likely exists also in fibroblasts, with the domain organization of the two membranes being inverted. The fact that in the fibroblast plasma membrane the raft and non-raft proteins diffuse with the same kinetics does, however, not contradict the existence of phase separation. Rather, the results can be explained on the basis of partition coefficients. From all we know, a limited set of proteins has the features required to be accommodated in the ordered lipid environment of a raft domain. While non-raft proteins that lack these features are largely excluded from rafts – that is, non-raft proteins have a low propensity to partition into the surrounding raft phase in the apical membrane of epithelial cells – raft proteins might have a preference for raft domains, but can easily partition into a less-ordered, non-raft environment – that is, raft proteins are not limited to raft domains in the plasma membrane of fibroblasts [28, 80, 81]. With the additional notion that raft domains in fibroblasts are believed to be small and highly dynamic, the differences between the long-range diffusion paths of raft and non-raft proteins in the fibroblasts plasma membrane become too small to be accessible to FRAP measurements.

1.7
Caveolae: Scaffolded Membrane Domains Rich in Raft Lipids

Caveolae were first defined morphologically by Palade, who observed plasma membrane invaginations in endothelial cells under the electron microscope [82]. He later named them "plasmalemmal vesicles" [83], implying that they would shuttle molecules across the cell. The name "caveolae" (little caves) was however coined two years later by Yamada, who described invaginations on the surface of gallbladder epithelial cells [84]. Although he did not distinguish between coated and uncoated invaginations, the name "caveolae" was later specifically attributed to flask-shaped invaginations of 50 to 100 nm diameter that were devoid of the clathrin-coat, but instead displayed a characteristic striated coat [85]. While research on clathrin-coated pits and vesicles was rapidly progressing, caveolae long remained elusive.

This was changed when, almost 40 years after the morphological description, caveolin was identified as the major protein constituent of caveolae [86, 87]. Subsequently, two additional caveolin genes were cloned, so that the original caveolin was from then on referred to as caveolin-1. Caveolin-2 was co-purified with caveolin-1 from adipocytes [88], and its expression pattern overlaps with that of caveolin-1. The two proteins are most abundant in endothelial cells, fibroblasts and adipocytes, and they form stable hetero-oligomeric complexes *in vivo* [89]. Caveolin-3 shows a high degree of sequence similarity with caveolin-1, but its expression is restricted to muscle cells in which there is low caveolin-1 expression [90]. Both caveolin-1 and -2 have a smaller β-isoforms in addition to the full-length α-isoform. Caveolin-1 assumes an unusual topology in that it is an integral membrane protein [91] but does not span the bilayer. Instead the central hydrophobic domain is thought to form a hairpin structure which inserts into the cytoplasmic leaflet, leaving both the N- and C-terminus in the cytoplasm [87].

A characteristic feature of caveolins is their propensity to form high molecular-weight homo- and hetero-oligomers. Highly stable caveolin-1 oligomers of 14 to 16 monomers, dissociating only upon harsh detergent treatment at elevated temperatures, were found to be assembled relatively rapidly after synthesis of caveolin-1 in the endoplasmic reticulum and prior to Golgi exit [92]. The domain responsible for the oligomerization was mapped to the N-terminus [93]. The N-terminus has also been shown to target caveolin-1 to caveolar invaginations at the plasma membrane, since its absence results in Golgi retention [94, 95]. This ensures that only caveolin oligomers, not monomers, are transported to the plasma membrane. In addition to homo-oligomerization, caveolin-1 can form similarly stable hetero-oligomers with caveolin-2, which are localized mainly to plasma membrane caveolae [89]. In the absence of caveolin-1, caveolin-2 is not able to oligomerize and is retained in the Golgi in the form of monomers and dimers [96–98], again indicating that only the oligomeric form is transported to the plasma membrane.

The fact that caveolin-1 immunostaining decorated the striated coat around plasma membrane caveolae [86], together with the observation that it self-assembled into filaments *in vitro* [92] indicated that it indeed was an integral coat component. Since then, the function of caveolae became very closely linked to the function of caveolin, and it was shown that formation of the stable plasma membrane invaginations depended on caveolin expression. Cells not expressing caveolin-1 (e.g., lymphocytes) lacked cell-surface caveolae, and the expression of caveolin-1 in these cells was sufficient to induce their formation [99]. Quantification of the number of caveolin-1 molecules per caveolae by fluorescence intensity distribution measurements revealed that the uniform size of caveolae as seen by electron microscopy results from a quantal assembly mechanism in which 144 ± 39 caveolin-1 molecules are incorporated into a single caveola [100]; caveolin-2 was not assessed in this study. Caveolin-1 filaments had previously been proposed to assemble from heptamers, measuring 10 nm in diameter [101]. If this model were true, then 144 caveolin-1 molecules would form a filament of roughly 200 nm length, enough to surround an invagination of 50–100 nm diameter with a circumference of 150–300 nm once. The structure and composition of the caveolar coat are far from being understood (see also Chapter 2) but, most likely, caveolin-1 is not the only coat component. Other open questions are, where is the coat assembled and what is the assembly mechanism?

Caveolin-1 has been shown to bind cholesterol and the ganglioside GM1, both *in vitro* and *in vivo* [102, 103]. Cholesterol-binding occurs with high affinity, resisting even harsh detergent treatments [103]. The lipid composition of caveolae is thus similar to that of lipid rafts, and it can be extrapolated that the caveolar membrane should also display properties of a liquid-ordered phase. However, a detailed lipid composition of isolated caveolae is still lacking. The strong interaction with two *bona fide* lipid raft components predisposes caveolin-1 for the role as a raft-clustering agent. Similar to clustered rafts, caveolae have been proposed to function as signaling platforms [104] (see also Chapters 5, 6, and 11). The clear parallels in lipid composition and the partial co-purification of lipid raft and caveolar components in DRMs [105, 106], or in membranes of low buoyant density [107], has often led to an equation of the two membrane systems. However, we will continue to refer to caveolae as plasma membrane invaginations scaffolded by the caveolin-coat. The stable membrane curvature of caveolae could be a result of two contributions. Curvature could be induced by: (1) the high cholesterol concentration [108]; and (2) the insertion of caveolin-1 into the cytoplasmic leaflet of the bilayer, which would increase the surface area of the cytoplasmic leaflet relative to that of the exoplasmic leaflet and thus promote inward bending of the membrane. This stabilization of a curved membrane structure and the presence of caveolins would distinguish caveolae functionally from lipid rafts.

1.8
Caveolae and Lipid Rafts in Membrane Traffic

Membrane traffic mediates the exchange of components between the different cellular organelles. Membrane proteins and lipids are synthesized in the endoplasmic reticulum and from there are transported to their subcellular sites of action [109, 110]. While peripheral membrane proteins as well as single lipids bound to lipid transfer proteins can shuttle between different membranes via the cytoplasm or through contacts between membranes [4], most membrane turnover is mediated by vesicular traffic. Directed vesicular transport involves several regulated steps:

- lateral sorting of membrane components according to their destination (i.e., the concentration of cargo following the same pathway and its segregation from cargo following different pathways);

- stabilization of a membrane domain destined for trafficking;
- bending of the membrane domain into the shape of a vesicle or tubule;
- pinching off from the donor compartment;
- traffic through the cytoplasm by passive diffusion or motor-protein-mediated transport along microtubules or actin filaments;
- fusion with the acceptor compartment; and
- release of the cargo.

The best-understood sorting mechanism for transmembrane proteins employs recyclable protein coats, such as clathrin-, COPI- or COPII-coats [111, 112] (Fig. 1.1, left panel). In this case the cargo proteins contain specific sorting signals in their cytoplasmic domains, which are bound by adaptor molecules, to which the coat proteins are recruited. Oligomerization of the coats leads to bending of the membrane domain into a vesicle, which is pinched off by the action of the GTPase dynamin and released into the cytosol. Here the coat disassembles, enabling the vesicle to fuse with its target membrane. This protein-driven mechanism operates by active inclusion of certain components and is not very efficient at excluding.

For other sorting events in membrane traffic, the lipid bilayer itself has been proposed to play the decisive role, and proteins only regulate what lipids can do on their own [113]. From theoretical considerations and model membrane studies it is known that if phases with different properties coexist in the same membrane, then the mismatch of interactions at the phase boundary leads to the so-called "line tension" – the two-dimensional equivalent of surface tension. Multiplied with the length of the phase boundary it gives rise to the "line energy". One way to minimize line energy is therefore to minimize the contact between phases. In the case of domains in cell membranes, this can be achieved by fusion of many small domains into one large domain, and bending the domain out of the surrounding bulk membrane [114]. The bending energy needed to curve the membrane as the domain buds out counteracts the line energy. As the bending energy increases and the line energy decreases, the domain reaches a stable curvature when the sum of the two energies is minimal. For small domains this can be when the domain is still connected to the bulk membrane, but above a critical domain size budding becomes energetically favorable. This mechanism is termed "domain-induced budding" (Fig. 1.1, right panel) and is initially achieved purely by lipid-driven phase separation [114]. However, in order to attain directionality in the budding process (i.e., budding towards the cytoplasm in most cases in cells) and also kinetics that are compatible with the cell's needs, proteins will have to control this process.

The fact that lipids are unevenly distributed between the two surfaces, the apical and the basolateral membrane domains, of epithelial cells [70] together with the finding that newly synthesized glucosyl-ceramide upon leaving the Golgi complex becomes two- to three-fold enriched in the apical versus the basolateral plasma membrane [115], has led to the proposal that lipids are also sorted by vesicular traffic. Interactions between glycosphingolipids and apical proteins were postulated to aid the assembly of sphingolipid microdomains in the Golgi that would concentrate apical cargo as the first step in vesicle formation [70]. This mechanism has two important features which distinguish it from the coat-mediated sorting:

- It also allows for the sorting of lipids.
- It works by actively excluding cargo that does not belong into the pathway and thus prevents the transported membrane from being diluted with inadequate material.

It has been shown previously, that basolateral proteins are excluded from the apical membrane [116], whereas the converse is not true [69, 117]. Physiologically this is sensible, since the apical membrane facing the lumen of an organ must be extremely resistant to external aggression by bile salt detergents, digestive enzymes or low pH, and its composition must therefore be tightly controlled. Whilst it is known that basolateral delivery depends on the interaction with adaptor proteins [118], domain-induced budding seems to be a mechanism ideally suited for delivery to the apical membrane.

Since these microdomains, or rafts, are believed to be small and dynamic, they must be clustered by proteins such as multivalent ligands or caveolin in order to be able to form a bud and later a vesicle or tubule. In apical raft delivery this has been postulated to be mediated by lectins or other multivalent cargo receptors [119, 120]. Raft and caveolar endocytosis is triggered by multivalent cargo, the best described being Simian virus 40 and cholera toxin [121–124], both of which bind several GM1 molecules [125]. Here, the caveolar coat is not necessary for the membrane bending or vesicle formation, since rafts can endocytose upon clustering by a virus or toxin and be delivered to specific destinations in the cell without caveolin [124]. In fact, the internalization has been shown to be faster in the absence of caveolin [126]. Caveolin might thus not be necessary for the endocytic event as such, but rather add another level of regulation to this pathway, which is required for the efficient sorting of some ligands [127].

Indeed, caveolae membrane traffic does display special features that set it apart from other membrane traffic mechanisms. Caveolae were previously believed to be static structures [128], simply increasing the cell-surface area and keeping raft

Fig. 1.1 Two paradigms of cargo sorting and vesicle formation ▶ in membrane traffic: inclusion due to sorting signals followed by coat-driven budding (left), or exclusion due to phase separation and domain-induced budding (right). In the left column, proteins containing the appropriate cytoplasmic sorting signals (regardless of if they are residing in a raft or non-raft domain) are bound by adaptor proteins, on which the coat proteins assemble. For the clathrin-coat, membrane bending and subsequent budding is believed to be driven by a conformational change in the coat protein. In the right column, raft proteins are clustered by oligomerizing ligands or cytoplasmic scaffolding proteins, thereby excluding the group of non-raft proteins. Membrane bending and budding is driven by the need to minimize the line energy acting at the domain boundary.

Coat-mediated budding   Domain-induced budding

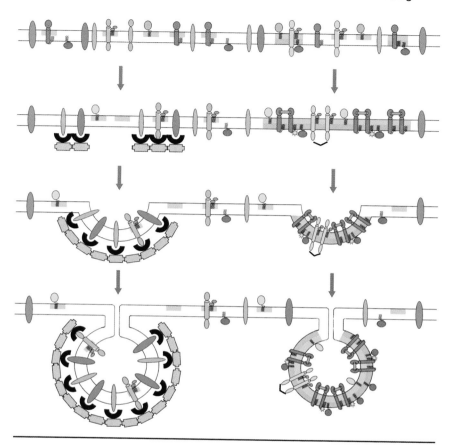

	non-raft domain			oligomerizing ligand
	raft domain in exoplasmic leaflet			
	raft domain in cytoplasmic leaflet			transmembrane raft protein, phosphorylated on cytoplasmic side
	GPI-anchored protein			
	doubly acylated protein			two different non-raft transmembrane proteins
	transmembrane raft protein, bound to glycosphingolipid			cytoplasmic crosslinking scaffold
				adaptor protein
	doubly acylated transmembrane raft protein			coat protein

membrane available on the cell surface. Recently, it became evident that even in unstimulated fibroblasts and epithelial cells, 30% of the caveolae undergo local kiss-and-run cycles with the plasma membrane in which they pinch off and fuse again close to the original site [100]. Upon receiving a trigger for endocytosis, caveolae switch from this short-range cycling to long-range cycling, resulting in an intermixing of cell-surface and intracellular caveolar vesicle pools and transport to caveosomes or endosomes [100]. During the trafficking event, the caveolar coat seems to stabilize the clustered raft domain within the bilayer, so that it stays intact even after fusion with the acceptor compartment and can be re-used for multiple rounds of membrane trafficking [127]. Cargo release at the target compartment must therefore also follow different principles than in the clathrin-coated vesicle traffic where the coat disassembles before fusion. Caveolae apparently keep their cargo sequestered, until its release is triggered by a compartment-specific cue. Cholera toxin is released upon encounter of a low pH environment in early endosomes, but stays sequestered in caveolae in the neutral environment at the plasma membrane or in caveosomes. This type of membrane traffic seems especially suited for the sorting of non-membrane spanning cargo, in particular glycosphingolipid-binding ligands [127].

The vesicle fusion machinery on the target compartment also has been proposed to be organized into domains of different lipid composition. The apical t-SNARE syntaxin 3 was proposed to reside in raft domains [129]. More recent investigations have claimed that indeed different SNAREs are compartmentalized in the plasma membrane with the help of lipid domains, with syntaxin 3 residing in raft domains, syntaxin 2 being excluded from raft domains, and syntaxin 4 being equally distributed between the two [130]. In polarized epithelial cells, syntaxin 4 resides on the basolateral surface, whereas syntaxin 2 and 3 are localized to the apical surface [131]. The data would thus imply, that there could be two pathways trafficking to the apical side of epithelial cells – one raft- and one non-raft pathway. Indeed, it was previously observed that two different apical proteins, sucrase-isomaltase and lactase-phlorizin-hydrolase, use separate containers for transport to the apical membrane of Madin-Darby canine kidney (MDCK) cells, and the existence of two different pathways was proposed [132].

Research on rafts and caveolae is entering a new phase. The technologies that have been used to study these membrane domains are being revised, and new technologies must be developed. If rafts are small and dynamic, many of the standard techniques that have been employed to visualize them (e.g., FRET, single particle tracking, FRAP in most cases) can not provide anything else but negative results because they are not suited for the size and time resolution needed. Another critical point is the purification methods used to isolate rafts or caveolae. The two were often confused with each other since they were supposed to co-fractionate when isolated based on detergent insolubility or light buoyant density. It is now accepted that these fractions are useful to obtain information about the proteins found in them, but since they form during the purification process, they can not be assumed to represent an equivalent of any pre-existing cellular domain, neither rafts nor caveolae [10]. Instead, new approaches have been taken – for example, to isolate plasma membrane fragments with small antibody-coated beads [133]. Techniques such as this must be developed in order to obtain pure raft and caveolae fractions that can be used to analyze their lipid and protein composition. With the new mass spectroscopic techniques it should then be possible to compare the lipidome of rafts and caveolae with each other to determine how similar they actually are, and also to compare them with the lipidome of the plasma membrane. Only then will we have a chance to assess properly the involvement of lipids in processes such as raft dynamics, raft clustering, and to address the special functions of caveolae.

Abbreviations

DRM	detergent-resistant membrane
FRAP	fluorescence recovery after photobleaching
FRET	Förster's resonance energy transfer
GFP	green fluorescent protein
GPI	glycosyl-phosphatidyl-inositol
GUV	giant unilamellar vesicles
LUV	large unilamellar vesicles
MDCK	Madin-Darby canine kidney
MLV	multilamellar vesicles
PC	phosphatidylcholine
PE	phosphatidylethanolamine
PI(3)P	phosphatidylinositol-3'-phosphate
PLAP	placental alkaline phosphatase
PS	phosphatidylserine
SM	sphingomyelin
T_m	melting temperature

References

1 Danielli, J. F. and H. Davson, A contribution to the theory of permeability of thin films. *J. Cell. Comp. Physiol.* 1935; 5: 495–508.

2 Singer, S. J. and G. L. Nicolson, The fluid mosaic model of the structure of cell membranes. *Science* 1972; 175(23): 720–731.

3 Devaux, P. F. and R. Morris, Transmembrane asymmetry and lateral domains in biological membranes. *Traffic* 2004; 5(4): 241–246.

4 Holthuis, J. C. and T. P. Levine, Lipid traffic: floppy drives and a superhighway. *Nat. Rev. Mol. Cell. Biol.* 2005; 6(3): 209–220.

5 Allan, D., Mapping the lipid distribution in the membranes of BHK cells (mini-review). *Mol. Membr. Biol.* 1996; 13(2): 81–84.

6 Tran, D., et al., Ligands internalized through coated or noncoated invaginations follow a common intracellular pathway. *Proc. Natl. Acad. Sci. USA* 1987; 84(22): 7957–7961.

7 Gillooly, D. J., C. Raiborg, and H. Stenmark, Phosphatidylinositol 3-phosphate is found in microdomains of early endo-

somes. *Histochem. Cell. Biol.* 2003; 120(6): 445–453.

8 Fratti, R. A., et al., Interdependent assembly of specific regulatory lipids and membrane fusion proteins into the vertex ring domain of docked vacuoles. *J. Cell Biol.* 2004; 167(6): 1087–1098.

9 Brown, D. A. and E. London, Functions of lipid rafts in biological membranes. *Annu. Rev. Cell. Dev. Biol.* 1998; 14: 111–136.

10 Lichtenberg, D., F. M. Goni, and H. Heerklotz, Detergent-resistant membranes should not be identified with membrane rafts. *Trends Biochem. Sci.* 2005; 30(8): 430–436.

11 Simons, K. and E. Ikonen, Functional rafts in cell membranes. *Nature* 1997; 387(6633): 569–572.

12 Munro, S., Lipid rafts: elusive or illusive? *Cell* 2003; 115(4): 377–388.

13 Edidin, M., The state of lipid rafts: from model membranes to cells. *Annu. Rev. Biophys. Biomol. Struct.* 2003; 32: 257–283.

14 Simons, K. and W. L. Vaz, Model systems, lipid rafts, and cell membranes. *Annu. Rev. Biophys. Biomol. Struct.* 2004; 33: 269–295.

15 Ipsen, J. H., et al., Phase equilibria in the phosphatidylcholine-cholesterol system. *Biochim. Biophys. Acta* 1987; 905(1): 162–172.

16 Ipsen, J. H., O. G. Mouritsen, and M. J. Zuckermann, Theory of thermal anomalies in the specific heat of lipid bilayers containing cholesterol. *Biophys. J.* 1989; 56(4): 661–667.

17 Miao, L., et al., From lanosterol to cholesterol: structural evolution and differential effects on lipid bilayers. *Biophys. J.* 2002; 82(3): 1429–1444.

18 Xu, X., et al., Effect of the structure of natural sterols and sphingolipids on the formation of ordered sphingolipid/sterol domains (rafts). Comparison of cholesterol to plant, fungal, and disease-associated sterols and comparison of sphingomyelin, cerebrosides, and ceramide. *J. Biol. Chem.* 2001; 276(36): 33 540–33 546.

19 Leventis, R. and J. R. Silvius, Use of cyclodextrins to monitor transbilayer movement and differential lipid affinities of cholesterol. *Biophys. J.* 2001; 81(4): 2257–2267.

20 Dietrich, C., et al., Lipid rafts reconstituted in model membranes. *Biophys. J.* 2001; 80(3): 1417–1428.

21 de Almeida, R. F., A. Fedorov, and M. Prieto, Sphingomyelin/phosphatidylcholine/cholesterol phase diagram: boundaries and composition of lipid rafts. *Biophys. J.* 2003; 85(4): 2406–2416.

22 Veatch, S. L. and S. L. Keller, Separation of liquid phases in giant vesicles of ternary mixtures of phospholipids and cholesterol. *Biophys. J.* 2003; 85(5): 3074–3083.

23 Silvius, J. R., Fluorescence energy transfer reveals microdomain formation at physiological temperatures in lipid mixtures modeling the outer leaflet of the plasma membrane. *Biophys. J.* 2003; 85(2): 1034–1045.

24 McConnell, H. M. and M. Vrljic, Liquid-liquid immiscibility in membranes. *Annu. Rev. Biophys. Biomol. Struct.* 2003; 32: 469–492.

25 Wang, T. Y. and J. R. Silvius, Cholesterol does not induce segregation of liquid-ordered domains in bilayers modeling the inner leaflet of the plasma membrane. *Biophys. J.* 2001; 81(5): 2762–2773.

26 Huang, J. and G. W. Feigenson, A microscopic interaction model of maximum solubility of cholesterol in lipid bilayers. *Biophys. J.* 1999; 76(4): 2142–2157.

27 Schroeder, R., E. London, and D. Brown, Interactions between saturated acyl chains confer detergent resistance on lipids and glycosylphosphatidylinositol (GPI)-anchored proteins: GPI-anchored proteins in liposomes and cells show similar behavior. *Proc. Natl. Acad. Sci. USA* 1994; 91(25): 12 130–12 134.

28 Kahya, N., D. A. Brown, and P. Schwille, Raft partitioning and dynamic behavior of human placental alkaline phosphatase in giant unilamellar vesicles. *Biochemistry* 2005; 44(20): 7479–7489.

29 Dietrich, C., et al., Partitioning of Thy-1, GM1, and cross-linked phospholipid analogs into lipid rafts reconstituted in supported model membrane monolayers. *Proc. Natl. Acad. Sci. USA* 2001; 98(19): 10 642–10 647.

30 Benting, J., et al., Acyl and alkyl chain length of GPI-anchors is critical for raft association in vitro. *FEBS Lett.* 1999; 462(1–2): 47–50.

31 Wang, T. Y., R. Leventis, and J. R. Silvius, Partitioning of lipidated peptide sequences into liquid-ordered lipid domains in model and biological membranes. *Biochemistry* 2001; 40(43): 13031–13040.

32 McIntosh, T. J., A. Vidal, and S. A. Simon, Sorting of lipids and transmembrane peptides between detergent-soluble bilayers and detergent-resistant rafts. *Biophys. J.* 2003; 85(3): 1656–1666.

33 Estronca, L. M., et al., Solubility of amphiphiles in membranes: influence of phase properties and amphiphile head group. *Biochem. Biophys. Res. Commun.* 2002; 296(3): 596–603.

34 Spiegel, S., et al., Direct visualization of redistribution and capping of fluorescent gangliosides on lymphocytes. *J. Cell Biol.* 1984; 99(5): 1575–1581.

35 Harder, T., et al., Lipid domain structure of the plasma membrane revealed by patching of membrane components. *J. Cell Biol.* 1998; 141(4): 929–942.

36 Gidwani, A., D. Holowka, and B. Baird, Fluorescence anisotropy measurements of lipid order in plasma membranes and lipid rafts from RBL-2H3 mast cells. *Biochemistry* 2001; 40(41): 12422–12429.

37 Gaus, K., et al., Visualizing lipid structure and raft domains in living cells with two-photon microscopy. *Proc. Natl. Acad. Sci. USA* 2003; 100(26): 15554–15559.

38 Pralle, A., et al., Sphingolipid-cholesterol rafts diffuse as small entities in the plasma membrane of mammalian cells. *J. Cell Biol.* 2000; 148(5): 997–1008.

39 Prior, I. A., et al., Direct visualization of Ras proteins in spatially distinct cell surface microdomains. *J. Cell Biol.* 2003; 160(2): 165–170.

40 Zacharias, D. A., et al., Partitioning of lipid-modified monomeric GFPs into membrane microdomains of live cells. *Science* 2002; 296(5569): 913–916.

41 Lommerse, P. H., et al., Single-molecule imaging of the H-ras membrane-anchor reveals domains in the cytoplasmic leaflet of the cell membrane. *Biophys. J.* 2004; 86(1 Pt 1): 609–616.

42 Kenworthy, A. K. and M. Edidin, Distribution of a glycosylphosphatidylinositol-anchored protein at the apical surface of MDCK cells examined at a resolution of <100 A using imaging fluorescence resonance energy transfer. *J. Cell Biol.* 1998; 142(1): 69–84.

43 Kenworthy, A. K., N. Petranova, and M. Edidin, High-resolution FRET microscopy of cholera toxin B-subunit and GPI-anchored proteins in cell plasma membranes. *Mol. Biol. Cell* 2000; 11(5): 1645–1655.

44 Glebov, O. O. and B. J. Nichols, Lipid raft proteins have a random distribution during localized activation of the T-cell receptor. *Nat. Cell Biol.* 2004; 6(3): 238–243.

45 Fra, A. M., et al., Detergent-insoluble glycolipid microdomains in lymphocytes in the absence of caveolae. *J. Biol. Chem.* 1994; 269(49): 30745–30748.

46 Varma, R. and S. Mayor, GPI-anchored proteins are organized in submicron domains at the cell surface. *Nature* 1998; 394(6695): 798–801.

47 Sharma, P., et al., Nanoscale organization of multiple GPI-anchored proteins in living cell membranes. *Cell* 2004; 116(4): 577–589.

48 Kusumi, A., I. Koyama-Honda, and K. Suzuki, Molecular dynamics and interactions for creation of stimulation-induced stabilized rafts from small unstable steady-state rafts. *Traffic* 2004; 5(4): 213–230.

49 Anderson, R. G. and K. Jacobson, A role for lipid shells in targeting proteins to caveolae, rafts, and other lipid domains. *Science* 2002; 296(5574): 1821–1825.

50 Dietrich, C., et al., Relationship of lipid rafts to transient confinement zones detected by single particle tracking. *Biophys. J.* 2002; 82(1 Pt 1): 274–284.

51 Schutz, G. J., et al., Properties of lipid microdomains in a muscle cell membrane visualized by single molecule microscopy. *EMBO J.* 2000; 19(5): 892–901.

52 Fujiwara, T., et al., Phospholipids undergo hop diffusion in compartmentalized cell membrane. *J. Cell Biol.* 2002; 157(6): 1071–1081.

53 Lafont, F., et al., Annexin XIIIb associates with lipid microdomains to function in apical delivery. *J. Cell Biol.* 1998; 142(6): 1413–1427.

54 Cheong, K. H., et al., VIP17/MAL, a lipid raft-associated protein, is involved in apical transport in MDCK cells. *Proc. Natl. Acad. Sci. USA* 1999; 96(11): 6241–6248.

55 Simons, K. and D. Toomre, Lipid rafts and signal transduction. *Nat. Rev. Mol. Cell. Biol.* 2000; 1(1): 31–39.

56 Gri, G., et al., The inner side of T cell lipid rafts. *Immunol. Lett.* 2004; 94(3): 247–252.

57 Pyenta, P. S., D. Holowka, and B. Baird, Cross-correlation analysis of inner-leaflet-anchored green fluorescent protein co-redistributed with IgE receptors and outer leaflet lipid raft components. *Biophys. J.* 2001; 80(5): 2120–2132.

58 Harder, T. and K. R. Engelhardt, Membrane domains in lymphocytes – from lipid rafts to protein scaffolds. *Traffic* 2004; 5(4): 265–275.

59 Kahya, N., et al., Probing lipid mobility of raft-exhibiting model membranes by fluorescence correlation spectroscopy. *J. Biol. Chem.* 2003; 278(30): 28 109–28115.

60 Pierce, S. K., Lipid rafts and B-cell activation. *Nat. Rev. Immunol.* 2002; 2(2): 96–105.

61 Holowka, D., et al., Lipid segregation and IgE receptor signaling: A decade of progress. *Biochim. Biophys. Acta* 2005; in press.

62 Horejsi, V., Lipid rafts and their roles in T-cell activation. *Microbes Infect.* 2005; 7(2): 310–316.

63 He, H. T., A. Lellouch, and D. Marguet, Lipid rafts and the initiation of T cell receptor signaling. *Semin. Immunol.* 2005; 17(1): 23–33.

64 Douglass, A. D. and R. D. Vale, Single-molecule microscopy reveals plasma membrane microdomains created by protein-protein networks that exclude or trap signaling molecules in T cells. *Cell* 2005; 121(6): 937–950.

65 Magee, A. I., J. Adler, and I. Parmryd, Cold-induced coalescence of T-cell plasma membrane microdomains activates signalling pathways. *J. Cell Sci.* 2005; 118(Pt 14): 3141–3151.

66 Veatch, S. L. and S. L. Keller, Seeing spots: Complex phase behavior in simple membranes. *Biochim. Biophys. Acta* 2005; in press.

67 Hammond, A. T., et al., Crosslinking a lipid raft component triggers liquid ordered-liquid disordered phase separation in model plasma membranes. *Proc. Natl. Acad. Sci. USA* 2005; 102(18): 6320–6325.

68 Herzlinger, D. A. and G. K. Ojakian, Studies on the development and maintenance of epithelial cell surface polarity with monoclonal antibodies. *J. Cell Biol.* 1984; 98(5): 1777–1787.

69 Balcarova-Stander, J., et al., Development of cell surface polarity in the epithelial Madin-Darby canine kidney (MDCK) cell line. *EMBO J.* 1984; 3(11): 2687–2694.

70 Simons, K. and G. van Meer, Lipid sorting in epithelial cells. *Biochemistry* 1988; 27(17): 6197–6202.

71 Danielsen, E. M. and G. H. Hansen, Lipid rafts in epithelial brush borders: atypical membrane microdomains with specialized functions. *Biochim. Biophys. Acta* 2003; 1617(1–2): 1–9.

72 Barenholz, Y. and T. E. Thompson, Sphingomyelins in bilayers and biological membranes. *Biochim. Biophys. Acta* 1980; 604(2): 129–158.

73 Meder, D., et al., Phase coexistence and connectivity in the apical membrane of polarized epithelial cells. Proc. Natl. Acad. Sci USA, in press.

74 Kenworthy, A. K., et al., Dynamics of putative raft-associated proteins at the cell surface. *J. Cell Biol.* 2004; 165(5): 735–746.

75 Feder, T. J., et al., Constrained diffusion or immobile fraction on cell surfaces: a new interpretation. *Biophys. J.* 1996; 70(6): 2767–2773.

76 Bouchaud, J. P. and A. Georges, Comment on "Stochastic pathway to anomalous diffusion". *Phys. Rev. A* 1990; 41(2): 1156–1157.

77 Vaz, W. L. and P. F. Almeida, Phase topology and percolation in multi-phase lipid bilayers: is the biological membrane a domain mosaic? *Curr. Opin. Struct. Biol.* 1993; 3: 482–488.

78 Almeida, P. F., W. L. Vaz, and T. E. Thompson, Lateral diffusion and percolation in two-phase, two-component lipid bilayers. Topology of the solid-phase domains in-plane and across the lipid bilayer. *Biochemistry* 1992; 31(31): 7198–7210.

79 Coelho, F. P., W. L. Vaz, and E. Melo, Phase topology and percolation in two-component lipid bilayers: a Monte Carlo approach. *Biophys. J.* 1997; 72(4): 1501–1511.

80 Abreu, M. S., M. J. Moreno, and W. L. Vaz, Kinetics and thermodynamics of association of a phospholipid derivative with lipid bilayers in liquid-disordered and liquid-ordered phases. *Biophys. J.* 2004; 87(1): 353–365.

81 Shogomori, H., et al., Palmitoylation and intracellular domain interactions both contribute to raft targeting of linker for activation of T cells. *J. Biol. Chem.* 2005; 280(19): 18931–18942.

82 Palade, G. E., Fine structure of blood capillaries. *J. Appl. Physiol.* 1953; 24: 1424.

83 Bruns, R. R. and G. E. Palade, Studies on blood capillaries. I. General organization of blood capillaries in muscle. *J. Cell Biol.* 1968; 37(2): 244–276.

84 Yamada, E., The fine structure of the gall bladder epithelium of the mouse. *J. Biophys. Biochem. Cytol.* 1955; 1(5): 445–458.

85 Peters, K. R., W. W. Carley, and G. E. Palade, Endothelial plasmalemmal vesicles have a characteristic striped bipolar surface structure. *J. Cell Biol.* 1985l 101(6): 2233–2238.

86 Rothberg, K. G., et al., Caveolin, a protein component of caveolae membrane coats. *Cell* 1992; 68(4): 673–682.

87 Dupree, P., et al., Caveolae and sorting in the trans-Golgi network of epithelial cells. *EMBO J.* 1993; 12(4): 1597–1605.

88 Scherer, P. E., et al., Caveolin isoforms differ in their N-terminal protein sequence and subcellular distribution. Identification and epitope mapping of an isoform-specific monoclonal antibody probe. *J. Biol. Chem.* 1995; 270(27): 16395–16401.

89 Scherer, P. E., et al., Cell-type and tissue-specific expression of caveolin-2. Caveolins 1 and 2 co-localize and form a stable hetero-oligomeric complex in vivo. *J. Biol. Chem.* 1997; 272(46): 29337–29346.

90 Tang, Z., et al., Molecular cloning of caveolin-3, a novel member of the caveolin gene family expressed predominantly in muscle. *J. Biol. Chem.* 1996; 271(4): 2255–2261.

91 Kurzchalia, T. V., et al., VIP21, a 21-kD membrane protein is an integral component of trans-Golgi-network-derived transport vesicles. *J. Cell Biol.* 1992; 118(5): 1003–1014.

92 Monier, S., et al., VIP21-caveolin, a membrane protein constituent of the caveolar coat, oligomerizes in vivo and in vitro. *Mol. Biol. Cell* 1995; 6(7): 911–927.

93 Sargiacomo, M., et al., Oligomeric structure of caveolin: implications for caveolae membrane organization. *Proc. Natl. Acad. Sci. USA* 1995; 92(20): 9407–9411.

94 Luetterforst, R., et al., Molecular characterization of caveolin association with the Golgi complex: identification of a cis-Golgi targeting domain in the caveolin molecule. *J. Cell Biol.* 1999; 145(7): 1443–1459.

95 Machleidt, T., et al., Multiple domains in caveolin-1 control its intracellular traffic. *J. Cell Biol.* 2000; 148(1): 17–28.

96 Scherer, P. E., et al., Identification, sequence, and expression of caveolin-2 defines a caveolin gene family. *Proc. Natl. Acad. Sci. USA* 1996; 93(1): 131–135.

97 Mora, R., et al., Caveolin-2 localizes to the Golgi complex but redistributes to plasma membrane, caveolae, and rafts when co-expressed with caveolin-1. *J. Biol. Chem.* 1999; 274(36): 25708–25717.

98 Parolini, I., et al., Expression of caveolin-1 is required for the transport of caveolin-2 to the plasma membrane. Retention of caveolin-2 at the level of the Golgi complex. *J. Biol. Chem.* 1999; 274(36): 25718–25725.

99 Fra, A. M., et al., De novo formation of caveolae in lymphocytes by expression of VIP21-caveolin. *Proc. Natl. Acad. Sci. USA* 1995; 92(19): 8655–8659.

100 Pelkmans, L. and M. Zerial, Kinase-regulated quantal assemblies and kiss-and-run recycling of caveolae. *Nature* 2005; 436(7047): 128–133.

101 Fernandez, I., et al., Mechanism of caveolin filament assembly. *Proc. Natl. Acad. Sci. USA* 2002; 99(17): 11193–11198.

102 Fra, A. M., et al., A photo-reactive derivative of ganglioside GM1 specifically cross-links VIP21-caveolin on the cell surface. *FEBS Lett.* 1995; 375(1–2): 11–14.

103 Murata, M., et al., VIP21/caveolin is a cholesterol-binding protein. *Proc. Natl. Acad. Sci. USA* 1995; 92(22): 10339–10343.

104 Lisanti, M. P., et al., Caveolae, caveolin and caveolin-rich membrane domains: a signalling hypothesis. *Trends Cell Biol.* 1994; 4(7): 231–235.

105 Brown, D.A. and J.K. Rose, Sorting of GPI-anchored proteins to glycolipid-enriched membrane subdomains during transport to the apical cell surface. *Cell* 1992; 68(3): 533–544.

106 Sargiacomo, M., et al., Signal transducing molecules and glycosyl-phosphatidylinositol-linked proteins form a caveolin-rich insoluble complex in MDCK cells. *J. Cell Biol.* 1993; 122(4): 789–807.

107 Smart, E.J., et al., A detergent-free method for purifying caveolae membrane from tissue culture cells. *Proc. Natl. Acad. Sci. USA* 1995; 92(22): 10104–10108.

108 Bacia, K., P. Schwille, and T. Kurzchalia, Sterol structure determines the separation of phases and the curvature of the liquid-ordered phase in model membranes. *Proc. Natl. Acad. Sci. USA* 2005; 102(9): 3272–3277.

109 Rodriguez-Boulan, E., G. Kreitzer, and A. Musch, Organization of vesicular trafficking in epithelia. *Nat. Rev. Mol. Cell. Biol.* 2005; 6(3): 233–247.

110 Mellman, I., Membranes and sorting. *Curr. Opin. Cell Biol.* 1996; 8(4): 497–498.

111 Salama, N.R. and R.W. Schekman, The role of coat proteins in the biosynthesis of secretory proteins. *Curr. Opin. Cell Biol.* 1995; 7(4): 536–543.

112 Kreis, T.E., M. Lowe, and R. Pepperkok, COPs regulating membrane traffic. *Annu. Rev. Cell. Dev. Biol.* 1995; 11: 677–706.

113 Schuck, S. and K. Simons, Polarized sorting in epithelial cells: raft clustering and the biogenesis of the apical membrane. *J. Cell Sci.* 2004; 117(Pt 25): 5955–5964.

114 Lipowsky, R., Domain-induced budding of fluid membranes. *Biophys. J.* 1993; 64: 1133–1138.

115 van Meer, G., et al., Sorting of sphingolipids in epithelial (Madin-Darby canine kidney) cells. *J. Cell Biol.* 1987; 105(4): 1623–1635.

116 Fuller, S.D. and K. Simons, Transferrin receptor polarity and recycling accuracy in "tight" and "leaky" strains of Madin-Darby canine kidney cells. *J. Cell Biol.* 1986; 103(5): 1767–1779.

117 Pfeiffer, S., S.D. Fuller, and K. Simons, Intracellular sorting and basolateral appearance of the G protein of vesicular stomatitis virus in Madin-Darby canine kidney cells. *J. Cell Biol.* 1985; 101(2): 470–476.

118 Folsch, H., et al., A novel clathrin adaptor complex mediates basolateral targeting in polarized epithelial cells. *Cell* 1999; 99(2): 189–198.

119 Paladino, S., et al., Protein oligomerization modulates raft partitioning and apical sorting of GPI-anchored proteins. *J. Cell Biol.* 2004; 167(4): 699–709.

120 Delacour, D., et al., Galectin-4 and sulfatides in apical membrane trafficking in enterocyte-like cells. *J. Cell Biol.* 2005; 169(3): 491–501.

121 Parton, R.G., B. Joggerst, and K. Simons, Regulated internalization of caveolae. *J. Cell Biol.* 1994; 127(5): 1199–1215.

122 Pelkmans, L., J. Kartenbeck, and A. Helenius, Caveolar endocytosis of simian virus 40 reveals a new two-step vesicular-transport pathway to the ER. *Nat. Cell. Biol.* 2001; 3(5): 473–483.

123 Kirkham, M., et al., Ultrastructural identification of uncoated caveolin-independent early endocytic vehicles. *J. Cell Biol.* 2005; 168(3): 465–476.

124 Damm, E.M., et al., Clathrin- and caveolin-1-independent endocytosis: entry of simian virus 40 into cells devoid of caveolae. *J. Cell Biol.* 2005; 168(3): 477–488.

125 Tsai, B., et al., Gangliosides are receptors for murine polyoma virus and SV40. *EMBO J.* 2003; 22(17): 4346–4355.

126 Le, P.U., et al., Caveolin-1 is a negative regulator of caveolae-mediated endocytosis to the endoplasmic reticulum. *J. Biol. Chem.* 2002; 277(5): 3371–3379.

127 Pelkmans, L., et al., Caveolin-stabilized membrane domains as multifunctional transport and sorting devices in endocytic membrane traffic. *Cell* 2004; 118(6): 767–780.

128 van Deurs, B., et al., Caveolae: anchored, multifunctional platforms in the lipid ocean. *Trends Cell Biol.* 2003; 13(2): 92–100.

129 Lafont, F., et al., Raft association of SNAP receptors acting in apical trafficking in Madin-Darby canine kidney cells. *Proc. Natl. Acad. Sci. USA* 1999; 96(7): 3734–3738.

130 Pombo, I., J. Rivera, and U. Blank, Munc18-2/syntaxin3 complexes are spatially separated from syntaxin3-containing

SNARE complexes. *FEBS Lett.* 2003; 550(1–3): 144–148.

131 Low, S. H., et al., Differential localization of syntaxin isoforms in polarized Madin-Darby canine kidney cells. *Mol. Biol. Cell* 1996; 7(12): 2007–2018.

132 Jacob, R. and H. Y. Naim, Apical membrane proteins are transported in distinct vesicular carriers. *Curr. Biol.* 2001; 11(18): 1444–1450.

133 Harder, T. and M. Kuhn, Selective accumulation of raft-associated membrane protein LAT in T cell receptor signaling assemblies. *J. Cell Biol.* 2000; 151(2): 199–208.

2
The Forces that Shape Caveolae

Pierre Sens and Matthew S. Turner

2.1
Introduction

Caveolae are Ω-shaped invaginations of the plasma membrane, found in many types of cells [1]. Caveolae are enriched in cholesterol, and have a membrane composition similar to that of lipid rafts [2]. In addition, caveolae show a high concentration of the protein caveolin, a hairpin-structured membrane protein possessing a hydrophobic domain [32 amino acids (AA), flanked by two hydrophilic termini (N-terminal: 101 AA, C-terminal: 43 AA)] [3]. Both termini of caveolin extend from the cytosolic side of the membrane, conferring a strong asymmetrical structure to the caveolar domain. The goal of this chapter is to provide an overview of the possible physical effects that can stem from both of these characteristics of caveolae, namely the composition difference with the rest of the plasma membrane ("raft-aspect") and their patent asymmetry ("hairy-aspect").

Although Caveolae were first observed more than 50 years ago, many of their properties and functions remain unknown. Caveolae formation seems to require the presence of the protein caveolin [4] and is very dependent on the cholesterol level in the cell [5]. There is also evidence that caveolin is coupled to other types of membrane deformation (e. g., tubular structures in endothelial cells [6]). These are strong indications that at least some biological functions of caveolae rely heavily upon their biophysical properties. Plasma membranes typically resist bending, and the formation of membrane invaginations requires the action of mechanical forces on the membrane. Even though caveolae are very complex biochemical objects, they are bound to obey the laws of physics. We must therefore understand the origin of the forces at play in the formation of the invaginations if we are to understand how, and why, caveolae form. As we make progress towards this we may gain important insights into the biological functions of caveolae. Indeed, since caveolae are inherently coupled to the mechanical state of the plasma membrane, one may envision that the cell has taken advantage of this coupling, and may use caveolae as mechano-sensors or mechano-regulators for the plasma membrane. Before discussing these possibilities in Section 2.6, we will first review some of the physical concepts behind the formation and structure of membrane domains and how this relates to the physical properties of membrane proteins.

The description present ed relies on coarse-grained physical models where the molecular structure of the membrane and proteins is only taken into account in an approximate way. This is justified by the fact that caveolae (of size ~100 nm) are much larger than the size of the individual caveolin proteins and of the thickness of the plasma membrane (~5 nm). This physical description is based on the well-known properties of fluid bilayer membranes, described in Section 2.2. Following this, two different points of view are taken to describe the formation and invagination of caveolae. In Section 2.3, caveolae are regarded as membrane domains that are chemically immiscible in the plasma membrane. This neglects effects associated directly with the details of domain composition. It is assumed there that membrane phase separation into domains does n't depend on the mechanical properties of the membrane, although the domain shape might. This description somewhat overlooks the importance of the protein caveolin in the formation of caveolae. In an attempt to approximate the complexity of the biological membrane, theoretical physicists have studied the behavior of membrane inclusions, and in particular how protein aggregation is coupled to membrane deformation, and vice-versa. These models are briefly overviewed in Section 2.4, and applied to the particular case of caveolin aggregation in caveolar membranes in Section 2.5, by taking some account of the protein structure. The final section includes a discussion of how such a description relates to the "life" of caveolae at the plasma membrane of cells. Finally, we speculate on further possible biological functions of caveolae.

2.2
Physical Modeling of Lipid Membranes

Mathematical models of deformable, fluid membranes have been available for many years [7,8], and have been successfully compared with experimental results, both on artificial [9] and biological [10] membranes. At the most fundamental level these theories rely on the single basic principle underlying statistical mechanics: that the probability of observing a given membrane deformation depends on the energy change involved in making this deformation [11]. The higher the energy, the less likely the deformation. Statistical mechanics tells us that the probability p_i of an event i is related to its energy F_i according to:

$$p_i \sim \exp\left[-\frac{F_i}{k_B T_m}\right] \tag{1}$$

This probability compares the deformation energy F_i to some energy source in the system. This energy is written F to remind us that it is a *free energy* and therefore includes changes in entropy, as well as internal and chemical energies [12]. Reactions that reduce the entropy of the system are disfavored in the same way as are those that involve a spontaneous increase in the energy by, for example, disrupting chemical bonds. Strictly speaking, Eq. (1) only holds for (sub)systems that are at equilibrium but this can often be a reasonable approximation, for example for small patches of membrane that can move and relax quickly, even though it may be inappropriate for the cell as a whole. In passive systems, the only energy source comes from the thermal fluctuations of energy $k_B T$, where k_B is the Boltzmann constant and T is the temperature (in Kelvin). Biological systems are called "active", because chemical energy, coming from, for example, ATP hydrolysis, can be harnessed by specific enzymes (molecular motors) to perform mechanical work. The cell membrane is generally the site of many active processes, including cytoskeleton polymerization and ion pumping. One may adopt the approach that these active processes provide an effective "membrane" temperature $T_m > T$ [13], and it is this that appears in Eq. (1).

In practice, much information can be obtained by the study of membrane deformations that minimize the membrane energy (those having the higher probability to occur). One contribution to membrane energy can arise from any change in the area of the cell, which must act against tension in the membrane. This is reminiscent of the work required to deform a child's balloon, for example by pinching a small patch of its surface between the fingers. As with any interface, a lipid membrane bears a "surface tension" (denoted γ throughout), which is the energy cost per unit area associated with decreasing the membrane area. However, while the surface tension observed at a water air interface is of the order 10^{-1} J m^{-2}, and typically dominates any other type of deformation energy, the surface tension of lipid bilayers can be extremely low (10^{-8} J m^{-2} in very floppy artificial systems, and $\sim 10^{-5}$ J m^{-2} for the plasma membrane). As the surface tension is low, other modes of deformation can also play an important role. One such mode is the energy associated with bending the membrane. A symmetrical bilayer membrane prefers to be flat, so that both monolayers have the same structure. Bending the membrane one way or the other breaks this symmetry, and costs an energy which varies quadratically with the membrane curvature (deformation) C. This is fundamentally analogous to the fact that the energy of an ideal spring varies with the square of its extension (known as Hooke's law), and is ultimately the reason why any flexible material that is bent will spring back into its original shape. If the membrane is asymmetrical, and cell membranes are indeed rather asymmetrical, it may prefer a non-zero curvature. This means that the membrane energy might be minimized by, and the membrane therefore most happy with, a non-zero curvature. This curvature is called the "spontaneous curvature" C_0. In this case, the deformation energy is again quadratic, but now is the difference between the membrane's (local) curvature and its spontaneous curvature. This can also be identified with a version of Hooke's law. While the membrane tension tells us how much the energy increases when the membrane area is increased, the energy increase caused by a deviation from the preferred membrane curvature is controlled by the "bending rigidity", conventionally denoted κ. Adding the curvature energy to the energy of membrane tension, the total energy of a patch of membrane of area S, with a curvature C is

$$F = \gamma S + \frac{1}{2} \kappa S(C - C_0)^2 \tag{2}$$

A Typical value for the bending rigidity of biomembranes [10] is $\kappa = 20\,k_B T$. It is convenient to measure energies in units of the thermal energy scale which, at room temperature is, $k_B T = 4 \times 10^{-21}$ J. Thus, 1 kJ mol$^{-1} = 0.4\,k_B T$.

In this chapter, we will be mostly concerned by the flask-shaped membrane deformations mimicking the caveolae (Fig. 2.1). For simplicity, we will assimilate the invagination to a spherical cap of constant curvature. In practice, there exists a membrane neck connecting the concave central cap to the flat surrounding membrane. Specialized proteins are likely to be present near the caveolae neck [14], and this is not included in the present models. From Eq. (2), the energy of a spherical membrane (with no spontaneous curvature), is $F_{sphere} = (\gamma S + 8\pi\kappa)$. The energy of large patches is dominated by membrane tension, and the energy of small patches by membrane rigidity. Clearly, this has strong consequences for the stability of membrane invaginations in general, and of caveolae in particular. Indeed, small invaginations all have the same energy ($\sim 8\pi\kappa$), which is dominated by the bending energy of the membrane. Large invaginations on the other hand, have an energy which increases with their size ($\sim \gamma S$), and are much less likely to be observed. The cross-over size between small and large invaginations in the physical sense corresponds to an area $S \sim 8\pi\kappa/\gamma$. Choosing a bending rigidity $\kappa \sim 20 k_B T$ and a surface tension $\gamma \sim 10^{-5}$ J m^{-2}, the cross-over size corresponds to a sphere of radius $R \sim$ 120 nm. The fact that this scale is close to the typical size scale of the invaginations is very encouraging for our physical approach. It indicates that even such simple physical arguments can reveal a competition between different physical energies (and hence forces) that could give rise to invaginations with roughly the observed size.

Of course biological membranes have a complexity that is not reflected in the seminal elastic model of Eq. (2). In particular, the complex lipid composition (up to 25 different lipid species), the inclusion of a host of membrane proteins ($\sim 30\%$ of the whole genome), and the support of the membrane cytoskeleton. The question of how to incorporate the two former features will form the subject of most of the following text. The cytoskeleton provides a visco elastic scaffold to the cell, and is able to exert direct forces to the membrane. Cytoskeletal anchoring of the plasma membrane is crucial to the membrane's mechanical behavior. The breaking of

Fig. 2.1 Sketch of a spherical membrane cap. The membrane curvature C is roughly constant over the deformed area S which has radius of curvature (the radius of the circle passing through the cap) 1/C, as shown. Inset: the bilayer structure of a lipid membrane.

some anchoring sites upon cell deformation and membrane extension is a major component of the energy cost of such deformations. In particular, cytoskeleton anchoring can account for up to 75% of the measured tension of cell membranes [15]. Here, we adopt the philosophy that the cytoskeleton acts to maintain the plasma membrane under tension, but does not exert direct forces to pull flask-shaped invaginations from the membrane. In fact, we will find that a consistent physical explanation of invagination can be constructed without the cytoskeleton playing any direct role in the formation of caveolae.

2.3
Caveolae as Invaginated Lipid Rafts

Caveolae are one example of lipid domains in the cell membrane [2]. These domains and other lipid "rafts" are characterized by a high concentration of cholesterol and saturated lipids. Although many controversies exist regarding the size and lifetime of lipid rafts, the morphology of caveolae seems much better defined. One likely reason for this is the stabilization of these membrane domains by the protein caveolin, and in particular the fact that they are invaginated. In this section, we present some general physical arguments concerning the behavior of membrane domains in a flexible, fluid lipid bilayer [16], without discussing the origin of their formation. Here, we assume that the phase separation is driven by chemical incompatibility between the raft and the non-raft phase, regardless of the mechanical state of the membrane. In Physical terms, chemical incompatibility can be accounted for by an energy cost of creating an interface between the two phases. Since the membrane is in two dimensions, the interface between the two phases is a line, and the immiscibility parameter is a "line tension", termed σ. For a given domain size, the line energy is the smallest when the interface is smallest, meaning that we can expect domains to be circular with a radius $R = \sqrt{S/\pi}$ (S is the domain area). Unless the line tension is very small, in which case the rafts are very small and their shape can fluctuate significantly. This signifies that they are only weakly phase separating from the non-raft membrane and are close to dissolving back into it.

Figure 2.2 illustrates how chemical incompatibility alone can have a strong influence on the domain shape. Indeed, a flat domain (Fig. 2.2a) has a large interface with its surrounding, costing a line energy of order σR. If the domain is large, this can be quite a large energy, and may cause the domain to bud off the membrane in an attempt to reduce the size of the interface to the membrane neck connecting the bud to the rest of the membrane. On the other hand, an invaginated domain costs the energy of bending the membrane into a spherical shape. The bending energy of a sphere is proportional to the bending rigidity of the membrane κ, and it has the remarkable feature that it does not depend on the size of the sphere for a symmetrical domain (it is equal to $8\pi\kappa$). Since the line energy increases with domain size, and the bending energy does not, there is a critical domain size for which we can expect the domain to invaginate spontaneously [16] (Fig. 2.2c). The

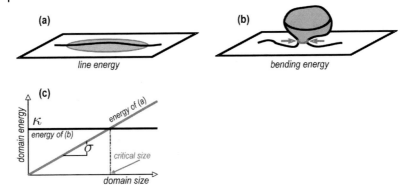

Fig. 2.2 Invagination of a membrane domain (in gray) due to chemical incompatilibity. (a) A flat domain has a large line energy, due to a large interface with the surrounding membrane. (b) An invaginated domain has a small interface, but is accompanied with a bending energy. (c) Comparison of the energy of a flat domain (sloping line) and of an invaginated domain (horizontal line). The invagination is favored for domains larger than a critical size, estimated to be of order 100 nm.

domain size at which this occurs is of the order $R \sim 4\kappa/\sigma$. The actual value of the physical parameters κ and σ vary from membrane to membrane, but we have a good idea of the order of magnitude of such parameters. The bending rigidity of biological membrane is typically of the order $\kappa \sim 20k_BT$. The line tension arises from unfavorable contacts at the molecular scale (the size of a lipid molecule, or the thickness of the bilayer). It is estimated to be of the order $\sigma \sim k_BT/nm$, although its actual value is very sensitive to the nature of the two phases in contact (in a raft, it is the contact between liquid-ordered and-liquid disordered lipid phases). Using those numbers, the critical size for domain invagination is $R = 80$ nm (corresponding to a spherical bud of radius 40 nm). Caveolae are precisely in this range of size, which is a good indication that the physical phenomena of membrane bending energy and raft line energy play a crucial role in caveolae formation and stability.

One possible picture of the formation of caveolae is the following [16] (see Fig. 2.2). Imagine a given amount of caveolin, cholesterol, and raft-forming lipids (in particular sphingolipids), dispersed in the cell membrane. With time, these various components diffuse into the membrane and find each other, forming growing membrane domains. Although the rate of this phase separation might be quite slow [17], domains should eventually grow to a large size if they are not perturbed by other dynamical phenomena at the cell membrane, and even more so if the presence of caveolin promotes the phase separation. Membrane recycling, endocytosis, and exocytosis might perturb domain growth, and may be invoked to explain the small size of the non-caveolae rafts observed in vivo (see [17].) When domains grow beyond the critical size discussed above (Fig. 2.2), they are at their lowest energy N and therefore most stable N when invaginated rather than flat.

Such a scenario is still qualitatively valid if the membrane supports a tension and the domain has a spontaneous curvature. In this case, however, the critical budding size depends upon the membrane tension. Indeed, work against membrane tension must be performed to invaginate a domain, and this stabilizes the flat shape. As a result, this simple theory applied to caveolae would predict that the size of the invagination increases with membrane tension. However, caveolae have very similar sizes across several cell types that can, presumably, bear different membrane tensions. As will be seen in Section 2.5, this indicates that the structure of the protein caveolin might play a crucial role in controlling the size of the invaginated domains.

2.4
Membrane Inclusions

Membrane proteins have hydrophobic regions inserted within the lipid bilayer, and this insertion may perturb the bilayer structure. For example, a mismatch in thickness between the hydrophobic core of the protein and that of the bilayer has an associated energy cost. It implies either that some hydrophobic residues are left unshielded from contact with water, or that the membrane (or the protein) changes its thickness to obtain a good match [18]. The consequence of hydrophobic mismatch may be protein clustering, as shown in Figure 2.3a,b. Clustering may occur even in the absence of direct (specific) interaction between the proteins, as the result of an effective attraction mediated by the membrane. As shown in Figure 2.3a,b, the membrane order is locally perturbed in the vicinity of the inclusion (the figure shows a local stretching of the lipid tails, to accommodate the hydrophobic thickness of the membrane). Bringing two inclusions together reduces the membrane area that needs to be perturbed and hence reduces the energy of membrane deformation. The result of this is an effective force that brings the proteins together.

An important phenomenon in the context of caveolae and their asymmetric membranes is when protein clustering is coupled to a change of membrane morphology. This can be expected for very asymmetric proteins, or for peripheral proteins that mostly extend on one side of the membrane. Such asymmetric membrane proteins can be thought of as imprinting a local spontaneous curvature (the C_0 term in Eq. (2) to the neighboring membrane (Fig. 2.3c). The membrane is locally curved near the protein, which again leads to a frustration of the bilayer order. As it is the case for hydrophobic mismatch, some of the frustration can be released if the proteins aggregate. In this case however, the concentration of a large number of proteins over a limited membrane area leads to a morphological change of the membrane, which adopts the preferred curvature of the proteins (Fig. 2.3d). As will be discussed in Section 2.5, this phenomenon, called "curvature instability" in the physics literature [19], is likely to play an important part in the formation of caveolae. The caveolin proteins found in caveolae are very good candidates for such large morphological changes for two reasons. On the one hand, both their hydro-

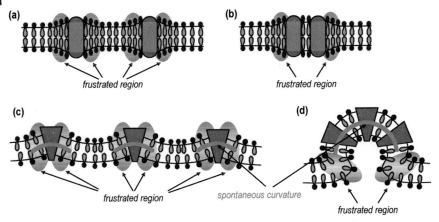

Fig. 2.3 Sketch of the aggregation of membrane proteins induced by an hydrophobic mismatch. (a) The mismatch imposes a perturbation of the bilayer structure around the protein. (b) The aggregation of two such proteins reduces the area of the perturbed membrane, and is energetically favorable. (c,d) Sketch of the aggregation of membrane proteins induced by an asymmetric coupling with the membrane. The asymmetric membrane perturbation around each inclusion (c), is reduced by protein aggregation (d), which induce a large-scale deformation in the membrane region with high protein density.

phobic termini face the cytoplasm, which makes their interaction with the neighboring membrane very asymmetric. A similar situation can to some extent be reproduced in artificial systems, by mixing bilayer-forming lipids with hydrophilic polymers (typically polyethylene glycol) with a hydrophobic anchor attached. Lipid membranes with a grafted (but mobile) polymer chain can be obtained in such manner, and it has been shown theoretically [20], and observed experimentally [21], that such a membrane can exhibit a phase separation. Another reason to expect membrane deformation near caveolin proteins is the fact that they are known to form homo-oligomers of about 15 proteins. This is due to specific biochemical interactions between caveolin via a short section of the N-terminal cytoplasmic domain, quite close to the transmembrane domain [3]. As shown in Section 2.5, this oligomerization may have much to do with the success of caveolin in aggregating and promoting membrane invagination. By concentrating the caveolin, oligomerization also concentrates the effect of the membrane asymmetry over a small membrane area, creating a large asymmetric pressure.

2.5
Caveolae as a Thermodynamic Phase Separation of Membrane Proteins

Simple mixtures of two or more material components can reside in a variety of states or "phases". The simplest of these is the mixed state, when all components are evenly mixed throughout the system. However, if molecules of one component have a sufficiently large mutual attraction for one another, or equivalently a sufficiently large repulsion from the remainder, they can "phase separate". There can then be large regions that are rich in this component suspended in a background which contains relatively little of it. It is this effect that causes oil to de-mix from water at room temperature but it is a far more generic effect than is often realized. It is now clear that there are components in the plasma membranes of cells that phase separate, for example, into caveolae. This is a slightly unusual phenomenon in that the phase-separated domains are typically only 100 nm across rather than macroscopic in size, but the principle is the same.

There is now good evidence that caveolin proteins form homo-oligomers [3] containing approximately 15 molecules. Whilst this is not a necessary feature for the generation of bending forces, which require only a molecular asymmetry between the two sides of the membrane, it may act to amplify those forces by increasing the density of interacting cytoplasmic domains (see Fig. 2.4).

It has been suggested [22] that the mechanism by which caveolin homo-oligomers form is reminiscent of micellization on a membrane. Usual in spherical surfactant micelles are formed by the aggregation of amphiphilic molecules which experience a mutual attraction between their hydrophobic tails [8]. Such micellar aggregates do not grow indefinitely because of the packing and stretching con-

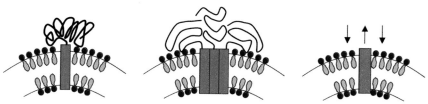

Fig. 2.4 Sketch indicating the origin of the forces that act to bend the membrane near an asymmetric membrane protein (left), or homo-oligomer thereof (center), with domains extending on one (cytoplasmic) side only. The cytoplasmic domains may be entirely disordered, resembling a random coil (as shown), or may contain some folded structure(s) forced into dense contact within the oligomer. In any case these domains exert forces on the membrane. Even disordered coils have their configurational entropy restricted by the presence of the membrane. This restriction is large for a planar membrane but is reduced if the interface bends away from the coils, leaving more room in which to fluctuate. This means that the proteins exert forces that give rise to "bending moments" (as shown, right).

straints of their tails. The same is true of caveolin. It has been determined that there is an attractive interaction between N-terminal segments of caveolin [3] and, as the aggregate grows, an increasing number of the caveolins enjoy such contacts. Eventually the repulsive forces between the greatly confined cytoplasmic domains is enough just to balance the force of attraction experienced by the next caveolin molecule that seeks to join the aggregate and, at this point, the optimal size has been reached. For caveolin oligomers this size appears to be ~15 molecules. Given the size of the cytoplasmic domains this indicates that the N-terminal attractive domains probably give rise to a substantial attraction, perhaps of the order of $10k_BT$ [22]. This, in turn, results in substantial repulsive forces between the cytoplasmic domains in the oligomers which acts to "amplify" the bending forces indicated in Figure 2.4.

In the same way that there exists a critical micelle concentration (cmc) in surfactant systems there is a similar concentration at which caveolin oligomers will start to form. For simplicity we denote this the cmc. Above this concentration there will be a few single caveolin molecules on the membrane at concentrations equal to that of the cmc, with the remainder forming as many oligomers (micelles) as are required to incorporate all the caveolin. Given that caveolins experience a substantial attraction, their cmc is probably so low that oligomers will always form at physiological concentrations. However, there is another scale of self assembly which also, in its way, involves a concentration that resembles a cmc. This is a critical budding concentration (cbc) which lies above the cmc. Below the cbc all oligomers exist on a roughly flat membrane, whilst above it the flat membrane supports oligomers at, or very close to the cbc, while the remainder of the oligomers form buds that each have an area fraction of oligomers $\varphi^* > \varphi_{cbc}$. As more oligomers are added to the membrane, more N but similar N buds are formed. We are able to establish the cbc by comparing the free energy of a membrane bearing buds to one which does not. In the following section it will be assumed implicitly that the cbc is exceeded and hence buds form.

A free inclusion, as shown in Figure 2.4 (left and center panels), is one which is not anchored to any external structure such as the cytoskeleton. In this case it is further possible to prove that there can be no net overall force acting to move the membrane up or down, nor torques which tilt it left or right. This is a direct consequence of Newton's third law: The membrane cannot experience a force (or torque) without another body or structure experiencing one that is equal and opposite. If there is no such structure there can be no such forces. This leaves the bending moment shown in Figure 2.4 (right panel) as the dominant mechanism for local membrane deformation [23]. The inclusion pushes down on the membrane with its "arms" and pulls up with its "body", but it is not connected to any other structure.

We propose to investigate how an asymmetric inclusion such as the protein caveolin (or an oligomer thereof) can generate a local curvature in the membrane, and how this curved membrane can then provide an environment preferred by other identical curvature-sensitive caveolin molecules. Whilst this approach has the advantage of providing a formal method for calculating the size of a caveolae bud directly from physical arguments, it suffers from the limitation that several parameters are known only to within an order of magnitude. Its utility should therefore be understood in the following terms:

- It represents a check on whether invaginations of 100 nm diameter might possibly be driven by the physical process described. In particular, since we find that this is indeed plausible, it provides a mechanism for the formation of caveolae that explicitly does not involve cytoskeletal forces playing any significant role.
- Such a model is then able to predict how the stability and size of the invaginations will vary with the control parameters, for example, surface tension, membrane rigidity and the tendency of any inclusions to curve the membrane. We are then able to compare these predictions with experiments involving several mutant caveolins.

Whilst an exact calculation of these bending forces is difficult there is one calculation that can at least give us an indication of the magnitude of such forces. This, involves treating the cytoplasmic tails as random coils. In this case there are well-established rules from the theory of polymers [24,25] that allow these bending forces to be calculated exactly [20,23,26]. The basic principle is that the chains gain more configurational entropy if they locate next to a convex surface rather than a flat one. This is formally equivalent to saying that each caveolin oligomer imprints a local spontaneous curvature C_0 on the membrane, which is of order $C_0 \sim f_0/\kappa$, where f_0 is a characteristic force exerted on the membrane by the cytoplasmic tails ("arms") of the caveolin oligomer, of the order $10pN$ [22].

One final physical "ingredient" is required in order to complete our model for the formation of caveolae. It is necessary to include the effect of mixing n caveolin oligomers, each of areas s, and hence area fraction $\varphi = ns/S$, on the surface of a caveolae. Simplistically, we view the surface of the caveolae as being made up of two components, caveolin oligomers (with fraction φ) surrounded by the rest of the caveolar membrane (with fraction $1-\varphi$). The energy of the membrane deformation is given by Eq. (2), where the spontaneous curvature of the bud increases with the density of caveolin, and is equal to $C_0\varphi$. Assuming that these components have no interactions of longer range than a, then this is a classical two-component ideal mixture. The free energy of mixing of this fluid is well known [12,22], contains similar contributions from the oligomer and non-oligomer membrane patches, and has the natural feature that it is very costly to remove all of either component. Indeed, the energy required to do this actually increases without bound as φ or $1 - \varphi \rightarrow 0$. For inclusions that interact with one another the interaction energy includes a contribution that scales like the density of oligomer – oligomer interactions ($\sim \varphi^2$).

The formation of buds is controlled by a variety of physical processes that have been introduced above. These can be combined into a single equation for the free energy per caveolin oligomer on a caveolae of radius R containing oligomers with area fraction φ. This merely encodes mathematically all of the physical contributions to the energy discussed earlier in this section. These are:

- The existence of a spontaneous curvature, indicating that energy is gained when

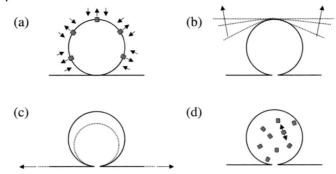

Fig. 2.5 The origin of the contributions to total free energy. (a) Energy is gained by bending the membrane in response to the bending moments exerted by the caveolin oligomers. (b) There is an energy cost when the membrane is bent away from its preferred shape: flat in the absence of caveolin and at precisely the preferred (spontaneous) curvature when they are present. (c) There is an energy cost when the area of the sphere is removed from the cell membrane against surface tension. (d) There is an energy cost associated with both mixing of and interactions between inclusions on the sphere surface. The latter increases with the area fraction of buds.

the bud, with curvature 1/R bends in response to the bending moments of the oligomers; this is the only effect which drives bending of the membrane.

- The energy cost of bending a membrane away from its preferred shape. If there are no oligomers, the membrane would like to remain flat. When it forms a bud it need not always have a curvature exactly equal to its spontaneous curvature and this, similarly, costs bending energy.
- The energy cost of drawing the area of the bud away from the remainder of the cell membrane into the bud; this involves doing work against the membrane tension γ.
- Finally, the repulsion between caveolin oligomers and the mixing energy must be included. The origin of all of these contributions is sketched in Figure 2.5.

The preferred caveolae state can be obtained by identifying the minimum of this free energy which, in turn, yields predictions for the preferred caveolae bulb radius R^* and oligomer density φ^* (see Fig. 2.6). The invagination radius decreases with increasing caveolin density, so that the curvature of the bud approaches the spontaneous curvature of the caveolar membrane: $C^* = C_0\varphi^*$.

These results follow from the same model for the bud as a nearly-closed sphere attached to the membrane by a small neck, as was introduced in Section 2.4. We find that a physical description of caveolae can yield predictions for such observable quantities as the caveolae radius R that are in good agreement with observations. In this model we find that the primary reason why caveolae form is because of the coupling between membrane curvature and protein density: proteins accu-

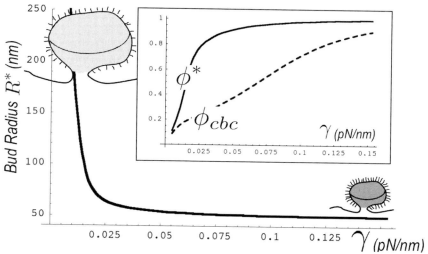

Fig. 2.6 Variation of the preferred radius of the caveolar bulb R with surface tension of the membrane. The size of the caveolae reduces with increasing tension for small tensions, but at larger tensions reaches a preferred value that is rather insensitive to tension. The two sketches of the calveolar bulb indicate this, with darker shading representing higher density of caveolin. Inset: The variation of the critical budding concentration of inclusions, expressed as the area fraction φ_{cbc}, and the area fraction of oligomers on buds, φ^*. For all but the smallest tensions our simple two-component model predicts that the caveolae should be almost entirely covered with caveolin oligomers, at a concentration $\varphi^* s^-$ that is always above that of the surrounding membrane between caveolae $\varphi_{cbc} s^-$.

mulate to a curved membrane (bud), stabilizing its shape and thereby attracting more proteins. If the formation of a curved membrane is too energetically costly because of a high surface tension, the domains are destabilized [22].

Also, we can again return to make contact with caveolae as lipid rafts. The consensus seems to be that these are the only rafts for which the identity and stability is not controversial. They are large, comparatively easy to observe, and very stable. We take this as evidence that the particular membrane curvature of caveolae stabilizes the phase separation into buds, a mechanism which is entirely consistent with the results of our physical analysis of their stability. Further evidence for a coupling between caveolae and membrane curvature can be found in the fact that an increase of the number of caveolae can enhance other types of membrane deformation, namely endothelial capillary tubule formation [6].

Finally, our theory provides a framework with which to seek to understand caveolae formation in mutant caveolin systems [27]. Mutants lacking the mutually attractive domain of the N-terminus are still able to drive membrane invagination, but with a much larger size $R \approx 1$ µm. This is consistent with the fact that the force exerted by isolated proteins should be an order of magnitude smaller than the force exerted by oligomers which results in a 10-fold increase in bud radius. Other mutants lacking the mutually attractive C-terminus also form larger buds. We would understand this as being due to a weaker oligomer – oligomer attraction, resulting in a lower density of caveolin in caveolae andtherefore larger buds.

The origin of the striated texture observed on the surface of caveolae [1], which superficially resembles tree bark, is still not understood. It may be that such structures are due to the spatial organization of caveolin oligomers on the surface of these "gnarly buds". If this is the case it may not be immediately obvious how circularly symmetric oligomers can organize themselves into asymmetric phases consisting of long, linear structures. However, it is now known that caveolin proteins also interact via the distal regions of their C-termini tails [3]. This attraction, together with a purely physical, membrane-mediated, longer-range repulsion that it is possible o estimate [23] could lead to a phase separation of the caveolin oligomers with caveolin-dense regions (stripes) coexisting with a caveolin-poor surface. Such phenomena have been studied in physically similar systems [28], and a reasonable conclusion would be that these structures may occur naturally as a result of a balance between a short ranged (C-terminal) attraction and a longer-ranged (membrane deformation-mediated) repulsion.

2.6
Caveolae and Membrane Tension: Mechano-Sensitivity and Mechano-Regulation

So far, we have two possible mechanisms by which invaginated membrane domains may form at the plasma membrane. The raft model of Section 2.3 tells us that a phase separation in the membrane promotes membrane curvature because of chemical immiscibility, the driving force is the domain line tension. The curvature instability model of Section 2.5, takes the point of view that membrane curvature promotes the phase separation because of the aggregation of proteins into patches of preferred curvature, the driving force being the protein spontaneous curvature. In both cases, the tendency to membrane invagination must overcome the membrane tension, which favors a smooth, flat membrane, and in both cases, increasing the membrane tension may lead to the flattening of the invagination. Figure 2.7 shows the effect of membrane tension on the energy of flat and invaginated domains for the raft model. At low tension, chemical incompatibility and the asymmetry of the membrane conspire to promote domain invagination, the budded state being the most stable state. At large tension, budding the domain costs too much energy, and invaginated domains flatten. Flat caveolae have indeed been reported in the literature [29], although they appear much less common than their invaginated counterparts. Figure 2.7 shows that an additional complexity arises from the fact that there is an energy barrier between the flat and budded states. This means that intermediate states (such as the hemispherical state – $\beta = 0.5$ of Fig. 2.7) are very unfavorable. This fact has two very important physical consequences. On the one hand, this means that the transition from invaginated

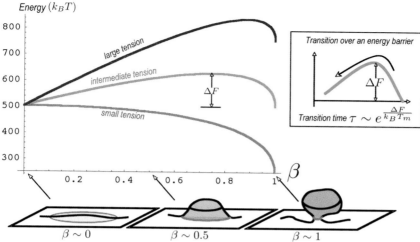

Fig. 2.7 Variation of the energy of a domain as a function of the domain shape for different membrane tension. The shape is characterized by a single parameter β, which vanishes for a flat domain and is equal to unity for a fully budded domain (corresponding to a closed sphere, a state that can be attained only if the domain endocytoses). The energy plot shows the domain energy (in k_BT unit) for a domain of size R = 100 nm, of line energy $\sigma = k_BT$ nm, and of bending rigidity $\varkappa$ = 20 k_BT. The energy is shown for three different membrane tensions. Under low tension (red), the domain tends to bud to minimize contact with the surrounding phase, and the

minimum of energy is for $\beta = 1$. As the membrane tension increases (green), the energy of the budded domain increases with respect to the energy of the flat domain. At even higher tension, the flat domain becomes the minimum of energy. Flattening the invagination requires an energy barrier (ΔF) to be exceeded. The transition over an energy barrier (inset) is activated by thermal fluctuations, and requires a time that increases exponentially with the height of the barrier (see text). The higher the membrane tension, the lesser the time needed to operate the flattening of the invagination.

to flat domains does not occur continuously. Instead, the domains will abruptly snap open when the membrane tension is raised to a sufficient value. We argue below that interesting biological functions for caveolae could stem from this physical fact. Furthermore, we have seen in Eq. (1) that states of high energy are exponentially unlikely, which means that the passage of a barrier ΔF requires an appropriate thermal fluctuation. This is a rare event which occurs only after a time proportional to $e^{\Delta F/k_BT_m}$. This means that the response of caveolae to a mechanical perturbation is sensitive to the time scale over which this perturbation occurs.

A new putative function of caveolae at the plasma membrane emerges from these physical considerations, in addition to their supposed role in cell signaling and cholesterol transport (to cite only a few). Specifically, this is a possible role in cell mechano-sensitivity and mechano-regulation. Although direct experimental evidence of such role is lacking at this time, Figure 2.7 provides a clear picture of the effect that membrane tension should have on caveolae. The one remaining question at this stage is the level of membrane tension required to affect caveolae morphology. We are able to relate this tension to relevant physical parameters of the caveolar membrane, such as the line tension, bending rigidity, and spontaneous curvature [22,30]. The expected values for these parameters leads to the identification of a characteristic membrane tension that can be observed in cells. At present, however, these parameters are not known with sufficient precision for the theory to produce quantitatively precise predictions.

We may however investigate some biological consequences of the disruption of caveolae at high membrane tension. In that respect, the scenarios presented in Sections 2.5 and 2.3 are somewhat different. If the very formation of the caveolin raft is coupled with membrane curvature (which is what the thermodynamic model of Section 2.5 predicts), increasing the membrane tension will lead not only to flattening of the invagination but also to dispersion of the caveolin aggregate. One can relate this phenomenon to a putative function of caveolae in cell signaling, which is to hold signaling components inactive until they are released and activated by an appropriate stimulus [31]. The thermodynamical model of Section 2.5 suggests that an increase in the mechanical tension of the cell membrane could provide such a stimulus. If, on the other hand, the phase separation leading to caveolin aggregates is independent of the shape of the membrane, the caveolin rafts will remain regardless of the membrane mechanical tension. Their morphology will however change upon tension increase, as is described Figure 2.7.

The morphological changes of caveolae with the tension of the plasma membrane provides the basis for mechanical regulation at the cell membrane. It is known that the tension of a cell increases if it is mechanically perturbed [32], and that cells have developed regulatory mechanisms to accommodate mechanical perturbations [32,33]. Caveolae might play a role in this mechanism, and many pathologies associated with caveolin seem to involve the mechanical behavior of the cell. One can cite their involvement in various muscular diseases [34], and defects in vascular relaxation and contractility in mice deficient of caveolin-1 [4]. There is an increase of the number of caveolae in Duchènne muscular dystrophy [35], and such an increase has also been observed in cells subjected to long-lasting shear stress [36]. Furthermore, there exists evidence that caveolin can contribute significantly to cell-cycle regulation [37], and cell entry into mitosis can be inhibited by artificially maintaining a high level of caveolin prior to mitosis. One can argue on the basis of physical arguments that the coexistence of flat and invaginated membrane domains regulates cell membrane tension [30]. Figure 2.8 shows that the mechanism of a perturbation of the cell membrane area can be buffered by the flattening and invagination of domains. By this mechanism, caveolin expression could regulate and buffer the membrane tension of cells by controlling the number of caveolae at the cell membrane. Along with many other factors, this could be one reason why caveolin is down-regulated prior to mitosis [37], as a means low-

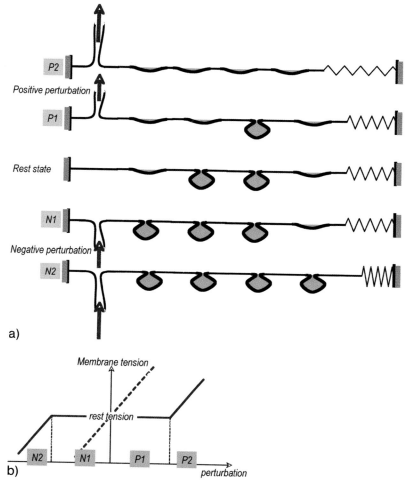

Fig. 2.8 The possible involvement of caveolae in mechanical regulation at the cell membrane. (Left) A mechanical perturbation is said to be positive if membrane area is taken out, and negative if it is put in. In the absence of invaginations, such perturbation would influence the membrane tension (visualized as a spring of various length), increasing it for positive perturbation, and decreasing it for negative perturbation. The presence of membrane invaginations, for which caveolae are a good candidate, allow buffering of the changes in membrane tension, as positive perturbations flatten the invagination (P1) prior to tension increase (P2), and negative perturbation leads to more invagination (N1), before it starts affecting the tension (N2). (Right) Variation of membrane tension with perturbation in the absence of invagination (dashed line), and with invagination (solid line). The membrane reservoir in the invagination helps keep the tension unaltered.

ering membrane tension by releasing the membrane area stored in caveolae, thereby assisting cell division. This is consistent with the fact that caveolin-1 knockout mice show an increased rate of cellular proliferation [4].

Compensatory pathways exist for cells lacking caveolin that do not exhibit caveolae at their plasma membranes [4]. In order to investigate further the possible role of caveolae in tension regulation, one potentially promising line of research might be to perturb (e.g. mechanically) cells that do have caveolae, and to observe the effect of that perturbation on caveolae before any alternative regulatory mechanisms can have a significant effect.

2.7
Conclusions

Fluid membranes can be described using physical laws. The membrane has some tension which resists the formation of invaginations of finite area. The area of each invagination must be removed from the rest of the cell membrane under tension in order to form a bud. The membrane has a rigidity which parameterizes the stiffness of the membrane. Patches (rafts) on the membrane which have a distinct chemical composition also experience a line tension that acts at the interface of the patch with the rest of the membrane. This line tension acts to minimize the length of the contact line and tends either to make the domain circular or to form a bud, with a much reduced contact region near the neck of the bud. Finally, membrane inclusions such as caveolin that are distributed asymmetrically in the membrane can always be expected to make the membrane curve. It is argued that the predominantly random coil of the N-terminal section of caveolin acts to bend the membrane away from it and hence favors the formation of endo, rather than exo, buds. These physical ingredients can be combined in simple theories to understand when, and if, caveolae-like invaginations should be stable and, if so, at what length scales. The characteristic scales that arise from comparing surface tension and line tension with rigidity both are in the 100 nm range, and thereby provide an early hint that a balance between the various physical effects listed above could be expected to give rise to invaginations similar to caveolae. We describe how this can be analyzed in more detail, leading to a theory for the stability of the buds under variation of surface tension. We find that buds of a single characteristic size stabilized by line tension can act as mechanical tension regulators and how these could very effectively buffer the cell's tension in the physiological range.

Abbreviations

AA	amino acid
cms	critical micelle concentration
cbc	critical budding concentration

References

1 Rothberg, K. G., J. E. Heuser, W. C. Donzell, Y. S. Ying, J. R. Glenney, and R. G. Anderson. Caveolin, a protein component of caveolae membrane coats. *Cell* **68**, 673–682 (1992).

2 Simons, K., and E. Ikonen. Functional rafts in cell membranes. *Nature* **387**, 569–572 (1997).

3 Schlegel, A., D. Volonté, J. A. Engelman, F. Galbiati, P. Mehta, X. L. Zhang, P. E. Scherer, and M. P. Lisanti. Crowded little caves: structure and function of caveolae. *Cell Signal* **10**, 457–463 (1998).

4 Drab, M., P. Verkade, M. Elger, M. Kasper, M. Lohn, B. Lauterbach, J. Menne, C. Lindschau, F. Mende, F. C. Luft, A. Schedl, H. Haller, and T. V. Kurzchalia. Loss of caveolae, vascular dysfunction, and pulmonary defects in caveolin-1 gene-disrupted mice. *Science* **293**, 2449 (2001).

5 Hailstones, D., L. S. Sleer, R. G. Parton, and K. K. Stanley. Regulation of caveolin and caveolae by cholesterol in MDCK cells. *J. Lipid Res.* **39**, 369–379 (1998).

6 Liu, J., X. B. Wang, D. S. Park, and M. P. Lisanti. Caveolin-1 expression enhances endothelial capillary tubule formation. *J. Biol. Chem.* **277**, 10661–10668 (2002).

7 Helfrich, W., and Servus R. *Nuovo Cimento D* **3**, 137 (1984).

8 Safran, S. A. *Statistical Thermodynamics of Surfaces, Interfaces and Membranes.* Perseus, Cambridge, MA (1994).

9 Evans, E., and Rawicz, W. Entropy-driven tension and bending elasticity in condensed-fluid membranes. *Phys. Rev. LEtt.* **64**, 2094–2097 (1990).

10 Brochard, F., and J. F. Lennon. *J. Physique (Paris)* **36**, 1035 (1975).

11 Chaikin, P. M., and T. C. Lubensky. *Principles of condensed matter physics.* Cambridge University Press, Cambridge UK (1995).

12 Reichl, L. E. *A modern course in statistical physics.* Edward Arnold, London (1980).

13 Gov, N. S., and S. A. Safran. Red blood cell membrane fluctuations and shape controlled by ATP-induced cytoskeletal. Defects *Biophys. J.* **88**, 1859–1874 (2005).

14 Oh, P., D. P. McIntosh, and J. E. Schnitzer. Dynamin at the neck of caveolae mediates their budding to form transport vesicles by GTP-driven fission from the plasma membrane of endothelium. *J. Cell Biol.* **141**, 101–114 (1998).

15 Sheetz, M. P. Cell control by membrane-cytoskeleton adhesion, *Nat. Rev. Mol. Cell Biol.* **2**, 392–396 (2001).

16 Lipowsky, R. (1992) Budding of membranes induced by intramembrane domains *J. Phys. II France* **2**, 1825–1840. Lipowsky, R. Domain-induced budding of fluid membranes *Biophys. J.* **64**, 1133–1138 (1993).

17 Turner, M. S., P. Sens, and N. D. Socci. Recycling and the control of raft-like membrane domains *Phys. Rev. Let.* (Submitted).

18 Mouritsen, O., and M. Bloom. *Biophys. J.* **46**, 141 (1984); *Annu. Rev. Biophys. Biomol. Struct.* **22**, 145 (1993).

19 Leibler, S. Curvature instability in membranes. *Journal de Physique I* **47**, 507–516 (1986).

20 Lipowsky, R. Bending of membranes by anchored polymers. *Europhys. Lett.* **30**, 197–202 (1995).

21 Szleifer, I., O. V. Gerasimov, and D. H. Thomson. Spontaneous liposome formation induced by grafted poly(ethylene oxide) layers. *Proc. Natl. Acad. Sci. USA* **95**, 1032–1037 (1998).

22 Sens, P., and M. S. Turner. Theoretical Model for the Formation of Caveolae and Similar Membrane Invagination. *Biophys. J.* **86**, 1–9 (2004).

23 Evans, A., M. S. Turner, and P. Sens. Interactions between proteins bound to biomembranes. *Phys. Rev. E.* **67** 041907 (2003).

24 Doi, M., and S. F. Edwards. *The Theory of Polymer Dynamics.* Oxford University Press, Oxford UK (1984).

25 de Gennes, P. G. *Scaling Concepts in Polymer Physics.* Cornell University Press, Ithaca (1979).

26 Bickel, T., C. Jeppesen, and C. M. Marques. Local entropic effects of polymers grafted to soft interfaces. *Eur. Phys. J. E* **4**, 33–43 (2001).

27 Li, S., F. Galbiati, D. Volonte, M. Sargiacomo, J. A. Engelman, K. Das, P. E. Scherer, and M. P. Lisanti. Mutational analysis of caveolin induced vesicle formation.

Expression of caveolin-1 recruits caveolin-2 to caveolae membranes. *FEBS Lett.* **434**, 127–134 (1998).

28 Sear, R. P., S. W. Chung, G. Markovich, W. M. Gelbart, and J. R. Heath. Spontaneous patterning of quantum dots at the air-water interface. *Phys. Rev. E.* **59**, R6255–R6258 (1999).

29 Prescott, L., and M. W. Brightman. The sarcolemma of *Aplysia* smooth muscle in freeze-fracture preparations. *Tissue Cell* **8**, 248–258 (1976).

30 Sens, P., and M. S. Turner. Budded membrane microdomains as regulators for cellular tension (2005).

31 Parton, R. G. Life without caveolae. *Science* **293**, 2404 (2001).

32 Raucher, D., and M. P. Sheetz. Characteristics of a membrane reservoir buffering membrane tension, *Biophys. J.* **77**, 1992–2002 (1999).

33 Morris, C. E., and U. Homann. Cell surface area regulation and membrane tension *J. Membrane Biol.* **179**, 79–102 (2000).

34 Woodman, S. E., F. Sotgia, F. Galbiati, C. Minetti, and M. P. Lisanti. Caveolinopathies: mutations in caveolin-3 cause four distinct autosomal dominant muscle diseases. *Neurology* **62**, 538–543 (2004).

35 Repetto, S., M. Bado, P. Broda, G. Lucania, E. Masetti, F. Sotgia, I. Carbone, A. Pavan, E. Bonilla, G. Cordone, M. P. Lisanti, and C. Minetti. Increased number of caveolae and caveolin-3 overexpression in Duchènne muscular dystrophy. *Biochem. Biophys. Res. Commun.* **261**, 547–550 (1999).

36 Park, H., Y.-M. Go, P. L. St.John, M. C. Maland, M. P. Lisanti, D. R. Abrahamson, and H. Jo. *Plasma membrane cholesterol is a key molecule in shear-dependent activation of extracellular signal-regulated kinase. J. Biol. Chem.* **273**, 32304–32311 (1998).

37 Fielding, C. J., A. Bist, and P. E. Fielding. Intracellular cholesterol transport in synchronized human skin fibroblasts. *Biochemistry* **38**, 2506–2513 (1999).

3
The Biophysical Characterization of Lipid Rafts

Pranav Sharma, Rajat Varma, and Satyajit Mayor

3.1
Introduction: The Fluid Mosaic Model and Membrane Domains

In an influential review in the early 1970s, Singer and Nicolson summarized the available information on the property of the lipid bilayer, and proposed a "fluid mosaic" model of the plasma membrane [1]. These authors suggested that biological membranes are two-dimensional fluids of lipids, in which integral membrane proteins are dissolved; peripheral proteins are attached to the surface of the membrane and protein milieu (Fig. 3.1). Lipids and proteins were proposed to have unrestricted lateral mobility, but restricted transverse mobility. These considerations were construed to result in a homogeneous distribution of lipids and proteins in biological membranes. However, the spatial and temporal inhomogeneity of lipids, while not explicitly advocated, was certainly not ruled out. In fact, domain models of cell membranes, as mosaic rather than fluid, have existed for a long time, based primarily on the properties of lipids in artificial liposome membranes [2,3]. The fluid-mosaic model of Singer and Nicolson also considered the possibility of small membrane domains in the fluid cell membrane bilayer. However, all these models of cell membranes did not focus on relating any specific biological functions that required domain formation.

3.2
The Origin of the Raft Hypothesis

Membrane heterogeneities resurfaced primarily as a necessity to explain a specific biological observation of preferential sorting of glycosphingolipids to apical membranes in polarized epithelial cells [4]. This idea was finally developed into a notion of lipid rafts by Simons and coworkers, and was centered on cholesterol-containing domains as the cornerstone of the raft model of life in a living cell membrane [5] (Fig. 3.2A).

Lipid rafts were hypothesized as specialized regions of cell membrane where sphingolipids and cholesterol come together as a result of chemical affinity and/or

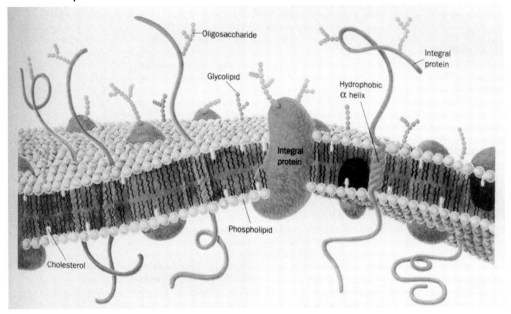

Fig. 3.1 The fluid-mosaic model of the plasma membrane. In this famous model, Singer and Nicholson summarized experimental observations from studying diffusion processes in cell and artificial membranes to suggest that proteins are dissolved in a two-dimensional fluid. They also considered the possibility of small membrane domains (~100 nm at most) in the fluid cell membrane bilayer.

their preferential packing. These regions could include or exclude other lipids and proteins, and this specific segregation was proposed to mediate their biological function [5]. Lipid rafts have been implicated in a variety of functions such as sorting, endocytosis, signaling, and cell migration [6]. Although lipid rafts are implicated in many fundamental biological functions, there is significant confusion in their definition, evidence for their existence, and their precise role in biological function. Numerous models to explain their structure and function have been proposed and are summarized in Figure 3.2.

Lipid rafts have been studied and defined with a variety of techniques, and this has resulted in various terminologies such as 'microdomains', detergent-insoluble glycolipid/glycosphingolipid-enriched complexes/membranes (DIGs), and detergent-resistant membranes (DRMs). In order to avoid confusion, the term "lipid rafts" in this chapter will be used henceforth as a general description of lipid-based membrane heterogeneity, and wherever necessary followed by the method used to define it.

This chapter focuses on the biophysical tools that have been used to examine membrane heterogeneities.

a)

b)

c)

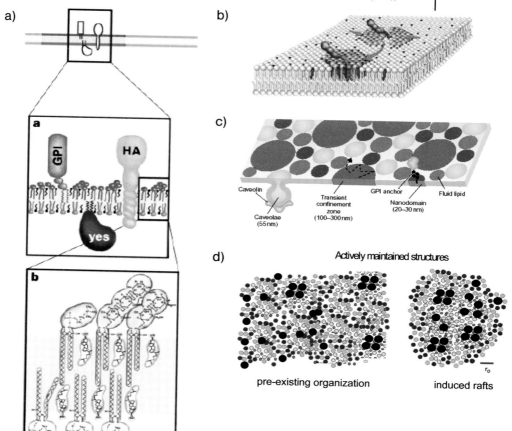

d)

Caveolin

Transient
confinement
zone
(100–300 nm)

Caveolae
(55 nm)

GPI anchor

Nanodomain
(20–30 nm)

Fluid lipid

Actively maintained structures

pre-existing organization

induced rafts

Fig. 3.2 Current raft models. (A) The most commonly cited hypothesis for membrane rafts proposed by K. Simons (Dresden, Germany) [5] depicts rafts that are relatively large structures (~50 nm), enriched in cholesterol and sphingolipid (SL), with which proteins are likely to associate. (B) Anderson and Jacobson visualize rafts as lipid shells which are small, dynamic molecular-scale assemblies in which "raft" proteins preferentially associate with certain types of lipids [83]. The recruitment of these "shells" into functional structures could be a dynamic and regulated process. (C) Another point of view is that a large fraction of the cell membrane is raft-like and exists as a "mosaic of domains"; cells regulate the amount of the different types of domains via a cholesterol-based mechanism [84]. (D) Actively generated spatial and temporal organization of raft components. A different picture that is consistent with data from GPI-anchored protein studies in living cells suggest that pre-existing lipid assemblies are small and dynamic, and coexist with monomers [30]. They are actively induced to form large-scale stable "rafts". Black circles = GPI-anchored proteins; red and pink circles = non-raft-associated lipids; yellow circles = raft-associated lipids; green = cholesterol. Scale bar = ~5 nm. (Reprinted with permission from [30].)

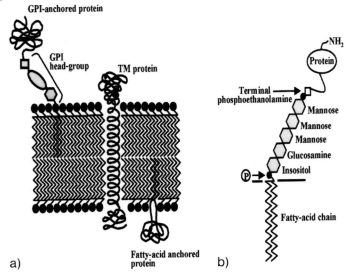

Fig. 3.3 (A) Membrane topology of GPI-anchored proteins in comparison to transmembrane (TM) proteins and fatty-acid linked proteins. (B) Core residues of the GPI-anchor. (Reprinted with permission from [7].)

3.3
The Role of Lipid-Anchored Proteins in the Development of the Membrane Raft Hypothesis

Before reverting to the heart of the matter, it is useful to examine why glycosyl-phosphatidylinositol (GPI)-anchored proteins have been used as markers for rafts. GPI-APs are a class of extracytoplasmic proteins that undergo a post-translational lipid modification that results in the exchange of an often perfectly competent hydrophobic transmembrane protein anchor with a glycolipid, the GPI-anchor [7] (Fig. 3.3). The GPI-anchor is the sole anchor by which most of these proteins attach to membranes, and often is required for targeting to plasma membrane after their synthesis and post-translational lipid modification in the endoplasmic reticulum (ER) [8]. Diverse proteins are GPI-anchored, and thus the GPI-anchor has been implicated in providing functions such as specific sorting in the secretory and endocytic pathway [7,9], and signaling [6,10–12]. In addition, in most cells almost all of the GPI-anchored proteins are present in DRMs. The requirement for maintenance of specific lipid composition for these special sorting and signaling characteristics, and the fact that the GPI-anchor did not extend beyond the first leaflet of the bilayer, provided the impetus to examine the distribution of GPI-anchored proteins in cell membranes as indicators of lipid-based heterogeneity markers. Similar arguments are applicable to other lipid-tethered proteins where the lipid anchor appears to specific sorting and signaling specificity to the lipid-tethered proteins in question [13].

3.4

The Case For and Against DRMs as Evidence for "Rafts" in Cell Membranes

For a long time, the existence of DRMs was thought to reflect "lipid rafts" in biological membranes, and this is still one of the most widely used methods to define lipid rafts. This was despite the notion that many membrane-associated proteins and lipids interacting with the cytoskeleton directly or via complexes could be resistant to detergent extraction [14,15]. Studies examining the interaction of detergent with membranes are about as old as models that predicted the fluid nature of biological membranes [16]. Membranes of Semliki Forest virus were treated with different detergents, and various stages of virus membrane dissociation (following detergent treatment) were investigated for understanding virus function [17–19]. Simons and coworkers, following their studies on the preferential apical transport of some proteins and glycosphingolipids [4], suggested that there may be a correlation between apical transport of these proteins and glycosphingolipids. This makes apical sorting of GPI-APs along with glycosphingolipids among the first biological function proposed for lipid rafts. Simons and coworkers proposed that glycosphingolipid-enriched patches might act as a sorting platforms for proteins that are preferentially sorted to apical compartments. In addition, GPI-APs and several sphingolipids were shown to become resistant to cold Triton-X 100 solubilization (also referred to as DRMs) in the trans-Golgi network (TGN) before their delivery to apical membranes in polarized epithelial cells [20,21]. The roots of the widespread use of cold nonionic detergent as an evidence of membrane inhomogeneities or lipid rafts (thus referred to as DRMs or DIGs) and its link to biological function may be partially traced to this seminal study. Brown and Rose showed that the cold detergent-insoluble complexes from lysates of polarized Madin-Darby canine kidney (MDCK) cells contained moderate amounts of apically delivered protein human placental alkaline phosphatase (PLAP) along with other GPI-APs. These detergent-insoluble membranes were concentrated in glycosphingolipids, but proteins destined for delivery to basolateral compartments were missing. This led the authors to speculate that these cold detergent-insoluble complexes could form the sorting platforms, as suggested by Simons and coworkers, for the apical delivery of PLAP.

The idea of DRMs as a biochemical purification of a specific membrane domain in living cells was reinforced from the studies investigating the phase behavior of lipids in membranes. Constituent lipids determine the state of membrane; lipids with saturated long acyl chains exists in the "gel state" with restricted lateral mobility and long range order because they are able to tightly pack the hydrocarbon chains of the lipids, whereas lipids with unsaturated (kinked) acyl chains exist as a "liquid crystalline state" with faster lateral mobility because they are unable to pack in the same fashion. Clearly, thermal effects determine in which state(s) these lipids may exist, and also the phase diagram of coexisting phases [22]. Extensive studies with artificial lipid membranes has suggested that lipids in the liquid crystalline state can exist in a liquid-disordered (l_d) or liquid-ordered (l_o) state [23], differentiated only by local order parameter. A lo state is characterized by a gel-like short-range local order but liquid crystalline state-like translational mobility. Sphingolipids with saturated long acyl chains and short rigid cholesterol undergo preferential packing into l_o phases [24,25]. The arguments that biological membranes contain patches of lo domains in otherwise ld membranes are supported by the following observations:

1. There is a coexistence of l_o and l_d phases in model membranes.
2. Model membranes known to be in l_o state are insoluble in cold, nonionic detergent (e. g., Triton X-100), and the physical state of model membranes treated with cold detergent were similar to that of the l_o state.
3. A fraction of the lipids in biological membranes are insoluble in cold nonionic detergent.

This physical picture provided the much-needed rationale to relate the existence of these detergent-insoluble complexes to 'rafts' in cell membranes, leading to a flood of reports investigating the components of cold detergent-insoluble membranes and linking them with biological function; indeed, several studies on the "proteome" of DRMs are also available today [26,27]. Even to date, detergent insolubility remains the most widespread method of identifying association with lipid rafts.

Despite numerous studies involving detergent insolubility on cells and artificial membranes, there remains a lack of understanding of phase behavior, composition, and also physical principles governing the association of lipids in the membranes of living cells. It would be difficult to consider the treatment of membranes with detergent as being nondisruptive. However, the phenomena of detergent insolubility could result from the chemical interaction (or possibly lack of it) of certain lipids with detergents. So, the interpretation of this technique rests heavily on the premise that detergent insolubility reflects some "chemical interaction" between lipids that existed in live cells prior to detergent treatment. This "chemical interaction" needs to be over and above the chemical interaction of various lipids to the detergent itself. To date, we lack a direct correlation between live cell lipid raft/ microdomain organization and the resulting detergent-insoluble complexes. In the absence of any clear understanding of the relationship between "a priori" live cell organization and resulting phenomena of cold detergent insolubility, the suggestion that cold detergent insolubility reflects presence of some organization on living cell is, at best, speculative.

Support for these suspicions came from the studies of Heerklotz [28], who examined the phase transitions and phase structures of model lipid membranes using microcalorimetry and solid state nuclear magnetic resonance (NMR) [28]. When examining vesicles composed of an equimolar mixture of 1-palmitoyl-2-oleoyl-*sn*-glycero-3-phosphocholine (PC), egg sphingomyelin (SM) and cholesterol, Heerklotz did not find any significant fraction of membrane in ordered state at 37 °C. However, the addition of increasing amounts of the detergent Triton X-100, or a lowering of the temperature, promoted the formation of ordered domains in these membranes, which were resistant to subsequent detergent extraction procedure. Hence, instead of reflecting upon the ordering of lipids in membrane, Triton X-100 could cause the formation of such ordered domains. In a follow-up study, Heer-klotz et al. showed that very small transition energies are required to induce changes in the size and abundance of ordered domains in artificial model membrane systems [29]. Hence, the perturbations caused by incorporating detergents could result in artifacts, especially in studies involving artificial lipid membranes. In biological membranes with complex lipid mixtures and proteins, there is a possibility of some component(s) acting as a stabilizer of the lipid domains, but the use of detergents to probe this situation is fraught with the concerns raised above. At best, DRM-association reveals a biochemical propensity that may be associated with ordered lipid domains [9,30].

3.5
Why Are Biophysical Studies Useful for Understanding Lipid Rafts?

Given the large size (larger than the limit of resolution of light microscopy) of membrane heterogeneities observed in artificial model membranes, one would expect to observe them in biological membranes with reasonable ease. However, even with the spectrum of protein- and lipid-related techniques available, ranging from electron microscopy, optical tweezers and single molecule studies to biochemical detection, the direct visualization of lipid rafts has been elusive. An association of proteins expected to be present in lipid rafts or DRMs is not detectable by using biochemical procedures such as SDS-PAGE, which indicates that an association between raft constituents – if present – is weak, noncovalent, and/or transient.

Within the resolution of light microscopy, DRM constituents such as GPI-anchored proteins appear to be diffusely distributed [31], indicating that if segregated "raft" structures exist they must be smaller than the resolution of light microscopy (at best 200 nm). Studying the distribution of GPI-anchored proteins by electron microscopy (EM), which has the correct scale of detection, also failed to detect any clustering of lipid raft constituents [31–33]. Elaborate fixation procedures and the efficiency of labeling with electron-dense tags might be possible causes of this loss of detection sensitivity [34]. As each technique is scrutinized for its suitability for raft detection, it has become clear that these structures – if they exist – are extremely difficult to visualize and/or detect in direct manner.

In the absence of any other option, indirect methods remain in widespread use to define the constituents and structure of lipid rafts; biophysical studies hold the promise of understanding lipid rafts. In the following sections a variety of different biophysical techniques used to study lipid rafts are discussed, together with an idea of their impact on our understanding of "raft" structures in living cell membranes.

The biophysical techniques used to examine the organization of lipid-based components may be divided into two types:
- those based on studying the diffusion characteristics of membrane components, based on the assumptions that raft-association will be detected as a change in

local membrane viscosity, or will generate large-sized entities that should show deviations from diffusive behavior attributable to monomer diffusion; and

- those based on detecting enhanced proximity between raft-associated molecules.

3.6
Diffusion-Based Measurements

Two main types of diffusion measurement have been analyzed, namely single molecule-based methods such as single-particle tracking (SPT), and ensemble-based methods such as fluorescence recovery after photobleaching (FRAP) or fluorescence correlation spectroscopy (FCS).

3.6.1
Single-Molecule Studies

Single-particle tracking studies, which involves observing the motion of a single molecule tagged with nanometer-sized colloidal gold or fluorescent dye [35], has been used to elucidate the fine structure of biological membranes (Fig. 3.4). Sheets and coworkers used video-enhanced bright field microscopy on 40-nm colloidal gold labeled to antibodies against Thy-1 or cholera toxin B (CtxB) subunit to study the movement of Thy-1 or GM1 respectively, in C3H 10T1/2 fibroblasts [36]. They divided the observed motion of molecules into four categories: fast diffusion; slow diffusion; confined diffusion; and stationary at 6.6 s time scale (200 frames at video rate of 30 frames per second). While significantly higher fraction of Thy-1 and GM1 showed confined diffusion (37% and 35%, respectively), only 16% of fluorescein phosphatidylethanolamine (fl-PE; phospholipid analogue) molecules displayed confined diffusion. Moreover, the treatment of cells with a glycosphingolipid inhibitor (which reduced the glycosphingolipid level by ~40%) reduced the fraction of Thy-1 (28%) molecules undergoing confined diffusion. This indicates a role of glycosphingolipids in the reduced mobility of Thy-1. At this timescale of 6.6 s, Thy-1 and GM1 were found in transient confinement zones (TCZs) averaging 325 to 370 nm in diameter. At the 60 s observation window, Thy-1 and GM1 were confined to TCZs for 7–9 s, with an average diameter of between 260 and 330 nm. Interestingly, the extraction with cold Triton X-100 did not affect either fraction of molecules showing confined diffusion or diameter of confined region. The authors concluded that these confined reasons might be *in-vivo* correlates of detergent-insoluble complexes. The same group conducted a further characterization [37] and found that the lipid analogues 1,2-dio-leoyl-*sn*-glycero-3-phosphoethanolamine-fluorescein (FL-DOPE) and 1,2-dipalmitoyl-*sn*-glycero-3-phosphoethanolamine-fluorescein (FL-DPPE) spent significantly less time in TCZs compared to Thy-1 and GM1. For Thy-1, the confinement times were significantly reduced upon cholesterol depletion. The authors investigated the mobility of Thy-1 within the TCZs at a higher time resolution, by capturing data using a high-speed

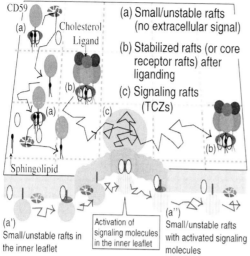

Fig. 3.4 Single-molecule tracking of membrane molecules suggests a model of a plasma membrane that resembles a partitioned fluid supported by a cytoskeleton mesh. High-speed tracking of single molecules in cell membranes reveals an unexpected behavior of diffusing particles which suggests the plasma membrane is a fluid that is partitioned by a membrane cytoskeleton fence. Using this technique, Kusumi et al. identified three types of lipidic structures that formed in the plasma membrane [85]. Type (a) is prevalent in the absence of extracellular stimulation; these are small (perhaps consisting of several molecules) and unstable (the lifetimes may be less than 1 ms), and may be the type that monomeric GPI-anchored proteins associate with [78]. Type (b) may appear when receptor molecules form oligomers upon liganding or crosslinking. The receptors may be GPI-anchored receptors or transmembrane receptors with some affinity to cholesterol and saturated alkyl chains. Oligomerized receptors may then induce small but stable rafts around them, perhaps due to the slight reduction in the thermal motion around the cluster and the subsequent assembly of cholesterol. Given the rather stable oligomerization of the receptor molecules, the type (b) raft may be stable for minutes, although the associated raft-constituent molecules may be exchanged frequently between the raft and the bulk domains. Type (c) structures may be formed around these receptor rafts. (Image reprinted with permission from [85].)

digital video camera (500 frames per second for up to 10 s). The diffusion coefficient within TCZs was reduced by a factor of ~2 compared to the one outside of the TCZs. In another study, the diffusion of GPI and transmembrane-anchored forms of neural cell adhesion molecule (NCAM) was studied in NIH-3T3 fibroblasts [38]. Surprisingly, a similar confinement was shown for GPI as well as the transmembrane forms of NCAMs.

Schutz et al. used the single-particle tracking of lipid labeled with fluorescent dye, a method referred to as "single dye tracing" [39]. In this approach, dilute quantities of Cy5-labeled, saturated lipid probe 1,2-dimyristol-*sn*-glycero-3-phosphoethanolamine (DMPE-Cy5) and a mono-unsaturated lipid probe DOPE-Cy5 were introduced into human coronary artery smooth muscle (HASM) cells. The single dye tracing data indicated rapid and confined diffusion for DMPE-Cy5 with a long residence time and a confinement area in the order of ~600–700 nm. By contrast, DOPE-Cy5 displayed a relatively unconfined diffusion within the membrane.

Pralle et al. examined the viscous drag of GPI and transmembrane-anchored proteins in regions much smaller than TCZs (as defined by video-based single-particle tracking experiments [40]). These authors performed high-resolution particle tracking with a bead (labeled with antibody as well as a fluorophore) held by laser trap and bound to membrane protein, and then observed the amplitude of fluctuations of a 2-mm bead in a laser trap of defined spring constant. The amplitude of fluctuations in turn may be related to the local viscosity by the Saffman-Delbruk model of diffusion in two dimensions [41]. The authors reported that raft proteins (by cold detergent-insolubility criterion) such as hemagglutinin (HA), PLAP or chimeric YFPGLGPI (a GPI-anchored protein containing the signal sequence of lactase-phlorizin hydrolase (LPH) fused to yellow fluorescent protein; YFP) experienced an approximately three-fold higher viscous drag than non-raft LYFPGT46 (YFP ectodomain fused to the transmembrane domain of the LDL receptor). Cholesterol depletion resulted in a significant decrease in the viscous drag of HA and GPI-APs, whereas viscous drag of LYFPGT46 was unchanged after cholesterol depletion. By applying the Saffman-Delbruck model for diffusion in biological membranes, Pralle et al. estimated the size of rafts as being ~26 ± 13 nm. However, the application of this theory to membrane diffusion in an heterogeneous environment is fraught with complications, and even if applicable the extremely insensitive relationship between particle size and diffusion coefficient [Diffusion coefficient $\infty \ln (1/R)$] makes the estimation of size inaccurate.

Kusumi et al. [42] presented a comprehensive review of the various factors that might influence the diffusion of a protein in the plasma membrane (Fig. 3.4). These authors suggested that there might be two different types of raft in the plasma membrane: (1) steady-state rafts or "reserve rafts" that exist at all times; and (2) "clustered rafts", which are more stable long-lived structures that might be created when processes such as signaling are initiated. Kusumi et al. also defined all possible physical interactions that take place between lipids and proteins that would give rise to segregation and, most importantly, associated lifetimes to each of these processes that are critical when designing any type of experiment to detect such structures. For many years Kusumi's group has focused its efforts on understanding the diffusion of proteins in membranes, by using single-particle tracking [43]. This technology allows single particles to be tracked at a time resolution of 25 ms, whereupon most proteins and lipids are seen not to undergo free unrestricted diffusion but rather to diffuse freely into small compartments between 30 and 250 nm in size that are bounded by cytoskeletal "fences". The proteins and lipids cross these fences at a frequency ranging from 1 to 25 ms, depending on the cell type [43]. Such a phenomenon is called "hop diffusion", and the frequency with which molecules hop from one compartment to the other is called the "rate of hop diffusion". Both theoretical models and experiments appear to coincide in this understanding of the structure of the cell membrane where the plasma membrane is actively partitioned by the cytoskeleton that it rests on into membrane skeleton pickets and fences.

When such experiments were performed on GPI-anchored proteins, the latter were found to have a rate of hop diffusion that was indistinguishable from that of phospholipids [42]. Surface scanning resistance (SSR) measurements are performed by coating a bead with antibodies to a receptor on the cell surface, and this bead is held by a laser trap while the stage is scanned in two dimensions [44]. The resistance felt by the bead is reflective of the barriers to diffusion present on the cell surface, and can be used to determine the linkages of the receptor to the cytoskeleton. SSR measurements performed on Qa-2 (GPI-anchored MHC class I) revealed that, using a low concentration of antibodies on the bead, the barriers encountered by the bead were similar to that observed by a monomeric GPI-AP [45]. When a higher concentration of antibody was used, it resulted in cross-linking of Qa-2 and the barriers observed were indicative of an association with a transmembrane protein that has linkage with the actin cytoskeleton. This result was surprising, and questioned most existing models of rafts. The authors interpreted their results by saying that these were the representatives of reserve rafts that consisted of a very small number of GPI-anchored proteins having a hop diffusion rate of 25 ms on average. If the fraction of molecules that resided in aggregated species was small, then in single-particle measurements the probability of labeling those species is also lowered and it becomes difficult to obtain statistically significant data on those events.

As indicated above, by using single-particle tracking, albeit at a lower time resolution, Jacobson and coworkers reported a phenomenon for raft-like molecules. They found that GPI-anchored proteins – but not other transmembrane proteins – underwent slow diffusion in small zones that were 200 nm in size [36,38, 86], called TCZs. Kusumi and coworkers clarified that these TCZs could not be compared to the membrane compartments that they observed because the time resolution of the two techniques was very different [42]. It is also possible that due to the inability to have single antibody per gold particle, Jacobson and co-workers might have observed diffusion of small clustered molecules. The issue of multi-valency of the tagging particle remains a matter of great concern in the correct interpretation of results from these techniques [46].

3.6.2
Fluorescence Recovery After Photobleaching

Fluorescence recovery after photobleaching (FRAP) is a well-established technique which is used to study the lateral mobility and fluorescence dynamics of proteins in membranes [47,48]. After labeling of the surface molecules with a fluorescent tag, a defined micrometer-sized area on the cell membrane is photobleached (irreversible photo-destruction) within a very short time, using a focused laser beam. This is followed by an observation of the recovery of fluorescence in the bleached area (by diffusion of fluorescent molecules from neighboring regions). Two parameters may be obtained from a rigorous analysis of the data: (1) the rate(s) of recovery, which results in an estimation of a rate of diffusion; and (2) the immobile fraction. The rates of fluorescence recovery are used to estimate the diffusion constants, whereas the discrepancy between fluorescence intensity before photo-bleaching and after complete recovery of fluorescence provides the fraction of im-mobile molecules [48]. Although this procedure does not throw light on the mo-tion of individual molecules, one clear advantage of FRAP over single molecule methods is its superior statistical confidence resulting from the averaging of large number of diffusion events. Since the technique results in the destruction of fluor-ophores to achieve the measurement, there are issues regarding the damage caused by this photobleaching phenomenon. In addition, the time scales and sen-sitivity of the technique are limited by instrumentation, and the many different models of diffusion may be used to explain the recovery characteristics. A prior physical picture of the diffusion process is usually essential in deciphering the data [49–51].

In one of the earliest FRAP studies of DRM-associated proteins, Ishihara et al. showed that although Thy-1 exhibited a diffusion constant similar to that of labeled lipids, while up to 50% of the protein was immobile on the surface of various cell types [52]. Hannan et al. [53] also showed the presence of an immobile fraction of GPI-APs on the surface of MDCK cells. When placed in perspective of recent developments in the picket-fence model, this immobile fraction would include the proteins which diffused within pickets but were restricted in mobility at larger timescales. Moreover, the results did not provide the immobile fraction of "non-raft" protein for comparison. Oliferenko et al. [54] performed FRAP measure-ments on a transmembrane-anchored lipid raft (DRM-associated) marker CD44 expressed in EpH4 cells (polarized mammary epithelial cells). These authors found that CD44 was significantly immobilized compared to a transferrin receptor (TfR), which is not present in lipid rafts (recovery after saturation being ~19% and ~50%, respectively). Cholesterol depletion and treatment with latranaculin A (an actin-disrupting agent) led to comparatively higher mobile fractions of CD44 (28% and 40% recovery respectively compared to ~19% for untreated CD44). Oliferenko et al. took these results as evidence of the presence of CD44 in lipid rafts, but the alternative possibility of CD44 being retained by pickets and fences better than TfR (perhaps through selective interaction) could not be ruled out. Cholesterol deple-tion and actin disruption could merely perturb pickets and fences by acting on the cytoskeleton [55]. Shvartsman et al. investigated the diffusion of influenza HA tagged with various anchors [56], and found that DRM-associated wild-type and GPI-anchored forms of HA diffused more slowly than an HA mutant that was not associated with the DRMs. However, the diffusion became comparable following the depletion of cholesterol from the cells. In cells that coexpressed the wild-type and GPI-anchored forms of HA, the patching of one form by using antibodies slowed down the diffusion of the other, thus indicating the anchor- (and hence raft-) dependent interaction between the two forms.

Using FRAP, Henis and coworkers [57,58] examined the lateral diffusion con-stants of wild-type and activated H-Ras and K-Ras (lipid-linked small GTPases which associate with the inner leaflet of the membrane). Whilst wild-type H-Ras was found to a greater extent in DRMs, the other isoforms (wild-type K-Ras, acti-vated H-Ras and activated K-ras) were not at all detergent-insoluble, suggesting a functional potential of the "lipid raft" association [59]. Interestingly, these authors did not report any significant difference in the lateral mobility of any of the proteins. Only wild-type H-Ras showed an increased lateral mobility upon cholesterol depletion. Moreover, the lateral mobility of activated H-Ras and K-Ras increased with expression level in a saturable manner, whereas the lateral mobility of wild-type H-Ras was independent of its expression level. These complicated results again highlighted the lack of a precise understanding of detergent insolubility. A more comprehensive understanding of the nature of the domains that these small-molecule GTPases occupy was reviewed recently [13].

3.6.3
Fluorescence Correlation Spectroscopy

Fluorescence correlation spectroscopy (FCS) provides information on the diffusion of fluorescently tagged molecules by observing the correlation of fluorophore fluctuation through a small optically delimited detection volume [60–65]. The resultant fluorescence fluctuations provide an autocorrelation curve, which could be used to calculate diffusion constant of the molecules. Whilst FCS retains the statistical advantages of FRAP, it can be performed with dilute fluorophores and with relatively less laser power. This makes it more suitable for live cell studies, with lesser photo-damage and lower fluorophore concentrations, closer to that of endogenous molecules [60,63,66].

Korlach et al. used giant unilamellar vesicles (GUVs) containing various mixtures of dilauroyl phosphatidylcholine (DLPC), dipalmitoyl phosphatidylcholine (DPPC) and cholesterol. These authors imaged coexisting phases (resulting from phase separation) with confocal fluorescence microscopy using differential probe partitioning of fluorescent probes 1,1'-dieicosanyl-3,3,3',3'-tetramethylindocarbocyanine perchlorate (DiI-C20) and 2-(4,4-difluoro-5,7-dimethyl-4-bora-3a,4a-diaza-s-indacene-3-pentanoyl)-1-hexadecanoyl-*sn*-glycero-3-phosphocholine (Bodipy-PC). The identified phases were characterized by measuring translational diffusion of DiI-C20 by FCS measurements. The probe displayed fast mobility in fluid membrane phases, and slower mobility in ordered membrane phases. Cholesterol was found to induce changes in coexisting phase domains. In binary mixtures of DLPC/cholesterol, the fluid phase of DLPC that contained a higher cholesterol content displayed slower diffusion coefficients for DiI-C20. However, by confocal fluorescence microscopy these phases appears identical.

In a similar study, Kahya et al. studied phases in GUVs prepared from ternary mixtures of 1,2-dioleoyl-*sn*-glycero-3-phosphocholine (DOPC), SM and cholesterol [67]. DiI-C18 was largely excluded from the SM-rich regions, in which the raft marker ganglioside GM1 was localized when visualized with CtxB subunit. The cholesterol content was found to be critical for the phase separation into a liquid-disordered, DOPC-enriched phase exhibiting high probe mobility and a dense, liquid-ordered, SM-enriched phase. The addition of cholesterol led to increased probe mobility for the liquid-disordered, DOPC/cholesterol mixture and decreased probe mobility for the liquid-ordered, SM/cholesterol mixture. Bacia et al. performed FCS on a raft marker GM1 probed with fluorescently labeled CtxB subunit and compared it with a non-raft marker dialkylcarbocyanine (DiI) [68]. In homogeneous GUVs, both probes displayed slightly different diffusion (attributed to factors other than membrane composition). Both probes also showed significantly different diffusion in GUVs that contained a raft lipid mixture (unsaturated phosphatidylcholine, cholesterol and SM). CtxB-GM1 diffused significantly more slowly than DiI, consistent with its presence in liquid-ordered domains. The depletion of cholesterol by methyl-β-cyclodextrin (mbCD) resulted in an increased mobility of CtxB-GM1, consistent with the disruption of liquid-ordered domains. Similarly, CtxB-GM1 displayed extremely slow diffusion compared to DiI in rat basophilic leukemia (RBL) cells. However, there was no increase in the mobility of CtxB-GM1 by depletion of cholesterol using mβCD. In contrast, disruption of the cytoskeleton by treatment with latrunculin A resulted in a higher mobility of CtxB-GM1. The authors speculated that these results could arise if some skeleton rafts remained associated with the cytoskeleton after cholesterol depletion, but they did not conduct an experiment in which cholesterol was depleted along with cytoskeleton disruption. A further increase in mobility could have suggested a hierarchical organization of CtxB-GM1 into cholesterol- and cytoskeleton-dependent structures. Bacia et al. also showed that the SNARE proteins syntaxin and synaptobrevin, when reconstituted into GUVs, were preferentially present in liquid-ordered phases. Interestingly, Lang et al. showed that syntaxin does not co-patch with typical raft markers such as GPI-linked proteins, and does not co-fractionate with DRMs [69], whereas others showed that SNAREs are highly enriched in DRMs [70,71]. Although these results related to DRM association are ambiguous, they demonstrate the gap between data obtained from model membranes and from biological membranes. In an interesting follow-up study, Bacia et al. examined the role of sterol structure in phase separation in GUVs [72]. Sterol structure was shown not only to influence phase separation but also to cause remarkable differences in the curvatures of GUVs. Whereas both cholesterol and lophenol induced positive curvature and outward budding of liquid-ordered phases, lanosterol and cholesteryl sulfonate treatment resulted in a negative curvature and inward budding of liquid-ordered phases.

One of the major criticisms of diffusion-based studies is lack of understanding of diffusion process in membranes with complex lipid mixtures, though a recent study conducted by Hac et al. showed some progress in this direction [73]. These authors studied diffusion in two-component binary lipid membranes as a function of composition (fraction of two lipids) and temperature. They performed Monte Carlo simulations using the thermodynamic properties of lipid mixtures (measured by calorimetry) to predict FCS autocorrelation profiles resulting from diffusion in the lipid mixtures. The predicted FCS data agreed very well with data obtained experimentally. Although biological membranes are far more complex than a two-component system, these studies at least provided some ground rules for an understanding of diffusion in biological membranes.

3.7
Proximity Measurements

Proximity measurements between two or more fluorophore-tagged molecules using the well-understood characteristics of fluorescence – namely energy transfer (Foerster's resonance energy transfer; FRET) – is another popular method of determining whether molecules are brought into nanometer proximity of each other.

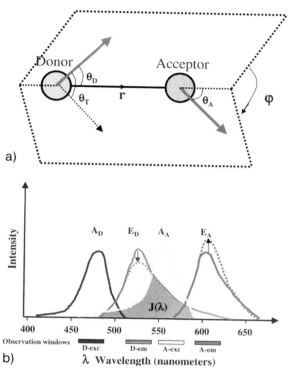

Fig. 3.5 Schematic depiction of the fluorescence resonance energy transfer process and its implementation. (A) Orientation of donor and acceptor transition dipoles. The relative angle between the two transition dipole is responsible for depolarization of fluorescence upon energy transfer. (B) Overlap integral $J(\lambda)$ between the donor emission (E_D) and acceptor absorption spectra (A_A). A_D and E_A are the donor absorption and acceptor emission spectra, respectively. Arrows depict decrease in donor emission and increase in acceptor emission intensities upon energy transfer. Observation windows show excitation and emission wavelength bandwidths for a typical imaging experiment, indicating the potential for cross-talk between the different imaging channels. D = donor; A = acceptor; exc = excitation; em = emission. (Reprinted with permission from [86].)

FRET may be theoretically described as an interaction between a dipole (excited state of a fluorophore) and an induced dipole (nearby ground-state fluorophore). This interaction decays extremely sharply with distance $(1/R6)$, which provides this technique with the characteristics of a spectroscopic ruler in a typical range of 1 to 10 nm for organic fluorophores [74]. Since there is a transfer of energy between an excited-state fluorophore (donor) and a ground-state fluorophore (acceptor), the detection of this phenomenon may be related to changes in donor characteristics (donor lifetime, bleaching rate, or net fluorescence emission intensity or anisotropy) or acceptor characteristics (emission intensity or anisotropy) (for a review, see [75]). In the detection of "rafts" – which are defined by this technique as an anomalous proximity between fluorophore-tagged molecules – two types of FRET experiments have been carried out, with differing results. In hetero-FRET, the donor and acceptor are of different molecular and spectral characteristics, whereas in homo-FRET the donor and acceptor are the same species. In all cases the extent of energy transfer was dependent upon spectral overlap between the donor and acceptor species, the distance between dipoles, and the orientation of dipoles with respect to each other (Fig. 3.5).

3.7.1
Proximity Measurement Using Homo-FRET

Homo-FRET measures the loss of fluorescence anisotropy, resulting from the FRET process. It is a relatively less well-known approach to FRET, and is also referred to as depolarization-FRET [74,75]. In this type of FRET, fluorescence emission excited by polarized light is measured for the extent of loss of fluorescence anisotropy using appropriately placed excitation and emission polarizers (Fig. 3.6). Due to a finite spread of allowed angular dependence between the donor and acceptor fluorophores, there is a significant transfer of energy between those donor and acceptor fluorophores that are *not* aligned to each other, and this results in an instantaneous loss of emission anisotropy. This loss can be measured in the steady state as a change in anisotropy of fluorescence emission in the presence or absence of nearby fluorophores, or alternatively in the time domain (during the lifetime of the fluorophore) as a rapid decay of emission anisotropy.

Using this technique in the steady-state measurement, Varma and Mayor [76] demonstrated the presence of lipid-dependent protein clusters on the surface of living cells. Since the extent of depolarization (or loss of anisotropy) resulting from FRET is dependent on distance (limited by R_0; [74]), increasing depolarization would be seen with increasing concentration. Using this assay, Varma and Mayor showed that fluorophore-tagged Folate Receptor (FR-GPI; a model GPI-AP) is organized in clusters maintained by cholesterol levels in the membrane, whereas the same FR ecto-domain – when linked to two different transmembrane domains – showed random organization. Cholesterol depletion led to a disruption of the clusters formed by FR-GPI. Later, Sharma and coworkers showed that GFP anchored to cell membranes via a GPI-anchor (GFP-GPI) and mYFP-GPI (mYFP is monomeric version of YFP; [77]) were also organized in cholesterol-dependent sub-reso-

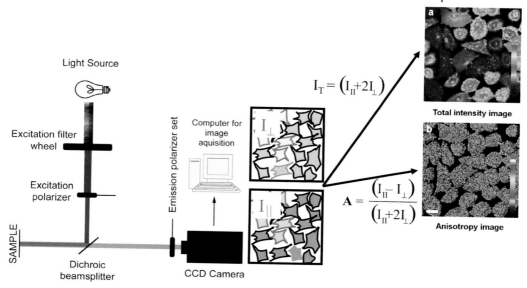

Fig. 3.6 Imaging set-up used to measure steady-state anisotropy. Parallel ($I_{\parallel}$) and perpendicular ($I_{\perp}$) fluorescence intensity images are obtained using a set of excitation and emission polarizers. The perpendicular and parallel intensity images thus obtained are processed mathematically using software to obtain anisotropy and total intensity images.

lution clusters, showing that mere GPI-anchoring could result into this sub-resolution clustering [78].

Although steady-state anisotropy measurement is a valuable tool for the study of sub-resolution nanometer-scale homotypic interactions of molecules in living cells, time-resolved data provide additional information that is not available from steady-state measurements. Steady-state anisotropy reports a time-averaged picture of the fluorescence anisotropy displayed by the molecules in a population. It is difficult to interpret the multiple states/possibilities that could result in this average value for the population. It is worthwhile considering the possibility of the existence of dimers (for simplicity) in a population. Steady-state anisotropy measurements would be capable of reporting homo-FRET between dimers, but they would not allow any distinction to be made between the multiple possibilities that could result in particular homo-FRET efficiency. In a situation where a homo-FRET efficiency of 50% is recorded, this could result either from 50% FRET efficiencies between all molecules, or 100% FRET efficiencies between half of the molecules. Steady-state anisotropy measurements would not be able to distinguish between the two possibilities. Time-resolved anisotropy measurements would provide the distinct decay profile for each of the above distributions, and also provide an estimate of the fraction of molecules in the clustered organization. Moreover, anisotropy decay rates associated with FRET can also be used to estimate the inter-fluorophore distances. In addition to FRET distances, time-resolved anisotropy is also capable of resolving multiple sources of depolarization arising from segmental motion or the rotation of a molecule. Hence, time-resolved anisotropy measurements provide additional information related to the fraction of molecules in cluster and intermolecular distances between molecules undergoing FRET.

Sharma and coworkers performed homo-FRET detection with time-resolved anisotropy measurements to obtain further information on the structure of GPI-AP organization [78]. Time-resolved anisotropy measurements on GFP-GPI and mYFP-GPI expressed in living cells showed that they were present in extremely high-density clusters, with ~20–40% of molecules present in the clusters and the remainder as monomers. The estimated structure of GFP-GPI clusters (with ~30% of molecules in clusters) was verified with results obtained with FR-GPI using the method of anisotropy photobleaching (for a description, see [78]). However, neither method could provide an estimate of cluster size. Sharma et al. also developed a novel tool to estimate cluster size at nanometer scale that required the measurement of homo- as well as hetero-FRET efficiencies. GPI-APs display significant homo-FRET, but hetero-FRET was not detected between GPI-APs using multiple methods of detection. In order to explain this discrepancy, Sharma et al. performed theoretical modeling of hetero-FRET efficiencies. Initially, they calculated the efficiency of hetero-FRET for variable donor:acceptor ratios, cluster sizes and fractions of molecules in clusters. The calculations showed that small clusters with a lesser fraction of molecules accounted for the lack of hetero-FRET. As expected from theoretical calculations, the formation of heptamers of GPI-APs by aerolysin toxin [79] resulted in hetero-FRET detection. This methodology provides an upper bound on the cluster size (less than four molecules). The challenge now lies in using other techniques to detect these clusters. Using this information, FCS is a likely candidate if a suitable model for the diffusion of different species can be incorporated into theoretical analyses of the correlation function.

3.7.2
Proximity Measurement Using Hetero-FRET

Another FRET technique which has been used extensively to detect proximities between fluorophores is that of hetero-FRET [80]. Several hetero-FRET methods exist (see Fig. 3.5), and most have been applied to study GPI-anchored proteins (for a review, see [75]). In the early studies, Kenworthy and Edidin [80], when examining FRET between donor and acceptor labeled antibodies against 5′-nucleotidase (5′-NT; a GPI-AP), reported that most proteins on the surface of fixed cells were monomers. These authors overexpressed the large quantities of proteins in MDCK cells and found that FRET, as reported by the acceptor photobleaching method (measuring donor dequenching after photobleaching of acceptor), was dependent on the density of the labeled acceptors. A comparison of data with theoretical predictions for FRET in membranes ruled out any significant clustering between 5′-NT. In order to address the discrepancy between their results and those of

Varma and Mayor, Kenworthy et al. investigated FRET between FR-GPI in unfixed living cells [81] and failed to detect any significant clustering. These authors also examined FRET between either glycosphingolipid GM1 (as probed by the binding of fluorophore-labeled CtxB) or GM1 and GPI-AP. Although FRET was detected in each case (indicating the presence of these molecules in proximity to each other), the data ruled out any significant clustering as predicted by theoretical modeling. It is interesting to note however, that Kenworthy et al. also failed to detect any significant dimerization of CD59 as reported by Hatanaka et al. using cross-linking and biochemical (PAGE) detection [82]. However, all of these results showing a lack of hetero-FRET detection were consistent with the predictions of hetero-FRET modeling described by Sharma et al. [78]. Taken together, the results of these studies provide a complex picture of GPI-anchored protein organization, and also generate new tools and concepts for an understanding of the organization of "raft" components in membranes.

3.8
Conclusions

Although it is easy to lose one's way when interpreting the many biophysical approaches of analyzing the existence of lipid rafts, few conclusions could be drawn without significant dissent. Model membrane studies are vital in understanding lipid-lipid and lipid-protein interaction, but there is still a long way to go in understanding multicomponent complex biological membranes. This could be analogous to the "three-body problem" where the gravitational interaction of three masses is surprisingly difficult to solve. In the light of information that small transition energies could bring about remarkable structural changes, there may be serious problems in extending model membrane studies to biological membranes. This includes all model membrane studies which support the concept of "detergent-insoluble" complexes to describe lipid rafts. Although diffusion-based studies provide valuable live cell data, they have several drawbacks. It is not easy to interpret results from diffusion data due to a poor understanding of: (1) the diffusion of molecules in complex biological membranes; (2) the ultrastructure of biological membranes; and (3) interaction of the cytoskeleton with biological membranes. Diffusion data might provide a valuable time-kinetics, though it is difficult to deduce structural information from diffusion data with current theoretical understanding. Although homo-FRET-based studies provide an excellent source of structural information on proximity relationships derived by lipidic interactions, the relatively longer time scales of measurement mask the temporal information. In the absence of any ideal "sub-resolution ultra-fast imaging" technique, it is desirable to study chosen model raft components in a model cellular system with available biophysical techniques, and appropriate functional consequences.

Abbreviations

AP	anchored protein
CtxB	cholera toxin B
DIG	detergent-insoluble glycolipid
DiI	dialkylcarbocyanine
DLPC	dilauroyl phosphatidylcholine
DPPC	dipalmitoyl phosphatidylcholine
DRM	detergent-resistant membrane
EM	electron microscopy
ER	endoplasmic reticulum
FCS	fluorescence correlation spectroscopy
FL-DOPE	1,2-dio-leoyl-*sn*-glycero-3-phosphoethanolamine-fluorescein
FL-DPPE	1,2-dipalmitoyl-*sn*-glycero-3-phosphoethanolamine-fluorescein
fl-PE	fluorescein phosphatidylethanolamine
FRAP	fluorescence recovery after photobleaching
FRET	Foerster's resonance energy transfer
GPI	glycosyl-phosphatidylinositol
GUV	giant unilamellar vesicle
HA	hemagglutinin
HCASM	human coronary artery smooth muscle
LPH	lactase-phlorizin hydrolase
mβCD	methyl-β-cyclodextrin
MDCK	Madin-Darby canine kidney
NCAM	neural cell adhesion molecule
NMR	nuclear magnetic resonance
5'-NT	5'-nucleotidase
PAGE	polyacrylamide gel electrophoresis
PC	phosphocholine
PLAP	placental alkaline phosphatase
RBL	rat basophilic leukemia
SM	sphingomyelin
SPT	single-particle tracking
SSR	surface scanning resistance
TCZ	transient confinement zone
TfR	transferrin receptor
TGN	trans-Golgi network
YFP	yellow fluorescent protein

References

1 Singer, S. J. and G. L. Nicolson. The fluid mosaic model of the structure of cell membranes. *Science* 1972; 175(23): 720–731.

2 Jain, M. K. and H. B. White, III. Long-range order in biomembranes. *Adv. Lipid Res.* 1977; 15: 1–60.

3 Klausner, R. D., et al. Lipid domains in membranes. Evidence derived from structural perturbations induced by free fatty acids and lifetime heterogeneity analysis. *J. Biol. Chem.* 1980; 255(4): 1286–1295.

4 Simons, K. and G. van Meer. Lipid sorting in epithelial cells. *Biochemistry* 1988; 27(17): 6197–6202.

5 Simons, K. and E. Ikonen. Functional rafts in cell membranes. *Nature* 1997; 387(6633): 569–572.

6 Simons, K. and D. Toomre. Lipid rafts and signal transduction. *Nat. Rev. Mol. Cell. Biol.* 2000; 1(1): 31–39.

7 Chatterjee, S. and S. Mayor. The GPI-anchor and protein sorting. *Cell. Mol. Life Sci.* 2001; 58(14): 1969–1987.

8 Udenfriend, S. and K. Kodukula. How glycosylphosphatidylinositol-anchored membrane proteins are made. *Annu. Rev. Biochem.* 1995; 64: 563–591.

9 Mayor, S. and H. Riezman. Sorting GPI-anchored proteins. *Nat. Rev. Mol. Cell. Biol.* 2004; 5(2): 110–120.

10 Robinson, P. J. Signal transduction via GPI-anchored membrane proteins. *Adv. Exp. Med. Biol.* 1997; 419: 365–370.

11 Tsui-Pierchala, B. A., et al. Lipid rafts in neuronal signaling and function. *Trends Neurosci.* 2002; 25(8): 412–417.

12 Horejsi, V., et al. GPI-microdomains: a role in signalling via immunoreceptors. *Immunol. Today* 1999; 20(8): 356–361.

13 Parton, R. G. and J. F. Hancock. Lipid rafts and plasma membrane microorganization: insights from Ras. *Trends Cell Biol.* 2004; 14(3): 141–147.

14 Gonen, A., P. Weisman-Shomer, and M. Fry. Cell adhesion and acquisition of detergent resistance by the cytoskeleton of cultured chick fibroblasts. *Biochim. Biophys. Acta* 1979; 552(2): 307–321.

15 Streuli, C. H., B. Patel, and D. R. Critchley. The cholera toxin receptor ganglioside GM remains associated with Triton X-100 cytoskeletons of BALB/c-3T3 cells. *Exp. Cell Res.* 1981; 136(2): 247–254.

16 Helenius, A. and K. Simons. Solubilization of membranes by detergents. *Biochim. Biophys. Acta* 1975; 415(1): 29–79.

17 Simons, K., A. Helenius, and H. Garoff. Solubilization of the membrane proteins from Semliki Forest virus with Triton X-100. *J. Mol. Biol.* 1973; 80(1): 119–133.

18 Becker, R., A. Helenius, and K. Simons. Solubilization of the Semliki Forest virus membrane with sodium dodecyl sulfate. *Biochemistry* 1975; 14(9): 1835–1841.

19 Helenius, A., et al. Solubilization of the Semliki Forest virus membrane with sodium deoxycholate. *Biochim. Biophys. Acta* 1976; 436(2): 319–334.

20 Brown, D. A. and J. K. Rose. Sorting of GPI-anchored proteins to glycolipid-enriched membrane subdomains during transport to the apical cell surface. *Cell* 1992; 68(3): 533–544.

21 Brown, D. A. Interactions between GPI-anchored proteins and membrane lipids. *Trends Cell Biol.* 1992; 2(11): 338–343.

22 Yeagle, P. *The Membranes of Cells.* 2nd edn. San Diego, CA: Academic Press, 1993.

23 Lamaze, C., et al. Interleukin 2 receptors and detergent-resistant membrane domains define a clathrin-independent endocytic pathway. *Mol. Cell* 2001; 7(3): 661–671.

24 Brown, D. A. and E. London. Functions of lipid rafts in biological membranes. *Annu. Rev. Cell Dev. Biol.* 1998; 14: 111–136.

25 London, E. and D. A. Brown. Insolubility of lipids in Triton X-100: physical origin and relationship to sphingolipid/cholesterol membrane domains (rafts). *Biochim. Biophys. Acta* 2000; 1508(1–2): 182–195.

26 Shaw, A. R. and L. Li. Exploration of the functional proteome: lessons from lipid rafts. *Curr. Opin. Mol. Ther.* 2003; 5(3): 294–301.

27 Foster, L. J., C. L. De Hoog, and M. Mann. Unbiased quantitative proteomics of lipid rafts reveals high specificity for signaling factors. *Proc. Natl. Acad. Sci. USA* 2003; 100(10): 5813–5818.

28 Heerklotz, H. Triton promotes domain formation in lipid raft mixtures. *Biophys. J.* 2002; 83(5): 2693–2701.

29 Heerklotz, H., et al. The sensitivity of lipid domains to small perturbations demonstrated by the effect of Triton. *J. Mol. Biol.* 2003; 329(4): 793–799.

30 Mayor, S. and M. Rao. Rafts: scale-dependent, active lipid organization at the cell surface. *Traffic* 2004; 5(4): 231–240.

31 Mayor, S., K. G. Rothberg, and F. R. Maxfield. Sequestration of GPI-anchored proteins in caveolae triggered by cross-linking. *Science* 1994; 264(5167): 1948–1951.

32 Mayor, S. and F. R. Maxfield. Insolubility and redistribution of GPI-anchored proteins at the cell surface after detergent treatment. *Mol. Biol. Cell* 1995; 6(7): 929–944.

33 Parton, R. G., B. Joggerst, and K. Simons. Regulated internalization of caveolae. *J. Cell Biol.* 1994; 127(5): 1199–1215.

34 Maunsbach, A. Immunolabeling and staining of ultrathin sections in biological electron microscopy. In: Celis, J. (Ed.). *Cell Biology: A Laboratory Handbook.* Academic Press: San Diego, CA, 1998.

35 Sheets, E. D., R. Simson, and K. Jacobson. New insights into membrane dynamics from the analysis of cell surface interactions by physical methods. *Curr. Opin. Cell Biol.* 1995; 7(5): 707–714.

36 Sheets, E. D., et al. Transient confinement of a glycosylphosphatidylinositol-anchored protein in the plasma membrane. *Biochemistry* 1997; 36(41): 12449–12458.

37 Dietrich, C., et al. Relationship of lipid rafts to transient confinement zones detected by single particle tracking. *Biophys. J.* 2002; 82(1 Pt 1): 274–284.

38 Simson, R., et al. Structural mosaicism on the submicron scale in the plasma membrane. *Biophys. J.* 1998; 74(1): 297–308.

39 Schutz, G. J., et al. Properties of lipid microdomains in a muscle cell membrane visualized by single molecule microscopy. *EMBO J.* 2000; 19(5): 892–901.

40 Pralle, A., et al. Sphingolipid-cholesterol rafts diffuse as small entities in the plasma membrane of mammalian cells. *J. Cell Biol.* 2000; 148(5): 997–1008.

41 Saffman, P. G. and M. Delbruck. Brownian motion in biological membranes. *Proc. Natl. Acad. Sci. USA* 1975; 72(8): 3111–3113.

42 Kusumi, A., I. Koyama-Honda, and K. Suzuki. Molecular dynamics and interactions for creation of stimulation-induced stabilized rafts from small unstable steady-state rafts. *Traffic* 2004; 5(4): 213–230.

43 Kusumi, A., et al. Paradigm shift of the plasma membrane concept from the two-dimensional continuum fluid to the partitioned fluid: high-speed single-molecules tracking of membrane molecules. *Annu. Rev. Biophys. Biomol. Struct.* 2005; 34: 351–378.

44 Suzuki, K., R. E. Sterba, and M. P. Sheetz. Outer membrane monolayer domains from two-dimensional surface scanning resistance measurements. *Biophys. J.* 2000; 79(1): 448–459.

45 Suzuki, K. and M. P. Sheetz. Binding of cross-linked glycosylphosphatidylinositol-anchored proteins to discrete actin-associated sites and cholesterol-dependent domains. *Biophys. J.* 2001; 81(4): 2181–2189.

46 Ritchie, K. and A. Kusumi. Single-particle tracking image microscopy. *Methods Enzymol.* 2003; 360: 618–634.

47 Edidin, M. In: Damjanovich, S., Edidin, M., Szollosi, J., Tron, L. (Eds.). *Mobility and Proximity in Biological Membranes.* CRC: Boca Raton, Florida, 1994: 109–135.

48 Reits, E. A. and J. J. Neefjes. From fixed to FRAP: measuring protein mobility and activity in living cells. *Nat. Cell. Biol.* 2001; 3(6): E145-E147.

49 Houtsmuller, A. B. and W. Vermeulen. Macromolecular dynamics in living cell nuclei revealed by fluorescence redistribution after photobleaching. *Histochem. Cell. Biol.* 2001; 115(1): 13–21.

50 Lippincott-Schwartz, J. and G. H. Patterson. Development and use of fluorescent protein markers in living cells. *Science* 2003; 300(5616): 87–91.

51 Lippincott-Schwartz, J., N. Altan-Bonnet, and G. H. Patterson. Photobleaching and photoactivation: following protein dynamics in living cells. *Nat. Cell. Biol.* 2003; Suppl: S7-S14.

52 Ishihara, A., Y. Hou, and K. Jacobson. The Thy-1 antigen exhibits rapid lateral diffusion in the plasma membrane of rodent lymphoid cells and fibroblasts. *Proc. Natl. Acad. Sci. USA* 1987; 84(5): 1290–1293.

53 Hannan, L. A., et al. Correctly sorted molecules of a GPI-anchored protein are clustered and immobile when they arrive at the apical surface of MDCK cells. *J. Cell Biol.* 1993; 120(2): 353–358.

54 Oliferenko, S., et al. Analysis of CD44-containing lipid rafts: recruitment of annexin II and stabilization by the actin cytoskeleton. *J. Cell Biol.* 1999; 146(4): 843–854.

55 Edidin, M. Patches, posts and fences: proteins and plasma membrane domains. *Trends Cell Biol.* 1992; 2(12): 376–380.

56 Shvartsman, D. E., et al. Differently anchored influenza hemagglutinin mutants

display distinct interaction dynamics with mutual rafts. *J. Cell Biol.* 2003; 163(4): 879–888.

57 Niv, H., et al. Activated K-Ras and H-Ras display different interactions with saturable nonraft sites at the surface of live cells. *J. Cell Biol.* 2002; 157(5): 865–872.

58 Niv, H., et al. Membrane interactions of a constitutively active GFP-Ki-Ras 4B and their role in signaling. Evidence from lateral mobility studies. *J. Biol. Chem.* 1999; 274(3): 1606–1613.

59 Prior, I. A., et al. GTP-dependent segregation of H-ras from lipid rafts is required for biological activity. *Nat. Cell. Biol.* 2001; 3(4): 368–375.

60 Bulseco, D. A. and D. E. Wolf. Fluorescence correlation spectroscopy: molecular complexing in solution and in living cells. *Methods Cell Biol.* 2003; 72: 465–498.

61 Berland, K. M. Fluorescence correlation spectroscopy: a new tool for quantification of molecular interactions. *Methods Mol. Biol.* 2004; 261: 383–398.

62 Haupts, U., et al. Dynamics of fluorescence fluctuations in green fluorescent protein observed by fluorescence correlation spectroscopy. *Proc. Natl. Acad. Sci. USA* 1998; 95(23): 13573–13578.

63 Koppel, D. E., et al. Dynamics of fluorescence marker concentration as a probe of mobility. *Biophys. J.* 1976; 16(11): 1315–1329.

64 Schwille, P., J. Korlach, and W. W. Webb. Fluorescence correlation spectroscopy with single-molecule sensitivity on cell and model membranes. *Cytometry* 1999; 36(3): 176–182.

65 Rigler, R. Fluorescence correlations, single molecule detection and large number screening. Applications in biotechnology. *J. Biotechnol.* 1995; 41(2–3): 177–186.

66 Korlach, J., et al. Characterization of lipid bilayer phases by confocal microscopy and fluorescence correlation spectroscopy. *Proc. Natl. Acad. Sci. USA* 1999; 96(15): 8461–8466.

67 Kahya, N., et al. Probing lipid mobility of raft-exhibiting model membranes by fluorescence correlation spectroscopy. *J. Biol. Chem.* 2003; 278(30): 28109–28115.

68 Bacia, K., et al. Fluorescence correlation spectroscopy relates rafts in model and native membranes. *Biophys. J.* 2004; 87(2): 1034–1043.

69 Lang, T., et al. SNAREs are concentrated in cholesterol-dependent clusters that define docking and fusion sites for exocytosis. *EMBO J.* 2001; 20(9): 2202–2213.

70 Chamberlain, L. H., R. D. Burgoyne, and G. W. Gould. SNARE proteins are highly enriched in lipid rafts in PC12 cells: implications for the spatial control of exocytosis. *Proc. Natl. Acad. Sci. USA* 2001; 98(10): 5619–5624.

71 Xia, F., et al. Disruption of pancreatic beta-cell lipid rafts modifies Kv2.1 channel gating and insulin exocytosis. *J. Biol. Chem.* 2004; 279(23): 24685–24691.

72 Bacia, K., P. Schwille, and T. Kurzchalia. Sterol structure determines the separation of phases and the curvature of the liquid-ordered phase in model membranes. *Proc. Natl. Acad. Sci. USA* 2005; 102(9): 3272–3277.

73 Hac, A. E., et al. Diffusion in two-component lipid membranes – a fluorescence correlation spectroscopy and Monte Carlo simulation study. *Biophys. J.* 2005; 88(1): 317–333.

74 Lakowicz, J. R. *Principles of Fluorescence Spectroscopy.* 2nd edn. Kluwer Academic/Plenum Publishers, 1999.

75 Krishnan, R. V., R. Varma, and S. Mayor. Fluorescence methods to probe nanometer-scale organization of molecules in living cell membranes. *J. Fluorescence* 2001; 11(3): 211–226.

76 Varma, R. and S. Mayor. GPI-anchored proteins are organized in submicron domains at the cell surface. *Nature* 1998; 394(6695): 798–801.

77 Zacharias, D. A., et al. Partitioning of lipid-modified monomeric GFPs into membrane microdomains of live cells. *Science* 2002; 296(5569): 913–916.

78 Sharma, P., et al. Nanoscale organization of multiple GPI-anchored proteins in living cell membranes. *Cell* 2004; 116(4): 577–589.

79 Fivaz, M., et al. Differential sorting and fate of endocytosed GPI-anchored proteins. *EMBO J.* 2002; 21(15): 3989–4000.

80 Kenworthy, A. K. and M. Edidin. Distribution of a glycosylphosphatidylinositol-anchored protein at the apical surface of

MDCK cells examined at a resolution of <100 Å using imaging fluorescence resonance energy transfer. *J. Cell Biol.* 1998; 142(1): 69–84.

81 Kenworthy, A. K., N. Petranova, and M. Edidin. High-resolution FRET microscopy of cholera toxin B-subunit and GPI- anchored proteins in cell plasma membranes. *Mol. Biol. Cell* 2000; 11(5): 1645–1655.

82 Hatanaka, M., et al. Cellular distribution of a GPI-anchored complement regulatory protein CD59: homodimerization on the surface of HeLa and CD59-transfected CHO cells. *J. Biochem. (Tokyo)* 1998; 123(4): 579–586.

83 Anderson, R. G. and K. Jacobson. A role for lipid shells in targeting proteins to caveolae, rafts, and other lipid domains. *Science* 2002; 296(5574): 1821–1825.

84 Maxfield, F. R. Plasma membrane microdomains. *Curr. Opin. Cell Biol.* 2002; 14(4): 483–487.

85 Subczynski, W. K. and A. Kusumi. Dynamics of raft molecules in the cell and artificial membranes: approaches by pulse EPR spin labeling and single molecule optical microscopy. *Biochim. Biophys. Acta* 2003; 1610(2): 231–243.

86 Jacobson, K., and Dietrich. Looking at Lipid rafts? *Trends Cell Biol.* 1999; 9 (3): 87–91.

4

The Role of Caveolae and Noncaveolar Rafts in Endocytosis

Bo van Deurs, Frederik Vilhardt, Maria Torgersen, Kirstine Roepstorff, Anette M. Hommelgaard, and Kirsten Sandvig

4.1
Introduction

Endocytosis is involved in multiple cellular processes, including the uptake of transport proteins, uptake of "opportunistic ligands" such as bacterial and plant toxins and viruses, attenuation of signaling activity, receptor recycling and resensitization, down-regulation of cell contacts during epithelial-to-mesenchymal transition, antigen uptake and processing in MHC class II-expressing cells, transcytosis and delivery of antibodies to the newborn baby, and synaptic function. About 15–20 years ago it was frequently – and persistently – claimed that only one endocytic mechanism existed, namely the one mediated by clathrin-coated pits and vesicles. However, in studies in which clathrin-dependent uptake was inhibited by potassium depletion and acidification of the cytosol, it became clear that clathrin-independent endocytic mechanisms also must be taken into consideration [1–6]. That different forms of clathrin-independent endocytosis exist is now well-established. Thus, although the clathrin-mediated endocytic machinery is by far the most well-studied type of endocytosis [7–9], a plethora of clathrin-independent endocytic mechanisms also appears in today's literature; however, the underlying molecular machinery is far from being clarified [10–16]. One such clathrin-independent endocytic mechanism can involve caveolae.

Caveolae are small, 50- to 70-nm membrane invaginations that are present on the plasma membrane of many different cell types [17]. Caveolae are often clustered within a short stretch of the plasma membrane, and they can even form large, sometimes branched invaginations deeply into the cytoplasm (Fig. 4.1). *In vivo*, caveolae are particularly abundant in adipocytes, endothelial cells, fibroblasts and smooth muscle cells, but they are also found in, for instance, the basal layer of epithelial cells in stratified epithelia [18]. In contrast, they are scarce or absent in hematopoietic cells and neurons, for example. *In vitro*, the presence of caveolae is more unpredictable because cultured cells do not always reflect the caveolin/caveolae status of the tissue of origin. In addition, the caveolin/caveolae status of the cells of origin is often unknown, not least when cells derive from cancers [17].

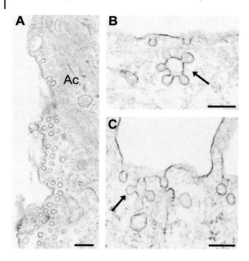

Fig. 4.1 Electron micrographs of human myoepithelial cells grown in a chemically defined medium in the absence of insulin. Under these conditions the cells stop proliferating and express a differentiated phenotype including distinct bundles of actin filaments (shown as Ac in panel A) and numerous caveolae. In the presence of insulin, the cells do not show these characteristics but proliferate (see [19]). Note the deeply invaginated caveolae clusters in panels B and C (arrows). Scale bars = 200 nm.

Moreover, cells may express cav-1 without having structurally identifiable caveolae (our unpublished results). Also, the culture conditions may influence whether caveolae are frequent or absent in one and the same cell line [19] (Fig. 4.1).

Caveolae are a subset of lipid rafts which, in addition to an enrichment in cholesterol and sphingolipids, are characterized by the protein caveolin. There are three members of the caveolin family, caveolin-1 and −2, which are (co)expressed in many cell types, and caveolin-3 that is specific for muscle cells. Caveolin-1 and caveolin-2 exist in different isoforms. The caveolins form a characteristic hairpin loop into the membrane lipid bilayer, exposing both the N- and C-termini to the cytoplasm. In the N-terminal region the caveolin scaffolding domain is responsible for the interaction with numerous other proteins. The C-terminal region is attached to the membrane by palmitoyl anchors. Expression of caveolin-1 can be sufficient to generate caveolae, although other factors than caveolin may be involved. For instance, in polarized epithelial cells such as intestinal Caco-2 cells, expression of caveolin-1 results in formation of caveolae only at the basolateral surface [20].

Caveolae seem to represent a kind of multifunctional platform as they have been implicated in such different functions as cholesterol transport, calcium transport and homeostasis, signaling, regulation of endothelial nitric oxide synthase (eNOS) activity, and tumor suppression [17,21–27]. In addition, it has been debated over the years whether caveolae are also involved in endocytosis, although the many other functions of caveolae would contradict such a role. Historically, the reason for believing that caveolae could be involved in endocytosis comes from their characteristic, invaginated shape as seen in the electron microscope and, more recently, because dynamin, a GTP-binding protein involved in the formation of clathrin-coated vesicles, has been found in association with caveolae [28,29] (see Section 4.8). Since caveolae also bind a variety of ligands that become internalized (e.g., cholera toxin; see Section 4.5), it is tempting to conclude – by analogy to clathrin-coated pits – that they are endocytic, although the question of whether they are actually able to pinch off and deliver material to intracellular compartments has often been ignored. Recent studies, including electron microscopy (EM) and live cell digital imaging, strongly indicate that the answer to the question of whether caveolae are endocytic structures or not, is far from a simple "yes" or "no", but more complex [30]. Therefore, in the present chapter we will treat these aspects of caveolar biology and present a working model that includes the various findings and speculations (see Section 4.10).

4.2
Caveolae are Largely Immobile, Nonendocytic Membrane Domains

In the discussion of whether caveolae are endocytic structures, or not, it is important to distinguish between constitutive endocytosis and stimulated endocytosis. Similarly, frequency and time are also important parameters in relation to endocytic processes. Hence, if a certain endocytic mechanism operates rarely and very slowly it does not add much to the cell's total internalization of membrane, receptors and ligands. Moreover, such a mechanism can be very difficult to document.

It was shown recently that caveolae, in contrast to clathrin-coated pits, are not involved in efficient, constitutive endocytosis in nonstimulated cells [31]. This was in part documented by using photobleaching approaches on different cell lines expressing N- and C-terminally green fluorescent protein (GFP)-tagged caveolin-1 (GFP-tagged caveolin). Caveolin which was found to be incorporated into caveolae at the plasma membrane was highly immobile, whilst some intracellular, caveolin-1-associated structures were dynamic.

The basic idea of using GFP-tagged caveolin fusion proteins and photobleaching techniques such as fluorescence recovery after photobleaching (FRAP) to evaluate whether caveolae are involved in efficient, constitutive endocytosis operating as a parallel internalization mechanism to that of clathrin-coated pits is as follows. Fluorescent caveolin becomes incorporated in caveolae at the plasma membrane, as well as in presumptive caveolar endocytic and recycling vesicles. If caveolae are involved in efficient, constitutive endocytosis, then there will be a rapid turnover of caveolae at the plasma membrane. If a group of fluorescent caveolae at the plasma membrane is bleached, then it will be rapidly replaced by new fluorescent caveolae, a process that is reflected in a rapid recovery of fluorescence intensity in the bleached field of interest. Alternatively, if caveolae are immobile structures at the plasma membrane – that is, there is no internalization/recycling or lateral mobility of caveolin/caveolae taking place – then the bleached field of interest will remain bleached over time. A prerequisite indeed is that the expressed fluorescent caveolin behaves as endogenous caveolin, namely that it becomes associated with caveolae and that it does not change the amount of caveolae at the plasma membrane. This was tested by using quantitative immunogold labeling electron microscopy [31]. Moreover, no differences were found between results obtained with N- and C-terminally tagged caveolin-1.

FRAP experiments applying bleaching fields over both the cell periphery/plasma membrane and the interior of HeLa cells, A431 cells, and Madin-Darby canine kidney (MDCK) cells revealed that the fluorescence recovery at the plasma membrane was very low compared to that of the interior of the cells [31]. This means that caveolin-associated membrane inside the cell (for instance, associated with the trans-Golgi network (TGN) or caveosomes; see Section 4.7) is mobile, whereas caveolae at the plasma membrane are highly immobile. Thus, the experiments revealed that the mobile fraction of fluorescent caveolin associated with internal structures was about 80%, which is quite comparable to the value obtained for other membrane proteins moving without constraints [32]. However, the mobile fraction of fluorescent caveolin associated with caveolae at the plasma membrane was as low as about 5–20%, a value comparable to that of E-cadherin after this adhesion molecule has become trapped by the actin cytoskeleton to form immobile structures [33]. Also, the low diffusion coefficient obtained for caveolae-associated fluorescent caveolin was in the same order of magnitude as that of E-cadherin.

An alternative approach to FRAP in the study of the mobility of a fluorescent fusion protein is that of fluorescence loss in photobleaching (FLIP). Here, a certain region of interest is exposed to several bleaching cycles, and the fluorescence intensity in the region of interest as well as of the entire cell is measured. When FLIP is applied to a fluorescent-caveolin-expressing cell it is striking that there is basically no fluorescence recovery in the region after the first bleaching cycle, and the fluorescence intensity of the entire cell falls very slowly [31]. Importantly, in particular the fluorescence signal deriving from caveolae at the plasma membrane (seen as strongly fluorescent dots or elongated structures at the rim of the cells; the resolution of the confocal microscope does not allow distinction to be made between single caveolae and clusters of caveolae) was hardly influenced by the bleaching cycles. This confirms the FRAP data, and further stresses that caveolin/ caveolae are highly immobile. When, for comparison, FLIP was applied to GFP-Rab7-expressing cells, a completely different result was obtained. Thus, within each bleaching cycle large amounts of GFP-Rab7 diffused into the bleaching region, and the fluorescence level of the entire cell fell continuously. In fact, the GFP-Rab7-expressing cells could be completely fluorescence-depleted by FLIP [31]. This is in agreement with Rab7's properties as a small, mobile GTPase that rapidly switches between being membrane-associated and, after GTP hydrolysis, cytosolic [34].

Like noncaveolar rafts, caveolae are cholesterol-based structures, and cholesterol depletion with methyl-β-cyclodextrin (mβCD) leads to the disappearance of caveolae [35–37]. When cholesterol is removed from fluorescent caveolin-expressing cells, FLIP revealed a gradual disappearance of the distinct caveolin fluorescence at the plasma membrane. Thus, caveolin exhibits an increased mobility after cholesterol depletion, possibly due to a loss of caveolae. Also, a much more efficient removal of fluorescence from the bleaching region was obtained compared to control cells [31]. These findings support the notion that cholesterol plays an important role in the maintenance of caveolar integrity.

Moreover, the actin cytoskeleton may help to stabilize caveolae at the plasma membrane [38,39]. Thus, we have shown previously by using a yeast two-hybrid system that the actin-binding protein filamin is a binding partner for caveolin-1. Activation of Rho leads to reorganization of the actin cytoskeleton and subsequently to the reorganization of caveolae [39]. This was further substantiated in FLIP studies of fluorescent caveolin-expressing cells treated with the actin-depolymerizing drug cytochalasin D. Here, the normal fluorescent staining of caveolae at the plasma membrane was perturbed and caveolae began to move laterally and to cluster in the plasma membrane [31].

Taken together, the results of these studies show that plasma membrane-associated caveolin-1 is a highly immobile molecule, and that caveolae are not involved in efficient constitutive endocytosis. Furthermore, the actin cytoskeleton plays an important role in keeping caveolae immobilized. However, it should be emphasized that this immobility of caveolae in the normal steady-state situation is not incompatible with a role of caveolin and caveolae in endocytosis under special conditions where profound changes of the actin cytoskeleton takes place (see Section 4.4). This makes the unraveling of caveolar function even more intriguing.

4.3
Caveolae May Show Local, Short-Range Motility: A Role in Transendothelial Transport?

In the above-mentioned bleaching studies a special FRAP protocol was included in which the entire interior of the cells was bleached, leaving only a narrow, fluorescent rim of GFP-tagged caveolin at the cell periphery [31]. These FRAP experiments highlighted two important points:

- The total fluorescence intensity of the peripheral rim including caveolae at the plasma membrane decreased only very slowly, further supporting the notion that caveolae are not becoming efficiently internalized (see also Section 4.6).
- There was a lively activity of the fluorescent caveolae at the cell periphery, although they did not disappear from the periphery (see Ref. [31], Fig. 5, online movie).

Whether this reflects that caveolae (or groups of caveolae) actually pinch off and refuse with the plasma membrane without really moving away from the subplasmalemmal zone (for example, because they are tethered by the actin cytoskeleton), or it reflects movements in the plasma membrane with its population of caveolae as such, was not clear. However, such continuous recycling of caveolae immediately beneath the plasma membrane was recently demonstrated [40].

A short-range motility and fission-fusion processes may be highly relevant in order to understand the function of caveolae in transendothelial transport, or transcytosis. In endothelial transcytosis [41] caveolae are thought to give rise to free vesicles at one (lumenal or ablumenal) pole and thereafter move to and fuse with the opposite pole, thereby being involved in the exchange of macromolecules between the blood and the connective tissue. Although it is widely accepted, a major problem with the concept of transendothelial transcytosis in its strict meaning is that truly free, caveolar vesicles have been difficult or impossible to demonstrate ultrastructurally, both in conventionally fixed and rapidly frozen tissue [42–44]. However, considering that the distance between the lumenal and ablumenal membranes in the flattened endothelial cell is often around 200 nm, a short-range motility of the 50–70 nm caveolae or chains of caveolae and their apparent ability to fuse and detach again might explain how caveolae could be involved in transendothelial transport by a "kiss-and-run" activity, even without ever pinching off to form free, endocytic vesicles [17]. Such a process would most likely have to be highly regulated. In fact, the caveolar membrane and the endothelial cell cytoplasm contain the required molecular machinery [28,45,46], and transendothelial transport of albumin has been shown to require interaction of the albumin-docking protein pg60 with caveolin and activation of G_i-coupled Src kinase signaling [47]. Unfortunately, recent studies on caveolin-1-deficient mice have not clarified the role of caveolae in transendothelial transport. Thus, although lacking caveolae, these mice do not show any marked reduction in the transport of albumin [48,49]. This is most likely because caveolae also plays a more indirect role in vascular permeability. Vasorelaxation and permeability is regulated by eNOS, which is interacting with, and negatively regulated by, caveolin associated with endothelial caveolae [50]. In caveolin knockout mice, the microvasculature has even been reported to be hyperpermeable because of "opened" intercellular spaces and tight junctions apparently caused by uncontrolled release of and signaling via nitric oxide [51]. This hyperpermeability blurs any possible reduction in the caveolae-mediated transendothelial transport in the knockout mice.

4.4
An Internalization Wave of Caveolae can be Stimulated by Virus

Studies on the entry of simian 40 (SV40) virus by Pelkmans and coworkers [52–54] have documented that caveolae can actually play a role in nonconstitutive endocytosis. Thus, after binding of SV40 virus to the cell surface via the MHC class I molecule, the virus particles move laterally in the plasma membrane to end up in caveolae. Although these caveolae are initially immobile, the virus initiates a complex signaling cascade leading to a profound disorganization of the cortical actin cytoskeleton and a transient recruitment of the GTP-binding protein dynamin known to be involved in membrane fission (see Section 4.8). Importantly, without SV40-stimulation, less than 10 % of the caveolae were associated with dynamin. These changes, in turn, resulted in a wave of incoming caveolar vesicles containing virus where reorganized actin filaments formed "tails" necessary for internalization of the SV40-containing caveolae [53]. Subsequently, the virus was delivered to caveosomes (see Section 4.7) and transported further downstream to the endoplasmic reticulum (ER). However, a delay of several hours then occurs before caveolin returns from the caveosomes to the plasma membrane in vesicles now devoid of virus particles [52].

It is interesting to note that antibody-induced crosslinking of MHC class I molecules (the SV40 receptor) results in an accumulation of MHC class I clusters in "small uncoated surface invaginations" identical to caveolae, as reported 25 years ago by Huet and coworkers. No clusters were found in clathrin-coated pits. From the caveolae-like invaginations the clusters were apparently internalized and delivered to lysosomes [55]. It is therefore tempting to speculate that it is the same underlying mechanism that is responsible for caveolae-mediated uptake of SV40 virus particles after their binding to MHC class I and of MHC class I clusters generated by antibody crosslinking.

Echovirus 1 is also taken up by caveolae, and binds to the collagen receptor $\alpha_2\beta_1$ integrin [56]. Interestingly, recent studies revealed that $\alpha_2\beta_1$ is localized to non-caveolar rafts, but that antibody crosslinking clustered $\alpha_2\beta_1$ in caveolae, which subsequently became internalized and delivered the integrin to caveosome-like structures. This internalization is dependent on protein kinase Cα activity [57]. In the same study it was revealed that αV integrin clusters are not taken up by caveolae, but via clathrin-coated pits and vesicles. The common human polyomavirus BK also seems to become internalized by caveolae [58]. It should be stressed, however, that several types of virus are internalized in a clathrin-dependent manner, the classical example being Semliki Forest virus [59], although other recent examples include rubella virus [60] and bovine viral diarrhea virus (a pest virus) [61].

In an ultrastructural study, Parton and co-workers [62] found that the treatment of cells with the phosphatase inhibitor okadaic acid leads to aggregation and subsequent internalization of caveolae, and that the process is dependent on an intact actin cytoskeleton since treatment with cytochalasin D could prevent it. These results suggest that okadaic acid somehow induces a reorganization of actin. The okadaic acid-induced internalization of caveolae was later confirmed by FLIP studies on fluorescent caveolin-expressing cells. Thus, after okadaic acid treatment, plasma membrane caveolin/caveolae gradually disappear from the plasma membrane and aggregate in the perinuclear region, and the mobility of caveolin clearly increased so that the repeated bleaching cycles almost completely extracted the entire cellular fluorescence signal [31].

Finally, a rather special example of a caveolin/caveolae-stimulated internalization should be mentioned. Thus, FimH-expressing *Escherichia coli* are, via binding of the bacteria to CD48 on macrophages and mast cells, apparently able to recruit and cluster caveolae, eventually leading to the formation of intracellular, bacteria-containing compartments [63,64].

4.5
Role of Caveolae in Endocytosis of Cholera Toxin

In addition to the recent studies on internalization of virus mentioned above, studies on cholera toxin (CT) uptake have also been important for the ongoing discussion of the role of caveolae in endocytosis. CT belongs to a large group of protein toxins with enzymatically active A-moieties, and B-moieties that act as ligands and bind to cell-surface components. These toxins must be endocytosed before they exert their toxic effect(s). In the case of CT, the B-moieties bind to the ganglioside GM1 and, following internalization and transport via the Golgi complex to the ER, the A-moiety is translocated to the cytosol where it affects the activity of adenylyl cyclase [11].

Although clathrin-mediated and clathrin- and caveolin-independent endocytosis can play a role in the uptake of CT [65–69], this does not in any way exclude a role of caveolae as well, and it is widely believed that caveolae or caveolae-like structures are the major vehicle for CT internalization and the subsequent delivery to the TGN [70–74]. The main reason for this is that CT binds to GM1, which is in part present in caveolae [68,75]. However, the consequences of caveolae-mediated CT/GM1 internalization for the cell's steady-state balance of membrane-associated caveolin and caveolae have generally been ignored. In principle, two possibilities for CT-stimulated internalization of caveolae exist. Binding of CT to GM1 may induce a wave of caveolae internalization as described above for SV40 and okadaic acid, leading to down-regulation of caveolae at the plasma membrane. Alternatively, CT could induce a constitutive internalization mechanism for caveolae including an efficient recycling of caveolae or caveolin back to the plasma membrane. This would not lead to a depletion of the plasma membrane pool of caveolae, but requires a rapid replacement of those CT-containing caveolae that become internalized with new, empty caveolae.

The first report of a major role for caveolae in CT endocytosis was an ultrastructural study published in 1982 by Montesano et al. [72]. Here, the authors used CT-B chain (CT-B)-gold and found that the conjugate preferentially bound to caveolae at 2 °C. Interestingly, they noticed an increase in CT-B-gold in caveolae relative to CT-B-gold bound to noncaveolar plasma membrane over time at 37 °C. These observations were originally interpreted as the result of an up-concentration of CT in endocytic caveolae. However, an alternative explanation could be selective internalization of CT bound to the noncaveolar plasma membrane. In fact, CT/GM1 in caveolae could represent an immobilized fraction of the ligand-receptor complex. In the study by Montesano et al., CT-B-gold was only found very rarely, if ever, in clathrin-coated pits. However, other studies have documented small, but significant amounts of CT-B-gold [68], as well as biotin-GM1 detected by antibiotin antibodies conjugated to gold [75] in clathrin-coated pits. CT-B-HRP has also been localized to clathrin-coated pits [66]. Parton [68] was in fact very careful not to draw too far-reaching conclusions based on the preferential localization of CT-B to caveolae, and stressed that at least some GM1 must be internalized by clathrin-coated pits. We would like to emphasize that the finding that only minimal CT-B can be observed at any given time point in clathrin-coated pits does not exclude a significant role for the coated pits in CT-B uptake. Thus, clathrin-coated pits are highly dynamic structures with a half-life of minutes at the cell surface [8], and CT-B may continuously move into newly formed clathrin-coated pits to become efficiently internalized. This is in agreement with the findings that clathrin-dependent endocytosis can account for about 50% of CT internalization [66,76].

Several uptake mechanisms have been described for CT and these may – to some extent – be cell type-dependent. Thus, CT can be internalized both by clathrin-dependent and -independent mechanisms, and the effect of cholesterol-binding drugs (nystatin, filipin, cyclodextrin) on CT-internalization varies [65–67,71,77,78]. In studies with dominant negative mutants of epsin and eps15 (molecules required for clathrin-mediated endocytosis), Nichols et al. [67] found that a proportion of CT-B is internalized by clathrin-coated pits. Moreover, Shogomori and Futerman [65] reported that although CT-B is present in detergent-insoluble rafts or microdomains, it becomes internalized by a raft-independent mechanism, presumably via clathrin-coated pits. The same is true for the epidermal growth factor receptor [79]. Recently, Hansen et al. [69] showed that CT bound to GM1 localized to a detergent-insoluble, raft-like fraction of the enterocyte brush border membrane, and was subsequently internalized by a cholesterol-independent, but clathrin-dependent mechanism. It could be argued that uptake mediated by clathrin-coated pits would not lead to delivery of cargo to the TGN. However, Shiga toxin, which binds to globotriasylceremide (Gb3), is internalized via clathrin-coated pits and vesicles by an as-yet unknown mechanism [80] and subsequently transported to the TGN and the ER [81]. In accordance with this, expression of antisense clathrin heavy chain inhibits the toxicity of Shiga toxin [82]. Interestingly, Shiga toxin-HRP, like CT-B-HRP, also accumulates in caveolae at 37 °C (our unpublished data). It should be noted that ligands taken up from caveolae and clathrin-coated pits can ultimately be located in the same endosome (see Section 4.7).

In our attempts to characterize the endocytic mechanisms of CT uptake [66], Caco-2 cells were transfected with caveolin, leading to the formation of basolateral caveolae in the otherwise caveolae/caveolin-negative, highly polarized cell line [20]. This did not change the uptake or effect of CT. Furthermore, treatment of the cav-1-expressing Caco-2 cells with the cholesterol-binding drug filipin only reduced internalization of CT slightly (<20%), suggesting that although caveolae may be involved in CT endocytosis, they do not play a major role. In contrast, cholesterol-depletion with mβCD, a treatment that both removes caveolae and inhibits the formation of deeply invaginated clathrin-coated pits and subsequently coated vesicle formation [37,83], resulted in a 30–40% reduction in CT uptake [66], indicating that coated pits/vesicles also play a role, though not exclusive, in CT uptake. Similarly, in baby hamster kidney (BHK) cells expressing antisense clathrin heavy chain [84], endocytosis of CT was reduced by about 50%. Moreover, in HeLa cells expressing the dominant-negative dynamin mutant K44A, a 50–70% reduction in CT uptake was seen [66]. In these cells both endocytosis mediated by caveolae and by clathrin-coated pits/vesicles are inhibited, as well as possible caveolin- and clathrin-independent mechanisms that may depend on dynamin. In BHK and HeLa cells, in which either antisense clathrin or the dominant-negative dynamin mutant was expressed, CT is still internalized after cholesterol depletion with mβCD [85]. In a recent report it was similarly shown that the overexpression of dominant mutants that inhibit clathrin-, caveolin- or Arf6-dependent endocytic pathways does not prevent CT uptake and trafficking to the Golgi and ER, or CT cytotoxicity.

Interestingly, even under conditions where all three endocytic pathways were inhibited simultaneously, CT has a toxic effect [86]. Importantly, it must be borne in mind that the blocking of one or more pathways may lead to up-regulation of other pathways that are normally quiescent [87], or it may induce new pathways [88]. Taken together, these results suggest that CT can be internalized by caveolae and clathrin-coated pits/vesicles as well as by one or more mechanism not involving these structures. However, caveolae do not seem to play a major role in the uptake.

In order to further analyze the importance of caveolae in CT-uptake, and not least to evaluate the internalization efficiency of CT bound to GM1 inside and outside caveolae, we incubated HeLa cells with red fluorescent CT-B on ice and subsequently at 37 °C for various periods of time (between 0 and 120 min), followed by fixation and immunocytochemical detection of caveolae using an antibody against endogenous caveolin-1. A partial co-localization of CT-B and caveolin on the cell surface following labeling at 0 °C was seen. However, upon heating to 37 °C, CT-B was internalized and gradually accumulated in the perinuclear region. After 30 min and more, some – but not all – of the internalized CT-B was co-localized with TGN38, a marker of the TGN (Fig. 4.2A), while a small fraction of CT was still seen at the plasma membrane where it apparently co-localized with caveolin. Interestingly, during this CT-B uptake, no change in the distribution of endogenous caveolin was detected, irrespective of the time of CT-B incubation. At all time points (0–120 min) the peripheral rim of caveolae remained stable. In blind experiments, where the microscope operator only examined caveolin in the confocal microscope and was unaware of the incubation time with CT-B at 37 °C, no difference between the time points could be established. Similarly, no differences in the distribution of caveolae could be observed when cells were incubated with the holotoxin (CT A+B chain) (our unpublished data).

Since the individual cells bound CT-B to varying degrees, and some were unlabeled, such cells could serve as internal controls for a changed pattern in the distribution of endogenous caveolin stimulated by CT-B binding. Importantly, at all incubation times the caveolar localization was the same, irrespective of the GM1 expression level of the cell and consequently the degree of CT-B binding (Fig. 4.2B). Taken together, these data strongly indicate that CT-B uptake does not cause a synchronized wave of caveolae internalization. To further analyze the effect of CT-B uptake on the distribution of caveolae, we expressed GFP-tagged caveolin-1 fusion proteins [31] in HeLa cells and human skin fibroblasts. When these cells were incubated with CT-B on ice and subsequently incubated at 37 °C for various periods (0–120 min), and then fixed and examined in the confocal microscope, results similar to those with endogenous caveolin were obtained: CT-B became internalized and accumulated in the TGN over time, while the pattern of caveolar expression was unchanged – no wave of incoming caveolae or caveolin stimulated by CT-B was observed (Fig. 4.2C and D). When the pattern of CT-B internalization in cells expressing GFP-tagged caveolin was compared to that of nontransfected, neighboring cells in the same culture, no differences were seen (Fig. 4.2C). Thus, the expression of GFP-tagged caveolin does not influence CT-B uptake and transport.

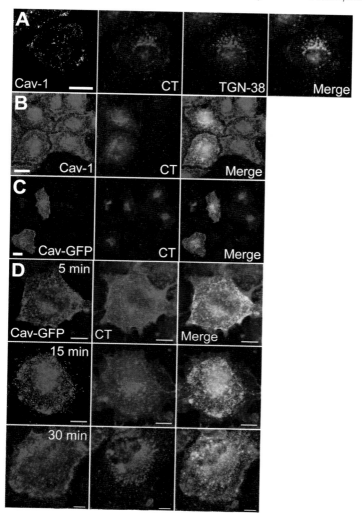

Fig. 4.2 (A) HeLa cells were labeled with Alexa 594 CT-B (red) on ice for 1 h, washed, and incubated at 37 °C for 2 h to allow internalization of CT-B. The cells were subsequently fixed and immunolabeled for endogenous caveolin-1 (white) and TGN-38 (green). After 2 h, the majority of CT-B has been internalized to the TGN. (B) HeLa cells were allowed to internalize CT-B for 2 h, as described above. The cells were subsequently fixed and immunolabeled for endogenous caveolin-1 (green). The panel shows two cells expressing GM1 that have internalized CT-B, and adjacent cells that have not internalized CT-B. The cellular distribution of caveolin-1 is the same, irrespective of whether the cells have internalized CT-B. (C) HeLa cells transfected with Cav-GFP were allowed to internalize CT-B for 2 h, as described above. The panel shows two transfected cells and adjacent, nontransfected cells. The pattern of internalized CT-B is the same in transfected and nontransfected cells. (D) HeLa cells transfected with Cav-GFP and incubated with CT-B for 5 to 30 min at 37 °C. While CT-B moves from the cell surface to the perinuclear region (the TGN), the distribution of Cav-GFP-labeled caveolae is not changed. Scale bars = 20 μm.

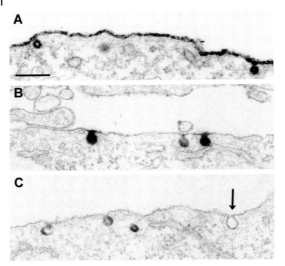

Fig. 4.3 Electron micrographs of BHK cells incubated with a CT-B-HRP conjugate. (A) Cells were incubated at 0 °C with the conjugate, which is seen all over the cell surface including some caveolae. (B,C) Cells have been incubated with the conjugate at 0 °C for 1 h, then washed and further incubated for 30 min at 37 °C. Very little or no labeling is seen at the cell surface, except in caveolae, which are heavily labeled. Such images suggest that the CT-B-HRP has become internalized by a caveolae-independent mechanism. However, on very rare occasions unlabeled caveolae can be seen (arrow in C). These caveolae most likely are formed after the surface-associated CT-B-HRP conjugate was internalized, and may represent a substitution for a rare caveola that has been involved in conjugate uptake. Scale bar = 200 nm.

Next, the internalization of CT-B in relation to caveolae was followed over time in HeLa cells and human skin fibroblasts by photobleaching techniques (our unpublished results). For this purpose, cells expressing GFP-tagged caveolin were preincubated for 1 h at 4 °C with CT-B, washed and further incubated for 5–10 min in CT-B-free medium at 37 °C on stage to stabilize the culture. The cells were then exposed to a modified FRAP protocol where the entire cytoplasm was bleached in both the red and the green channels, leaving only the most peripheral rim of fluorescence corresponding to the plasma membrane (see also Ref. [31]). Fluorescence recovery in the cytoplasm was then followed over time. The rationale of this type of experiment is that if CT-B binding stimulates caveolae to become constitutively internalized and replaced by a recycling mechanism, then the GFP-tagged caveolae at the plasma membrane should disappear and be replaced by caveolae which are not labeled – that is, the peripheral fluorescence should decrease and the intracellular fluorescence increase. It was, however, striking that although CT-B appeared in vesicles in the bleached interior of the cells, GFP-tagged caveolin did not, but rather remained at the cell periphery. These findings strongly suggest that (GFP-tagged) caveolae are not efficiently internalized and recycled in response to CT-binding but are more likely stable, plasma membrane-associated structures.

These findings were further supported by EM observations on HeLa cells showing that even after 30–120 min of CT-B-HRP internalization, caveolae were often distinctly labeled by CT-B-HRP although the remaining plasma membrane was unlabeled (Fig. 4.3). This emphasizes that at time points where the main, mobile GM1/CT-B fraction has been internalized by a caveolae-independent mechanism(s), a nonmobile fraction is still present on the cell surface, trapped in the caveolae. It was also possible by using EM to detect the internalized CT-B-HRP in the TGN [17]. The number of caveolae at the cell surface of cells pulse-chased with CT-B-HRP for 30 min at 37 °C was the same as in control cells not exposed to CT-B-HRP (our unpublished results).

Furthermore, since it has been reported that expression of the K44A dominant-negative dynamin-1 mutant inhibits caveolae-mediated internalization of CT-B in endothelial cells [28], we also quantified the number of caveolae in HeLa K44A cells expressing the mutant – that is, in cells grown without tetracycline. Interestingly, although expression of the dynamin mutant leads to a two- to three-fold increase in the number of clathrin-coated pits at the cell surface as expected [66], the number of caveolae at the cell surface was unchanged, indicating that caveolae are not constitutively internalized by a dynamin-dependent mechanism. In K44A cells grown both in the presence or absence of tetracycline and incubated for 30 min at 37 °C with CT-B-HRP, practically all caveolae were labeled (our unpublished observations).

4.6
A Small Fraction of Caveolae may become Constitutively Internalized

Clearly, the possibility cannot be excluded that a few caveolae (or clusters of caveolae) pinch off occasionally and therefore participate in the delivery of CT and other molecules to intracellular compartments, although this must – in terms of endocytic activity – be relatively insignificant. Recent studies conducted by Kirkham et al. [76] showed that a very small fraction (or a subpopulation) of caveolae is actually internalized constitutively. These authors developed an ultrastructural assay which made it possible to quantitate free, budded caveolae versus surface-connected caveolae. For this, they used CT-B-HRP as an endocytic marker, and quenched the HRP reaction of labeled structures connected to the cell surface with ascorbic acid, which is membrane-impermeable. This was combined with an immunolabeling protocol that allowed them to show that truly free caveolae-like vesicles containing the HRP reaction product were in fact caveolae. In this way, it was shown that about 2% of the total population of caveolae bud off per minute.

Interestingly, the internalization of prion proteins that are GPI-anchored also appears to be a rather slow or inefficient process that can be mediated by caveolae [89]. Thus, in an immunogold labeling pulse-chase experiment it was found that approximately 90% of the caveolae at the plasma membrane that were labeled after a 10-min period were still labeled after a 50-min chase; only about 10% of all caveolae were internalized per hour. This slow internalization may be constitutive, although it cannot be excluded that it is somehow stimulated by the prion proteins because the caveolae-mediated pathway was not observed for several other GPI-anchored proteins [89].

In our FRAP experiments in which the interior of the cells were bleached, only leaving a narrow, fluorescent zone of GFP-tagged caveolin structures, the fluorescence disappeared only very slowly from the peripheral zone (see Fig. 5t in Ref. [31]). Based on extrapolations of such data, the fluorescence would disappear completely from the periphery within about 3 h. Taken together, the described EM and FRAP data are consistent with a very slow, constitutive internalization of caveolae.

4.7
Caveosomes: Intracellular Caveolin-Associated Structures

In addition to reaching the TGN, internalized CT is also found in caveosomes [90], the organelle reached by internalized SV40 virus [52]. The caveosome is a non-acidic, caveolin-associated compartment that does not stain for EEA1, a marker of early endosomes reached by the clathrin-dependent endocytic pathway. Moreover, caveosomes do not accumulate Lysotracker, a lysosomal marker, and they do not stain for TGN46 and mannosidase II, both of which are Golgi markers [52]. Evidence that the clathrin-dependent endosome pathway and the caveolin-dependent caveosome pathway somehow merge are accumulating [91,92]. Moreover, in studies with SV40 virus and CT it was recently reported that these caveolar markers are transported by a Rab5-dependent pathway to early endosomes and that early endosomes and caveosomes may even communicate via this Rab5 pathway [91]. An important difference between the two ligands is that the Rab5-dependent step is required for CT transport to the Golgi complex, but not for SV40 entry into the ER.

These studies further stress the important notion that because a certain ligand initially is seen in caveolae, and later on also in intracellular compartments associated with caveolin, the ligand has not necessarily been internalized and transported to the compartment by caveolae. For instance, transforming growth factor beta (TGFβ) was found to localize to both rafts/caveolae and clathrin-coated pits at the cell surface [93]. Moreover, after internalization, TGFβ was seen in caveolin-positive vesicles as well as in vesicles staining for EEA1. It was therefore concluded that two endocytic pathways for TGFβ were operating in parallel: one mediated by clathrin-coated pits and vesicles and leading to endosomes and subsequently to TGFβ signaling; and one mediated by rafts/caveolae leading to caveolin-positive vesicles (caveosomes?) involved in receptor degradation and turnover. However, caveolae could in fact bind TGFβ without being involved in endocytosis, and all internalized receptors could have been taken up by endocytic noncaveolar rafts or clathrin-dependent endocytosis, leading to endosomes. These endosomes, in turn, may exchange material with caveolin-positive vesicles or even with caveosomes via intracellular, caveolin-associated carrier vesicles.

4.8
The Role of Dynamin in Caveolar Function

From the sections above, it is clear that dynamin is central in the discussions on caveolar endocytosis, and this GTP-binding protein therefore warrants further attention in this chapter. It is well established that dynamin plays a role in the final scission of clathrin-coated vesicles to form free endocytic vesicles [94,95], and it has also been reported to be important for the fission of caveolae [28,29]. However, the role of dynamin associated with caveolae can be complex. Dynamin is an actin-interacting protein which, for example, binds to cortactin. Indeed, recently dynamin was found to be involved in the regulation of actin polymerization during micropinosome comet formation – that is, the formation of rapidly moving vesicles propelled forward by an actin treadmilling machine [96]. Additionally, caveolin interacts with the actin cytoskeleton via filamin, and reorganization of the actin cytoskeleton leads to redistribution of caveolae [39]. Depolymerization of the actin cytoskeleton with cytochalasin D leads to an increase in caveolar mobility, and it has therefore been suggested that the normal immobility of caveolae is due to an anchoring role of actin filaments [31]. Dynamin could be a partner in such stabilization of caveolae. As mentioned above (see Section 4.4), Pelkmans et al. [53] found a pronounced SV40 virus-induced reorganization of the actin cytoskeleton and showed that dynamin is transiently recruited to SV40 virus-containing caveolae, which are subsequently internalized. Hence, it could be speculated that the internalization of caveolae, induced for instance by SV40 virus or okadaic acid [62], leads to a reorganization of the actin cytoskeleton mediated by dynamin. In fact, cytochalasin D inhibits the okadaic acid-stimulated uptake of caveolae [62], and there is an increasing body of evidence that actin plays a key role in endocytosis [62,97–99]. Therefore, the possible association of dynamin with caveolae does not *per se* indicate that these caveolae are going to pinch off unless other processes such as actin reorganization have also been initiated in response to a specific stimulation. In agreement with this and, as pointed out above, we found no accumulation of caveolae at the plasma membrane in cells expressing dominant-negative dynamin, as would have been expected if dynamin was constitutively mediating scission of caveolae (our unpublished observations).

4.9
Caveolin Immobilizes Rafts/Caveolar Invaginations

In addition to the actin cytoskeleton, which seems to be involved in the immobility of caveolae (see Section 4.2), caveolin-1 itself apparently immobilizes caveolae. Thus, Le et al. [100] and Nabi and Le [14] suggested that lipid rafts can invaginate in a cholesterol-dependent but caveolin-independent way to give rise to caveolae-like invaginations of the plasma membrane, which become rapidly internalized in a dynamin-dependent way. Such endocytic raft structures may then be immobilized by caveolin-1 and only become internalized after specific stimulation (e. g., virus binding). Pang et al. [77] recently showed that the content of GM1 varies among cells, and that cells with a low GM1 content also had a relatively low CT uptake which was independent of caveolin-1 expression.

It remains an open question as to whether there exist subpopulations of caveolae, or a subpopulation of caveolae-like invaginations with so little caveolin that it cannot be immobilized, but rather is endocytic [12]. Such a subpopulation could account for the small fraction of caveolae that appears to become constitutively internalized (see Section 4.6).

As mentioned above (see Section 4.5), CT-B can be internalized by mechanisms that are caveolin-, clathrin- and dynamin-independent [66]. Although such an endocytic mechanism (or several mechanisms) is far from well characterized, it is clear that for instance other protein toxins may enter cells in such a manner [11]. It should be noted that caveolin-, clathrin- and dynamin-independent endocytosis is not necessarily dependent on lipid rafts [37], but one such internalization pathway could be via a noncaveolar, raft-based and cholesterol-dependent mechanism [101,102]. For example, in a study on lymphocytes it was found that after ligand stimulation the interleukin-2 receptor became internalized in a clathrin- and caveolin-independent, but dynamin-dependent way via detergent-resistant membrane domains [102]. It should be stressed, however, that noncaveolar rafts, which do not form characteristic, regular, 50- to 70-nm invaginations during their pinching-off [14,100] (in contrast to caveolae or caveolae-like invaginated rafts) are poorly defined morphologically. This indeed makes the study of a possible role of noncaveolar rafts in endocytosis difficult. Several years ago we identified small, uncoated endocytic vesicles which differed from coated pits/vesicles and caveolae ultrastructurally [103]. In a recent study, Kirkham et al. [76] found that CT was mainly internalized in a clathrin-, caveolin-, and dynamin-independent way by means of uncoated tubular or ring-shaped structures, as identified ultrastructurally. These structures also contained GPI-anchored proteins. That uptake of this type of protein can occur independently of clathrin, caveolin and dynamin is in agreement with our study of a GPI-anchored diphtheria toxin receptor [104]. The mechanism reported by Kirkham et al. [76] was operating both in primary fibroblasts from wild-type and cav-1$^{-/-}$(cav-1-null) mice. Moreover, it was recently reported also that SV40 virus can be rapidly internalized in both cav-1-null and wild-type fibroblasts in a caveolin-, clathrin- and dynamin-independent manner [105].

The special caveolar lipid-environment appears to be of functional importance for caveolae-mediated endocytosis. Thus, increasing the cellular cholesterol level increases caveolae-mediated uptake of albumin and lactosylceramide. A similar effect is seen after the addition of exogenous lactosylceramide or GM1. In fact, the balance between the cellular amount of caveolin and glycosphingolipids may be of vital importance for the ability of caveolae to pinch off. In control cells, increasing the amount of caveolin-1 leads to a decrease in the caveolar-mediated endocytosis of albumin. In contrast, increasing both the amount of caveolin-1 and glycosphingolipid leads to an increased endocytosis of albumin, presumably because in the latter case the correct balance between caveolin-1 and glycosphingolipids is maintained [106].

4.10
A 2005 Consensus Model for Caveolar Endocytosis

Based on the various findings presented here, we propose the following model for a role of caveolae and noncaveolar rafts in endocytosis (see also Ref. [30]). Noncaveolar lipid rafts, perhaps smaller than caveolae, fuse laterally and form preendocytic domains that may pinch off by both dynamin-dependent and -independent mechanisms. Such rafts may also become associated with caveolin. This association leads to a stable, defined curvature and size of the raft, and to a reduced ability to pinch off. The newly formed caveolae become associated with the actin cytoskeleton via filamin and are now immobilized. However, a small fraction of these caveolae may actually become constitutively internalized, perhaps as a means of caveolin turnover, either because they have not been sufficiently immobilized by the actin cytoskeleton and/or they contain too little caveolin. Molecules present in such caveolae may therefore become internalized. Moreover, caveolae may be involved in local, short-range motility, possibly including fission and fusion processes. Finally, in some cases – for example, after virus stimulation – a signaling cascade may be initiated, leading to reorganization of the actin cytoskeleton and recruitment of dynamin, and a subsequent wave of internalized caveolae, which are only very slowly replaced. Considering all the other functions ascribed to caveolin/caveolae at the plasma membrane (see Section 4.1), such a massive, long-lasting down-regulation of caveolae can, however, hardly be considered a physiologically desirable situation for the cell.

Acknowledgments

The studies referred to in this chapter from the authors' laboratories have been supported by the Danish and Norwegian Cancer Societies, the Danish Medical Research Council, the Norwegian Research Council for Science and Humanities, The Novo Nordisk Foundation, The John and Birthe Meyer Foundation, the Jahre Foundation, and Jeanette and Søren Bothners Legacy.

Abbreviations

BHK   baby hamster kidney
CT   cholera toxin
EM   electron microscopy
eNOS   endothelial nitric oxide synthase
ER   endoplasmic reticulum
FLIP   fluorescence loss in photobleaching
FRAP   fluorescence recovery after photobleaching
Gb3   globotriasylceremide
GFP   green fluorescent protein
mβCD   methyl-β-cyclodextrin
MDCK   Madin-Darby canine kidney
TGFβ transforming growth factor beta
TGN   trans-Golgi network

References

1. Larkin, J.M., Brown, M.S., Goldstein, J.L., Anderson, R.G.W., *Cell* 1983, 33, 273–285.
2. Larkin, J.M., Donzell, W.C., Anderson, R.G.W., *J. Cell. Physiol.* 1985, 124, 372–378.
3. Moya, M., Dautry-Varsat, A., Goud, B., Louvard, D., Boquet, P., *J. Cell Biol.* 1985, 101, 548–559.
4. Sandvig, K., Olsnes, S., Petersen, O.W., van Deurs, B., *J. Cell Biol.* 1987, 105, 679–689.
5. Madshus, I.H., Sandvig, K., Olsnes, S., van Deurs, B., *J. Cell. Physiol.* 1987, 131, 14–22.
6. van Deurs, B., Petersen, O.W., Olsnes, S., Sandvig, K., *Int. Rev. Cytol.* 1989, 117, 131–177.
7. Merrifield, C.J., Feldman, M.E., Wan, L., Almers, W., *Nature Cell Biol.* 2002, 4, 691–698.
8. Marsh, M., McMahon, H.T., *Science* 1999, 285, 215–220.
9. Higgins, M.K., McMahon, H.T., *Trends Biochem. Sci.* 2002, 27, 257–263.
10. Johannes, L., Lamaze, C., *Traffic* 2002, 3, 443–451.
11. Sandvig, K., van Deurs, B., *Annu. Rev. Cell Dev. Biol.* 2002, 18, 1–24.
12. Nichols, B., *J. Cell Sci.* 2003, 116, 4707–4714.
13. Helms, J.B., Zurzolo, C., *Traffic* 2004, 5, 247–254.
14. Nabi, I.R., Le, P.U., *J. Cell Biol.* 2003, 161, 673–677.
15. Conner, S.D., Schmid, S.L., *Nature* 2003, 422, 37–44.
16. Kirkham, M., Parton, R., *Biochim. Biophys. Acta* 2005, 1745, 273–286.
17. van Deurs, B., Roepstorff, K., Hommelgaard, A.M., Sandvig, K., *Trends Cell Biol.* 2003, 13, 92–100.
18. Fujimoto, T., Nakade, S., Miyawaki, A., Mikoshiba, K., Ogawa, K.J., *Cell. Biol.* 1992, 119, 1507–1513.
19. Petersen, O.W., Hansen, S.H., Laursen, I., van Deurs, B., *Eur. J. Cell Biol.* 1989, 50, 500–509.
20. Vogel, U., Sandvig, K., van Deurs, B., *J. Cell Sci.* 1998, 111, 825–832.
21. Fielding, C.J., Fielding, P.E., *Adv. Drug Deliv. Rev.* 2001, 49, 251–264.
22. Fielding, C.J., Fielding, P.E., *Biochem. Soc. Trans.* 2004, 32, 65–69.
23. Ikonen, E., Parton, R.G., *Traffic* 2000, 1, 212–217.
24. Isshiki, M., Anderson, R.G., *Cell Calcium* 1999, 26, 201–208.
25. Chini, B., Parenti, M., *J. Mol. Endocrinol.* 2004, 32, 325–338.
26. Cohen, A.W., Hnasko, R., Schubert, W., Lisanti, M.P., *Physiol. Rev.* 2004, 84, 1341–1379.

27 Tortelote, G. G., Valverde, R. H., Lemos, T., Guilherme, A., Einicker-Lamas, M., Vieyra, A., *FEBS Lett.* 2004, 576, 31–35.

28 Oh, P., McIntosh, D. P., Schnitzer, J. E., *J. Cell Biol.* 1998, 141, 101–144.

29 Henley, J. R., Krueger, E. W. A., Oswald, B. J., McNiven, M. A., *J. Cell Biol.* 1998, 141, 85–99.

30 Hommelgaard, A. M., Roepstorff, K., Vilhardt, F., Torgersen, M. L., Sandvig, K., van Deurs, B., *Traffic* 2005, 6, 720–724.

31 Thomsen, P., Roepstorff, K., Stahlhut, M., van Deurs, B., *Mol. Biol. Cell* 2002, 13, 238–250.

32 Kenworthy, A. K., Nichols, B. J., Remmert, C. L., Hendrix, G. M., Kumar, M., Zimmerberg, J., Lippincott-Schwartz, J., *J. Cell Biol.* 2004, 165, 735–746.

33 Adams, C. L., Chen, Y. T., Smith, S. J., Nelson, W. J., *J. Cell Biol.* 1998, 142, 1105–1119.

34 Bucci, C., Thomsen, P., Nicoziani, P., McCarthy, J., van Deurs, B., *Mol. Biol. Cell* 2000, 11, 467–480.

35 Chang, W. J., Rothberg, K. G., Kamen, B. A., Anderson, R. G. W., *J. Cell Biol.* 1992, 118, 63–69.

36 Hailstone, D., Sleer, L. S., Parton, R. G., Stanley, K. K.. *J. Lipid Res.* 1998, 39, 369–379.

37 Rodal, S. K., Skretting, G., Garred, O., Vilhardt, F., van Deurs, B., Sandvig, K., *Mol. Biol. Cell* 1999, 10, 961–974.

38 Mundy, D. I., Machleidt, T., Ying, Y., Anderson, R. G. W., Bloom, G. S., *J. Cell Sci.* 2002, 115, 4327–4339.

39 Stahlhut, M., van Deurs, B., *Mol. Biol. Cell* 2000, 11, 325–337.

40 Pelkmans, L., Zerial, M., *Nature* 2005, 436, 128–133.

41 Simionescu, M., Gafencu, A., Antohe, F., *Microsc. Res. Tech.* 2002, 57, 269–288.

42 Frøkjær-Jensen, J., *Prog. Appl. Microcirc.* 1983, 1, 17–34.

43 Frøkjær-Jensen, J., Wagner, R. C., Andrews, S. B., Hagman, P., Reese, T. S., *Cell Tissue Res.* 1988, 254, 17–24.

44 Bundgaard, M., Hagman, P., Crone, C., *Microvasc. Res.* 1983, 25, 358–368.

45 Predescu, S. A., Predescu, D. A., Palade, G. E., *Mol. Biol. Cell* 2001, 12, 1019–1033.

46 Schnitzer, J. E., Liu, J., Oh, P., *J. Biol. Chem.* 1995, 270, 14 399–14404.

47 Minshall, R. D., Tiruppathi, C., Vogel, S. M., Niles, W. D., Gilchrist, A., Hamm, H. E., Malik, A. B., *J. Cell Biol.* 2000, 150, 1057–1069.

48 Drab, M., Verkade, P., Elger, M., Kasper, M., Lohn, M., Lauterbach, B., Menne, J., Lindschau, C., Mende, F., Luft, F. C., Schedl, A. S., Haller, H., Kurzchalia, T. V., *Science* 2001, 293, 2449–2452.

49 Razani, B., Engelman, J. A., Wang, X. B., Schubert, W., Zhang, X. L., Marks, C. B., Macaluso, F., Russell, R. G., Li, M., Pestell, R. G., Di Vizio, D., Hou, H., Jr., Kneitz, B., Lagaud, G., Christ, G. J., Edelmann, W., Lisanti, M. P., *J. Biol. Chem.* 2001, 276, 38121–38138.

50 Goligorsky, M. S., Li, H., Brodsky, S., Chen, J., *Am. J. Physiol.* 2002, 283, F1-F10.

51 Schubert, W., Frank, P. G., Woodman, S. E., Hyogo, H., Cohen, D. E., Chow, C. W., Lisanti, M. P., *J. Biol. Chem.* 2002, 277, 40091–40098.

52 Pelkmans, L., Kartenbeck, J., Helenius, A., *Nature Cell Biol.* 2001, 3, 473–483.

53 Pelkmans, L., Puntener, D., Helenius, A., *Science* 2002, 296, 535–539.

54 Pelkmans, L., Helenius, A., *Traffic* 2002, 3, 311–320.

55 Huet, C., Ash, J. F., Singer, S. J., *Cell* 1980, 21, 429–438.

56 Marjomäki, V. S., Pietianen, V., Matilainen, H., Upla, P., Ivaska, J., Nissinen, L., Reunanen, H., Huttunen, P., Hyypia, T., Heino, J., *J. Virol.* 2002, 76, 1856–1865.

57 Upla, P., Marjomäki, V. S., Kankaanpaa, P., Ivaska, J., Hyypia, T., van der Goot, F. G., Heino, J., *Mol. Biol. Cell* 2004, 15, 625–636.

58 Eash, S., Querbes, W., Atwood, W. J., *J. Virol.* 2004, 78, 11 583–11590.

59 Helenius, A., Kartenbeck, J., Simons, K., Fries, E., *J. Cell Biol.* 1980, 84, 404–420.

60 Kee, S. H., Cho, E. J., Song, J. W., Park, K. S., Baek, L. J., Song, K., *J. Microbiol. Immunol.* 2004, 48, 823–829.

61 Grummer, B., Grotha, S., Greiser-Wilke, I. J., *Vet. Med. B Infect. Dis. Vet. Public Health* 2004, 51, 427–432.

62 Parton, R. G., Joggerst, B., Simons, K., *J. Cell Biol.* 1994, 127, 1199–1215.

63 Shin, J.-S., Abraham, S. N., *Immunology* 2001, 102, 2–7.

64 Shin, J.-S., Gao, Z., Abraham, S. N., *Science* 2000, 289, 785–788.

65 Shogomori, H., Futerman, A. H., *J. Biol. Chem.* 2001, 276, 9182–9188.

66 Torgersen, M. L., Skretting, G., van Deurs, B., Sandvig, K., *J. Cell Sci.* 2001, 114, 3737–3747.

67 Nichols, B. J., Kenworthy, A. K., Polishchuk, R. S., Lodge, R., Roberts, T. H., Hirschberg, K., Phair, R. D., Lippincott-Schwartz, J., *J. Cell Biol.* 2001, 153, 529–541.

68 Parton, R. G., *J. Histochem. Cytochem.* 1994, 42, 155–166.

69 Hansen, G. H., Dalskov, S. M., Rasmussen, C. R., Immerdal, L., Niels-Christiansen, L.-L., Danielsen, E. M., *Biochemistry* 2005, 44, 873–882.

70 Puri, V., Watanabe, R., Singh, R. D., Dominguez, M., Brown, J. C., Wheatley, C. L., Marks, D. L., Pagano, R. E., *J. Cell Biol.* 2001, 154, 535–547.

71 Orlandi, P. A., Fishman, P. H., *J. Cell Biol.* 1998, 141, 905–915.

72 Montesano, R., Roth, J., Robert, A., Orci, L., *Nature* 1982, 296, 651–653.

73 Matveev, S., Li, X., Everson, W., Smart, E. J., *Adv. Drug Deliv. Rev.* 2001, 49, 237–250.

74 Norkin, L. C., *Adv. Drug Deliv. Rev.* 2001, 49, 301–315.

75 Möbius, V., Herzog, V., Sandhoff, K., Schwarzmann, G., *J. Histochem. Cytochem.* 1999, 47, 1005–1014.

76 Kirkham, M., Fujita, A., Chadda, R., Nixon, S. J., Kurzchalia, T. V., Sharma, D. K., Pagano, R. E., Hancock, J. F., Mayor, S., Parton, R. G., *J. Cell Biol.* 2005, 168, 465–476.

77 Pang, H., Le, P. U., Nabi, I. R., *J. Cell Sci.* 2004, 117, 1421–1430.

78 Singh, R. D., Puri, V., Valiyaveettil, J. T., Marks, D. L., Bittman, R., Pagano, R. E., *Mol. Biol. Cell* 2003, 14, 3254–3265.

79 Roepstorff, K., Thomsen, P., Sandvig, K., van Deurs, B., *J. Biol. Chem.* 2002, 277, 18954–18960.

80 Sandvig, K., Olsnes, S., Brown, J. E., Petersen O. W., van Deurs, B., *J. Cell Biol.* 1989, 108, 1331–1343.

81 Sandvig, K., Garred, Ø., Prydz, K., Kozlov, J. V., Hansen, S. H., van Deurs, B., *Nature* 1992, 358, 510–511.

82 Sandvig, K., Grimmer, S., Lauvrak, S. U., Torgersen, M. L., Skretting, G., van

Deurs, B., Iversen, T. G., *Histochem. Cell. Biol.* 2002, 117, 131–141.

83 Subtil, A., Hémar, A., Dautry-varsat, A. J., *Cell Sci.* 1994, 107, 3461–3468.

84 Iversen, T.-G., Skretting, G., van Deurs, B., Sandvig, K., *Proc. Natl. Acad. Sci. USA* 2003, 100, 5175–5180.

85 Sandvig, K., Spilsberg, B., Lauvrak, S. U., Torgersen, M. L., Iversen, T.-G., van Deurs, B., *Int. J. Med. Microbiol.* 2004, 293, 483–490.

86 Massol, R. H., Larsen, J. E., Fujinaga, Y., Lencer, W. I., Kirchhausen, T., *Mol. Biol. Cell* 2004, 15, 3631–3641.

87 Damke, H., Baba, T., van der Bliek, A. M., Schmid, S. L., *J. Cell Biol.* 1995, 131, 69–80.

88 Llorente, A., Lauvrak, S. U., van Deurs, B., Sandvig, K., *J. Biol. Chem.* 2003, 278, 35850–35855.

89 Peters, P. J., Mironov, A., Peretz, D., van Donselaar, E., Leclerc, E., Erpel, S., DeArmond, S. J., Burton, D. R., Williamson, R. A., Vey, M., Prusiner, S. B., *J. Cell Biol.* 2003, 162, 703–717.

90 Nichols, B. J., *Nature Cell Biol.* 2002, 4, 374–378.

91 Pelkmans, L., Burli, T., Zerial, M., Helenius, A., *Cell* 2004, 118, 767–780.

92 Sharma, D. K., Choudhury, A., Singh, R. D., Wheatley, C. L., Marks, D. L., Pagano, R. E., *J. Biol. Chem.* 2003, 278, 7564–7572.

93 Di Guglielmo, G. M., Le Roy, C., Goodfellow, A. F., Wrana, J. L., *Nature Cell Biol.* 2003, 5, 410–421.

94 Hill, E., van Der Kaay, J., Downes, C. P., Smythe, E., *J. Cell Biol.* 2001, 152, 309–323.

95 Sever, S., Damke, H., Schmid, S. L., *Traffic* 2000, 1, 385–392.

96 Orth, J. D., Krueger, E. W., Cao, H., McNiven, M. A., *Proc. Natl. Acad. Sci. USA* 2002, 99, 167–172.

97 Jeng, R. L., Welch, M. D., *Curr. Biol.* 2001, 11, R691-R694.

98 Schafer, D. A., *Curr. Opin. Cell Biol.* 2002, 14, 76–81.

99 Yarar, D., Waterman-Storer, C. M., Schmid, S. L., *Mol. Biol. Cell* 2005, 16, 964–975.

100 Le, P. U., Guay, G., Altschuler, Y., Nabi, I. R., *J. Biol. Chem.* 2002, 277, 3371–3379.

101 Ros-Baro, A., Lopez-Iglesias, C., Peiro, S., Bellido, D., Palacin, M., Zorzano, A., Camps, M., *Proc. Natl. Acad. Sci. USA* 2001, 98, 12050–12055.

102 Lamaze, C., Dujeancourt, A., Baba, T., Lo, C.G., Benmerah, A., Dautry-Varsat, A., *Mol. Cell* 2001, 7, 661–671.

103 Hansen, S.H., Sandvig, K., van Deurs, B., *J. Cell Biol.* 1991, 113, 731–741.

104 Skretting, G., Torgersen, M.L., van Deurs, B., Sandvig, K., *J. Cell Sci.* 1999, 112, 3899–3909.

105 Damm, E.M., Pelkmans, L., Kartenbeck, J., Mezzacasa, A., Kurzchalia, T., Helenius, A., *J. Cell Biol.* 2005, 168, 477–488.

106 Sharma, D.K., Brown, J.C., Choudhury, A., Peterson, T.E., Holicky, E., Marks, D.L., Simari, R., Parton, R.G., Pagano, R.E., *Mol. Biol. Cell* 2004, 15, 3114–3122.

5
Role of Cholesterol in Signal Transduction from Caveolae

Christopher J. Fielding and Phoebe E. Fielding

5.1
Introduction

Caveolae are free cholesterol/sphingolipid (FC/SPH)-rich microdomains of the cell surface that are assembly sites for many transmembrane signaling complexes. Other proteins associated with caveolae include the transporters of some small ligands (glucose, inorganic ions) and catalysts of cell FC homeostasis. The highest levels of caveolae are found in differentiated primary cells, including pulmonary type-1 cells, adipocytes, endothelial cells, smooth muscle cells, and fibroblasts. In blood lymphocytes and many transformed and cancer cell lines, caveolae are sparse or may be completely absent.

While there is no broadly accepted nomenclature, many investigators now recognize two classes of FC/SPH-rich microdomains, caveolae and lipid rafts (Fig. 5.1) [1–3]. Caveolae are invaginated, and contain unique structural proteins (caveolins) that play an essential role in maintaining membrane curvature (see Chapter 2). The mean diameter of caveolar pits is ~60–80 Å. A second class of proteins (dynamins) is present in the necks of caveolae [4], but these are also present in other structures, such as clathrin-coated pits. The central role of caveolins-[particularly caveolin-1, the largest (22 kDa) caveolin-family protein] in maintaining the structure of caveolae is shown by their disappearance from the cell surface if the expression of caveolin is knocked down in wild-type cells [5]. This is confirmed by the absence of caveolae from caveolin-1 −/− cells [6,7]. The structural significance of FC in caveolae is shown by the flattening that first occurs when the plasma membrane is FC-depleted [8,9]. The caveolin skeleton remains at the cell surface. Caveolae reappear when FC is replaced in the plasma membrane. Additional loss of FC may be followed by disassembly of caveolin multimers [10]. Whilst the transfer of caveolin between the cell surface and intracellular pools can be demonstrated using inhibitors of microtubule assembly, it is unclear whether this normally occurs.

Under physiological conditions the caveolin skeleton at the surface of living cells appears to be relatively long-lived. Individual caveolae can be identified at the cell surface over periods of hours or days [11]. In contrast, FC and signaling proteins

Lipid Rafts and Caveolae. Christopher J. Fielding
Copyright © 2006 WILEY-VCH Verlag GmbH & Co. KGaA, Weinheim
ISBN: 3-527-31261-7

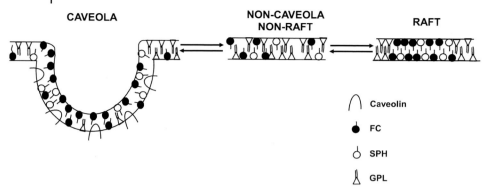

CAVEOLA   **NON-CAVEOLA NON-RAFT**   **RAFT**

Caveolin

FC

SPH

GPL

Fig. 5.1 The equilibrium between invaginated caveolae and planar lipid rafts. The model suggests that interconversion of lipid rafts and caveolae proceeds via equilibration in free-cholesterol (FC)-poor microdomains of the plasma membrane.

move in and out of caveolae much more rapidly (in some cases over a few minutes) in response to signal transduction, mitosis, and cell migration [12,13]. Caveolae are defined here as invaginated cell-surface microdomains stabilized with caveolin whose association with more labile complexes of lipids and other proteins responds to physiological stimuli. Almost all research investigations into the relationship between caveolin and FC have focused on caveolin-1.

Lipid rafts have a similar diameter to caveolae, but are planar and lack caveolin (see Fig. 5.1). Most studies of lipid rafts have been carried out in cells that lack appreciable levels of caveolin or caveolae; however, even in cells rich in caveolae, some caveolin-free lipid rafts are probably present. Glycosylphosphatidylinositol (GPI)-anchored proteins are enriched in lipid rafts, and reduced or absent in caveolae [1,2,14]. The lifetime of lipid rafts appears to be orders of magnitude less than that of caveolae. Single molecules of GPI-anchored protein move between rafts with a $t_{1/2}$ of seconds or minutes (see Chapter 3), though rafts incorporating multi-protein signaling complexes may be more stable. FC/SPH-rich microdomains with physical properties similar to those of lipid rafts form spontaneously in synthetic lipid bilayers to an extent dependent on the levels of FC and SPH, and reflecting the separation of a FC-rich liquid-ordered (L_o) phase [15–17]. In addition to GPI-anchored proteins, many acylated proteins are raft-associated. It seems likely that acylation is an important promoter of the association of signaling proteins in FC/SPH-rich raft membrane domains.

Much less is known of the organization of lipids in caveolae, but almost certainly there are significant differences from that in lipid rafts. In particular, it is not clear that the lipids of caveolae represent a L_o phase. This need not imply that there is no exchange of lipids between caveolae and rafts, but it could involve equilibration with non-raft membrane microdomains (see Fig. 5.1). The properties of caveolae and lipid rafts are reviewed in Chapters 2, 3, and 7. Here, the focus is on the regulatory role of FC, and in particular its interaction with signaling proteins and caveolin.

5.2
Lipids of Caveolae

The lipid composition of caveolae has been determined in only a few cases. The results of early studies in this area are difficult to interpret due to the presence of the detergents that are now recognized to modify the native distribution of lipids and proteins in membrane fractions [18]. A second problem has been the combination of caveolae and lipid rafts in a FC/SPH-rich "lipid raft" plasma membrane fraction, in which the contribution of caveolin-containing vesicles was undetermined. An additional variable has been the extent to which a "rim" of circumferential membrane and "neck" joining the caveolar bulb to the cell surface was included with the membrane "bowl" which made up the rest of the caveolar surface [1]. Recently, techniques for detergent-free isolation of caveolae from the cell surface have been described [19]. One detailed recent report is of the composition of caveolae from primary rat adipocytes [18]. These were purified from a total plasma membrane fraction by gradient ultracentrifugation, and then by immunoprecipitation with caveolin antibody.

Caveolae contain significantly higher levels of FC and sphingomyelin than do unfractionated plasma membranes. That of glycerophospholipids is essentially unchanged, so the total number of lipid molecules per unit area is increased (Fig. 5.2). The level of gangliosides is higher in caveolae than in plasma mem-

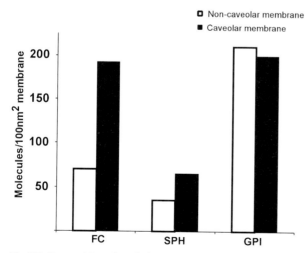

Fig. 5.2 Composition of total plasma membrane and purified caveolae from rat adipocytes. Data are expressed per 100 nm² plasma membrane (from [18]). FC = free cholesterol; SPH = sphingolipids; GPL = glycerophospholipids.

branes overall, though it represents only a small part (about 1%) of the total sphingolipid present. The major ganglioside of adipocytes is GM3. The same has been found for other differentiated peripheral cells rich in caveolae. GM1, though often identified as a specific marker for caveolae by its reaction with cholera toxin, in primary adipocytes was enriched only 2.6-fold in this fraction.

Additional analyses were reported from a line of human epidermal carcinoma (KB) cells stably transfected with mouse caveolin-1 cDNA [20]. The membrane fraction in this study was not immunopurified, and so probably included some caveolin-free lipid rafts. Nevertheless, as in the adipocyte study, the caveola-enriched fraction of KB cells contained increased levels of FC and sphingomyelin, relative to the rest of the plasma membrane. An unexpected finding was the enrichment there of arachidonyl ethanolamine plasmalogens, though this was also found in the raft fraction from a control, caveolin-free KB cell line.

Another unexpected finding was the rapidity with which FC moved between caveolae and other microdomains or extracellular acceptors in response to signal transduction [21]. FC was transferred readily to either cyclodextrin, a synthetic extracellular FC acceptor, or lipid-poor high-density lipoprotein, prebeta-HDL [22,23]. Dehydroergosterol, a fluorescent sterol marker for FC, was transferred more rapidly from of a caveola-rich fraction of fibroblast-derived l-cells than from other membrane domains [24]. In synthetic membranes, the effect of lowering FC is to decrease membrane stiffness and increase diffusion rates from the bilayer [25,26]. In contrast, FC depletion from caveola-rich membranes, which are linked to the sub-skeleton via the actin-family protein filamin [27] led to increased membrane stiffness [28,29].

Further evidence for a unique organization of FC in caveolae was presented in a recent study of the water permeability of caveolae from rat lung. This was 5- to 10-fold greater than that of noncaveolar membranes of comparable lipid composition [30]. Aquaporin has been reported in lung caveolae [31], but aquaporin did not significantly stimulate water flux in caveolae in this study [30]. If confirmed with caveolae from other cells, this observation could help to explain the rapid changes in FC in caveolae to physiological stimuli [21] compared to the stability of their caveolin skeleton [11]. FC-FC bonds within caveolae appear to be weaker than in other membrane microdomains.

Taken together, these data suggest that the organization of FC in caveolae and lipid rafts is fundamentally different. FC and SPH are enriched in both (relative to other membrane fractions), but within caveolae FC is labile not stabilized and the lipid bilayer is more, rather than less, permeable to water. The key factor may be that caveolin binds FC directly [31–33]. If this is correct, the properties of FC in lipid rafts would be determined mainly by its interaction with other lipids particularly SPH; in caveolae, they would be determined mainly by caveolin [13,33].

In addition to the major lipid classes (FC, sphingolipids, glycerolipids), caveolae also contain relatively high levels (compared to other plasma membrane fractions) of signaling lipids, including phosphatidic acid, diglyceride, ceramide and asialogangliosides. Most of these are probably generated *in situ* since caveolae are enriched in phospholipase D2 [34], lipid phosphate phosphohydrolase [35], sphingomyelinase and ceramidase [36,37] and sialidase [38] While the primary role of these lipids appears to be in signaling, some may also act locally to regulate the composition and properties of caveolae. Ceramide generated by extracellular bacterial sphingomyelinase reduced the interaction of FC and caveolin [39]; however, whether the low levels of bioactive lipids present under physiological conditions would be sufficient for such effects to be significant remains uncertain.

5.3
Proteins in Caveolae

Caveolar membranes contain one or more members of small (18–22 kDa), highly conserved proteins of the caveolin family of which caveolin-1 is the major structural protein of caveolae in cells other than striated muscle. It is present in two isoforms that may represent different gene transcripts [40]. The longer (α) isoform is the major species in most cells. A second family member (caveolin-2) plays a role at the cell surface that is secondary, because caveolae are not detected in caveolin-1 $-/-$ cells, despite the expression of caveolin-2 [41]. Caveolin-3 is the major caveolin of striated muscle cells [42]. A central domain in each caveolin (represented by residues 110–132 in caveolin-1) is highly hydrophobic. Both N- and C-termini are cytoplasmic [43]. This suggests that the protein penetrates (but does not traverse) the plasma membrane bilayer.

In fixed membranes from rat adipocytes or human fibroblasts, myc-tagged caveolin-1 was present in the necks but not the bulbs of caveolae [44]. In contrast, in quick-frozen unfixed membranes from 3T3-L1 mouse fibroblastic cells, caveolin-1 was identified as a belt around the caveolar bulb, but was absent from the neck that joins it to the plasma membrane [10]. In both cell lines, the depletion of membrane FC with an extracellular acceptor (cyclodextrin) led to disassembly of caveolin multimers and flattening.

The caveolin(82–101) domain has been implicated in self-recognition of caveolin monomers, leading to assembly of a supportive structural basketwork. Based on an estimate of the predicted α-helical content of the caveolin-1 peptide including residues 79–96, it was proposed that filaments made up of caveolin heptamers formed a basketwork surrounding the caveola [45]. However, short peptides can readily assume many different conformations, and secondary structure predictions for the 79–96 aa region in the context of the full primary sequence suggest a more complex structural situation. Other evidence discussed below suggests the presence of significant tertiary structure within the N-terminal half of caveolin-1. High-resolution three-dimensional structural analysis of caveolin will almost certainly be needed to distinguish these alternatives.

The composition of multi-protein complexes containing caveolin in living cells remains a contentious issue. Several dozens of proteins covering a wide range of functions at the cell surface have been identified at one time or another in purified membranes containing caveolae. It has been difficult to prove the existence of many of these in caveolae in living cells. Several factors have contributed to this situation. In earlier research, the range of factors that could modify native complexes in plasma membrane fractions, including detergents and cross-linking antibodies, was not fully appreciated. Major differences between cell lines in the protein composition of caveolae also were not recognized. Proteins in caveolae in primary cells may be found in caveolin-free lipid rafts or nonraft membrane domains in transformed and continuous cell lines, many of which express few, if any, caveolae [46–48]. Growth conditions can have major effects on the structure of caveolae, and on the distribution of caveolin between caveolae and other microdomains [49]. Expression of caveolin in cell lines that are normally caveolin-deficient (e.g., FRT cells) may lead to the appearance of only a few cell-surface caveolae; most of the caveolin expressed accumulates on intracellular membrane vesicles [50]. The sum of these factors means that the distribution of membrane proteins between caveolae and other cell-surface domains, and the influence of FC, is highly dependent on the cell or tissue used, technical details of fractionation, and the conditions of analysis.

This being said, certain classes of signaling proteins in tissues and primary cells have been repeatedly shown, by using several different techniques, to be reliably caveola-associated. The following criteria have been used in this chapter to assess if a multi-protein complex including caveolin represents a *bona fide* caveolar complex: co-localization with caveolin at the cell surface by confocal microscopy; recovery in caveolar vesicles in the absence of detergents; co-precipitation with caveolin antibodies from caveolae; and competitive displacement by caveolin peptides.

In addition to caveolin, caveolae contain other structural proteins which are insufficient by themselves to support membrane invagination, but are possibly important for the biological properties of these domains. Flotillins are a conserved protein family first identified as co-precipitates with caveolin in cells that had been extracted with Triton X-100 and octyl glucoside. Most recent research identifies these proteins mainly in association with GPI-anchored proteins in caveolin-free lipid rafts [51]. Annexins are Ca^{2+}-binding proteins. Annexin-2 forms a stable cytoplasmic chaperone complex with caveolin-1 in mammalian cells in culture and in zebrafish *in vivo* (see Chapter 8). However, the inclusion of these proteins in caveolae at the cell surface has not yet been conclusively shown.

It is a characteristic of many differentiated peripheral cells that mitosis is strongly dependent on the activity of protein growth factors. These serve as ligands for transmembrane receptors. The protein kinase activity of these receptors initiates signaling cascades that terminate in the activation of nuclear transcription factors. The anchorage-independent growth of virally-transformed and cancer cells reflects their independence from exogenous growth factors, consistent with the frequent reduction of caveolin in cancer cells, and the role proposed for caveolae in growth control and cell attachment [49,52]. Hyperplasia reported in multiple tissues in caveolin-1 −/− mice [6,7] similarly reflects the impairment of normal growth regulation.

Transmembrane signaling kinases have been localized to caveolae in many different peripheral cell lines, using many different criteria. Receptor proteins for the platelet-derived, epidermal and vascular endothelial growth factors (PDGF, EGF,

VEGF) co-purified with the caveolar membrane fraction, and were co-precipitated with caveolin-1 antibodies. PDGFR co-purified with caveolae in 3T3 cells [53,54], normal human fibroblasts [55] and human vascular smooth muscle cells [50]. EGFR co-purified with caveolae in primary human fibroblasts [55] and in a mouse fibroblast (3T3) line [56], but not laryngeal (Hep-2) or epidermal (A431) cancer cell lines [57,58]. VEGFR co-purified with caveolae and caveolin in both bovine aortic and human umbilical endothelial cells [59–61].

Additional evidence of a structural and functional association of caveolin with growth factors comes from studies of its (Y14)-phosphorylation, mediated by non-receptor c-Src family kinases, which are themselves substrates for the tyrosine kinase activities of PDGFR, EGFR, and VEGFR (see Chapter 6). These data provide strong support for the existence of functional complexes between caveolin-1, trans-membrane kinases, and nonreceptor signaling kinases such as c-Src and Fyn in living cells [62]. Membrane transporter proteins are also frequently recovered in preparations of caveolae. Glucose (Glut-4) transporters were localized to caveolae in 3T3 cells [63]. Potassium (K+(KATP), Na+, and Ca^{2+} channels were found in this fraction in SMC [64,65].

ATP-binding cassette transporter-A1 (ABCA1) ferries phospholipids and possibly FC across cell membranes, but it was not found with caveolin in detergent-extracted membranes [66]. However, the opposite result was more recently obtained, under detergent-free conditions, using the plasma membrane fraction of rat endothelial cells, after purification with caveolin antibody [67]. These contrasting data illustrate the ambiguity in protein composition data of caveolae from detergent-treated membranes.

Another recent study showed that a second ABC transporter (p-glycoprotein) can regulate the distribution of FC across the membrane bilayer [68]. The localization of p-glycoprotein to caveolae in primary tissues and cells has been shown in several studies. [47,69,70]. In contrast, in 2780AD ovarian carcinoma cells (which lack caveolae completely), p-glycoprotein was recovered with lipid rafts [71].

Several other proteins able to modify the level of plasma membrane FC have been identified less consistently in caveolae. Scavenger receptor BI (SR-BI) catalyzes the selective uptake of cholesteryl esters and FC from HDL. It also plays a key physiological role in supplying substrate for steroid hormone production by adrenal and gonadal cells. SR-BI was identified in the caveolae of both overexpressing Chinese hamster ovary (CHO) cells and mouse adrenal (Y1) cells on the basis of immunofluorescence co-localization [72]. A second study using SV-40 transformed human fibroblasts (WI38-VA13 cells) found little SR-BI in caveolae; the majority of this protein was in microvilli of the cell surface [73]. The transformed cells contained relatively few caveolae. In adrenal cells *in vivo*, SR-BI was mainly associated with a novel class of double-membrane channels associated with microvilli containing few, if any, caveolae [74]. The association of SR-BI with caveolae, when present, remains unsettled at this time. In contrast, the beta-subunit of ATP synthase, identified as a high-density lipoprotein (HDL) binding protein, was localized to caveolae, and immunoprecipitated with caveolin [75]. These data, and that relating to ABCA1 [67], suggest that caveolae may be able to regulate their own FC content.

One particularly well-characterized complex of caveolar lipids and proteins is that of FC with caveolin and endothelial nitric oxide synthase (eNOS) Numerous studies have shown the co-purification of eNOS and caveolin, and its inhibition of this activity by caveolin peptide [76–80] (see also Chapter 11).

Several proteins which control growth and differentiation by other pathways are also present in caveolae. These include receptors for bone morphogenetic proteins [81] and the cell-surface receptor proteins for estrogen and vitamin D, identical to the transcription factors regulated by these hormones in the nucleus [82,83].

To summarize, the distribution of proteins between different cell-surface domains in living cells is not maintained after detergent extraction. Even in the absence of detergents, the distribution of these proteins in continuous cell lines may be modified from that found in intact tissues and primary cells. Nevertheless, a subset of proteins is reproducibly associated with caveolae in tissues and primary cells. These include transmembrane signaling kinases, eNOS, and some membrane transporters. These caveola-associated proteins are characterized both by caveolin-binding, and a marked dependence on FC. The structural and functional relationship between these properties, and its implications, are considered in the following sections.

5.4
The Caveolin Scaffold Hypothesis

The scaffold hypothesis is a widely cited early interpretation of the link between caveolin and caveola-associated proteins [84]. This hypothesis proposes that proteins associated *in vivo* with caveolin can be identified by a "scaffold recognition" sequence that is responsible for their co-assembly, and identifies the protein-protein contact domain. Based on the selectivity of a peptide library, the scaffold sequence motif was identified as -$\Phi xx\Phi xxxx\Phi$-, $\Phi xxxx\Phi$ xxΦ- or -$\varphi x\varphi xxxx\varphi$- where Φ is an aromatic amino acid (F, W, or Y) and x is any residue. The orientation of the signature aromatic amino acids in these linear motifs varies, depending on whether it forms part of a loop, beta-sheet or alpha-helical sequence within the tertiary structure of the native protein.

In terms of this definition, caveolin itself contains a scaffold sequence or rather, two overlapping sequences (Fig. 5.3A). One of these overlaps a sequence (-K_{96}YW-FYR-) which is implicated in membrane binding ("membrane attachment sequence") [85]. GFP-caveolin peptide lacking this sequence retains about 50% of membrane binding. One scaffold sequence is mainly predicted as helix, the other as beta-sheet. The cav(82–101) domain also includes a "cholesterol recognition amino acid consensus (CRAC-1)" sequence -L/V(x_{1-4})Y (x_{1-4})K/R- [86] that partially overlaps the "scaffold" sequences.

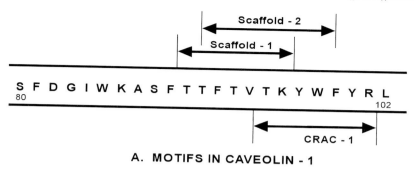

A. MOTIFS IN CAVEOLIN - 1

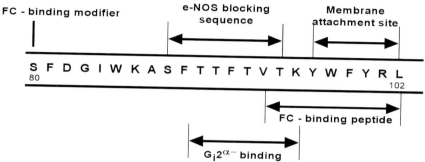

B. FUNCTIONAL SEQUENCES IN CAVEOLIN - 1

Fig. 5.3 (A) Location of predicted scaffold motifs and FC recognition sites of the cav(82–101) domain of human caveolin-1 (from [84,86]). (B) Location of amino acid residues needed for association G1α, eNOS, and FC with caveolin (from [80,82,85,96]).

5.4.1
Does the Scaffold Motif in Signaling Proteins that are Present in Caveolae Represent the Contact Site of these Proteins with Caveolin?

In the eNOS complex with caveolin (which is perhaps the best-studied example), the scaffold sequence is -F_{347}SAAPFSGW-. This was recently identified as part of an internal loop stabilizing the heme prosthetic group [87], and so it is unlikely to be accessible to caveolin [80]. -F_{656}SYVNPQF- in protein kinase C is within a closed conformation of the V5/C3/4 domain [88]. The scaffold sequence in endothelin receptor-A (ER-A, -WPFDHNDFGVF-) is part of extracellular loop-1 [89]. Since caveolin lacks an extracellular domain [43], the scaffold motif in ER-A cannot represent a functional protein-protein contact site. In other cases, structural information is inadequate to assign the location of the scaffold motif within the three-dimensional structure of the protein. Overall, however, the experimental data are lacking that, in a native complex of caveolar proteins, the "scaffold sequence" identifies a site that binds caveolin.

Table 5.1 Peptide contributions to free-cholesterol (FC)-binding sites.

Protein	Sequence	Reference
NPC2[a]	-V97KEEYPSIK-	91
StARD4[a]	-L210ANFYSDLRK-	92
RORα[a]	-L285ETCQYLR-	93
Benzodiazepine receptor[b]	-L150NYCVWR-	94
HIV-1 Nef[b]	-L HPEYYK-	95
Caveolin-1[b]	-V93TKYWFYR-	96

[a] From X-ray crystallography.
[b] From FC or sterol analogue-binding.

Another test of the scaffold hypothesis for signaling proteins can be made. Does the presence or absence of a scaffold sequence predict whether a cell membrane protein binds to caveolin? In Table 5.1, the frequency of scaffold sites was seen to be one per 541 amino acids within the primary sequence of caveola-associated signaling proteins. However, a quite similar incidence (one in 493 residues) was present in lipid-associated proteins not associated with caveolin or caveolae (NPC-1, HMG-CoA reductase, lecithin:cholesterol acyltransferase, acyl CoA cholesterol acyltransferase, clathrin heavy chain) (sequences data from GenBank). This finding argues strongly against the diagnostic significance of the scaffold motif in signaling proteins.

Two rather different questions relate the F,W,Y-rich "scaffold" sequences in caveolin.

- Is the domain of caveolin that includes these sequences the contact site with signaling proteins in caveolae?
- If so, are the aromatic amino acids that define the scaffold sequence necessary for this contact?

There can be little doubt that the central domain of caveolin (cav82–101) is somehow important in both promoting protein-protein and protein-lipid associations in caveolae. Evidence supporting this includes its ability both *in vitro* [90] and *in vivo* [78] to compete with caveolin to affect signal protein binding and activity (Table 5.1). But is it the pattern of three aromatic residues that is important?

Inconsistent with the scaffold hypothesis, alanine-scanning mutagenesis showed that an intact scaffold sequence was not required for caveolin-derived peptides to bind to G1α [84]. Within the cav(82–101) domain, only residues -F_{92}TVT- were needed for binding activity (Fig. 5.3B). Nor was a complete scaffold sequence required to compete with caveolin in displacing eNOS [80]. In a third case, that of adenyl cyclase [90], a different pattern of amino acids, including elements of the FC recognition site, was needed for caveolin binding.

Though information of this same kind is needed for additional proteins, the data so far argue against the significance of a meaningful "scaffold sequence." Proteins bound to caveolin are no more likely to include a scaffold sequence than other proteins. The scaffold sequences in caveolin appears to be parts of a broader pattern of amino acids within the cav(82–101) domain responsible both for the association of caveolin with signaling proteins, and with FC.

5.5
FC Binding by Proteins Including Caveolin

In contrast to reviews of protein-protein and protein-DNA binding, very few studies have been made of the structural aspects of FC binding to proteins. The sum of evidence available suggests that FC lies within a hydrophobic cleft or tunnel, the sides of which are composed of several different hydrophobic sequences organized by the tertiary structure of the native protein. A positively charged amino acid (K or R) may contribute to a "charge clamp" stabilizing the 3β-OH group. Whilst the volume of FC has been estimated at 741 $Å^3$ [91], its binding cavity is usually about twice as large. There is evidence in some instances that FC itself induces significant changes in the shape and size of this cavity. In the case of many of the FC-binding proteins for which a tertiary structure has been established, one of the hydrophobic sequences contributing to the FC-binding cavity conforms to the "cholesterol recognition" consensus motif (-V/L_{x1-4} Y_{x1-4} K/R-) [86] (Table 5.1).

The caveolin central domain (cav82–101) also contains a cholesterol recognition sequence (CRAC-1) (Fig. 5.3B) that binds FC [96]. The isolated peptide also binds FC from FC/phosphatidylcholine vesicles to an extent that exceeds FC solubility in the lipid bilayer. This result, based on tryptophan fluorescence and NOESY data, indicates the ability of the peptide to induce macromolecular order in FC, possibly by stabilizing FC-FC links [97]. The sequence required for FC binding (-V94TKYWFYR-) abuts the residues in cav(82–101) needed for interaction with signal proteins Gi2α [80] and eNOS [76]. A key question considered later is whether the binding of protein and FC to the same domain is complementary or competitive.

Although residues 94–101 within the caveolin(83–102) peptide promote binding with synthetic FC-containing liposomes, it seems likely that additional hydrophobic residues contribute to membrane binding by caveolin *in vivo*. Phosphorylation at S80 has a substantial effect on FC binding [50], suggesting a role for neighboring hydrophobic residues within the sequence -S80FDGLW-. In contrast, phosphorylation at Y14 completely inhibited FC binding, which may indicate that the short hydrophobic sequence -L13YTV- may also contribute. Though the data remain limited, it seems likely that the structural basis of FC binding in caveolin resembles that in other proteins.

Do other proteins present in caveolae bind FC? A number of caveolin-associated proteins crosslink to the photoactivable FC analogue FCBP [13], and many caveolin-associated proteins including eNOS and PDGFR include one or more "cho-

Table 5.2 Effects of FC depletion (↓) and cav (82–101) on activities of caveolar proteins.

Activity	Effect of FC ↓	Addition of cav (82–101)	Reference(s)
Neutral ceramidase	↑		109
Adenyl cyclase	↓	↓	90
Ca^{2+}-act K^+ channel	↑		64
TGFbeta-1 receptor	↑		110
Ca^{2+}-dependent PLA2	↓	↓	111, 112
Ca^{2+}-ATPase	↓		113
ERK1/2	↓		114
p-glycoprotein	↓		115
Agonist stim cAMP accum	↑		116
Insulin receptor	↓		117
eNOS	↓	↓	80, 118
PKCα translocation	↓	↓	119, 120

FC was depleted from cultured cells with beta-methyl cyclodextrin. Cav (82–101) was determined either *in vitro* in cultured cell homogenates, or *in vivo* as a complex with a cell-permeable antennopedia peptide.

lesterol recognition" motifs within the primary sequence, though at present experimental data showing if these sequences are involved in FC binding are lacking.

5.6
FC in Caveolae: Effects of Depletion and Loading

It is characteristic of proteins in caveolae that their activities are very sensitive to membrane levels of FC. In some cases these activities are increased, in other cases inhibited, when FC is depleted (Table 5.2). Addition of the cav(82–101) peptide – either *in vitro* or *in vivo* – spliced to an antennopedia (AP) "Trojan peptide" [78] also affects the activity of caveola-associated signaling proteins. In those examples where comparative data are available, the addition of peptide (at 10–100 µM) in each case mimics the effect of FC depletion. Is this coincidence, or informative about the role of FC in this system?

One way to look at the role of FC in caveolar signaling is to modify the level of FC, and to determine the effects of this on the activity of caveola-associated proteins. Much of the research on the influence of FC on caveolae has been carried out with cyclodextrins, cyclic oligosaccharides containing six to eight α-1,4-linked-glycopyranoside units enclosing a central hydrophobic tunnel [98]. These bind

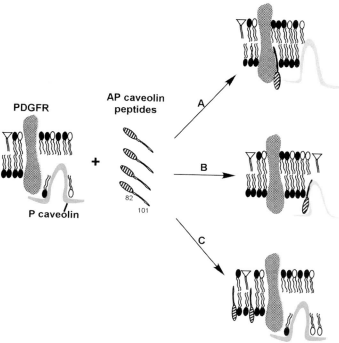

Fig. 5.4 Alternative mechanisms for the effects of caveolin(82–101) peptide on functional multiprotein complexes in caveolae. Mechanisms shown: A = displacement of caveolin from signaling kinase (PDGFR) by anteonnopedia (AP)-linked caveolin(82–101) peptide. B = displacement of PDGFR from its association with caveolin by AP peptide binding to caveolin. C = the same AP-peptide acting as a sink for caveolar FC.

small hydrophobic molecules in a reaction depending on the replacement of core water molecules by the organic ligand. β-Methyl and β-hydroxypropyl cyclodextrins have an internal cavity of ~0.8 nm. They interact with FC, but not with other common membrane lipids. Consequently, FC-free cyclodextrins are effective and selective receptor-independent acceptors of cell FC by diffusion. Conversely, pre-formed cyclodextrin-FC complexes, or low-density lipoprotein (LDL), can donate FC to increase levels of FC-rich microdomains, including caveolae. Decreased FC mediated by cyclodextrin led to the dissociation of signaling proteins from caveolae, disassembly of caveolin multimers [10] and eventually, to a reduction in the rate of caveolin synthesis by transcriptional down-regulation [99]. In human primary fibroblasts and smooth muscle cells the chronic effects of FC loading included an increase in cell-surface caveolae by transfer of caveolin from intracellular pools [49], increased endocytosis of FC-rich vacuoles [100] and, over time, the induction of caveolin synthesis at the transcriptional level by a FC-sensitive promoter site [101,102]. In human primary endothelial cells, an increase in caveolin at the cell surface in response to LDL was drawn mainly from intracellular pools [103]. These data suggest that the presence of FC is closely linked to both the structure and function of caveolae.

Three different mechanisms could give rise to the displacement by caveolin peptide(82–101) of signaling proteins from their complex with caveolin (Fig. 5.4):

1. Caveolin peptide(82–101) competes with the target kinase, binding caveolin and generates free kinase.
2. Caveolin peptide(82–101) competes with caveolin to bind the target kinase.
3. Caveolin peptide(82–101) binds FC competitively, displacing it from caveolin, secondarily dissociating the caveolin-kinase complex.

Since peptides cav(1–101) and cav(1–79) polymerize similarly *in vitro* [45], FC-binding to cav (82–101) [96] is unlikely to play a direct role in caveolin self-assembly. These data argue against the first hypothesis. Since the cav(82–101) peptide mimics caveolin and, like the full-length protein, binds FC, it is difficult to envisage a mechanism by which cav(82–101) would reverse the effect of native caveolin. Other evidence supports the hypothesis that cav(82–101) may mimic cyclodextrin by binding FC competitively. The relatively high concentrations of this freely internalized peptide required for maximal effect (50–100 µM) would be adequate to bind significant amounts of plasma membrane FC. F_{92} of intact caveolin is necessary for the effect of peptide on eNOS [80], and the same residue is required for FC binding [96]. We suggest that the scaffold peptide cav(82–101) may act at least in part to competitively sequester caveolar FC.

5.7
FC Changes in Caveolae: Effects of Signal Transduction

The metabolic effects of chronic changes in the FC content of the caveolae can be explained in terms of competition between binding of protein and binding of FC to overlapping sequences within a central (resides 82–101) domain of caveolin, However the content of FC in caveolae also responds both spatially and temporally to physiological changes at the cell surface, in particular to the binding of protein growth factors. Could these changing FC levels be involved in regulating the magnitude and duration of signal transduction and possibly, in the case of branching pathways, its selectivity?

The mechanism of signal transduction via protein growth factors and transmembrane receptor kinases is well understood in outline. Ligand binding is coupled to dimerization of the receptor protein, receptor autophosphorylation, and induction of its activity with downstream kinases, particularly proteins of the c-Src family (see Chapter 6). This leads to dissociation of signaling proteins from the cell surface and eventually, to transcriptional activation of a specific pattern of genes important in mitosis. A consistent feature of ACTH, PDGF, -EGF, VEGF, insulin and insulin-like growth factor-mediated signaling is that receptor autophosphorylation is followed by the generation of p(Y_{14})caveolin, the synthesis of which is

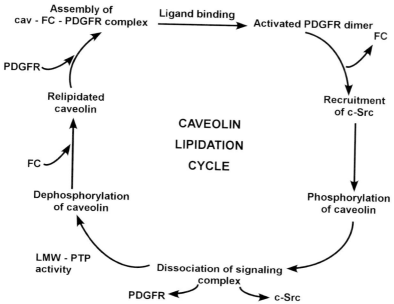

Fig. 5.5 A multistage caveolin lipidation cycle to explain the roles of FC at different points in signal transduction from caveolae. LMW-PTP = low molecular-weight phosphotyrosine phosphatase (from [121]).

mediated by c-Src or a Src-family kinase such as Fyn [50,104–108]. This observation provides *prima facie* evidence for the existence of signaling complexes containing bound caveolin.

In the case of PDGFR, signal transduction was recently shown to be associated with a loss of FC binding to caveolin, assayed either by co-purification of ^{3}H-FC with caveolin, or by the formation of stable crosslinks between caveolin and a photoactivable FC analogue, FCBP [50]. A comparable change occurs when VEGF activates its receptor in human aortic endothelial cells, and confirms that the association of FC with caveolin is quite labile. Even though <1% of caveolin was associated with PDGFR, a maximum of 70–80% of caveolin-associated FC was lost in the course of signal transduction. This is consistent with the concept that FC bound to caveolin has higher-order effects on membrane FC in caveolae. Reassembly of the PDGFR signaling complex requires the re-establishment of FC levels in the caveola (Fig. 5.5). Studies of the time course of signaling in the presence and absence of inhibitors of specific kinases and phosphatases, and substitution within caveolae of mutant caveolins with altered polarity and FC binding properties, were carried out.

The yield of caveolin-associated ^{3}H-FC or -FCBP under different conditions was assayed. Recovery of the FC content of caveolae following exposure to PDGF took 30–40 min at 37 °C. The cell became responsive again to PDGF only after the FC content of its caveolae was completely recovered. If the activity of the caveola-associated low molecular-weight phosphotyrosine phosphatase was inhibited by hydrogen peroxide [121], p(Y_{14})caveolin accumulated and the caveola did not recover its reactivity with PDGF. If caveolin(S80A), which binds FC more tightly than the native protein [50] was overexpressed, then although PDGF bound normally to its receptor, FC was not displaced from this caveolin, and the signal was not propagated from the PDGF receptor (PDGFR) to c-Src and to caveolin. These data suggest that, at different steps, FC has positive and negative roles. The presence of FC is required for the assembly of the transmembrane signaling complex; after ligand binding, loss of FC is required for signal transduction. Following signal transduction, FC re-enters the caveola. These observations are incorporated into Fig. 5.5:

1. A signaling complex containing at a minimum caveolin, FC, a transmembrane receptor kinase, a Src-family non-receptor kinase is first assembled within caveolae. At least in SMC, caveolin is constitutively phosphorylated at S_{80}, influencing FC binding to the cav(82–101)
2. Addition of ligand leading to receptor and downstream receptor kinase activation displaces FC from its binding site. Mutant Caveolin(S80A), which cannot be phosphorylated, does not release FC and signal transduction is inhibited.
3. Loss of FC from caveolin precedes p(Y_{14})-caveolin synthesis mediated by c-Src or Src-family kinase. Since the level of p-caveolin, which is normally low, is dynamically regulated by caveolar LMW-PTP, the rise in p-caveolin which follows the loss of FC must be the result of either the dissociation of this phosphatase, or its inhibition *in situ*. These alternatives have not yet been distinguished. p-Caveolin synthesis in response to PDGF was not associated with any detectable disassembly of caveolin oligomers, or withdrawal of caveolin from the cell surface. This is in contrast to what occurs when p(Y_{14})-caveolin is chronically increased – for example by vanadate, a nonspecific phosphotyrosine phosphatase inhibitor.
4. After dissociation of both FC and downstream kinases, LMW-PTP is reactivated, and reduces p-caveolin levels to baseline. Levels of total caveolin continue unchanged.
5. FC levels in caveolae (and those of FCBP in cells equilibrated with this photoactivable FC analogue) are restored only after p-caveolin is hydrolyzed. In cells exposed to peroxide, phosphocaveolin levels were maintained at their maximum; FC was not restored to caveolae, and the cells remained insensitive to PDGF.
6. Finally (at ca. 30 min following initial exposure to PDGF) the cell regains responsiveness to ligand.

These data indicate that the overall equilibrium between FC-associated and FC-free caveolin in caveolae is influenced by phosphorylation of both receptor protein and caveolin at different points in the signaling reaction.

5.8
Summary

FC binding to caveolin plays important structural and functional roles in caveolae. Structurally, it is needed to maintain the invaginated form of these microdomains. Functionally, FC sensitively regulates the activity of caveolin-associated proteins including signaling kinases, transporters and eNOS. At the molecular level, these effects are mediated by competition between adjacent caveolin-protein and caveolin-FC binding sites.

Abbreviations

ABCA1	ATP-binding cassette transporter-A1
AP	antennopedia
CHO	Chinese hamster ovary
CRAC	cholesterol recognition amino acid consensus
EGF	epidermal growth factor
eNOS	endothelial nitric oxide synthase
ER-A	endothelin receptor-A
FC/SPH	free cholesterol/sphingolipid
GPI	glycosylphosphatidylinositol
HDL	high-density lipoprotein
PDGF	platelet-derived growth factor
PDGFR	PDGF receptor
SR-BI	scavenger receptor BI
VEGF	vascular endothelial growth factor

References

1 Schnitzer JE, McIntosh DP, Dvorak AM, Liu J and Oh P (1995) Separation of caveolae from associated microdomains of GPI-anchored proteins. *Science* 269, 1435–1439.

2 Abrami L, Fivaz M, Kobayashi T, Kinoshita T, Parton RG and van der Groot FG (2001) Cross-talk between caveolae and glycosylphosphatidylinositol-rich domains. *J. Biol. Chem.* 276, 30729–30736.

3 Sowa G, Pypaert M and Sessa WC (2001) Distinction between signaling mechanisms in lipid rafts vs caveolae. *Proc. Natl. Acad. Sci. USA* 98, 14072–14077.

4 Oh P, McIntosh DP and Schnitzer JE (1998) Dynamin at the neck of caveolae mediates their budding to form transport vesicles by GTP-driven fission from the plasma membrane of endothelium. *J. Cell Biol.* 141, 101–114.

5 Griffoni C, Spisni E, Santi S, Riccio M, Guarnieri T and Tomasi V (2000) Knockdown of caveolin-1 by antisense oligonucleotides impairs angiogenesis in vitro and in vivo. *Biochem. Biophys. Res. Commun.* 276, 756–761.

6 Drab M, Verkade P, Elger M, Kasper M, Lohn M, Lauterbach B, Menne J, Lindschau C, Mende F, Luft FRC, Schedl A, Haller H, Kurzchalia TV (2001) Loss of caveolae, vascular dysfunction, and pulmonary defects in caveolin-1 gene disrupted mice. *Science* 293, 2449–2452.

7 Razani B, Engelman JA, Wang XB, Schubert W, Zhang XL, Marks CB, Macaluso F, Russell RG, Li M, Pestell RG, Di Vizio D, Hou H, Kneitz B, Lagaud G, Christ GJ, Edelmann W and Lisanti MP (2001) Caveolin-1 null mice are viable but show evidence of hyperproliferative and vascular abnormalities. *J. Biol. Chem.* 276, 38121–38138.

8 Parpal S, Karlsson M, Thorn H, Stralfors P (2001) Cholesterol depletion disrupts caveolae and insulin receptor signaling for metabolic control via insulin receptor substrate-1, but not for mitogen-activated protein kinase control. *J. Biol. Chem.* 276, 9670–9678.

9 Dreja K, Volstedlind M, Vinten J, Tranum-Jensen J, Hellstrand P and Sward K (2002) Cholesterol depletion disrupts caveolae and differentially impairs agonist-induced arterial contraction. *Arterioscler. Thromb. Vasc. Biol.* 22, 1267–1272.

10 Westermann M, Steiniger F and Richter W (2005) Belt-like localization of caveolin in deep caveolae and its redistribution after cholesterol depletion. *Histochem. Cell Biol.* May 12, e-pub.

11 Thomsen P, Roepstorff K, Shahlhut M and van Deurs B (2002) Caveolae are highly immobile plasma membrane microdomains, which are not involved in constitutive endocytic trafficking. *Mol. Cell Biol.* 13, 238–250.

12 Liu P, Wang P, Michaely P, Zhu M and Anderson RGW (2000) Presence of oxidized cholesterol in caveolae uncouples active platelet-derived growth factor receptors from tyrosine kinase substrates. *J. Biol. Chem.* 275, 31648–31654.

13 Fielding PE, Russel JS, Spencer TA, Hakamata H, Nagao K and Fielding CJ (2002) Sterol efflux to apolipoprotein A-1 originates from caveolin-rich microdomains and potentiates PDGF-dependent protein kinase activity. *Biochemistry* 41, 4929–4937.

14 Kirkham M, Fujita A, Chadda R, Nixon SJ, Kurzchalia TV, Sharma DK, Pagano RE, Hancock JF, Mayor S and Parton RG (2005) Ultrastructural identification of uncoated caveolin-independent early endocytic vesicles. *J. Cell Biol.* 168, 465–476).

15 Dietrich C, Volovyk ZN, Levi M, Thompson NL and Jacobson K (2001) Partitioning of Thy-1, GM1 and cross-linked phospholipid analogs into lipid rafts reconstituted in supported model membrane monolayers. *Proc. Natl. Acad. Sci. USA* 98, 10642–10647.

16 Dietrich C, Bagatolli LA, Vovovyk ZN, Thompson NL, Levi M, Jacobson K and Gratton E (2001) *Biophys. J.* 3, 1417–1428.

17 Sheets ED, Lee GM, Simson R and Jacobson K (1997) Transient confinement of a glycophosphatidylinositol-anchored protein in the plasma membrane. *Biochemistry* 41, 12449–12458.

18 Ortegren U, Karlsson M, Blazic N, Blomqvist M, Nystrom FH, Gustavsson J, Fredman P and Stralfors P (2004) Lipids and glycosphingolipids in caveolae and surrounding plasma membrane of primary adipocytes. *Eur. J. Biochem.* 271, 2028–2036.

19 Smart EJ, Ying YS, Mineo C, Anderson RGW (1995) A detergent-free method for purifying caveolae membrane from tissue culture cells. *Proc. Natl. Acad. Sci. USA* 92, 10104–10108.

20 Pike LJ, Han X, Chung KN and Gross RW (2002) Lipid rafts are enriched in arachidonic acid and plasmenylethanolamine and their composition is independent of caveolin-1 expression: a quantitative electrospray ionization/mass spectrometric analysis. *Biochemistry* 41, 2075–2088.

21 Fielding CJ and Fielding PE (2004) Membrane cholesterol and the regulation of signal transduction. *Biochem. Soc. Trans.* 32, 65–69.

22 Dreja K, Voldstedlund M, Vinten J, Tranum-Jernsen J, Hellstrand P and Sward K (2002) Cholesterol depletion disrupts caveolae and differentially impairs agonist-induced arterial contraction. *Arterioscler. Thromb. Vasc. Biol.* 22, 1267–1272.

23 Fielding PE and Fielding CJ (1995) Plasma membrane caveolae mediate the efflux of cellular free cholesterol. *Biochemistry* 34, 14288–14292.

24 Gallegos AM, McIntosh AL, Atshaves BP and Schroeder F (2004) Structure and cholesterol domain dynamics of an enriched caveolae/lipid raft isolate. *Biochem. J.* 382, 451–461.

25 Song J and Waugh RE (1993) Bending rigidity of SOPC membranes containing cholesterol. *Biophys. J.* 64, 1967–1970.

26 Lundback JA, Birn P, Girsshman J, Hansen AJ and Anderson OS (1996) Membrane stiffness and channel function. *Biochemistry* 35, 3825–3830.

27 Stahlhut M and van Deurs B (2000) Identification of filamin as a novel ligand for caveolin-1: evidence for the organization of caveolin-associated membrane domains by the actin cytoskeleton. *Mol. Biol. Cell* 11, 325–337.

28 Kwik J, Boyle S, Fooksman D, Margolis L, Sheetz MP and Edidin M (2003) Membrane cholesterol, lateral mobility, and the phosphatidylinositol 4,5-bisphosphate-dependent organization of cell actin. *Proc. Natl. Acad. Sci. USA* 24, 13964–13969.

29 Byfield FJ, Aranda-Espinoza H, Romanenko VG, Rothblat GH and Levitan I (2004) Cholesterol depletion increases membrane stiffness of aortic endothelial cells. *Biophys. J.* 87, 3336–3343.

30 Hill WG, Almasri E, Ruiz WG, Apodaca G and Zeidel ML (2005) Water and solute permeability of rat lung caveolae: high permeabilities explained by acyl chain unsaturation. *Am. J. Physiol. Cell Physiol.* 289, C33-C41.

31 Schnitzer JE and Oh P (1996) Aquaporin-1 in plasma membrane and caveolae provides mercury-sensitive water channels across lung endothelium. *Am. J. Physiol.* 270, H416-H422.

32 Murata M, Peranen J, Schriener R, Wieland F, Kurzchalia TV and Simons K (1995) VIP21/caveolin is a cholesterol-binding protein. *Proc. Natl. Acad. Sci. USA* 92, 10339–10343.

33 Li S, Song KS and Lisanti MP (1996) Expression and characterization of recombinant caveolin. Purification by polyhistidine tagging and cholesterol-dependent incorporation into defined lipid membranes. *J. Biol. Chem.* 271, 568–573.

34 Cho CH, Lee CS, Chang M, Jang IH, Kin SJ, Hwang I, Ryu SH, Lee CO and Koh GY (2004) Localization of VEGFR-2 and PLD-2 in endothelial caveolae is involved in VEGF-induced phosphorylation of MEK and ERK. *Am. J. Physiol.* 286, H1881–H1888.

35 Nanjundan N and Possmayer F (2001) Pulmonary lipid phosphate phosphohydrolase in plasma membrane signaling platforms. *Biochem. J.* 358, 637–646.

36 Veldman RJ, Maestre N, Aduib OM, Medin JA, Salvayre R and Levade T (2001) A neutral sphingomyelinase residues in sphingolipid-enriched microdomains and is inhibited by the caveolin-scaffolding domain: potential implications in tumor necrosis factor signaling. *Biochem. J.* 355, 859–868.

37 Romiti E, Meacci E, Tanzi G, Becciolini L, Mitsutake S, Farnararo M, Ito M and Bruni P (2001) Localization of neutral ceramidase in caveolin-enriched light membranes of murine endothelial cells. *FEBS Lett.* 506, 163–168.

38 Wang Y, Yamaguchi K, Wada T, Hata K, Zhao X, Fujimoto T and Miyagi T (2002) A close association of the ganglioside-specific sialidase Neu3 with caveolin in membrane microdomains. *J. Biol. Chem.* 277, 26252–26259.

39 Yu C, Alterman M and Dobrowsky RT (2005) Ceramide displaces cholesterol from lipid raft membranes and decreases the association of the cholesterol binding protein caveolin-1. *J. Lipid Res.* May, e-pub.

40 Kogo H and Fujimoto T (2000) Caveolin-1 isoforms are encoded by distinct mRNAs. Identification of mouse caveolin-1 mRNA variants caused by alternative transcription initiation and splicing. *FEBS Lett.* 465, 119–123.

41 Prolini I, Sargiacomo M, Galbiati F, Rizzo G, Grignani F, Engelman JA, Okamoto T, Ikezu T, Scherer PE, Mora R, Rodriguez-Boulan E, Peschle C and Lisanti MP (1999) Expression of caveolin-1 is required for the transport of caveolin-2 to the plasma membrane. Retention of caveolin-2 at the level of the Golgi complex. *J. Biol. Chem.* 274, 25718–25725.

42 Way M and Parton RG (1995) M-caveolin, a muscle-specific caveolin-related protein. *FEBS Lett.* 376, 108–112.

43 Dupree P, Parton RG, Raposo G, Kurzchalia TV and Simons K (1993) Caveolae and sorting in the trans-Golgi network of epithelial cells. *EMBO J.* 12, 1597–1605.

44 Thorn H, Stenkula KG, Karlsson M, Ortegren U, Nystrom FH, Gustavsson J and Stralfors P. Cell surface orifices of caveolae and localization of caveolin to the necks of caveolae in adipocytes. *Mol. Biol. Cell* 14, 3967–3976.

45 Fernandez I, Ying Y, Albanesi J and Anderson RGW (2002) Mechanism of caveolin filament assembly. *Proc. Natl. Acad. Sci. USA* 99, 11193–11198.

46 Koleske AJ, Baltimore D and Lisanti MP (1995) Reduction of caveolin and caveolae in oncogenically transformed cells. *Proc. Natl. Acad. Sci. USA* 92, 1381–1385.

47 Lavie Y, Fiucci G and Liscovitch M (1998) Up-regulation of caveolae and caveolar constituents in multi-drug resistant cancer cells. *J. Biol. Chem.* 273, 32380–32383.

48 Lee SW, Reimer CL, Oh P, Campbell DB and Schnitzer JE (1998) Tumor cell growth inhibition by caveolin re-expression in human breast tumor cells. *Oncogene* 16, 1391–1397.

49 Thyberg J (2002) Caveolae and cholesterol distribution in vascular smooth muscle cells of different phenotypes. *J. Histochem. Cytochem.* 50, 185–195.

50 Fielding PE, Chau P, Liu D, Spencer TA and Fielding CJ (2004) Mechanism of platelet-derived growth factor-dependent caveolin-1 phosphorylation: relationship to sterol binding and the role of serine-80. *Biochemistry* 43, 2578–2586.

51 Stuermer CA and Plattner H. (2005) The 'lipid raft' microdomain proteins reggie-1 and reggie-2 (flotillins) are scaffolds for protein integration and signaling. *Biochem. Soc. Symp.* 72, 109–118.

52 Fielding CJ, Bist A and Fielding PE (1999) Intracellular cholesterol transport in synchronized human skin fibroblasts. *Biochemistry* 38, 2506–2513.

53 Yamamoto M, Toya Y, Jensen RA and Ishikawa Y (1999) Caveolin is an inhibitor of platelet-derived growth factor receptor signaling. *Exp. Cell Res.* 247, 380–388.

54 Matveev SV and Smart EJ (2002) Heterologous desensitization of EGF receptors and PDGF receptors by sequestration in caveolae. *Am. J. Physiol.* 282, C935–C946.

55 Liu P, Ying Y, Ko YG and Anderson RGW (1996) Localization of platelet-derived growth factor-stimulated phosphorylation cascade to caveolae. *J. Biol. Chem.* 271, 10299–10303.

56 Park WY, Cho KA, Park JS, Kim DI and Park SC (2001) Attenuation of EGF signaling in senescent cells by caveolin. *Ann. N. Y. Acad. Sci.* 928, 79–84.

57 Ringerike T, Blystad FD, Levy FO, Madshus IH and Stang E (2002) Cholesterol is important in control of EGF receptor kinase activity but EGF receptors are not concentrated in caveolae. *J. Cell Sci.* 115, 1331–1340.

58 Ringerike T, Blystad FD, Levy FO, Madshus IH and Stang E (2002) Cholesterol is important in control of EGF receptor kinase activity but EGF receptors are not concentrated in caveolae. *J. Cell Sci.* 115, 1331–1340.

59 Labrecque L, Royal I, Surprenant DS, Patterson S, Gingras D and Beliveau R (2003) Regulation of vascular endothelial growth factor receptor-2 activity by caveolin-1 and plasma membrane cholesterol. *Mol. Biol. Cell* 14, 334–347.

60 Ikeda S, Ushio-Fukai M, Zuo L, Tojo T, Dikalov S, Patrushev NA and Alexander RW (2005) Novel role for ARF6 in vascular endothelial growth factor-induced signaling and angiogenesis. *Circ. Res.* 96, 467–475.

61 Cho CH, Lee CS, Chang M, Jang IH, Kim SJ, Hwang I, Ryu SH, Lee CO and Koh GY (2004) Localization of VEGFR-2 and PLD2 in endothelial caveolae is involved in VEGF-induced phosphorylation of MEK and ERK. *Am. J. Physiol.* 286, H1881–H1888.

62 Sanguinetti AR, Caoi H, Mastick CC (2003) Fyn is required for oxidative and hyperosmotic-stress-induced tyrosine phosphorylation of caveolin-1. *Biochem. J.* 376, 159–168.

63 Shigematsu S, Watson RT, Khan AH and Pessin JE (2003) The adipocyte plasma membrane caveolin functional/structural organization is necessary for the efficient endocytosis of GLUT-4. *J. Biol. Chem.* 278, 10683–10690.

64 Wang XL, Ye D, Peterson TE, Cao S, Shah VH, Katusic ZS, Sieck GC and Lee HC (2005) Caveolae targeting and regulation of large conductance Ca(2+)-activated K+ channels in vascular endothelial cells. *J. Biol. Chem.* 280, 11656–11664.

65 Sampson LJ, Hayabuchi Y, Standen NB and Dart C (2004) Caveolae localize protein kinase A signaling to arterial ATP-sensitive potassium channels. *Circ. Res.* 95, 1012–1018.

66 Mendez AJ, Lin G, Wade DP, Lawn RM and Oram JF (2001) Membrane domains distinct from cholesterol/sphingomyelin-rich rafts are involved in the ABCA1-me-

diated lipid secretory pathway. *J. Biol. Chem.* 276, 3158–3166.

67 Chao WT, Tsai SH, Lin YC, Lin WW and Yang VC (2005) Cellular localization and interaction of ABCA1 and caveolin-1 in aortic endothelial cells after HDL incubation. *Biochem. Biophys. Res. Commun.* 332, 743–749.

68 Garrigues A, Escargueil AE and Orlowski S (2002) The multidrug transporter, P-glycoprotein, actively mediates cholesterol redistribution in the cell membrane. *Proc. Natl. Acad. Sci. USA* 99, 10 347–10 352.

69 Demeule M, Jodoin J, Gingras D and Beliveau R (2000) P-glycoprotein is localized in caveolae in resistant cells and in brain capillaries. *FEBS Lett.* 466, 219–224.

70 Jodoin J, Demeule M, Fenart L, Cecchelli R, Farmer S, Linton KJ, Higgins CF and Beliveau R (2003) *J. Neurochem.* 87, 1010–1023.

71 Hinrichs JW, Klappe K, Hummel I and Kok JW (2004) ATP-binding cassette transporters are enriched in non-caveolar detergent-insoluble glycosphingolipid-enriched membrane domains (DIGs) in human multidrug-resistant cancer cells. *J. Biol. Chem.* 279, 5734–5738.

72 Babitt J, Trigatti B, Rigotti A, Smart EJ, Anderson RGW, Xu S and Krieger M (1997) Murine SR-BI, a high density lipoprotein receptor that mediates selective lipid uptake, is N-glycosylated and fatty acylated and colocalizes with plasma membrane caveolae. *J. Biol. Chem.* 272, 13242–13249.

73 Peng Y, Akmentin W, Connelly MA, Lund-Katz S, Phillips MC and Williams DL (2004) Scavenger receptor BI (SR-BI) clustered on microvillar extensions suggests that this plasma membrane domain is a way station for cholesterol trafficking between cells and high density lipoproteins. *Mol. Biol. Cell* 15, 384–396.

74 Azhar S, Nomoto A and Reaven E (2002) Hormonal regulation of adrenal microvillar channel formation. *J. Lipid Res.* 43, 861–871.

75 Chatenay-Rivauday C, Cakar ZP, Jeno P, Kuzmenko ES and Fiedler K (2004) Caveolae: biochemical analysis. *Mol. Biol. Rep.* 31, 67–84.

76 Garcia-Cardena G, Fan R, Stern DF, Liu J and Sessa WC (1996) Endothelial nitric oxide synthase is regulated by tyrosine phosphorylation and interacts with caveolin-1. *J. Biol. Chem.* 271, 27237–27240.

77 Ghosh S, Gachhui R, Crooks C, Wu C, Lisanti MP and Stuehr DJ (1998) Interaction between caveolin-1 and the reductase domain of endothelial nitric oxide synthase. Consequences for catalysis. *J. Biol. Chem.* 273, 22267–22271.

78 Bucci M, Gratton JP, Rudic RD, Acevedo L, Roviezzo F, Cirino G and Sessa WC (2000) In vivo delivery of the caveolin-1 scaffolding domain inhibits nitric oxide synthesis and reduces inflammation. *Nature Med.* 6, 1362–1267.

79 Gratton JP, Fontana J, O'Connor DS, Garcia-Cardena G, McCabe TJ and Sessa WC (2000) Reconstitution of an endothelial nitric oxide synthase (eNOS), hsp90, and caveolin-1 complex in vitro. Evidence that hsp90 facilitates calmodulin-stimulated displacement of eNOS from caveolin-1. *J. Biol. Chem.* 275, 22268–22272.

80 Bernatchez PN, Bauer PM, Yu J, Prendergast JS, He P and Sessa WC (2005) Dissecting the molecular control of endothelial NO synthase by caveolin-1 using cell-permeable peptides. *Proc. Natl. Acad. Sci. USA* 102, 761–766.

81 Nohe A, Keating E, Underhill TM, Knaus P and Pedersen NO (2005) Dynamics and interaction of caveolin-1 isoforms with BMP-receptors. *J. Cell Sci.* 118, 643–650.

82 Razandi M, Oh P, Pedram A, Schnitzer J and Levin ER (2002) Ers associate with and regulate the production of caveolin: implications for signaling and cellular actions. *Mol. Endocrinol.* 16, 100–115.

83 Huhtakangas JA, Olivera CJ, Bishop JE, Zanello LP and Norman AW (2004) The vitamin D receptor is present in caveolae-enriched plasma membranes and binds 1-alpha,25(OH)2-vitamin D in vivo and in vitro. *Mol. Endocrinol.* 18, 2660–2671.

84 Couet J, Li S, Okamoto T, Ikezu T and Lisanti MP (1997) Identification of peptide and protein ligands for the caveolin-scaffolding domain. Implications for the interaction of caveolin with caveolae-associated proteins. *J. Biol. Chem.* 272, 6525–6533.

85 Woodman SE, Schlegel A, Cohen AW and Lisanti MP (2002) Mutational analysis identifies a short atypical membrane

attachment sequence (KYWFYR) within caveolin-1. *Biochemistry* 41, 3790–3795.

86 Jamin N, Neumann JM, Ostuni MA, Vu TK, Yao ZX, Murail S, Robert JC, Giatzakis C, Papadopoulos V and Lacapere JJ (2005) Characterization of the cholesterol recognition amino acid consensus sequence of the peripheral-type benzodiazepine receptor. *Mol. Endocrinol.* 19, 588–594.

87 Raman CS, Li H, Martasek P, Kral V, Masters BS and Poulos TL (1998) Crystal structure of constitutive endothelial nitric oxide synthase: a paradigm for pterin function involving a novel metal center. *Cell* 95, 939–950.

88 Bornancin F and Parker PJ (1997) Phosphorylation of protein kinase C-alpha on serine 657 controls the accumulation of active enzyme and contributes to its phosphatase-resistant state. *J. Biol. Chem.* 272, 3544–3549.

89 Orry AJ and Wallace BA (2000) Modelling and docking the endothelin G-protein-coupled receptor. *Biophys. J.* 79, 3083–3094.

90 Toya Y, Schwencke C, Couet J, Lisanti MP and Ishikawa Y (1998) Inhibition of adenyl cyclase by caveolin peptides. *Endocrinology* 139, 2025–2031.

91 Friedland N, Lious HL, Lobel P, Stock AM (2003) Structure of a cholesterol-binding protein deficient in Niemann-Pick type C2 disease. *Proc. Natl. Acad. Sci. USA* 100, 2512–2517.

92 Romanowski MJ, Soccio RE, Breslow JL and Burley SK (2002) Crystal structure of the *Mus musculus* cholesterol-regulated START protein 4 (StarD4) containing a StAR-related lipid transfer domain. *Proc. Natl. Acad. Sci. USA* 99, 6949–6954.

93 Kallen JA, Schaeppi JM, Bitsch F, Geisse S, Geiser M, Delhon I and Fournier B (2002) X-ray structure of the hROR alpha LBD at 1.63Å: structural and functional data that cholesterol or a cholesterol derivative is the natural ligand of RORalpha. *Structure* 10, 1697–1707.

94 Jamin N, Neumann JM, Ostuni MA, Vu TK, Yao ZX, Murail S, Robert JC, Giatzakis C, Papadopoulos V and Lacapere JJ (2005) Characterization of the cholesterol recognition amino acid consensus se-

quence of the peripheral-type benzodiazepine receptor. *Mol. Endocrinol.* 19, 588–594.

95 Zheng YH, Plemenitas A, Fielding CJ and Peterlin BM (2003) Nef increases the synthesis of and transports cholesterol to lipid rafts and HIV-1 progeny virus. *Proc. Natl. Acad. Sci. USA* 100, 8460–8465.

96 Epand RM, Sayer BG and Epand RF (2005) Caveolin scaffolding region and cholesterol-rich domains in membranes. *J. Mol. Biol.* 345, 339–350.

97 Harris JS, Epps DE, Davio SR and Kezdy FJ (1995) Evidence for transbilayer, tail-to-tail cholesterol dimmers in dipalmitoylglycerophosphocholine liposomes. *Biochemistry* 34, 3851–3857.

98 Jensen KJ and Brask J (2005) Carbohydrates in peptide and protein design. *Biopolymers.* May 31, e-pub.

99 Hailstones D, Sleer LS, Parton RG and Stanley KK (1998) Regulation of caveolin and caveolae by cholesterol in MDCK cells. *J. Lipid Res.* 39, 369–379.

100 Sharma DK, Brown JC, Choudhury A, Peterson TE, Holicky E, Marks DL, Simari R, Parton RG and Pagano RE (2004) Selective stimulation of caveolar endocytosis by glycosphingolipids and cholesterol. *Mol. Cell. Biol.* 15, 3114–3122.

101 Fielding CJ, Bist A and Fielding PE (1997) Caveolin mRNA levels are up-regulated by free cholesterol and down-regulated by oxysterols in fibroblast monolayers. *Proc. Natl. Acad. Sci. USA* 94, 3753–3758.

102 Bist A, Fielding PE and Fielding CJ (1997) Two sterol regulatory element-like sequences mediate up-regulation of caveolin gene transcription in response to low density lipoprotein free cholesterol. *Proc. Natl. Acad. Sci. USA* 94, 10693–10698.

103 Zhu Y, Liao HL, Wang N, Yuan Y, Ma KS, Verna L and Stemerman MB (2000) Lipoprotein promotes caveolin-1 and Ras translocation to caveolae: role of cholesterol in endothelial signaling. *Arterioscler. Thromb. Vasc. Biol.* 20, 2465–2470.

104 Colonna C and Podesta EJ (2005) ACTH-induced caveolin-1 tyrosine phosphorylation is related to podosome assembly in Y1 adrenal cells. *Exp. Cell Res.* 304, 432–442.

105 Lee H, Volonte D, Galbiati F, Iyengar P, Lublin DM, Bregman DB, Wilson MT, Campos-Gonzalez R, Bouzahzah B, Pestell RG, Scherer PE and Lisanti MP (2000) constitutive and growth factor-regulated phosphorylation of caveolin-1 occurs at the same site (Tyr-14) in vivo. *Mol. Endocrinol.* 14, 1750–1775.

106 Labrecque L, Nyalendo C, Langlois S, Durocher Y, Roghi C, Murphy G, Gingras D and Beliveau R (2004) Sr-c-mediated tyrosine phosphorylation of caveolin-1 induces its association with membrane type 1 matrix metalloproteinase. *J. Biol. Chem.* 279, 52132–52140.

107 Maggi D, Biedi C, Segat D, Barbero D, Panetta D and Cordera R (2002) IGF-1 induces caveolin 1 tyrosine phosphorylation and translocation in the lipid rafts. *Biochem. Biophys. Res. Commun.* 295, 1085–1089.

108 Kimura A, Mora S, Shigematsu S, Pessin JE and Saltiel AR (2002) The insulin receptor catalyzes the tyrosine phosphorylation of caveolin-1. *J. Biol. Chem.* 277, 30153–30158.

109 Romiti E, Meacci E, Donati C, Formigli L, Zecchi-Orlandini S, Farnararo M, Ito M and Bruni P (2003) Neutral ceramidase secreted by endothelial cells is released in part associated with caveolin-1. *Arch. Biochem. Biophys.* 417, 27–33.

110 Stehr M, Estrada CR, Khoury J, Danciu TE, Sullivan MP, Peters CA, Solomon KR, Freeman MR and Adam RM (2004) Caveolae are negative regulators of transforming growth factor-beta1 signaling in urethral smooth muscle cells. *J. Urol.* 172, 2451–2455.

111 Graziani A, Bricko V, Carmignani M, Graier WF and Groschner K (2004) Cholesterol- and caveolin-rich membrane domains are essential for phospholipase A2-dependent EDHF formation. *Cardiovasc. Res.* 64, 234–242.

112 Gaudreault SB, Chabot C, Gratton JP and Poirier J (2004) The caveolin scaffolding domain modifies 2-amino-3-hydroxy-5-methyl-4-isoxazole propionate receptor binding properties by inhibiting phospholipase A2 activity. *J. Biol. Chem.* 279, 356–362.

113 Tortelote GG, Valverde RH, Lemos T, Guilherme A, Einicker-Lamas M and Vieyra A (2004) The plasma membrane Ca^{2+} pump from proximal kidney tubules is exclusively localized and active in caveolae. *FEBS Lett.* 576, 31–35.

114 Zeidan A, Broman J, Hellstrand P and Sward K (2003) Cholesterol dependence of vascular ERK1/2 activation and growth in response to stretch: role of endothelin-1. *Arterioscler. Thromb. Vasc. Biol.* 23, 1528–1534.

115 Troost J, Lindenmaier H, Haefeli WE and Weiss J (2004) Modulation of cellular cholesterol alters p-glycoprotein activity in multidrug-resistant cells. *Mol. Pharmacol.* 66, 1332–1339.

116 Rybin VO, Xu X, Lisanti MP and Steinberg SF (2000) Differential targeting of beta-adrenergic receptor subtypes and adenyl cyclase to cardiomyocyte caveolae. A mechanism to functionally regulate the cAMP signaling pathway. *J. Biol. Chem.* 275, 41447–41457.

117 Parpal S, Karlsson M, Thorn H and Stralfors P (2001) Cholesterol depletion disrupts caveolae and insulin receptor signaling for metabolic control via insulin receptor substrate-1, but not for mitogen-activated protein kinase control. *J. Biol. Chem.* 276, 9670–9678.

118 Blair A, Shaul PW, Yuhanna IS, Conrad PA and Smart EJ (1999) Oxidized low density lipoprotein displaces endothelial nitric oxide synthase (eNOS) from plasmalemmal caveolae and impairs eNOS activation. *J. Biol. Chem.* 274, 32512–32519.

119 Niggli V, Meszaros AV, Oppliger C and Tornay S (2004) Impact of cholesterol depletion on shape changes, actin reorganization, and signal transduction in neutrophil-like HL-60 cells. *Exp. Cell Res.* 296, 358–368.

120 Taggart MJ, Leavis P, Feron O and Morgan KG (2000) Inhibition of PKCalpha and rhoA translocation in differentiated smooth muscle by a caveolin scaffolding domain peptide. *Exp. Cell Res.* 258, 72–81.

121 Caselli A, Taddei ML, Manao G, Camici G and Ramponi G (2001) Tyrosine-phosphorylated caveolin is a physiological substrate of the low M(r) phosphotyrosine phosphatase. *J. Biol. Chem.* 276, 18849–18854.

6

Phosphorylation of Caveolin and Signaling from Caveolae

Cynthia Corley Mastick, Amy Sanguinetti, Haiming Cao, and Suhani Thakker

6.1
Introduction

Caveolae are specialized invaginated domains of the plasma membrane that act as organizing centers for signaling molecules. Caveolae are formed in membranes by the caveolins, a family of three related gene products (caveolins-1, -2, and -3) [1–4]. Caveolins form homo- and hetero-oligomers that make up the characteristic striated coat of caveolae [5]. Expression of caveolin is necessary and sufficient to induce cell-surface caveolae [6–8]. In addition to their role as coat proteins that drive the invagination of caveolae, the caveolins are also cholesterol-binding proteins, and caveolae are highly enriched in cholesterol, glycolipids and sphingolipids, forming a distinctive domain in the membrane. Lipid-modified signaling molecules, including the tandemly acylated Src-family kinases, are enriched in these structures due to their affinity for the lipid composition of these domains. However, cholesterol-enriched lipid-ordered domains, or "rafts" also form independently of caveolae [9]. The caveolins direct the composition of the signaling complexes organized in caveolae by acting as scaffolding proteins that bind to specific signaling molecules, which include Ga_{q11}, endothelial nitric oxide synthase (eNOS), and Src-family kinases [10–13].

In addition to organizing signaling complexes, the caveolins also participate directly in signaling cascades as substrates for both tyrosine and serine/threonine kinases. Caveolin-1 is phosphorylated on a single tyrosine residue (Tyr14) in the amino-terminus of the protein. This residue is constitutively phosphorylated at low levels in most cell types, and its phosphorylation increases in response to a number of stimuli, including insulin and insulin mimetics (IGF-1, sulfonylureas, phosphoinositolglycan), angiotensin II, endothelin-1, adrenocorticotropin (ACTH), platelet-derived growth factor (PDGF), vascular endothelial growth factor (VEGF), and epidermal growth factor (EGF) (in cells expressing very high levels of the EGF receptor or expressing mutant forms of the EGF receptor) [14–27]. Phosphorylation at Tyr14 is also increased in response to cellular stresses, including shear stress, apoptotic stress, ultraviolet radiation, oxidative stress, and osmotic shock [24,28–34], in response to integrin activation (i.e., during plating and spreading on

Lipid Rafts and Caveolae. Christopher J. Fielding
Copyright © 2006 WILEY-VCH Verlag GmbH & Co. KGaA, Weinheim
ISBN: 3-527-31261-7

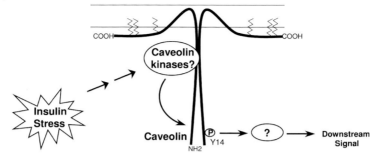

Fig. 6.1 Signaling pathways leading to and from caveolin phosphorylation. Hypothesis to be explored: insulin and stress activate a caveolin-directed tyrosine kinase localized in the caveolae. Upon activation, this kinase phosphorylates caveolin-1 on Tyr14 (pY14). This leads to activation of downstream signaling cascades.

fibronectin) [24,34], and when caveolae are triggered to internalize [35–37]. In response to some stimuli, such as insulin, oxidative stress and osmotic shock, the increase in caveolin phosphorylation is robust and sustained, whilst in response to other stimuli, such as shear stress, PDGF and VEGF, the increase is less intense and is transient. Caveolin-1 is also phosphorylated on up to five serine/threonine residues in response to various stimuli [26,31,38,39]. Caveolin-2 is phosphorylated on two tyrosine residues in its amino-terminal domain, Tyr 19 and Tyr27 [40–43]. Tyr27 in caveolin-2 falls within an amino acid sequence (YADP) that is very similar to Tyr14 in caveolin-1 (YTVP), and phosphocaveolin-2 is found in complexes with phosphocaveolin-1. Caveolin-3 lacks a site for tyrosine phosphorylation in its amino-terminal domain, and it has not been reported to be phosphorylated on either tyrosine or serine.

The goals of our research in this area have been to: 1) trace the signal transduction pathways that lead to caveolin tyrosine phosphorylation; and 2) identify signaling cascades that lie downstream of caveolin phosphorylation. These two areas will form the focus of this chapter (Fig. 6.1). In a very satisfying way, the investigations in these two areas have come together to provide a very clear picture of at least one of the roles of caveolin phosphorylation and caveolae in cells.

6.2
Signaling Pathways Leading to Caveolin Tyrosine Phosphorylation

6.2.1
Caveolins-1 and -2 are Phosphorylated in Response to Insulin in Adipocytes

Whilst caveolae are found in many tissues, they are particularly abundant in lung epithelial cells, endothelial cells, muscle cells, and adipocytes [1,3,4]. In adipocytes, they cover a significant fraction (ca. 30%) of the total inner cell surface of the plasma membrane [44]. In addition, the expression of caveolins-1 and -2 increases approximately 20-fold upon adipocyte differentiation, with a concomitant 10-fold increase in cell-surface caveolae [15,45,46]. Consistent with an important role for caveolae in adipocyte function, adipose tissue is significantly disrupted in caveolin-1 knockout animals [47–49].

Early studies on isolated caveolin-enriched cell fractions had implicated caveolae in cellular signaling [50–54]. The abundance of caveolae in adipocytes and muscle – two of the major target tissues for insulin – together with their potential role in signaling, suggested that they might play a role in insulin signal transduction. To investigate this, a simple question was asked: Does stimulation of adipocytes with insulin lead to an increase in the phosphorylation of any proteins associated with caveolae? It was found that, in adipocytes, insulin stimulates the tyrosine phosphorylation of three proteins in caveolae: caveolin-1, caveolin-2, and a 29-kDa caveolin-associated protein [14,15]. These three proteins are found in SDS-resistant complexes and can be co-immunoprecipitated. Caveolin phosphorylation shows two additional interesting properties. The first is that it shows specificity for insulin, and does not occur in adipocytes in response to two other growth factors, PDGF and EGF, despite the expression of active receptors for all three growth factors in these cells. This is interesting because stimulation of glucose metabolism also shows specificity for insulin in these cells. Insulin stimulates glucose transport, glycogen synthesis, and lipogenesis ten to hundreds of fold, while EGF and PDGF have no effect on these processes [55]. The second interesting property of insulin-stimulated caveolin phosphorylation is that it is cell type- dependent: it occurs only in the fully differentiated 3T3-L1 adipocytes, not in the preadipocytes, despite the expression of both caveolin and active insulin receptor in both cell types. In fact, caveolin is not phosphorylated in response to insulin in fibroblast cells engineered to express high levels of the insulin receptor. Differentiation dramatically increases the insulin responsiveness of glucose metabolism in these cells [56]. Unlike phosphorylation of the caveolins, the 29-kDa caveolin-associated protein was phosphorylated in response to PDGF as well as in response to insulin, and this phosphorylation occurred in both adipocytes and preadipocytes [14,20]. At present, the identity of this protein is unknown, but this result indicates that other growth factors also signal through tyrosine phosphorylation of caveolar proteins.

6.2.2
The Caveolins are not Direct Substrates of the Insulin Receptor

Insulin binding to its receptor at the cell surface causes a conformational change in the intracellular domain of the receptor, leading to auto-transphosphorylation of the receptor. This autophosphorylation in turn activates the kinase domain, leading to the phosphorylation of direct substrates, including insulin receptor substrate-1 (IRS-1). Since the insulin receptor is associated with caveolae [14,57,58], it was possible that caveolin was a direct substrate of the insulin receptor itself. Several lines of evidence indicate that this is not the case, however [14,15]. First, although caveolin co-fractionates with the insulin receptor, caveolin is phosphory-lated *in vitro* under conditions where the insulin receptor in these fractions is completely inactive (i. e., in the absence of insulin). Therefore, caveolin co-purifies with a caveolin-tyrosine kinase that is not the insulin receptor. A second line of evidence comes from the differentiation dependence of caveolin phosphorylation. Both adipocytes and preadipocytes express caveolin-1, and caveolin-1 co-purifies with caveolin-directed tyrosine kinase activity in both cell types. Adipocytes and preadipocytes both express active insulin receptors that phosphorylate direct sub-strates such as IRS-1 equally well. The insulin receptor co-fractionates with cav-eolins in both cell types. However, insulin stimulates caveolin phosphorylation only in adipocytes, not in preadipocytes. The cell type dependence of caveolin phosphorylation strongly indicates that the insulin receptor is not the insulin-stimulated caveolin tyrosine kinase, and that differentiation leads to the expression of signaling molecules that lie downstream of the insulin receptor and couple activation of the insulin receptor to activation of the caveolin tyrosine kinase.

6.2.3
Src-Family Kinases and Stress-Induced Caveolin Phosphorylation

Signal transduction via transmembrane receptor tyrosine kinases often involves the activation of additional downstream kinases, both serine/threonine-directed and tyrosine-directed. A number of studies have implicated Src-family kinases in tyrosine phosphorylation of caveolin-1. Caveolin-1 was originally identified as a major tyrosine-phosphorylated protein in v-Src-transformed cells [1,39,59,60]. Cav-eolin is also highly phosphorylated in cells that overexpress c-Src or c-Fyn, and is one of the most prominent phosphoproteins detected in these cells [15,16,31,61]. Caveolin-1 binds to and co-purifies with Src-family kinases [10,52,62,63]. Further-more, caveolin-1 can be directly phosphorylated by Src and Fyn *in vitro* [16,64]. These data indicated that Src and Fyn are caveolin tyrosine kinases in cells.

Caveolin-1 is phosphorylated in response to a number of cellular stresses, in-cluding shear stress, oxidative stress, and osmotic shock [24,28–32,34]. These stresses also activate Src-family kinases, including both Src and Fyn [31,34,65–67]. While overexpression of either kinase is sufficient to cause caveolin tyrosine phos-phorylation under basal conditions, overexpression of Fyn also caused significant hyperphosphorylation of caveolin-1 in response to stress [31]. Therefore, whilst overexpression can activate Fyn to some extent, stress clearly activates the kinase. These data indicate that Fyn is part of the signaling cascade leading to caveolin tyrosine phosphorylation in response to stress. Consistent with this, expression of kinase-inactive Src blocked caveolin phosphorylation in response to osmotic shock [29]. Furthermore, the small molecule Src-family kinase inhibitors SU6656, PP2, and PD180970 inhibited both oxidative stress and osmotic shock-induced caveolin phosphorylation, indicating that both require activation of a Src-family kinase [31]. Shear stress-induced caveolin phosphorylation was blocked by the small molecule Src-family kinase inhibitor PP1, and enhanced by inactivation of Csk, a negative regulator of Src-family kinases [34]. Consistent with the inhibitor data, both oxidative stress and osmotic shock-induced caveolin phosphorylation were blocked in SYF$^{-/-}$ cells, a cell line derived from a knockout animal deficient in three Src-family kinases: Src, Yes, and Fyn [31]. These data show that stress-induced caveolin phosphorylation requires activation of a Src-family kinase.

Using cell lines derived from single kinase knockout mice (Src$^{-/-}$, Yes$^{-/-}$, and Fyn$^{-/-}$), it was found that expression of Fyn is required for both oxidative stress and osmotic shock-induced caveolin phosphorylation, while expression of Src and Yes are not [31]. In fact, phosphorylation in the Src$^{-/-}$ cells was even higher than that observed in the cells from wild-type mice. This correlated with an increase in Fyn expression in these cells relative to wild-type cells. Heterologous expression of Fyn was sufficient to restore oxidative stress-induced caveolin phosphorylation in both the Fyn$^{-/-}$ and SYF$^{-/-}$ cells, indicating that Fyn can promote the phosphorylation of caveolin in the absence of Src or Yes. Therefore, Fyn expression is both necessary and sufficient for stress-induced caveolin phosphorylation.

Both Src and Fyn can directly phosphorylate caveolin, and both are activated in response to stress, but only Fyn is required for stress-induced caveolin phosphorylation. These data suggest that the Src that is activated in response to stress is localized to a compartment that does not contain caveolin [31]. Fyn is targeted to caveolae/lipid rafts due to tandem acylation by myristate and palmitate. Co-localization of dually acylated proteins such as Lyn or Fyn with caveolin has recently been confirmed using fluorescence resonance energy transfer (FRET) [63]. In contrast to Fyn, Src is only singly acylated with myristate. Singly acylated proteins have less affinity for membranes and do not co-purify with caveolae/lipid rafts [52,68]. The behavior of singly acylated proteins, such as Src, was not determined in the FRET experiment. However, Src can bind directly to caveolin [10]. The present data suggest that there are distinct signaling complexes containing caveolin and Fyn or caveolin and Src that are differentially activated in response to stress. In the context of cellular stress, Fyn – but not Src – is a caveolin tyrosine kinase. However, Src may phosphorylate caveolin under other types of stimuli, for example during cell attachment and spreading on fibronectin [24].

6.2.4
Non-Receptor Tyrosine Kinases and Insulin-Induced Caveolin Phosphorylation

Significant data had linked activation of Src-family kinases to caveolin phosphorylation. Therefore, it was initially hypothesized that a Src-family kinase was the insulin-stimulated caveolin-tyrosine kinase in adipocytes. Consistent with this, treatment of isolated caveolar fractions with Src-family kinase inhibitors blocked caveolin phosphorylation *in vitro*, indicating that the caveolin kinase activity that co-purifies with caveolin is a Src-family kinase (CCM, unpublished observation; [16]). (These inhibitors did not block Src-family kinase activation in intact adipocytes as measured by kinase autophosphorylation. In contrast, inhibition of autophosphorylation was readily detectable in fibroblasts. This is a common problem in adipocytes. Compounds that are sufficiently lipophilic to cross membranes are often sequestered within the prominent fat droplets in these cells.) The most abundant Src-family kinase that co-purifies with caveolin-1 in adipocytes is Fyn [14,15,69]. Fyn is activated in response to insulin via Src-homology 2 (SH2) domain-mediated binding to IRS-1 [70]. To determine if Fyn was involved in insulin-stimulated caveolin tyrosine phosphorylation, Fyn was overexpressed in adipocytes [15]. Overexpression of Fyn was sufficient to induce caveolin tyrosine phosphorylation under basal conditions, and hyperphosphorylation of caveolin-1 in response to insulin. These results verify that Fyn is activated in response to insulin, and that it is part of the signaling cascade leading to caveolin tyrosine phosphorylation in response to insulin. However, differentiation does not change the level of expression of Fyn, and Fyn co-localizes with caveolin-1 in both pre-adipocytes and adipocytes. Furthermore, overexpression of Fyn in fibroblasts did not increase basal caveolin phosphorylation or reconstitute insulin-stimulated phosphorylation. These data indicate that, while Fyn is a part of the insulin-stimulated caveolin phosphorylation pathway in adipocytes, differentiation induces the expression of an additional protein or proteins required for caveolin tyrosine phosphorylation.

An additional line of evidence suggested that a second non-receptor tyrosine kinase may be involved in caveolin phosphorylation. The phosphorylation site on caveolin-1 (Tyr14, L-**Y**-T-V-P) is not in the context of a consensus Fyn phosphorylation site (I/L-**Y**-D/E-X-L). Tyr14 lies within the motif I/L-**Y**-X-X-P, a consensus Abl phosphorylation site [71,72]. Tyr27 in caveolin-2 falls within a similar sequence (E-**Y**-A-D-P). It has not been determined whether insulin activates Abl in adipocytes, although several known Abl substrates are phosphorylated in response to insulin, including Crk, Cbl, and Dok [73,74]. In addition, the Crk binding partner CAS is dephosphorylated in response to insulin, consistent with Abl activation [75]. Importantly, differentiation of 3T3-L1 fibroblasts into adipocytes leads to a large increase in Abl expression (CCM, unpublished observation), which may account for the cell type dependence of insulin-stimulated caveolin phosphorylation.

6.2.5
Abl is a Caveolin Kinase

To determine initially whether Abl phosphorylates caveolin, a fibroblast cell line expressing a temperature-sensitive form of v-Abl was used [76]. A temperature-sensitive form of v-Abl was necessary because constitutively active v-Abl leads to loss of expression of both caveolin-1 and -2 after only a few days [76,77]. (Expression of v-Src also causes down-regulation of caveolin [60,77]; however, this down-regulation is secondary to cellular transformation, and is not caused by phosphorylation of caveolin [76].) Caveolin-1 was one of the strongest phosphotyrosine signals detected in these cells after activation of the kinase. Caveolin-1 was also one of the most prominent phosphoproteins detected in primary human fibroblast cells overexpressing c-Abl. Caveolin-2 co-immunoprecipitated with caveolin-1, and was also phosphorylated under both of these conditions. Abl can directly phosphorylate caveolin-1 *in vitro* and in a yeast expression system [76,78]. The phosphorylation of caveolin-1 by Abl required Tyr14 and did not occur on a fusion protein in which this residue was changed to phenylalanine, indicating that the consensus Abl phosphorylation site is the only site in caveolin-1 phosphorylated by Abl.

To verify that Abl phosphorylates caveolin, fibroblast cell lines derived from an Abl knockout mouse (Abl$^{-/-}$) were utilized. The same cells reconstituted with Abl served as controls (Abl$^+$). Although, insulin does not stimulate caveolin phosphorylation in fibroblasts, caveolin is phosphorylated in response to oxidative stress in these cells [28,29]. Oxidative stress activates Abl [79,80]; therefore, oxidative stress-induced phosphorylation was a good system initially to test the requirement for Abl in caveolin phosphorylation [32].

Abl was required for oxidative stress-induced caveolin phosphorylation. Caveolin was not phosphorylated in response to oxidative stress in the Abl$^{-/-}$ cells, but phosphorylation was restored in the Abl$^+$ cells. In contrast to caveolin, many other proteins were phosphorylated on tyrosine in the Abl$^{-/-}$ cells, indicating that these cells still respond to oxidative stress, but that phosphorylation of Abl substrates is specifically lost. The only site of tyrosine phosphorylation of caveolin-1 in response to oxidative stress is Tyr14, the consensus Abl phosphorylation site. Therefore, expression of Abl is necessary for phosphorylation of caveolin-1 on tyrosine in response to oxidative stress, and the only site of tyrosine phosphorylation is a consensus Abl site. Additionally, overexpression of Abl is sufficient to induce caveolin phosphorylation in some cell types, and purified Abl phosphorylates caveolin at Tyr14 *in vitro*. These data indicate that c-Abl is also a stress-induced caveolin-tyrosine kinase.

6.2.6
Abl and Fyn Cooperate in the Caveolin Phosphorylation Signaling Pathway

The data indicate that expression of both Abl and Fyn is required for stress-induced caveolin phosphorylation. To verify that both Fyn and Abl are required for caveolin phosphorylation in the same cell, the effect of Src-family kinase inhibitors on caveolin phosphorylation in the Abl$^{-/-}$ and Abl$^+$ cells was analyzed. Pretreatment of the Abl$^+$ cells with SU6656 abolished oxidative stress-induced caveolin phosphorylation, indicating that both Abl and Src-family kinases are required in this pathway in a single cell.

One mechanism to explain the requirement for both Abl and Fyn would be that they act sequentially in a linear pathway. For example, Fyn might activate Abl, and Abl may be the caveolin kinase (Stress → Fyn → Abl → cav-P). Consistent with this model, previous studies had shown that Src-family kinase activation leads to Abl activation in a kinase cascade, and that both Fyn and Src can directly phosphorylate Abl *in vitro* [81]. If Fyn does not directly phosphorylate caveolin, then this model predicts that Fyn overexpression-induced caveolin phosphorylation would require Abl expression as well. To test this, Fyn was overexpressed in Abl$^+$ or Abl$^{-/-}$ fibroblasts. As was observed in fibroblasts from wild-type mice, overexpression of Fyn was sufficient to induce caveolin phosphorylation in the Abl$^+$ cells. However, inconsistent with a linear pathway from Fyn through Abl, Fyn-induced caveolin phosphorylation was even higher in the Abl$^{-/-}$ cells than in the Abl$^+$ cells, indicating that Abl actually negatively regulates Fyn under basal conditions. Therefore, overexpression of Fyn can bypass the requirement for Abl in caveolin phosphorylation. These results indicate that Fyn directly phosphorylates caveolin-1 and does not require Abl as an intermediary.

In an alternative linear pathway, Abl could be required for Fyn activation (Stress → Abl → Fyn → cav-*P*). Inconsistent with this model, however, oxidative stress-induced activation of Fyn does not require expression of Abl. While overexpression of Fyn was sufficient to induce caveolin phosphorylation, oxidative stress significantly increased this phosphorylation to very high levels in the Fyn overexpressing cells, indicating further activation of the kinase. This hyperphosphorylation occurred in both the Abl^+ and $Abl^{-/-}$ cells. To test if Src-family kinase activity is required downstream of Abl, the effect of Src-family kinase inhibitors on Abl-induced caveolin phosphorylation was examined. While SU6656 blocked Fyn overexpression-induced caveolin phosphorylation, Abl-induced phosphorylation was unaffected. These results indicate that Abl, like Fyn, acts directly on caveolin and does not require activation of a downstream Src-family kinase.

6.2.7
Model of the Interaction of Fyn and Abl in Caveolin Phosphorylation

Expression of both Abl and Fyn is necessary for caveolin phosphorylation, and overexpression of either is sufficient to induce caveolin phosphorylation. Therefore, the caveolin phosphorylation pathway represents a newly identified signaling cascade involving both Abl and Fyn. Signaling complexes involving both Src-family kinases and Abl have also been identified in a number of other systems [82–89]. Whilst both Abl and Fyn can phosphorylate caveolin directly, it is believed that Fyn and Abl act synergistically to induce sustained, high-level phosphorylation of caveolin-1. Our model is that Fyn activity is required for the efficient recruitment of Abl to the caveolae, and that Abl is required for sustained phosphorylation of caveolin (Fig. 6.2). In this model, activation of Fyn that is resident in the caveolae leads to phosphorylation of caveolin-1 at Tyr14. This phosphorylation creates a binding site for the SH2 protein binding domain of Abl (consensus binding site, pY-X-X-P), and recruitment of Abl into the complexes (domain structure of Abl: SH3, SH2, kinase domain, tail). Abl then phosphorylates adjacent caveolin molecules in the complex. In this way, the phosphorylation when both kinases are activated is significantly greater than either alone. Overexpression of Abl causes activation of Abl and inefficient phosphorylation of caveolin-1, which leads to the recruitment of Abl into caveolae and more efficient phosphorylation. Overexpression of Fyn bypasses an inherent limitation on the level of caveolin phosphorylation that can normally be catalyzed by Fyn alone (see below). This model may also explain why some stimuli lead to only transient phosphorylation of caveolin, while others lead to sustained phosphorylation of caveolin. Whilst all activate Src-family kinases in caveolae and initiate caveolin phosphorylation, they may differ in their ability to activate and translocate Abl to the caveolae. Our investigations into the signaling cascades that lie downstream of caveolin phosphorylation strongly sup-

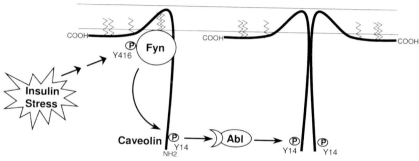

Fig. 6.2 Fyn and Abl are caveolin tyrosine kinases. Insulin and stress activate the Src-family kinase Fyn and autophosphorylation of the kinase (pY416). Fyn is localized to lipid rafts via tandem acylation and to caveolae through direct binding to caveolin. Upon activation, Fyn phosphorylates caveolin-1 on Tyr14. Tyrosine phosphorylation promotes SH2 domain-mediated binding of Abl. This in turn leads to the phosphorylation of adjacent caveolin molecules.

port this model, and give significant insights into the reason that caveolin phosphorylation by Fyn alone is self-limited and requires the activation of two non-receptor tyrosine kinases, Fyn and Abl, for sustained high level phosphorylation to occur.

6.3
Signaling Pathways Downstream of Caveolin Tyrosine Phosphorylation

With the exception of sites within the activation loops of kinases themselves, the function of tyrosine phosphorylation is to promote protein-protein interactions, particularly through SH2 protein-binding domains. This in turn leads to the activation of downstream signaling cascades. Therefore, phosphorylation of caveolin on tyrosine is likely to be an intermediate step in a signaling cascade occurring within caveolae. Caveolin-1 phosphorylated at Tyr14 would serve as a docking site for SH2 domain-containing proteins and would recruit proteins into caveolae to activate downstream signaling cascades (Fig. 6.3).

In order to identify proteins that bind to phosphorylated caveolin-1, a 3T3-L1 adipocyte cDNA library was screened using a novel yeast dihybrid screen [78]. The Gal4-based yeast two-hybrid system was modified to perform a phosphotyrosine-dependent dihybrid protein interaction screen. Then, a kinase (Abl) was introduced into the two-hybrid system to phosphorylate the bait protein (caveolin-1), after which screening was carried out for phosphorylation-dependent protein interactions. Using this system to screen an adipocyte cDNA library, three proteins were identified that interact with the amino-terminus of caveolin-1: JAB1, TRAF2, and Csk. Of these three proteins, only Csk contains an SH2 domain.

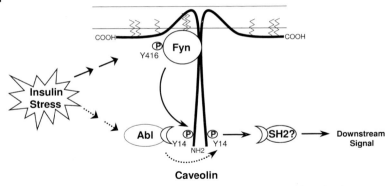

Fig. 6.3 Activation of signaling cascades downstream of caveolin phosphorylation. Extracellular signals (insulin and stress) activate caveolin kinases (Fyn and Abl). This leads to phosphorylation of caveolin-1 on Tyr14. Tyrosine phosphorylation promotes SH2 domain-mediated protein interactions. This in turn leads to activation of downstream signaling cascades within the caveolae.

6.3.1
Csk Binds to Phosphocaveolin

Based on the initial screen, positive proteins could interact with caveolin-1 in a phosphorylation-dependent or independent manner. In order to counter-screen for phosphorylation-dependent interactions, the positive clones were transformed back into yeast that expressed caveolin-1 alone, caveolin-1 and Abl, or the phosphorylation mutant caveolin-1/Y14F and Abl. Only the interaction of Csk with caveolin-1 was completely dependent on phosphorylation. TRAF2 also bound to non-phosphorylated caveolin-1, although phosphorylation of caveolin-1 increased the binding of TRAF2 to caveolin-1 approximately three-fold. The proteasome subunit JAB1 interacted with caveolin-1 in a phosphorylation-independent manner.

Previous studies had shown that TRAF2 and caveolin-1 form a complex that recruits the tumor necrosis factor-alpha (TNFa) receptor after ligand binding [90]. Therefore, focus was centered on Csk. The interaction of Csk with phosphocaveolin in mammalian cells was verified. Phosphocaveolin co-immunoprecipitated with Csk in cells expressing v-Abl, and was one of only two major tyrosine-phosphorylated proteins bound to Csk in these cells [78]. The other phosphoprotein was paxillin, a multi-domain focal adhesion protein known to bind to Csk through an SH2 domain-phosphotyrosine interaction. Phosphocaveolin also co-immunoprecipitated with Csk in untransfected cells and this association increased after induction of oxidative stress or shear stress, and in adipocytes after stimulation with insulin [24,34,78,91]. Csk interacted only with caveolin phosphorylated on Tyr14, and did not bind to non-phosphorylated caveolin. Csk is one of only two proteins that are known to bind specifically to phosphorylated caveolin-1; the SH2 domain-containing protein Grb7 is the other [16]. Only Csk has been shown to interact with caveolin-1 in a regulated manner in cells.

6.3.2
Regulation of Src-Family Kinases by Csk

Phosphorylation of caveolin is an ideal mechanism to recruit Csk to its substrates (the Src-family kinases) that are highly enriched in the caveolae. Csk is a negative regulator of Src-family kinases [92]. Csk phosphorylates Src-family kinases at an inhibitory tyrosine (Tyr527 in Src). When this residue is phosphorylated, it binds to the SH2 domain in the amino-terminus of the kinase, folding it into an inactive conformation (domain structure of Src-family kinases: SH3, SH2, kinase domain, regulatory tail with Csk phosphorylation site). The Src-family kinases can be reactivated either through dephosphorylation of this residue, or by displacement of the C-terminal tail by another phosphoprotein. However, the Src-family kinases are lipid-modified and localized to the plasma membrane, while Csk is largely free in the cytosol. Csk must be specifically targeted to its substrates in membranes via an SH2-domain-mediated interaction with a tyrosine-phosphorylated protein. In brain and lymphocytes, Csk is recruited to lipid rafts in the plasma membrane through binding to a transmembrane protein called Cbp that is constitutively phosphorylated on tyrosine [93,94]. Binding to phosphorylated Cbp also activates Csk. Phosphocaveolin also targets Csk to its substrates in the plasma membrane. Src-family kinases are highly enriched in caveolae, both through their lipid modifications and through direct binding to the "scaffolding domain" of the caveolins. Therefore, phosphocaveolin is an ideal targeting subunit for Csk. Significantly, caveolin phosphorylation is stimulated in response to extracellular signals. In contrast, Cbp is constitutively phosphorylated, and only transiently dephosphorylated in response to T-cell activation. Regulated phosphorylation of caveolin represents a novel mechanism for the regulation of Src-family kinases by extracellular signals through the recruitment and activation of Csk.

6.3.3
Feedback Inhibition of Fyn Through Activation of Csk

These data support the following model (Fig. 6.4). Activation of Fyn in caveolae by insulin or stress leads to phosphorylation of caveolin-1 on Tyr14, which leads to the recruitment of Csk, and phosphorylation and inhibition of resident Src-family kinases. This feedback mechanism is supported by a number of observations [24,31]. Oxidative stress simultaneously activates Src-family kinases and their negative regulator Csk. Induction of oxidative stress leads to concomitant increases in both active site and Csk inhibitory site phosphorylation of Fyn in many cell types. Basal Csk activity varied from cell type to cell type, but was very low in fibroblasts from wild-type mice and absent from fibroblasts from Csk knockout mice. However, basal Src-family kinase activity was low in all cases. Therefore, Src-family kinases are maintained in an inactive conformation in fibroblasts through a

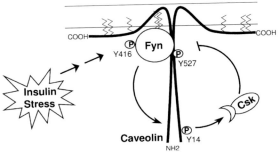

Fig. 6.4 Phosphocaveolin recruits Csk to the caveolae, attenuating Fyn. Csk (c-terminal Src kinase) is a negative regulator of Src-family kinases. Csk must be targeted to its substrates in membranes via an SH2 domain-mediated interaction with a tyrosine-phosphorylated protein. This activates Csk, leading to phosphorylation of Src-family kinases at their inhibitory site (pY527) and attenuation of their activity. Csk binds specifically to phosphocaveolin only after stimulation with insulin or oxidative stress, and is activated under these conditions.

mechanism that is independent of Csk phosphorylation. In contrast to basal activity, oxidative stress-induced Src-family kinase activity was much greater in $Csk^{-/-}$ cells than in $Csk^{+/+}$ cells, indicating that loss of Csk activity leads to dysregulation of the Src-family kinases, but only after activation. Therefore, Csk plays a modulatory, not a strictly regulatory role for Src-family kinases in these cells. This is in marked contrast to the mechanism of regulation of Src-family kinases described in lymphocytes. In these cells, Src-family kinases are constitutively phosphorylated by Csk, and activated by dephosphorylation of this site [95].

6.3.4
Phosphocaveolin in the Loop

Csk must be recruited to its substrates via SH2-mediated binding to a tyrosine-phosphorylated targeting protein. A number of observations implicate phosphocaveolin in the feedback inhibition of Src-family kinases [24,31]. Src-family kinases are highly enriched in caveolae, due to both acylation and direct binding to caveolin. Caveolin-1 is phosphorylated in response to stimuli that activate Fyn, including oxidative stress and insulin, and stress-induced phosphorylation of caveolin requires Fyn. Stress-induced caveolin phosphorylation is self-limiting and attenuated by Csk: caveolin is phosphorylated to a much greater extent in $Csk^{-/-}$ cells than in the $Csk^{+/+}$ cells. Csk binds specifically to phosphocaveolin, which is one of only two tyrosine-phosphorylated proteins associated with Csk in fibroblasts and adipocytes. Association with Csk increases significantly in response to either insulin or stress. These data indicate that binding to phosphocaveolin is a major mechanism for the regulation of Csk in response to stress and insulin. Therefore, the role of caveolin phosphorylation in signal transduction becomes a question of the role that regulation of caveolar Src-family kinase activity plays in signal transduction.

6.3.5
Src-Family Kinases, Csk and Actin Remodeling

Src-family kinases are essential for cell proliferation, differentiation, and adhesion [96]. However, uncontrolled Src-family kinase activity leads to constitutive activation of mitogenic pathways, tumor promotion, and loss of cell attachment. Therefore, tight regulation of Src-family kinase activity is essential. The requirement for tight control of Src-family kinase activity is readily apparent in the regulation of actin/cell surface/extracellular matrix adhesions [97–100]. Both Src and Fyn are translocated to newly forming focal contacts during cell spreading. Src-family kinase activity is essential for the maintenance of these structures: inhibition of Src-family kinase activity leads to disassembly of adhesions. Paradoxically, constitutively active forms of Src also disrupt cell adhesion, and therefore the activity of Src in focal adhesions must be carefully regulated. During cell spreading there is an initial disruption of plasma membrane-actin attachments to allow membrane extension at the leading edge of the cell, followed by assembly of focal contacts and actin filaments behind the leading edge. Src-family kinases are activated at the cell edge during the initial stage of cell spreading to transiently relieve actin-induced tension at the plasma membrane, but must then be attenuated to allow actin reassembly. Attenuation occurs through phosphorylation by Csk. Csk-deficient cells exhibit unregulated Src-family kinase activity, hyperphosphorylation of actin-associated substrate proteins, impaired stress fiber formation and defects in cell adhesion [97]. Interestingly, anti-sense-mediated suppression of caveolin expression results in similar phenotypes, including elevated Src-family kinase activity and loss of cell adhesion [7,101].

6.3.6
Phosphocaveolin is Enriched at Sites of Attachment of the Actin Cytoskeleton to the Plasma Membrane

Significant data links caveolae and caveolins to the actin cytoskeleton [102,103]. In confluent, quiescent cells and in tissues, caveolin-1 is primary localized to the plasma membrane. The caveolin-1 at cell surface is tethered to the actin cytoskeleton [104,105]. Caveolin binds to actin through filamin, a protein that regulates cortical actin assembly [106]. Agents that disrupt the actin cytoskeleton cause rapid internalization of caveolin [105]. Caveolin-1 also redistributes in response to shear stress and during cell migration [30,32,107–109]. The muscle specific isoform caveolin-3 is also bound to actin, and loss of caveolin-3 causes a form of muscular dystrophy due to defects in the anchoring of the actin cytoskeleton to the plasma membrane [110,111].

Phosphocaveolin is ideally localized to act as the mediator between Src activation and Csk-induced inactivation in the regulation of actin assembly. Phosphocaveolin

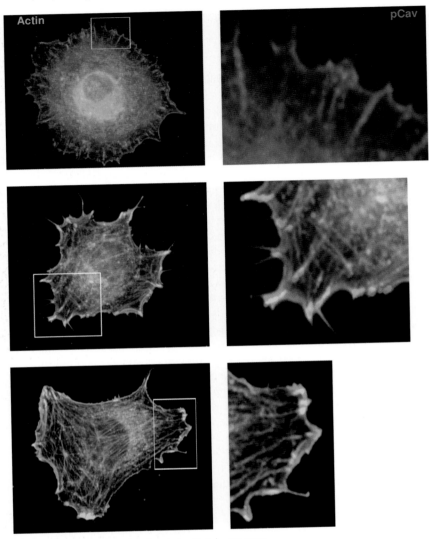

Fig. 6.5 Caveolin is phosphorylated at actin/plasma membrane attachment sites. Fibroblast cells plated onto fibronectin for 5 min (top) or 15 min. Actin is labeled with FITC-phalloidin (green). Phosphocaveolin is labeled with anti-PY14 antibody and Cy3-labeled secondary antibody (red). The boxed portions in the right-hand panels are shown enlarged on the left.

is highly enriched at or near focal adhesions at the ends of the actin stress fibers [18,24,27,29,32,34,35,109]. In migrating non-confluent cells, caveolin is cleared from the leading edge of the cell and is found predominantly in vesicles at the trailing edge of the cell. However, phosphocaveolin is highly enriched near forming focal adhesions at the cell edge in actively migrating cells, or in cells spreading on fibronectin. Double labeling with phalloidin showed that caveolin phosphorylation occurs at the ends of bundles of actin fibers at the edge of the cell (Fig. 6.5). The enrichment of phosphocaveolin near focal adhesions and the tight association of caveolin with cortical actin indicate that phosphorylation of caveolin may regulate the actin cytoskeleton through Csk-mediated inhibition of Src-family kinases. Consistent with a link between caveolin, Src-family kinases, and the actin cytoskeleton, integrin signaling through Fyn requires expression of caveolin-1 [62,101].

6.3.7
Abl in the Loop

Our data indicate that activation of Fyn in caveolae would be sufficient to induce caveolin tyrosine phosphorylation, although this phosphorylation is expected to be self-limiting and transient due to feedback inhibition through Csk. Both Abl and Fyn are required for robust, sustained caveolin phosphorylation. Our current model is that Fyn and Abl act synergistically in the phosphorylation of caveolin (Fig. 6.6). Extracellular stimuli such as insulin or stress activate Fyn in caveolae, which phosphorylates caveolin. This leads to the recruitment of Csk, attenuates Fyn, and limits the extent of phosphorylation of caveolin. At the same time, these signals activate Abl which translocates into caveolae where it also phosphorylates caveolin. Abl is not regulated by Csk, and remains active in these complexes, main-

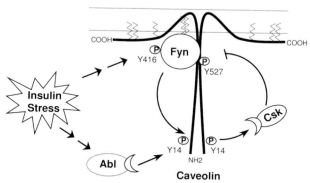

Fig. 6.6 Abl kinase is required for stable phosphorylation of caveolin. Both Abl and Fyn are required for caveolin phosphorylation. Both are caveolin tyrosine kinases and directly phosphorylate it *in vitro*. Both are activated by oxidative stress. Fyn is resident in caveolae and may be required for the activation or recruitment of Abl to caveolae. Recruitment of Csk to phosphocaveolin would attenuate Fyn activity, leading to transient caveolin phosphorylation. Since Abl is not inhibited by Csk, recruitment to or activation of Abl in caveolae would induce stable phosphorylation of caveolin-1.

taining a high level of caveolin phosphorylation. In the absence of Abl, caveolin phosphorylation is limited in extent, and is transient. Recruitment/activation of Abl is required for high-level, sustained phosphorylation of caveolin-1, and sustained inhibition of Src-family kinases. This represents a novel mechanism for the attenuation of Src-family kinase activity by Abl: phosphorylation of a scaffolding protein (caveolin) and recruitment of Csk. Paxillin, a substrate of both Abl and Src, is likely to organize a similar regulatory complex by binding to Abl, Src, and Csk [112]. Csk is recruited only after phosphorylation of paxillin.

Interestingly, Fyn and Abl are required for opposing stress-induced pathways in cells. Activation of Fyn is required for the induction of survival pathways [66,113], whereas activation of Abl induces cell death [114]. Activation of Fyn and Abl are also temporally different. Fyn is activated rapidly (within minutes), while Abl activation takes longer (maximum activation after 30 minutes). Low-level exposure to oxidative stress (low concentration or short duration) stimulates survival pathways, while higher exposures induce apoptotic pathways [115]. It is possible that low-level exposures stimulate only Fyn, hence survival pathways, while higher exposures are required to activate Abl and apoptotic pathways. Abl-induced recruitment of Csk to complexes containing Src-family kinases would be a mechanism to ensure that survival pathways are turned off, allowing apoptosis to proceed. Counterregulatory effects of Abl and Fyn have been observed in a number of additional signaling pathways [84,88,89], and negative regulatory circuits involving Abl, Fyn, and their substrates have been identified genetically in second-site repressor screens in *Drosophila* [82,83]. Currently, an Abl-specific inhibitor STI571 (Gleevec) is used in patients to treat chronic myelogenous leukemia. Therefore, counterregulatory complexes containing Src-family kinases and Abl have important therapeutic implications, particularly in the treatment of cancer.

6.3.8
Abl and Actin Remodeling

Abl and Src-family kinases also have opposing effects on the actin cytoskeleton (Abl stabilizes/Src destabilizes) and cell migration (Abl inhibits/ Src promotes). Signaling complexes that regulate focal adhesions are known to contain Abl and Src-family kinases, as well as substrates for both kinases [85–87]. Abl, Fyn and their substrates are associated with signaling complexes that organize N-WASP and Arp2/3 at the cell membrane. As members of this complex, Abl and Fyn play opposing roles in regulating actin assembly and remodeling. Fyn recruits and activates N-WASP and ARP2/3 which initiates actin polymerization. Abl inhibits actin polymerization by phosphorylating and inhibiting enabled (Ena) and activating profilin. Abl also strengthens focal contacts by inhibiting their breakdown through an unidentified mechanism. This is may be due to inhibition of Fyn through recruitment of Csk. Transient Src-family kinase activity is required for focal adhesion turnover and membrane extension during actin remodeling. Caveolin phosphorylation and recruitment of Csk represent a mechanism through which temporal and spatial regulation of Src-family kinase activity could be achieved during cell migration to allow transient activation then rapid Csk-induced inactivation of Src-family kinases. Stimulation of caveolin phosphorylation through recruitment/activation of Abl would inhibit Src-family kinase activity at focal contacts, stabilizing these structures.

6.3.9
Insulin-Induced Actin Remodeling, GluT4 Translocation, and Caveolae

Adipocytes are terminally differentiated and are not dividing. They are also not migrating or spreading on the extracellular matrix, and they do not have well-formed stress fibers. Therefore, what is the significance of caveolin phosphorylation and Csk-induced attenuation of Src-family kinase activity in response to insulin in these cells? Insulin increases glucose transport in fat and muscle cells by stimulating the translocation of GluT4 from intracellular vesicles to the plasma membrane. Insulin induces cortical actin remodeling which is required for Glut4 translocation [116,117]. Therefore, the regulation of cortical actin assembly is a key process in the stimulation of glucose transport by insulin. In a manner analogous to cell migration, cortical actin remodeling would require that the tension between the cell surface and the actin cytoskeleton first be transiently relieved, followed by rapid formation of new initiation sites for actin assembly at the membrane. Based on other modes of actin remodeling, it is likely that Src-family kinases and Csk play roles in insulin-induced actin remodeling in adipocytes.

In adipocytes, caveolin is co-localized with actin in unique complexes at the cell surface [118,119]. Disruption of these complexes, either through expression of dominant-negative forms of caveolin or by treatment with cyclodextran, blocks insulin-stimulated cortical actin assembly and GluT4 translocation [120]. Insulin-stimulated caveolin phosphorylation would activate Csk close to sites of cortical actin assembly, which would modulate the insulin-induced actin remodeling. Consistent with this, other stimuli that induce GluT4 translocation also stimulate caveolin phosphorylation, including endothelin-1, angiotensin II, and osmotic stress [14,15,18,28,32].

6.3.10
The Role of Caveolin Phosphorylation in Cells

Our current hypothesis is that caveolin organizes signaling complexes containing Fyn, Csk, and Abl that regulate cortical actin remodeling. Caveolin phosphorylation is required for the recruitment of both Csk and Abl into the complexes, which leads to negative regulation of the Src-family kinases that are resident in the caveolae. When the phosphorylation of caveolin is catalyzed by the Src-kinases themselves, this is a mechanism for the transient activation/rapid Csk-induced attenuation of Src-kinases through feedback inhibition. When the caveolin is phosphorylated by Abl, this regulatory mechanism would inhibit activation of a specific pool of Src family kinases. This regulatory complex involves the following three steps (Fig. 6.7):

*1)   Signals activate Fyn leading to phosphorylation of substrates
    including caveolin-1.*

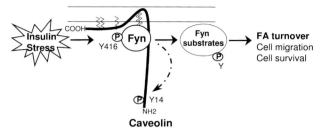

2)   Caveolin phosphorylation recruits Csk and attenuates Fyn activity.

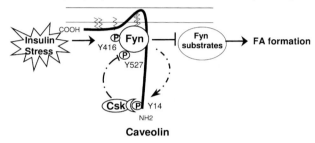

*3)   Prolonged signals activate/recruit Abl leading to prolonged caveolin
    phosphorylation and attenuation of Fyn.*

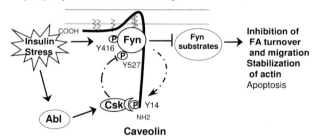

Fig. 6.7 Caveolin organizes signaling complexes with Fyn, Csk
and Abl that regulate cortical actin remodeling.

1. Insulin or stress activates Fyn that is resident in the caveolae. This leads to the
   phosphorylation of specific Fyn substrates involved in focal adhesion turnover,
   cell migration, and cell survival.
2. It also leads to the phosphorylation of caveolin-1 at Tyr14. Caveolin phosphorylation recruits Csk, which attenuates Fyn activity. The transient activation of
   Fyn allows for the transient release of actin from the plasma membrane. Fyn
   must be then be inactivated to allow subsequent reformation of actin contact
   sites.
3. Prolonged signals activate/recruit Abl, leading to high-level, sustained phosphorylation of caveolin and sustained attenuation of Fyn. This leads to inhibi-

tion of focal adhesion turnover and inhibition of cell migration, stabilization of actin, and can lead to apoptosis.

This model links caveolin phosphorylation to two pathways known to be impacted by caveolin expression: actin assembly/cell migration and control of cell growth.

6.4
Summary

Two signaling molecules required for caveolin phosphorylation have been identified: Fyn and Abl. The data suggest a novel mechanism for the attenuation of Src-kinase activity by Abl: stable tyrosine phosphorylation of a scaffolding protein (caveolin-1) and recruitment of a negative regulator of Src-family kinase activity (Csk). The unexpected complexity of this pathway has important implications for treatment of diseases, including cancer and diabetes.

Three binding partners for phosphocaveolin have been identified: TRAF2, Grb7, and Csk. The identification of Csk as a binding partner for phosphorylated caveolin-1 led to a unique model for the function of caveolae in cells. It also demonstrated the utility of a powerful new technique to identify novel phosphotyrosine-directed protein interactions.

A novel feedback mechanism for Src-family kinase regulation has been identified: recruitment and activation of Csk by Src-family kinase substrates such as caveolin-1. Recruitment and activation of Abl in the complex induces sustained activation of Csk and attenuation of Src-family kinase activity, consistent with the counter-regulatory effects of these kinases. This previously undescribed, but simple, mechanism can explain a number of well-studied observations, including transient activation of Src-family kinases in forming focal contacts, and the counter-regulatory effects of Abl and Src-family kinases in cell growth, migration, and actin polymerization.

A novel role for caveolae and caveolin tyrosine phosphorylation in cells was proposed: regulation of cortical actin assembly and/or remodeling. The caveolin-1/Csk/Src family kinase/Abl signaling complex may be involved in transmitting signals to the actin cytoskeleton (i.e., from integrins or oxidative stress) or transmitting signals from the actin cytoskeleton (i.e., from shear or osmotic stress).

Abbreviations

ACTH   adrenocorticotropin
EGF   epidermal growth factor
eNOS   endothelial nitric oxide synthase
FRET   fluorescence resonance energy transfer
IGF-1   insulin-like growth factor-1
IRS-1   insulin receptor substrate-1

PDGF   platelet-derived growth factor
SDS   sodium dodecyl sulfate
SH2   Src-homology 2
TNFα   tumor necrosis factor-alpha
VEGF   vascular endothelial growth factor

References

1 Glenney, J. R., and D. Soppet (1992). Sequence and expression of caveolin, a protein component of caveolae plasma membrane domains phosphorylated on tyrosine in Rous sarcoma virus-transformed fibroblasts. *Proc. Natl. Acad. Sci. USA* 89, 10517–10521.

2 Scherer, P. E., Tang, Z., Chun, M., Sargiacomo, M., Lodish, H. F., and Lisanti, M. P. (1995). Caveolin isoforms differ in their N-terminal protein sequence and subcellular distribution. *J. Biol. Chem.* 270, 16395–16401.

3 Scherer, P. E., Okamoto, T., Chun, M., Nishimoto, I., Lodish, H. F., and Lisanti, M. P. (1996). Identification, sequence, and expression of caveolin-2 defines a caveolin gene family. *Proc. Natl. Acad. Sci. USA* 93, 131–135.

4 Tang, Z., Scherer, P. E., Okamoto, T., Song, K., Chu, C., Kohtz, D. S., Nishimoto, I., Lodish, H. F., and Lisanti, M. P. (1996). Molecular cloning of caveolin-3, a novel member of the caveolin gene family expressed predominantly in muscle. *J. Biol. Chem.* 271, 2255–2261.

5 Scheiffele, P., Verkade, Fra, M., Virta, Simons, and Ikonen (1998). Caveolin-1 and -2 in the exocytic pathway of MDCK cells. *J. Cell Biol.* 140, 795–806.

6 Fra, A. M., Williamson, E., Simons, K., and Parton, R. G. (1995). De novo formation of caveolae in lymphocytes by expression of VIP21-caveolin. *Proc. Natl. Acad. Sci. USA* 92, 8655–8659.

7 Drab, M., Verkade, P., Elger, M., Kasper, M., Lohn, M., Lauterbach, B., Menne, J., Lindschau, C., Mende, F., Luft, F. C., Schedl, A., Haller, H., and Kurzchalia, T. V. (2001). Loss of caveolae, vascular dysfunction, and pulmonary defects in caveolin-1 gene-disrupted mice. *Science* 9, 2449–2452.

8 Razani, B., Engelman, J. A., Wang, X. B., Schubert, W., Zhang, X. L., Marks, C. B., Macaluso, F., Russell, R. G., Li, M., Pestell, R. G., Di Vizio, D., Hou, H., Jr., Kneitz, B., Lagaud, G., Christ, G. J., Edelmann, W., and Lisanti, M. P. (2001). Caveolin-1 null mice are viable but show evidence of hyperproliferative and vascular abnormalities. *J. Biol. Chem.* 276, 38121–38138.

9 Kurzchalia, T. V., and Parton, R. G. (1999). Membrane microdomains and caveolae. *Curr. Opin. Cell Biol.* 11, 424–431.

10 Li, S., Couet, J., and Lisanti, M. P. (1996). Src tyrosine kinases, Galpha subunits, and H-Ras share a common membrane-anchored scaffolding protein, caveolin. Caveolin binding negatively regulates the auto-activation of Src tyrosine kinases. *J. Biol. Chem.* 271, 29182–29190.

11 Garcia-Cardena, G., Fan, R., Stern, D. F., Liu, J., and Sessa, W. C. (1996). Endothelial nitric oxide synthase is regulated by tyrosine phosphorylation and interacts with caveolin-1. *J. Biol. Chem.* 271, 27237–27240.

12 Okamoto, T., Schlegel, A., Scherer, P. E., and Lisanti, M. P. (1998). Caveolins, a family of scaffolding proteins for organizing "preassembled signaling complexes" at the plasma membrane. *J. Biol. Chem.* 273, 5419–5422.

13 Oh, P., and Schnitzer, J. E. (2001). Segregation of heterotrimeric G proteins in cell surface microdomains. G(q) binds caveolin to concentrate in caveolae, whereas G(i) and G(s) target lipid rafts by default. *Mol. Biol. Cell* 12, 685–698.

14 Mastick, C. C., Brady, M. J., and Saltiel, A. R. (1995). Insulin stimulates the tyrosine phosphorylation of caveolin. *J. Cell Biol.* 129, 1523–1531.

15 Mastick, C. C., and Saltiel, A. R. (1997). Insulin-stimulated tyrosine phosphorylation of caveolin is specific for the differentiated adipocyte phenotype in 3T3-L1 cells. *J. Biol. Chem.* 272, 20706–20714.

16 Lee, H., Volonte, D., Galbiati, F., Iyengar, P., Lublin, D. M., Bregman, D. B., Wilson, M. T., Campos-Gonzalez, R., Bouzahzah, B., Pestell, R. G., Scherer, P. E., and Lisanti, M. P. (2000). Constitutive and growth factor-regulated phosphorylation of caveolin-1 occurs at the same site (Tyr-14) in vivo: identification of a c-Src/Cav-1/Grb7 signaling cassette. *Mol. Endocrinol.* 14, 1750–1775.

17 Kim, Y. N., Wiepz, G. J., Guadarrama, A. G., and Bertics, P. J. (2000). Epidermal growth factor-stimulated tyrosine phosphorylation of caveolin-1. Enhanced caveolin-1 tyrosine phosphorylation following aberrant epidermal growth factor receptor status. *J. Biol. Chem.* 275, 7481–7491.

18 Ushio-Fukai, M., Hilenski, L., Santanam, N., Becker, P., Ma, Y., Griendling, K., and RW, A. (2001). Cholesterol depletion inhibits epidermal growth factor receptor transactivation by angiotensin II in vascular smooth muscle cells: Role of cholesterol-rich microdomains and focal adhesions in angiotensin II signaling. *J. Biol. Chem.* 276, 48269–48275.

19 Muller, G., Jung, C., Wied, S., Welte, S., and Frick, W. (2001). Insulin-mimetic signaling by the sulfonylurea glimepiride and phosphoinositolglycans involves distinct mechanisms for redistribution of lipid raft components. *Biochemistry* 40, 14603–14620.

20 Newcomb, L. F., and Mastick, C. C. (2002). Src family kinase-dependent phosphorylation of a 29-kDa caveolin-associated protein. *Biochem. Biophys. Res. Commun.* 290, 1447–1453.

21 Kim, Y. N., Dam, P., and Bertics, P. J. (2002). Caveolin-1 phosphorylation in human squamous and epidermoid carcinoma cells: dependence on ErbB1 expression and Src activation. *Exp. Cell Res.* 280, 134–147.

22 Hua, H., Munk, S., and Whiteside, C. I. (2003). Endothelin-1 activates mesangial cell ERK1/2 via EGF-receptor transactivation and caveolin-1 interaction. *Am. J. Physiol. Renal Physiol.* 284, F303-F312.

23 Labrecque, L., Royal, I., Surprenant, D. S., Patterson, C., Gingras, D., and Beliveau, R. (2003). Regulation of vascular endothelial growth factor receptor-2 activity by caveolin-1 and plasma membrane cholesterol. *Mol. Biol. Cell* 14, 334–347.

24 Cao, H., Sanguinetti, A. R., and Mastick, C. C. (2004). Oxidative stress activates both Src-kinases and their negative regulator Csk and induces phosphorylation of two targeting proteins for Csk: caveolin-1 and paxillin. *Exp. Cell Res.* 294, 159–171.

25 Podar, K., Shringarpure, R., Tai, Y. T., Simoncini, M., Sattler, M., Ishitsuka, K., Richardson, P. G., Hideshima, T., Chauhan, D., and Anderson, K. C. (2004). Caveolin-1 is required for vascular endothelial growth factor-triggered multiple myeloma cell migration and is targeted by bortezomib. *Cancer Res.* 64, 7500–7506.

26 Fielding, P. E., Chau, P., Liu, D., Spencer, T. A., and Fielding, C. J. (2004). Mechanism of platelet-derived growth factor-dependent caveolin-1 phosphorylation: relationship to sterol binding and the role of serine-80. *Biochemistry* 43, 2578–2586.

27 Colonna, C., and Podesta, E. J. (2005). ACTH-induced caveolin-1 tyrosine phosphorylation is related to podosome assembly in Y1 adrenal cells. *Exp. Cell Res.* 304, 432–442.

28 Aoki, T., Nomura, R., and Fujimoto, T. (1999). Tyrosine phosphorylation of caveolin-1 in the endothelium. *Exp. Cell Res.* 253, 629–636.

29 Volonte, D., Galbiati, F., Pestell, R. G., and Lisanti, M. P. (2001). Cellular stress induces the tyrosine phosphorylation of caveolin-1 (Tyr(14)) via activation of p38 mitogen-activated protein kinase and c-Src kinase. Evidence for caveolae, the actin cytoskeleton, and focal adhesions as mechanical sensors of osmotic stress. *J. Biol. Chem.* 276, 8094–8103.

30 Rizzo, V., Morton, C., DePaola, N., Schnitzer, J. E., and Davies, P. F. (2003). Recruitment of endothelial caveolae into mechanotransduction pathways by flow conditioning in vitro. *Am. J. Physiol. Heart Circ. Physiol.* 285, H1720–H1729.

31 Sanguinetti, A. R., Cao, H., and Corley Mastick, C. (2003). Fyn is required for ox-

idative- and hyperosmotic-stress-induced tyrosine phosphorylation of caveolin-1. *Biochem. J.* 376, 159–168.

32 Sanguinetti, A. R., and Mastick, C. C. (2003). c-Abl is required for oxidative stress-induced phosphorylation of caveolin-1 on tyrosine 14. *Cell Signal.* 15, 289–298.

33 Navakauskiene, R., Treigyte, G., Gineitis, A., and Magnusson, K. E. (2004). Identification of apoptotic tyrosine-phosphorylated proteins after etoposide or retinoic acid treatment. *Proteomics* 4, 1029–1041.

34 Radel, C., and Rizzo, V. (2005). Integrin mechanotransduction stimulates caveolin-1 phosphorylation and recruitment of Csk to mediate actin reorganization. *Am. J. Physiol. Heart Circ. Physiol.* 288, H936–H945.

35 Brown, G., Rixon, H. W., and Sugrue, R. J. (2002). Respiratory syncytial virus assembly occurs in GM1-rich regions of the host-cell membrane and alters the cellular distribution of tyrosine phosphorylated caveolin-1. *J. Gen. Virol.* 83, 1841–1850.

36 Minshall, R. D., Sessa, W. C., Stan, R. V., Anderson, R. G., and Malik, A. B. (2003). Caveolin regulation of endothelial function. *Am. J. Physiol. Lung Cell Mol. Physiol.* 285, L1179–L1183.

37 Shajahan, A. N., Tiruppathi, C., Smrcka, A. V., Malik, A. B., and Minshall, R. D. (2004). Gbetagamma activation of Src induces caveolae-mediated endocytosis in endothelial cells. *J. Biol. Chem.* 279, 48055–48062.

38 Sargiacomo, M., Scherer, P. E., Tang, Z. L., Casanova, J. E., and Lisanti, M. P. (1994). In vitro phosphorylation of caveolin-rich membrane domains: identification of an associated serine kinase activity as a casein kinase II-like enzyme. *Oncogene* 9, 2589–2595.

39 Nomura, R., and Fujimoto, T. (1999). Tyrosine-phosphorylated caveolin-1: immunolocalization and molecular characterization. *Mol. Biol. Cell* 10, 975–986.

40 Lee, H., Park, D. S., Wang, X. B., Scherer, P. E., Schwartz, P. E., and Lisanti, M. P. (2002). Src-induced phosphorylation of caveolin-2 on tyrosine 19. Phospho-caveolin-2 (Tyr(P)19) is localized near focal adhesions, remains associated with lipid rafts/caveolae, but no longer forms a high molecular mass hetero-oligomer with caveolin-1. *J. Biol. Chem.* 277, 34556–34567.

41 Kiss, A. L., Botos, E., Turi, A., and Mullner, N. (2004). Ocadaic acid treatment causes tyrosine phosphorylation of caveolin-2 and induces internalization of caveolae in rat peritoneal macrophages. *Micron* 35, 707–715.

42 Wang, X. B., Lee, H., Capozza, F., Marmon, S., Sotgia, F., Brooks, J. W., Campos-Gonzalez, R., and Lisanti, M. P. (2004). Tyrosine phosphorylation of caveolin-2 at residue 27: differences in the spatial and temporal behavior of phospho-Cav-2 (pY19 and pY27). *Biochemistry* 43, 13694–13706.

43 Zaas, D. W., Duncan, M. J., Li, G., Wright, J. R., and Abraham, S. N. (2005). Pseudomonas invasion of type I pneumocytes is dependent on the expression and phosphorylation of caveolin-2. *J. Biol. Chem.* 280, 4864–4872.

44 Robinson, L. J., Pang, S., Harris, D. S., Heuser, J., and James, D. E. (1992). Translocation of glucose transporter (GLUT4) to the cell surface in permeabilized 3T3-L1 adipocytes: effects of ATP, insulin, and GTPgS and localization of GLUT4 to clathrin lattices. *J. Biol. Chem.* 117, 1181–1196.

45 Scherer, P. E., Lisanti, M. P., Baldini, G., Sargiacomo, M., Mastick, C. C., and Lodish, H. F. (1994). Induction of caveolin during adipogenesis and association of GLUT4 with caveolin-rich vesicles. *J. Cell Biol.* 127, 1233–1243.

46 Kandror, K. V., Stephens, J. M., and Pilch, P. F. (1995). Expression and compartmentalization of caveolin in adipose cells: coordinate regulation with and structural segregation from GLUT4. *J. Cell Biol.* 129, 999–1006.

47 Razani, B., Combs, T. P., Wang, X. B., Frank, P. G., Park, D. S., Russell, R. G., Li, M., Tang, B., Jelicks, L. A., Scherer, P. E., and Lisanti, M. P. (2002). Caveolin-1-deficient mice are lean, resistant to diet-induced obesity, and show hypertriglyceridemia with adipocyte abnormalities. *J. Biol. Chem.* 277, 8635–8647.

48 Cohen, A. W., Razani, B., Wang, X. B., Combs, T. P., Williams, T. M., Scherer, P. E., and Lisanti, M. P. (2003). Caveolin-

1-deficient mice show insulin resistance and defective insulin receptor protein expression in adipose tissue. *Am. J. Physiol. Cell Physiol.* 285, C222–C235.

49 Cohen, A. W., Razani, B., Schubert, W., Williams, T. M., Wang, X. B., Iyengar, P., Brasaemle, D. L., Scherer, P. E., and Lisanti, M. P. (2004). Role of caveolin-1 in the modulation of lipolysis and lipid droplet formation. *Diabetes* 53, 1261–1270.

50 Lisanti, M. P., Scherer, P. E., Tang, Z., and Sargiacomo, M. (1994). Caveolae, caveolin and caveolin-rich membrane domains: a signalling hypothesis. *Trends Cell Biol.* 4, 231–235.

51 Chun, M., Liyanage, U. K., Lisanti, M. P., and Lodish, H. F. (1994). Signal transduction of a G protein-coupled receptor in caveolae: colocalization of endothelin and its receptor with caveolin. *Proc. Natl. Acad. Sci. USA* 91, 11728–11732.

52 Shenoy-Scaria, A. M., Dietzen, D. J., Kwong, J., Link, D. C., and Lublin, D. M. (1994). Cysteine3 of Src family protein tyrosine kinase determines palmitoylation and localization in caveolae. *J. Cell Biol.* 126, 353–363.

53 Chang, W. J., Ying, Y. S., Rothberg, K. G., Hooper, N. M., Turner, A. J., Gambliel, H. A., De Gunzburg, J., Mumby, S. M., Gilman, A. G., and Anderson, R.G. (1994). Purification and characterization of smooth muscle cell caveolae. *J. Cell Biol.* 126, 127–138.

54 Schnitzer, J. E., Oh, P., Jacobson, B. S., and Dvorak, A.M. (1995). Caveolae from luminal plasmalemma of rat lung endothelium: microdomains enriched in caveolin, Ca(2+)-ATPase, and inositol trisphosphate receptor. *Proc. Natl. Acad. Sci. USA* 92, 1759–1763.

55 Wiese, R. J., Mastick, C. C., Lazar, D. F., and Saltiel, A. R. (1995). Activation of mitogen-activated protein kinase and phosphatidylinositol 3'-kinase is not sufficient for the hormonal stimulation of glucose uptake, lipogenesis, or glycogen synthesis in 3T3-L1 adipocytes. *J. Biol. Chem.* 270, 3442–3446.

56 Brady, M., Bourbonais, F., and Saltiel, A. (1998). The activation of glycogen synthase by insulin switches from kinase inhibition to phosphatase activation during

adipogenesis in 3T3-L1 cells. *J. Biol. Chem.* 273, 14063–14066.

57 Smith, R. M., Harada, S., Smith, J. A., Zhang, S., and Jarett, L. (1998). Insulin-induced protein tyrosine phosphorylation cascade and signalling molecules are localized in a caveolin-enriched cell membrane domain. *Cell Signal.* 10, 355–362.

58 Gustavsson, J., Parpal, S., Karlsson, M., Ramsing, C., Thorn, H., Borg, M., Lindroth, M., Peterson, K. H., Magnusson, K. E., and Stralfors, P. (1999). Localization of the insulin receptor in caveolae of adipocyte plasma membrane. *FASEB J.* 13, 1961–1971.

59 Glenney, J. R. (1989). Tyrosine Phosphorylation of a 22-kDa protein is correlated with transformation by Rous Sarcoma Virus. *J. Biol. Chem.* 264, 20163–20166.

60 Ko, Y. G., Liu, P., Pathak, R. K., Craig, L. C., and Anderson, R.G. W. (1998). Early effects of pp60(v-src) kinase activation on caveolae. *J. Cell. Biochem.* 71, 524–535.

61 Lee, H., Woodman, S. E., Engelman, J. A., Volonte, D., Galbiati, F., Kaufman, H. L., Lublin, D. M., and Lisanti, M. P. (2001). Palmitoylation of caveolin-1 at a single site (Cys-156) controls its coupling to the c-Src tyrosine kinase: targeting of dually acylated molecules (GPI-linked, transmembrane, or cytoplasmic) to caveolae effectively uncouples c-Src and caveolin-1 (TYR-14). *J. Biol. Chem.* 276, 35150–35158.

62 Wary, K. K., Mariotti, A., Zurzolo, C., and Giancotti, F. G. (1998). A requirement for caveolin-1 and associated kinase Fyn in integrin signaling and anchorage-dependent cell growth. *Cell* 94, 625–634.

63 Zacharias, D. A., Violin, J. D., Newton, A. C., and Tsien, R. Y. (2002). Partitioning of lipid-modified monomeric GFPs into membrane microdomains of live cells. *Science* 296, 913–916.

64 Li, S., Seitz, R., and Lisanti, M. P. (1996). Phosphorylation of caveolin by Src tyrosine kinases. *J. Biol. Chem.* 271, 3863–3868.

65 Abe, J., Takahashi, M., Ishida, M., Lee, J. D., and Berk, B. C. (1997). c-Src is required for oxidative stress-mediated activation of big mitogen-activated protein kinase 1. *J. Biol. Chem.* 272, 20389–20394.

66 Abe, J., Okuda, M., Huang, Q., Yoshizumi, M., and Berk, B. C. (2000). Reactive oxygen species activate p90 ribosomal S6 kinase via Fyn and Ras. *J. Biol. Chem.* 275, 1739–1748.

67 Kapus, A., Di Ciano, C., Sun, J., Zhan, X., Kim, L., Wong, T. W., and Rotstein, O. D. (2000). Cell volume-dependent phosphorylation of proteins of the cortical cytoskeleton and cell-cell contact sites. The role of Fyn and FER kinases. *J. Biol. Chem.* 275, 32289–32298.

68 Alland, L., Peseckis, S. M., Atherton, R. E., Berthiaume, L., and Resh, M. D. (1994). Dual myristylation and palmitylation of Src family member p59fyn affects subcellular localization. *J. Biol. Chem.* 269, 16701–16705.

69 Muller, G., Jung, C., Wied, S., Welte, S., Jordan, H., and Frick, W. (2001). Redistribution of glycolipid raft domain components induces insulin-mimetic signaling in rat adipocytes. *Mol. Cell. Biol.* 21, 4553–4567.

70 Sun, X. J., Pons, S., Asano, T., Myers, M. G., Glasheen, E., and White, M. F. (1996). The Fyn tyrosine kinase binds IRS-1 and forms a distinct signaling complex during insulin stimulation. *J. Biol. Chem.* 271, 10583–10587.

71 Songyang, Z., and Cantley, L. C. (1995). Recognition and specificity in protein tyrosine kinase-mediated signalling. *Trends Biochem. Sci.* 20, 470–475.

72 Cujec, T. P., Medeiros, P. F., Hammond, P., Rise, C., and Kreider, B. L. (2002). Selection of v-Abl tyrosine kinase substrate sequences from randomized peptide and cellular proteomic libraries using mRNA display. *Chem. Biol.* 9, 253–264.

73 Beitner-Johnson, D., and LeRoith, D. (1995). Insulin-like growth factor-I stimulates tyrosine phosphorylation of endogenous c-Crk. *J. Biol. Chem.* 270, 5187–5190.

74 Lin, W. H., Huang, C. J., Liu, M. W., Chang, H. M., Chen, Y. J., Tai, T. Y., and Chuang, L. M. (2001). Cloning, mapping, and characterization of the human sorbin and SH3 domain containing 1 (SORBS1) gene: a protein associated with c-Abl during insulin signaling in the hepatoma cell line Hep3B. *Genomics* 74, 12–20.

75 Sorokin, A., and Reed, E. (1998). Insulin stimulates the tyrosine dephosphorylation of docking protein p130cas (Crk-associated substrate), promoting the switch of the adaptor protein crk from p130cas to newly phosphorylated insulin receptor substrate-1. *Biochem. J.* 334, 595–600.

76 Mastick, C. C., Sanguinetti, A. R., Knesek, J. H., Mastick, G. S., and Newcomb, L. F. (2001). Caveolin-1 and a 29-kDa caveolin-associated protein are phosphorylated on tyrosine in cells expressing a temperature-sensitive v-Abl kinase. *Exp. Cell Res.* 266, 142–154.

77 Koleske, A. J., Baltimore, D., and Lisanti, M. P. (1995). Reduction of caveolin and caveolae in oncogenically transformed cells. *Proc. Natl. Acad. Sci. USA* 92, 1381–1385.

78 Cao, H., Courchesne, W. E., and Corley Mastick, C. (2002). A phosphotyrosine-dependent dihybrid protein interaction screen reveals a role for phosphorylation of caveolin-1 on tyrosine 14: recruitment of C-terminal Src kinase. *J. Biol. Chem.* 277, 8771–8774.

79 Sun, X., Majumder, P., Shioya, H., Wu, F., Kumar, S., Weichselbaum, R., Kharbanda, S., and Kufe, D. (2000). Activation of the cytoplasmic c-Abl tyrosine kinase by reactive oxygen species. *J. Biol. Chem.* 275, 17237–17240.

80 Sun, X., Wu, F., Datta, R., Kharbanda, S., and Kufe, D. (2000). Interaction between protein kinase C delta and the c-Abl tyrosine kinase in the cellular response to oxidative stress. *J. Biol. Chem.* 275, 7470–7473.

81 Plattner, R., Kadlec, L., DeMali, K. A., Kazlauskas, A., and Pendergast, A. M. (1999). c-Abl is activated by growth factors and Src family kinases and has a role in the cellular response to PDGF. *Genes Dev.* 13, 2400–2411.

82 Gertler, F. B., Hill, K. K., Clark, M. J., and Hoffmann, F. M. (1993). Dosage-sensitive modifiers of Drosophila abl tyrosine kinase function: prospero, a regulator of axonal outgrowth, and disabled, a novel tyrosine kinase substrate. *Genes Dev.* 7, 441–453.

83 Gertler, F. B., Comer, A. R., Juang, J. L., Ahern, S. M., Clark, M. J., Liebl, E. C., and Hoffmann, F. M. (1995). enabled, a

dosage-sensitive suppressor of mutations in the Drosophila Abl tyrosine kinase, encodes an Abl substrate with SH3 domain-binding properties. *Genes Dev.* 9, 521–533.

84 Shishido, T., Akagi, T., Ouchi, T., Georgescu, M. M., Langdon, W. Y., and Hanafusa, H. (2000). The kinase-deficient Src acts as a suppressor of the Abl kinase for Cbl phosphorylation. *Proc. Natl. Acad. Sci. USA* 97, 6439–6444.

85 Lanier, L. M., and Gertler, F. B. (2000). From Abl to actin: Abl tyrosine kinase and associated proteins in growth cone motility. *Curr. Opin. Neurobiol.* 10, 80–87.

86 Krause, M., Sechi, A. S., Konradt, M., Monner, D., Gertler, F. B., and Wehland, J. (2000). Fyn-binding protein (Fyb)/SLP-76-associated protein (SLAP), Ena/vasodilator-stimulated phosphoprotein (VASP) proteins and the Arp2/3 complex link T cell receptor (TCR) signaling to the actin cytoskeleton. *J. Cell Biol.* 149, 181–194.

87 Small, J. V., Stradal, T., Vignal, E., and Rottner, K. (2002). The lamellipodium: where motility begins. *Trends Cell Biol.* 12, 112–120.

88 Furstoss, O., Dorey, K., Simon, V., Barila, D., Superti-Furga, G., and Roche, S. (2002). c-Abl is an effector of Src for growth factor-induced c-myc expression and DNA synthesis. *EMBO J.* 21, 514–524.

89 Arnaud, L., Ballif, B. A., Forster, E., and Cooper, J. A. (2003). Fyn tyrosine kinase is a critical regulator of Disabled-1 during brain development. *Curr. Biol.* 13, 9–17.

90 Feng, X., Gaeta, M. L., Madge, L. A., Yang, J. H., Bradley, J. R., and Pober, J. S. (2001). Caveolin-1 associates with TRAF2 to form a complex that is recruited to tumor necrosis factor receptors. *J. Biol. Chem.* 276, 8341–8349.

91 Duxbury, M. S., Ito, H., Ashley, S. W., and Whang, E. E. (2004). CEACAM6 cross-linking induces caveolin-1-dependent, Src-mediated focal adhesion kinase phosphorylation in BxPC3 pancreatic adenocarcinoma cells. *J. Biol. Chem.* 279, 23176–23182.

92 Howell, B. W., and Cooper, J. A. (1994). Csk suppression of Src involves movement of Csk to sites of Src activity. *Mol. Cell. Biol.* 14, 5402–5411.

93 Kawabuchi, M., Satomi, Y., Takao, T., Shimonishi, Y., Nada, S., Nagai, K., Tarakhovsky, A., and Okada, M. (2000). Transmembrane phosphoprotein Cbp regulates the activities of Src-family tyrosine kinases. *Nature* 404, 999–1003.

94 Takeuchi, S., Takayama, Y., Ogawa, A., Tamura, K., and Okada, M. (2000). Transmembrane phosphoprotein Cbp positively regulates the activity of the carboxyl-terminal Src kinase, Csk. *J. Biol. Chem.* 275, 29183–29186.

95 Torgersen, K. M., Vang, T., Abrahamsen, H., Yaqub, S., Horejsi, V., Schraven, B., Rolstad, B., Mustelin, T., and Tasken, K. (2001). Release from tonic inhibition of T cell activation through transient displacement of C-terminal Src kinase (Csk) from lipid rafts. *J. Biol. Chem.* 276, 29313–29318.

96 Thomas, S. M., and Brugge, J. S. (1997). Cellular functions regulated by Src family kinases. *Annu. Rev. Cell. Dev. Biol.* 13, 513–609.

97 Thomas, S. M., Soriano, P., and Imamoto, A. (1995). Specific and redundant roles of Src and Fyn in organizing the cytoskeleton. *Nature* 376, 267–271.

98 Fincham, V. J., and Frame, M. C. (1998). The catalytic activity of Src is dispensable for translocation to focal adhesions but controls the turnover of these structures during cell motility. *EMBO J.* 17, 81–92.

99 Arthur, W. T., Petch, L. A., and Burridge, K. (2000). Integrin engagement suppresses RhoA activity via a c-Src-dependent mechanism. *Curr. Biol.* 10, 719–722.

100 Li, L., Okura, M., and Imamoto, A. (2002). Focal adhesions require catalytic activity of Src family kinases to mediate integrin-matrix adhesion. *Mol. Cell. Biol.* 22, 1203–1217.

101 Wei, Y., Yang, X., Liu, Q., Wilkins, J. A., and Chapman, H. A. (1999). A role for caveolin and the urokinase receptor in integrin-mediated adhesion and signaling. *J. Cell Biol.* 144, 1285–1294.

102 van Deurs, B., Roepstorff, K., Hommelgaard, A. M., and Sandvig, K. (2003). Caveolae: anchored, multifunctional platforms in the lipid ocean. *Trends Cell Biol.* 13, 92–100.

103 Navarro, A., Anand-Apte, B., and Parat, M. O. (2004). A role for caveolae in cell migration. *FASEB J.* 18, 1801–1811.

104 Thomsen, P., Roepstorff, K., Stahlhut, M., and van Deurs, B. (2002). Caveolae are highly immobile plasma membrane microdomains, which are not involved in constitutive endocytic trafficking. *Mol. Biol. Cell* 13, 238–250.

105 Mundy, D. I., Machleidt, T., Ying, Y. S., Anderson, R. G., and Bloom, G. S. (2002). Dual control of caveolar membrane traffic by microtubules and the actin cytoskeleton. *J. Cell Sci.* 115, 4327–4339.

106 Stahlhut, M., and van Deurs, B. (2000). Identification of filamin as a novel ligand for caveolin-1: evidence for the organization of caveolin-1-associated membrane domains by the actin cytoskeleton. *Mol. Biol. Cell* 11, 325–337.

107 Isshiki, M., Ando, J., Yamamoto, K., Fujita, T., Ying, Y., and Anderson, R. G. (2002). Sites of Ca(2+) wave initiation move with caveolae to the trailing edge of migrating cells. *J. Cell Sci.* 115, 475–484.

108 Boyd, N. L., Park, H., Yi, H., Boo, Y. C., Sorescu, G. P., Sykes, M., and Jo, H. (2003). Chronic shear induces caveolae formation and alters ERK and Akt responses in endothelial cells. *Am. J. Physiol. Heart Circ. Physiol.* 285, H1113-H1122.

109 Beardsley, A., Fang, K., Mertz, H., Castranova, V., Friend, S., and Liu, J. (2005). Loss of caveolin-1 polarity impedes endothelial cell polarization and directional movement. *J. Biol. Chem.* 280, 3541–3547.

110 Minetti, C., Sotgia, F., Bruno, C., Scartezzini, P., Broda, P., Bado, M., Masetti, E., Mazzocco, M., Egeo, A., Donati, M. A., Volonte, D., Galbiati, F., Cordone, G., Bricarelli, F. D., Lisanti, M. P., and Zara, F. (1998). Mutations in the caveolin-3 gene cause autosomal dominant limb-girdle muscular dystrophy. *Nat. Genet.* 18, 365–368.

111 Hagiwara, Y., Sasaoka, T., Araishi, K., Imamura, M., Yorifuji, H., Nonaka, I., Ozawa, E., and Kikuchi, T. (2000). Caveolin-3 deficiency causes muscle degeneration in mice. *Hum. Mol. Genet.* 9, 3047–3054.

112 Turner, C. E. (2000). Paxillin interactions. *J. Cell Sci.* 113, 4139–4140.

113 Abe, J., and Berk, B. C. (1999). Fyn and JAK2 mediate Ras activation by reactive oxygen species. *J. Biol. Chem.* 274, 21003–21010.

114 Kumar, S., Bharti, A., Mishra, N. C., Raina, D., Kharbanda, S., Saxena, S., and Kufe, D. (2001). Targeting of the c-Abl tyrosine kinase to mitochondria in the necrotic cell death response to oxidative stress. *J. Biol. Chem.* 276, 17281–17285.

115 Martindale, J. L., and Holbrook, N. J. (2002). Cellular response to oxidative stress: signaling for suicide and survival. *J. Cell Physiol.* 192, 1–15.

116 Tong, P., Khayat, Z. A., Huang, C., Patel, N., Ueyama, A., and Klip, A. (2001). Insulin-induced cortical actin remodeling promotes GLUT4 insertion at muscle cell membrane ruffles. *J. Clin. Invest.* 108, 371–381.

117 Kanzaki, M., and Pessin, J. E. (2001). Insulin-stimulated GLUT4 translocation in adipocytes is dependent upon cortical actin remodeling. *J. Biol. Chem.* 276, 42436–42444.

118 Kanzaki, M., and Pessin, J. E. (2002). Caveolin-associated filamentous actin (Cav-actin) defines a novel F-actin structure in adipocytes. *J. Biol. Chem.* 277, 25867–25869.

119 Parton, R. G., Molero, J. C., Floetenmeyer, M., Green, K. M., and James, D. E. (2002). Characterization of a distinct plasma membrane macrodomain in differentiated adipocytes. *J. Biol. Chem.* 277, 46769–46778.

120 Watson, R. T., Shigematsu, S., Chiang, S. H., Mora, S., Kanzaki, M., Macara, I. G., Saltiel, A. R., and Pessin, J. E. (2001). Lipid raft microdomain compartmentalization of TC10 is required for insulin signaling and GLUT4 translocation. *J. Cell Biol.* 154, 829–840.

7

Role of Lipid Microdomains in the Formation of Supramolecular Protein Complexes and Transmembrane Signaling

György Vámosi, Andrea Bodnár, György Vereb, János Szöllősi, and Sándor Damjanovich

7.1
Introduction

The plasma membrane is the theater of all kinds of material and information exchange between a cell and its environment – that is, the "outer world". The plasma membrane is basically a lipid bilayer that accommodates a significant number of proteins with diverse structures and tasks necessary for the proper function of cells. Concepts about the architecture of the plasma membrane have changed dramatically through the past decades. The "rigid membrane" concept was replaced by the Singer-Nicolson (S-N) fluid mosaic membrane model in 1972, which postulated the random distribution and free lateral mobility of proteins in the unstructured lipid environment [1]. Construction of the S-N model was greatly advanced by the classical experiment of Frye and Edidin, which demonstrated intermixing of distinct molecular species in the plasma membrane of heterokaryons of human and murine lymphocytes [2]. Although the S-N model was able to explain many phenomena taking place in the cell membrane, it had a limited validity. First of all, it was mostly applicable to the quasi-symmetric circulating blood cells. It has been well known for a long time that cells built into solid tissues are frequently polarized as required by their physical environment and biological function, a most extreme example being the organization of brush border cells, into two discrete regions – the apical and the basolateral – with distinct functions and thus different lipid and protein composition. The picture of "freely moving proteins in the uniform lipid sea" was challenged by experimental observations suggesting the locally restricted mobility of proteins in the lipid bilayer [3,4]. Data indicating the existence of hierarchically built protein complexes even in non-polarized cells also contradicted the S-N model [5,6]. As for the concept of "uniform lipid sea", an important step forward was the discovery of sphingolipid- and cholesterol-enriched lipid domains – that is, lipid rafts – constituting a proof that phase-separation of lipids observed in model membranes also occurs in the more complex plasma membrane of living cells [7,8]. All these observations led to the "membrane microdomain" concept, namely the compartmentalization/organization of membrane proteins and lipids into nonrandom, well-defined, yet dynamic structures, which exist at different time and size scales.

7.1.1
Lateral organization of membrane proteins

According to our present knowledge, lateral arrangement of membrane components – whether proteins or lipids – is a general phenomenon, which is essential
for the proper functioning of both the individual molecules and the whole of the
plasma membrane. Processes associated with the plasma membrane (e.g., signal
transduction, protein sorting, etc.) demand the cooperation of various membrane
proteins and are often accompanied by dynamic rearrangement of the two-dimensional macromolecular patterns at the cell surface. The structured, and at the same
time dynamic, nature of the plasma membrane allows accumulation of relevant
molecules in particular membrane areas whilst excluding others, thus preventing
their interaction [9–11].

The basic organization level of membrane proteins is defined by their molecular
association/physical proximity, and is referred to as nanometer- or small-scale
clusters [6]. These clusters can be formed either in a homologous or heterologous
fashion; that is, their molecular components can be either identical or distinct. The
generalized occurrence of such protein complexes was initially proposed in the
early 1980s, based on the preferential accommodation of the genetically determined membrane-spanning α-helices of proteins into distinct membrane microdomains [12]. This assumption has been supported by a considerable amount of
experimental data. A major asset in studying small-scale protein assemblies was
the adaptation of fluorescence resonance energy transfer (FRET) to cellular systems (see Section 7.2).

Different types of small-scale protein patterns can be distinguished in the
plasma membrane [5]:
- In many cases, a given "functional unit" comprises several components/sub-
  units (e.g., in multi-chain immune recognition receptor complexes [13]).
- External stimuli can also induce cluster formation through reorganization of
  membrane proteins in the plane of the plasma membrane (e.g., ligand-evoked
  aggregation of the epidermal growth factor receptor [14]).
- Apart from the aforesaid examples, where the individual components are either
  preassembled or come together upon ligand binding/external stimuli, co-localization of apparently unrelated proteins can also be observed in many cases (e.g.,
  association of the insulin receptor and major histocompatability complex (MHC)
  I glycoproteins [15,16]). Revealing the co-localization of such proteins may call
  our attention to their potential functional relationship.

Beyond the small-scale protein associations (i.e., colocalization on the 1- to 10-nm
scale), clustering of membrane proteins at a second hierarchical level can also be
observed in many cases [5,11,17]. These so-called large-scale clusters can be several
hundred nanometers in diameter and could contain tens to thousands of proteins.
Some of the biophysical methods applicable for studying large-scale protein clusters are summarized in Section 7.2.

7.1.2
Factors controlling the organization of membrane proteins

The mosaic-like organization of lipid structures – that is, the assembly of lipids with similar physico-chemical character (saturation, length, etc.) – into distinct domains [4] plays an important role in the formation of both small- and large-scale protein assemblies. The lipid domain structure of the plasma membrane may cause selective accumulation of membrane proteins (or their exclusion from distinct membrane areas) through preferential interaction of the membrane-interacting region of a given protein with a select class of lipids [18]. Lipid rafts, enriched in cholesterol and glycosphingolipids, are a special type of lipid domains [4,7]. Lipid rafts were shown to accumulate a set of membrane proteins as well as cytosolic signaling elements, and were proposed to act as specialized signaling compartments [13,19–23]. There are several vehicles that may help target proteins into lipid rafts:

- a shell of annular lipids encasing the transmembrane segment of proteins [24];
- the addition of a GPI-anchor or saturated acyl chains via post-translational modification [25–28]; and
- interactions with proteins having a high affinity to the lipid raft environment.

Rafts are complex and dynamic structures which vary both in size and protein content [10]. By enabling the dynamic association/reassociation of proteins residing within the same domain, lipid rafts provide a platform for their functional cooperation. The dynamic exchange of components between rafts with different composition (or between raft and non-raft regions) as well as the aggregation of smaller rafts, raft "microdomains" into "macrodomains" also play an important role in the spatiotemporal organization of plasma membrane-associated processes taking place in lipid rafts [29].

In addition to lipid domains, cells have other means by which they can control the formation and maintenance of specific assemblies of membrane proteins (for reviews, see [3,5,11,30]). Protein-protein interactions – for example, between the transmembrane α-helices – may also contribute to the stability of protein clusters and membrane microdomains [31]. Vesicular transport mechanisms can produce selective accumulation of membrane proteins by means of "directed" transport of vesicular components to a given membrane region [32,33]. The cytoskeleton may act either by actively directing redistribution of proteins in the plasma membrane, or by restricting their motion and trapping them in a given membrane area by barriers formed from joint structures of the membrane and the cytoskeleton [34]. The assembly of lipid rafts into macrodomains is also governed by the actin cytoskeleton (see [29] and references therein). The free diffusion of membrane proteins can also be hindered by interaction with elements of different cytosolic signaling elements (e. g., G-proteins, kinases). These factors are not independent of each other and may act in concert to generate supramolecular structures in the plasma membrane.

In this chapter selected examples for the existence of hierarchically built protein complexes are provided. Their regulation by the lipid domain structure of the plasma membrane and the functional consequences of the formation of protein clusters in transmembrane signaling will also be discussed.

7.2
Biophysical Strategies for Studying the Lateral Organization of Membrane Proteins

Cell-surface proteins display non-random distribution patterns ranging in size from a few nanometers to microns. Here, we describe some widely used fluorescence-based biophysical methods that can be used to study the different hierarchical levels of the lateral organization and interactions of membrane proteins. Classical biochemical and immunological methods (chemical cross-linking, co-immunoprecipitation, detergent resistance analysis, etc.) provide valuable information on the interaction of membrane proteins, but have several drawbacks. First, with these methods proteins cannot be studied in their native environment. Second, the use of conventional extraction and isolation procedures inherent to these techniques may also disrupt protein-protein interactions, or may induce the formation of artificial protein aggregates. These methods provide information only on the bulk properties of interactions, without resolving cell-to-cell or subcellular variations. On the other hand, fluorescence-based observations of appropriately labeled molecules allow the detection of interactions with a subcellular resolution. Fluorescence detection is sensitive (down to the level of single molecules under select conditions), relatively non-destructive, and specific due to the high affinity of interaction between commonly used markers (specific antibodies, toxins, etc.) and their targets. Genes tailored to code for proteins carrying a fluorescent tag (GFP and its spectral variants) are routinely used to report on the subcellular distribution of proteins.

7.2.1
Determination of Domain Size and Overlap between Fluorescence Distributions using Fluorescence Microscopy

The lateral distribution of cell-surface proteins and their co-localization in membrane microdomains can be studied by digital imaging microscopy with a resolution of 200–300 nm, as set by Abbe's law [35]. The application of confocal laser scanning microscopy or multiphoton excitation [36] greatly improves image sharpness and contrast by excluding photons arising from out-of-focus planes. This resolution is not sufficient to directly indicate molecular associations; however, it allows the observation of overlap/segregation between different protein clusters or lipid microdomains. Quantitative analysis of the size of clusters/microdomains can be derived from the spatial autocorrelation function of the fluorescence intensity distribution [39]. Using this approach, cluster sizes of predominantly raft-localized proteins IL-2Rα, HLA I and II, as well as GPI-anchored proteins CD48, were determined to be ~600–700 nm, which coincided well with cluster sizes determined from electron microscopic analysis of immunogold-labeled samples. These domain sizes correlated well with the mean barrier-free path measured for the MHC I glycoprotein and its truncation mutants [37], as well as dimensions of confinement zones derived from single particle tracking in which E-cadherin or epidermal growth factor receptor (EGFR) molecules could freely diffuse [38]. Disruption of lipid rafts by cholesterol extraction blurred the boundaries of protein clusters and extended their diameter to ~1000 nm [39].

The extent of overlap between clusters of different membrane proteins and lipid microdomains can be characterized by the cross-correlation coefficient of the pixel intensities of individual fluorescence distributions [11,39,40]. For a pair of images x and y, the cross-correlation coefficient is calculated as:

$$C = \frac{\sum_{i,j} \left(x_{ij} - \langle x \rangle \right)\left(y_{ij} - \langle y \rangle \right)}{\sqrt{\sum_{i,j}\left(x_{ij} - \langle x \rangle \right)^2 \sum_{i,j}\left(y_{ij} - \langle y \rangle \right)^2}} \tag{7.1}$$

where x_{ij} and y_{ij} are fluorescence intensities at pixel coordinates i,j in images x and y, and <x>, <y> are the mean intensities. The theoretical maximum is $C = 1$ for identical images, and a value of 0 implies independent localization of the labeled molecules.

7.2.2
Fluorescence Resonance Energy Transfer (FRET)

Techniques utilizing Förster-type FRET offer convenient tools for mapping the spatial distribution and molecular vicinity relations of membrane proteins on live cells *in situ*, without any major interference with the physiological condition of the cells. Several techniques have been developed to measure FRET on cell surfaces [5,41–43].

FRET is a process wherein energy is transferred non-radiatively from an excited donor fluorophor to a nearby acceptor via dipole-dipole coupling [44]. In order for FRET to occur, it is necessary that the dipole moments of the dyes have a proper relative orientation and the emission spectrum of the donor and the absorption spectrum of the acceptor molecule overlap with each other [45]. From the point of view of biological applications, the most important property of FRET is that its rate is inversely proportional to the sixth power of the donor-acceptor distance; hence, it is a sensitive tool for the determination of inter- or intramolecular distances in the 1- to 10-nm range, and can be applied as a "spectroscopic ruler" [46]. The efficiency of FRET, E, is defined as the fraction of excitation quanta transferred from the donor to the acceptor, which can be expressed as:

$$E = \frac{k_{FRET}}{k_f + k_{nf} + k_{FRET}} = \frac{R_o^6}{R_o^6 + R^6} \tag{7.2}$$

where R is the donor-acceptor distance, R_o is the so-called Förster distance, at which the FRET efficiency is 50 % for the given donor-acceptor pair, and k_{FRET}, k_f and k_{nf} are the rate constants of de-excitation by FRET, fluorescence emission and non-radiative processes other than FRET, respectively. R_o is usually 5–10 nm, which defines the distance range for which FRET is applicable. In practice, the detection of FRET is based on the measurement of one or more of the following physical parameters: a) the decreased intensity of the donor (donor quenching); b) the enhanced emission of the acceptor (sensitized emission); c) the decreased fluorescence lifetime of the donor; d) the increased fluorescence anisotropy of the donor; or e) the decreased photobleaching rate of the donor.

Measurement of FRET by microscopy provides subcellular mapping of protein-protein interactions, allowing the visual identification of compartments/organelles where the interactions of interest take place (for a review, see [47]). Without going into detail, the most commonly used FRET microscopic methods are described below.

Based on the simultaneous detection of three (or in the case of using auto-fluorescence correction, four) fluorescence intensities (autofluorescence, donor and acceptor channels and FRET channel) at each pixel, and using appropriate controls for determining the spectral spillover between the channels, FRET efficiency can be measured even at rather low expression levels [48].

With the acceptor photobleaching technique, the extent of donor quenching due to FRET is detected in a fairly simple way [49,50]. If the acceptor is irreversibly photodestroyed by selective illumination at the acceptor's absorption wavelength, the intensity of the donor increases, and from the extent of increase E can be calculated:

$$E = 1 - \frac{I_{DA}}{I_D} \tag{7.3}$$

where I_{DA} and I_D are the background-corrected donor fluorescence intensities with and without acceptor – that is, before and after photobleaching. The advantage of the method is its simplicity and its requirement for only donor-acceptor double-labeled samples.

The donor photobleaching (pbFRET) method exploits the increased resistivity of the donor to photobleaching in the presence of acceptor. Photobleaching is initiated from the excited state. FRET reduces the fluorescence lifetime of the donor; that is, the dye spends less time in the excited state, resulting in an elongated photobleaching time constant:

$$E = 1 - \frac{T_D}{T_{DA}} \tag{7.4}$$

where T_D and T_{DA} are the photobleaching time constants of the donor in the absence and presence of acceptor, respectively [50,51].

The fluorescence lifetime of the donor can be directly measured by using the imaging version of phase fluorimetry, fluorescence lifetime imaging microscopy

(FLIM) [52]. Lifetime is a fairly robust parameter, which makes FLIM an attractive method in spite of its relatively complex instrumentation.

Although FRET microscopy has a clear advantage in providing subcellular information on interactions at microscopic resolution, it requires large numbers of cells to be evaluated to provide statistically valid data, and this is both time-consuming and labor-intensive. To determine small quantitative changes in protein-protein interactions, at least several hundreds or thousands of cells must be evaluated. A suitable alternative is that of flow cytometric cell-by-cell FRET measurement, which provides the mean FRET efficiency for each cell in the analyzed population [53,54]. The high number of cells that can be analyzed by flow cytometry provides excellent statistics, high accuracy, and reproducibility.

7.2.3
Fluorescence Cross-Correlation Spectroscopy: Analysis of Protein Co-Mobility

Most FRET methods are limited to recording a static picture – a "snapshot" of molecular proximities of the labeled biomolecules – without being able to report on the temporal stability of molecular interactions. Co-localization at the nanometer scale as revealed by FRET does not necessarily mean that the studied proteins form stable complexes with one another. The co-mobility – that is, the joint diffusive motion of proteins – is an evidence for their stable interaction, and this can be investigated by using the dynamic method of fluorescence cross-correlation spectroscopy (FCCS), the two-channel version of fluorescence correlation spectroscopy (FCS). A recent compilation on the theory and applications of FCS can be found in a publication edited by two pioneers of the technique, Rigler and Elson [55].

In FCS, a laser beam focused to a subfemtoliter volume element excites fluorophores diffusing across the sensitive volume (a prolate ellipsoid defined by the surface at which the detection efficiency drops to e^{-2} times the value at the center), giving rise to a fluctuating fluorescence signal. The rate of fluctuations is related to the mobility of the fluorescing molecules (i.e., the diffusion coefficient). Typically, the intensity autocorrelation function is calculated from the intensity versus time signal (either on-line by a dedicated correlator card or off-line), and this function is fitted according to model functions assuming different mechanisms of diffusion and accounting for various photophysical processes (singlet-triplet transition, dark state formation, photobleaching) or chemical reactions (e.g., protonation) taking place in the system. For a system with n different species diffusing in 2D (the plane of the plasma membrane) labeled with dyes undergoing singlet-triplet transition [56], the autocorrelation function is as follows:

$$G(\tau) = \frac{\langle \delta F(t) \cdot \delta F(t+\tau) \rangle}{\langle F \rangle^2} = \frac{\int_0^T \delta F(t) \cdot \delta F(t+\tau) \, dt}{\langle F \rangle^2} = \frac{1}{N} \cdot \frac{1 - \Theta_{tr} + \Theta_{tr} e^{-\tau/\tau_{tr}}}{1 - \Theta_{tr}} \cdot \sum_i \phi_i \left(1 + \frac{\tau}{\tau_i}\right)^{-1} \quad (7.5)$$

The left part of the equation is the definition of the autocorrelation function: the square brackets refer to averaging the expression over the duration T of the measurement, the variable τ is the lag time (the time difference between the samples taken from the F(t) curve), $\langle F \rangle$ is the mean fluorescence intensity over the studied time interval, and $\delta F(t) = F(t) - \langle F \rangle$ is the deviation of the actual fluorescence intensity from the mean. N is the mean number of molecules in the sensitive volume, Θ_{tr} is the fraction of molecules in the triplet state, τ_{tr} is the phosphorescence lifetime, τ_i is the diffusion time (the mean dwell time of a molecule in the sensitive volume) and φ_i is the weight of the ith species. The diffusion time is inversely proportional to the diffusion coefficient D_i:

$$D_i = \omega_{xy}^{\,2} \big/ 4\,\tau_i \tag{7.6}$$

with ω_{xy} indicating the lateral radius of the sensitive volume.

Thus, the parameters of major importance derived from the autocorrelation function regarding protein-protein interactions are the diffusion coefficient and the local concentration of the labeled molecules. The value of D decreases if the labeled proteins form aggregates or interact with the cytoskeleton. Another good measure of the aggregation (homo-association) state of the studied proteins is the fluorescence intensity of the jointly diffusing units, which is simply the ratio $\langle F \rangle / N$.

The diffusion coefficient has only a weak dependence on the molecular weight ($D \propto MW^{-1/3}$); thus, in a relatively heterogeneous system such as the plasma membrane of a live cell it is not always possible to distinguish between monomeric and dimeric states.

In FCCS, two molecular species are labeled with preferably distinctly excitable and detectable fluorophores. In case the two molecular species are associated, their joint diffusive motion will result in parallel fluctuations of the fluorescence intensities $F_a(t)$ and $F_b(t)$ in the two detection channels. In this case, the cross-correlation function $G^x(\tau)$ (see Eq. 7.7) has a nonzero amplitude $G^x(0)$, which is proportional to the concentration c_{ab} of the complexed fraction of molecular species "a" and "b" (see Eq. 7.8):

$$G^x(\tau) = \frac{\langle \delta F_a(t) \cdot \delta F_b(t+\tau) \rangle}{\langle F_a \rangle \langle F_b \rangle} \tag{7.7}$$

$$G^x(0) \propto \frac{c_{ab}}{V_{eff}\left(c_{a,tot}\right)\left(c_{b,tot}\right)} \tag{7.8}$$

where $c_{a,tot}$ and $c_{b,tot}$ are the total concentrations of molecules a and b in free state or in complex, and V_{eff} is the so-called effective volume. The actual form of the cross-correlation function also depends on the geometrical parameters of the laser foci and the diffusion properties of the different molecular species [57,58].

7.2.4
Atomic Force Microscopy (AFM)

In the version of this technique applied to cellular imaging, a needle with a sharp tip (radius of curvature 10–50 nm) is scanned over the cell surface at a pressing force on the order of 0.1 to 10 pN, and the height of the needle is recorded at each position, thus generating a topographic image of the soft cell surface. The major advantage of AFM as compared to other microscopic techniques is that it provides a better resolution than optical microscopy and yet allows the observation of living cells, which is impossible with electron microscopy. In order to study the cell-surface distribution of specific membrane proteins by AFM, immunogold labeling was applied to provide specificity. This approach was successfully applied to study distinct hierarchical levels of the cell surface distribution of class I and class II MHC molecules in immunocompetent cells [59,60].

7.2.5
Scanning Near-Field Optical Microscopy (SNOM)

This technique combines the enhanced lateral and vertical resolution character-istic of AFM with simultaneous measurements of topographic and optical signals. SNOM can achieve a spatial resolution beyond the diffraction limit by scanning a sub-wavelength-sized aperture, confining the excitation beam to the close prox-imity of the sample. The resolution depends on the size of the aperture and the distance between the probe and the sample, rather than on the wavelength. The most commonly used SNOM probe is an aluminum-coated tapered optical fiber with an aperture <100 nm, positioned very close to the surface (~10 nm). The position of the probe is controlled by a piezo-electric stand, and the light emitted by the sample is collected either by an objective or through the same optical fiber. SNOM can simultaneously map topographic and optical properties with high spa-tial resolution, has single molecule sensitivity, and is relatively noninvasive. In addition, by using fluorescent labels it can provide a high level of molecular speci-ficity. SNOM detected a highly patchy distribution of some fluorescent lipid ana-logues reflecting a lipid domain structure in fixed, dried cells [61]. The sizes of these patches were consistent with the sizes of domains implied by measurements of lateral diffusion with fluorescence photobleaching recovery. SNOM was also used to observe clustering of fluorescently labeled membrane receptors; clusters of platelet-derived growth factor (PDGF) receptors down to 80–100 nm diameter were observed on glioblastoma cells [50], and activation-dependent clustering of ErbB2 was revealed on breast tumor cells [62].

7.3
The Immunological Synapse

One of the best-characterized examples of specialized signaling domains where the dynamic assembly of both small- and large-scale protein associations have a crucial role, is the contact region formed between a T cell and a target or an antigen-presenting cell (APC), termed the immunological synapse (IS) [63,64]. Formation of the IS is initiated by recognition of the peptide antigen presented in complex with MHC glycoproteins on the APC or target cell by the T cell receptor complex (TCR) on the appropriate T cell [65,66]. Recognition of the antigen causes the redistribution of numerous molecules in both cells and leads to the formation of well-defined junctional structures at the interface of the two cells. Participation of the TCR along with adhesion and co-stimulatory molecules, co-receptors and associated cytosolic signaling elements on T cells as well as recruitment of MHC-peptide complexes and adhesion molecules on APCs can be observed in all ISs [67–69]. Supramolecular organization of these molecules is generated by their clustering/segregation at both the micrometer and submicrometer (nanometer) scale. ISs mature through discrete stages characterized by high-order temporal and spatial cooperation of multiple elements (membrane proteins, signaling molecules) required for appropriate function [66–68].

Involvement of lipid rafts in T cell signaling in general, and in the IS formation in particular, has been extensively studied and firmly established [19,29,70,71]. It is hypothesized that upon synapse formation small, individual rafts are assembled into raft macrodomains in a process regulated by the actin cytoskeleton [29]. Assembly of raft macrodomains occurs in three stages. Engagement of TCR initiates signals for actin polymerization followed by actin- and myosin-dependent migration of rafts to the site of cell signaling. Raft microdomains coalesce and, as a consequence, signaling proteins residing in discrete domains are now proximal within the same microenvironment, which enhances their interactions and amplifies the initial signals resulting in further raft assembly and signal amplification. The cascade continues until arrested by stop signals, which might include protein tyrosine phosphatases [29].

Despite the common features, ISs display diversity both in function and architecture, depending on the nature of interacting cells and as a consequence, that of the interacting molecular partners [67–69,72]. In the prototypic "bull-eye" structure, a central supramolecular activation cluster (cSMAC) containing TCR and MHC-peptide is surrounded by a pSMAC (peripheral SMAC) of adhesion molecules [63,64,73,74]. The "secretory synapse" formed between cytotoxic T cells (CTLs) and their targets has a double cSMAC containing the secretory apparatus juxtaposed with the TCR cluster [75]. The formation of several small, distinct TCR clusters instead of a large, single one (multifocal synapses) or nonclustered, diffuse distribution of TCR (nonsegregated IS) in the contact zone was also detected in many cases [69,72]. Dynamic contacts allowing migration (amoeboid movement) of T cells across the surface of the counterpart cells are presumably nonsegregated but at the same time mobile structures (migratory synapses) [76].

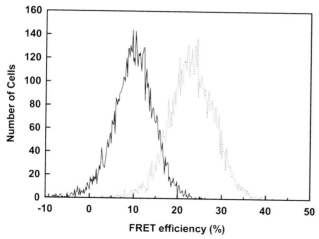

Fig. 7.1 Measurement of MHC I homoasso-ciation on OCM-3 uveal melanoma cells. The solid line denotes the distribution of FRET efficiency values between MHC I molecules measured by flow cytometry on a cell-by-cell basis. MHC I was targeted by Cy3- and Cy5-conjugated L368 mAbs specific for β2-micro-globulin (β2m, light chain of MHC I). The positive FRET value (peaking at ~10%) indicates homoassociation of MHC I. As a positive control, the intramolecular FRET efficiency between the heavy chain of MHC I and β2m targeted by Cy3-W6/32 and Cy5-L368 mAbs, respectively, was also determined (dotted line).

The IS may fulfill numerous functions with varying importance for a particular cell-cell interaction [67,68]. For example, it may enhance and/or prolong signaling, integrate different signaling pathways, direct granule release and cytokine secretion, terminate signaling processes, and balance enhancing and terminating signals.

Whereas antigen-induced redistribution of the relevant molecules on T cells has been extensively characterized (for reviews, see [63,67–69,72]), much less is known about the behavior of MHC and adhesion molecules or the mechanisms controlling their accumulation on target cells or APCs. Therefore, in the following section focus is centered on data regarding the distribution of MHC as well as intracellular adhesion molecules (ICAM-1) on APCs and target cells.

By using FRET and lateral diffusion (single particle tracking) experiments, clustering (self-association) of MHC I glycoproteins was observed at the surface of various human cell types [77–80] (see Fig. 7.1). A recent detergent-solubility analysis of their self-association properties also confirmed that homotypic association is an inherent property of MHC I (and MHC II) molecules [81], in accordance with earlier observations of their spontaneous clustering after reconstitution into liposome model systems [82]. Electron and scanning force microscopic experiments also disclosed the nonrandom (clusterized) organization of MHC I molecules at a higher hierarchical level: immunogold-labeled MHC I molecules were observed to form domains of several hundred nanometers diameter [59]. The degree of MHC I oligomerization showed good correlation with the expression of free MHC I heavy chains [lacking β2-microglobulin (β2m); "FHC"]: both of these were significant on activated or transformed/tumor cells [83]. The two forms of heavy chains participated in common small- and large-scale clusters at the surface of human B cells, as revealed by FRET and SNOM experiments [84]. Culturing cells with β2m resulted in a decreased homotypic association of intact MHC I heterodimers and their reduced co-clustering with free heavy chains [84]. According to these data, FHCs likely have an important contribution to MHC I clustering: their involvement seems to stabilize MHC I clusters and *vice versa*, their functionally active conformation, which is still capable of rebinding β2m, may also be stabilized by participation in these clusters [83,84]. Otherwise, FHCs would undergo irreversible denaturation and become functionally inactive and/or would be either internalized or released in a soluble form from the cell surface [85,86].

Clustered cell-surface distribution and anomalous diffusion of MHC II glycoproteins as well as their heteroassociation with MHC I were also reported in numerous cell types, including APCs [77,87–89]. Atomic force and electron microscopic data showed that MHC II molecules form homoclusters not only on the nanometer scale attainable by FRET, but also at a higher hierarchical level, in the micrometer distance range [60]. Electron microscopy revealed that a fraction of MHC II molecules was heteroclustered with MHC I at the same hierarchical level [60]. Molecular associations were detected between the ICAM-1 adhesion molecules and MHC glycoproteins at the surface of human T and B lymphoma cell lines [77,90]. In addition, a high degree of ICAM-1 self-association was found on HUT102 B2 human T lymphoma cells [77]. The above-mentioned association motifs of ICAM-1 and MHC glycoproteins were also observed on uveal melanoma and colon carcinoma cells. Interferon (IFN)-γ changed the expression levels of MHC and ICAM-1 molecules as well as inducing the re-arrangement of their spatial distribution/association patterns on these cells [78,91].

Since clustering of MHC and ICAM-1 molecules could be observed in the IS [64,74], it is reasonable to assume that in vivo formation of the aforesaid association patterns of MHC I, MHC II and ICAM-1 proteins may promote IS formation, and their high local concentration can significantly increase the avidity of APC-T cell interaction [63,92]. Indeed, diminishing MHC I oligomerization on target cells by β2m treatment considerably reduced the efficiency of activation and effector function of allospecific cytotoxic T lymphocytes [84]. This hypothesis is also supported by studies with soluble MHC:peptide multimers (dimers, trimers or tetramers) showing that aggregation of MHC molecules may significantly increase the efficiency of activation/immune response of T cells [93–95].

Although to a different extent, constitutive or inducible association of MHC glycoproteins and ICAM-1 molecules with lipid rafts could be observed in various cell types [39,78,90,96–101]. Disruption of lipid raft integrity with filipin or methyl-β-cyclodextrin caused dispersion of large-scale MHC clusters [39,97] and translocation of MHC to the soluble membrane fractions [90,96]. Dissociation of small-scale MHC II clusters was also detected upon cholesterol depletion [97]. These data

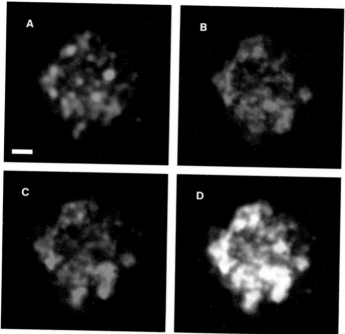

Fig. 7.2 Triple co-localization of lipid rafts, ICAM-1 and MHC I on OCM-3 human uveal melanoma cells, as detected by CLSM. Lipid rafts were labeled by Alexa Fluor 488-conjugated cholera toxin B subunit (panel A). ICAM-1 (panel B) and MHC I (panel C) molecules were targeted by Alexa 546-MEM111 and Cy5-W6/32 mAbs, respectively. Membrane areas where two or three membrane species co-localize are indicated with mixed colors in the overlay image (panel D). The pairwise cross-correlation coefficients between the fluorescence distributions indicate a high level of co-localization between the observed markers: $C_{AB} \sim 0.7$, $C_{AC} \sim 0.7$, $C_{BC} = 0.65$. The applied colors are pseudocolors. (Scale bar = 2 μm.)

indicate that lipid raft association is one of the underlying mechanisms responsible for MHC clustering.

Co-localization of MHC I and ICAM-1 could be observed within lipid rafts of colon carcinoma and uveal melanoma cells [78,91] (Fig. 7.2). On human B lymphoblastoid cells, physical association of MHC I and ICAM-1 could be detected both in detergent-insoluble and in detergent-soluble membranes [90]. The disruption of raft integrity resulted in a significant loss of MHC I and ICAM-1 from the raft fraction, but their association was still detectable, implying that this interaction does not critically depend on the structure of rafts.

The accommodation of MHC and ICAM-1 in lipid rafts has important functional consequences in the process of antigen presentation. Lipid raft-assisted compartmentation of MHC II was shown to enhance the efficiency of antigen presentation to CD4+ T cells [96,97,102]. This effect was more prominent at low antigen doses, suggesting that rafting MHC domains are critical for T cell activation by rare MHC II-peptide complexes and less important when the antigen density is high [96,97,102,103]. It was also demonstrated that APC lipid rafts, raft-associated relevant MHC II-peptide complexes and even immunologically irrelevant MHC II molecules accumulate at the IS [103]. Upon maturation of the IS, relevant MHC II-peptide complexes were sorted to the central region of the interface, while irrelevant MHC II molecules were excluded from this site [103]. Similar to T cells, remodeling of the APC surface after the initial TCR signal seems to be also cytoskeleton-dependent [97].

Co-clustering of ICAM-1 with MHC I in lipid rafts of B lymphoblastoid cells was also shown to facilitate efficient presentation of viral peptides to CTLs [90]. Raft accommodation of MHC I-ICAM-1 assemblies enabled specific recruitment of Src kinases harbored in lipid rafts to these complexes. Since activity of Src kinases along with preserved integrity of rafts was critical for the CTL response, it can be suggested that engagement of raft-included MHC I and ICAM-1 initiates intracellular signaling, leading to the concomitant migration of rafts and MHC I-ICAM-1 assemblies to the area of the initial target cell-CTL contact [90]. This mechanism could provide the linkage between antigen recognition and early immunological synapse formation [90,92].

7.4
Voltage-Gated K$^+$ Channels in Lipid Rafts: Possible Involvement in Local Regulatory Processes

Kv1.3 channels [104,105], the dominant voltage-gated potassium channels of T lymphocytes, play key roles in the control of membrane potential and calcium signaling, thereby affecting signal transduction pathways leading to the antigen-induced activation of these cells [106,107].

Activation of T cells through the TCR generates an oscillatory Ca^{2+} signal, which is created by a release from the Ca^{2+}-storage compartments of the endoplasmic reticulum (ER) triggered by IP_3 and consequential Ca^{2+} influx from the extracellular space [108]. The depolarizing Ca^{2+} influx must be counterbalanced by the activation of K$^+$ channels, clamping the membrane potential at negative values and thereby providing a sufficient driving force for further Ca^{2+} entry. Voltage-gated K$^+$ (Kv) channels form highly K$^+$-selective pores that are conformationally switched open or closed by changes in membrane voltage [109]. In addition to the classical synapse-forming molecules, recently we described the recruitment of Kv1.3 to the immunological synapse [110], which may be mediated by its association with lipid rafts [111,112]. Elevation of the cholesterol content of the membrane modulated the gating properties of these channels [111]. By using confocal laser scanning microscopy (CLSM) and FRET, we have demonstrated clustering of Kv1.3 channels and their co-localization with the TCR/CD3 complex in Jurkat cells and human peripheral CTLs [110,113], indicating a possible crosstalk between the TCR signaling complex and Kv1.3. In nonengaged CTLs, small patches containing Kv1.3 and

TCR/CD3 complexes were evenly distributed on the cell surface, whereas they were both enriched at the IS formed at the CTL-target cell interface while maintaining their molecular proximity [110]. This is in accordance with biochemical studies suggesting the interaction of Kv1.3 channels with protein kinases, Lck and PKC, as well as various adaptor molecules, such as hDlg, PSD-95 (95 kDa post-synaptic density protein), Kvβ2, ZIP1 (PKC-ζ-interacting protein 1) and ZIP2, and the co-receptor CD4 (for reviews, see [107,114,115]). Physical association of Kv1.3 channels with the TCR might underline the importance of previous findings, in which regulation of Kv1.3 function by protein tyrosine kinase- and PKC-dependent phosphorylation was described. Besides the possibility of Kv1.3 channel regulation during formation of the IS, and the consequent modulation of Ca^{2+} signaling, localization of Kv1.3 in the IS raises the possibility of reciprocal regulation of IS function by nearby Kv1.3 [115]. For example, conformational changes in membrane proteins driven by the membrane potential might affect the antigen-recognition process [11,116], or local K^+ efflux through Kv1.3 might activate the function of β_1-integrin, a possible determinant of the stability of the immunological synapse [117].

In addition to Kv1.3 channels, a whole class of voltage-gated Kv K^+ channels are targeted to lipid rafts, a finding which bridges a gap between classical molecular immunology and electrophysiology (for a review, see [112]).

7.5
Cell Fusion as a Tool for Studying Dynamic Behavior of Protein Clusters

Whereas the Frye-Edidin experiment proved the lateral redistribution of membrane proteins on the micrometer scale [2], due to technical limitations, it could not resolve whether intermixing of proteins results from the movement of large-scale clusters with constant protein composition or instead, proteins could be exchanged between clusters at the molecular level by dynamic association-dissociation events (dynamically changing composition). In order to address this question, the classical experiment was repeated with some modifications [118]. Intermixing of membrane proteins was studied on homokaryons of human lymphoblasts where, before fusion, the two cells were labeled separately with antibodies (or their Fab fragments) carrying spectrally distinct fluorophores targeting the proteins of interest. The process of intermixing was monitored by simultaneous application of photobleaching FRET and SNOM techniques, which provided a resolution power well beyond that of the original experiment and allowed us to explore the dynamic behavior of both hierarchical levels of protein clusters (see Section 7.2).

As noted in Section 7.3, clustering of MHC glycoproteins is well-characterized and has an important role in antigen presentation [59,60,83,84,102]. Both small- and large-scale clusters of MHC I were found to be dynamic: dissociation and re-association of small-scale protein complexes and reformation of large-scale associations took place after the fusion of cells that were labeled with fluorescein- and rhodamine-conjugated Fab fragments against MHC I heavy chains. The redistribution of micrometer-scale clusters preceded that of the small-scale clusters, corroborating the hierarchical organization of MHC I [118].

Large-scale homoclusters of MHC II were as dynamic as those of MHC I. Small- and large-scale heteroclusters of MHC I and MHC II also showed dynamic behavior in cell fusion experiments. At the same time, small-scale associations of MHC II were static as revealed by FRET: intermixing of components did not take place between nanometer-scale clusters of MHC II even 80 minutes after fusion [118]. This may be explained by the molecular structure of MHC II which, in its functional dimer form, has two membrane-spanning α-helical transmembrane domains. It can be hypothesized, that hydrophobic interactions between these domains are strong enough to prevent the mixing of small-scale clusters of MHC II [17].

One may picture this situation as overlapping large-scale clusters of MHC I and MHC II containing dynamic small-scale homoclusters of MHC I and static small-scale clusters of MHC II. Although the small-scale homoclusters of MHC II are not dynamic, they engage in dynamic small-scale association with MHC I [118].

There was no difference in the behavior of transferrin receptors and the GPI-anchored CD48 protein, representatives of nonraft- and raft-associated proteins, respectively. Therefore, it could be concluded that the lipid microenvironment, on its own, does not determine the dynamic properties of protein associations. Forces resulting in protein clustering, whether they are related to membrane trafficking or to microdomain formation, do not generally inhibit the dynamic exchange of protein components between protein clusters, if the clusters reside in the same type of microdomain [118].

As a conclusion, one can say that in the composition of both small- and large-scale membrane protein clusters dynamism is the rule, rather than the exception. Whereas preformed large-scale homoclusters of proteins are generally not associated in a static manner, and exchange of components between like clusters is usually observed, tight interactions in the small-scale associations of some proteins could completely block the exchange of these molecules between nanometer-sized clusters [118].

7.6
Lipid Rafts as Platforms for Cytokine Receptor Assembly and Signaling

Interleukin-2 (IL-2) and -15 (IL-15) are substantially involved in controlling T cell homeostasis and function [119,120,121]. Their receptors comprise three distinct components: while the α-chains are cytokine-specific, the β- and $γ_c$-subunits are employed by both IL-2 and IL-15. In addition, the so-called common $γ_c$-chain is the component of a series of other cytokine receptors – that is, the members of the $γ_c$ cytokine receptor family (IL-4, IL-7, IL-9, and IL-21). As a result of combining various subunits, several forms of receptor complexes with different affinities may exist at the cell surface. Heterodimerization of the intracellular domains of the β- and $γ_c$-chains was found critical for one set of signaling events shared by both cytokines. In this case the two cytokines activate similar signaling pathways involving Janus kinase (JAK1 and JAK3)-assisted tyrosine phosphorylation of downstream signaling molecules (e.g., STAT3 and STAT5). Sharing of common receptor subunits explains the redundancy in the biological actions of IL-2 and IL-15 (e.g., stimulation of T cell proliferation) [119,120]. In addition to the shared functions, they can also exhibit opposing contributions to T-cell-mediated immunity [119,120]. Since IL-2 plays a pivotal role in activation-induced cell death (AICD), it is critical in the elimination of self-reactive T cells and so in peripheral self-tolerance. At the same time, IL-15 manifests anti-apoptotic actions and inhibits IL-2-mediated AICD. IL-2 and IL-15 play opposing roles in the control of the homeostasis of $CD8^+$ memory phenotype T cells. IL-15 provides potent and selective stimulation of memory phenotype $CD8^+$ T cells *in vivo*, whereas IL-2 inhibits the persistence of these cells.

FRET data suggested that, in contrast to the earlier "sequential subunit-organization" (affinity conversion) model proposing ligand-induced association of initially separate subunits [122], the three chains of the high-affinity IL-2R (IL-2Rαβγ$_c$) complex are preassembled in the plasma membrane of human T lymphoma cells even in the absence of IL-2 [123]. Binding of IL-2 or IL-15 was reported to differentially modulate the conformation of the receptor complex: addition of IL-2 made the heterotrimer more compact, while IL-15 loosened the interaction/proximity between the IL-2Rα and γ$_c$-chains [123]. A similar preassembly of the heterotrimeric IL-15R (IL-15Rαβγ$_c$), as well as the molecular proximity of IL-15Rα and IL-2Rα was demonstrated on human T cells expressing all the elements of the IL-2/IL-15 receptor system [98] (Fig. 7.3). Whereas neither IL-2, nor IL-15 affected the molecular association of the two α-chains, the interaction between the β- and IL-15Rα subunits became tighter upon IL-15 treatment, as indicated by FRET measurements. Based on these data, a heterotetrameric model of the IL-2/IL-15R complex can be envisaged: binding of IL-2 or IL-15 rearranges the subunits to form the appropriate αβγ$_c$ high-affinity receptor complex, while the other α-chain rotates or moves away from the site of cytokine-receptor interaction. FRET experiments also indicated the homodimeric/oligomeric molecular association of IL-15Rα [98]. Homoassociation of IL-2Rα may also occur in T lymphoma cells, although in a cell type-dependent manner [124].

It was shown by using biophysical (FRET and CLSM) and biochemical approaches that IL-2/IL-15R subunits are mainly partitioned into lipid rafts in the plasma membrane of human T lymphoma cells [39,79,98] (see Fig. 7.3). These rafts contained, among others, GM1 gangliosides, the GPI-anchored CD48 protein and a major fraction of MHC glycoproteins. At the same time the domains containing transferrin receptors (coated pits) were clearly distinct from GM1-containing lipid rafts (Fig. 7.4).

In addition, the high-affinity IL-2R was shown to be resistant to cold detergent extraction both in murine and human T lymphoma cells [79,125]. It was also demonstrated that the integrity of lipid rafts has a crucial role in organizing the lateral distribution of IL-2R and it is also essential for IL-2-mediated signaling [39,79]. Disruption of the native structure of lipid rafts by cholesterol extraction resulted in

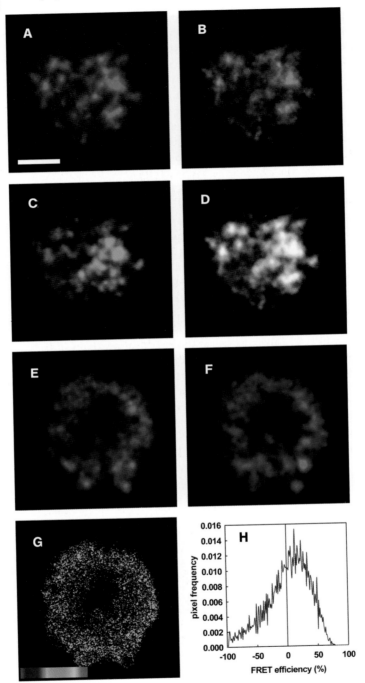

the dispersion of the above raft components and simultaneously abrogated STAT3/STAT5 tyrosine phosphorylation related to IL-2 signaling [39,79]. This suggests that raft integrity is critical in keeping the intracellular domains of the β- and γ$_c$-chains together with the docked JAKs and STATs in a proper, juxtaposed position. Upon cholesterol depletion, the size of lipid rafts increased and the boundaries of the microdomains became fuzzier – that is, the compactness and cohesion within the microdomain declined [39]. This implies that the lipid microenvironment, in particular cholesterol, might be an important factor in maintaining the integrity of signaling complexes. Lipid rafts may promote the formation and cytokine-specific modulation of IL-2R/IL-15R complexes and β- and γ$_c$-subunit "switching" between IL-2 and IL-15 receptors as well.

Marmor and Julius proposed a different mode of IL-2R signal regulation by rafts, based on observations on murine T cells [126]. Whereas IL-2Rα was also found constitutively enriched in lipid rafts, the β- and γ$_c$-chains, along with JAK1 and JAK3 kinases, were found mostly in the detergent-soluble membrane fractions. IL-2-mediated assembly of the high-affinity receptor complex as well as activation of JAKs occurred exclusively in the soluble fractions. As a consequence, disruption of lipid raft integrity did not impair IL-2R-induced signaling. It was proposed that sequestration of IL-2Rα within raft domains of murine T cells hampers its interactions and regulates IL-2 signaling through impeding its interaction with the signaling βγ$_c$ heterodimer.

A third mechanism for raft-assisted IL-2 signaling is outlined by Goebel et al. [127]. Using biochemical approaches, these authors demonstrated selective enrichment of IL-2/15Rβ chains, but not cytokine-specific α-chains or γ$_c$-chains, in lipid rafts of phytohemagglutinin (PHA)-activated human peripheral T cells. IL-2 stimulation was accompanied by a partial translocation of the β-chains along with the associated signaling molecules (JAK1, lck, Grb-2) to the soluble membrane fraction. Furthermore, disruption of lipid raft integrity attenuated IL-2 signaling.

◀ **Fig. 7.3** Co-localization of IL-15Rα and IL-2Rα in lipid rafts of FT7.10 T lymphoma cells. (Panels A-D): Confocal microscopic images of the distribution of IL-15Rα (panel A, Cy3-anti-FLAG), IL-2Rα (panel B, Cy5–7G7 B6) and GM1 ganglioside, a lipid raft marker (panel C, labeled by Alexa Fluor 488-cholera toxin B). In the overlay image (panel D) those pixels appearing in white represent co-localization of all three molecules. Confocal sections were recorded from the cover slip-proximal surface of the cell. Pairwise correlation coefficients between the different channels were fairly high ($C_{AB} = 0.79$, $C_{AC} = 0.59$, $C_{BC} = 0.67$), referring to substantial overlap between the lateral distributions of the studied molecules. (Scale bar = 2 μm.) Panels E-H: Acceptor photobleaching FRET measure- ment: Confocal images of IL-15Rα (panel E) and IL-2Rα (panel F) recorded before acceptor photobleaching (see Section 7.2 for a description of FRET microscopic methods). Receptor subunits were targeted by Cy3–7A4 24 (donor) and Cy5-anti-Tac (acceptor) mAbs. Panel G shows the pixel-by-pixel FRET efficiency map between IL-15Rα and IL-2Rα as determined from the donor images taken before and after photobleaching. The color code ranges between FRET efficiency values of 0 (purple) to 100% (red). Pixels with fluorescence intensities lower than the background threshold are displayed in black. Panel H shows the frequency distribution histogram of FRET efficiencies in the individual pixels. The mean FRET efficiency value was 17%.

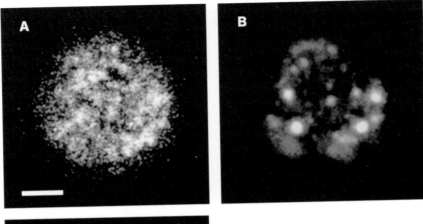

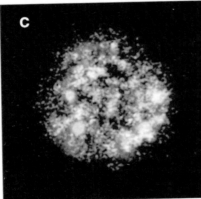

Fig. 7.4 Confocal laser scanning microscopy (CLSM) images of the distribution of transferrin receptors and GM1 gangliosides. Transferrin receptors (B), which are enriched in coated pits, were co-localized poorly with GM1 gangliosides segregated into lipid rafts (A). The distinctness of the distributions (C) clearly indicated segregation of the two types of membrane domains. The correlation coefficient between the images was C = 0.22. Transferrin receptors were labeled by Cy3-MEM75 mAbs, and GM1 was targeted by Cy5-cholera toxin B.

These authors suggested that sequestration of the β-chains in rafts prior to IL-2 stimulation controls the specific cytokine responsiveness, since it ensures that pairing with the more "promiscuous" γ_c-chains only takes place upon binding of the appropriate ligand [127].

Association of IL-2 receptors with detergent-resistant membrane microdomains was also reported to define a clathrin-independent endocytotic pathway [128].

Incongruence observed in the raft association of the IL-2/IL-15R system could indicate that composition of rafts as well as partition of a given protein between the raft and non-raft membrane regions can exhibit cell- or species-specificity [79,127]. Whether the observed discrepancies are only due to the different experimental approaches or they are caused by real differences in the observed systems (and if yes, what is the cause of distinct localization: post-translational modification, lipid composition or protein-protein interactions) is yet to be determined.

Flow cytometric FRET experiments revealed the co-localization of the IL-2/IL-15R system and MHC I molecules in the plasma membrane of cells of human T lymphoma/leukemia origin [39,79,98]. Although the exact role of this co-localiza-

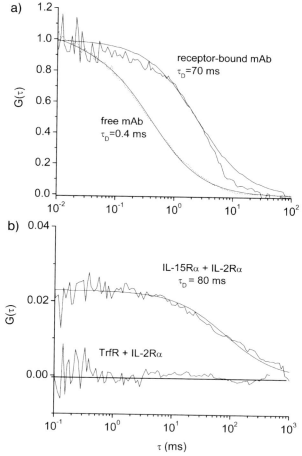

Fig. 7.5 Mobility and co-mobility measurements by FCS and FCCS. (A) Normalized autocorrelation curves detected from Cy5-tagged anti-Tac Fabs free in solution or bound to IL-2Rα subunits on Kit 225 K6 T lymphoma cells. The diffusion time of the antibody decreased by an order of magnitude upon receptor binding. (B) Cross-correlation curve measured on Kit 225 FT 7.10 cells between IL-2Rα and IL-15Rα (labeled with Cy5-anti-Tac Fab and Alexa 488 anti-FLAG mAbs, respectively). The nonzero cross-correlation amplitude suggests that at least a certain fraction of the proteins form stable complexes for at least the duration of the diffusion time. As a negative control, cross-correlation between transferrin receptors (Trfr) and IL-2Rα was determined on K6 cells yielding a flat correlation curve, which is indicative of no interaction. Receptors were labeled by Alexa 488-MEM75 mAb and Cy5-anti-Tac Fab, respectively.

tion has not yet been elucidated, a regulatory tyrosine phosphorylation cross-talk, as suggested earlier for the class I MHC-insulin receptor interaction [15], cannot be excluded [39,79]. Association of the IL-2/IL-15R with MHC II glycoproteins was also demonstrated. Co-localization of the elements of the IL-2/IL-15R system with MHC glycoproteins also takes place in lipid rafts, as revealed by confocal microscopy [39,98].

FRET assays do not report on the dynamics and stability of protein-protein interactions. By using FCCS, it was shown that α subunits of IL-2R and IL-15R diffused together at least for several tens of milliseconds – the time window of an FCCS experiment (Fig. 7.5). Similar stable association was detected between MHC I and IL-2Rα or IL-15Rα chains [98]. On the other hand, no cross-correlation could be detected between IL-2Rα and coated pit-located transferrin receptor molecules (Fig. 7.5).

An interesting consequence of these results follows from the relative expression levels of the studied molecules. The ratio of the amount of IL-15Rα, IL-2Rα and MHC I is ~1:10:50–100 on the Kit 225 FT7.10 T lymphoma cells used in the FCCS experiments. If complexes of 1:1 stoichiometry were formed between IL-15Rα and MHC I, then the out-of-complex fraction of MHC I molecules would suppress the cross-correlation amplitude below the detection level (see Eq. 7.8). This suggests that higher-order aggregates of MHC class I molecules float together with IL-2 and IL-15 receptors in large supramolecular complexes in the plasma membrane. These results are in accordance with previous data on the homoassociation of MHC I molecules detected by FRET and electron microscopy/atomic force microscopy (see Section 7.3) [59,83].

Our observations suggest the possibility of a supramolecular complex of MHC, ICAM-1 molecules and cytokine receptor subunits that could include all members of the γ_c cytokine receptor family in addition to IL-2Rα and IL-15Rα, in particular, IL-4Rα, IL-7Rα, IL-9Rα and IL-21Rα. Such an association in a lipid raft-accommodated supercomplex could provide one explanation for the functional competition among cytokines that has been observed on the simultaneous addition of IL-2 and IL-4 to lymphocytes. Furthermore, the definition of such a supercomplex of cytokine receptors would also add to our understanding of the regulation of lymphocyte proliferation and effector immune responses that are mediated by these pivotal γ_c-associated cytokines.

7.7
Organization and Function of Receptor Tyrosine Kinases is Linked to Lipid Microdomains

Receptor tyrosine kinases are prominent examples of the proteins involved in cell signaling that form molecular associations and superstructures in the cell membrane. Cooperative interactions between or among receptor tyrosine kinases play a pivotal role in signal transduction. This includes homo- and hetero-dimerizations as well as potentially higher-order associations, which may be either dependent or independent of ligands. In addition to protein-protein interactions, lipid micro-domains also play an important role in the organization of superstructures. The EGF receptor, the insulin receptor, the PDGF receptor, vascular endothelial growth factor (VEGF) and nerve growth factor (NGF) receptors have been shown to be localized to low density, cholesterol-rich membrane domains. In all cases, signaling by these receptors can be modulated by changes in cellular cholesterol content. Thus, raft localization appears to be of functional importance to these receptors (for a review, see [129]).

One of the best-studied receptors in this respect is the EGF receptor which belongs to the type I family of transmembrane receptor tyrosine kinases. In addition to EGFR or ErbB1, the other members of the family are ErbB2 (HER2 or Neu), ErbB3 and ErbB4 [130–133]. Within a given tissue, these receptors are rarely expressed alone, but are found in various combinations. Members of the family display various degrees and combinations of homo- and hetero-associations at the cell surface, depending on their relative expression levels. ErbB2 is an orphan receptor: no soluble physiological ligand, specific to ErbB2, has been detected so far. Despite this fact, ErbB2 participates actively in ErbB receptor combinations, and receptor complexes including the ErbB2-ErbB3 dimer which appears to be more potent in mitogenic activity than any other combination [130–134]. Recently, a molecular model was built for the nearly full-length ErbB2 dimer based on the X-ray or nuclear magnetic resonance (NMR) structures of extracellular, transmembrane and intracellular domains, and intramolecular distances determined by FRET. Favorable dimerization interactions were predicted for the extracellular, transmembrane and protein kinase domains which may act in a coordinated fashion in ErbB2 homodimerization, or alternatively in ErbB heterodimerizations [135].

Molecular-scale physical associations among ErbB family members have been studied using classical biochemical [136,137], molecular biological and biophysical methods [48,62,138,139]. When isolated from cells, members of the ErbB family self-associate (homoassociate) and associate with other family members (hetero-associate) [136]. However, experiments on isolated proteins are inherently unable to detect interactions in cellular environments *in vivo* and *in situ*, and cannot detect heterogeneity within or among cells. FRET measurements detected dimerization of ErbB1 receptors in fixed [138,140] and living cells [140]. FRET was also applied to monitor the association pattern of ErbB2 in breast tumor cells [48,62,138,139]. There was considerable homoassociation of ErbB2 and heteroassociation of ErbB2 with EGFR in quiescent breast tumor cells. ErbB2 homoassociation was enhanced by EGF treatment in SKBR-3 cells and in the BT474 subline BT474M1 with high tumorigenic potential, whereas the original BT474 line was resistant to this effect. These differences correlated well with EGFR expression. Since these measurements were performed with flow cytometry, one single FRET efficiency value was obtained for each cell analyzed. In order to reveal heterogeneity in the homo-association pattern of ErbB2 within a single cell, one of the microscopic FRET approaches had to be utilized. Donor photobleaching FRET microscopy was used to visualize FRET efficiency within single cells with spatial resolution limited only by diffraction in the optical microscope [48,50,141]. This allows detailed analysis of the spatial heterogeneity of molecular interactions. Donor pbFRET measurements showed that ErbB2 homoassociation was also heterogeneous in unstimulated breast tumor cells; and membrane domains with erbB2 homoassociation had mean diameters of less than 1 μm [62,142]. It was not clear whether the domain size was imposed by the optical resolution limit of wide-field microscopy in the X-Y plane or whether it originated from the actual size of ErbB2 aggregates.

In order to refine the size estimate of domains containing ErbB2 molecules, it was necessary to use SNOM [50,143,144]. This technique is not limited by diffraction optics, and can readily image objects in the 0.1 to 1 μm range, including sub-μm lipid and protein clusters in the plasma membrane [4] (see Section 7.2). ErbB2 was concentrated in irregular membrane patches with a mean diameter of approximately 500 nm, containing up to 1000 ErbB2 molecules in nonactivated SKBR-3 and MDA453 human breast tumor cells. The mean cluster diameter increased to 600–900 nm when SKBR-3 cells were treated with EGF, heregulin or a partially agonistic anti-erbB2 antibody. The increase in cluster size was inhibited by an EGFR-specific tyrosine kinase inhibitor, suggesting that EGFR was somehow involved in organizing this ErbB2 superstructure. Since the domain size was larger than the resolution limit of confocal microscopy (200–300 nm in the X-Y plane), we were able to confirm the SNOM results with confocal laser scanning microscopy (Fig. 7.6) [142].

The role of lipid rafts in the organization of these EGFR and ErbB2-containing superstructures has also been revealed in further experiments. The size of lipid rafts was investigated with dye-labeled cholera toxin B (CTX-B) subunit, which binds to the glycosphingolipid GM1 ganglioside. In order to study the role of lipid rafts in the homoassociation patterns of ErbB2, confocal microscopic studies were performed. The signal from one laser beam was used to monitor lipid rafts, and signals excited by the other two laser beams to reveal the homoassociation pattern of ErbB2. Observations suggest that similarly to ErbB1 [129], ErbB2 is localized mostly in GM1-enriched membrane domains, that are distinct from caveolae. However, there is a negative correlation between ErbB2 homoassociation and the local density of the lipid raft marker CTX-B. This environment could alter the association properties of ErbB2. Since stimulating ErbB2 increases the size of ErbB2 clusters [142] and lipid rafts [139], the amount of ErbB2 concentrated in rafts is very likely related to the function of the protein. Localization of ErbB2 in lipid rafts is dynamic, since it can be dislodged from rafts by cholera toxin-induced raft crosslinking [139]. Upon crosslinking with CTX-B, GM1 leaves ErbB protein clusters behind and migrates into caveolae. The association properties and biological activity of ErbB2 excluded from rafts differ from those inside rafts. For example, internalization of ErbB2 mediated by 4D5 (the parent murine version of trastuzumab, a monoclonal anti-ErbB2 antibody used in breast cancer therapy) is blocked in CTX-B-pretreated cells, while its antiproliferative effect is not. A role of lipid rafts in limiting autoactivation of the ErbB signaling system is supported by the increased tyrosine phosphorylation of Shc after removing ErbB proteins from rafts by CTX-B treatment. On the other hand, lipid rafts are also responsible for

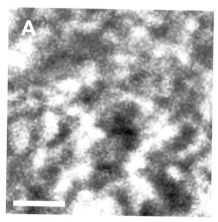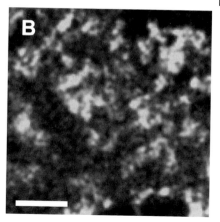

Fig. 7.6 Scanning near-field optical microscopy (SNOM) and confocal laser scanning microscopy (CLSM) images of TAMRA-4D5-labeled ErbB2 receptors on SKBR-3 cells. SKBR-3 cells grown on glass coverslips were labeled on ice using TAMRA-conjugated 4D5 monoclonal anti-ErbB2 antibody Fab fragments. (A) For SNOM, a custom-built shared aperture instrument was used on formaldehyde-fixed, dehydrated, air-dried samples [142]. (B) 1-mm optical sections of live cells were obtained in CLSM with a Zeiss LSM 410 instrument. Fluorescence intensity is displayed in pseudocolor. (Scale bar = 2 μm.)

maintaining ErbB proteins in a growth factor-responsive state. This is supported by the following results:

- Neither EGF, nor heregulin are able to activate Shc if ErbB proteins are removed from lipid rafts.
- The formation of heregulin-responsive ErbB2/ErbB3 heterodimers and heregulin-induced ErbB2 tyrosine phosphorylation decrease if ErbB proteins are removed from lipid rafts.

These results emphasize that alterations in the local environment of ErbB2 strongly influence its association properties, which are reflected in its biological activity and in its behavior as a target for therapy [139].

The results of several studies have implied that integrins and growth factor receptors cooperate in tumor formation, and have demonstrated the existence of integrin-growth factor receptor complexes leading to a decreased threshold of transmembrane signaling [145–147]. Similar to ErbB2, integrins were shown to be raft-associated [148]. Cooperative signaling between ErbB proteins and integrins [146,149] is a common feature of invasive cancer cells, and association of β_1-integrin with ErbB2 proteins could provide a framework in which tumor cell metastasis might be better understood. FRET and confocal microscopic measurements demonstrated an association between ErbB2 and β_1-integrin in the nanometer range and on the scale of membrane microdomains, respectively. Lipid rafts showed a substantial overlap with both ErbB2- and β_1-integrin-rich microdomains [150]. These results corroborated the existence of molecular interactions between ErbB2 and β_1-integrins and their association with lipid rafts. Interestingly, although ErbB2-positive but trastuzumab-resistant breast and gastric cancer cell lines were found to express a substantially higher amount of β_1-integrin than corresponding trastuzumab lines, there was no significant difference among them in the trastuzumab-induced tyrosine phosphorylation of ErbB2, which was probably caused by the weak functional interaction between the two proteins.

In summary, there is ample evidence for the role of local factors, for example, the lipid environment, other receptor tyrosine kinases and integrins, in influencing receptor tyrosine kinase activity and consequential modulation of the ability of these molecules in driving cellular functions. In addition to a more thorough understanding of the complexity of the receptor tyrosine kinase signaling networks, experiments linking lipid rafts and receptor function may facilitate the development of more efficient therapeutic strategies targeting receptor tyrosine kinases [150].

Acknowledgments

G. Vámosi and A. Bodnár contributed equally to this manuscript. These studies were supported by the following grants: OTKA TS40773, T48745, T42618, F46497; T38037; T43061; ETT 602/2003, 603/2003; 524/2004; 532/2004; NATO Life Science and Technology Collaborative Linkage Grant 980200, EU FP6 LSHB-CT-2004–503467; Bolyai János Research Fellowships (to G. Vámosi and A. Bodnár) and Békési Fellowship (to G. Vereb).

Abbreviations

$\beta 2m$	β2-microglobulin
AFM	atomic force microscopy
AICD	activation-induced cell death
APC	antigen-presenting cell
CLSM	confocal laser scanning microscopy
cSMAC	central supramolecular activation cluster
CTL	cytotoxic T cell
CTX-B	cholera toxin B
EGFR	epidermal growth factor receptor
ER	endoplasmic reticulum
FCCS	fluorescence cross-correlation spectroscopy
FCS	fluorescence correlation spectroscopy
FHC	free heavy chain
FLIM	fluorescence lifetime imaging microscopy
FRET	fluorescence resonance energy transfer
ICAM	intracellular adhesion molecule

IFN	interferon
IL	interleukin
IS	immunological synapse
JAK	janus kinase
MHC	major histocompatibility complex
NGF	nerve growth factor
NMR	nuclear magnetic resonance
pbFRET	photobleaching FRET
PDGF	platelet-derived growth factor
PHA	phytohemagglutinin
pSMAC	peripheral supramolecular activation cluster
SNOM	scanning near-field optical microscopy
TCR	T-cell receptor
VEGF	vascular endothelial growth factor

References

1 S. J. Singer, G. L. Nicolson. The fluid mosaic model of the structure of cell membranes. *Science* 1972, *175*, 720–731.

2 L. D. Frye, M. Edidin. The rapid intermixing of cell surface antigens after formation of mouse-human heterokaryons. *J. Cell Sci.* 1970, *7*, 319–335.

3 M. Edidin. Patches and fences: probing for plasma membrane domains. *J. Cell Sci. Suppl.* 1993, *17*, 165–169.

4 M. Edidin. Lipid microdomains in cell surface membranes. *Curr. Opin. Struct. Biol.* 1997, *7*, 528–532.

5 S. Damjanovich, R. J. Gáspár, C. Pieri. Dynamic receptor superstructures at the plasma membrane. *Q. Rev. Biophys.* 1997, *30*, 67–106.

6 S. Damjanovich, J. Matkó, L. Mátyus, G. Szabò, Jr., J. Szöllősi, J. C. Pieri, T. Farkas, R. Gáspár, Jr. Supramolecular receptor structures in the plasma membrane of lymphocytes revealed by flow cytometric energy transfer, scanning force- and transmission electron-microscopic analyses. *Cytometry* 1998, *33*, 225–233.

7 K. Simons, E. Ikonen. Functional rafts in cell membranes. *Nature* 1997, *387*, 569–572.

8 K. Simons, W. L. Vaz. Model systems, lipid rafts, and cell membranes. *Annu. Rev. Biophys. Biomol. Struct.* 2004, *33*, 269–295.

9 G. Vereb, L. Mátyus, L. Bene, G. Panyi, Z. Bacsó, M. Balázs, J. Matkó, J. Szöllősi, R. Jr. Gáspár, S. Damjanovich. Plasma membrane bound macromolecules are dynamically aggregated to form nonrandom codistribution patterns of selected functional elements. Do pattern recognition processes govern antigen presentation and intercellular interactions? *J. Mol. Recognit.* 1995, *8*, 237–246.

10 M. Edidin. Shrinking patches and slippery rafts: scales of domains in the plasma membrane. *Trends Cell Biol.* 2001, *11*, 492–496.

11 G. Vereb, J. Szöllősi, J. Matkó, P. Nagy, T. Farkas, L. Vígh, L. Mátyus, T. A. Waldmann, S. Damjanovich. Dynamic, yet structured: The cell membrane three decades after the Singer-Nicolson model. *Proc. Natl. Acad. Sci. USA* 2003, *100*, 8053–8058.

12 S. Damjanovich, B. Somogyi, L. Trón. Macromolecular dynamics and information transfer. *Adv. Physiol. Sci.* 1981, *30*, 9–15.

13 J. Matkó, J. Szöllősi. Landing of immune receptors and signal proteins on lipid rafts: a safe way to be spatio-temporally coordinated? *Immunol. Lett.* 2002, *82*, 3–15.

14 R. Zidovetzki, Y. Yarden, J. Schlessinger, T. M. Jovin. Rotational diffusion of epider-

mal growth factor complexed to cell surface receptors reflects rapid microaggregation and endocytosis of occupied receptors. *Proc. Natl. Acad. Sci. USA* 1981, *78*, 6981–6985.

15 T. S. Ramalingam, A. Chakrabarti, M. Edidin. Interaction of class I human leukocyte antigen (HLA-I) molecules with insulin receptors and its effect on the insulin-signaling cascade. *Mol. Biol. Cell.* 1997, *8*, 2463–2474.

16 J. Reiland, M. Edidin. Chemical cross-linking detects association of insulin receptors with four different class I human leukocyte antigen molecules on cell surfaces. *Diabetes* 1993, *42*, 619–625.

17 S. Damjanovich, L. Mátyus, L. Damjanovich, L. Bene, A. Jenei, J. Matkó, R. Gáspár, J. Szöllősi. Does mosaicism of the plasma membrane at molecular and higher hierarchical levels in human lymphocytes carry information on the immediate history of cells? *Immunol. Lett.* 2002, *82*, 93–99.

18 J. F. Tocanne, L. Cezanne, A. Lopez, B. Piknova, V. Schram, J. F. Tournier, M. Welby. Lipid domains and lipid/protein interactions in biological membranes. *Chem. Phys. Lipids* 1994, *73*, 139–158.

19 V. Horejsi. The roles of membrane microdomains (rafts) in T cell activation. *Immunol. Rev.* 2003, *191*, 148–164.

20 V. Horejsi. Membrane rafts in immunoreceptor signaling: new doubts, new proofs? *Trends Immunol.* 2002, *23*, 562–564.

21 D. C. Hoessli, S. Ilangumaran, A. Soltermann, P. J. Robinson, B. Borisch, U. D. Nasir. Signaling through sphingolipid microdomains of the plasma membrane: the concept of signaling platform. *Glycoconj. J.* 2000, *17*, 191–197.

22 H. A. Lucero, P. W. Robbins. Lipid rafts-protein association and the regulation of protein activity. *Arch. Biochem. Biophys.* 2004, *426*, 208–224.

23 X. L. Yang, W. C. Xiong, L. Mei. Lipid rafts in neuregulin signaling at synapses. *Life Sci.* 2004, *75*, 2495–2504.

24 R. G. Anderson, K. Jacobson. A role for lipid shells in targeting proteins to caveolae, rafts, and other lipid domains. *Science* 2002, *296*, 1821–1825.

25 T. Harder, K. Simons. Caveolae, DIGs, and the dynamics of sphingolipid-cholesterol microdomains. *Curr. Opin. Cell Biol.* 1997, *9*, 534–542.

26 D. A. Brown. Interactions between GPI-anchored proteins and membrane lipids. *Trends Cell Biol.* 1992, *2*, 338–343.

27 M. D. Resh. Membrane targeting of lipid modified signal transduction proteins. *Subcell. Biochem.* 2004, *37*, 217–232.

28 M. D. Resh. Fatty acylation of proteins: new insights into membrane targeting of myristoylated and palmitoylated proteins. *Biochim. Biophys. Acta* 1999, *1451*, 1–16.

29 W. Rodgers, D. Farris, S. Mishra. Merging complexes: properties of membrane raft assembly during lymphocyte signaling. *Trends Immunol.* 2005, *26*, 97–103.

30 A. Kusumi, Y. Sako. Cell surface organization by the membrane skeleton. *Curr. Opin. Cell Biol.* 1996, *8*, 566–574.

31 M. A. Lemmon, D. M. Engelman. Specificity and promiscuity in membrane helix interactions. *Q. Rev. Biophys.* 1994, *27*, 157–218.

32 Q. Tang, M. Edidin. Vesicle trafficking and cell surface membrane patchiness. *Biophys. J.* 2001, *81*, 196–203.

33 L. A. Gheber, M. Edidin. A model for membrane patchiness: lateral diffusion in the presence of barriers and vesicle traffic. *Biophys. J.* 1999, *77*, 3163–3175.

34 K. Ritchie, A. Kusumi. Role of the membrane skeleton in creation of microdomains. *Subcell. Biochem.* 2004, *37*, 233–245.

35 J. Pawley. *Handbook of biological confocal microscopy*. Plenum Press, New York, 1995.

36 W. R. Zipfel, R. M. Williams, W. W. Webb. Nonlinear magic: multiphoton microscopy in the biosciences. *Nat. Biotechnol.* 2003, *21*, 1369–1377.

37 M. Edidin, M. C. Zuniga, M. P. Sheetz. Truncation mutants define and locate cytoplasmic barriers to lateral mobility of membrane glycoproteins. *Proc. Natl. Acad. Sci. USA* 1994, *91*, 3378–3382.

38 A. Kusumi, Y. Sako, M. Yamamoto. Confined lateral diffusion of membrane receptors as studied by single particle tracking (nanovid microscopy). Effects of calcium-induced differentiation in cultured epithelial cells. *Biophys. J.* 1993, *65*, 2021–2040.

39 G. Vereb, J. Matkó, G. Vámosi, S. M. Ibrahim, E. Magyar, S. Varga, J. Szöllősi, A. Jenei, R. J. Gáspár, T. A. Waldmann, S. Damjanovich. Cholesterol-dependent clustering of IL-2Ralpha and its colocalization with HLA and CD48 on T lymphoma cells suggest their functional association with lipid rafts. *Proc. Natl. Acad. Sci. USA* 2000, *97*, 6013–6018.

40 G. Vereb, J. Szöllősi, S. Damjanovich, J. Matkó. Exploring membrane microdomains and functional protein clustering in live cells with flow and image cytometric methods. *Reviews in Fluorescence*, Kluwer Academic/Plenum Publishers, New York, 2004, pp. 105–152.

41 S. Damjanovich, L. Bene, J. Matkó, L. Mátyus, Z. Krasznai, G. Szabo, C. Pieri, R. J. Gáspár, J. Szöllősi. Two-dimensional receptor patterns in the plasma membrane of cells. A critical evaluation of their identification, origin and information content. *Biophys. Chem.* 1999, *82*, 99–108.

42 J. Szöllősi, S. Damjanovich, L. Mátyus. Application of fluorescence resonance energy transfer in the clinical laboratory: routine and research. *Cytometry* 1998, *34*, 159–179.

43 G. Vereb, J. Matkó, J. Szöllősi. Cytometry of fluorescence resonance energy transfer. *Methods Cell Biol.* 2004, *75*, 105–152.

44 T. Förster. Zwischenmolekulare Energiewanderung und Fluoreszenz. *Ann. Phys.* 1948, *2*, 55–75.

45 R. M. Clegg. Fluorescence resonance energy transfer (FRET). In: *Fluorescence Imaging Spectroscopy and Microscopy*, Wiley, John & Sons, Inc., New York, 1996, pp. 179–252.

46 L. Stryer, R. P. Haugland. Energy transfer: a spectroscopic ruler. *Proc. Natl. Acad. Sci. USA* 1967, *58*, 719–726.

47 E. A. Jares-Erijman, T. M. Jovin. FRET imaging. *Nat. Biotechnol.* 2003, *21*, 1387–1395.

48 P. Nagy, G. Vámosi, A. Bodnár, S. J. Lockett, J. Szöllősi. Intensity-based energy transfer measurements in digital imaging microscopy. *Eur. Biophys. J.* 1998, *27*, 377–389.

49 P. I. Bastiaens, I. V. Majoul, P. J. Verveer, H. D. Soling, T. M. Jovin. Imaging the intracellular trafficking and state of the AB5 quaternary structure of cholera toxin. *EMBO J.* 1996, *15*, 4246–4253.

50 G. Vereb, C. K. Meyer, T. M. Jovin, Novel microscope-based approaches for the investigation of protein-protein interactions in signal transduction. In: *Interacting Protein Domains, their Role in Signal and Energy Transduction.* Springer-Verlag, New York, 1997, pp. 49–52.

51 T. M. Jovin, D. J. Arndt-Jovin, FRET microscopy: digital imaging of fluorescence resonance energy transfer. Application in cell biology. In: *Cell Structure and Function by Microspectrofluorometry.* Academic Press, San Diego, 1989, pp. 99–117.

52 R. M. Clegg, O. Holub, C. Gohlke. Fluorescence lifetime-resolved imaging: measuring lifetimes in an image. *Methods Enzymol.* 2003, *360*, 509–542.

53 L. Trón, J. Szöllősi, S. Damjanovich, S. H. Helliwell, D. J. Arndt-Jovin, T. M. Jovin. Flow cytometric measurements of fluorescence resonance energy transfer on cell surfaces. Quantitative evaluation of the transfer efficiency on a cell by cell basis. *Biophys. J.* 1984, *45*, 939–946.

54 Z. Sebestyén, P. Nagy, G. Horváth, G. Vámosi, R. Debets, J. W. Gratama, D. R. Alexander, J. Szöllősi. Long wavelength fluorophores and cell-by-cell correction for autofluorescence significantly improves the accuracy of flow cytometric energy transfer measurements on a dual-laser benchtop flow cytometer. *Cytometry* 2002, *48*, 124–135.

55 R. Rigler, E. S. Elson. *Fluorescence Correlation Spectroscopy. Theory and Applications.* Springer Verlag, Berlin, Heidelberg, New York, Barcelona, Hong Kong, London, Milan, Paris, Singapore, Tokyo, 2001.

56 J. Widengren, Ü. Mets, R. Rigler. Fluorescence correlation spectroscopy of triplet state in solution: A theoretical and experimental study. *J. Phys. Chem.* 1995, *99*, 13368–13379.

57 K. Bacia, I. V. Majoul, P. Schwille. Probing the endocytic pathway in live cells using dual-color fluorescence cross-correlation analysis. *Biophys. J.* 2002, *83*, 1184–1193.

58 T. Weidemann, M. Wachsmuth, M. Tewes, K. Rippe, J. Langowski. Analysis of ligand binding by two-colour fluorescence cross-correlation spectroscopy. *Single Molecules* 2002, *3*, 49–61.

59 S. Damjanovich, G. Vereb, A. Schaper, A. Jenei, J. Matkó, J. P. Starink, G. Q. Fox, D. J. Arndt-Jovin, T. M. Jovin. Structural hierarchy in the clustering of HLA class I molecules in the plasma membrane of human lymphoblastoid cells. *Proc. Natl. Acad. Sci. USA* 1995, *92*, 1122–1126.

60 A. Jenei, S. Varga, L. Bene, L. Mátyus, A. Bodnár, Z. Bacsó, C. Pieri, R. J. Gáspár, T. Farkas, S. Damjanovich. HLA class I and II antigens are partially co-clustered in the plasma membrane of human lymphoblastoid cells. *Proc. Natl. Acad. Sci. USA* 1997, *94*, 7269–7274.

61 J. Hwang, L. A. Gheber, L. Margolis, M. Edidin. Domains in cell plasma membranes investigated by near-field scanning optical microscopy. *Biophys. J.* 1998, *74*, 2184–2190.

62 P. Nagy, L. Bene, M. Balázs, W. C. Hyun, S. J. Lockett, N. Y. Chiang, F. Waldman, B. G. Feuerstein, S. Damjanovich, J. Szöllősi. EGF-induced redistribution of erbB2 on breast tumor cells: flow and image cytometric energy transfer measurements. *Cytometry* 1998, *32*, 120–131.

63 S. K. Bromley, W. R. Burack, K. G. Johnson, K. Somersalo, T. N. Sims, C. Sumen, M. M. Davis, A. S. Shaw, P. M. Allen, M. L. Dustin. The immunological synapse. *Annu. Rev. Immunol.* 2001, *19*, 375–396.

64 A. Grakoui, S. K. Bromley, C. Sumen, M. M. Davis, A. S. Shaw, P. M. Allen, M. L. Dustin. The immunological synapse: a molecular machine controlling T cell activation. *Science* 1999, *285*, 221–227.

65 K. H. Lee, A. D. Holdorf, M. L. Dustin, A. C. Chan, P. M. Allen, A. S. Shaw. T cell receptor signaling precedes immunological synapse formation. *Science* 2002, *295*, 1539–1542.

66 M. F. Krummel, M. M. Davis. Dynamics of the immunological synapse: finding, establishing and solidifying a connection. *Curr. Opin. Immunol.* 2002, *14*, 66–74.

67 D. M. Davis, M. L. Dustin. What is the importance of the immunological synapse? *Trends Immunol.* 2004, *25*, 323–327.

68 J. Jacobelli, P. G. Andres, J. Boisvert, M. F. Krummel. New views of the immunological synapse: variations in assembly and

function. *Curr. Opin. Immunol.* 2004, *16*, 345–352.

69 A. Trautmann, S. Valitutti. The diversity of immunological synapses. *Curr. Opin. Immunol.* 2003, *15*, 249–254.

70 T. Harder. Lipid raft domains and protein networks in T-cell receptor signal transduction. *Curr. Opin. Immunol.* 2004, *16*, 353–359.

71 H. T. He, A. Lellouch, D. Marguet. Lipid rafts and the initiation of T cell receptor signaling. *Semin. Immunol.* 2005, *17*, 23–33.

72 P. Friedl, J. Storim. Diversity in immune-cell interactions: states and functions of the immunological synapse. *Trends Cell Biol.* 2004, *14*, 557–567.

73 A. Kupfer, S. J. Singer. The specific interaction of helper T cells and antigen-presenting B cells. IV. Membrane and cytoskeletal reorganizations in the bound T cell as a function of antigen dose. *J. Exp. Med.* 1989, *170*, 1697–1713.

74 C. R. Monks, B. A. Freiberg, H. Kupfer, N. Sciaky, A. Kupfer. Three-dimensional segregation of supramolecular activation clusters in T cells. *Nature* 1998, *395*, 82–86.

75 J. C. Stinchcombe, G. Bossi, S. Booth, G. M. Griffiths. The immunological synapse of CTL contains a secretory domain and membrane bridges. *Immunity* 2001, *15*, 751–761.

76 P. Friedl, E. B. Brocker. TCR triggering on the move: diversity of T-cell interactions with antigen-presenting cells. *Immunol. Rev.* 2002, *186*, 83–89.

77 L. Bene, M. Balázs, J. Matkó, J. Most, M. P. Dierich, J. Szöllősi, S. Damjanovich. Lateral organization of the ICAM-1 molecule at the surface of human lymphoblasts: a possible model for its co-distribution with the IL-2 receptor, class I and class II HLA molecules. *Eur. J. Immunol.* 1994, *24*, 2115–2123.

78 L. Bene, A. Bodnár, S. Damjanovich, G. Vámosi, Z. Bacsó, J. Aradi, A. Berta, J. Damjanovich. Membrane topography of HLA I, HLA II, and ICAM-1 is affected by IFN-gamma in lipid rafts of uveal melanomas. *Biochem. Biophys. Res. Commun.* 2004, *322*, 678–683.

79 J. Matkó, A. Bodnár, G. Vereb, L. Bene, G. Vámosi, G. Szentesi, J. Szöllősi, R.

Gáspár, V. Horejsi, T. A. Waldmann, S. Damjanovich. GPI-microdomains (membrane rafts) and signaling of the multichain interleukin-2 receptor in human lymphoma/leukemia T cell lines. *Eur. J. Biochem.* 2002, *269*, 1199–1208.

80 P. Smith, I. Morrison, K. Wilson, N. Fernandez, R. Cherry. Anomalous diffusion of major histocompatibility complex class I molecules on HeLa cells determined by single particle tracking. *Biophys. J.* 1999, *76*, 3331–3344.

81 K. Triantafilou, M. Triantafilou, K. M. Wilson, N. Fernandez. Human major histocompatibility molecules have the intrinsic ability to form homotypic associations. *Hum. Immunol.* 2000, *61*, 585–598.

82 A. Chakrabarti, J. Matkó, N. A. Rahman, B. G. Barisas, M. Edidin. Self-association of class I major histocompatibility complex molecules in liposome and cell surface membranes. *Biochemistry* 1992, *31*, 7182–7189.

83 J. Matkó, Y. Bushkin, T. Wei, M. Edidin. Clustering of class I HLA molecules on the surfaces of activated and transformed human cells. *J. Immunol.* 1994, *152*, 3353–3360.

84 A. Bodnár, Z. Bacsó, A. Jenei, T. M. Jovin, M. Edidin, S. Damjanovich, J. Matkó. Class I HLA oligomerization at the surface of B cells is controlled by exogenous β_2-microglobulin: implications in activation of cytotoxic T lymphocytes. *Int. Immunol.* 2003, *15*, 331–339.

85 S. Demaria, R. Schwab, S. Gottesman, Y. Bushkin. Soluble β_2-microglobulin-free class I heavy chains are released from the surface of activated and leukemia cells by a metalloprotease. *J. Biol. Chem.* 1994, *269*, 6689–6694.

86 W. Pickl, W. Holter, J. Stöckl, O. Majdic, W. Knapp. Expression of LA45 reactive β_2-microglobulin free HLA class I a-chains on activated T cells is regulated by internalization, constitutive and protein kinase C inducible release. *Tissue Antigens* 1996, *48*, 15–21.

87 W. F. Wade, J. H. Freed, M. Edidin. Translational diffusion of class II major histocompatibility complex molecules is constrained by their cytoplasmic domains. *J. Cell Biol.* 1989, *109*, 3325–3331.

88 K. M. Wilson, I. E. Morrison, P. R. Smith, N. Fernandez, R. J. Cherry. Single particle tracking of cell-surface HLA-DR molecules using R-phycoerythrin labeled monoclonal antibodies and fluorescence digital imaging. *J. Cell Sci.* 1996, *109 (Pt 8)*, 2101–2109.

89 J. Szöllõsi, S. Damjanovich, M. Balázs, P. Nagy, L. Trón, M. J. Fulwyler, F. M. Brodsky. Physical association between MHC class I and class II molecules detected on the cell surface by flow cytometric energy transfer. *J. Immunol.* 1989, *143*, 208–213.

90 T. Lebedeva, N. Anikeeva, S. A. Kalams, B. D. Walker, I. Gaidarov, J. H. Keen, Y. Sykulev. Major histocompatibility complex class I-intercellular adhesion molecule-1 association on the surface of target cells: implications for antigen presentation to cytotoxic T lymphocytes. *Immunology* 2004, *113*, 460–471.

91 Z. Bacsó, L. Bene, L. Damjanovich, S. Damjanovich. INF-γ rearranges membrane topography of MHC-I and ICAM-1 in colon carcinoma cells. *Biochem. Biophys. Res. Commun.* 2002, *290*, 635–640.

92 T. Lebedeva, M. L. Dustin, Y. Sykulev. ICAM-1 co-stimulates target cells to facilitate antigen presentation. *Curr. Opin. Immunol.* 2005, *17*, 251–258.

93 J. Boniface, J. Rabinowitz, C. Wülfing, J. Hampl, Z. Reich, J. Altman, R. Kantor, C. Beeson, H. McConnell, M. Davis. Initiation of signal transduction through the T cell receptor requires the multivalent engagement of peptide/MHC ligands. *Immunity* 1998, *9*, 459–466.

94 J. Cochran, T. Cameron, L. Stern. The relationship of MHC-peptide binding and T cell activation probed using chemically defined MHC class II oligomers. *Immunity* 2000, *12*, 241–250.

95 M. A. Daniels, S. C. Jameson. Critical role for CD8 in T cell receptor binding and activation by peptide/major histocompatibility complex multimers. *J. Exp. Med.* 2000, *191*, 335–345.

96 H. A. Anderson, E. M. Hiltbold, P. A. Roche. Concentration of MHC class II molecules in lipid rafts facilitates antigen presentation. *Nat. Immunol.* 2000, *1*, 156–162.

97 I. Gombos, C. Detre, G. Vámosi, J. Matkó. Rafting MHC-II domains in the APC (presynaptic) plasma membrane and the thresholds for T-cell activation and immunological synapse formation. *Immunol. Lett.* 2004, *92*, 117–124.

98 G. Vámosi, A. Bodnár, G. Vereb, A. Jenei, C. K. Goldman, J. Langowski, K. Tóth, L. Mátyus, J. Szöllősi, T. A. Waldmann, S. Damjanovich. IL-2 and IL-15 receptor α-subunits are coexpressed in a supramolecular receptor cluster in lipid rafts of T cells. *Proc. Natl. Acad. Sci. USA* 2004, *101*, 11082–11087.

99 M. Wadehra, H. Su, L. K. Gordon, L. Goodglick, J. Braun. The tetraspan protein EMP2 increases surface expression of class I major histocompatibility complex proteins and susceptibility to CTL-mediated cell death. *Clin. Immunol.* 2003, *107*, 129–136.

100 R. W. Tilghman, R. L. Hoover. E-selectin and ICAM-1 are incorporated into detergent-insoluble membrane domains following clustering in endothelial cells. *FEBS Lett.* 2002, *525*, 83–87.

101 J. Goebel, K. Forrest, D. Flynn, R. Rao, T. L. Roszman. Lipid rafts, major histocompatibility complex molecules, and immune regulation. *Hum. Immunol.* 2002, *63*, 813–820.

102 N. J. Poloso, P. A. Roche. Association of MHC class II-peptide complexes with plasma membrane lipid microdomains. *Curr. Opin. Immunol.* 2004, *16*, 103–107.

103 E. M. Hiltbold, N. J. Poloso, P. A. Roche. MHC class II-peptide complexes and APC lipid rafts accumulate at the immunological synapse. *J. Immunol.* 2003, *170*, 1329–1338.

104 G. Panyi, Z.-F. Sheng, L.-W. Tu, C. Deutsch. C-type inactivation of a voltage-gated K^+ channel occurs by a cooperative mechanism. *Biophys. J.* 1995, *69*, 896–904.

105 G. Panyi, C. Deutsch. Assembly and suppression of endogenous Kv1.3 channels in human T cells. *J. Gen. Physiol.* 1996, *107*, 409–420.

106 G. Panyi, G. Vámosi, A. Bodnár, R. Gáspár, S. Damjanovich. Looking through ion channels: recharged concepts in T-cell signaling. *Trends Immunol.* 2004, *25*, 565–569.

107 G. Panyi, Z. Varga, R. Gáspár. Ion channels and lymphocyte activation. *Immunol. Lett.* 2004, *92*, 55–66.

108 R. S. Lewis. Calcium signaling mechanisms in T lymphocytes. *Annu. Rev. Immunol.* 2001, *19*, 497–521.

109 P. C. Biggin, T. Roosild, S. Choe. Potassium channel structure: domain by domain. *Curr. Opin. Struct. Biol.* 2000, *10*, 456–461.

110 G. Panyi, G. Vámosi, Z. Bacsó, M. Bagdany, A. Bodnár, Z. Varga, R. Gáspár, L. Mátyus, S. Damjanovich. Kv1.3 potassium channels are localized in the immunological synapse formed between cytotoxic and target cells. *Proc. Natl. Acad. Sci. USA* 2004, *101*, 1285–1290.

111 P. Hajdu, Z. Varga, C. Pieri, G. Panyi, R. Gáspár, Jr. Cholesterol modifies the gating of Kv1.3 in human T lymphocytes. *Pflugers Arch.* 2003, *445*, 674–682.

112 J. R. Martens, K. O'Connell, M. Tamkun. Targeting of ion channels to membrane microdomains: localization of KV channels to lipid rafts. *Trends Pharmacol. Sci.* 2004, *25*, 16–21.

113 G. Panyi, M. Bagdany, A. Bodnár, G. Vámosi, G. Szentesi, A. Jenei, L. Mátyus, S. Varga, T. A. Waldmann, R. Gáspár, S. Damjanovich. Colocalization and nonrandom distribution of Kv1.3 potassium channels and CD3 molecules in the plasma membrane of human T lymphocytes. *Proc. Natl. Acad. Sci. USA* 2003, *100*, 2592–2597.

114 K. G. Chandy, H. Wulff, C. Beeton, M. Pennington, G. A. Gutman, M. D. Cahalan. K^+ channels as targets for specific immunomodulation. *Trends Pharmacol. Sci.* 2004, *25*, 280–289.

115 J. Matkó. K^+ channels and T-cell synapses: the molecular background for efficient immunomodulation is shaping up. *Trends Pharmacol. Sci.* 2003, *24*, 385–389.

116 L. Bene, J. Szöllősi, M. Balázs, L. Mátyus, R. Gáspár, M. Ameloot, R. E. Dale, S. Damjanovich. Major histocompatibility complex class I protein conformation altered by transmembrane potential changes. *Cytometry* 1997, *27*, 353–357.

117 M. Levite, L. Cahalon, A. Peretz, R. Hershkoviz, A. Sobko, A. Ariel, R. Desai, B. Attali, O. Lider. Extracellular K^+ and opening of voltage-gated potassium channels activate T cell integrin function: physical and functional association between Kv1.3 channels and β1 integrins. *J. Exp. Med.* 2000, *191*, 1167–1176.

118 P. Nagy, L. Mátyus, A. Jenei, G. Panyi, S. Varga, J. Matkó, J. Szöllősi, R. Gáspár, T. M. Jovin, S. Damjanovich. Cell fusion experiments reveal distinctly different association characteristics of cell-surface receptors. *J. Cell Sci.* 2001, *114*, 4063–4071.

119 T. A. Waldmann, S. Dubois, Y. Tagaya. Contrasting roles of IL-2 and IL-15 in the life and death of lymphocytes: implications for immunotherapy. *Immunity* 2001, *14*, 105–110.

120 T. A. Fehniger, M. A. Cooper, M. A. Caligiuri. Interleukin-2 and interleukin-15: immunotherapy for cancer. *Cytokine Growth Factor Rev.* 2002, *13*, 169–183.

121 T. A. Fehniger, M. A. Caligiuri. Interleukin 15: biology and relevance to human disease. *Blood* 2001, *97*, 14–32.

122 S. Kondo, A. Shimizu, Y. Saito, M. Kinoshita, T. Honjo. Molecular basis for two different affinity states of the interleukin 2 receptor: affinity conversion model. *Proc. Natl. Acad. Sci. USA* 1986, *83*, 9026–9029.

123 S. Damjanovich, L. Bene, J. Matkó, A. Alileche, C. K. Goldman, S. Sharrow, T. A. Waldmann. Preassembly of interleukin 2 (IL-2) receptor subunits on resting Kit 225 K6 T cells and their modulation by IL-2, IL-7, and IL-15: a fluorescence resonance energy transfer study. *Proc. Natl. Acad. Sci USA* 1997, *94*, 13134–13139.

124 D. M. Eicher, S. Damjanovich, T. A. Waldmann. Oligomerization of IL-2Rα. *Cytokine* 2002, *17*, 82–90.

125 D. C. Hoessli, M. Poincelet, E. Rungger-Brandle. Isolation of high-affinity murine interleukin 2 receptors as detergent-resistant membrane complexes. *Eur. J. Immunol.* 1990, *20*, 1497–1503.

126 M. D. Marmor, M. Julius. Role for lipid rafts in regulating interleukin-2 receptor signaling. *Blood* 2001, *98*, 1489–1497.

127 J. Goebel, K. Forrest, L. Morford, T. L. Roszman. Differential localization of IL-2- and –15 receptor chains in membrane rafts of human T cells. *J. Leukoc. Biol.* 2002, *72*, 199–206.

128 C. Lamaze, A. Dujeancourt, T. Baba, C. G. Lo, A. Benmerah, A. Dautry-Varsat. Inter-leukin 2 receptors and detergent-resistant membrane domains define a clathrin-independent endocytic pathway. *Mol. Cell* 2001, *7*, 661–671.

129 L. J. Pike. Growth factor receptors, lipid rafts and caveolae: An evolving story. *Biochim. Biophys. Acta* 2005.

130 P. Nagy, A. Jenei, S. Damjanovich, T. M. Jovin, J. Szöllősi. Complexity of signal transduction mediated by ErbB2: clues to the potential of receptor-targeted cancer therapy. *Pathol. Oncol. Res.* 1999, *5*, 255–271.

131 A. Citri, K. B. Skaria, Y. Yarden. The deaf and the dumb: the biology of ErbB-2 and ErbB-3. *Exp. Cell Res.* 2003, *284*, 54–65.

132 Y. Yarden, M. X. Sliwkowski. Untangling the ErbB signalling network. *Nat. Rev. Mol. Cell. Biol.* 2001, *2*, 127–137.

133 G. Vereb, P. Nagy, J. W. Park, J. Szöllősi. Signaling revealed by mapping molecular interactions: implications for ErbB-targeted cancer immunotherapies. *Clin. Appl. Immunol. Rev.* 2002, *2*, 169–186.

134 M. X. Sliwkowski, J. A. Lofgren, G. D. Lewis, T. E. Hotaling, B. M. Fendly, J. A. Fox. Nonclinical studies addressing the mechanism of action of trastuzumab (Herceptin). *Semin. Oncol.* 1999, *26*, 60–70.

135 P. Bagossi, G. Horváth, G. Vereb, J. Szöllősi, J. Tőzsér. Molecular modeling of nearly full-length ErbB2 receptor. *Biophys. J.* 2005, *88*, 1354–1363.

136 E. Tzahar, H. Waterman, X. Chen, G. Levkowitz, D. Karunagaran, D. Lavi, B. J. Ratzkin, Y. Yarden. A hierarchical network of interreceptor interactions determines signal transduction by Neu differentiation factor/neuregulin and epidermal growth factor. *Mol. Cell. Biol.* 1996, *16*, 5276–5287.

137 M. X. Sliwkowski, G. Schaefer, R. W. Akita, J. A. Lofgren, V. D. Fitzpatrick, A. Nuijens, B. M. Fendly, R. A. Cerione, R. L. Vandlen, K. L. Carraway, III. Coexpression of erbB2 and erbB3 proteins reconstitutes a high affinity receptor for heregulin. *J. Biol. Chem.* 1994, *269*, 14661–14665.

138 T. W. Gadella, Jr., T. M. Jovin. Oligomerization of epidermal growth factor receptors on A431 cells studied by time-resolved fluorescence imaging microscopy. A stereochemical model for tyrosine ki-

nase receptor activation. *J. Cell Biol.* 1995, *129*, 1543–1558.

139 P. Nagy, G. Vereb, Z. Sebestyén, G. Horváth, S. J. Lockett, S. Damjanovich, J. W. Park, T. M. Jovin, J. Szöllősi. Lipid rafts and the local density of ErbB proteins influence the biological role of homo- and heteroassociations of ErbB2. *J. Cell Sci.* 2002, *115*, 4251–4262.

140 T. W. Gadella, Jr., R. M. Clegg, T. M. Jovin. Fluorescence lifetime imaging microscopy: Pixel-by-pixel analysis of phase-modulation data. *Bioimaging* 1994, *2*, 139–159.

141 P. I. Bastiaens, T. M. Jovin. Microspectroscopic imaging tracks the intracellular processing of a signal transduction protein: fluorescent-labeled protein kinase C beta I. *Proc. Natl. Acad. Sci. USA* 1996, *93*, 8407–8412.

142 P. Nagy, A. Jenei, A. K. Kirsch, J. Szöllősi, S. Damjanovich, T. M. Jovin. Activation-dependent clustering of the erbB2 receptor tyrosine kinase detected by scanning near-field optical microscopy. *J. Cell Sci.* 1999, *112 (Pt 11)*, 1733–1741.

143 E. Monson, G. Merritt, S. Smith, J. P. Langmore, R. Kopelman. Implementation of an NSOM system for fluorescence microscopy. *Ultramicroscopy* 1995, *57*, 257–262.

144 A. K. Kirsch, C. K. Meyer, T. M. Jovin, Integration of optical techniques in scanning probe microscopes: the scanning near-field optical microscope (SNOM). In: *Proceedings of NATO Advanced Research Workshop: Analytical Use of Fluorescent Probes in Oncology*, Plenum Press, New York, 1996, pp. 317–323.

145 F. G. Giancotti, E. Ruoslahti. Integrin signaling. *Science* 1999, *285*, 1028–1032.

146 S. Miyamoto, H. Teramoto, J. S. Gutkind, K. M. Yamada. Integrins can collaborate with growth factors for phosphorylation of receptor tyrosine kinases and MAP kinase activation: roles of integrin aggregation and occupancy of receptors. *J. Cell Biol.* 1996, *135*, 1633–1642.

147 F. Wang, V. M. Weaver, O. W. Petersen, C. A. Larabell, S. Dedhar, P. Briand, R. Lupu, M. J. Bissell. Reciprocal interactions between β1-integrin and epidermal growth factor receptor in three-dimensional basement membrane breast cultures: a different perspective in epithelial biology. *Proc. Natl. Acad. Sci. USA* 1998, *95*, 14821–14826.

148 B. Leitinger, N. Hogg. The involvement of lipid rafts in the regulation of integrin function. *J. Cell Sci.* 2002, *115*, 963–972.

149 M. A. Adelsman, J. B. McCarthy, Y. Shimizu. Stimulation of β1-integrin function by epidermal growth factor and heregulin-β has distinct requirements for erbB2 but a similar dependence on phosphoinositide 3-OH kinase. *Mol. Biol. Cell* 1999, *10*, 2861–2878.

150 M. Mocanu, Z. Fazekas, M. Petrás, P. Nagy, Z. Sebestyén, J. Isola, J. Timar, J. W. Park, G. Vereb, J. Szöllősi. Associations of ErbB2, β1-integrin and lipid rafts on Herceptin (Trastuzumab) resistant and sensitive tumor cell lines. *Cancer Lett.* 2005, *227*, 201–212.

8

Caveolin and its Role in Intracellular Chaperone Complexes

William V. Everson and Eric J. Smart

8.1
Caveolae and Caveolin-1

Our understanding of plasma membrane microdomains in general, and of caveolae and lipid rafts in particular, has grown tremendously during the past few years. One important paradigm shift occurred with the clear demonstration that two very similar domains exist on the plasma membrane called caveolae and lipid rafts [1,2]. Caveolae in most cells and tissues are defined by the presence of a 22-kDa protein called caveolin-1, whereas lipid rafts are defined by the presence of glycosyl-phosphatidylinositol (GPI)-anchored proteins such as CD55. Caveolae and lipid rafts are similar in that both types of domain are enriched in cholesterol, sphingomyelin, and signaling proteins [3]. However, caveolae contain significantly more cholesterol than lipid rafts, and it is this high relative concentration of cholesterol that is thought to be responsible for the invaginated morphology of caveolae in some cell types [4,5]. In contrast, caveolae that are depleted of cholesterol can lose their invaginated morphology and flatten within the plane of the plasma membrane [6]. Thus, the contents of caveolin and cholesterol in cells appear to be critical elements in the formation, number and morphology of caveolae. The localization of caveolin-1 in caveolae is critical in the organization of caveolae, and this is a combined result of the effect of caveolin on the cholesterol content, organization of the membrane lipid components, and the effect of caveolin as it forms oligomers and is able to bind to and scaffold other proteins.

Few studies have been conducted in which the levels and distribution of caveolin-1 and the absolute content of cholesterol within caveolae have been analyzed. Variation has been observed in the content of caveolin in caveolin-expressing cells and tissues that differ by more than two orders of magnitude. Quite clearly, a "caveolin-containing" cell that has a relative 100-fold enrichment of caveolin compared to another "caveolin- containing" cell is quite likely to have a dramatically different organization of caveolae, a different proportion of caveolae within the plasma membrane, and a different distribution of caveolin-organized domains within other intracellular membranes causing variation in caveolin's role in the regulation of trafficking and signaling pathways. However, few studies have taken

Lipid Rafts and Caveolae. Christopher J. Fielding
Copyright © 2006 WILEY-VCH Verlag GmbH & Co. KGaA, Weinheim
ISBN: 3-527-31261-7

into account the heterogeneity and functional differences between distinct cell types. In a parallel argument, cells in which caveolin expression has been lost or ablated in culture will respond differently, reflecting the alteration of steady-state equilibria between caveolae domains, lipid rafts, and phospholipids regions of the plasma membrane and intracellular membranes. Thus, some signaling or trafficking pathways normally regulated by caveolin may show little impact of caveolin disruption due to compensatory activation of secondary pathways localized to lipid rafts or even phospholipids domains. A number of ligands that initiate signaling in caveolae can be internalized by clathrin-mediated endocytosis, although in caveolin-expressing cells the rapid caveolae-mediated endocytic pathway dominates under normal physiologic conditions. This also holds true for membrane components. Overexpression of caveolin-1 changed the uptake of specific glycosphingolipids and shifted GM1 from the clathrin endocytic pathway to a caveolae-endocytic pathway [7]. The abolition of GPI synthesis to cause cell depletion of GPI-anchored proteins resulted in an increase in caveolae at the cell surface, indicating that some type of inverse relationship existed between the amount of lipid rafts and caveolae expressed on the cell surface [8]. The manipulation of total cell cholesterol content with cyclodextrin has been shown to have profound effects on caveolae organization and localization of caveolae-associated proteins, including caveolin-1. The effects of cyclodextrin require careful measurement of caveolae cholesterol content before and after treatment to determine whether such effects either disrupt caveolae or deplete the entire plasma membrane surface of cholesterol [9]. Physiological manipulations, such as the addition of lipoproteins which bind to receptors and alter cholesterol distribution in caveolae, result in changes in caveolae cholesterol and caveolin content, and change caveolae signaling and trafficking as a consequence [10,11]. These studies document the importance of careful quantitative analysis of the level of expression of caveolin protein and the mass of cholesterol in the cell as a whole, and within the caveolae compartment specifically, to demonstrate the physiological relevance of altered caveolae cholesterol levels to the change that occurs in a specific pathway or activity. Otherwise, the change could be due to alterations in cholesterol levels in noncaveolae membrane domains which cause a change in a pathway associated with these domains.

Because of the steady-state interactions between caveolae and other membrane domains, the merging of endocytic pathways and capacity for redundancy in endocytosis, and redundancy in signal transduction that has been identified since the first null mouse without an obvious phenotype was produced, care must be taken in interpreting the results of gross manipulations which alter protein and lipid content of cells and caveolae. In particular, studies in cells in which caveolin is absent, or in which the expression has been ablated, must be carefully evaluated. Several studies have been published from which conclusions have been drawn using negative data about the role (or lack of role) of caveolae and caveolin in a particular pathway, without having incorporated controls to ensure that the model system being employed is physiologically relevant or evaluation of changes in the activity of compensatory, overlapping, or redundant pathways.

8.2
Caveolin Protein Structure, Domains, and Membrane Interactions

Three caveolins have been identified in mammalian cells, termed caveolin-1, −2, and −3. Caveolin-1 and −2 are co-expressed in a wide range of tissues, exhibiting high expression in lung, vascular tissue, fibroblasts and adipocytes, whereas caveolin-3 shows limited expression and is the dominant caveolin in striated muscle. Caveolin-1, a 21- to 24-kDa protein, is a major integral membrane component of caveola membranes (Fig. 8.1). Caveolin-1 contains an additional N-terminal 27 amino acids (aa) that are not found in caveolin-3, and is also 16 amino acids longer than caveolin-2. Thus, all three caveolins resolve at distinct molecular weights by sodium dodecylsulfate-polyacryamide gel electrophoresis (SDS-PAGE). The predicted secondary structure of caveolin contains an N-terminal cytoplasmic region, a membrane-associated domain, and a cytosolic C-terminal tail. All three caveolins exhibit a similar structure, with the N- and C-terminal ends of the protein in the cytoplasm flanking a ~20 aa hydrophobic domain that forms a hairpin in the membrane. Several regions of caveolin-1 have been identified that mediate interactions

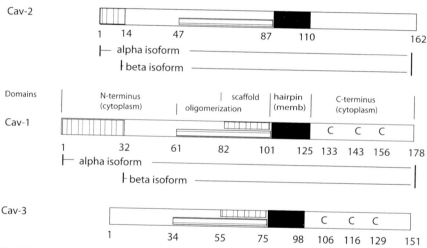

Fig. 8.1 Caveolin protein structure and domains. The distinct functional domains in caveolin-1 (Cav-1) are shown graphically and labeled as described in the text. Both caveolin-1 and caveolin-2 have alternative splice sites and exist as full-length alpha and truncated beta isomers. Domains showing potential conservation based on primary sequence homology are aligned for caveolin-3 (below Cav-1) and caveolin-2 (above Cav-1). Caveolin-3 shows high sequence homology in the hairpin, oligomerization, scaffolding and C-terminal cytoplasmic domains, including conservation of the position of three cysteines that are acylated in caveolin-1, as discussed in the text. Caveolin-2 shows homology in the hairpin domain and the N-terminal half of the oligomerization domain, but differs significantly in the primary sequence of the scaffolding domain and the C-terminal cytoplasmic domain. All three caveolins contain unique sequences in the N-terminal region that aligns with the first 50 amino acids of caveolin-1.

with itself and other proteins. The N-terminal membrane proximal region (residues 61–101) of caveolin-1 is sufficient to mediate the formation of caveolin homo-oligomers, and a portion of this controls exit from the Golgi [12]. A part of this region (residues 82–101) has been termed the "scaffolding domain", and mediates the putative interaction of caveolin-1 with signaling molecules such as small GTP-binding proteins, Src family tyrosine kinases, and endothelial nitric oxide synthase (eNOS) [13,14]. Other domains within caveolin have also been reported to interact with and serve as scaffolds to bind signaling molecules to caveolae [15].

Caveolin-1 has three cysteines, caveolin-2 has five cysteines, and caveolin-3 has eight cysteines. Caveolin-1 and –3 are both highly homologous at the protein level, with conservation of the location of the three cysteines C-terminal to the hairpin domain that we have shown are functionally acylated in caveolin-1 (discussed below). Caveolin-2 shows much less homology, and none of its cysteines aligns with the cysteines in caveolin-1. It is not known whether caveolin-2 or caveolin-3 are acylated proteins. The potential role of acylation in the control of membrane interactions of caveolin-1 are discussed below, but the acylation and potential functions associated with acylation in caveolin-2 or caveolin-3 remain to be elucidated.

8.3
Caveolin Expression and Localization in the Cell

Subcellular fractionation, immunofluorescence microscopy and electron microscopy with immunogold labeling methods have each been used to examine the localization of caveolin-1 in different tissues. Early studies isolated caveolae and lipid rafts based on the resistance of these cholesterol- and sphingolipid-rich domains to solubilization in cold buffers containing Triton X-100 detergent and the light buoyancy of the fractions on sucrose gradients. A nondetergent methods was developed that is based on sequential density gradient centrifugation, in which the plasma membrane is first isolated, after which the caveolae and noncaveolae domains are separated on a second density gradient. An analysis of the purity and enrichment of the final caveolae fraction showed that this method yields a high-purity fraction, enriched in caveolae, and containing minimal contaminants (< 5 %) from other organelle fractions [16]. In contrast, when detergents such as 0.1 % Triton X-100 are used with density gradient centrifugation to isolate membranes enriched in cholesterol and sphingolipids, the buoyant fractions have been shown to be a mixture of membranes from multiple organelles. Moreover, during the isolation procedure mixing of the lipids and artifactual associations of proteins has been shown to occur. A rigorous technique to isolate caveolae from lung tissue by using cationic colloidal silica particles showed that starting with the plasma membrane and avoiding the use of detergent eliminates many of the contaminants originating from intracellular membranes when detergent-based fractionation methods are used [17].

The analysis of caveolae distribution within cells has been carried out using subcellular fractionation with calculation of relative recoveries of material in different fractions, and by immunomicroscopic methods and gene manipulation techniques. When the overall distribution of caveolin was examined to determine where caveolin is localized by either confocal microscopy or subcellular fractionation by these more rigorous methods, a substantial quantity of caveolin was found to be associated with the intracellular membranes, and caveolin-1 has been shown to be present at some level within most subcellular fractions.

Several studies have identified technical issues that must be considered in the immunolocalization of caveolin and caveolae-associated proteins. It is well known that epitopes in proteins can be masked by interactions of the protein with other proteins, macromolecules such as lipids and membrane surfaces. It appears that this technical issue is very important in studies on proteins that associate with cholesterol-/sphingolipid-rich membranes or surfaces rich in neutral lipids. Several published studies have reported apparently conflicting results with regard to the expression or localization of caveolae in cells or tissues. Some of the first commercially available antibodies against caveolin-1 were known to recognize epitopes that were easily hidden when caveolin localized to different intracellular sites. Methods such as brief treatment with SDS have been employed to allow for antigen retrieval [18], giving antibodies access to epitopes in caveolin on intracellular membranes in leukocytes. Some apparent discrepancies in these relative expression or localization studies can be explained by the differences in epitope accessibility dependent on fixation, permeabilization, and the antibody detection methods employed. A recent study expanded this point to show that a number of current commercially available antibodies that are in wide use differ in their abilities to bind to caveolin at distinct sites, and that individual antibodies show distinct localization patterns under different fixation and permeabilization conditions [19]. Again, this study highlighted the importance of careful evaluation of negative data and the danger of making sweeping conclusions based on negative evidence. Confirmation of data interpretation by employment of two or more alternative approaches – for example, subcellular fractionation, combined with either immunomicroscopic methods or genetic studies with expression of mutant proteins in cells or animals – are critical when studies are carried out to evaluate the localization of caveolin and its relevance to regulation of signaling and trafficking pathways.

Because of the close association between caveolin and cholesterol- and sphingolipid-rich domains, the presence of caveolin in most subcellular fractions and organelles suggests that specialized membrane domains may be important functional units in many organelles and subcellular fractions. This is in addition to the prominent roles that have been identified for caveolae in the plasma membrane in the regulation of signal transduction and rapid endocytosis. Much remains to be investigated to define the functions of these domains within distinct organelles, or those involved in specialized trafficking between intracellular organelles based on either protein or lipid organization of these domains. The results of these studies clarify the point that negative data alone may be of little value, and that a combination of antibodies with several methods for fixation, antigen unmasking and detection of caveolins may be required to evaluate the total distribution of caveolin-1 within the cell.

8.4
Caveolin Expression and Localization Varies Depending on the Physiological State of Cells in Culture

The localization of caveolin in cells has been shown to be dependent on culture conditions, growth state, and the degree of confluence. In studies in which caveolin has been expressed in cells lacking caveolae, such as lymphocytes [20] or cancer cells [21], caveolin-1 expression resulted in its localization to the plasma membrane, the formation of caveolae, and the redistribution of other caveolae-specific proteins to these newly formed caveolae. The level of expression and distribution of caveolin-1 in isolated versus confluent endothelial cells is dramatically different. As cells approach confluence, caveolin and cholesterol accumulate at the lateral borders of endothelial cells, along with other caveolin-associated proteins and signaling molecules, including annexin II and other caveolae-localized proteins [22]. The organization of caveolae and associated proteins in these lateral membranes has been well defined in venular endothelial cells (Fig. 8.2). In confluent venular endothelial cells and intact veins, a large tubular vesicular network forms from endosomes originating from caveolae. This system has been extensively characterized and identified as being critical in transcytosis and leukocyte extravasation, and is termed the vesicular vacuolar organelle (VVO). The VVO represents an extensive set of tubules and vesicles that are connected, dynamic, and extend to take up approximately 18% of the total volume of the cytoplasm [23–25]. Several studies have linked caveolin and caveolae to macromolecule transport across the endothelium [26,27]. The structure and regulation of caveolae and its associated structures such as the VVO may be important in the functions of caveolin *in vivo* in control of vessel permeability and leukocyte migration. There is much that remains to be investigated using appropriate models, as well as studies in intact vessels and animals.

Both caveolin-1 and caveolin-2 exhibit widespread tissue distribution and extensive co-localization within the cell [28–31]. Both are found distributed in association with the plasma membrane and with intracellular membranes associated with several organelles in cells. Caveolin-1 and caveolin-2 also exhibit coordinate changes in their tissue-specific expression. For example, ablation of caveolin-1 in the mouse resulted in the widespread down-regulation of caveolin-2 in all of the tissues in which caveolin-1 was expressed [31]. Mutations in either caveolin-1 or caveolin-2 cause both proteins to mis-localize and accumulate with newly formed lipid bodies localized in the perinuclear region of the cell [32,33]. An intriguing study in cells lacking both caveolin-1 and -2 (LnCaP cells) showed that the formation of caveolae required expression of both caveolin-1 and caveolin-2, and that the localization of caveolin-1 to the cell surface required phosphorylation of caveolin-2 at specific sites [21]. However, the caveolin-2 null mouse shows normal caveolin-1 expression and normal caveolae in many tissues [34]. These data are intriguing, and suggest that much remains to be defined in the specific function, role and interactions between caveolin-1 and -2 in the regulation of caveolae organization and associated functions.

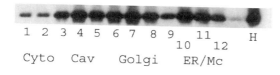

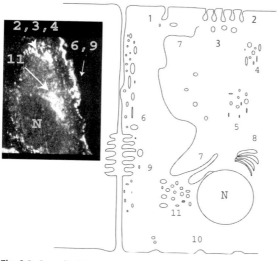

Fig. 8.2 Caveolin-1 is present in multiple subcellular locations. Top panel: a typical immunoblot from subcellular fractions isolated from confluent human umbilical vein endothelial cells (HUVEC). Twelve fractions were collected and an aliquot, matched for recovery to compare the amount of caveolae in different fractions, loaded into lanes 1–12 (light to dense fractions). The first two fractions represent the cytosol (the fraction loaded). Caveolin was present in fractions 1–2 corresponding to the cytosol (Cyto), fractions 3–5 which contain the plasma membrane and caveolae (Cav), fractions 6–8 which contain the Golgi (Golgi), fractions 9–11 which contain the endoplasmic reticulum and microsomes (ER/Mc), fraction 12 which contains the nuclear pellet (not labeled), and the lane containing the homogenate (H). Bottom panel: a schematic of caveolin-1-positive membranes and vesicles in a "typical" HUVEC. Caveolin localizes to the apical plasma membrane in small clusters and large clusters of caveolae (1, 2), to vesicles near clusters of caveolae (3), to multiple clusters of vesicles within the cytosol which may correspond to early endosomes (4), a sorting or recycling compartment(s) (5), vesicles clustered in the perinuclear region (11), to the vesicular vacuolar organelle (VVO) which comprises a large volume in the cytosol adjacent to the lateral membrane, to regions within lateral membranes (6), regions of the ER (7) and Golgi (8), and domains within the basal membrane including focal adhesions (10). Inset: the inset in the bottom panel shows a single confocal "slice" obtained from confluent HUVEC following immunostaining with caveolin-1 antibody followed by Cy3 fluorophore conjugated to a second antibody. The location of the nucleus is indicated (N), and regions with intense staining are marked which correspond to caveolin-positive membranes and vesicles in large clusters adjacent to the plasma membrane (2,3,4), the lateral membrane and VVO (6,9), and the perinuclear vesicles (11).

8.5
Caveolin-1 Expression Confers a New Level of Regulation

Caveolin-1 association with a number of proteins can be inhibitory. Likewise, caveolin expression in tissues in which its expression is normally low results in the formation of caveolae. The presence of caveolin then causes docking of signaling proteins, inhibition where proteins were previously constitutively active, and induction of regulatory pathways where they were absent, as a result. For example, expression of caveolin in hepatocytes causes down-regulation of lipid uptake in the liver [35], a tissue that is normally active in the uptake of high-density lipoprotein (HDL), leading to higher circulating levels of lipoproteins as a result. Loss of caveolin in cancer removes a regulatory structure, and the inhibitory activity that caveolin-1 confers to a number of signaling proteins, resulting in overactivation of growth signaling. Dysregulation of caveolin-1 is associated with an overactivation of growth signals in breast [36,37], and prostate cancers [38–40]. Several of the growth-signaling pathways which are constitutively turned on in prostate cancer, are found to be associated, and regulated, within caveolae in normal cells. A number of other proteins have also been suggested to be inhibited by the direct binding of caveolin-1.

8.6
Caveolae Cholesterol and Caveolin Localization to Caveolae

Soon after caveolin was first cloned, studies with filipin – an antibiotic that specifically binds cholesterol [41–43] showed that filipin-cholesterol complexes were enriched in nonclathrin-coated endosomes and regions of membrane corresponding to caveolae. This raised the question of how and why cholesterol was enriched in caveolae. Experimental manipulation of caveolae cholesterol by the addition of bacterial cholesterol oxidase to the media of cells was used to investigate this question [6,44]. Cholesterol oxidase caused rapid oxidation of cholesterol in caveolae, leading to cholesterol dispersal and the rapid internalization of caveolin-1 [6]. The removal of cholesterol oxidase from the media allowed the re-formation of caveolae, and both caveolin-1 and cholesterol were restored to caveolae in the plasma membrane over a period of about 90 minutes. Immunolocalization studies showed that caveolin-1 moved rapidly out of the caveolae, and was subsequently found on vesicles in the endoplasmic reticulum-Golgi-intermediate-compartment (ER-GIC), a region between the Golgi and the endoplasmic reticulum (ER) [6]. This identified a very rapid pathway connecting the plasma membrane to a region adjacent to the ER, as caveolin totally redistributed within 30 seconds following the addition of bacterial cholesterol oxidase. Temperature shifting and inhibitors were employed to define a cycle of caveolin-1 movement from cell-surface caveolae into the cell and back to the cell surface. Caveolin-1 rapidly translocated first to the rough ER (within 30 seconds), then slowly over 15–20 minutes to the ER-GIC, to the Golgi, before finally returning to surface caveolae. An investigation of cholesterol changes during the same time course showed that cholesterol followed a similar pattern of movement out of the caveolae, followed by a slow return to the caveolae, suggesting that caveolin-1 and cholesterol were linked together in a cycle. These studies were among the first to reveal a caveolin-trafficking cycle between cell-surface caveolae and the ER-Golgi membranes, for the transport of both caveolin and cholesterol between the plasma membrane and these perinuclear organelles.

8.7
Caveolin and Cholesterol Cross Membranes During Trafficking

During the process of vesicle trafficking, membrane topology is normally conserved – that is, material found in the extracellular (exofacial) leaflet of the plasma membrane is topologically conserved. For example, it remains associated with the exofacial leaflet during endocytosis and after fusion with organelles. The exofacial leaflet is thus the inner leaflet of vesicles and the interior leaflet of organelles such as the ER. Proteins and lipids associated with the cytofacial leaflet (cytoplasmic side) remain associated with the cytofacial leaflet of endocytic vesicles, and upon fusion remain localized with the cytoplasmic leaflet. Surprisingly, during translocation of caveolin and cholesterol between the plasma membrane and the ER, caveolin-1 "flips" across the membrane from the cytofacial leaflet and becomes associated with the exofacial leaflet of the ER [6,45] rather than the cytosolic leaflet.

Early studies which identified caveolin as a transmembrane protein may have been based on this same process of flipping, as this appears to occur when caveolin is newly synthesized. Initially, caveolin is transported to the cell surface with cholesterol, but then appears outside the cell, and is subsequently found localized in the cytofacial leaflet of the plasma membrane in caveolae. This suggests that caveolin-1 has a role in cholesterol trafficking across membranes from one leaflet to another, and that this flipping function is active at multiple membranes where cholesterol is transported. Another protein family has been identified that exhibits this same flipping behavior; this family – the engrailed family of homeoproteins – associates with caveolae when expressed in COS cells [46,47]. The engrailed protein, as well as other homeodomain proteins, contains a short domain that has been identified as a potential flip domain, which may allow their crossing from one layer to the other in membranes rich in cholesterol [46,47]. Robenek et al. have recently further characterized the crossing of caveolin-1 from one to another during endocytosis using ultrathin cryosectioning, freeze fracture, and immunogold labeling [45]. During the cycling of caveolin between the plasma membrane and intracellular sites, caveolin switches from the cytofacial leaflet to the exofacial leaflet, and is exclusively localized within the exofacial leaflet in the ER [45]. As mentioned above, overexpression of caveolins or expression of specific caveolin mutants causes formation of lipid droplets marked by caveolin localized to the ER, as lipids accumulated and budded off from the cytofacial leaflet due to the accumulation of caveolins at the ER [32,33]. Another study extended these observations to examine the relationship between caveolin-1 and lipid droplet biogenesis originating in association with the ER [48]. Caveolin-1 was found localized to the surface of droplets, and also extensively localized to the interior of the droplets, which exhibited a highly organized lamellar structure. However, caveolin-1 was localized strictly in association with the exofacial leaflet of the ER. The model of lipid budding as lipids accumulate and aggregate within the cytofacial leaflet would result in droplets lacking caveolin. There may be differences due to cell type, and droplets produced for different functional reasons may involve different pathways in their formation. Lipid droplets that are transient, rapidly induced and critical to inflammatory prostaglandin production are likely to differ from lipid droplets in adipocytes. The specific proteins and mechanisms regulating their formation and breakdown are also likely to differ. Much remains to be defined before we understand the basic mechanisms regulating lipid storage and specialized lipid-metabolizing organelles, and caveolin has been localized to both types of droplets in specific cell types.

8.8
Two Chaperone Complexes Regulate a Caveola-Cholesterol Trafficking Cycle

In addition to organizing cholesterol in caveolae, caveolin has been found to play a specific role in nonvesicular cholesterol trafficking in cells. A direct role for caveolin in trafficking newly synthesized cholesterol from the ER to the plasma membrane was shown in cells which lacked caveolin and in which caveolin was re-expressed. Radiolabeled tracers and blockers of cholesterol transport were used to show that caveolin and cholesterol trafficked together from intracellular sites to cell-surface caveolae [49]. A subsequent study revealed that a chaperone complex ferries newly synthesized cholesterol from the ER through the cytosol to plasma membrane caveolae [50]. This chaperone complex was isolated from the cytosol, distinct from any caveola membrane, plasma membrane, intracellular membrane or vesicle fraction. The complex was shown to be comprised of cholesterol, caveolin-1 and three additional proteins – cyclophilin A (cypA), cyclophilin 40 (cyp40), and heat shock protein 56 (hsp56). The activity of this complex could be inhibited by compounds which bind to and inhibit the function of hsp56 (rapamycin) or interact with cyclophilins (cyclosporine). Either of these inhibitors prevented the formation of the chaperone complex and blocked cholesterol movement from the Golgi to plasma membrane caveolae.

The linkage between caveolin movement in and out of caveolae to caveolae cholesterol homeostasis led to the subsequent identification of a second chaperone complex which regulates transport of newly delivered cholesterol into the cell. This second complex consists of cholesteryl ester, caveolin-1, cypA, cyp40, and annexin II [10]. HDL can deliver cholesteryl ester to caveolae via scavenger receptor BI (SR-BI). Cholesteryl ester is then transported via this complex into the cell, where it can be converted to cholesterol and transported back to the cell surface to caveolae via the first chaperone complex. These two complexes provide a nonvesicle pathway which can regulate cholesterol uptake and delivery from caveolae in fibroblasts and other caveolin-1-containing cells, but not in cells such as hepatocytes, which normally contain minimal caveolin-1.

8.9
Caveolae Linked to Nongenomic Actions and Uptake of Estrogen

The initial paradigm of sex hormone action in the cell begins with the delivery of sex hormones to the cell surface, passage across the plasma membrane, interaction with a receptor localized in the cytosol, and transport of the hormone-receptor complex to the nucleus, where the sex hormone-bound receptor acts to alter specific gene transcription. During the early 1990s, a few studies showed that the initial model proposing that the steroid receptor was the cytosolic chaperone for these hydrophobic compounds (which do not diffuse readily through an aqueous environment) was in fact incorrect, since the majority of the estrogen receptors were found exclusively in the nucleus. The initial studies which observed estrogen receptors within the cytosol were due to an artifact that occurred during processing [51,52]. In the absence of ligand, the receptor had a lowered binding affinity for DNA, causing the receptor to leak out of the nucleus. Thus, the initial steps that were posited to explain uptake and transportation across the cytosol to the nucleus no longer had a mechanistic explanation. Additionally, to date, there is still no mechanism in place to account for the initial uptake of sex hormone by cells, or to explain how sex hormones cross the plasma membrane to enter the cell, or what regulates delivery to the nucleus or sites of nongenomic action. A number of recent studies have begun to fill in this gap, however. The first point to be made was that caveolae mark cholesterol-rich membranes which are organized into a network in the cell, providing an organized set of membranes through which other sterols can "diffuse". The second point was the discovery that the estrogen receptor is found associated with caveolae at the plasma membrane [53–55]. The third point is the recent finding that activation of nitric oxide by sex hormones requires a specific pool of estrogen which is tightly associated with HDL [14]. Estrogen is tightly bound specifically with HDL, and HDL from female mice – but not male mice – activates eNOS. The activation of eNOS is linked to HDL binding to SR-BI and SR-BI-mediated delivery of estrogen to caveolae. This study was the first to identify caveolae as a putative site of uptake of estrogen into endothelial cells. The results of these studies, taken together, define an emerging new paradigm of sex hormone delivery to cells and transport of sex hormones from the plasma membrane to specific intracellular organelles which initiate in caveolae. The role of intracellular caveolin-associated membranes in estrogen trafficking within the cell remains to be elucidated. This emerging paradigm of the first steps in estrogen delivery to cells may represent a new paradigm for the uptake of some other sterols. Recently, vitamin D was shown to bind to a pool of the nuclear vitamin D receptor, which localizes to caveolae in the intestine [56,57]. Thus, the initial interaction of vitamin D with cells and many of its nongenomic actions appears to extend this emerging model of sex hormone uptake to a model that may be important in a broader context of other sterols. In addition, it might also provide novel insights into the uptake and action of other lipophilic hormones, vitamins, and nutrients.

8.10
Protein Acylation and Caveolae

Acylation of proteins has been linked to caveolae localization, presumably due to the direct interaction of acyl chains by intercalation into the organized lipid of caveolae membranes. Site-directed mutational analysis of eNOS acylation shows the role of two-site acylation in caveolae association and regulation of eNOS activation in caveolae [58]. eNOS is myristoylated during post-translational processing and acylated by covalent attachment of fatty acids at the N-terminus and at a specific cysteine. Silencing of each of these acylation sites inhibited eNOS activity to one-tenth of the activity of wild-type eNOS, and silencing of both acylations is synergistic, resulting in one-hundredth of the activity. The loss of acylation resulted in a loss of association of eNOS with caveolae to the same extent as the loss of activity.

Caveolin itself is acylated at three cysteines, and acylation has been shown to be important in the interaction and organization of caveolin and other proteins with caveolae [59,60]. Acylation is also important in the interaction of caveolin-1 with cholesterol in chaperone complexes. Site-directed mutagenesis studies have revealed that two of the three acylation sites – Cys143 and Cys156 – are required for formation and activity of the chaperone complex that delivers cholesterol from the Golgi to caveolae [61]. The third acylation, at Cys133, is essential for the formation and activity of the chaperone complex that internalizes cholesterol ester into cells [10].

A number of studies have shown that acylation of proteins is a factor in raft association of proteins and in raft signaling. The Src family of protein tyrosine kinases has been found to contain a number of different acyl groups, with stearate and oleate derivatives showing decreased affinity for rafts compared to the myristoylated forms [62]. Enzymes have been identified which can de-acylate lipid raft-associated proteins, such as a recently cloned lysophospholipase/acyl thioesterase [63]. We have observed heterogeneity in the acylation of several caveolin-associated proteins (unpublished observations). The mechanisms and roles of acylation in the overall organization and dynamics of caveolae are fruitful areas for further exploration.

8.11
Scavenger Receptors Localize to Caveolae

CD36 has been localized to lipid rafts in several tissues, and we and others have shown CD36 to be localized within endothelial caveolae. CD36 has a putative role in the control of hypertension, and in angiogenesis [64,65]. CD36 in striated muscle caveolae appears to be important in the uptake and accumulation of fatty acids, in both skeletal muscle and heart [66,67]. Scavenger receptor class B, Type I is an 82-kDa glycosylated plasma membrane protein that is closely related to CD36 [68–72]. SR-BI is a transmembrane protein with short cytoplasmic N-terminal and C-terminal cytoplasmic domains, two transmembrane domains, and a large extracellular domain comprising the majority of the protein [69,71,72]. SR-BI is a receptor for HDLs and has broad ligand-binding specificity. In addition to HDL, SR-BI binds native low-density lipoprotein (LDL), oxidized LDL, acetylated LDL, and anionic phospholipids, but not the many polyanions that are bound by the type-A scavenger receptors [73–75]). SR-BI is a physiological receptor for HDL and also plays a role in regulating plasma cholesterol levels; however, the function of SR-BI in cells other than hepatic or steroidogenic cells is not well understood. We have recently shown that SR-BI has additional roles in endothelial cells, regulating HDL-mediated delivery of estrogen to cells [14], and regulating HDL-mediated inhibition of a cell apoptosis pathway involving eNOS [76].

8.12
Cholesterol Homeostasis Regulates Caveolin Localization and Organization of other Proteins in Caveolae

The cycle of cholesterol movement between cell-surface caveolae and intracellular pools rich in cholesterol contributes to caveolae cholesterol homeostasis. This cycle is controlled in a complex fashion that can involve scavenger receptors (SR-BI and CD-36), lipoproteins, and even sex hormones [11,14,65,77,78]. Many studies using methyl-beta-cyclodextrin have documented that cholesterol depletion and repletion cause major changes in the organization of caveolae, caveolin-1 localization to caveolae, or redistribution to intracellular sites, and resultant effects on numerous signaling proteins that are found in association with caveolae or bound to caveolae by caveolin-1. A recent report has shown that shear stress induction of eNOS activity is also susceptible to disruption of caveolae cholesterol, either by methyl-beta cyclodextrin depletion, or by cyclosporine A inhibition of caveolin-1-cypA interaction [79]. This indicates that disruption of this chaperone complex cycle contributes to the endothelial pathogenesis which leads to hypertension induced by cyclosporine.

8.13
Chaperone Complexes Involved in Cholesterol Transport in Specialized Tissues

The intestine has a major role in the overall regulation of systemic cholesterol levels. We have identified a third chaperone complex that is involved in the net uptake and transport of cholesterol in the intestine [80]. Annexin II and caveolin-1 form a chaperone complex with cyp40 and cypA that binds cholesterol in the intestine. Ablation of annexin II or caveolin-1 in the zebrafish disrupted cholesterol uptake. Further, the drug ezetimibe decreased cholesterol levels in the circulation by disrupting intestinal cholesterol transport. Ezetimibe also disrupted this novel annexin II-caveolin-cholesterol chaperone complex. However, the interaction of annexin II with caveolin-1 in this intestinal complex is quite different from the two chaperone complexes described previously. Annexin II and caveolin-1 appear to form a heterodimeric band which is stable to heat, SDS and reducing agents, and was also immunoreactive against both annexin II and caveolin-1 and resolved as a complex at 55–58 kDa on SDS gels. This band, after digestion and analysis, yielded several peptides corresponding to regions of each individual protein, and its size was consistent with that of a heterodimeric complex. This novel complex is not limited to zebrafish, however. In mouse intestine, a band that corresponds to this heterodimeric complex, along with immunoreactive bands corresponding to the monomeric forms of each protein were also found. Recently, another protein – NPC1 like 1 protein, has been found in intestine, and shown to regulate intestinal cholesterol and sitosterol uptake [81,82]. NPC-1 fibroblasts (which lack functional NPC-1, the first protein in this family) show a block in cholesterol transport causing accumulation of cholesterol-rich late endosomes [83]. In these cells, both caveolin and annexin II exhibit elevated expression and accumulation with cholesterol in late endosomes. Further studies will be needed to determine the relationship between these two overlapping pathways and their roles in intestinal cholesterol trafficking.

8.14
Caveolin is Linked to Additional Sterol and Lipid Uptake and Trafficking Pathways

Several additional studies have indicated new roles for caveolin and associated proteins in the intracellular transport of cholesterol and the specific uptake of lipids. Caveolin-1 and SCP-2 directly interact in L-type fibroblasts, and co-localize both at the plasma membrane and in the cytosol [84]. The interplay between these nonvesicle trafficking pathways and vesicle-mediated transport in control of cholesterol trafficking and caveolae structure and organization will provide fruitful ground for further exploration.

8.15
Conclusions

Over a decade ago, caveolin was identified as a marker of caveolae and was found to be present in most cell types. Investigations of caveolae and lipid rafts over the past decade have resulted in more than 3500 publications which have brought tremendous change to our understanding of the organization of membranes and the functional organization of signaling and trafficking pathways within the cell. A new paradigm of the cell membrane consisting of multiple functional and structural domains has replaced the simple phospholipid bilayer model. This has also brought a conceptual paradigm shift of examining the integration of pathways linked through caveolae across the whole cell. The next frontier will involve the progression to models that are sufficiently sophisticated to provide a mechanistic understanding of the integration of pathways across tissues and organ systems. These investigations will be aided by use of cell- and tissue-specific knockout and knockin models which will, in turn, lead to a new level of integration in our understanding of the molecular events underlying diseases such as diabetes, inflammation, vascular disease, and cancer.

Abbreviations

cyp40	cyclophilin 40
cypA	cyclophilin A
eNOS	endothelial nitric oxide synthase
ER	endoplasmic reticulum
ER-GIC	endoplasmic reticulum-Golgi-intermediate-compartment
GPI	glycosyl-phosphatidylinositol
HDL	high-density lipoprotein
hsp	heat shock protein
HUVEC	human umbilical vein endothelial cells
LDL	low-density lipoprotein
PM	plasma membrane
SDS-PAGE	sodium dodecylsulfate-polyacryamide gel electrophoresis
SR-BI	scavenger receptor BI
VVO	vesicular vacuolar organelle

References

1 Hooper NM. Detergent-insoluble glycos-phingolipid/cholesterol-rich membrane domains, lipid rafts and caveolae (review). *Mol. Membr. Biol.* 16: 145–156, 1999.

2 Iwabuchi K, Handa K, Hakomori S. Separation of glycosphingolipid-enriched microdomains from caveolar membrane characterized by presence of caveolin. *Methods Enzymol.* 312: 488–494, 2000.

3 Smart EJ, Graf GA, McNiven MA, Sessa WC, Engelman JA, Scherer PE, Okamoto T, Lisanti MP. Caveolins, liquid-ordered domains, and signal transduction. *Mol. Cell. Biol.* 19: 7289–7304, 1999.

4 Rothberg KG, Heuser JE, Donzell WC, Ying Y, Glenney JR, Anderson RGW. Caveolin, a protein component of caveolae membrane coats. *Cell* 68: 673–682, 1992.

5 Rothberg KG, Ying Y, Kamen BA, Anderson RGW. Cholesterol controls the clustering of the glycophospholipid-anchored membrane receptor for 5-methyltetrahydrofolate. *J. Cell Biol.* 111: 2931–2938, 1990.

6 Smart EJ, Ying YS, Conrad PA, Anderson RG. Caveolin moves from caveolae to the Golgi apparatus in response to cholesterol oxidation. *J. Cell Biol.* 127: 1185–1197, 1994.

7 Singh RD, Puri V, Valiyaveettil JT, Marks DL, Bittman R, Pagano RE. Selective caveolin-1-dependent endocytosis of glycosphingolipids. *Mol. Biol. Cell* 14: 3254–3265, 2003.

8 Abrami L, Fivaz M, Kobayashi T, Kinoshita T, Parton RG, van der Goot FG. Cross-talk between caveolae and glycosylphosphatidylinositol-rich domains. *J. Biol. Chem.* 276: 30729–30736, 2001.

9 Smart EJ, Anderson RG. Alterations in membrane cholesterol that affect structure and function of caveolae. *Methods Enzymol.* 353: 131–139, 2002.

10 Uittenbogaard A, Everson WV, Matveev SV, Smart EJ. Cholesteryl ester is transported from caveolae to internal membranes as part of a caveolin-annexin II lipid-protein complex. *J. Biol. Chem.* 277: 4925–4931, 2002.

11 Uittenbogaard A, Shaul PW, Yuhanna IS, Blair A, Smart EJ. High density lipoprotein prevents oxidized low density lipoprotein-induced inhibition of endothelial nitric-oxide synthase localization and activation in caveolae. *J. Biol. Chem.* 275: 11278–11283, 2000.

12 Machleidt T, Li WP, Liu P, Anderson RG. Multiple domains in caveolin-1 control its intracellular traffic. *J. Cell Biol.* 148: 17–28, 2000.

13 Ghosh S, Gachhui R, Crooks C, Wu C, Lisanti MP, Stuehr DJ. Interaction between caveolin-1 and the reductase domain of endothelial nitric-oxide synthase. Consequences for catalysis. *J. Biol. Chem.* 273: 22267–22271, 1998.

14 Gong MC, Wilson ME, Kelly T, Su W, Dressman J, Kincer JF, Matveev S, Guo L, Guerin TM, Li X-A, Zhu W, Uittenbogaard A, Smart EJ. HDL-associated estradiol stimulates endothelial NO synthase and vasodilation in an SR-BI-dependent manner. *J. Clin. Invest.* 111: 1579–1587, 2003.

15 Yao Q, Chen J, Cao H, Orth JD, McCaffery JM, Stan RV, McNiven MA. Caveolin-1 interacts directly with dynamin-2. *J. Mol. Biol.* 348: 491–501, 2005.

16 Smart EJ, Ying YS, Mineo C, Anderson RG. A detergent-free method for purifying caveolae membrane from tissue culture cells. *Proc. Natl. Acad. Sci. USA* 92: 10104–10108, 1995.

17 Schnitzer JE, McIntosh DP, Dvorak AM, Liu J, Oh P. Separation of caveolae from associated microdomains of GPI-anchored proteins. *Science* 269: 1435–1439, 1995.

18 Robinson JM, Vandre DD. Antigen retrieval in cells and tissues: enhancement with sodium dodecyl sulfate. *Histochem. Cell. Biol.* 116: 119–130, 2001.

19 Pol A, Martin S, Fernandez MA, Ingelmo-Torres M, Ferguson C, Enrich C, Parton RG. Cholesterol and fatty acids regulate dynamic caveolin trafficking through the Golgi complex and between the cell surface and lipid bodies. *Mol. Biol. Cell* 16: 2091–2105, 2005.

20 Fra AM, Williamson E, Simons K, Parton RG. De novo formation of caveolae in lymphocytes by expression of VIP21-caveolin. *Proc. Natl. Acad. Sci. USA* 92: 8655–8659, 1995.

21 Sowa G, Pypaert M, Fulton D, Sessa WC. The phosphorylation of caveolin-2 on serines 23 and 36 modulates caveolin-1-dependent caveolae formation. *Proc. Natl. Acad. Sci. USA* 100: 6511–6516, 2003.

22 Corvera S, DiBonaventura C, Shpetner HS. Cell confluence-dependent remodeling of endothelial membranes mediated by cholesterol. *J. Biol. Chem.* 275: 31414–31421, 2000.

23 Dvorak AM, Feng D. The vesiculo-vacuolar organelle (VVO). A new endothelial cell permeability organelle. *J. Histochem. Cytochem.* 49: 419–432, 2001.

24 Dvorak AM, Kohn S, Morgan ES, Fox P, Nagy JA, Dvorak HF. The vesiculo-vacuolar organelle (VVO): a distinct endothelial cell structure that provides a transcellular pathway for macromolecular extravasation. *J. Leukoc. Biol.* 59: 100–115, 1996.

25 Feng D, Nagy JA, Dvorak HF, Dvorak AM. Ultrastructural studies define soluble macromolecular, particulate, and cellular transendothelial cell pathways in venules, lymphatic vessels, and tumor-associated microvessels in man and animals. *Microsc. Res. Tech.* 57: 289–326, 2002.

26 Bauer PM, Yu J, Chen Y, Hickey R, Bernatchez PN, Looft-Wilson R, Huang Y, Giordano F, Stan RV, Sessa WC. Endothelial-specific expression of caveolin-1 impairs microvascular permeability and angiogenesis. *Proc. Natl. Acad. Sci. USA* 102: 204–209, 2005.

27 Stan RV. Structure and function of endothelial caveolae. *Microsc. Res. Tech.* 57: 350–364, 2002.

28 Mora R, Bonilha VL, Marmorstein A, Scherer PE, Brown D, Lisanti MP, Rodriguez-Boulan E. Caveolin-2 localizes to the Golgi complex but redistributes to plasma membrane, caveolae, and rafts when co-expressed with caveolin-1. *J. Biol. Chem.* 274: 25708–25717, 1999.

29 Parolini I, Sargiacomo M, Galbiati F, Rizzo G, Grignani F, Engelman JA, Okamoto T, Ikezu T, Scherer PE, Mora R, Rodriguez-Boulan E, Peschle C, Lisanti MP. Expression of caveolin-1 is required for the transport of caveolin-2 to the plasma membrane. Retention of caveolin-2 at the level of the Golgi complex. *J. Biol. Chem.* 274: 25718–25725, 1999.

30 Scherer PE, Lewis RY, Volonte D, Engelman JA, Galbiati F, Couet J, Kohtz DS, van Donselaar E, Peters P, Lisanti MP. Cell-type and tissue-specific expression of caveolin-2. Caveolins 1 and 2 co-localize and form a stable hetero-oligomeric complex in vivo. *J. Biol. Chem.* 272: 29337–29346, 1997.

31 Scherer PE, Okamoto T, Chun M, Nishimoto I, Lodish HF, Lisanti MP. Identification, sequence, and expression of caveolin-2 defines a caveolin gene family. *Proc. Natl. Acad. Sci. USA* 93: 131–135, 1996.

32 Ostermeyer AG, Paci JM, Zeng Y, Lublin DM, Munro S, Brown DA. Accumulation of caveolin in the endoplasmic reticulum redirects the protein to lipid storage droplets. *J. Cell Biol.* 152: 1071–1078, 2001.

33 Pol A, Luetterforst R, Lindsay M, Heino S, Ikonen E, Parton RG. A caveolin dominant negative mutant associates with lipid bodies and induces intracellular cholesterol imbalance. *J. Cell Biol.* 152: 1057–1070, 2001.

34 Razani B, Wang XB, Engelman JA, Battista M, Lagaud G, Zhang XL, Kneitz B, Hou H, Christ GJ, Edelmann W, Lisanti MP. Caveolin-2 deficient mice show evidence of severe pulmonary dysfunction without disruption of caveolae. *Mol. Biol. Cell* 22: 2329–2344, 2002.

35 Frank PG, Pedraza A, Cohen DE, Lisanti MP. Adenovirus-mediated expression of caveolin-1 in mouse liver increases plasma high-density lipoprotein levels. *Biochemistry* 40: 10892–10900, 2001.

36 Bouras T, Lisanti MP, Pestell RG. Caveolin-1 in breast cancer. *Cancer Biol. Ther.* 3: 931–941, 2004.

37 Yang G, Truong LD, Timme TL, Ren C, Wheeler TM, Park SH, Nasu Y, Bangma CH, Kattan MW, Scardino PT, Thompson TC. Elevated expression of caveolin is associated with prostate and breast cancer. *Clin. Cancer Res.* 4: 1873–1880, 1998.

38 Mouraviev V, Li L, Tahir SA, Yang G, Timme TM, Goltsov A, Ren C, Satoh T, Wheeler TM, Ittmann MM, Miles BJ, Amato RJ, Kadmon D, Thompson TC. The role of caveolin-1 in androgen insensitive prostate cancer. *J. Urol.* 168: 1589–1596, 2002.

39 Pramudji C, Shimura S, Ebara S, Yang G, Wang J, Ren C, Yuan Y, Tahir SA, Timme TL, Thompson TC. In situ prostate cancer gene therapy using a novel adenoviral vector regulated by the caveolin-1 promoter. *Clin. Cancer Res.* 7: 4272–4279, 2001.

40 Thompson TC, Timme TL, Li L, Goltsov A. Caveolin-1, a metastasis-related gene that promotes cell survival in prostate cancer. *Apoptosis* 4: 233–237, 1999.

41 Montesano R, Mossaz A, Vassalli P, Orci L. Specialization of the macrophage plasma membrane at sites of interaction with opsonized erythrocytes. *J. Cell Biol.* 96: 1227–1233, 1983.

42 Montesano R, Vassalli P, Orci L. Structural heterogeneity of endocytic membranes in macrophages as revealed by the cholesterol probe, filipin. *J. Cell Sci.* 51: 95–107, 1981.

43 Orci L, Montesano R, Meda P, Malaisse-Lagae F, Brown D, Perrelet A, Vassalli P. Heterogeneous distribution of filipin-cholesterol complexes across the cisternae of the Golgi apparatus. *Proc. Natl. Acad. Sci. USA* 78: 293–297, 1981.

44 Conrad PA, Smart EJ, Ying Y, Anderson RWG, Bloom GS. Caveolin cycles between plasma membrane caveolae and the Golgi complex by microtubule-dependent and microtubule-independent steps. *J. Cell Biol.* 131: 1421–1433, 1995.

45 Robenek MJ, Schlattmann K, Zimmer KP, Plenz G, Troyer D, Robenek H. Cholesterol transporter caveolin-1 transits the lipid bilayer during intracellular cycling. *FASEB J.* 17: 1940–1942, 2003.

46 Joliot A, Maizel A, Rosenberg D, Trembleau A, Dupas S, Volovitch M, Prochiantz A. Identification of a signal sequence necessary for the unconventional secretion of Engrailed homeoprotein. *Curr. Biol.* 8: 856–863, 1998.

47 Joliot A, Trembleau A, Raposo G, Calvet S, Volovitch M, Prochiantz A. Association of Engrailed homeoproteins with vesicles presenting caveolae-like properties. *Development* 124: 1865–1875, 1997.

48 Robenek MJ, Severs NJ, Schlattmann K, Plenz G, Zimmer KP, Troyer D, Robenek H. Lipids partition caveolin-1 from ER membranes into lipid droplets: updating the model of lipid droplet biogenesis. *FASEB J.* 18: 866–868, 2004.

49 Smart EJ, Ying Y, Donzell WC, Anderson RG. A role for caveolin in transport of cholesterol from endoplasmic reticulum to plasma membrane. *J. Biol. Chem.* 271: 29427–29435, 1996.

50 Uittenbogaard A, Ying Y, Smart EJ. Characterization of a cytosolic heat-shock protein-caveolin chaperone complex. Involvement in cholesterol trafficking. *J. Biol. Chem.* 273: 6525–6532, 1998.

51 King WJ, Greene GL. Monoclonal antibodies localize oestrogen receptor in the nuclei of target cells. *Nature* 307: 745–747, 1984.

52 Welshons WV, Lieberman ME, Gorski J. Nuclear localization of unoccupied oestrogen receptors. *Nature* 307: 747–749, 1984.

53 Chambliss KL, Shaul PW. Rapid activation of endothelial NO synthase by estrogen: evidence for a steroid receptor fast-action complex (SRFC) in caveolae. *Steroids* 67: 413–419, 2002.

54 Chambliss KL, Yuhanna IS, Mineo C, Liu P, German Z, Sherman TS, Mendelsohn ME, Anderson RG, Shaul PW. Estrogen receptor alpha and endothelial nitric oxide synthase are organized into a functional signaling module in caveolae. *Circ. Res.* 87: E44-E52, 2000.

55 Kim HP, Lee JY, Jeong JK, Bae SW, Lee HK, Jo I. Nongenomic stimulation of nitric oxide release by estrogen is mediated by estrogen receptor alpha localized in caveolae. *Biochem. Biophys. Res. Commun.* 263: 257–262, 1999.

56 Huhtakangas JA, Olivera CJ, Bishop JE, Zanello LP, Norman AW. The vitamin D receptor is present in caveolae-enriched plasma membranes and binds 1 alpha,25(OH)$_2$-vitamin D3 in vivo and in vitro. *Mol. Endocrinol.* 18: 2660–2671, 2004.

57 Norman AW, Olivera CJ, Barreto Silva FR, and Bishop JE. A specific binding protein/receptor for 1alpha,25-dihydroxyvitamin D(3) is present in an intestinal caveolae membrane fraction. *Biochem. Biophys. Res. Commun.* 298: 414–419, 2002.

58 Shaul PW, Smart EJ, Robinson LJ, German Z, Yuhanna IS, Ying Y, Anderson RG, Michel T. Acylation targets emdothelial nitric-oxide synthase to plasmalemmal caveolae. *J. Biol. Chem.* 271: 6518–6522, 1996.

59 Galbiati F, Volonte D, Meani D, Milligan G, Lublin DM, Lisanti MP, Parenti M. The dually acylated NH$_2$-terminal domain of gi1alpha is sufficient to target a green fluorescent protein reporter to caveolin-enriched plasma membrane domains. Palmitoylation of caveolin-1 is required for the recognition of dually acylated g-protein alpha subunits in vivo. *J. Biol. Chem.* 274: 5843–5850, 1999.

60 Shenoy-Scaria AM, Dietzen DJ, Kwong J, Link DC, Lublin DM. Cysteine3 of Src family protein tyrosine kinase determines palmitoylation and localization in caveolae. *J. Cell Biol.* 126: 353–363, 1994.

61 Uittenbogaard A, Smart EJ. Palmitoylation of caveolin-1 is required for cholesterol binding, chaperone complex formation, and rapid transport of cholesterol to caveolae. *J. Biol. Chem.* 275: 25595–25599, 2000.

62 Liang JS, Distler O, Cooper DA, Jamil H, Deckelbaum RJ, Ginsberg HN, Sturley SL. HIV protease inhibitors protect apolipoprotein B from degradation by the proteasome: A potential mechanism for protease inhibitor-induced hyperlipidemia. *Nature Med.* 7: 1327–1331, 2001.

63 Wang A, Johnson CA, Jones Y, Ellisman MH, Dennis EA. Subcellular localization and PKC-dependent regulation of the human lysophospholipase A/acyl-protein thioesterase in WISH cells. *Biochim. Biophys. Acta* 1484: 207–214, 2000.

64 Febbraio M, Hajjar DP, Silverstein RL. CD36: a class B scavenger receptor involved in angiogenesis, atherosclerosis, inflammation, and lipid metabolism. *J. Clin. Invest.* 108: 785–791, 2001.

65 Kincer JF, Uittenbogaard A, Dressman J, Guerin TM, Febbraio M, Guo L, Smart EJ. Hypercholesterolemia promotes a CD36-dependent and endothelial nitric oxide synthase-mediated vascular dysfunction. *J. Biol. Chem.* 277: 23525–23533, 2002.

66 Bastie CC, Hajri T, Drover VA, Grimaldi PA, Abumrad NA. CD36 in myocytes channels fatty acids to a lipase-accessible triglyceride pool that is related to cell lipid and insulin responsiveness. *Diabetes* 53: 2209–2216, 2004.

67 Nozaki S, Tanaka T, Yamashita S, Sohmiya K, Yoshizumi T, Okamoto F, Kitaura Y, Kotake C, Nishida H, Nakata A, Nakagawa T, Matsumoto K, Kameda-Takemura K, Tadokoro S, Kurata Y, Tomiyama Y, Kawamura K, Matsuzawa Y. CD36 mediates long-chain fatty acid transport in human myocardium: complete myocardial accumulation defect of radiolabeled long-chain fatty acid analog in subjects with CD36 deficiency. *Mol. Cell. Biochem.* 192: 129–135, 1999.

68 Acton S, Rigotti A, Landschulz KT, Xu S, Hobbs HH, Krieger M. Identification of scavenger receptor SR-BI as a high density lipoprotein receptor. *Science* 271: 518–520, 1996.

69 Acton SL, Scherer PE, Lodish HF, Krieger M. Expression cloning of SR-BI, a CD36-related class B scavenger receptor. *J. Biol. Chem.* 269: 21003–21009, 1994.

70 Babitt J, Trigatti B, Rigotti A, Smart EJ, Anderson RG, Xu S, Krieger M. Murine SR-BI, a high density lipoprotein receptor that mediates selective lipid uptake, is N-glycosylated and fatty acylated and colocalizes with plasma membrane caveolae. *J. Biol. Chem.* 272: 13242–13249, 1997.

71 Connelly MA, Klein SM, Azhar S, Abumrad NA, Williams DL. Comparison of class B scavenger receptors, CD36 and scavenger receptor BI (SR-BI), shows that both receptors mediate high density lipoprotein-cholesteryl ester selective uptake but SR-BI exhibits a unique enhancement of cholesteryl ester uptake. *J. Biol. Chem.* 274: 41–47, 1999.

72 Trigatti B, Rigotti A, Krieger M. The role of the high-density lipoprotein receptor SR-BI in cholesterol metabolism. *Curr. Opin. Lipidol.* 11: 123–131, 2000.

73 Azhar S, Leers-Sucheta S, Reaven E. Cholesterol uptake in adrenal and gonadal tissues: the SR-BI and 'selective' pathway connection. *Front. Biosci.* 8: 998–1029, 2003.

74 Krieger M. Charting the fate of the 'good cholesterol': identification and characterization of the high-density lipoprotein receptor SR-BI. *Annu. Rev. Biochem.* 68: 523–558, 1999.

75 Varban ML, Rinninger F, Wang N, Fairchild-Huntress V, Dunmore JH, Fang Q, Gosselin ML, Dixon KL, Deeds JD, Acton SL, Tall AR, Huszar D. Targeted mutation reveals a central role for SR-BI in hepatic selective uptake of high density lipoprotein cholesterol. *Proc. Natl. Acad. Sci. USA* 95: 4619–4624, 1998.

76 Li XA, Guo L, Dressman JL, Asmis R, Smart EJ. A novel ligand-independent apoptotic pathway induced by scavenger receptor class B, type I and suppressed by endothelial nitric-oxide synthase and high density lipoprotein. *J. Biol. Chem.* 280: 19087–19096, 2005.

77 Chikani G, Zhu W, Smart EJ. Lipids: potential regulators of nitric oxide generation. *Am. J. Physiol. Endocrinol. Metab.* 287: E386-E389, 2004.

78 Everson WV, Smart EJ. Influence of caveolin, cholesterol, and lipoproteins on nitric oxide synthase. implications for vascular

disease. *Trends Cardiovasc. Med.* 11: 246–250, 2001.

79 Lungu AO, Jin ZG, Yamawaki H, Tanimoto T, Wong C, Berk BC. Cyclosporin A inhibits flow-mediated activation of endothelial nitric oxide synthase via altering cholesterol content in caveolae. *J. Biol. Chem.* e-pub, 2004.

80 Smart EJ, deRose RA, Farber SA. Annexin 2-caveolin 1 complex is a target of ezetimibe and regulates intestinal cholesterol transport. *Proc. Natl. Acad. Sci. USA* 101: 3450–3455, 2004.

81 Davis HR, Jr., Zhu LJ, Hoos LM, Tetzloff G, Maguire M, Liu J, Yao X, Iyer SP, Lam MH, Lund EG, Detmers PA, Graziano MP, Altmann SW. Niemann-Pick C1 Like 1 (NPC1L1) is the intestinal phytosterol and cholesterol transporter and a key modulator of whole-body cholesterol homeostasis. *J. Biol. Chem.* 279: 33586–33592, 2004.

82 Garcia-Calvo M, Lisnock J, Bull HG, Hawes BE, Burnett DA, Braun MP, Crona JH, Davis HR, Jr., Dean DC, Detmers PA, Graziano MP, Hughes M, Macintyre DE, Ogawa A, O'Neill K A, Iyer SP, Shevell DE, Smith MM, Tang YS, Makarewicz AM, Ujjainwalla F, Altmann SW, Chapman KT, Thornberry NA. The target of ezetimibe is Niemann-Pick C1-Like 1 (NPC1L1). *Proc. Natl. Acad. Sci. USA* 102: 8132–8137, 2005.

83 Garver WS, Hossain GS, Winscott MM, and Heidenreich RA. The Npc1 mutation causes an altered expression of caveolin-1, annexin II and protein kinases and phosphorylation of caveolin-1 and annexin II in murine livers. *Biochim. Biophys. Acta* 1453: 193–206, 1999.

84 Zhou M, Parr RD, Petrescu AD, Payne HR, Atshaves BP, Kier AB, Ball JM, Schroeder F. Sterol carrier protein-2 directly interacts with caveolin-1 in vitro and in vivo. *Biochemistry* 43: 7288–7306, 2004.

9

The Roles of Caveolae and Caveolin in Cell Shape, Locomotion, and Stress Fiber Formation

Sang Chul Park and Kyung A. Cho

9.1
Introduction

Molecular mechanistic studies of senescent phenotypes such as morphological alteration and deterioration in physiological function have led to the finding that the caveolin molecule might play a prime determinant role in the bimodal nature of the aging process [1,2]. The defective endocytosis system in the aged organism, which is due to an imbalance or dysregulation of the signal transduction system for the entry and relay of signals, was seen to be the basis of the gate theory of aging, with special emphasis being placed on the role of prime modulator molecules to determine the senescent phenotype [3]. Although having been proposed previously as a candidate for a prime modulator molecule [4], caveolin has more recently been suggested as being a possible determinant of the morphological adjustment of senescent cells via modulation of the cytoskeleton, as well as having a role as a functional modulator [5].

Various cellular processes such as differentiation, apoptosis, migration, transformation and cellular senescence require morphological changes with cytoskeletal rearrangement. In this context, a new proposal has been made that caveolins might play a role in morphological determination via actin remodeling through the modulation of polarity and Rho GTPase activity [6,7]. Thus, the activity of caveolin as a modulator of polarity and Rho GTPase activity might provide a novel – albeit somewhat intriguing – approach to study the crosstalk of cellular function and structure relationships.

9.2
Caveolin and Polarity

Animal cells adopt a vast diversity of shapes, ranging from the relatively simple-looking columnar epithelial cell to the highly complex branched structure of a neuron. Shape and migration are highly dependent on the external environmental conditions for the directional cues that drive intracellular polarity. All eukaryotic

Lipid Rafts and Caveolae. Christopher J. Fielding
Copyright © 2006 WILEY-VCH Verlag GmbH & Co. KGaA, Weinheim
ISBN: 3-527-31261-7

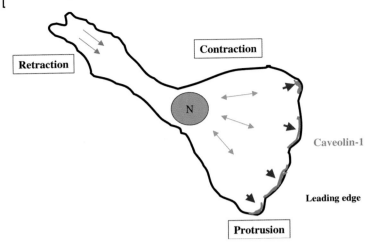

Fig. 9.1 Cellular motility. Cells move through the polarized and dynamic re-organization of the actin cytoskeleton, involving a protruding force at the front (blue arrows), combined with a contractile force in the cell body (green double-headed arrows). Caveolin-1 (red) accumulates at the leading edge and involves polarization during cell movement. N = nucleus.

cells are able to polarize in response to cues at the plasma membrane, for example during the budding of yeast, asymmetrical cell division, and mammalian cell differentiation [8].

Caveolin-1 may play an important role in cell motility because it exhibits anterior-posterior polarization during cell migration. Caveolin-1 was found to accumulate at the leading edge of cultured fibroblasts [9] and human umbilical vein smooth muscle cells [10]. Caveolae and lipid rafts also exhibit pronounced polarity during cell migration (Fig. 9.1), with raft-associated ganglioside GM1 being found at the leading edge of human adenocarcinoma MCF-7 cells, when stimulated with insulin growth factor-1 (IGF-1) [11]. Endothelial cells (ECs) exhibit a polarized distribution of caveolin-1 when traversing a filter pore [12]. In these cells, caveolin-1 seems to be released from the caveolar structure in the cell rear and to be re-localized at the cell front; this is in contrast to the situation that occurs during planar movement, when caveolin-1 is concentrated at the rear of endothelial cells, co-localized with caveolae. Phosphorylation of the Tyr14 residue of caveolin-1 is also required for polarization of the protein during transmigration [12]. Therefore, the localization and phosphorylation of caveolin might play a crucial role in the polarity of cellular morphological changes, although the molecular mechanism involved is, as yet, unclear.

9.3
Caveolin and Rho-family GTPases

Rho GTPases participate in the regulation of polarity, microtubule dynamics and cell shape, the latter property being regulated by the Rho GTPases adjusting the organization of the actin cytoskeleton. For example, Cdc42 induces filopodia, Rac induces lamellipodia, and Rho induces focal adhesion and associated stress fibers [13] (Fig. 9.2).

Rho GTPases are a group of molecular switches which control complex cellular processes. They cycle between two conformational states: one state is bound to GTP (the "active" state), and the other state is bound to GDP (the "inactive" state), although both states hydrolyze GTP to GDP. The active GTPases recognize target proteins and generate a response until GTP hydrolysis returns the switch to the GDP state.

In order to drive the processes in precise fashion, the activities of Rho GTPases

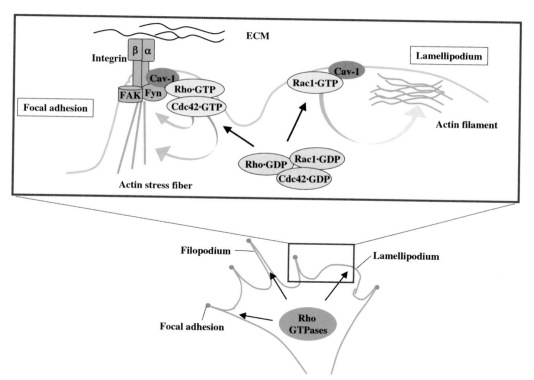

Fig. 9.2 Rho GTPases and caveolae. Rho GTPases induce morphological changes via the formation of filopodia, lamellipodia, focal adhesion and actin stress fiber. Rho GTPases are recruited into the caveolae, where their activities are regulated by caveolin-1. Caveolin-1 can interact with the integrin α subunit and Fyn, leading to stable focal adhesion formation.

must be tightly controlled spatiotemporally within the cells. Recent studies have suggested that the function of Rho GTPases may be deeply related with caveolae or lipid rafts. In endothelial cells, sucrose gradient density centrifugation studies have revealed that a significant proportion of RhoA and Cdc42 are localized within caveolae-enriched membrane domains. Moreover, caveolin-1 is directly bound with RhoA but not with Cdc42 [6]. In neonatal rat cardiomyocytes, the initiation and transduction of stretch-induced RhoA and Rac1 activation requires caveolar compartment [7]. However, in unstretched cardiomyocytes RhoA and Rac1 were detected in both the caveolae and noncaveolar fractions. RhoA and Rac1 was activated within 4 minutes by stretching, then inactivated after 15 minutes, and subsequently became dissociated from the caveolae. In addition, treatment with methyl-β-cyclodextrin (mβCD), a caveolae-disrupting agent, inhibits the stretching-induced RhoA and Rac1 activation [7]. Moreover, integrins influence the targeting of Rac and Rho GTPases to the plasma membrane via lipid raft or caveolae and their coupling to downstream effector molecules [14]. In migrating cells, integrins interact with caveolae or lipid rafts to mobilize the activated GTP-bound Rac and Rho to the plasma membrane.

As illustrated in Figure 9.2, caveolin-1 is involved in the regulation of cellular morphological changes via the modulation of Rho GTPases activity. Senescent human diploid fibroblasts (HDFs) show an altered cellular morphology of flattened and enlarged cell shape, in contrast to the small, spindle shape of young cells. In senescent HDFs, the activities of Rac1 and Cdc42 are significantly increased, and overexpression of active Rac1 and Cdc42 in young HDFs resulted in senescence-like morphological changes. We have observed that the active forms of Rac1 and Cdc42 are localized in caveolae and interact directly with caveolin-1 in senescent HDFs [5]. Interestingly, it has been suggested that caveolin-1 is required for filopodia formation, which may enhance the invasive ability of lung adenocarcinoma cells, though the level of caveolin itself is relatively low [15]. These results suggest that caveolin might involve the determination of cell shape and migration through polarity arrangement and the regulation of Rho GTPases activity.

9.4
Caveolin and Focal Adhesion Complex

When cells come into contact with the extracellular matrix (ECM), they usually extend filopodia. Then, integrins located at the tip of filopodia bind to the ECM and initiate the formation of focal adhesions. Actin-rich lamellipodia are then generated as the cell spreads on the ECM [16]. As the integrins bind to the ECM they become clustered in the plane of the cell membrane and associate with the cytoskeletal and signaling complex that promote the assembly of actin filaments. The reorganization of actin filaments into larger stress fibers in turn causes more clustering of integrins, thus enhancing the matrix binding and organization by integrins in a positive feedback system. As a consequence, the ECM proteins, integrins and cytoskeletal proteins assemble into aggregates on each side of the membrane, these aggregates being termed "focal adhesions". Several integrins have been found to associate laterally with caveolin-1, at least in primary cells (see Fig. 9.2) [17,18]. Although the biochemical nature of this interaction is not yet clear, inhibition of caveolin expression suppresses the formation of focal adhesions and actin stress fibers [5,17].

Integrins activate a variety of protein tyrosine kinases, including focal adhesion kinase (FAK), which may be recruited and acquire tyrosine kinase activity by its interaction with integrins. Subsequently, FAK can phosphorylate other cytoskeletal proteins. In addition to the activation of FAK, some β_1 and α_v integrins can activate the tyrosine kinase Fyn and the adapter protein Shc. In this pathway, caveolin-1 appears to function as a membrane adaptor, which couples the integrin α-subunit to Fyn [19]. In senescent HDFs, the inhibition of caveolin-1 expression can disrupt focal adhesion and actin stress fiber, most likely due to the de-phosphorylation of FAK [5]. In NIH-3T3 cells, caveolin-2 undergoes Src-induced phosphorylation on Tyr19, which is localized near to the focal adhesion, and remains associated with the caveolae [20].

9.5
The Dynamics of Caveolin and Actin

Ultrastructural and biochemical analyses have implicated the actin cytoskeleton as having a role in caveolae function [21–24]. Caveolin is also involved in dynamic actin remodeling in endocytosis or molecular trafficking.

In adipocytes, the stimulation of glucose uptake by insulin is achieved via the translocation of intracellular glucose transporter 4 (GLUT4) to the cell-surface membrane. Insulin-induced GLUT4 translocation in adipocytes requires dynamic actin remodeling at the inner surface of the plasma membrane (cortical actin) and in the perinuclear region [25]. In particular, the treatment of adipocytes with the actin-depolymerizing agents cytochalasin D and latrunculin A or B, and the actin-stabilizing agent jasplakinolide, all lead to the inhibition of insulin-stimulated GLUT4 translocation [25–29].

Caveolin-1 mediates the translocation of GLUT4 through direct binding with actin filaments in adipocytes. In differentiated adipocytes, the stress fiber F-actin becomes small patches of punctate actin that are co-localized with the caveolin-positive clusters. In adipocytes, caveolin-actin structures are disrupted by mβCD (which in caveolae causes cholesterol depletion) [30]. Taken together, these results suggest that, in adipocytes, caveolin-1 may play an important role in the transloca-tion of GLUT4 through direct binding with actin.

The F-actin cross-linking protein filamin was identified as being a ligand for caveolin-1 by using a yeast two-hybrid screen [31]. The N-terminus of caveolin-1 binds to both nonmuscle and muscle filamin, indicating that such interaction might not be cell type-specific. Caveolin-1 is present in filamin-positive patches at the plasma membrane, and is co-aligned with actin stress fibers upon Rho stimula-tion. Filamin plays a role in cell locomotion and mechanoprotection, and also as a cytoskeletal linker for transmembrane proteins such as integrins and glycoprotein I complex in platelets. Therefore, the interaction of caveolin-1 with filamin supports one of the possibilities that caveolin-1 is linked to the cortical actin cytoskeleton via filamin.

Caveolin-1, in addition, can indirectly regulate actin remodeling by the activation of Rho family small GTP-binding protein TC10 upon insulin-stimulation in adipocytes. The translocation of GLUT4 requires both phosphatidylinositol (PI) 3-kinase-dependent pathways for activation of Akt [32–34], and a PI3-kinase-independent pathway for the activation of TC10 [35–37]. Recently, both PI3-kinase and TC10 have been reported as being involved in the regulation of actin cytoskeleton rearrangement in various cell types [25,38,39]. TC10 is mainly localized to the caveolae, and subsequently caveolin-1-enriched caveolae are required for the activation of TC10 through a CAP-Cbl signaling pathway [35,36]. Insulin stimulates the phosphorylation of another insulin receptor substrate, the proto-oncogene c-Cbl [40]. Once phosphorylated, Cbl can recruit the SH2-containing adapter protein CrkII to caveolae along with the guanine nucleotide exchange factor C3G. The latter then appears to activate TC10 [35]. Although the action of TC10 remains unknown, a potential clue towards understanding its physiological function comes from the role of Rho proteins in modulation of the actin cytoskeleton. The inhibition of Rho function with toxin B, or expression of the amino-terminal domain of TC10, disrupts the adipocyte actin cytoskeleton and inhibits GLUT4 translocation. Moreover, the dominant-negative mutant of TC10 disrupts caveolae-associated F-actin structures in adipocytes [41]. The disruption of caveolae with cholesterol-depleting drugs or by overexpression of the inhibitory forms of caveolin-1 completely blocks TC10 activation, as well as the stimulation of glucose transport by insulin [36]. However, direct evidence for an interaction between TC10 and caveolin-1 remains vague.

9.6
Caveolae-Dependent Endocytosis via Actin Stress Fiber

Recently, caveolae-mediated endocytosis has been implicated in the internalization of certain membrane components, extracellular ligands, bacterial toxins, and several nonenveloped viruses [42,43]. Simian virus 40 (SV40) utilizes endocytosis through caveolae to achieve infectious entry into host cells [44,45]. After binding to the caveolae, the virus particles induce the transient breakdown of actin stress fibers. Actin is then recruited to virus-loaded caveolae as actin patches are responsible sites for actin "tail" formation. Latrunculin A (an actin monomer-sequestering drug) and jasplakinolide (an actin polymer-stabilizing drug) both reduced virus internalization by 60–65% during the later stages of the entry process [46]. This result suggests that actin might function as a scaffold to restrict the lateral mobility of the caveolae. These events are dependent upon the presence of cholesterol and the activation of tyrosine kinases, which phosphorylate proteins in caveolae. SV40 particles induce tyrosine phosphorylation of proteins at virus-loaded caveolae, and thereby inhibition of tyrosine kinases inhibits the caveolae- mediated internalization of the virus. These findings indicate that the phosphorylation of caveolae proteins is essential for the formation of caveolae-derived endocytic vesicles and for viral infection into the cell [46]. Therefore, it is possible that tyrosine phosphorylation of caveolae-associated proteins might trigger the recruitment of components for F-actin assembly [46,47].

9.7
Summary

The roles of caveolin and caveolae in a variety of cellular processes have been reassessed. In particular, responsibility for the regulation of cellular shape determination, migration and stress fiber formation has been reviewed. The mode of cellular polarity can be partially explained by the recruitment and polarization of intracellular caveolin, which might be responsible in turn for cellular motility (Fig. 9.3). Likewise, the interaction of caveolin with Rho GTPases might affect the

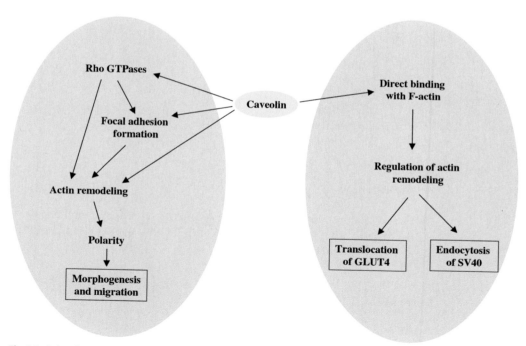

Fig. 9.3 Role of caveolin-1 via actin remodeling. Caveolin-1 may involve in morphological changes or migration via regulation of Rho GTPases, focal adhesion formation or actin remodeling. For molecular trafficking, caveolin can interact with F-actin or filamin. These interactions may play a crucial role in the translocation of GLUT4 in adipocytes or endocytosis of viruses.

relevant activities for microtubule dynamics, actin remodeling and migration, resulting in cellular morphological changes as well as locomotive activity. Moreover, caveolin's interaction with the focal adhesion kinase complex and actin cytoskeletal structures resulted in the modulation of molecular trafficking for many biologically active molecules. These findings of caveolin function led us to explain, in part, the bimodal nature of changes in structure and function in senescent phenotypes. In this context, the role of caveolin as a determinant of structural change in the senescent cell highlighted the novel modality for the modulation of age-related morphological alteration as well as functional deterioration through the simple adjustment of caveolin status.

In conclusion, it is possible that the status of caveolin – via its interaction with actin cytoskeletal structures, focal adhesion kinase complex and Rho GTPases – may affect a variety of cellular processes such as signaling modulation, viral infectivity, hormone sensitivity, transformability, invasiveness and neuronal capacity, among a broad spectrum of cellular phenomena.

Abbreviations

EC	endothelial cell
ECM	extracellular matrix
FAK	focal adhesion kinase
GLUT4	glucose transporter 4
HDF	human diploid fibroblast
IGF-1	insulin growth factor-1
mβCD	methyl-β-cyclodextrin
PI	phosphatidylinositol
SV40	Simian virus 40

Acknowledgements

This work has been supported by the grants from the Korea Science and Engineering Foundation (RII-2002-097-05001-0 and RII-2002-097-00001-0) and the Korea Research Foundation for Health Science.

References

1 W. Y. Park, K. A. Cho, J. S. Park, D. I. Kim, S. C. Park, *J. Biol. Chem.* 2000, 275(27), 20847–20852.

2 K. A. Cho, S. C. Park, *Mech. Ageing. Dev.* 2005, 126(1), 105–110.

3 E. J. Yeo, S. C. Park, *Mech. Ageing. Dev.* 2002, 123(12), 1563–1578.

4 K. A. Cho, S. J. Ryu, J. S. Park, I. S. Jang, J. S. Ahn, K. T. Kim, S. C. Park, *J. Biol. Chem.* 2003, 278(30), 27789–27795.

5 K. A. Cho, S. J. Ryu, Y. S. Oh, J. H. Park, J. W. Lee, H. P. Kim, K. T. Kim, I. S. Jang, S. C Park, *J. Biol. Chem.* 2004, 279(40), 42270–42278.

6 D. Gingras, F. Gauthier, S. Lamy, R. R. Desrosiers, R. Beliveau, *Biochem. Biophys. Res. Commun.* 1998, 247, 888–893.

7 S. Kawamura, S. Miyamoto, J. H. Brown, *J. Biol. Chem.* 2003, 278, 31111–31117.

8 M. Vicente-Manzanares, F. Sanchez-Madrid, *Dev. Immunol.* 2000, 7(2–4), 51–65.

9 K. G. Rothberg, J. E. Heuser, W. C. Donzell, Y. S. Ying, J. R. Glenney, R. G. Anderson, *Cell* 1992, 68, 673–682.

10 S. S. Okada, J. E. Tomaszewski, E. S. Barnathan, *Exp. Cell. Res.* 1995, 217, 180–187.

11 S. Manes, E. Mira, C. Gomez-Mouton, R. A. Lacalle, P. Keller, J. P. Labrador, A. C. Martinez, *EMBO J.* 1999, 18, 6211–6220.

12 M. O. Parat, B. Anand-Apte, P. L. Fox, *Mol. Biol. Cell.* 2003, 14, 3156–3168.

13 A. Hall, *Science* 1998, 279, 509–514.

14 A. F. Palazzo, C. H. Eng, D. D. Schlaepfer, E. E. Marcantonio, G. G. Gundersen, *Science* 2004, 303, 836–839.

15 C. C. Ho, P. H. Huang, H. Y. Huang, Y. H. Chen, P. C. Yang, S. M. Hsu, *Am. J. Pathol.* 2002, 161, 1647–1656.

16 F. G. Giancotti, E. Ruoslahti, *Science* 1999, 285(5430), 1028–1032.

17 K. K. Wary, F. Mainiero, S. J. Isakoff, E. E. Marcantonio, F. G. Giancotti, *Cell* 1996, 87, 733–743.

18 Y. Wei, X. Yang, Q. Liu, J. A. Wilkins, H. A Chapman, *J. Cell. Biol.* 1999, 144, 1285–1294.

19 K. K. Wary, A. Mariotti, C. Zurzolo, F. G. Giancotti, *Cell* 1998, 94, 625–634.

20 H. Lee, D. S. Park, X. B. Wang, P. E. Scherer, P. E. Schwartz, M. P. Lisanti, *J. Biol. Chem.* 2002, 277, 34556–34567.

21 P. Rohlich, A. C. Allison, *J. Ultrastruct. Res.* 1976, 57, 94–103.

22 B. van Deurs, K. Nilausen, *J. Cell. Biol.* 1982, 94, 279–286.

23 R. G. Parton, B. Joggerst, K. Simons, *J. Cell. Biol.* 1994, 127, 1199–1215.

24 T. Fujimoto, *Seikagaku* 1995, 67, 1396–1401.

25 M. Kanzaki, J. E. Pessin, *J. Biol. Chem.* 2001, 276, 42436–42444.

26 T. Tsakiridis, P. Tong, B. Matthews, E. Tsiani, P. J. Bilan, A. Klip, G. P. Downey, *Microsc. Res. Tech.* 1999, 47, 79–92.

27 Z. A. Khayat, P. Tong, K. Yaworsky, R. J. Bloch, A. Klip, *J. Cell. Sci.* 2000, 113 (Pt 2), 279–290.

28 W. Omata, H. Shibata, L. Li, K. Takata, I. Kojima, *Biochem. J.* 2000, 346 (Pt 2), 321–328.

29 P. Tong, Z. A. Khayat, C. Huang, N. Patel, A. Ueyama, A. Klip, *J. Clin. Invest.* 2001, 108, 371–381.

30 M. Kanzaki, M. Furukawa, W. Raab, J. E. Pessin, *J. Biol. Chem.* 2004, 279, 30622–30633.

31 M. Stahlhut, B. van Deurs, *Mol. Biol. Cell.* 2000, 11, 325–337.

32 K. Kotani, W. Ogawa, M. Matsumoto, T. Kitamura, H. Sakaue, Y. Hino, K. Miyake, W. Sano, K. Akimoto, S. Ohno, M. Kasuga, *Mol. Cell. Biol.* 1998, 18, 6971–6982.

33 Q. Wang, R. Somwar, P. J. Bilan, Z. Liu, J. Jin, J. R. Woodgett, A. Klip, *Mol. Cell. Biol.* 1999, 19, 4008–4018.

34 M. L. Standaert, G. Bandyopadhyay, L. Perez, D. Price, L. Galloway, A. Poklepovic, M. P. Sajan, V. Cenni, A. Sirri, J. Moscat, A. Toker, R. V. Farese, *J. Biol. Chem.* 1999, 274, 25308–25316.

35 S. H. Chiang, C. A. Baumann, M. Kanzaki, D. C. Thurmond, R. T. Watson, C. L. Neudauer, I. G. Macara, J. E. Pessin, A. R. Saltiel, *Nature* 2001, 410, 944–948.

36 R. T. Watson, S. Shigematsu, S. H. Chiang, S. Mora, M. Kanzaki, I. G. Macara, A. R. Saltiel, J. E. Pessin, *J. Cell. Biol.* 2001, 154, 829–840.

37 A. Baumann, V. Ribon, M. Kanzaki, D. C. Thurmond, S. Mora, S. Shigematsu, P. E. Bickel, J. E. Pessin, A. R. Saltiel, *Nature* 2000, 407, 202–207.

38 G. A. Murphy, P. A. Solski, S. A. Jillian, P. Perez de la Ossa, P. D. Eustachio, C. J. Der, M. G. Rush, *Oncogene* 1999, 18, 3831–3845.

39 C. Vignal, M. De Toledo, F. Comunale, A. Ladopoulou, C. Gauthier-Rouviere, A. Blangy, P. Fort, *J. Biol. Chem.* 2000, 275, 36457–36464.

40 V. Ribon, A. R. Saltiel, *Biochem. J.* 1997, 324 (Pt 3), 839–845.

41 M. Kanzaki, J. E. Pessin, *J. Biol. Chem.* 2002, 277, 25867–25869.

42 B. Razani, M. P. Lisanti, *Exp. Cell. Res.* 2001, 271, 36–44.

43 L. Pelkmans, A. Helenius, *Traffic* 2002, 3, 311–320.

44 H. A. Anderson, Y. Chen, L. C. Norkin, *Mol. Biol. Cell.* 1996, 7, 1825–1834.

45 D. Stang, J. Kartenbeck, R. G. Parton, *Mol. Biol. Cell.* 1997, 8, 47–57.

46 L. Pelkmans, D. Puntener, A. Helenius, *Science* 2002, 296, 535–539.

47 A. E. Engqvist-Goldstein, D. G. Drubin, *Annu. Rev. Cell. Dev. Biol.* 2003, 19, 287–332.

10

Lipid Rafts in Trafficking and Processing of Prion Protein and Amyloid Precursor Protein

Daniela Sarnataro, Vincenza Campana, and Chiara Zurzolo

10.1
Introduction

Extensive evidence has accumulated in recent years that several human disorders have the same molecular basis, namely, a change in the conformation of a protein. These disorders have been named "conformational diseases" [1], and the most important among them are prion and Alzheimer diseases. Prion diseases have been proposed to be caused by the transconformation of the cellular prion protein PrP^c into a protease-resistant and readily aggregated isoform (PrP^{Sc}) which accumulates in the brain. However, controversy exists regarding exactly where and how in the cell this conversion occurs. Conversely, in Alzheimer's disease (AD) mutations in genes encoding three different proteins, amyloid precursor protein (APP) and presenilins 1 and 2 have been shown to lead to the overproduction and accumulation in the brain of the amyloid peptide Aβ that converts from a soluble form into amyloid fibrils. During its biogenesis, APP undergoes sequential enzymatic cleavages, and a critical question for understanding the pathogenesis of Alzheimer's disease is where, and at what rate, Aβ is produced in neurons. In the case of prion diseases, it has been postulated that missorting of APP or altered intracellular trafficking of Aβ could play a key role in the pathogenesis of AD (2,3).

Lipid rafts, which are small membrane patches of highly ordered saturated lipids and cholesterol, have been proposed to play a role in the biogenesis of both these neurodegenerative disorders because they might represent a preferential site for the formation of the pathological forms of the prion protein and amyloidogenic Aβ. Thus, for both conformational diseases it appears that the intracellular trafficking of PrP^c and APP, and their association with rafts, have a predominant role in their related pathogenesis. Here, we review the latest findings on these two fundamental aspects.

Lipid Rafts and Caveolae. Christopher J. Fielding
Copyright © 2006 WILEY-VCH Verlag GmbH & Co. KGaA, Weinheim
ISBN: 3-527-31261-7

10.2
Lipid Rafts and Caveolae

10.2.1
Biochemical Properties and Functions

Lipid rafts have been defined as islands of highly ordered saturated lipids and cholesterol that are laterally mobile in the plane of a more disordered fluid bilayer of largely unsaturated lipids [4–6]. Because of their ability to segregate functional proteins, lipid rafts have been proposed to play a central role in many cellular processes, including intracellular signaling and protein and lipid sorting [4,5]. In particular, Simons and Ikonen in 1997 postulated that, in polarized epithelial cells, rafts can act as sorting platforms for inclusion of proteins into apical post-trans-Golgi network (TGN) sorting vesicles. Later studies subsequently provided evidence for the role of lipid rafts in signaling, as in the case of IgE receptor (FcRI) and T-cell antigen receptor (TCR) [7,8].

Association with detergent-resistant membranes (DRM) is a useful criterion to estimate whether a protein associates with lipid rafts [6]. After solubilization of membranes or cells with Triton X-100 at 4 °C, raft-associated proteins and lipids remain insoluble and can then be floated to low density by sucrose density gradient centrifugation. If cholesterol is extracted by using methyl-β-cyclodextrin (mβCD) or is complexed by saponin, the raft proteins usually (but not always) become detergent-soluble [9].

Constitutive raft residents include glycophosphatidylinositol (GPI)-anchored proteins (e. g., the prion protein), double acylated proteins (e. g., tyrosine kinases of the Src family), palmitate-anchored proteins and transmembrane proteins (e. g., β-secretase; BACE) [5].

One source of confusion in the field of rafts has been the inter-relationship between rafts and caveolae. Indeed, for a long time these two terms have been used interchangeably. However, this issue has now been clarified by the analysis of caveolin knockout mice [10,11].

Caveolae appear as "smooth" uncoated-pits of 50- to 100-nm flask-shaped invaginations of the plasma membrane, originally identified by electron microscopy in a wide variety of tissues and cell types [12,13]. They represent a morphologically identifiable subset of lipid rafts identified by the coat protein, caveolin. Whilst the biochemical composition of lipid rafts and caveolae is thought to overlap, these microdomains are not equivalent [14].

Caveolar invagination is possibly driven by the polymerization of caveolins, of which there are three types: caveolin-1, -2, and -3. Caveolin-1 appears to have a central role in the formation of caveolae, because it was shown that cells without caveolin-1 lacked morphological caveolae, and that reintroduction of the protein was sufficient to generate caveolae [15,16].

Caveolae usually remain attached to the cell surface, but their internalization can be stimulated under certain conditions; for example, by Simian virus-40 (SV40) [17] or by treatment with the phosphatase inhibitor okadaic acid [18,19].

Both caveolae and rafts mediate the internalization of sphingolipids and sphingo-lipid-binding toxins, GPI-anchored proteins [20], and the autocrine motility factor (AMF).

Internalizations via caveolae or via lipid rafts are fundamentally similar processes, defined by their clathrin independence and sensitivity to cholesterol depletion. However, the cholesterol-dependent invagination of rafts occurs independently of caveolin-1 and of dynamin 2, a GTPase, localized at the neck of the caveolae [21] which regulates their internalization. Interestingly, in some cases caveolin-1 acts as a negative regulator of the budding of caveolar invaginations but caveolae become competent for endocytosis after specific signalling stimuli [22].

Caveolae/raft dysfunction has been implicated recently in the pathogenesis of different human diseases. Several groups of pathogens, including bacteria, prions, viruses, and parasites appear to hijack lipid rafts during internalization [23–25]. In this chapter, we illustrate the proposed role of lipid rafts in the trafficking and processing of PrP^c and APP and in the pathogenesis of their related diseases.

10.3
PrP^c and Prion Diseases

Transmissible spongiform encephalopathies (also known as prion diseases) have become an interesting example of how lipid rafts are involved in regulating protein trafficking and processing (for a review, see [26]). Prion diseases include a large group of neurodegenerative disorders including scrapie in sheep and goats, bovine spongiform encephalopathies, chronic wasting disease in deer and elk, and Creutzfeldt-Jakob disease (CJD) in humans [27–29]. These pathologies are caused by an agent consisting of a protein which is usually referred to as a prion ("proteinaceous infectious only") [27]. The prion diseases are often (but not always) characterized by the cerebral accumulation of a protease-resistant, misfolded isoform of the prion protein (PrP), the so-called PrP^Sc (for scrapie PrP), which is derived from the normal isoform of the cellular glycoprotein PrP^c (for cellular PrP) [27,30]. Compared to PrP^c, the PrP^Sc form has an increased content of β-sheet structures and is partially resistant to proteinase K digestion; therefore, it aggregates and accumulates in the brain [27]. Thus, this conformational change of PrP has been proposed to be the cause of the disease.

Prion diseases can be of infectious, sporadic and genetic origin. In the case of infectious diseases, a direct interaction between the pathogenic PrP^Sc template and the endogenous PrP^c substrate is proposed to drive the formation of nascent infectious misfolded prions [27]. In contrast, in the genetic forms of the diseases, mutations present in the gene of PrP^c, *Prpn* [27,31], can directly and spontaneously induce alterations in PrP^c conformation. The exact mechanism by which PrP^c is converted into PrP^Sc is not yet known, but several lines of evidence suggest that lipid rafts are involved [32,33].

PrP^c is a cell-surface GPI-anchored protein which is normally expressed in neurons and in a range of non-neuronal tissues, as well as leukocytes [34]. Human PrP is the product of a single gene which directs the synthesis of a protein containing 253 amino acids, with five octapeptide repeats near the N-terminus, two glycosylation sites and one disulfide bridge. The GPI-anchor, which attaches the protein to the outer surface of the cell membrane, allows its association with rafts.

The role of PrP^c remains unknown. In 1992, Weissmann's group [35] generated PrP^c-null mice and reported that PrP^c expression is dispensable for normal development and behavior. However, its conservation in different species infers some relevance in basic physiological processes. PrP^c has been proposed to be involved in several functions:

- copper/zinc transport or metabolism [36–38];
- protection from oxidative stress [38];
- cellular signalling [39,40];
- membrane excitability and synaptic transmission [41,42];
- neuritogenesis [43]; and
- apoptosis [44].

Strong evidence for PrP^c function derives from its interaction with different partners, ligands and/or effectors, such as laminin, BIP, GFAP, and Bcl-2 (for a review, see [45]), each of which can be relevant for the different proposed function of PrP^c.

Several studies support the possibility that PrP^c misfolding and/or misfunction correlate with defects in its trafficking and with its raft association. In particular, the intracellular localization of some pathological mutants of PrP^c, which cause inherited prion diseases, has been shown to be altered [31]. Therefore, in order to understand the mechanism of the disease it is important to understand the relationships between raft association, intracellular trafficking, proper protein folding, and the function of PrP^c.

10.3.1
The Site of PrP^c Conversion: The Role of Rafts in the Different Intracellular Compartments

A major unresolved question is where PrP^c-PrP^{Sc} transconformation occurs. Both PrP^c and PrP^{Sc} have been localized at the plasma membrane and have been shown to undergo endocytosis [46,47], so it is likely that the plasma membrane and/or the endolysosomal compartment participate in PrP^{Sc} formation. In addition, in the case of inherited diseases, pulse-chase experiments indicate that the pathological conversion of mutant PrP to the PrP^{Sc}-like conformer proceeds in a stepwise manner, via a series of identifiable biochemical intermediates, and that one of the earliest properties of PrP^{Sc} (i.e., resistance to cleavage by phosphatidylinositol phospholipase C) is acquired in the endoplasmic reticulum (ER) [31]. Moreover, the ER could also be implicated in the degradation of misfolded PrP mutants via the ER-associated degradation (ERAD) pathway [48–50].

Hence, the available data indicate that in the case of genetic prion diseases originating from PrP mutants (for a review, see [31]), the ER might be directly involved in protein transconformation and consequent PrP^{Sc} formation. Conversely, because in infected cells the stimulation of PrP^c retrograde transport results in an increase in the PrP^{Sc} form [51], we recently proposed [26] that in infectious diseases the ER could represent an amplification compartment for PrP^{Sc} produced earlier at other subcellular sites.

Detergent-resistant microdomains in the ER (ER-rafts) could also be involved in the folding of PrP^c [52]. Like neuronal cell lines, epithelial cells synthesize four different isoforms of PrP^c corresponding to the unglycosylated, monoglycosylated, immature diglycosylated, and mature diglycosylated isoforms. Interestingly, it was found that the immature diglycosylated precursor form of PrP^c was recovered in a DRM fraction in the ER. Using cholesterol- and sphingolipid-depleting drugs in concomitance with pulse-chase experiments, we were able to show that this earlier raft association was crucial for the correct folding of PrP. Indeed, a portion of the protein became misfolded in the ER when cholesterol was extracted [52].

The mechanism that underlies the specificity of cholesterol depletion for PrP^c misfolding could be explained in two ways:

- either cholesterol depletion could perturb the formation of specific DRMs present in the ER, leading to an interference of the association of the immature PrP^c isoform with rafts; or
- cholesterol itself could be directly involved in the folding of PrP^c by acting as a lipochaperone in the ER [53,54].

In contrast with the proposed role for the ER in prion conversion, the results of several studies have indicated that the conversion of PrP^c to a protease- and phospholipase-resistant state is an event that occurs after the protein has reached the cell surface [47,55,56]. Hence, the release of PrP^c from the cell surface by different methods [47,55,57] and exposure of PrP^c to different antibodies [57] prevents PrP^{Sc} formation in infected cells.

Therefore, the current evidence suggests that both the ER and the plasma membrane might be important sites for prion formation, and that they are differently involved in the genetic and infectious diseases. Whilst in the case of genetic prion diseases, the ER could be involved in the generation of PrP^{Sc} or PrP^{Sc}-like conformers from PrP mutants [31], in the case of infectious diseases, the first contact between physiological and pathological PrP isoforms could occur at the plasma membrane, although the transconformation might occur later after internalization.

After its transport to the plasma membrane, PrP^c is constitutively internalized and recycles back to the surface [31,46]. The endocytic recycling pathway is of interest from the standpoint of prion generation, since there is evidence that initial steps in the conversion of PrP^c into PrP^{Sc} may take place on the plasma membrane or following the internalization of PrP^c [47,51,55]. The route and mechanism of internalization of PrP^c are controversial because both caveolae and clathrin-coated pits have been shown to be involved (for a review, see [31,46]). Clathrin-coated pits appear to be primarily responsible for endocytic uptake of PrP^c. This conclusion is based on immunogold localization of PrP^c in these organelles by electron microscopy [58,59] and inhibition of PrP^c internalization by incubating cells in hypertonic sucrose, which disrupts clathrin lattices [58].

Because PrP^c lacks a cytoplasmic tail that could interact directly with adaptor proteins and clathrin [60], several candidate proteins have been proposed to be PrP-interacting partners mediating its internalization via the clathrin pathway. Specifically, a basic amino acid motif found in the N-terminal region of PrP^c [31,60,61] has been shown to be essential for coated pit localization and internalization. In contrast to these studies, the presence of PrP^c in caveolar-like domains (CLDs) has also been extensively reported [62,63]. In Chinese hamster ovary (CHO) cells, which express caveolin-1, PrP^c is enriched in caveolae both at the TGN and at the plasma membrane and in interconnecting chains of endocytic caveolae, but it is apparently absent in clathrin-coated pits and vesicles [64].

The initial recruitment of PrP^c to pre-endocytic membranes may therefore be a complex event which occurs by more than one mechanism. It is possible that PrP^c is internalized by default by clathrin-coated vesicles, and that caveolae or CLDs provide alternative internalization pathways occurring in particular cells or conditions.

These different mechanisms may provide a range of possibilities for protein conversion and pathological spreading. Indeed, both CLDs and clathrin-coated pits have been suggested to be involved in PrP^c to PrP^{Sc} transconformation [60,63], but until the internalization pathway of PrP^c is clarified it will be difficult to establish the involvement of one or the other pathway in transconformation.

The fact that most PrP^c molecules reside in raft domains does not argue against an association of the protein with coated-pits, because only a small fraction of the PrP^c molecules are undergoing endocytosis at any one time, and this fraction has probably left the raft domain to enter the coated pits. In this context, it has been demonstrated [60] that PrP^c, prior to endocytosis, leaves the detergent-insoluble raft environment to cluster, along with TfR (the prototypical transmembrane protein endocytosed by coated pits and excluded by lipid rafts) [65] in non-raft membranes. Thus, PrP^c on the cell surface rapidly traffics through two very different membrane environments, probably with different consequences for its conformational stability.

10.3.2
Role of Lipid Rafts in PrP^{Sc} Formation

Like other pathogens, infectious prions might use rafts to enter the cells and possibly to initiate and propagate the PrP^c to PrP^{Sc} conversion process that allows prion amplification [56,66–68]. Several lines of evidences suggest that rafts are candidate sites for the generation of PrP^{Sc} in infected cells:

- Both PrP^c and PrP^{Sc} are recovered in lipid rafts [68].
- Impairment of raft association by drugs that reduce intracellular levels of cholesterol decrease PrP^{Sc} formation in infected cells [33]; similarly, removal of PrP^c from rafts by exchanging its GPI anchor with a transmembrane domain prevents PrP^{Sc} formation [63].

- Infectious prion rods were found to contain two sphingolipids, GalCer and sphingomyelin [69], which are enriched in rafts, suggesting that selected raft lipids might interact with normal and/or pathogenic prion proteins. In particular, PrP^c and PrP^{Sc}-associated rafts appear to have different characteristics, being separated from each other by solubilization and flotation on density gradients [68].

These data suggest either the presence of different kinds of rafts or different characteristics of membrane association of the wild-type and pathological isoforms with the same raft-type. The exact mechanisms by which rafts could control the transconformation of PrP^c to PrP^{Sc} remains unknown, although different scenarios can be envisaged [26]:

1. Rafts could function as a platform by which PrP^c is transported to a specific compartment where the conformational change into PrP^{Sc} occurs (Fig. 10.1A). We have shown previously that in transfected cells, cholesterol- and sphingo-lipid-depleting drugs which impair PrP^c raft association do not impair its exocytic trafficking to the plasma membrane [70], but rather slow down PrP^c endo-cytic trafficking (D. Sarnataro, personal communication), suggesting that rafts could represent the cellular environment that regulates PrP^{Sc} biosynthesis during endocytosis.

2. Rafts might represent a container of indispensable machinery required for PrP^{Sc} formation, such as proteins/lipids, that facilitate the conversion process (Fig. 10.1B).

3. Rafts could represent a favorable environment for transconformation by facilitating a close encounter between the substrate (PrP^c) and the seed (PrP^{Sc}), and could act by concentrating PrP^c and PrP^{Sc} molecules within confined regions of the plasma membrane (Fig. 10.1C). The role of rafts as a "meeting place" between PrP^c and PrP^{Sc} is supported by the studies of Baron et al., who have shown that PrP^c to PrP^{Sc} transconformation occurs only when the two protagonists of the reaction are inserted into contiguous membranes [32].

4. Rafts might allow a direct interaction of sphingolipids and/or cholesterol with PrP^c and/or with PrP^{Sc}, which could affect the conformational stability of PrP^C (Fig. 10.1D). In this case, it is possible that different raft-resident lipids could act as molecular chaperones to facilitate the unfolding of one or more α-helices or the refolding into β-sheets of PrP^c. Alternatively, a change in the local environment (in terms of enrichment in specific lipids and proteins) could mediate this process.

10.3.3
Mechanism of Raft Action in Prion Conversion

It has been shown that direct cell-to-cell contact between infected cells and uninfected cells (i.e., with PrP^c and PrP^{Sc} being on opposite cell surfaces [71]), can efficiently induce the passage of prion infection between cells. The importance of this membrane environment in the conversion reaction has been underscored by

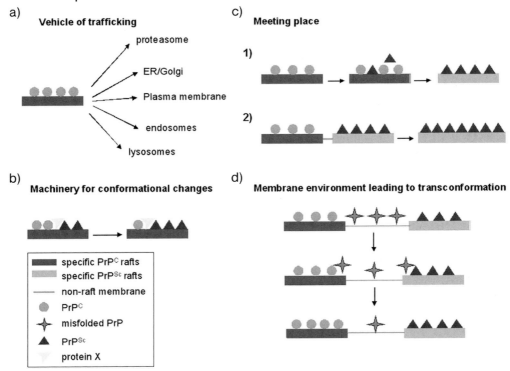

Fig. 10.1 Different models for the role of rafts in prion formation, based on the apparent implication of rafts in many features of prion protein trafficking. (A) Rafts may represent the vehicle of prion transport to the intracellular compartment (e. g., endoplasmic reticulum (ER), plasma membrane, endosomes-lysosomes, caveolae) where the conformational changes could occur. (B) Rafts may embody the cofactors (protein-X or lipid chaperones) of the transconformation machinery. (C) Rafts may represent: (1) the membrane location where PrP^c accumulates and where it encounters PrP^{Sc}; thus, the prion conversion reaction would be enhanced in these microdomains. Alternatively (2), rafts may represent a membrane environment accumulating both PrP^c and PrP^{Sc}; coalescence of these two specific prion rafts could favor and initiate prion conversion. (D) PrP^c conformation could be favored and stabilized by association with specific raft domains, so that when PrP^c exits them it is misfolded and might better interact with PrP^{Sc} and mediate transconformation.

several studies where specific lipids have been shown to play direct roles as chaperones in protein folding [72,73]. In particular, both PrP^c and PrP^{Sc} can bind to raft-like membranes enriched in cholesterol and sphingolipids [74]. In order to analyze the role of lipid rafts in this conformational transition, binding of both the α-helical-enriched structure (α-PrP) and the β-sheet-enriched form (β-PrP) to model lipid membranes was recently investigated [75]. The result of these studies indicate that binding to raft membranes results in a stabilization of α-helical structures,

PrP^C associates with rafts
early during its biosynthesis

Perturbation of this association promotes PrP misfolding...

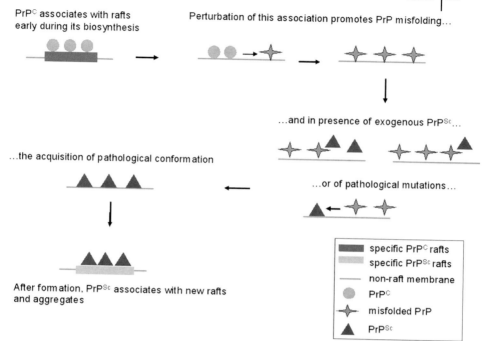

...and in presence of exogenous PrP^{Sc}...

...the acquisition of pathological conformation

...or of pathological mutations...

After formation, PrP^{Sc} associates with new rafts
and aggregates

specific PrP^C rafts
specific PrP^{Sc} rafts
non-raft membrane
PrP^C
misfolded PrP
PrP^{Sc}

Fig. 10.2 Model for PrP^c to PrP^{Sc} conversion in lipid rafts. PrP^c associates with specific rafts early during its biosynthesis. Perturbation of this membrane environment promotes PrP^c misfolding. Misfolded PrP, in the presence of PrP^{Sc} or of pathological mutants, can acquire the pathological conformation. Once formed, PrP^{Sc} can associate with new specific types of raft in which aggregation is favored.

while interaction with negatively charged lipid (non-raft) membranes increases β-sheet content [74].

This evidence for a "protective role" of rafts in the transconformation process is further reinforced by the fact that, in a non-cellular assay, PrP^c within isolated lipid rafts is highly resistant to conversion to PrP^{Sc} [32], and inhibition of sphingolipid synthesis in cells increases the rate of conversion of PrP^c [76].

Our own data on the destabilization of PrP^c folding in cholesterol depletion also support the hypothesis that the raft environment is necessary to stabilize the proper PrP^c conformation, therefore suggesting that transconformation occurs outside of the rafts, where PrP^c folding is destabilized and where misfolded PrP intermediates might be more prone to interact with PrP^{Sc} and to transconform (Fig. 10.2). However, the fact that recombinant β-PrP also has a high affinity for raft-like membranes [75] and that PrP^{Sc} is also found enriched in rafts [68] leads us to propose that, together with the protective role in prion transconformation, rafts could have a second role in promoting aggregation of PrP^{Sc}. In this scenario, PrP^{Sc} would form outside rafts in a non-protective environment but, once formed, PrP^{Sc}

would be able to reassociate with the rafts (perhaps different to the rafts where PrP^c is found), and this would favor its aggregation (Fig. 10.2).

This hypothesis is also supported by the data of Fantini et al. [77], who proposed that PrP^c can maintain a non-pathological conformation by interacting with lipid rafts through a sphingolipid-binding domain (V3-like domain). Interestingly, in the E200K PrP mutant, which undergoes PrP transconformation in familial CJD, this mutation abrogates sphingomyelin recognition. A similar sphingolipid-binding motif has also been identified in gp120 glycoprotein of HIV and in the β-amyloid peptide in Alzheimer's disease, suggesting a role of lipid rafts in the pathogenesis of these different diseases.

10.3.4
Role of Rafts in Proteolytic Attack on PrP^c

PrP^c is a complex multi-domain protein that contains potential toxic sequences (PrP^c 106–126) [78]. It has been shown that the PrP^c 106–126 peptide could trigger neurotoxicity and lead to an apoptotic response by insertion into membranes [79]. Like APP, PrP^c undergoes protein kinase C (PKC)-regulated proteolysis by identical proteases of the disintegrin family, which also inactivate the peptide.

Indeed, the normal cleavage of PrP^c, directed by ADAM10 (a disintegrin and metalloprotease) occurs inside the 106–126 "toxic" core of the protein, leading to the formation of a 11- to 12-kDa fragment referred to as N1. This processing also has a PKC-regulated counterpart regulated by the ADAM17. Interestingly, this cleavage site is inaccessible in PrP^{Sc}, where the toxic core of the protein remains uncleaved and might have a function in the production of the PrP^{Sc} aggregates [80].

PrP^c is the first example of a GPI-anchored protein that is a substrate of ADAM10 and 17, which are the β-secretase enzymes mediating APP cleavage [81,82]. The participation of these enzymes in the processing of PrP^c is quite unexpected because ADAM proteases are ectoenzymes (i.e., they have transmembrane activities), and substrates of disintegrins are generally transmembrane proteins (e.g., βAPP). Nevertheless, cleavage of both PrP^c and APP by ADAM10 and 17 takes place inside the toxic domains of these two proteins. Thus, this proteolytic attack could be viewed as an inactivating mechanism since it prevents the proteinaceous accumulation of Aβ and prion proteins often detected in affected brains.

To our knowledge, it has not yet been demonstrated whether the proteolytic attack on PrP^c occurs in lipid rafts, as has been postulated for APP (see below). However, this is an interesting possibility because in human embryonic kidney (HEK) cells a minor fraction of the ADAM10 immature proform was raft-associated [83] and another member of the metalloprotease family, ADAM19, has been found to be active in lipid rafts [84].

10.4
Alzheimer's Disease: The Role of Rafts in APP Trafficking and Processing

10.4.1
The "History" of APP Cleavage

The amyloid β-peptide (Aβ) is one of the hallmarks of AD. Aβ derives from a transmembrane protein, the amyloid precursor protein (APP) [85], through two sequential cleavages. APP is first cleaved by β-secretase BACE 1 (the β-site APP cleavage enzyme), in its luminal domain to generate a secreted ectodomain (sAPPβ) and a membrane-bound APP carboxyl terminal fragment (CTFβ). This 10-kDa C-terminal stub of APP is subsequently the substrate for β-secretase or presenilin 1 [86], which cleaves the transmembrane domain of APP to release two Aβ peptides of 40 and 42 amino acids [85].

In an alternative non pathogenic pathway, APP is cleaved within the Aβ sequence by α-secretase (belonging to the ADAM family of metalloproteases), which generates other secreted derivates known as sAPPα and APP CTFα. Like CTFβ, CTFα can be cleaved by γ-secretase yielding CTFγ and a fragment designated p3 [87]. Since α-cleavage cuts APP within the Aβ region it prevents Aβ formation and, as α- and β-cleavage compete for their substrate APP, it is crucial to understand the mechanism which regulates and controls the access of these enzymes to APP.

10.4.2
Intracellular Compartments and Aβ Generation: Involvement of Lipid Rafts

The broad intracellular distribution of the key proteins involved in Aβ generation has made it difficult to identify the intracellular site where this event occurs. APP is distributed predominantly in the TGN, but significant amounts of the protein are found at the cell surface and within endosomes [88]. BACE has been placed within the early endosomes and/or throughout the endosomal-lysosomal system [88,89], although a predominant TGN localization has also been reported [90,91]. Finally, recent evidence suggests that presenilins are located primarily not only in the ER and Golgi apparatus but also on the plasma membrane and in the endosomes [90–92]. In addition to these different localizations, many reports indicate that APP, β-secretase and presenilin 1 all reside in rafts [86,93–95]. These findings led to the proposal that lipid rafts may be a site for the proteolytic processing of APP [96,97] (Fig. 10.3A). However, the observation that APP is present in DRMs from brain tissue at levels no higher than several other non-DRM proteins questions the involvement of lipid rafts in APP proteolytic processing.

The conflicting reports about the presence of APP in DRMs could be explained by reasoning that APP in DRMs is rapidly processed such that the steady-state amount of raft-associated protein is lower than it would otherwise be expected. However, it is possible that APP cleavage occurs outside rafts but that, after its generation, the Aβ peptide rapidly translocates to the DRM after it is cleaved from APP because it has a high affinity for cholesterol [98] and ganglioside GM1

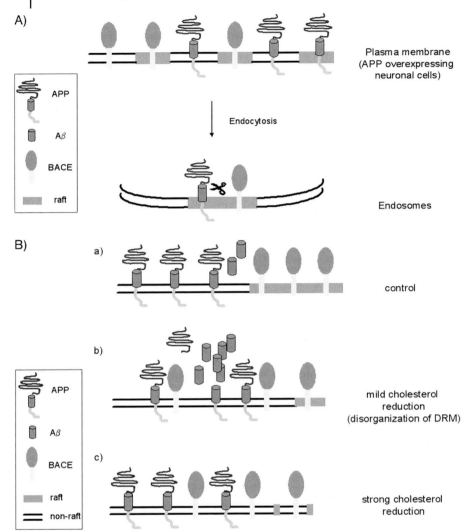

Fig. 10.3 Two different models for β-secretase processing of APP. (A) In neuronal APP-over-expressing cells, two cellular pools of both APP and BACE1 are present at the plasma membrane: one raft-associated and another outside rafts. Rafts are small and highly dispersed at the cell surface, and because they contain only a few proteins it is likely that APP and BACE1 are localized in separate rafts at the plasma membrane. Endocytosis is an essential step for APP- and BACE1-rafts to cluster and allow β-cleavage. In this model strong cholesterol depletion alters APP and BACE1 raft-association causing inhibition of Aβ formation. (B) In an alternative model, the β-cleavage of APP should occur outside lipid rafts, as APP is mainly distributed in non-raft domains (a). In this model, the amyloid-β is physiologically produced, but under mild cholesterol reduction (b) raft disorganization occurs and this process facilitates the close contact between APP and BACE1, leading to β-cleavage and a higher production of Aβ. Under strong cholesterol depletion (c), although BACE1 can more easily encounter APP, its activity is repressed because of raft disruption, and consequently Aβ production is inhibited.

[99,100], both of which are enriched in DRM [62,101] (Fig. 10.3B). Although depleting cells of cholesterol with mβCD has been shown to decrease the production of Aβ [102], this effect may not be entirely due to the disruption of lipid rafts, because such treatment also disrupts clathrin-coated pits [103] in which APP has been localized [104] (see below).

Rafts could also be involved in the formation of amyloid fibrils, that are one of the pathological hallmarks of AD [105]. The molecular mechanism of amyloid fibril formation involves a major conformational transition of Aβ, from α-helix to β-sheet [3], thus resembling the PrP^c-PrP^{Sc} transconformation. In the case of AD, the conformational change required for the conversion of soluble peptide into amyloid fibrils is modulated by pH, Aβ concentration and alteration in the primary sequence of Aβ. In addition, two raft lipids (GM1 and cholesterol) bind to Aβ and promote fibril formation [86,106]. Furthermore, synthetic lipid vesicles from bovine brain containing gangliosides such as GM1 bind to Aβ, inducing an increased amount of α-helix at pH 7 and β-sheet at pH 6 [107]. It has also been demonstrated that a conformationally altered form of Aβ, which acts as a "seed" for amyloid fibril formation, is generated in cholesterol-rich microdomains [108]. These findings support the view that lipid rafts could participate in the generation of Aβ, and that raft lipids could modulate its conformation.

Moreover, since a sphingolipid-binding domain similar to the V3-like domain of PrP has been identified in Aβ, APP and prion proteins might interact with lipid rafts by a common mechanism [109]. The molecular model proposed in Figure 10.1 to explain the role of lipid rafts in the PrP^c to PrP^{Sc} conversion might also apply for Aβ: in particular, evidence from biochemical, genetic and *in-vivo* studies has indicated that apolipoprotein E (apoE) seems to act as a pathological chaperone in AD amyloidogenesis, promoting fibril formation by inducing or stabilizing β-sheet conformation [3].

10.4.3
The Role of Rafts in β-Secretase Activity

A fraction of APP and BACE1 were shown to be associated with a raft population distinct from caveolae in a cholesterol-dependent manner. In particular, BACE1 activity decreases in cholesterol-depleted cells [93,95,102], while α-secretase activity increases after inhibition of β-secretase under these conditions. The decreased β-secretase activity after cholesterol depletion could be a result of the reduced amount of the substrate available for β-secretase cleavage. On the other hand, the increase in α-cleavage activity may derive from the fact that APP is present in two cellular pools, in equilibrium with each other – one that is raft-associated and leads to Aβ generation, and another that is outside rafts where the major amount of α-cleavage could take place. Cholesterol depletion would shift the partitioning of APP from the lipid rafts to the surrounding lipid bilayer, where it would become more accessible to α-cleavage (see below).

Interestingly, β-cleavage does not appear to be induced by partitioning of APP and BACE1 into rafts alone, but to be dependent on endocytosis [95]. However, the

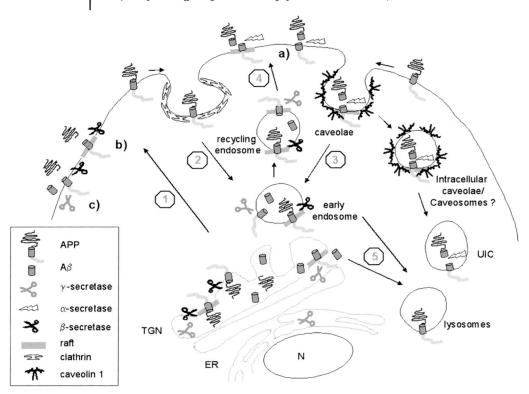

Fig. 10.4 APP cleaving pathways and cellular compartments involved in its processing. APP is a large type I transmembrane protein which is cleaved out sequentially by α-, β- and γ-secretase enzymes. Once synthesized in the ER, APP can follow distinct destinations in the cells. It can directly reach the plasma membrane ① from which it could be internalized via clathrin-coated pits ② or caveolae ③. After internalization from the plasma membrane, APP can be rapidly recycled back to the cell surface ④ or reach the lysosomes for degradation ⑤. *Plasma membrane*: APP can be processed by α- (a), β- (b) and γ-secretase (c) enzymes on the plasma membrane. Cell-surface lipid rafts seem to be involved in the α- and β-cleavage of APP, while γ-secretase activity seems to operate outside plasma membrane rafts (see text for discussion and Fig. 10.3A and B). *Caveolae*: APP has been localized in caveolae together with the CTFα fragment. Caveolae at the plasma membrane, intracellular form of caveolae or an unidentified intracellular compartment (UIC) could be the site for α-processing of APP.
Early/recycling endosomes: the early and/or recycling endosomes could represent the intracellular sites for both β- and γ-secretase cleavage of APP. Lipid rafts might be involved in these processing events. *Trans Golgi Network*: β- and γ-secretase enzymes are both present in this organelle. The TGN could represent the intracellular site for their activity on APP. The possible involvement of lipid rafts is discussed in the text.

exact cellular site of β-cleavage is not totally clear as it may occur during or after delivery to the cell surface, and/or during endocytosis [104,110–112] (Fig. 10.4).

In pulse-chase experiments, perturbation of clathrin-dependent and -independent endocytosis led to a decreased secretion of newly generated Aβ, while the α-cleavage was not affected [113,114]; this suggested that "most but not all" of the β-cleavage occurs after internalization. Furthermore, since cholesterol depletion is also known to decrease the rate of endocytosis [103], this also likely contributes to the decreased β-cleavage. The inhibition of β-cleavage by cholesterol depletion suggests that the processing of APP by BACE1 might critically depend on the lipid raft environment. Ehehalt et al. [95] proposed that rafts would have to cluster together to bring APP and BACE1 into the same raft environment in order for β-cleavage to occur. Hence, APP and BACE1 would meet after endocytosis by coalescence of BACE1- or APP-containing rafts within endosomes (see Fig. 10.3A). This hypothesis is supported by the fact that the induction of raft clustering at the cell surface with antibody cross-linking would allow β-cleavage to occur in patches containing both APP and BACE1 at the plasma membrane, and this could increase Aβ formation (Fig. 10.3) [95].

In contrast with these findings, Chyung and Selkoe [115] reported that when dynamin function was inhibited by the K44A mutant in HELA cells, the α-secretase cleavage products of APP increased in the membrane, as well as the *total* amount of secreted Aβ. This could be due to the fact that α-cleavage occurs on the cell surface [116,117].

To investigate further the significance of lipid rafts in APP β-processing, a GPI anchor has been added to BACE, replacing the transmembrane and C-terminal domains in order to target the enzyme exclusively to lipid rafts [118]. Expression of GPI-BACE substantially up-regulates the secretion of both sAPPβ and Aβ over the levels observed in cells overexpressing wild-type BACE. Furthermore, when lipid rafts were disrupted by depleting cellular cholesterol levels this effect was reversed. These results suggest that the processing of APP to the Aβ occurs mainly in lipid rafts, and that cholesterol levels are critically involved in regulating the access of α- and β-secretase to APP.

In another system (and with contrasting results) it has been reported that in neurons, APP does not seem to have the capacity to be incorporated into cholesterol-rich environments, even when overexpressed [119] (Fig. 10.3B, panel a). Furthermore, treatment leading to moderate reductions of neuronal cholesterol (Fig. 10.3B, panel b) in hippocampal membranes in culture resulted in increased APP β-cleavage, which is inconsistent with the occurrence of BACE1 cleavage of APP in DRMs. Conversely, a mild reduction of membrane cholesterol resulted in more BACE1 in the soluble fractions, higher BACE1-APP co-localization, and enhanced β-processing, whereas a strong cholesterol reduction (Fig. 10.3B, panel c) resulted in a significant fall in Aβ generation, as observed previously [95,102] (see also figure legend for description).

The discrepancy of these results with previous findings [95] could be explained by postulating that the latter data were obtained in cells that overexpressed APP and thus contained larger amounts of the protein in DRMs. Alternatively, in the overexpressing cells, more cleavage may have occurred as a result of excess APP in non-DRM domains, as suggested by Dotti et al. [119]. Consequently, further studies are required to understand the role of rafts in APP β-cleavage and the mechanism regulating the trafficking and clustering of APP and BACE1.

10.4.4
The Role of Caveolae/Lipid Rafts in α-Secretase Activity

Several reports support the view that α-secretase-mediated cleavage of APP occurs on the cell surface [116,117,120–122]. Furthermore, a recent report showed that in non-neuronal cells APP is enriched within caveolae and is physically associated by its cytoplasmic domain with caveolin-1 [97]. The C-terminal fragment resulting from APP processing by α-secretase is also localized within caveolae-enriched fractions. Importantly, in AD caveolae dysfunction may cause reduced activity of α-secretase and accumulation of toxic Aβ, and caveolin depletion by antisense oligonucleotides prevented α-cleavage. On the other hand, caveolin overexpression increased the α-secretase-mediated proteolysis of APP [97], strongly suggesting that α-cleavage could occur in caveolae (Fig. 10.4). However, proteinase inhibitors added to the cell surface had no effect on APP cleavage, indicating that the bulk of the processing takes place intracellularly [123–125]. Therefore, a second mechanism should exist that involves an intracellular compartment which may be independent of the plasma membrane caveolae. Alternatively, this phenomenon could be explained by the presence of an intracellular form of caveolae – that is, plasmalemmal vesicles. Thus, the α-secretase processing of APP could be regulated by the cycle of caveolae internalization and recycling. Because α-secretase cleavage occurs at both Leu17 and Val18 in the amyloid peptide [126], it is also possible to speculate on the existence of multiple α-secretases which cleave APP at distinct α-sites.

APP is known to transit through clathrin-coated pits and vesicles on its way to endosomes and lysosomes [127]. It is therefore conceivable that a pool of APP is localized in caveolae where α-secretase processing takes place, whereas the remaining intact APP may be cleared from the cell surface via clathrin-coated pits and targeted to endosomes and lysosomes for proteolysis (Fig. 10.4).

Furthermore, Kojro et al. [83] found that small amounts of the ADAM10 (with α-secretase activity on APP) immature proform were associated with rafts in human embryonic kidney (HEK) cells and that cholesterol depletion by mβCD increased α-secretase activity. Similarly, filipin treatment, which causes the destruction of caveolar structures, also led to a substantial increase in α-secretase activity.

These data indicate that only a "minor part" of APP could be cleaved by the α-secretase within lipid rafts or caveolae microdomains. Moreover, fluorescence anisotropy studies and biochemical assays [83] indicate that increased membrane fluidity and impaired APP internalization are responsible for the increased α-secretase activity after acute cholesterol depletion by treatment with mβCD. Specifically, increased membrane fluidity could increase the lateral movement of APP and the α-secretase activity within the membrane.

Ledesma et al. [128] have shown that plasmin (a serine protease), which is present exclusively in lipid rafts of hippocampal neurons in culture, participates in APP α-processing directly or through the activation of other proteases (i. e., ADAM 10 [129]). Reduced brain plasmin could be one cause of amyloid plaque formation, since first, plasmin levels are low in brains affected by AD and some aged humans, and second, activation of plasmin increases the α-processing of APP and decreases the levels of Aβ peptide [128].

Thus, the formation of amyloid plaques during senescence can be a consequence of a natural decrease in levels and/or activity of plasmin-mediated α-cleavage of APP. Genetic predisposition and environmental factors would determine who suffers down-regulation of plasmin throughout life.

10.4.4.1 The Role of Lipid Rafts in this Event

Ledesma et al. [130] have shown that AD hippocampi show a large disorganization of membrane lipid rafts and reduced plasmin activity. Raft disorganization could lead to AD due to a failure in the activation of a plasmin-mediated amyloid clearance pathway. Thus, these findings highlight the importance of correct membrane organization in the maintenance of amyloid clearance (see Fig. 10.3B).

Such hypotheses are in apparent contradiction with the idea that raft perturbation by cholesterol depletion may prevent AD by reducing the production of Aβ [95,102]. The amount of cholesterol removal and the different cell types used may explain the diverse results of rafts disruption. Hence, plasmin activity was lost when cholesterol reduction was no higher than 36% in human samples. In contrast, inhibition of Aβ production was observed in one case after acute removal of membrane cholesterol (60%) [102] (see Fig. 10.3B), and also in undifferentiated N2A cells [95]. From these data it is clear that the lack of proper rafts organization produces changes in different raft-mediated events that might be related to AD pathogenesis.

10.4.5
The Role of Caveolae/Rafts in γ-Secretase Activity

The γ-secretase complex was also shown to be associated with rafts [131,132], mainly in the late-Golgi and post-Golgi-derived vesicles as well as in recycling endosomes, but not in plasma membrane rafts [95,132,133].

A recent report showed that despite γ-secretase cleavage occurring in lipid rafts, γ-secretase catalytic activity is independent of the presence of cholesterol [133,134]. Indeed, although biochemical assays in neuronal cells showed mature γ-secretase to be associated with lipid rafts in a cholesterol-dependent manner when cholesterol was acutely depleted using mβCD, the quantities of Aβ produced were not altered.

In addition, it has been proposed that γ-cleavage of APP could also occur following endocytosis, resulting in the intracellular generation of Aβ that could be either retained in intracellular compartments or released from recycling endosomes [115]. This balance of intracellular versus cell-surface Aβ generation could be regulated by the half-life of APP at the cell surface.

The current data therefore support two different possibilities for APP γ-cleavage:

- γ-cleavage occurs within cholesterol-rich lipid rafts in an intracellular compartment such as early/recycling endosomes, late-Golgi and post-Golgi-derived vesicles; or
- γ-cleavage of APP occurs at the cell surface outside rafts (see Fig. 10.4).

10.4.6

The Contribution of Cholesterol and Sphingolipids in APP Processing

The cholesterol content of lipid rafts has been shown to contribute to the integrity of raft structure and the function of lipid rafts in signaling and membrane trafficking [4,135]. In addition, the results of several studies have shown that sphingolipids modulate raft functions [136,137].

A very recent report [138] examined the changes in APP processing and Aβ generation in sphingolipid-deficient cells, thus demonstrating the importance of sphingolipid levels for modulating APP processing. In particular, it has been shown that sphingolipid deficiency enhances sAPPα secretion via activation of the MAPK/ERK pathway, though the mechanism by which sphingolipid deficiency enhances ERK activity is as yet unknown. Interestingly, cholesterol depletion is reported to increase sAPPα secretion rates, although it is not known whether the MAPK/ERK pathway is involved in this cholesterol depletion-mediated pathway [83].

Furthermore, the possibility that cholesterol and sphingolipids depletion enhances APP α-cleavage in different ways cannot be excluded. Previous reports have shown that cholesterol depletion causes a decrease in β-cleavage activity and an increase in α-cleavage activity of APP [102]. In contrast, under conditions in which cholesterol levels are unchanged and lipid raft dysfunction is caused by sphingolipid depletion, the α-cleavage of APP is enhanced without affecting the β-cleavage activity of APP or the APP level in lipid rafts. These findings could suggest that sphingolipid depletion may enhance α-cleavage of APP without shifting the intracellular trafficking of APP from the "Aβ generation site" (lipid rafts) to the "Aβ nongeneration site" (outside rafts).

Therefore, cholesterol and sphingolipids may play different roles in affecting α- and β-cleavage of APP. Interestingly, also in the case of prion diseases, the effect of sphingolipid depletion on the formation of scrapie prion protein is opposite to that of cholesterol depletion [33,76].

10.5
Conclusions

In this chapter we have examined the intracellular routing and processing of PrP^c and APP, and have discussed the possible intracellular sites of prion conversion and Aβ generation. Because the intracellular trafficking and processing of prion proteins have crucial roles in prion conversion, it is believed that investigations of the different stages of intracellular trafficking and processing of prion proteins, together with an analysis of the cellular site involved in the conformational changes, will help to clarify the mechanisms which regulate prion formation.

Current data suggest that the ER might play a major role in the conversion of mutant PrP, whilst in the infectious diseases it is the transport of PrP^c to the plasma membrane and its subsequent internalization that appear to be requirements for conversion. Furthermore, lipid rafts with which both PrP^c and PrP^{Sc} are associated also appear to be fundamental for the conversion process. There are clear indications that rafts play an important role in stabilizing PrP^c conformation, thereby exerting a protective role for the disease (see Fig. 10.2). They also appear to play a crucial role in the pathogenesis of Alzheimer's disease.

In particular, current evidence indicates that APP α-cleavage could occur both at the cell surface and intracellularly. Although some of the α-secretases have been localized in caveolae, the majority of this cleavage seems to occur outside rafts. Nonetheless, it is clear that membrane and raft integrity play major roles in controlling the balance between α- and β-cleavage which compete for the same substrate. Indeed, a moderate or drastic cholesterol depletion could affect the levels of these cleavages in different ways, leading to an increment of one or the other secretase processing, and thereby either incrementing or reducing Aβ production (see Fig. 10.3B). The manner in which this occurs and the nature of the major players is not completely clear, however.

A more meticulous analysis of lipid raft composition, together with the application of new methods to investigate the specific location of PrP and APP/Aβ in living cells and to reveal conformational changes within the molecules should provide a better understanding of prion and Aβ generation. This will lead to a better understanding of the pathogenesis of prion and Alzheimer's diseases, and possibly also to the development of new drugs for the prevention and therapy of these conditions.

Acknowledgments

One of the authors (D. S.) is recipient of a fellowship from FIRB 2001, No. NE01S29H. Prion research in the Zurzolo laboratory is supported by EU grant QLK-CT-2002–81628, the Weizmann-Pasteur Foundation, the FRM grant and from Telethon (No. GGP04147).

Abbreviations

Aβ	amyloid β-peptide
AD	Alzheimer's disease
AMF	autocrine motility factor
apoE	apolipoprotein E
APP	amyloid precursor protein
BIP	immunoglobulin heavy chain binding protein
BACE	BETA-SITE APP cleavage enzyme
CHO	Chinese hamster ovary
CJD	Creutzfeldt-Jakob disease
CLD	caveolar-like domain
CTF	carboxyl terminal fragment

DRM   detergent-resistant membrane
ER   endoplasmic reticulum
ERAD   ER-associated degradation
GFAP   glial fibrillary ecidic protein
GPI   glycophosphatidylinositol
HEK   human embryonic kidney
HEK   human embryonic kidney
mβCD   methyl-β-cyclodextrin
PKC   protein kinase C
SV40   Simian virus-40
TCR   T-cell receptor
TGN   trans-Golgi network

References

1 Mann, D.M.A., Iwatsubo, T., Nochlin, D., et al. (1997) Amyloid deposition in chromosome 1-linked Alzheimer's disease: the Volga German families. *Ann. Neurol.* 41: 52–57.

2 Hsiao, K.K., Chapman, P., Nilsen, S., et al. (1996) Correlative memory deficits, Aβ elevation, and amyloid plaques in transgenic mice. *Science* 274: 99–102.

3 Soto, C. (1999) Alzheimer's and prion diseases as disorders of protein conformation: implication for the design of novel therapeutic approaches. *J. Mol. Med.* 77: 412–418.

4 Simons, K., Ikonen, E. (1997) Functional rafts in cell membranes. *Nature* 387: 569–572.

5 Simons, K., Toomre, D. (2000) Lipid rafts and signal transduction. *Nat. Rev. Mol. Cell. Biol.* 1(1): 31–39.

6 Brown, D.A., London, E. (1998) Functions of lipid rafts in biological membranes. *Annu. Rev. Cell. Dev. Biol.* 14: 111–136.

7 Janes, P.W., Ley, S.C., Magee, A.I., Kabouridis, P.S. (2000) The role of lipid rafts in T cell antigen receptor (TCR) signalling. *Semin. Immunol.* 12: 23–34.

8 Langlet, C., Bernard, A.M., Drevot, P., He, H.T. (2000) Membrane rafts and signaling by the multichain immune recognition receptors. *Curr. Opin. Immunol.* 12: 250–255.

9 London, E., Brown, D.A. (2000) Insolubility of lipids in Triton X-100: physical origin and relationship to sphingolipid/cholesterol membrane domains (rafts). *Biochim. Biophys. Acta* 1508: 182–195.

10 Drab, M., Verkade, P., Elger, M., Kasper, M., Lohn, M., Lauterbach, B., Menne, J., Lindschau, C., Mende, F., Luft, F.C., Schedl, A., Haller, H., Kurzchalia, T.V.(2001) Loss of caveolae, vascular dysfunction and pulmonary defects in caveolin-1 gene disrupted mice. *Science* 293: 2449–2452.

11 Capozza, F., Cohen, A.W., Cheung, M.W., Sotgia, F., Schubert, W., Battista, M., Lee, H., Frank , P.G., Lisanti, M.P. (2005) Muscle-specific interaction of caveolin isoforms: Differential complex formation between caveolins in fibroblastic vs. muscle cells. *Am. J. Physiol. Cell. Physiol.* 288: C677–91 EPUB 2004 Nov 17.

12 Palade, G.E. (1953) Fine structure of blood capillaries. *J. Appl. Physiol.* 24: 1424.

13 Parton, R.G. (2003) Caveolae – from ultrastructure to molecular mechanisms. *Nat. Rev. Mol. Cell. Biol.* 4: 162–167.

14 Liu, J., Oh, P., Horner, T., Rogers, R.A., Schnitzer, J.E. (1997) Organized endothelial cell surface signal transduction in caveolae distinct from glycosylphosphatidylinositol-anchored protein microdomains. *J. Biol. Chem.* 272: 7211–7222.

15 Fra, A.M., Williamson, E., Simons, K., Parton, R.G. (1995) De novo formation of caveolae in lymphocytes by expression of

VIP21-caveolin. *Proc. Natl. Acad. Sci. USA* 92: 8655–8659.

16 Lipardi, C., Mora, R., Colomer, V., Paladino, S., Nitsch, L., Rodriguez-Boulan, E., Zurzolo, C. (1998) Caveolin transfection results in caveolae formation but not apical sorting of glycosylphosphatidylinositol (GPI)-anchored proteins in epithelial cells. *J. Cell Biol.* 140(3): 617–626.

17 Pelkmans, L., Helenius, A. (2002) Endocytosis via caveolae. *Traffic* 3: 311–320.

18 Thomsen, P., Roepstorff, K., Stahlhut, M., van Deurs, B. (2002) Caveolae are highly immobile plasma membrane microdomains, which are not involved in constitutive endocytic trafficking. *Mol. Biol. Cell* 13: 238–250.

19 Parton, R.G., Joggerstam, B., Simons, K. (1994) Regulated internalization of caveolae. *J. Cell Biol.* 127: 1199–1215.

20 Mayor, S., Riezman, H. (2004) Sorting GPI-anchored proteins. *Nat. Rev. Mol. Cell. Biol.* 5(2): 110–120.

21 Oh, P., McIntosh, D.P., Schnitzer, J.E. (1998) Dynamin at the neck of caveolae mediates their budding to form transport vesicles by GTP-driven fission from the plasma membrane of endothelium. *J. Cell Biol.* 141: 101–114.

22 Nabi, I.R., Le, P.U. (2003) Caveolae/rafts-dependent endocytosis. *J. Cell Biol.* 161: 673–677.

23 van der Goot, F.G., Harder, T. (2001) Raft membrane domains: from a liquid-ordered membrane phase to a site of pathogen attack. *Semin. Immunol.* 13(2): 89–97.

24 Nichols, B.J., Lippincott-Schwartz, J. (2001) Endocytosis without clathrin-coats. *Trends Cell Biol.* 11: 406–412.

25 Conner, S.D., Schmid, S.L. (2003) Regulated portals of entry into the cell. *Nature* 422: 37–44.

26 Campana, V., Sarnataro, D., Zurzolo, C. (2005) The highways and byways of prion protein trafficking. *Trends Cell Biol.* 15(2): 102–111.

27 Prusiner, S.B. (1998) Prions. *Proc. Natl. Acad. Sci. USA* 95(23): 13363–13383.

28 Harris, D.A. (1999) Cellular biology of prion diseases. *Clin. Microbiol. Rev.* 12: 429–444.

29 Aguzzi, A., Heppner, F.L. (2000) Pathogenesis of prion diseases: a progress report. *Cell Death Differ.* 7: 889–902.

30 Chiesa, R., Harris, D.A. (2001) Prion disease: what is the neurotoxic molecule? *Neurobiol. Dis.* 8: 743–763.

31 Harris, D.A. (2003) Trafficking, turnover and membrane topology of PrP. *Br. Med. Bull.* 66: 71–85.

32 Baron, G.S., Wehrly, D., Dorward, D.W., Chesebro, B., Caughey, B. (2002) Conversion of raft associated prion protein to the protease-resistant state requires insertion of PrP-res (PrP(Sc)) into contiguous membranes. *EMBO J.* 21(5): 1031–1040.

33 Taraboulos, A., Scott, M.R.D., Semenov, A., Avraham, D., Laszlo, L., Prusiner, S.B. (1995) Cholesterol depletion and modification of COOH-terminal targeting sequence of the prion protein inhibit formation of the scrapie isoform. *J. Cell Biol.* 129(1): 121–132.

34 Aguzzi, A., Polymenidou, M. (2004) Mammalian prion biology: one century of evolving concepts. *Cell* 116(2): 313–327.

35 Bueler, H., Fischer, M., Lang, Y., Bluethmann, H., Lipp, H.P., DeArmond, S.J., Prusiner, S.B., Aevet, M., Weissmann, C. (1992) Normal development and behaviour of nice lacking the neuronal cell-surface PrP protein. *Nature* 356: 577–582.

36 Pauly, P.C., Harris, D.A. (1998) Copper stimulates endocytosis of the prion protein. *J. Biol. Chem.* 273(50): 33107–33110.

37 Watt, N.T., Hooper, N.M. (2003) The prion protein and neuronal zinc homeostasis. *Trends Biochem. Sci.* 28(8): 406–410.

38 Brown, D.R. (2001) Copper and prion disease. *Brain Res. Bull.* 55(2): 165–173.

39 Chiarini, L.B., Freitas, A.R., Zanata, S.M., Brentani, R.R., Martins, V.R., Linden, R. (2002) Cellular prion protein transduces neuroprotective signals. *EMBO J.* 21(13): 3317–3326.

40 Mouillet-Richard, S., Ermonval, M., Chebassier, C., Laplanche, JL., Lehmann, S., Launay, J.M., Kellermann, O. (2000) Signal transduction through prion protein. *Science* 289(5486): 1925–1928.

41 Mallucci, G.R., Ratte, S., Asante, E.A., Linehan, J., Gowland, I., Jefferys, J.G., Collinge, J. (2002) Post-natal knockout of prion protein alters hippocampal CA1 properties, but does not result in neurodegeneration. *EMBO J.* 21(3): 202–210.

42 Collinge, J., Whittington, M.A., Sidle, K.C., Smith, C.J., Palmer, M.S., Clarke, A.R., Jefferys, J.G. (1994) Prion protein is necessary for normal synaptic function. *Nature* 370(6487): 295–297.

43 Graner, E., Mercadante, A.F., Zanata, S.M., Forlenza, O.V., Cabral, A.L., Veiga, S.S., Juliano, M.A., Roesler, R., Walz, R., Minetti, A., Izquierdo, I., Martins, V.R., Brentani, R.R. (2000) Cellular prion protein binds laminin and mediates neuritogenesis. *Brain Res. Mol. Brain Res.* 76(1): 85–92.

44 Solforosi, L., Criado, J.R., McGavern, D.B., Wirz, S., Sanchez-Alavez, M., Sugama, S., DeGiorgio, L.A., Volpe, B.T., Wiseman, E., Abalos, G., Masliah, E., Gilden, D., Oldstone, M.B., Conti, B., Williamson, R.A. (2004) Cross-linking cellular prion protein triggers neuronal apoptosis in vivo. *Science* 303(5663): 1514–1516 (e-pub 2004 January 29).

45 Lee, K.S, Linden, R., Prado, M.A., Brentani, R.R., Martins, V.R. (2003) Towards cellular receptors for prions. *Rev. Med. Virol.* 13(6): 399–408.

46 Prado, M.A., Alves-Silva, J., Magalhaes, A.C., Prado, V.F., Linden, R., Martins, V.R., Brentani, R.R. (2004) PrPc on the road: trafficking of the cellular prion protein. *J. Neurochem.* 88(4): 769–781.

47 Borchelt, D.R., Taraboulos, A., Prusiner S.B. (1992) Evidence for synthesis of scrapie prion proteins in the endocytic pathway. *J. Biol. Chem.* 267(23): 16188–16199.

48 Zanusso, G., Petersen, R.B., Jin, T., Jing, Y., Kanoush, R., Ferrari, S., Gambetti, P., Singh, N. (1999) Proteasomal degradation and N-terminal protease resistance of the codon 145 mutant prion protein. *J. Biol. Chem.* 274(33): 23396–23404.

49 Nunziante, M., Gilch, S., Schatzl, H.M. (2003) Prion diseases: from molecular biology to intervention strategies. *Chembiochem* 4(12): 1268–1284.

50 Hegde, R.S., Rane, N.S. (2003) Prion protein trafficking and the development of neurodegeneration. *Trends Neurosci.* 26(7): 337–339.

51 Beranger, F., Mange, A., Goud, B., Lehmann, S. (2002) Stimulation of PrP(C) retrograde transport toward the endoplasmic reticulum increases accumulation of PrP(Sc) in prion-infected cells. *J. Biol. Chem.* 277(41): 38972–38977.

52 Sarnataro, D., Campana, V., Paladino, S., Stornaiuolo, M., Nitsch, L., Zurzolo, C. (2004) PrP(C) association with lipid rafts in the early secretory pathway stabilizes its cellular conformation. *Mol. Biol. Cell* 15(9): 4031–4042 (e-pub 2004, June 30).

53 Bogdanov, M., Dowhan, W. (1999) Lipid-assisted protein folding. *J. Biol. Chem.* 274(52): 36827–36830.

54 Sanders, C.R., Nagy, J.K. (2000) Misfolding of membrane proteins in health and disease: the lady or the tiger? *Curr. Opin. Struct. Biol.* 10(4): 438–442.

55 Caughey, B., Raymond, G.J. (1991) The scrapie-associated form of PrP is made from a cell surface precursor that is both protease- and phospholipase-sensitive. *J. Biol. Chem.* 266(27): 18217–18223.

56 Taraboulos, A., Raeber, A.J., Borchelt, D.R., Serban, D., Prusiner, S.B. (1992) Synthesis and trafficking of prion proteins in cultured cells. *Mol. Biol. Cell* 3(8): 851–863.

57 Supattapone, S. Nishina K., Rees J.R. (2002) Pharmacological approaches to prion research. *Biochem. Pharmacol.* 63(8): 1383–1388.

58 Shyng, S.L., Heuser, J.E., Harris, D.A. (1994) A glycolipid-anchored prion protein is endocytosed via clathrin-coated pits. *J. Cell Biol.* 125(6): 1239–1250.

59 Madore, N., Smith, K.L., Graham, C.H., Jen, A., Brady, K., Hall, S., Morris, R. (1999) Functionally different GPI proteins are organized in different domains on the neuronal surface. *EMBO J.* 18(24): 6917–6926.

60 Sunyach, C., Jen, A., Deng, J., Fitzgerald, K.T., Frobert, Y., Grassi, J., McCaffrey, M.W., Morris, R. (2003). The mechanism of internalization of glycosylphosphatidylinositol-anchored prion protein. *EMBO J.* 22(14): 3591–3601.

61 Lee, K.S., Magalhaes, A.C., Zanata, S.M., Brentani, R.R., Martins, V.R., Prado, M.A. (2001) Internalization of mammalian fluorescent cellular prion protein and N-terminal deletion mutants in living cells. *J. Neurochem.* 79(1): 79–87.

62 Vey, M., Pilkuhn, S., Wille, H., Nixon, R., DeArmond, S.J., Smart, E.J., Anderson, R.G., Taraboulos, A., Prusiner, S.B.

(1996) Subcellular colocalization of the cellular and scrapie prion proteins in caveolae-like membranous domains. *Proc. Natl. Acad. Sci. USA* 93(25): 14945–14949.

63 Kaneko, K., Vey, M., Scott, M., Pilkuhn, S., Cohen, F. E., Prusiner, S. B. (1997) COOH-terminal sequence of the cellular prion protein directs subcellular trafficking and controls conversion into the scrapie isoform. *Proc. Natl. Acad. Sci. USA* 94(6): 2333–2338.

64 Peters, P. J., Mironov, A., Jr., Peretz, D., van Donselaar, E., Leclerc, E., Erpel, S., DeArmond, S. J., Burton, D. R., Williamson, R. A., Vey, M., Prusiner, S. B. (2003) Trafficking of prion proteins through a caveolae-mediated endosomal pathway. *J. Cell Biol.* 162(4): 703–717.

65 Gacescu, R., Demaurex, N., Parton, R. G., Hunziker, W., Huber, L. A., Gruenberg, J. (2000) The recycling endosome of Madin-Darby canine kidney cells is a mildly acidic compartment rich in rafts component. *Mol. Biol. Cell* 11: 2775–2791.

66 Baron, G. S., Caughey, B. (2003) Effect of glycosylphosphatidylinositol anchor-dependent and -independent prion protein association with model raft membranes on conversion to the protease-resistant isoform. *J. Biol. Chem.* 278(17): 14883–14892 (e-pub 2003 February 19).

67 Botto, L., Masserini, M., Cassetti, A., Palestini, P. (2004) Immunoseparation of prion protein enriched domains from other detergent-resistant membrane fractions, isolated from neuronal cells. *FEBS Lett.* 557(1–3): 143–147.

68 Naslavsky, N., Stein, R., Yanai, A., Friedlander, G., Taraboulos, A. (1997) Characterization of detergent-insoluble complexes containing the cellular prion protein and its scrapie isoform. *J. Biol. Chem.* 272(10): 6324–6331.

69 Klein, T. R., Kirsch, D., Kaufmann, R., Riesner, D. (1998) Prion rods contain small amount of two host sphingolipids as revealed by thin-layer chromatography and mass spectrometry. *Biol. Chem.* 379: 655–666.

70 Sarnataro, D., Paladino, S., Campana, V., Grassi, J., Nitsch, L., Zurzolo, C. (2002) PrPC is sorted to the basolateral membrane of epithelial cells independently of its association with rafts. *Traffic* 3(11): 810–821.

71 Kanu, N., Imokawua, Y., Drechsel, D. N., Williamson, R. A., Birkett, C. R., Bostock, C. J., Brockes, J. P. (2002) Transfer of scrapie prion infectivity by cell contact in culture. *Curr. Biol.* 12: 523–530.

72 Bogdanov, M., Dowhan, W. (1999) Lipid-assisted protein folding. *J. Biol. Chem.* 274(52): 36827–36830.

73 Sanders, C. R., Nagy, J. K. (2000) Misfolding of membrane proteins in health and disease: the lady or the tiger? *Curr. Opin. Struct. Biol.* 10(4): 438–442.

74 Sanghera, N., Pinheiro, T. J. (2002) Binding of prion protein to lipid membranes and implications for prion conversion. *J. Mol. Biol.* 315(5): 1241–1256.

75 Critchley, P., Kazlauskaite, J., Eason, R., Pinheiro, T. J. (2004) Binding of prion proteins to lipid membranes. *Biochem. Biophys. Res. Commun.* 313(3): 559–567.

76 Naslavsky, N., Shmeeda, H., Friedlander, G., Yanai, A., Futerman, A. H., Barenholz, Y., Taraboulos, A. (1999) Sphingolipid depletion increases formation of the scrapie prion protein in neuroblastoma cells infected with prions. *J. Biol. Chem.* 274(30): 20763–20771.

77 Fantini, J., Garmy, N., Mahfoud, R., Yahi, N. (2002) Lipid rafts: structure, function and role in HIV, Alzheimer's and prion diseases. *Expert Rev. Mol. Med.* 2002: 1–22.

78 Forloni, G., Angeretti, N., Chiesa, R., Monzani, E., Salmona, M., Bugiani, O., Tagliavini, F. (1993) Neurotoxicity of a prion protein fragment. *Nature* 362: 543–546.

79 Ettaiche, M., Pichot, R., Vincent, J. P., Chabry, J. (2000) In vivo cytotoxicity of the prion protein fragment 106–126. *J. Biol. Chem.* 275: 36487–36490.

80 Jobling, M. F., Stewart, L. R., White, A. R., McLean, C., Friedhuber, A., Maher, F., Beyreuther, K., Masters, C. L., Barrow, C. J., Collins, S. J., Cappai, R. (1999) The hydrophobic core sequence modulates the neurotoxic and secondary structure properties of the prion peptide 106–126. *J. Neurochem.* 73(4): 1557–1565.

81 Turner, A. J., Hooper, N. (1999) Role for ADAM-family proteinases as membrane protein secretases. *Biochem. Soc. Trans.* 27: 255–259.

82 Nunan, J., Small, D. H. (2000) Regulation of APP cleavage by α-, β- and •-secretase. *FEBS Lett.* 483: 6–10.

83 Kojro, E., Gimpl, G., Lammich, S., Marz, W., Fahrenholz, F. (2001) Low cholesterol stimulates the nonamyloidogenic pathway by its effect on the α-secretase ADAM 10. *Proc. Natl. Acad. Sci. USA* 98(10): 5815–5820.

84 Wakatsuki, S., Kurisaki, T., Sehara-Fujisawa, A. (2004) Lipid rafts identified as locations of ectodomain shedding mediated by Meltrin beta/ADAM19. *J. Neurochem.* 89(1): 119–123.

85 Selkoe, D. J. (2001) Alzheimer's disease: genes, proteins, and therapy. *Physiol. Rev.* 81: 741–766.

86 Golde, T. E., Eckman, C. B. (2001) Cholesterol modulation as an emerging strategy for the treatment of Alzheimer's disease. *Drug Discov. Today* 6: 1049–1055.

87 Sisodia, S. S., St. George-Hyslop, P. H. (2002) gamma-Secretase, Notch, Abeta and Alzheimer's disease: where do the presenilins fit in? *Nat. Rev. Neurosci.* 3(4): 281–290.

88 Vassar, R., Bennett, B. D., Babu-Khan, S., Kahn, S., Mendiaz, E. A., Denis, P., Teplow, D. B., Ross, S., Amarante, P., Loeloff, R., Luo, Y., Fisher, S., Fuller, J., Edenson, S., Lile, J., Jarosinski, M. A., Biere, A. L., Curran, E., Burgess, T., Louis, J. C., Collins, F., Treanor, J, Rogers, G., Citron, M. (1999) Beta-secretase cleavage of Alzheimer's amyloid precursor protein by the transmembrane aspartic protease BACE. *Science* 286(5440): 735–741.

89 Capell, A., Steiner, H., Willem, M., Kaiser, H., Meyer, C., Walter, J., Lammich, S., Multhaup, G., Haass, C. (2000) Maturation and pro-peptide cleavage of beta-secretase. *J. Biol. Chem.* 275: 30849–30854.

90 Annaert, W. G., Levesque, L., Craessaerts, K., Dierinck, I., Snellings, G., Westaway, D., St. George-Hyslop, P., Cordell, B., Fraser, P., de Strooper, B. (1999) Presenilin 1 controls gamma-secretase processing of amyloid precursor protein in pre-Golgi compartments of hippocampal neurons. *J. Cell Biol.* 147: 277–294.

91 Zhang, J., Kang, D. E., Xia, W., Okochi, M., Mori, H., Selkoe, D. J., Koo, E. H. (1998) Subcellular distribution and turnover of presenilins in transfected cells. *J. Biol. Chem.* 273: 12436–12442.

92 Kaether, C., Lammich, S., Edbauer, D., Ertl, M., Rietdorf, J., Capell, A., Steiner, H., Haass, C. (2002) Presenilin-1 affects trafficking and processing of beta APP and is targeted in a complex with nicastrin to the plasma membrane. *J. Cell Biol.* 158: 551–561.

93 Riddell, D. R., Christie, G., Hussain, I., Dingwall, C.(2001) Compartmentalization of β-secretase (Asp2) into low-buoyant density, noncaveolar lipid rafts. *Curr. Biol.* 11: 1288–1293.

94 Burns, M., Duff, K. (2002) Cholesterol in Alzheimer's disease and tauopathy. *Ann. N. Y. Acad. Sci.* 977: 367–375.

95 Ehehalt, R., Keller, P., Haass, C., Thiele, C., Simons, K. (2003) Amyloidogenic processing of the Alzheimer beta-amyloid precursor protein depends on lipid rafts. *J. Cell Biol.* 160(1): 113–123.

96 Lee, S. J., Liyanage, U., Bickel, P. E., Xia, W., Lansbury, P. T., Kosik, K. S. (1998) A detergent-insoluble membrane compartment contains A beta in vivo. *Nat. Med.* 4: 730–734.

97 Ikezu, T., Trapp, B. D., Song, K. S., Schlegel, A., Lisanti, M. P., Okamoto, T. (1998) Caveolae, plasma membrane microdomains for α-secretase-mediated processing of the amyloid precursor protein. *J. Biol. Chem.* 273(17): 10485–10495.

98 Avdulov, N. A., Chochina, S. V., Igbavboa, U., Warden, C. S., Vassiliev, A. V., Wood, W. G. (1997) Lipid binding to amyloid beta-peptide aggregates: preferential binding of cholesterol as compared with phosphatidylcholine and fatty acids. *J. Neurochem.* 69: 1746–1752.

99 Choo-Smith, L. P., Garzon-Rodriguez, W., Glabe, C. G., Surewicz ,W. K. (1997) Acceleration of amyloid fibril formation by specific binding of Abeta-(1–40) peptide to ganglioside-containing membrane vesicles. *J. Biol. Chem.* 272: 22987–22990.

100 Matsuzaki, K., Horikiri, C. (1999) Interactions of amyloid beta-peptide (1–40) with ganglioside-containing membranes. *Biochemistry* 38: 4137–4142.

101 Brown, D. A., Rose, J. K. (1992) Sorting of GPI-anchored proteins to glycolipid-enriched membrane subdomains during transport to the apical cell surface. *Cell* 68: 533–544.

102 Simons, M., Keller, P., De Strooper, B., Beyreuther, K., Dotti, C. G., Simons, K. (1998) Cholesterol depletion inhibits the generation of beta-amyloid in hippocampal neurons. *Proc. Natl. Acad. Sci. USA* 95: 6460–6464.

103 Rodal, S. K., Skretting, G., Garred, O., Vilhardt, F., van Deurs, B., Sandvig, K. (1999) Extraction of cholesterol with methyl-beta-cyclodextrin perturbs formation of clathrin-coated endocytic vesicles. *Mol. Biol. Cell* 10: 961–974.

104 Koo, E. H., Squazzo, S. L. (1994) Evidence that production and release of amyloid beta protein involves the endocytic pathway. *J. Biol. Chem.* 269: 17386–17389.

105 Dumery, L., Bourdel, F., Soussan, Y., Fialkowsky, A., Viale, S., Nicolas, P., Reboud-Ravaux, M. (2001) Beta-amyloid protein aggregation: its implication in the physiopathology of Alzheimer's disease. *Pathol. Biol. (Paris)* 49: 72–85.

106 Kakio, A. (2002) Interactions of amyloid beta-protein with various gangliosides in raft-like membranes: importance of GM1 ganglioside-bound form as an endogenous seed for Alzheimer amyloid. *Biochemistry* 41: 7385–7390.

107 McLaurin, J. (1998) Structural transitions associated with the interaction of Alzheimer beta-amyloid peptides with gangliosides. *J. Biol. Chem.* 273: 4506–4515.

108 Mizuno, T., Nakata, M., Naiki, H., Michikawa, M., Wang, R., Haass, C., Yanagisawa, K. (1999) Cholesterol-dependent generation of a seeding amyloid β-protein in cell culture. *J. Biol. Chem.* 274: 15110–15114.

109 Mahfoud, R., Garmy, N., Maresca, M., Yahi, N., Puigserver, A., Fantini, J. (2002) Identification of a common sphingolipid-binding domain in Alzheimer, prion and HIV proteins. *J. Biol. Chem.* 277: 11292–11296.

110 Perez, R. G., Soriano, S., Hayes, D. J., Ostaszewski, B., Xia, W., Selkoe, D. J., Chen, X., Stokin, G. B., Koo, E. H. (1999) Mutagenesis identifies new signals for beta-amyloid precursor protein endocytosis, turnover and the generation of secreted fragments, including Abeta 42. *J. Biol. Chem.* 274: 18851–18856.

111 Huse, J. T., Pijak, D. S., Leslie, G. J., Lee, V. M., Doms, R. W. (2000) Maturation and endosomal targeting of beta-site amyloid precursor protein-cleaving enzyme. The Alzheimer's disease beta secretase. *J. Biol. Chem.* 275: 33729–33737.

112 Kamal, A., Almenar-Queralt, A., LeBlanc, J. F., Roberts, E. A., Goldstein, L. S. (2001) Kinesin-mediated axonal transport of a membrane compartment containing beta-secretase and presenilin-1 requires APP. *Nature* 414: 643–648.

113 Damke, H. T., Baba, T., Warnock, D. E., Shmid, S. L. (2004) Induction of mutant dynamin specifically blocks endocytic coated vesicle formation. *J. Cell Biol.* 127: 915–934.

114 Lanzetti, L., Rybin, V., Malabarba, M. G., Christoforidis, S., Scita, G., Zerial, M., Di Fiore, P. P. (2000) The Eps8 protein coordinates EGF receptor signalling through Rac and trafficking through Rab5. *Nature* 408: 374–377.

115 Chyung, J. H., Selkoe, D. J. (2003) Inhibition of receptor-mediated endocytosis demonstrates generation of amyloid beta-protein at the cell surface. *J. Biol. Chem.* 278(51): 51035–51043 (e-pub 2003 October 02).

116 Haass, C., Koo, E. H., Mellon, A., Hung, A. Y., Selkoe, D. J. (1992) Targeting of cell surface beta-amyloid precursor protein to lysosomes: alternative processing into amyloid-bearing fragments. *Nature* 357: 500–503.

117 Parvathy, S., Hussain, I., Karran, E. H., Turner, A. J., Hooper, N. M. (1999) Cleavage of Alzheimer's amyloid precursor protein by alpha-secretase occurs at surface of neuronal cells. *Biochemistry* 38: 9728–9734.

118 Cordy, J. M., Hussain, I., Dingwall, C., Hooper, N. M., Turner, A. J. (2003) Exclusively targeting beta-secretase to lipid rafts by GPI-anchor addition up-regulates beta-site processing of the amyloid precursor protein. *Proc. Natl. Acad. Sci. USA* 100: 11735–11740.

119 Abad-Rodriguez, J., Ledesma, M. D., Craessaerts, K., Perga, S., Medina, M., Delacourte, A., Dingwall, C., De Strooper,

B., Dotti, C. G. (2004) Neuronal membrane cholesterol loss enhances amyloid peptide generation. *J. Cell Biol.* 167: 953–960.

120 Koo, E. H., Park, L., Selkoe, D. J. (1993) Amyloid beta-protein as a substrate interacts with extracellular matrix to promote neurite outgrowth. *Proc. Natl. Acad. Sci. USA* 90: 4748–4752.

121 Sisodia, S. S. (1992) Beta-amyloid precursor protein cleavage by a membrane-bound protease. *Proc. Natl. Acad. Sci. USA* 89: 6075–6079.

122 Arribas, J., Lopez-Casillas, F., Massague, J. (1997) Role of the juxtamembrane domains of the transforming growth factor-alpha precursor and the beta-amyloid precursor protein in regulated ectodomain shedding. *J. Biol. Chem.* 272: 17161–17165.

123 De Strooper, B., Umans, L., Van Leuven, F., Van Den Berghe, H. (1993) Study of the synthesis and secretion of normal and artificial mutants of murine amyloid precursor protein (APP): cleavage of APP occurs in a late compartment of the default secretion pathway. *J. Cell Biol.* 121: 295–304.

124 Haass, C., Koo, E. H., Capell, A., Teplow, D. B., Selkoe, D. J. (1995) Polarized sorting of beta-amyloid precursor protein and its proteolytic products in MDCK cells is regulated by two independent signals. *J. Cell Biol.* 128: 537–547.

125 De Strooper, B., Van Leuven, F., Van den Berghe, H. (1992) Alpha 2-macroglobulin and other proteinase inhibitors do not interfere with the secretion of amyloid precursor protein in mouse neuroblastoma cells. *FEBS Lett.* 308(1): 50–53.

126 Selkoe, D. J. (1994) Cell biology of the amyloid beta-protein precursor and the mechanism of Alzheimer's disease. *Annu. Rev. Cell Biol.* 10: 373–403.

127 Nordstedt, C., Caporaso, G. L., Thyberg, J., Gandy, S. E., Greengard, P. (1993) Identification of the Alzheimer beta/A4 amyloid precursor protein in clathrin-coated vesicles purified from PC12 cells. *J. Biol. Chem.* 268(1): 608–612.

128 Ledesma, M. D., Da Silva, G. S., Crassaerts, K., Delacourte, A., De Strooper, B., Dotti, C. G. (2000) Brain plasmin enhances APP α-cleavage and is reduced in Alzheimer's disease brains. *EMBO Rep.* 1(6): 530–535.

129 Koike, H., Tomioka, S., Sorimachi, H., Saido, T. C., Maruyama, K., Okuyama, A., Fujisawa-Sehara, A., Ohno, S., Suzuki, K., Ishiura, S. (1999) Membrane-anchored metalloprotease MDC9 has an alpha-secretase activity responsible for processing the amyloid precursor protein. *Biochem. J.* 343: 371–375.

130 Ledesma, M. D., Abad-Rodriguez, J., Galvan C., Biondi E., Navarro, P., Delacourte, A., Dingwall, C., Dotti, C. G. (2003) Rafts disorganization leads to reduced plasmin activity in Alzheimer's disease brains. *EMBO Rep.* 4(12): 1190–1196.

131 Li, Y. M., Xu, M., Lai M. T., Huang, Q., Castro, J. L., DiMuzio-Mower, J., Harrison, T., Lellis, C., Nadin, A., Neduvelil J. G., et al. (2000) Photoactivated gamma-secretase inhibitors directed to the active site covalently label presenilin 1. *Nature* 405: 689–694.

132 Wahrle, S., Das, P., Nyborg, A. C., McLendon, C., Shoji, M., Kawarabayashi, T., Younkin, L. H., Younkin, S. G., Golde, T. E. (2002) Cholesterol-dependent gamma-secretase activity in buoyant cholesterol-rich membrane microdomains. *Neurobiol. Dis.* 9(1): 11–23.

133 Vetrivel, K. S., Cheng, H., Lin, W., Sakurai, T., Li, T., Nukina, N., Wong, P. C., Xu, H., Thinakaran, G. (2004) Association of •-secretase with lipid rafts in post-Golgi endosomes membranes. *J. Biol. Chem.* 279: 44945–44954.

134 Wada, S., Morishima-Kawashima, M., Qi, Y., Misono, H., Shimada, Y., Ohno-Iwashita, Y., Ihara, Y. (2003) Gamma-secretase activity is present in rafts but is not cholesterol-dependent. *Biochemistry* 42(47): 13977–13986.

135 Anderson, R. G., Jacobson, K. (2002) A role for lipid shells in targeting proteins to caveolae, rafts, and other lipid domains. *Science* 296(5574): 1821–1825.

136 Hanada, K., Izawa, K., Nishijima, M., Akamatsu, Y. (1993) Sphingolipid deficiency induces hypersensitivity of CD14, a glycosylphosphatidylinositol-anchored protein, to phosphatidylinositol-specific phospholipase C. *J. Biol. Chem.* 268: 13820–13823.

137 Hanada, K., Nishijima, M., Akamatsu, Y., Pagano, R. E. (1995) Both sphingolipids and cholesterol participate in the detergent insolubility of alkaline phosphatase, a glycosylphosphatidylinositol-anchored protein, in mammalian membranes. *J. Biol. Chem.* 270: 6254–6260.

138 Sawamura, N., Ko, M., Yu, W., Zou, K., Hanada, K., Suzuki, T., Gong, J. S., Yanagisawa, K., Michikawa, M. (2004) Modulation of amyloid precursor protein cleavage by cellular sphingolipids. *J. Biol. Chem.* 279(12): 11984–11991.

11
Caveolae and the Endothelial Nitric Oxide Synthase

Olivier Feron

11.1
Introduction

Nitric oxide (NO) is a multifaceted molecule which plays key roles in many biological situations [1]. Endothelial nitric oxide synthase (eNOS) is the major NOS isoform responsible for cardiovascular homeostasis. eNOS is a calmodulin-activated enzyme which consists of an oxygenase and a reductase domain containing binding sites for a variety of cofactors that promote electron transfer from one domain to the other, leading ultimately to the conversion of L-arginine to citrulline and NO [2] (Fig. 11.1).

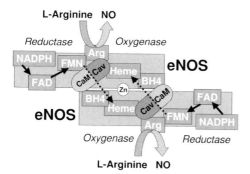

Fig. 11.1 Reciprocal regulation of the eNOS catalytic activity by caveolin (Cav) and calcium-bound calmodulin (CaM). eNOS is a two-domain enzyme consisting of a reductase domain containing binding sites for flavin mononucleotide (FMN), flavin adenine dinucleotide (FAD) and nicotinamide adenine dinucleotide phosphate hydrogen (NADPH) and an N-terminal oxygenase domain with binding sites for heme, L-arginine (Arg) and tetrahydrobiopterin (BH4). eNOS is active as a dimer: NADPH-derived electrons are transferred to the flavins and then to the heme (located on the vis-à-vis monomer) where O_2 can be recruited and catalyzes NO synthesis from L-arginine. Caveolin interaction with the eNOS oxygenase domain stabilizes the complex and prevents L-arginine binding, whereas caveolin interaction with the reductase domain antagonizes CaM binding and slows down electron transfer to the oxygenase domain, thereby inhibiting NO production.

Lipid Rafts and Caveolae. Christopher J. Fielding
Copyright © 2006 WILEY-VCH Verlag GmbH & Co. KGaA, Weinheim
ISBN: 3-527-31261-7

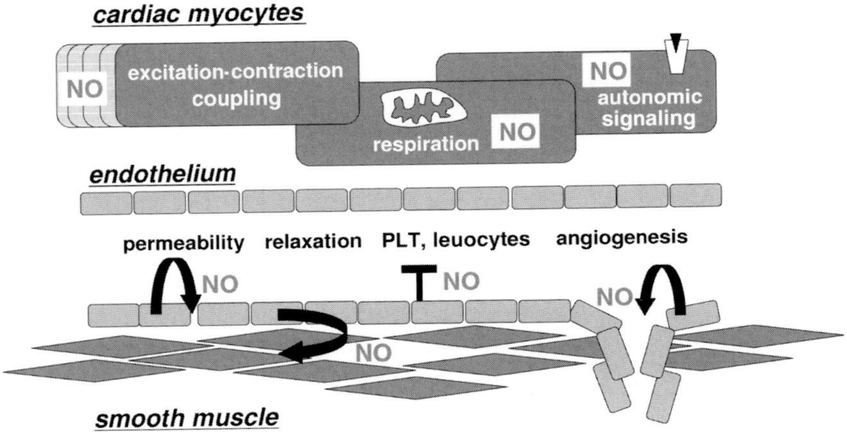

Fig. 11.2 The multiple roles of nitric oxide (NO) in the healthy heart. Endothelial cells in coronary arteries (as in other vascular beds) constitutively express endothelial nitric oxide synthase (eNOS) that regulates critical vascular functions such as contractility, permeability, leukocyte adhesion, platelet aggregation and angiogenesis through basal and stimulated NO production. In cardiac myocytes, both eNOS and nNOS are constitutively expressed and modulate key processes including excitation-contraction coupling, mitochondrial respiration, and receptor-mediated autonomic stimulation.

The principal source of NO within the normal myocardium is the endothelium of the coronary vasculature. Endothelial cells constitutively express the eNOS isoform, which generates NO in response to specific extracellular signals to regulate vascular smooth muscle tone and thrombogenicity, among other actions [3] (Fig. 11.2). In addition to coronary vascular (and endocardial) endothelium, both atrial and ventricular myocytes – including specialized pacemaker tissue – also express eNOS. Excitation-contraction coupling, modulation of autonomic signaling and mitochondrial respiration are more directly regulated by myocyte-produced NO [4] (see Fig. 11.2). Amazingly, the same molecule, NO, has been involved in many cardiovascular diseases [5]. A shift from finely regulated NO production by eNOS (and neuronal NOS, also expressed in cardiac myocytes) to a deregulated NO production by the inducible NOS isoform (iNOS) is, indeed, associated with a variety of heart diseases. The extent of NO release (e.g., limited for the two constitutive NOS and in large excess for iNOS) is thought to account for the differential effects on cardiac function. Recognition of the threshold above which NO becomes toxic is, however, unclear and certainly appears elusive when considering, for instance, the potential benefits of nitrates – medications which deliver large amounts of NO. A safer way of addressing the question of cytotoxic versus protective effects of NO is to emphasize the qualitative characteristics of NO release. Consequently, the following paragraphs will emphasize, by a series of examples, the developing consensual view according to which (in nonpathological states at least) NO exerts its regulatory roles by being produced at the right time in the right place.

11.2
Caveolin: A Scaffold for eNOS

Since NO is a very labile and highly reactive messenger molecule with autocrine and paracrine functions, the site of NO production should logically have a major influence on its biological activity. The discovery in 1996 of the location of eNOS in caveolae [6,7] was therefore viewed as the proof of concept that compartmentation of the enzyme is critical to fine-tune NO synthesis. This specific locale of eNOS had been suspected based on the double acylation process that characterizes eNOS: myristoylation on glycine (at position 2) and palmitoylation on two cysteines (at positions 15 and 26). In fact, by using cultured endothelial cells, eNOS was shown to be preferentially located in caveolae (versus the rest of the plasma membrane), with each acylation process enhancing the caveolar enrichment some 10-fold [6]. This discovery was rapidly followed by the identification of a tight regulation between eNOS and caveolin, the structural protein of caveolae. It has been reported that, in endothelial cells and cardiac myocytes, eNOS was quantitatively associated with caveolin-1 and caveolin-3, respectively [8]. The determinants of this interaction subsequently became the focus of studies conducted by several independent groups. It was shown, by exploring the differential effects of detergents, that although eNOS thiopalmitoylation is not absolutely required to induce formation of the caveolin-eNOS complex, acylation largely facilitates the interaction between both proteins [9]. The sequences involved in this mutual interaction were also identified, based on the studies of Lisanti et al., who found a region within the caveolin sequence that could act as a scaffold for many caveolar proteins [10].

This so-called "caveolin scaffolding domain" (CSD) is a region spanning 20 residues in the caveolin sequence (mapping to residues 81–101 in the human caveolin-1 sequence) [10]. Using a glutathione S-transferase (GST)-CSD fusion protein as a bait to select peptide ligands from a bacteriophage display library, Lisanti and colleagues identified a "caveolin binding motif" (CBM) that appeared to be present in whole or in part in many proteins located in caveolae ($\Phi X\Phi XXXX$ $\Phi XX\Phi$, where Φ represents an aromatic amino acid) [11]. That the interaction with caveolin involves these consensus sequences is, however, only documented for a few caveolar residents but among them, stands eNOS [12,13]. Several laboratories have indeed investigated the molecular determinants of the caveolin-eNOS interaction using *in-vitro* binding assay systems with GST fusion proteins (including deletion mutants) and an *in-vivo* yeast two-hybrid system [9,13–15]. The major conclusions from these studies are that eNOS and caveolin-1 interact directly rather than indirectly, and that this interaction involves multiple sites: the oxygenase and reductase domains of eNOS and the two cytoplasmic domains of caveolin-1. The CBM (sequence 350–358 FPAAPFSGW) that recognizes the CSD is located in the oxygenase domain of eNOS, between the heme and the calmodulin binding domains. This location is adjacent to a glutamate residue (Glu361) necessary for the binding of ʟ-arginine, which suggests that caveolin may interfere with heme iron reduction, similarly to ʟ-arginine-based NOS inhibitors (see Fig. 11.1).

This latter observation led us and others to investigate whether the caveolin-eNOS interaction was inhibitory. Like all known NO synthases, eNOS enzyme activity is dependent on calmodulin binding, the activation of which requires an increase in intracellular calcium. With the discovery of the caveolin-eNOS interaction, it appeared that calmodulin acts, in fact, as a direct allosteric competitor promoting the disruption of the heteromeric complex formed between eNOS and caveolin in a Ca^{2+}-dependent fashion [13,15,16] (Fig. 11.1). Both the CSD and the CBM domains were shown to be involved. Accordingly, peptides corresponding to the CSD domain were shown to interact directly with the enzyme and markedly inhibit NOS activity in endothelial cells [13]. Likewise, site-directed mutagenesis of the CBM was found to block the ability of caveolin-1 to suppress NO release in transfection experiments [12].

Using full-length eNOS or truncated enzyme which only expresses the oxygenase domain, studies conducted by Ghosh et al. [17] led to the establishment of a model, according to which caveolin interaction with the oxygenase domain helps to target the eNOS-caveolin complex to caveolae. In contrast, caveolin interaction with the reductase domain is primarily responsible for antagonizing calmodulin binding and for slowing electron transfer from the reductase, thus inhibiting heme iron reduction and NO synthesis (see Fig. 11.1).

11.3
The Caveolin-eNOS Regulatory Cycle

Consecutive to disruption of the caveolin-eNOS complex induced by agonist stimulation or shear stress, eNOS has been proposed to traffic intracellularly (Fig. 11.3). Prabhakar et al. showed that eNOS is de-palmitoylated after prolonged agonist stimulation, and is no longer selectively sequestered in the caveolae [18]. The acyl-protein thioesterase 1 (APT1) has, indeed, been shown specifically to promote eNOS depalmitoylation through a Ca^{2+}-calmodulin-dependent pathway [19]. The translocated enzyme then partitions into noncaveolar plasma/intracellular membranes, and also in the cytosol. The interaction of eNOS with Hsp90 and consecutive (de)phosphorylation (see below) is probably also involved in trafficking of the enzyme, but the molecular mechanisms underlying these processes are still not clearly delineated. By contrast, several lines of evidence have indicated that, subsequent to the translocation of the enzyme and after the decline in $[Ca^{2+}]_i$ to basal levels, eNOS may once again interact with caveolin and is then re-targeted to the caveolae, the process being accelerated (or stabilized) by enzyme palmitoylation [14]. The long-chain fatty acyl CoA synthetase was recently identified as a key modulator of eNOS re-palmitoylation [20]. Re-association of eNOS with caveolin could occur either at the plasma (caveolar) or perinuclear membrane levels, or

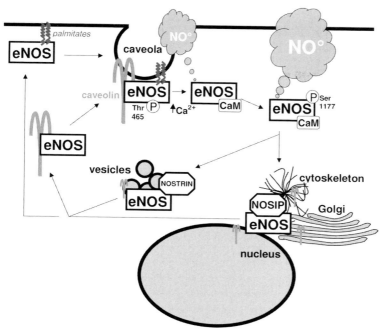

Fig. 11.3 The caveolin-eNOS regulatory cycle (see text for details). NOSIP = eNOS interacting protein; NOSTRIN = eNOS traffic inducer.

even in the cytosol through which caveolin complexes may shuttle between the caveolae and an internalized caveolar vesicle/trans-Golgi network (see Fig. 11.3).

The lag time between the agonist-induced disruption of the caveolin-eNOS interaction and the heterocomplex re-formation is thought to be nonexclusively associated with eNOS activation. Indeed, the arginine transporter CAT1 being located in the caveolae [21], the dissociation of the enzyme from its proximity as well as from several receptors/effectors localized in the caveolae [22,23], is likely to serve as a feedback mechanism for eNOS activation. Also, because NO activates molecular targets outside the endothelial cell, it seems likely that the intracellular locale of eNOS could affect the signaling roles of its product (e.g., the paracrine effects of NO), and thereby modulate the response to extracellular signals. NO finds, indeed, most of its targets in the proximal myocyte layers or circulating blood cells such as platelets and red cells. Similarly, it appears logical that the luminal surface of the endothelium, which is directly exposed to the blood flow and therefore expected to be sensitive to hemodynamic forces, would be a primary site for the documented flow-responsive eNOS activity.

The group of Müller-Esterl has identified, by using yeast two-hybrid screening, two new proteins named NOSIP ("eNOS interacting protein") and NOSTRIN ("eNOS traffic inducer") that specifically bind to the human eNOS oxygenase domain [24,25] (see Fig. 11.3). Although structurally unrelated, overexpression of both proteins in eNOS-expressing cells has similar effects: net dissociation of eNOS from the plasma membrane and inhibition of agonist-induced NO production. Some observations indicate that both effects are very likely to be related (e. g., NOSIP and NOSTRIN modulate eNOS enzyme activity by uncoupling eNOS from plasma membrane caveolae). For instance, NOSIP overexpression does not impact on eNOS activity measured *in vitro* using a citrulline assay. Also, eNOS binding sites for caveolin and NOSIP do overlap. Nonetheless, whether NOSTRIN and NOSIP promote eNOS translocation from the plasma membrane or inhibit the reverse transport (usually observed after prolonged stimulation) remains unknown.

Of note, although NOSIP and NOSTRIN share some of their functional features and are both particularly abundant in vascularized organs, they differ in other respects [24,25]. Accordingly, while NOSIP overexpression induces eNOS translocation to intracellular sites that co-localize with Golgi and cytoskeletal marker proteins (β-COP and tubulin, respectively), NOSTRIN overexpression largely targets the enzyme to vesicle-like structures spread all over the cytosol. Also, in endothelial cells, NOSIP is mostly found in the cytosol and the nucleus, whereas NOSTRIN is found exclusively in extranuclear locations and at the plasma membrane; in this context, a positive effect of NOSTRIN to address eNOS to the plasma membrane (caveolae) cannot be excluded.

Importantly, although this chapter is focused on the caveolin-related mode of regulation of eNOS activity, it should be emphasized that besides the protein-protein interactions detailed above, eNOS is also regulated by phosphorylations [26]. Among the putative phosphorylation sites within the eNOS sequence, two (Ser1177 and Thr495) are currently considered to be critical for eNOS activation. Ser1177 phosphorylation is proposed to improve electron flux through the enzyme and to increase its affinity for calmodulin, whereas dephosphorylation of Thr495 is thought to suppress the steric inhibition for calmodulin association to its binding site [26] (Fig. 11.3). Accordingly, the phosphorylation of eNOS on Ser1177 has been extensively documented as a major kinase-dependent mode of eNOS activation, whereas Thr495 has been reported to participate, when phosphorylated, in the tonic inhibition of eNOS activity. In addition, by directly examining changes in native eNOS post-translational regulation, we recently found that the scaffolding function of Hsp90 previously identified for Akt [27,28] also applied to the phosphatase calcineurin [29,30]. These Hsp90-driven protein-protein associations provide an explanation for the reciprocal regulation of eNOS on distant phosphorylation sites (e. g., Akt-dependent Ser1177 phosphorylation and calcineurin-mediated Thr495 dephosphorylation).

The regulation of eNOS activity/trafficking is very likely to result from the combination of its dynamic interaction with the different partners identified to date (including caveolin, NOSIP, NOSTRIN and Hsp90) and the phosphorylation pattern of the enzyme. In the following sections, the caveolin-eNOS interaction will be retained as the main thread, and reference will be made to other modes of regulation when necessary.

11.4
Lipoproteins and Caveolin-eNOS Interaction

The observations by Fielding et al. that, in human fibroblasts, high levels of cellular free cholesterol (FC) induce caveolin gene transcription [31,32] led us to examine whether a similar increase in caveolin abundance in endothelial cells could account for a reduction in NO production. Accordingly, we exposed endothelial cells to low-density lipoprotein (LDL)-cholesterol and found that both caveolin abundance and caveolin-eNOS complex formation were increased [33] (Fig. 11.4). Furthermore, NO release (under basal and stimulated conditions) was inhibited, thereby providing some insights for a new pathogenic mechanism linking hypercholesterolemia and endothelial dysfunction. A defect in the NO pathway is, indeed, viewed as a hallmark of endothelial dysfunction characterized by an impaired endothelium-dependent vasodilation and the unopposed influence of thrombogenic and proliferative factors on the vessel wall.

In parallel to these observations that cholesterol could lead to eNOS inhibition through the induction of caveolin expression, Blair et al. [34] documented that

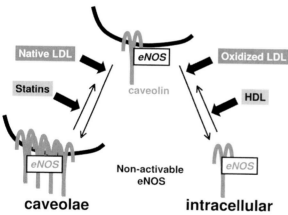

Fig. 11.4 Reversible lipoprotein-dependent regulation of caveolin-eNOS interaction. High levels of native LDL stimulate caveolin transcription and thereby promote the interaction of eNOS with the increased caveolin pool (left). The resulting inhibition of eNOS activity can be reversed by statins that, by inhibiting the endogenous synthesis of cholesterol in endothelial cells (as well as indirectly by reducing circulatory LDL-cholesterol), negatively impact on caveolin expression. The interaction of oxidized LDL (oxLDL) with the CD36 receptor located in caveolae leads to a marked depletion of caveolar cholesterol and to the translocation of caveolin and eNOS to intracellular compartments (see right), wherein basal and agonist-stimulated NO production are dramatically reduced. Conversely, HDL, through caveolar SRBI binding, provisions cholesterol esters to the cell, thereby reversing the deleterious effects of oxLDL.

oxidized LDL (oxLDL) caused the translocation of both eNOS and caveolin from caveolae to intracellular membranes (Fig. 11.4). These authors further documented that oxLDL, through class B CD36 receptor binding [35], act as acceptors of cholesterol, leading to marked depletion of caveolae cholesterol and redistribution of caveolin and eNOS (but not of other caveolar residents such as PKCα and ganglioside GM1). They also showed that when examining the pattern of eNOS activation upon exposure to acetylcholine, the dose-response curve was shifted to the right by 100-fold. A recent study by the Lisanti's group also documented that the loss of caveolin-1 (as observed in caveolin knockout mice) resulted in a dramatic down-regulation of CD36 and, importantly, conferred a significant protection against atherosclerosis in double apoE/caveolin knockout mice [36]. This latter study confirmed the findings of Kincer et al., who showed that in apoE/CD36 double knockout mice – in contrast to apoE knockout mice – the acetylcholine-evoked reduction in blood pressure is conserved (as well as the eNOS localization to caveolae) [37].

Whether such processes of native and oxLDL-dependent regulation of the caveolin-eNOS interaction are reversible was also addressed. Our group showed, both *in vitro* and *in vivo*, that hydroxymethylglutaryl coenzyme A (HMGCoA) reductase inhibitors (statins) could reduce caveolin abundance [38,39]. In cultured endothelial cells, the reduction in caveolin abundance obtained with atorvastatin was associated with a restoration of basal and agonist-stimulated eNOS activity (see Fig. 11.4) [38]. In dyslipidemic, apolipoprotein (apo) $E^{-/-}$ mice, the alterations in heart rate and blood pressure variabilities were corrected by chronic treatment with rosuvastatin [39]. Our findings also highlighted the therapeutic potential of statins in diseases other than hypercholesterolemia, such as hypertension or heart failure. Indeed, we showed that statins could decrease caveolin abundance in endothelial cells and in apoE$^{-/-}$ mice, independently of the extracellular and plasma load in LDL-cholesterol, respectively [38,39].

As for the oxLDL-mediated CD36-dependent alteration in caveolin-eNOS biology, the reversibility of the phenomenon was documented with high-density lipoprotein (HDL) that prevented both the depletion of caveolar cholesterol and the eNOS displacement from caveolae [37]. Amazingly, the provision of cholesterol esters by HDL binding to the scavenger receptor BI (and not the inhibition of cholesterol transfer from caveolae to oxLDL) was found to account for the correction of eNOS mislocalization and the restoration of the acetylcholine-induced activation of eNOS [40] (see Fig. 11.4). Of note, the eNOS stimulation by HDL was recently shown to involve Src-mediated signaling [41].

The conclusion to be drawn from the above studies is that both native LDL in excess and oxLDL contribute to the change in NO production, and therefore account for the many functional defects associated with NO deficiency. Although the oxidative stress paradigm is well established as a trigger of the atherosclerotic process, endothelial dysfunction occurs before the appearance of any ultrastructural change in the vessel wall. It may therefore be postulated that chronologically, chronic elevations in serum LDL-cholesterol and then lipoprotein oxidation contribute to caveolin-dependent alteration in NO signaling. Importantly, both phenomena appear reversible. Physiologically, the beneficial effects of HDL are clearly emphasized by several studies described herein. Moreover, the pharmacologically pleiotropic effects of statins can be expected (interestingly) at doses that do not necessarily require any reduction in LDL correction.

11.5
Angiogenesis and Caveolin-eNOS Interaction

In 1999, Lisanti and colleagues documented that caveolin-1 was down-regulated by angiogenic growth factors in subconfluent endothelial cells, but not when these cells were confluent [42]. These authors further showed that, in contrast, caveolin-1 protein levels were up-regulated during endothelial cell differentiation and that expression of caveolin-1 in confluent endothelial cells stimulated endothelial tube formation [43]. Although, the original observation that growth factor exposure can down-regulate caveolin expression in endothelial cells remains a matter of debate, the second set of data (e. g., the role of caveolin in endothelial differentiation/tube reorganization) was verified by other investigators (but only for the link between a reduction in caveolin abundance and the inhibition of angiogenesis). Indeed, Griffoni et al. found, using caveolin antisense technology, that a reduction in caveolin abundance reduced vessel formation in the chorioallantoic membrane assay [44].

Consecutively, we found that statins could stimulate tube formation from macrovascular endothelial cells cultured on Matrigel® through a decrease in caveolin abundance (and in its inhibitory interaction with eNOS) [27]. In microvascular endothelial cells, statins only marginally decreased the abundance of caveolin protein (that amounted to almost 10-fold the pool of caveolin in macrovascular endothelial cells), and therefore did not impact on the regulation of eNOS activity. In those endothelial cells, however, statins were shown to stimulate angiogenesis through eNOS phosphorylation on Ser1177 – a process which is facilitated by the recruitment of the chaperone protein hsp90 that acts as an adaptor between eNOS and the kinase. Still, caveolin overexpression or cell loading with caveolin scaffolding domain-derived peptides prevented the ability not only of statins but also of vascular endothelial growth factor (VEGF) to stimulate in-vitro angiogenesis (Fig. 11.5). These observations were further confirmed in a mouse model of angiogenesis (in tumors). In-vivo lipofection of a caveolin plasmid led, indeed, to the inhibition of both NO-mediated vasodilation and angiogenesis in tumors [45] (Fig. 11.5).

Paradoxically, we found that in aortic endothelial cells isolated from caveolin-1-deficient mice (Cav$^{-/-}$) (as well as Cav$^{+/-}$ mice), VEGF-induced NO production and endothelial tube formation were dramatically decreased when compared with Cav$^{+/+}$ endothelial cells (see Fig. 11.5). The VEGFR-2 mistargeting (due to the lack of caveolin in Cav$^{-/-}$ mice) was identified as the cause of the incapacity of VEGF to activate the downstream signaling cascades, including eNOS and ERK activation. This led to dramatic consequences in a model of adaptive angiogenesis obtained after femoral artery resection [46]. In fact, contrary to Cav$^{+/+}$ mice, both Cav$^{-/-}$ and

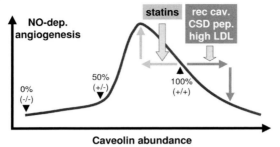

Fig. 11.5 Model of the regulation of angiogenesis by caveolin-eNOS interaction. Experimentally based relationship between the abundance of caveolin and the NO-dependent angiogenesis. Note the position of the "normal" or "physiological" (100% expression) caveolin phenotype within the bell-shaped pattern, emphasizing the anti-angiogenic effects of increasing caveolin abundance by recombinant (rec.) caveolin expression, caveolin scaffolding domain (CSD) peptides or LDL-cholesterol exposure as well as the pro-angiogenic effects of reducing caveolin abundance (upon statins) until a given threshold from which anti-angiogenic effects will be observed (similar to those obtained with caveolin overexpression).

Cav$^{+/-}$ mice failed to recover a functional vasculature, as authenticated by laser Doppler evaluation of the ischemic tissue perfusion and histochemical analyses. These data recapitulate the findings of Woodman et al., who found in Cav$^{-/-}$ mice a dramatic reduction in both vessel infiltration and density in tumor models of angiogenesis [47]. Interestingly, in aortic endothelial cells isolated from Cav$^{-/-}$ mice, we further documented that recombinant caveolin expression in endothelial cells helped to redirect the VEGFR-2 in caveolar membranes and to restore the VEGF/NO and VEGF/ERK signaling cascades. Amazingly, however, when (too-) elevated levels of recombinant caveolin were reached, VEGF exposure failed to activate ERK and eNOS [46], these findings being in good agreement with the experiments of caveolin transfection described above [45] (Fig. 11.5).

A model integrating the "compartmentalizing" effect of caveolin (e. g., receptor-effector coupling is either prevented or promoted when/where caveolin is down- or up-regulated) and the "inhibitory" hypothesis (e. g., inhibition proportional to caveolin levels) is described in Figure 11.5.

11.6
Vasodilation, Endothelial Permeability and Caveolin-eNOS Interaction

The role of caveolae in endothelium-dependent and NO-mediated vascular relaxation was documented in the original papers reporting the phenotype of caveolin-deficient mice by the groups of Kurzchalia and Lisanti [48,49]. These authors have, indeed, evaluated the NO-mediated vasorelaxing effects of acetylcholine on aortic rings precontracted with phenylephrine (an α1-adrenergic vasoconstrictor). Both groups reported a significantly greater relaxation in Cav-1 null aortic rings at all acetylcholine concentrations examined. Drab et al. further documented that, in primary culture of aortic vascular smooth muscle cells, the basal release of NO was one-third higher than in wild-type cells and the content of cyclic guanosine monophosphate (cGMP) was about three-fold higher in knockout animals [48]. Razzani et al. also found that, in the presence of the NOS inhibitor L-NAME, the increase in contractile response to phenylephrine was significantly greater in the Cav-1 null mice [49].

That eNOS becomes hyperactivated in the absence of caveolin-1 formed the basis for further studies exploring this paradigm in a variety of biological contexts, including agonist- and shear stress-induced vasoresponse as well as disease states. For example, Omura et al. reported that eicosapentaenoic acid stimulated NO production and the associated endothelium-dependent relaxation through stimulation of the dissociation of the caveolin-eNOS complex [50]. Similarly, increasing vascular flow (which is by far the main *in-vivo* trigger for vasodilation) was shown rapidly to activate caveolar eNOS by inducing calmodulin-dependent eNOS dissociation from caveolin [51]. By contrast, in a model of portal hypertension, Shah et al. [52] found that caveolin expression was significantly increased in liver sinusoids and venules, thereby leading to a significant reduction in NO production. An abnormal tight coupling between eNOS and caveolin was also identified by Murata et al. in a rat model of hypoxia-induced pulmonary hypertension (another disease state which is in part due to impaired bioactivity of vascular NO) [53]. These authors documented that, in the hypoxic pulmonary artery, the increased caveolin-eNOS interaction accounted for the impaired eNOS activity in either the presence or absence of carbachol. In yet another study, Pelligrino et al. attributed the defect in acetylcholine-induced vasodilation of ovariectomized rat pial arteries to caveolin. More exactly, they found that the endothelial dysfunction observed in these operated rats could be reversed by estradiol treatment through a reduction in endothelial caveolin-1 expression [54]. Finally, using isolated tumor arterioles mounted on a pressure myograph, we documented that local tumor irradiation induced NO-mediated vasorelaxation through not only an increase in the abundance of eNOS but also a decrease in caveolin-1 expression [55].

Besides vasodilation, caveolin-eNOS interaction has also been proposed to impact on vascular permeability. Caldwell et al. initially reported that VEGF increased endothelial cell permeability by an eNOS-dependent mechanism of transcytosis in caveolae and also, interestingly, that VEGF-R2 and eNOS co-localized with caveolin-1 in plasma membrane caveolae in retinal microvascular endothelial cells [56]. The same authors then documented that VEGF stimulated the translocation of eNOS, caveolin-1 and the VEGF receptor into the nucleus [57]. In the context of inflammation and tumor angiogenesis, Sessa's group also identified a role for caveolin in endothelial cell permeability. Accordingly, Bucci et al. used two experimental inflammatory models (subplantar administration of carrageenan and ear application of mustard oil) to examine the effects of the CSD on induced permeability [58]. These authors showed that the systemic administration of CSD-derived peptides fused with a cellular internalization sequence (derived from the Antennapedia homeodomain) suppressed acute inflammation and vascular leak to the same extent as the NOS inhibitor L-NAME. Gratton et al. showed that the same fusion peptide inhibited eNOS-dependent vascular leakage in tumors and consecutively delayed tumor progression in mice [59]; extravasation of plasma proteins is, indeed, known to contribute to the formation of a provisional matrix required to initiate neoangiogenesis.

Taken together, these data emphasize the key role of caveolin and caveolae in regulating smooth muscle relaxation and endothelial permeability. The results of several studies have also suggested that activated eNOS, as observed in inflammation, tumors or hypoxia (versus healthy tissues), is particularly sensitive to alterations in the caveolin pool, thereby opening new perspectives of treatments (using, for example, CSD-derived peptides).

11.7
Caveolin-3-eNOS Interaction in Cardiac Myocytes

To explore the dual roles of eNOS caveolar targeting in cardiac myocytes (e.g., compartmentation to facilitate activation upon agonist stimulation and inhibition of the eNOS catalytic activity in basal conditions), we refer to the paradigm of the muscarinic cholinergic NO-mediated regulation of heart rate. eNOS activated by muscarinic cholinergic agonists contributes to the so-called accentuated antagonism – that is, the ability of muscarinic cholinergic stimulation to attenuate β-adrenergic signaling in various models [4]. In order to examine the impact of eNOS compartmentation in caveolae of cardiac myocytes, we first used neonatal myocytes isolated from eNOS-deficient mouse, that were transfected with cDNA constructs encoding either the wild-type eNOS or a myristoylation-deficient eNOS mutant [23] (Fig. 11.6). These knock-in experiments provided us with myocytes expressing eNOS protein in either the caveolae or in the cytosolic compartment. In myocytes expressing wild-type eNOS, a muscarinic cholinergic agonist dramatically reduced the spontaneous heart beat rate (in a cGMP-dependent manner), whereas in the myr-eNOS myocytes the agonist failed to exert its negative chronotropic effect (Fig. 11.6). The second arm of the caveolae regulation (i.e., that caveolin-3 exerts inhibitory effects on myocyte eNOS) was demonstrated by documenting the blockade of muscarinic cholinergic agonist-induced negative chronotropic effects in cardiac myocytes loaded with caveolin-3 scaffolding domain-derived peptides.

Interestingly, a large fraction of sarcolemmal m2 muscarinic Cholinergic receptor (mAchR) was found to be targeted to cardiac myocyte caveolae upon agonist stimulation [60], thereby reinforcing the role of compartmentation in regulating NO signaling in myocyte. In a further study, we examined the impact of this translocation on the mAchR internalization process and the consecutive alteration in downstream NO signaling [22]. It was found that mAChR stimulation led to the

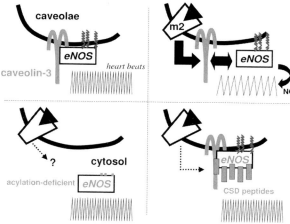

Fig. 11.6 The key roles of caveolin-3 and caveolae in the muscarinic cholinergic (mAchR) regulation of heart rate. Top left: Under basal conditions, caveolin-3 maintains eNOS in its inactivated state and thereby limits the negative chronotropic effects of NO. Top right: The m2 mAchR receptor targeting to caveolae upon agonist stimulation leads to the activation of eNOS through a local increase in intracellular calcium (the sarcoplasmic reticulum is in close vicinity to caveolae) and the consecutive disruption of the caveolin-3-eNOS heterocomplex: the myocyte beating rate is slowed (see representation of heart-beating chart recording). Bottom: Proof of principle that eNOS compartmentation in caveolae is critical for mAchR signaling in the heart [23]. Left: In cardiac myocytes expressing only recombinant myristoylation-deficient eNOS in the cytosol, the coupling between agonist-bound m2 mAchR receptor and the mutant eNOS is lost, and no effect on the myocyte beating rate can be observed. Right: When caveolin-3-derived peptides (corresponding to the CSD sequence) are introduced in myocytes, eNOS is inactivated by this excess inhibitory clamping, preventing activation of the m2mAchR signaling cascade and the associated negative chronotropism.

sequestration of mAchRs through caveolae fission through a dynamin-dependent GTP-driven process. Repeated stimulations of mAchRs led to a progressive increase in mAchR sequestration (via the detachment of caveolae from myocyte sarcolemma) and a concurrent stabilization of the inhibitory eNOS-caveolin complex. These findings suggested that caveolae fission may contribute to G-protein-coupled receptor desensitization and thereby terminate the (initially facilitated) NO signaling cascade.

11.8
Conclusions

In this chapter we have reviewed the multitude of evidence that the structural protein caveolin-1 and the caveolae themselves are essential for the control of NO production. Although caveolin-deficient mice are viable, there are today clear insights on the deregulation, in these mice, of many biological functions wherein NO is a key mediator or modulator, including angiogenesis [46,47], vasodilation [48,49], vascular permeability [61,62], lipid metabolism [36], and cardiac biology [63,64]. More specifically, we have documented that the caveolar compartmentation of eNOS plays a paradoxical role, both tonically repressing basal eNOS activity by the enzyme's interactions with caveolin, and also ensuring the efficient activation of the enzyme upon agonist stimulation.

No other caveolar protein resident has been so extensively studied as eNOS. Although many studies remain to be performed to understand the relevance of the specific locale of the dozens of molecules proposed to be associated with caveolin, it can be stated that among the responses to the many incoming signals integrated in the caveolar organelles, endothelial NO production appears as one of the major signal emanating from these signaling platforms.

Abbreviations

APT1	acyl-protein thioesterase 1
CaM	calmodulin
CBM	caveolin binding motif
CSD	caveolin scaffolding domain
eNOS	endothelial nitric oxide synthase
FC	free cholesterol
GST	glutathione S-transferase
HDL	high-density lipoprotein
HMGCoA	hexamethylglutaryl coenzyme A
iNOS	inducible NOS isoform
mAchR	muscarinic cholinergic
NO	nitric oxide
NOSIP	eNOS interacting protein
NOSTRIN	eNOS traffic inducer
oxLDL	oxidized low-density lipoprotein
VEGF	vascular endothelial growth factor

References

1 T. Michel, O. Feron, *J. Clin. Invest.* **1997**, *100*, 2146–2152.

2 D. J. Stuehr, J. Santolini, Z. Q. Wang, C. C. Wei, S. Adak, *J. Biol. Chem.* **2004**, *279*, 36167–36170.

3 L. J. Ignarro, *J. Physiol. Pharmacol.* **2002**, *53*, 503–514.

4 P. B. Massion, O. Feron, C. Dessy, J. L. Balligand, *Circ. Res.* **2003**, *93*, 388–398.

5 H. C. Champion, M. W. Skaf, J. M. Hare, *Heart Fail. Rev.* **2003**, *8*, 35–46.

6 P. W. Shaul, E. J. Smart, L. J. Robinson, Z. German, I. S. Yuhanna, Y. Ying, R. G. Anderson, T. Michel, *J. Biol. Chem.* **1996**, *271*, 6518–6522.

7 G. Garcia-Cardena, P. Oh, J. Liu, J. E. Schnitzer, W. C. Sessa, *Proc. Natl. Acad. Sci. USA* **1996**, *93*, 6448–6453.

8 O. Feron, L. Belhassen, L. Kobzik, T. W. Smith, R. A. Kelly, T. Michel, *J. Biol. Chem.* **1996**, *271*, 22810–22814.

9 O. Feron, J. B. Michel, K. Sase, T. Michel, *Biochemistry* **1998**, *37*, 193–200.

10 S. Li, J. Couet, M. P. Lisanti, *J. Biol. Chem.* **1996**, *271*, 29182–29190.

11 J. Couet, S. Li, T. Okamoto, T. Ikezu, M. P. Lisanti, *J. Biol. Chem.* **1997**, *272*, 6525–6533.

12 G. Garcia-Cardena, P. Martasek, B. S. Masters, P. M. Skidd, J. Couet, S. Li, M. P. Lisanti, W. C. Sessa, *J. Biol. Chem.* **1997**, *272*, 25437–25440.

13 J. B. Michel, O. Feron, K. Sase, P. Prabhakar, T. Michel, *J. Biol. Chem.* **1997**, *272*, 25907–25912.

14 O. Feron, F. Saldana, J. B. Michel, T. Michel, *J. Biol. Chem.* **1998**, *273*, 3125–3128.

15 J. B. Michel, O. Feron, D. Sacks, T. Michel, *J. Biol. Chem.* **1997**, *272*, 15583–15586.

16 H. Ju, R. Zou, V. J. Venema, R. C. Venema, *J. Biol. Chem.* **1997**, *272*, 18522–18525.

17 S. Ghosh, R. Gachhui, C. Crooks, C. Wu, M. P. Lisanti, D. J. Stuehr, *J. Biol. Chem.* **1998**, *273*, 22267–22271.

18 P. Prabhakar, H. S. Thatte, R. M. Goetz, M. R. Cho, D. E. Golan, T. Michel, *J. Biol. Chem.* **1998**, *273*, 27383–27388.

19 D. C. Yeh, J. A. Duncan, S. Yamashita, T. Michel, *J. Biol. Chem.* **1999**, *274*, 33148–33154.

20 M. T. Weis, J. L. Crumley, L. H. Young, J. N. Stallone, *Cardiovasc. Res.* **2004**, *63*, 338–346.

21 K. K. McDonald, S. Zharikov, E. R. Block, M. S. Kilberg, *J. Biol. Chem.* **1997**, *272*, 31213–31216.

22 C. Dessy, R. A. Kelly, J. L. Balligand, O. Feron, *EMBO J.* **2000**, *19*, 4272–4280.

23 O. Feron, C. Dessy, D. J. Opel, M. A. Arstall, R. A. Kelly, T. Michel, *J. Biol. Chem.* **1998**, *273*, 30249–30254.

24 J. Dedio, P. Konig, P. Wohlfart, C. Schroeder, W. Kummer, W. Muller-Esterl, *FASEB J.* **2001**, *15*, 79–89.

25 K. Zimmermann, N. Opitz, J. Dedio, C. Renne, W. Muller-Esterl, S. Oess, *Proc. Natl. Acad. Sci. USA* **2002**, *99*, 17167–17172.

26 I. Fleming, R. Busse, *Am. J. Physiol Regul. Integr. Comp Physiol* **2003**, *284*, R1-R12.

27 A. Brouet, P. Sonveaux, C. Dessy, S. Moniotte, J. L. Balligand, O. Feron, *Circ. Res.* **2001**, *89*, 866–873.

28 A. Brouet, P. Sonveaux, C. Dessy, J. L. Balligand, O. Feron, *J. Biol. Chem.* **2001**, *276*, 32663–32669.

29 C. Kupatt, C. Dessy, R. Hinkel, P. Raake, G. Daneau, C. Bouzin, P. Boekstegers, O. Feron, *Arterioscler. Thromb. Vasc. Biol.* **2004**, *24*, 1435–1441.

30 R. Rezzani, L. Rodella, C. Dessy, G. Daneau, R. Bianchi, O. Feron, *FEBS Lett.* **2003**, *552*, 125–129.

31 A. Bist, P. E. Fielding, C. J. Fielding, *Proc. Natl. Acad. Sci. USA* **1997**, *94*, 10693–10698.

32 C. J. Fielding, A. Bist, P. E. Fielding, *Proc. Natl. Acad. Sci. USA* **1997**, *94*, 3753–3758.

33 O. Feron, C. Dessy, S. Moniotte, J. P. Desager, J. L. Balligand, *J. Clin. Invest.* **1999**, *103*, 897–905.

34 A. Blair, P. W. Shaul, I. S. Yuhanna, P. A. Conrad, E. J. Smart, *J. Biol. Chem.* **1999**, *274*, 32512–32519.

35 A. Uittenbogaard, P. W. Shaul, I. S. Yuhanna, A. Blair, E. J. Smart, *J. Biol. Chem.* **2000**, *275*, 11278–11283.

36 P. G. Frank, S. E. Woodman, D. S. Park, M. P. Lisanti, *Arterioscler. Thromb. Vasc. Biol.* **2003**, *23*, 1161–1168.

37 J. F. Kincer, A. Uittenbogaard, J. Dressman, T. M. Guerin, M. Febbraio, L. Guo, E. J. Smart, *J. Biol. Chem.* **2002**, *277*, 23525–23533.

38 O. Feron, C. Dessy, J. P. Desager, J. L. Balligand, *Circulation* **2001**, *103*, 113–118.

39 M. Pelat, C. Dessy, P. Massion, J. P. Desager, O. Feron, J. L. Balligand, *Circulation* **2003**, *107*, 2480–2486.

40 I. S. Yuhanna, Y. Zhu, B. E. Cox, L. D. Hahner, S. Osborne-Lawrence, P. Lu, Y. L. Marcel, R. G. Anderson, M. E. Mendelsohn, H. H. Hobbs, P. W. Shaul, *Nat. Med.* **2001**, *7*, 853–857.

41 C. Mineo, I. S. Yuhanna, M. J. Quon, P. W. Shaul, *J. Biol. Chem.* **2003**, *278*, 9142–9149.

42 J. Liu, B. Razani, S. Tang, B. I. Terman, J. A. Ware, M. P. Lisanti, *J. Biol. Chem.* **1999**, *274*, 15781–15785.

43 J. Liu, X. B. Wang, D. S. Park, M. P. Lisanti, *J. Biol. Chem.* **2002**, *277*, 10661–10668.

44 C. Griffoni, E. Spisni, S. Santi, M. Riccio, T. Guarnieri, V. Tomasi, *Biochem. Biophys. Res. Commun.* **2000**, *276*, 756–761.

45 A. Brouet, J. DeWever, P. Martinive, X. Havaux, P. Bouzin, P. Sonveaux, O. Feron, *FASEB J.* **2005**, *19*, 602–604.

46 P. Sonveaux, P. Martinive, J. DeWever, Z. Batova, G. Daneau, M. Pelat, P. Ghisdal, V. Gregoire, C. Dessy, J. L. Balligand, O. Feron, *Circ. Res.* **2004**, *95*, 154–161.

47 S. E. Woodman, A. W. Ashton, W. Schubert, H. Lee, T. M. Williams, F. A. Medina, J. B. Wyckoff, T. P. Combs, M. P. Lisanti, *Am. J. Pathol.* **2003**, *162*, 2059–2068.

48 M. Drab, P. Verkade, M. Elger, M. Kasper, M. Lohn, B. Lauterbach, J. Menne, C. Lindschau, F. Mende, F. C. Luft, A. Schedl, H. Haller, T. V. Kurzchalia, *Science* **2001**, *293*, 2449–2452.

49 B. Razani, J. A. Engelman, X. B. Wang, W. Schubert, X. L. Zhang, C. B. Marks, F. Macaluso, R. G. Russell, M. Li, R. G. Pestell, D. Di Vizio, H. Hou, Jr., B. Kneitz, G. Lagaud, G. J. Christ, W. Edelmann, M. P. Lisanti, *J. Biol. Chem.* **2001**, *276*, 38121–38138.

50 M. Omura, S. Kobayashi, Y. Mizukami, K. Mogami, N. Todoroki-Ikeda, T. Miyake, M. Matsuzaki, *FEBS Lett.* **2001**, *487*, 361–366.

51 V. Rizzo, D. P. McIntosh, P. Oh, J. E. Schnitzer, *J. Biol. Chem.* **1998**, *273*, 34724–34729.

52 V. Shah, S. Cao, H. Hendrickson, J. Yao, Z. S. Katusic, *Am. J. Physiol. Gastrointest. Liver Physiol.* **2001**, *280*, G1209–G1216.

53 T. Murata, K. Sato, M. Hori, H. Ozaki, H. Karaki, *J. Biol. Chem.* **2002**, *277*, 44085–44092.

54 D. A. Pelligrino, S. Ye, F. Tan, R. A. Santizo, D. L. Feinstein, Q. Wang, *Biochem. Biophys. Res. Commun.* **2000**, *269*, 165–171.

55 P. Sonveaux, C. Dessy, A. Brouet, B. F. Jordan, V. Gregoire, B. Gallez, J. L. Balligand, O. Feron, *FASEB J.* **2002**, *16*, 1979–1981.

56 Y. Feng, V. J. Venema, R. C. Venema, N. Tsai, M. A. Behzadian, R. B. Caldwell, *Invest. Ophthalmol. Vis. Sci.* **1999**, *40*, 157–167.

57 Y. Feng, V. J. Venema, R. C. Venema, N. Tsai, R. B. Caldwell, *Biochem. Biophys. Res. Commun.* **1999**, *256*, 192–197.

58 M. Bucci, J. P. Gratton, R. D. Rudic, L. Acevedo, F. Roviezzo, G. Cirino, W. C. Sessa, *Nat. Med.* **2000**, *6*, 1362–1367.

59 J. P. Gratton, M. I. Lin, J. Yu, E. D. Weiss, Z. L. Jiang, T. A. Fairchild, Y. Iwakiri, R. Groszmann, K. P. Claffey, Y. C. Cheng, W. C. Sessa, *Cancer Cell* **2003**, *4*, 31–39.

60 O. Feron, T. W. Smith, T. Michel, R. A. Kelly, *J. Biol. Chem.* **1997**, *272*, 17744–17748.

61 W. Schubert, P. G. Frank, S. E. Woodman, H. Hyogo, D. E. Cohen, C. W. Chow, M. P. Lisanti, *J. Biol. Chem.* **2002**, *277*, 40091–40098.

62 W. Schubert, P. G. Frank, B. Razani, D. S. Park, C. W. Chow, M. P. Lisanti, *J. Biol. Chem.* **2001**, *276*, 48619–48622.

63 A. W. Cohen, D. S. Park, S. E. Woodman, T. M. Williams, M. Chandra, J. Shirani, D. S. Pereira, R. N. Kitsis, R. G. Russell, L. M. Weiss, B. Tang, L. A. Jelicks, S. M. Factor, V. Shtutin, H. B. Tanowitz, M. P. Lisanti, *Am. J. Physiol. Cell Physiol.* **2003**, *284*, C457–C474.

64 Y. Y. Zhao, Y. Liu, R. V. Stan, L. Fan, Y. Gu, N. Dalton, P. H. Chu, K. Peterson, J. Ross, Jr., K. R. Chien, *Proc. Natl. Acad. Sci. USA* **2002**, *99*, 11375–11380.

12

The Role of Caveolin-1 in Tumor Cell Survival and Cancer Progression

Dana Ravid and Mordechai Liscovitch

12.1
Introduction

Multifunctional adaptor proteins may have divergent actions in early versus late phases of cancer progression, playing both tumor-suppressing and tumor-promoting roles in a context-dependent manner. One such protein is the adaptor and caveolar coat protein caveolin-1, which is an essential structural constituent of plasma membrane caveolae (for a review, see [1,2]). The cellular localization of caveolin-1 is not limited to caveolae in all cells [3], and it exhibits diverse functions that go beyond its well-characterized role as a component of the caveolar coat (for a review, see [4]). Caveolin-1 was implicated in tumorigenesis because its expression is suppressed by oncogenic transformation, and little or no expression of caveolin-1 was initially found in various human tumors and cancer cell lines [5]. In addition, caveolin-1 has well-established growth-inhibitory properties, and it has been suggested to act as a tumor-suppressor protein [5]. However, a general tumor suppressor action cannot easily be reconciled with the fact that, in many other cancer cell lines and tumor specimens, the expression of caveolin-1 is high [6]. Furthermore, a positive correlation was often noted between the expression of caveolin-1 and the tumor cell grade and progression stage; in certain studies, the expression of caveolin-1 could be used to independently predict poor disease prognosis [6].

How can the divergent, cell type- and tumor stage-dependent changes in caveolin-1 be explained? Previous studies have indicated that in addition to its growth-inhibitory action, under certain circumstances caveolin-1 acts as a survival-promoting protein [7–14]. The differential expression of caveolin-1 in various tumor cells and specimens may thus be explained by the ability of caveolin-1 to exert both anti-proliferative and pro-survival effects. It was previously hypothesized that, during the early stages of cancer progression (when rapid proliferation is essential for clonal expansion), expression of caveolin-1 is down-regulated, thus suppressing its growth-inhibitory actions. Conversely, during the late, advanced stages of the disease (when survival and stress resistance are paramount), expression of caveolin-1 is up-regulated and it plays a pro-survival role [6,15]. In the following sections we

Lipid Rafts and Caveolae. Christopher J. Fielding
Copyright © 2006 WILEY-VCH Verlag GmbH & Co. KGaA, Weinheim
ISBN: 3-527-31261-7

shall re-evaluate this hypothesis in view of recent evidence that relates the expression and function(s) of caveolin-1 to cancer progression and tumor cell survival.

12.2
The Caveolin-1 Gene and its Regulation During Differentiation and Transformation

Caveolin-1, which was first identified as a ~22-kDa, tyrosine-phosphorylated protein in Rous sarcoma virus-transformed cells [16], was later found to be an essential constituent of caveolae [17–19]. The caveolar membrane system mediates certain transport processes, including transcytosis, potocytosis, and clathrin-independent endocytosis [20]. Caveolin-1 binds sphingolipids and cholesterol – lipids that are characteristic constituents of lipid rafts [4]. Caveolin-1 and caveolae are also involved in mediating cellular cholesterol efflux [19,21].

Caveolin-1 is a member of a gene family that also comprises caveolin-2 and caveolin-3. Caveolin-2 is co-expressed with caveolin-1 in many cell types, including mesenchymal, endothelial, epithelial, neuronal, and glial cells [22,23]. Together, caveolin-1 and caveolin-2 form hetero-oligomeric assemblies that constitute the filamentous caveolar coat [23,24]. Caveolin-3 is selectively expressed in skeletal and heart muscle cells, where it appears to substitute functionally for caveolin-1 [25].

Caveolin-1 interacts with numerous proteins via a caveolin "scaffolding" domain (CSD) that binds short-sequence motifs that are rich in aromatic amino acids [1,26,27]. The ability of caveolin-1 to interact with many raft-localized signaling proteins has indicated that it participates in signal transduction, and that its expression may have a profound effect on cell function and fate. Indeed, the expression of caveolin-1 is altered dynamically under different physiological conditions, clearly implicating it as a regulator of cell growth and survival.

The induction of differentiation up-regulates caveolin-1 in various cell types [3,28–32]. Up-regulation of caveolin-1 is also observed upon acquisition of cell senescence [33,34]. In contrast, caveolin-1 is down-regulated upon transformation of fibroblasts by oncogenes such as Bcr-Abl, v-Abl, H-Ras, Polyoma virus middle T and Crk1 [35], or Neu-T, c-Src-Y52F and Myc [36]. These data accorded well with the many growth-inhibitory effects of caveolin-1 (for reviews, see [5,6]) and its human chromosomal location near a locus (7q31.1/D7S522) that is deleted in several forms of cancers [37,38]. In addition, genetic knockout of caveolin-1 leads to hyperplasia of pulmonary endothelial cells and mammary gland epithelial cells [39,40] and results in increased sensitivity to oncogenic and carcinogenic stimuli [41,42]. Together, these data have led to the suggestion that caveolin-1 may act as a tumor-suppressor protein [5].

However, as discussed below, this simple hypothesis is unable to explain the complex pattern of caveolin-1 expression in human tumors and the full range of its actions in cancer cells.

12.3
Divergent Expression of Caveolin-1 in Human Cancer: The Case of Lung Cancer

The expression of caveolin-1 in different cancer cell lines and tumor samples was documented in numerous studies, and the picture that emerges from these studies is that caveolin-1 expression is highly divergent [6]. Whereas in many cases caveolin-1 expression is down-regulated, in other cancer cells elevated caveolin-1 levels are maintained. High expression of caveolin-1 in cancer cells was initially demonstrated in human multidrug resistant (MDR) cancer cells [43–45] and in mouse metastatic prostate cancer cells [46]. Evidence that has accumulated since these early studies seems to indicate that the expression of caveolin-1 often depends on the tumor's stage and grade. In fact, in most cases where this relationship was examined explicitly, a positive correlation was found between a high expression of caveolin-1 and advanced tumor cell grade and/or progression stage. Such was the case in cancers from the breast [46], prostate [46,47], lung [48,49], bladder [50], kidney [51,52] and pancreas [53,54]. Furthermore, in some cases, high expression of caveolin-1 was shown to be an independent predictor of poor disease prognosis [47,49,51–53,55–58].

The divergent pattern of caveolin-1 in human cancer is well represented in studies of lung cancer tumors and cell lines. Human lung adenocarcinoma- and small cell carcinoma-derived cell lines exhibited little or no caveolin-1 expression, in contrast to high levels of caveolin-1 expression observed in CaLu-1 lung squamous carcinoma cells [59]. However, when compared with normal human lung epithelia, four other lung squamous cell carcinoma lines expressed reduced levels of caveolin-1 [60]. In another study, low-level caveolin-1 expression was similarly found in cell lines derived from two lung adenocarcinomas, a bronchioalveolar carcinoma and a large-cell lung carcinoma, whereas non-small-cell lung carcinoma cell lines (Hop-62, Hop-92) highly expressed caveolin-1 [61]. More recently, it was found that about 95% of small-cell lung cancer (SCLC) cell lines exhibit low or no caveolin-1 expression, whereas a majority (76%) of non-SCLC lines retained high caveolin-1 expression [62].

The loss of caveolin-1 expression in SCLC and in primary non-SCLC was verified immunohistochemically in tumor samples [63,64]. Caveolin-1 expression was reported to be positively correlated with metastatic potential in a series of lung adenocarcinoma cell lines established by selection for increasing invasiveness [48]. The same study found that primary lung adenocarcinoma tumors are largely caveolin-1-negative, but there was a significant trend of increased caveolin-1 expression in metastatic lung tumors and in their lymph nodes metastases [48]. Caveolin-1 was prominently down-regulated in primary lung adenocarcinomas, as revealed by DNA microarray analysis [65,66].

Nevertheless, ~25% of lung adenocarcinomas still expressed high levels of caveolin-1 protein, although this study found no correlation of caveolin-1 expression with tumor stage or lymph node status [63]. Other analyses of primary lung squamous cell carcinoma specimens revealed that 26–30% were caveolin-1-positive [49,67]. In these studies there was a significant correlation between caveolin-1 expression and advanced pathologic stage [49,67].

Furthermore, there was a statistically significant decrease in five-year survival after complete resection of patients with caveolin-1-positive tumors [49]. Together, the above data are consistent with a suppression of caveolin-1 gene expression in primary lung tumors (in particular, SCLC). However, some lung tumors and lung cancer cell lines are caveolin-1-positive (notably non-small cell lung carcinoma), and there seems to be a positive correlation between caveolin-1 expression and advanced cancer pathologic stage or metastatic potential. Thus, the status of caveolin-1 in lung cancer is as complex as it is in other forms of cancer.

12.4
Actions of Caveolin-1 in Cancer Cells: Effects of Heterologous Expression and Genetic or Functional Suppression

12.4.1
Anti-Proliferative Activity of Caveolin-1

Heterologous expression of caveolin-1 in T47-D human mammary cancer cells results in a 50% decrease in growth rate and a three- to 10-fold reduction in anchorage-independent growth [68]. Inhibition of *in-vitro* anchorage-independent growth, a parameter that is highly correlated with *in-vivo* tumorigenesis [69], was similarly seen in MCF-7 human breast adenocarcinoma cells [11] and SCLC cells [62]. Caveolin-1 may therefore block a matrix-independent, intrinsic growth signal (e.g., a signal that emanates from an activated oncogene). Indeed, transient transfection with caveolin-1 reduces growth rates in human mammary tumor cells [11,68] and human ovarian carcinoma cells [70]. Accordingly, a mutant caveolin-1 (P132L), identified in about 16% of primary human breast cancer specimens [71], induces morphological transformation in NIH-3T3 cells and supports anchorage-independent growth of mutant-transfected cells [71]. P132L appears to act by causing missorting of normal caveolin-1, leading to its retention at a perinuclear compartment that is probably the Golgi apparatus [72]. It should be noted that the occurrence of the P132L mutation in mammary tumors awaits confirmation in non-Japanese breast cancer patients [73,74]. Further support for its growth-inhibitory action was obtained by analysis of heterozygous and homozygous caveolin-1 knockout mice. Retroviral inactivation of one of the caveolin-1 alleles results in loss of ca. 50% of caveolin-1 expression and enables anchorage-independent growth [75]. Likewise, genetic knockout of caveolin-1 results in hyperplasia of pulmonary endothelial cells and mammary gland epithelial cells [39,40]. Although spontaneous development of mammary or other tumors was not evident in caveolin-1-null mice [72], caveolin-1 gene knockout results in increased sensitivity to carcinogenic and oncogenic stimuli [41,42]. Mammary gland tumor-prone MMTV-PyMT mice exhibit accelerated formation of larger and higher-grade dysplastic foci [42]. Long-term mammary tumorigenesis in these mice was doubled and lung metastases were significantly increased [76]. Genetic disruption of caveolin-1 was shown also to cooperate with loss of the tumor suppressor INK4a. This study showed that double knockout of caveolin-1 and INK4a stimulates proliferation of mouse embryo fibroblasts, greatly increases transformation by an activated onco-gene (e.g., H-Ras-G12V; v-Src) and results in dramatic stimulation of tumor growth *in vivo* [77]. Taken together with the heterologous expression data, these results implicate caveolin-1 as an important anti-proliferative protein.

12.4.2
Pro-Apoptotic Activity of Caveolin-1

Caveolin-1 can also acts as a pro-apoptotic protein. This was originally observed in Rat-1 fibroblasts, where overexpression of caveolin 1 sensitizes the cells to both γ-irradiation and ceramide-induced cell death [78]. Elevated sensitivity to apoptotic stimuli was also reported in caveolin-1-transfected OVCAR-3 ovarian carcinoma cells [65] and T24 bladder cancer cells [79], and in mouse embryo fibroblasts that transgenically overexpress caveolin-1 [80]. Activation of caspase-3 was reported to occur in three OVCA ovarian cancer cell lines upon expression of caveolin-1 [70]. Supporting these data, caveolin-1 antisense-suppressed NIH-3T3 cells were re-ported to be more resistant to staurosporine-induced apoptosis [79]. Similarly, ret-roviral disruption of the caveolin-1 gene in L929 murine fibrosarcoma cells caused resistance to tumor necrosis factor-α (TNF-α)-, hydrogen peroxide- and staurospor-ine-induced apoptosis, whereas forced caveolin-1 expression sensitized HepG2 hu-man hepatocellular carcinoma cells to TNF-α [81]. Caveolin-1 expression also sen-sitizes HeLa human cervical carcinoma cells to sodium arsenite and hydrogen peroxide toxicity [82]. In addition, adenoviral overexpression of caveolin-1 was found to inhibit platelet-derived growth factor (PDGF)-induced proliferation of primary vascular smooth muscle cells (VSMCs), leading to apoptosis [83]. Col-lectively, the results of these studies indicate that the growth-inhibitory actions of caveolin-1 may sometimes be accompanied by a pro-apoptotic activity.

12.4.3
Survival-Promoting Activity of Caveolin-1

Several studies using either overexpression or antisense suppression techniques demonstrated that caveolin-1 may act as a positive regulator of cell survival in certain cancer cells. This was first shown in mouse and human prostate cancer cells, where expression of caveolin-1 protects the cells from androgen deprivation-induced apoptosis and c-Myc-induced apoptosis, respectively [7,10]. In the former case, caveolin-1 was secreted from the cells, upon testosterone treatment, acting as an autocrine or paracrine pro-survival factor [9]. Similarly, overexpression of cav-eolin-1 in LNCaP human prostate cancer cells significantly reduced thapsigargin-induced apoptosis [12]. The pro-survival action of caveolin-1 in prostate cancer cells was recently confirmed in the TRAMP mouse model, where caveolin-1 gene knockout attenuated tumor progression and metastasis *in vivo* and stimulated apoptosis of tumor-derived cells both *in vitro* and *in vivo* [84]. We have recently shown that caveolin-1 expression in MCF-7 cells results in inhibition of anoikis (detachment-induced apoptosis) [11] and of detachment-induced activation of p53 [13]. Interestingly, cellular resistance to anoikis was also recently shown to be caveolin-1-dependent in pancreatic adenocarcinoma cells [85]. Antisense inhibition of caveolin-1 expression sensitizes nonmalignant intestinal epithelial cells to anoikis [14]. Taken together, these data clearly indicate that caveolin-1 can promote cell survival upon environmental challenge in both normal and cancer cells.

12.5
Molecular Mechanisms Implicated in the Pro-Survival Action of Caveolin-1

The phosphoinositide 3-kinase (PI3K)/Akt cell survival pathway has recently emerged as a major target for regulation by caveolin-1 in a variety of cancer cells [12,13,86]. A possible role of caveolin-1 in PI3K/Akt pathway activation was shown in multiple myeloma cells which, unlike most other hematopoietic-derived cells, express high levels of caveolin-1 [86]. Caveolin-1 was found to co-localize in lipid rafts fractions, and to co-exist in an immunoprecipitable complex, with receptors for insulin-like growth factor-I (IGF-I) and interleukin-6 (IL-6). These cell survival-inducing factors stimulated c-Src-mediated phosphorylation of caveolin-1 on Tyr14 and its association with PI3K subunits. The disruption of lipid raft organization by cholesterol depletion resulted in a redistribution of caveolin-1 and PI3K, an inhibition of Tyr14 phosphorylation of caveolin-1, and an abrogated IGF-I- and IL-6-induced activation of Akt and survival, thus confirming that both caveolin-1 and intact caveolae are essential for these processes [86]. Consistent with this conclusion, transient expression of caveolin-1 in LNCaP human prostate cancer cells resulted in elevated Akt phosphorylation and activation and increased resistance to thapsigargin-induced apoptosis [12]. Similarly, stable expression of caveolin-1 in MCF-7 human breast cancer cells also resulted in elevated basal phosphorylation of Akt, concomitantly increasing cellular resistance to anoikis [13].

Interestingly, a correlation between caveolin-1 expression and Akt activation was also seen in HEK-293 human embryonic kidney cells [82] and L929 mouse fibrosarcoma cells [81] although, in the latter two cases, Akt activation was reported to sensitize the cells to the apoptotic stimuli.

The mechanisms whereby caveolin-1 regulates PI3K/Akt-mediated cell survival have yet to be fully elucidated. It is clear, however, that caveolin-1 may influence this important pathway by recruiting and/or modulating its various components at different levels. First, caveolin-1 may act at the receptor level, as shown in caveolin-1-expressing MCF-7 cells, in which IGF-I receptor expression is elevated [13]. In these cells, the up-regulation of IGF-I receptors is associated with enhanced IGF-I signaling to the Erk1/2 and PI3K/Akt pathways (Fig. 12.1). In endothelial cells, caveolin-1 promotes the nongenomic action of nuclear receptors such as the estrogen receptor-α (ERα), resulting in activation of Akt and endothelial nitric oxide synthase (eNOS) [87]. Whether a similar mechanism operates in steroid-dependent human cancers, such as breast cancer and prostate cancer, has yet to be determined. In endothelial cells, caveolin-1 similarly interacts with TNF-α receptors,

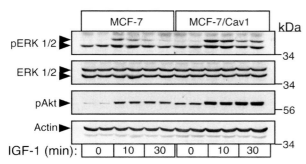

Fig. 12.1 Enhanced IGF-I-mediated signaling in caveolin-1-transfected MCF-7 breast adenocarcinoma cells. Cells were serum-starved for 24 h and then stimulated with 50 ng mL^{-1} human IGF-I for the indicated times. Cell lysates were resolved by SDS-PAGE and then blotted with antibodies to the active phospho-Erk1/2 (pErk1/2), Erk1/2, phospho-Akt (pAkt) and actin (loading control) as indicated. (Figure reprinted, with permission, from [13].)

allowing TNF-α-induced activation of Akt [88]. An essential role of caveolin-1 in $\alpha_v\beta_3$ integrin-dependent activation of PI3K and Akt upon mechanical stress was recently noted also in VSMC [89]. In these cells, caveolin-1 is additionally required for angiotensin II receptor transactivation of the EGF receptor after Rac1 and NADPH oxidase activation, resulting in Akt activation [90]. Caveolin-1 is part of a survival signaling complex comprising urokinase-type plasminogen activator receptor, integrin $\alpha_v\beta_3/\alpha_5\beta_1$ and the SFK Yes in vitronectin-attached endothelial cells [91].

As mentioned above, caveolin-1 recruits both regulatory and catalytic subunits of PI3K upon IGF-I and IL-6 stimulation in multiple myeloma cells [86]. Phosphoinositide-dependent protein kinase-1 (PDK1), which mediates Akt Thr308 phosphorylation was also found physically to interact with caveolin-1 [92]. However, in this case a caveolin-1 scaffolding peptide suppressed the self-phosphorylation and the *in-vitro* kinase activities of PDK1. These results are inconsistent with the data showing that caveolin-1 significantly increases the activity of PDK1 and Akt [12]. Chun and co-workers suggested that these differences may result from changes in both subcellular localization and in the affinity to caveolin-1 of PDK1 compared to other factors (such as the serine/threonine protein phosphatases) [92]. Integrin-linked kinase has been proposed to serve as an Akt Ser473-kinase, and was found to interact with caveolin-1 via a CSD-binding motif [93,94]. Intriguingly, another putative Akt Ser473 kinase, namely DNA-PK, is localized in part in lipid rafts, although in this case direct interaction with caveolin-1 has yet to be demonstrated [95].

Finally, caveolin-1 may regulate the PI3K/Akt pathway by affecting lipid and protein phosphatases that turn the pathway off. Interaction of caveolin-1 via its CSD with protein phosphatases that dephosphorylate phospho-Akt, namely PP1 and PP2A, results in their inhibition and in consequent activation of Akt in LNCaP cells [12]. Caveolin-1 is also associated with the tumor suppressor protein PTEN, a 3-phosphoinositide phosphatase that terminates the PI3K-dependent signal, although in this case the effect of caveolin-1 on PTEN activity has not been determined [96]. Interestingly, it was shown recently that caveolin-1 knockout up-regulates PTEN expression in TRAMP mouse prostate tumors, consistent with the inhibition of tumor progression caused by loss of caveolin-1 in this model [84].

The PI3K/Akt pathway is not the only survival pathway that is regulated by caveolin-1. Although caveolin-1 usually inhibits growth factor activation of the mitogenic Erk1/2 pathway, it is required for integrin-dependent activation of Erk1/2 through a complex that consists of Fyn, Shc, and Grb2 [97,98]. The Erk1/2 pathway promotes cell survival, at least in some cell types [99,100]. Caveolin-1 is similarly required for β_1-integrin-mediated signaling to Src kinases and focal adhesion kinase (FAK) and, consequently, β_1-integrin-dependent adhesion [101]. Caveolin-1 enables activation of c-Src upon cross-linking of the cell adhesion protein CECAM6 in BxPC3 human pancreatic adenocarcinoma cells, as well as c-Src-dependent tyrosine phosphorylation of FAK and the consequent inhibition of anoikis [85]. A positive regulatory role of caveolin-1 on survival signaling may also be implied by data showing that it interacts with a component of the TNF-α-NFκB pathway [102], and that it may inhibits a caveolae-resident neutral sphingomyelinase via its CSD sequence [103].

12.6
The Role of Tyr14 Phosphorylation in Caveolin-1-Mediated Signaling

Tyr14 resides within a consensus motif for c-Src and c-Abl phosphorylation, present in caveolin-1α (but not in caveolin-1β), that is phosphorylated in a constitutive manner in v-Src- and v-Abl-transformed cells [16,104,105]. Phosphorylation of Tyr14 in response to cell stimulation has emerged recently as a major switch in caveolin-1 physiological function. Tyr14 phosphorylation occurs in various cell types in response to extracellular signal molecules such as insulin [106], IGF-I [107], EGF [108], fibronectin [109], IL-6 [86], PDGF [110], VEGF [111], and adrenocorticotropic hormone (ACTH) [112]. In addition, Tyr14 phosphorylation occurs in response to cell stressors such as oxidants [113], hyperosmolarity and UV irradiation [114], DNA damage-inducing drugs [115], and denial of extracellular matrix attachment [14].

Although insulin-dependent Tyr14 phosphorylation was initially believed to be mediated by a Src-family kinase (SFK) [116], more recent studies have shown that insulin-dependent Tyr14 phosphorylation is insensitive to a general SFK inhibitor, and suggested instead that it is mediated by the insulin receptor directly [117]. In contrast, EGF-, IGF-I and IL-6-induced phosphorylation of Tyr14 were inhibited by the same SFK blocker [86,118]. Similarly, a SFK is clearly involved in hyperosmotic stress-induced Tyr14 phosphorylation, since it is strongly inhibited by a dominant-negative form of Src [114]. As noted above, exposure of primary human fibroblasts to oxidative stress causes Tyr14 phosphorylation, and the SFK Fyn was shown to be required for this response [119]. In the same cells, this phosphorylation event also depends on the presence of c-Abl [120]. The relationship between Fyn- and Abl-mediated phosphorylation of caveolin-1 is unclear, as both are required for oxidant-induced Tyr14 phosphorylation, but neither kinase is required for the action of the other, suggesting that Fyn and Abl do not participate in a linear signaling pathway [119]. It was proposed that low level of oxidative stress results in the activation of Fyn and Tyr14 phosphorylation, promoting cell survival, whereas Abl is activated (and phosphorylates caveolin-1) upon high level of oxidant exposure, leading to apoptosis [119].

What is the role of the phosphorylation of caveolin on Tyr14? The formation of a phosphotyrosine residue likely constitutes a binding site for proteins with Src homology 2 (SH2) and phosphotyrosine binding (PTB) domains. Such proteins, recruited upon Tyr14 phosphorylation, include Grb7 [105] and Csk [121,122]. The recruitment of Grb7 to pTyr14 was shown to greatly enhance anchorage-independent growth in cells co-transfected with Grb7, c-Src, and caveolin-1 [105]. Similarly, caveolin-1 transfection markedly increased EGF-stimulated cell migration and this, too, was dependent on the presence of a phosphorylatable Tyr14 [105]. The recruitment of Csk, which catalyzes the C-terminal phosphorylation of SFK and inhibits their activity, is likely a part of a negative regulatory loop wherein Csk limits or abrogates SFK activation in oxidant-stressed cells [122]. In accordance with this study, crosslinking of the GPI-anchored protein CECAM6 reduced caveolin-1 Tyr14 phosphorylation, forcing its dissociation from the Csk and thus inducing Src-dependent activation of FAK [85]. Recently, Tyr14 phosphorylation was found to mediate interaction of caveolin-1 with the membrane type I matrix metalloprotease and this interaction, in turn, was shown to correlate with the protease-induced cell migration [123]. This interesting finding resonates with the fact that pTyr14-caveolin-1 is localized in focal adhesions, as shown in Src-transfected cells [105,124], as well as cells exposed to hyperosmotic and oxidative stress [114,120], cells plated on a fibronectin matrix [109,122,124], and cells treated with ACTH [112]. In summary, although the precise mechanisms and role of Tyr14 phosphorylation has not been fully resolved, the evidence accumulated so far clearly implicates this event as critical to at least some of the physiological functions of caveolin-1. In this context, of particular interest are the differential actions of caveolin-1α and caveolin-1β, which could be related to the lack of the Tyr14 residue in the latter protein.

12.7
Stress-Induced Changes in Caveolin-1 Expression

New evidence shows that not only caveolin-1 may negatively regulate survival and apoptosis but also that stressful stimuli may, in turn, positively regulate caveolin-1 expression. This phenomenon was shown to occur in NIH-3T3 mouse fibroblasts exposed to subcytotoxic levels of hydrogen peroxide [34]. Significant up-regulation of caveolin-1 was observed in mouse macrophages exposed to various unrelated

apoptotic agents, including simvastatin, camptothecin, or glucose depriva-
tion [125]. In this case, caveolin-1 was found to co-localize with phosphatidylserine
on the cell surface of the apoptotic cells, thus serving as an indicator of macrophage apoptosis. Other stress signals that were reported to increase caveolin-1
protein levels included exposure to various cytostatic drugs in lung cancer
cells [45,126,127]. The acute up-regulation of caveolin-1 expression by chemother-
apeutic drugs may be related to the constitutively elevated caveolin-1 levels observed in MDR human cancer cell lines [44,45,128,129] and the correlation of cav-
eolin-1 expression with expression of the *MDR1* gene in leukemic bone marrow
leukocytes [130]. Another stress condition reported to induce caveolin-1 protein
levels in endothelial cells at G_0/G_1 cell-cycle phase is hypergravity stress [131]. In
the latter case, the up-regulation of caveolin-1 was associated with the redistribution of caveolin-1 to an intracellular compartment [131]. Recently, caveolin-1 protein levels were found to be significantly increased, in a time-dependent manner,
upon detachment of anoikis-resistant breast and MDR colon cancer cells [13]. A
related phenomenon was also shown by immunofluorescence staining of caveolin-
1 in kidneys of acute renal failure rats *in vivo*, where high-intensity caveolin-1
expression was observed in injured proximal tubules that were losing basement
membrane adhesion or were apoptotic, at one to four days after ischemia-reper-
fusion [132].

The mechanisms involved in the regulation of caveolin-1 expression is response
to stress are poorly understood. TNF-α- and IL-1-induced up-regulation of cav-
eolin-1 in breast and ovarian carcinoma cells is mediated by the NFκB pathway [133]. A more recent study provides strong evidence implicating FOXO transcription factors, known to be up-regulated upon oxidative stress, in the induction
of caveolin-1 [134]. Finally, p53 was also shown to act as a positive transcriptional
regulator of caveolin-1 expression [60,135].

Taken together, these data indicate that caveolin-1 expression is regulated by
various stress and apoptosis-inducing conditions, suggesting that caveolin-1 may
play an important role in the physiological stress response of both normal and
cancer cells. Additional experiments are required in order to determine the mechanisms involved in caveolin-1 regulation and whether caveolin was functioning as a
pro-survival protein or alternatively, causing apoptosis in these cells.

12.8
Concluding Remarks

The complex picture that emerges from the studies outlined above defies a simple
explanation and indicates, instead, that caveolin-1 plays different roles in early-
versus advanced-stage cancer cells. The growth-inhibitory actions of caveolin-1 are
well established, and involve direct inhibition of mitogenic signaling pathways. It
is likely that, during the early phase of cancer progression, caveolin-1 is down-
regulated in order to suppress its growth-inhibitory actions and to allow rapid
proliferation and clonal expansion.

Yet, it is clearly evident that caveolin-1 also exhibits pro-survival actions. We believe that these actions explain why the expression of caveolin-1 is often up-regulated at late, advanced stages of cancer, when tumor cell survival and stress resistance are of paramount importance. Although the PI3K/Akt pathway has been revealed as a major survival pathway targeted by caveolin-1, other pathways may also participate in mediating survival of malignant cells during advanced stages of cancer progression. The molecular mechanisms utilized by caveolin-1 to modulate the activity of these pathways have still to be fully elucidated. Likewise, an intriguing question – the answer to which remains obscure – is how advanced stage cancer cells manage to circumvent the anti-proliferative actions of caveolin-1.

The ability of caveolin-1 to effect both growth-inhibitory and survival-promoting activities provides a rational explanation for the divergent changes of caveolin-1 expression in different cancer cells and tumor specimens, and revises the currently dominant view of caveolin-1 as a primarily tumor-suppressor-like protein. Furthermore, the context-dependent dual functionality of caveolin-1 highlights the potential of multifunctional adaptor proteins to affect cancer cell phenotype in an unpredictable manner, thus underscoring the complexity of cancer cell biology.

Acknowledgments

The authors are grateful to all members of their group for many helpful discussions. This project was supported in part by a grant from the DKFZ/MOST, and is currently supported by a grant from the Philip Morris Foundation and by intramural grants from the Willner Center for Vascular Biology and the Center for Scientific Excellence. M. L. is the incumbent of the Harold L. Korda Professorial Chair in Biology.

Abbreviations

ACTH	adrenocorticotropic hormone
CSD	caveolin scaffolding domain
eNOS	endothelial nitric oxide synthase
ER-α	estrogen receptor-α
FAK	focal adhesion kinase
IGF-I	insulin-like growth factor-I
IL	interleukin
MDR	multidrug resistance/t
PDGF	platelet-derived growth factor
PDK1	phosphoinositide-dependent protein kinase-1
PI3K	phosphoinositide 3-kinase
PTB	phosphotyrosine binding
SCLC	small-cell lung cancer

SFK   Src family kinase(s)
SH2   Src homology 2
TNF-α   tumor necrosis factor-α
VSMC   vascular smooth muscle cells

References

1 Razani, B., Woodman, S. E., Lisanti, M. P. (2002) *Pharmacol. Rev.* 54, 431–467.

2 Parton, R. G. (2003) *Nat. Rev. Mol. Cell Biol.* 4, 162–167.

3 Li, W. P., Liu, P., Pilcher, B. K., Anderson, R. G. (2001) *J. Cell Sci.* 114, 1397–1408.

4 Liu, P., Rudick, M., Anderson, R. G. (2002) *J. Biol. Chem.* 277, 41295–41298.

5 Razani, B., Schlegel, A., Liu, J., Lisanti, M. P. (2001) *Biochem. Soc. Trans.* 29, 494–499.

6 Liscovitch, M., Burgermeister, E., Jain, N., Ravid, D., Shatz, M., Tencer, L. (2004) In: Mattson, M. P. (Ed.) *Membrane Microdomain Signaling. Lipid Rafts in Biology and Medicine.* Humana Press, Totowa, New Jersey, pp. 161–190.

7 Nasu, Y., et al. (1998) *Nat. Med.* 4, 1062–1064.

8 Li, L., et al. (2001) *Cancer Res.* 61, 4386–4392.

9 Tahir, S. A., et al. (2001) *Cancer Res.* 61, 3882–3885.

10 Timme, T. L., Goltsov, A., Tahir, S., Li, L., Wang, J., Ren, C., Johnston, R. N., Thompson, T. C. (2000) *Oncogene* 19, 3256–3265.

11 Fiucci, G., Ravid, D., Reich, R., Liscovitch, M. (2002) *Oncogene* 21, 2365–2375.

12 Li, L., Ren, C. H., Tahir, S. A., Ren, C., Thompson, T. C. (2003) *Mol. Cell. Biol.* 23, 9389–9404.

13 Ravid, D., Maor, S., Werner, H., Liscovitch, M. (2005) *Oncogene* 24, 1338–1347.

14 Loza-Coll, M. A., Perera, S., Shi, W., Filmus, J. (2005) *Oncogene* 24, 1727–1737.

15 Shatz, M., Liscovitch, M. (2004) *Leukemia Res.* 28, 907–908.

16 Glenney, J.R.J. (1989) *J. Biol. Chem.* 264, 20163–20166.

17 Glenney, J.R.J., Soppet, D. (1992) *Proc. Natl. Acad. Sci. USA* 89, 10517–10521.

18 Rothberg, K. G., Heuser, J. E., Donzell, W. C., Ying, Y. S., Glenney, J. R., Anderson, R. G. (1992) *Cell* 68, 673–682.

19 Smart, E. J., Graf, G. A., McNiven, M. A., Sessa, W. C., Engelman, J. A., Scherer, P. E., Okamoto, T., Lisanti, M. P. (1999) *Mol. Cell. Biol.* 19, 7289–7304.

20 Anderson, R.G.W. (1998) *Annu. Rev. Biochem.* 67, 199–225.

21 Fielding, C. J., Fielding, P. E. (2001) *Biochim. Biophys. Acta* 1529, 210–222.

22 Scherer, P. E., Okamoto, T., Chun, M., Nishimoto, I., Lodish, H. F., Lisanti, M. P. (1996) *Proc. Natl. Acad. Sci. USA* 93, 131–135.

23 Scherer, P. E., et al. (1997) *J. Biol. Chem.* 272, 29337–29346.

24 Scheiffele, P., Verkade, P., Fra, A. M., Virta, H., Simons, K., Ikonen, E. (1998) *J. Cell Biol.* 140, 795–806.

25 Galbiati, F., Razani, B., Lisanti, M. P. (2001) *Trends Mol. Med.* 7, 435–441.

26 Li, S., Couet, J., Lisanti, M. P. (1996) *J. Biol. Chem.* 271, 29182–29190.

27 Couet, J., Li, S., Okamoto, T., Ikezu, T., Lisanti, M. P. (1997) *J. Biol. Chem.* 272, 6525–6533.

28 Scherer, P. E., Lisanti, M. P., Baldini, G., Sargiacomo, M., Mastick, C. C., Lodish, H. F. (1994) *J. Cell Biol.* 127, 1233–1243.

29 Galbiati, F., et al. (1998) *Proc. Natl. Acad. Sci. USA* 95, 10257–10262.

30 Campbell, L., Hollins, A. J., Al-Eid, A., Newman, G. R., von Ruhland, C., Gumbleton, M. (1999) *Biochem. Biophys. Res. Commun.* 262, 744–751.

31 Mikol, D. D., Hong, H. L., Cheng, H. L., Feldman, E. L. (1999) *Glia* 27, 39–52.

32 Fuchs, S., Hollins, A. J., Laue, M., Schaefer, U. F., Roemer, K., Gumbleton, M., Lehr, C. M. (2003) *Cell Tissue Res.* 311, 31–45.

33 Park, W. Y., Park, J. S., Cho, K. A., Kim, D. I., Ko, Y. G., Seo, J. S., Park, S. C. (2000) *J. Biol. Chem.* 275, 20847–20852.

34 Volonte, D., Zhang, K., Lisanti, M. P., Galbiati, F. (2002) *Mol. Biol. Cell* 13, 2502–2517.

35 Koleske, A. J., Baltimore, D., Lisanti, M. P. (1995) *Proc. Natl. Acad. Sci. USA* 92, 1381–1385.

36 Engelman, J. A., et al. (1998) *J. Biol. Chem.* 273, 20448–20455.

37 Engelman, J. A., Zhang, X. L., Lisanti, M. P. (1998) *FEBS Lett.* 436, 403–410.

38 Fra, A. M., Mastroianni, N., Mancini, M., Pasqualetto, E., Sitia, R. (1999) *Genomics* 56, 355–356.

39 Drab, M., et al. (2001) *Science* 293, 2449–2452.

40 Razani, B., et al. (2001) *J. Biol. Chem.* 276, 38121–38138.

41 Capozza, F., Williams, T. M., Schubert, W., McClain, S., Bouzahzah, B., Sotgia, F., Lisanti, M. P. (2003) *Am. J. Pathol.* 162, 2029–2039.

42 Williams, T. M., et al. (2003) *Mol. Biol. Cell* 14, 1027–1042.

43 Lavie, Y., Liscovitch, M. (1997) *Mol. Biol. Cell* 8, 207a.

44 Lavie, Y., Fiucci, G., Liscovitch, M. (1998) *J. Biol. Chem.* 273, 32380–32383.

45 Yang, C.-P. H., Galbiati, F., Volonte, D., Horwitz, S. B., Lisanti, M. P. (1998) *FEBS Lett.* 439, 368–372.

46 Yang, G., et al. (1998) *Clin. Cancer Res.* 4, 1873–1880.

47 Yang, G., Truong, L. D., Wheeler, T. M., Thompson, T. C. (1999) *Cancer Res.* 59, 5719–5723.

48 Ho, C. C., Huang, P. H., Huang, H. Y., Chen, Y. H., Yang, P. C., Hsu, S. M. (2002) *Am. J. Pathol.* 161, 1647–1656.

49 Yoo, S. H., et al. (2003) *Lung Cancer* 42, 195–202.

50 Sanchez-Carbayo, M., Socci, N. D., Charytonowicz, E., Lu, M., Prystowsky, M., Childs, G., Cordon-Cardo, C. (2002) *Cancer Res.* 62, 6973–6980.

51 Campbell, L., Gumbleton, M., Griffiths, D. F. (2003) *Br. J. Cancer* 89, 1909–1913.

52 Joo, H. J., Oh, D. K., Kim, Y. S., Lee, K. B., Kim, S. J. (2004) *BJU Int.* 93, 291–296.

53 Suzuoki, M., et al. (2002) *Br. J. Cancer* 87, 1140–1144.

54 Terris, B., Blaveri, E., Crnogorac-Jurcevic, T., Jones, M., Missiaglia, E., Ruszniewski, P., Sauvanet, A., Lemoine, N. R. (2002) *Am. J. Pathol.* 160, 1745–1754.

55 Kato, K., et al. (2002) *Cancer* 94, 929–933.

56 Satoh, T., et al. (2003) *Cancer* 97, 1225–1233.

57 Horiguchi, A., Asano, T., Asakuma, J., Sumitomo, M., Hayakawa, M. (2004) *J. Urol.* 172, 718–722.

58 Yang, G., Timme, T. L., Frolov, A., Wheeler, T. M., Thompson, T. C. (2005) *Cancer* 103, 1186–1194.

59 Racine, C., Belanger, M., Hirabayashi, H., Boucher, M., Chakir, J., Couet, J. (1999) *Biochem. Biophys. Res. Commun.* 255, 580–586.

60 Razani, B., Altschuler, Y., Zhu, L., Pestell, R. G., Mostov, K. E., Lisanti, M. P. (2000) *Biochemistry* 39, 13916–13924.

61 Ross, D. T., et al. (2000) *Nat. Genet.* 24, 227–235.

62 Sunaga, N., et al. (2004) *Cancer Res.* 64, 4277–4285.

63 Wikman, H., et al. (2004) *J. Pathol.* 203, 584–593.

64 Belanger, M. M., Roussel, E., Couet, J. (2004) *Chest* 125(5), 106S.

65 Wiechen, K., et al. (2001) *Am. J. Pathol.* 159, 1635–1643.

66 Wikman, H., Kettunen, E., Seppanen, J. K., Karjalainen, A., Hollmen, J., Anttila, S., Knuutila, S. (2002) *Oncogene* 21, 5804–5813.

67 Kato, T., et al. (2004) *Cancer Lett.* 214, 121–128.

68 Lee, S. W., Reimer, C. L., Oh, P., Campbell, D. B., Schnitzer, J. E. (1998) *Oncogene* 16, 1391–1397.

69 Shin, S.-I., Freedman, V. H., Risser, R., Pollack, R. (1975) *Proc. Natl. Acad. Sci. USA* 72, 4435–4439.

70 Syed, V., Mukherjee, K., Lyons-Weiler, J., Lau, K. M., Mashima, T., Tsuruo, T., Ho, S. M. (2005) *Oncogene* 24, 1774–1787.

71 Hayashi, K., Matsuda, S., Machida, K., Yamamoto, T., Fukuda, Y., Nimura, Y., Hayakawa, T., Hamaguchi, M. (2001) *Cancer Res.* 61, 2361–2364.

72 Lee, H., Park, D. S., Razani, B., Russell, R. G., Pestell, R. G., Lisanti, M. P. (2002) *Am. J. Pathol.* 161, 1357–1369.

73 Sloan, E. K., Stanley, K. L., Anderson, R. L. (2004) *Oncogene* 23, 7893–7897.

74 Chen, S. T., Lin, S. Y., Yeh, K. T., Kuo, S. J., Chan, W. L., Chu, Y. P., Chang, J. G. (2004) *Int. J. Mol. Med.* 14, 577–582.

75 Zou, W., McDaneld, L., Smith, L. M. (2003) *Anticancer Res.* 23, 4581–4586.

76 Williams, T. M., et al. (2004) *J. Biol. Chem.* 279, 51630–51646.

77 Williams, T.M., et al. (2004) *J. Biol. Chem.* 279, 24745–24756.

78 Zundel, W., Swiersz, L.M., Giaccia, A. (2000) *Mol. Cell. Biol.* 20, 1507–1514.

79 Liu, J., Lee, P., Galbiati, F., Kitsis, R.N., Lisanti, M.P. (2001) *Am. J. Physiol. Cell Physiol.* 280, C823–C835.

80 Galbiati, F., Volonte, D., Liu, J., Capozza, F., Frank, P.G., Zhu, L., Pestell, R.G., Lisanti, M.P. (2001) *Mol. Biol. Cell* 12, 2229–2244.

81 Ono, K., Iwanaga, Y., Hirayama, M., Kawamura, T., Sowa, N., Hasegawa, K. (2004) *Am. J. Physiol. Lung Cell. Mol. Physiol.* 287, L201-L209.

82 Shack, S., Wang, X.T., Kokkonen, G.C., Gorospe, M., Longo, D.L., Holbrook, N.J. (2003) *Mol. Cell. Biol.* 23, 2407–2414.

83 Peterson, T.E., et al. (2003) *Arterioscler. Thromb. Vasc. Biol.* 23, 1521–1527.

84 Williams, T.M., et al. (2005) *J. Biol. Chem.* 280, 25134–25145.

85 Duxbury, M.S., Ito, H., Ashley, S.W., Whang, E.E. (2004) *J. Biol. Chem.* 279, 23176–23182.

86 Podar, K., et al. (2003) *J. Biol. Chem.* 278, 5794–5801.

87 Acconcia, F., Ascenzi, P., Bocedi, A., Spisni, E., Tomasi, V., Trentalance, A., Visca, P., Marino, M. (2005) *Mol. Biol. Cell* 16, 231–237.

88 D'Alessio, A., Al-Lamki, R.S., Bradley, J.R., Pober, J.S. (2005) *Am. J. Pathol.* 166, 1273–1282.

89 Sedding, D.G., et al. (2005) *Circ. Res.* 96, 635–642.

90 Zuo, L., Ushio-Fukai, M., Ikeda, S., Hilenski, L., Patrushev, N., Alexander, R.W. (2005) *Arterioscler. Thromb. Vasc. Biol.* 25, 1824–1830.

91 Cao, D.J., Guo, Y.L., Colman, R.W. (2004) *Circ. Res.* 94, 1227–1234.

92 Chun, J., Kwon, T., Lee, E.J., Hyun, S., Hong, S.K., Kang, S.S. (2005) *Biochem. Biophys. Res. Commun.* 326, 136–146.

93 Meyer, A., van Golen, C.M., Boyanapalli, M., Kim, B., Soules, M.E., Feldman, E.L. (2005) *Biochemistry* 44, 932–938.

94 Chun, J., Hyun, S., Kwon, T., Lee, E.J., Hong, S.K., Kang, S.S. (2005) *Cell Signal.* 17, 751–760.

95 Feng, J., Park, J., Cron, P., Hess, D., Hemmings, B.A. (2004) *J. Biol. Chem.* 279, 41189–41196.

96 Caselli, A., Mazzinghi, B., Camici, G., Manao, G., Ramponi, G. (2002) *Biochem. Biophys. Res. Commun.* 296, 692–697.

97 Wary, K.K., Mainiero, F., Isakoff, S.J., Marcantonio, E.E., Giancotti, F.G. (1996) *Cell* 87, 733–743.

98 Wary, K.K., Mariotti, A., Zurzolo, C., Giancotti, F.G. (1998) *Cell* 94, 625–634.

99 Martindale, J.L., Holbrook, N.J. (2002) *J. Cell. Physiol.* 192, 1–15.

100 Kohno, M., Pouyssegur, J. (2003) *Prog. Cell Cycle Res.* 5, 219–224.

101 Wei, Y., Yang, X., Liu, Q., Wilkins, J.A., Chapman, H.A. (1999) *J. Cell Biol.* 144, 1285–1294.

102 Feng, X., Gaeta, M.L., Madge, L.A., Yang, J.H., Bradley, J.R., Pober, J.S. (2001) *J. Biol. Chem.* 276, 8341–8349.

103 Veldman, R.J., Maestre, N., Aduib, O.M., Medin, J.A., Salvayre, R., Levade, T. (2001) *Biochem. J.* 355, 859–868.

104 Li, S., Seitz, R., Lisanti, M.P. (1996) *J. Biol. Chem.* 271, 3863–3868.

105 Lee, H., et al. (2000) *Mol. Endocrinol.* 14, 1750–1775.

106 Mastick, C.C., Brady, M.J., Saltiel, A.R. (1995) *J. Cell Biol.* 129, 1523–1531.

107 Maggi, D., Biedi, C., Segat, D., Barbero, D., Panetta, D., Cordera, R. (2002) *Biochem. Biophys. Res. Commun.* 295, 1085–1089.

108 Kim, Y.N., Wiepz, G.J., Guadarrama, A.G., Bertics, P.J. (2000) *J. Biol. Chem.* 275, 7481–7491.

109 Mettouchi, A., Klein, S., Guo, W., Lopez-Lago, M., Lemichez, E., Westwick, J.K., Giancotti, F.G. (2001) *Mol. Cell* 8, 115–127.

110 Fielding, P.E., Chau, P., Liu, D., Spencer, T.A., Fielding, C.J. (2004) *Biochemistry* 43, 2578–2586.

111 Podar, K., et al. (2004) *Cancer Res.* 64, 7500–7506.

112 Colonna, C., Podesta, E.J. (2005) *Exp. Cell Res.* 304, 432–442.

113 Vepa, S., Scribner, W.M., Natarajan, V. (1997) *Free Radic. Biol. Med.* 22, 25–35.

114 Volonte, D., Galbiati, F., Pestell, R.G., Lisanti, M.P. (2001) *J. Biol. Chem.* 276, 8094–8103.

115 Navakauskiene, R., Treigyte, G., Gineitis, A., Magnusson, K.E. (2004) *Proteomics* 4, 1029–1041.

116 Mastick, C. C., Saltiel, A. R. (1997) *J. Biol. Chem.* 272, 20706–20714.

117 Kimura, A., Mora, S., Shigematsu, S., Pessin, J. E., Saltiel, A. R. (2002) *J. Biol. Chem.* 277, 30153–30158.

118 Kim, Y. N., Dam, P., Bertics, P. J. (2002) *Exp. Cell Res.* 280, 134–147.

119 Sanguinetti, A. R., Cao, H., Corley Mastick, C. (2003) *Biochem. J.* 376, 159–168.

120 Sanguinetti, A. R., Mastick, C. C. (2003) *Cell Signal.* 15, 289–298.

121 Cao, H., Courchesne, W. E., Mastick, C. C. (2002) *J. Biol. Chem.* 277, 8771–8774.

122 Cao, H., Sanguinetti, A. R., Mastick, C. C. (2004) *Exp. Cell Res.* 294, 159–171.

123 Labrecque, L., Nyalendo, C., Langlois, S., Durocher, Y., Roghi, C., Murphy, G., Gingras, D., Beliveau, R. (2004) *J. Biol. Chem.* 279, 52132–52140.

124 Lee, H., Park, D. S., Wang, X. B., Scherer, P. E., Schwartz, P. E., Lisanti, M. P. (2002) *J. Biol. Chem.* 277, 34556–34567.

125 Gargalovic, P., Dory, L. (2003) *J. Lipid Res.* 44, 1622–1632.

126 Belanger, M. M., Roussel, E., Couet, J. (2003) *Anticancer Drugs* 14, 281–287.

127 Roussel, E., Belanger, M. M., Couet, J. (2004) *Anticancer Drugs* 15, 961–967.

128 Lavie, Y., Czarny, M., Liscovitch, M. (1997) *FASEB J.* 11, A1346.

129 Bender, F. C., Reymond, M. A., Bron, C., Quest, A. F. (2000) *Cancer Res.* 60, 5870–5878.

130 Pang, A., Wing, Y., Kwong, Y. L. (2004) *Leukemia Res.* 28, 973–977.

131 Spisni, E., Bianco, M. C., Griffoni, C., Toni, M., D'Angelo, R., Santi, S., Riccio, M., Tomasi, V. (2003) *J. Cell. Physiol.* 197, 198–204.

132 Mahmoudi, M., et al. (2003) *J. Pathol.* 200, 396–405.

133 Deregowski, V., Delhalle, S., Benoit, V., Bours, V., Merville, M. P. (2002) *Biochem. Pharmacol.* 64, 873–881.

134 van den Heuvel, A. P., Schulze, A., Burgering, B. M. (2005) *Biochem. J.* 385, 795–802.

135 Bist, A., Fielding, C. J., Fielding, P. E. (2000) *Biochemistry* 39, 1966–1972.

Index

a

AA *see* amino acid
Aβ *see* amyloid β-peptide
ABCA1 *see* ATP-binding cassette transporter-A1
Abl 129–130
– actin remodeling 130–131
– caveolin kinase 120, 129
– caveolin phosphorylation 121
acceptor, fluorescence correlation spectroscopy 59
acceptor channels, FRET 146
ACTH *see* adrenocorticotropic hormone
actin cytoskeleton
– attachment 127–129
– dynamics of caveolin 199–200
– dynamin 83
– endocytosis 73
– stabilisation 130
actin/plasma membrane attachment sites, phosphorylation 128
actin polymerization 131
actin remodeling 127
– Abl 130–131
– insulin-induced 131
activation, Csk 125–127
activation-induced cell death (AICD), lipid rafts 157
acylation, signal transduction 92
AD *see* Alzheimer's disease
ADAM10, metalloprotease 214
adaptor proteins, multifunctional 249
adhesion complex, focal 198–199
adhesion molecules, immunological synapse 151
adipocytes
– caveolin 199
– caveolin phosphorylation 117
– signaling pathways 117

adrenocorticotropic hormone (ACTH) 256–257
affinity conversion, lipid rafts 157
AFM *see* atomic force microscopy
aggregation, membrane proteins 32
aging, gate theory 195
aging process, caveolin 195
AICD *see* activation-induced cell death
Alzheimer's disease (AD) 205
– role of rafts 215–223
amino acid (AA), caveolins domains 25
amino-terminus, caveolin-1 123
amphiphilic dye, LAURDAN 5
amyloid β-peptide (Ab) 215–217
amyloid precursor protein (APP)
– cleavage 215–223
– processing 205–223
anchored protein (AP)
– GPI- 8, 54, 63, 92, 207, 214, 257
angiogenesis, caveolin-eNOS interaction 241–242
anisotropy, measurements 61
annular lipids, transmembrane signaling 143
anoikis, cellular resistance 253–254
anomalous diffusion, immunological synapse 152
antennopedia (AP) peptide 102
anti-proliferative activity, caveolin-1 252
antibodies, diffusion-based measurements 55
antigen-presenting cell, immunological synapse *see* APC
antisense suppression techniques, caveolin-1 253
AP *see also* antennopedia, *see* anchored protein
APC, immunological synapse 150
apical membrane
– basolateral protein exclusion 14
– epithelial cells 9–10

Lipid Rafts and Caveolae. Christopher J. Fielding
Copyright © 2006 WILEY-VCH Verlag GmbH & Co. KGaA, Weinheim
ISBN: 3-527-31261-7